Special Cutting Instructions

ISBN:

Title:

Author/Editor/Publisher:

Fold-outs:

Page	Turn and fold?

Notes:

Ethiopic Grammar

Ancient Language Resources

K. C. Hanson, Series Editor

Arno Poebel
Fundamentals of Sumerian Grammar/ Grundzüge der Sumerischen Grammatik

A. H. Sayce
Assyrian Grammar

Samuel A. B. Mercer
Introduction to Assyrian Grammar

The Student's Concise Hebrew-English Lexicon of the Bible

Heinrich Ewald
Syntax of the Hebrew Language of the Old Testament

S. R. Driver
A Treatise on the Use of the Tenses in Hebrew

M. H. Segal
A Grammar of Mishnaic Hebrew

William B. Stevenson
Grammar of Palestinian Jewish Aramaic

Carl Brockelmann
Lexicon Syriacum

J. Payne Smith
Compendious Syriac Dictionary

William Jennings
Lexicon to the Syriac New Testament

Eberhard Nestle
Syriac Grammar

Theodor Nöldeke
Compendius Syriac Grammar

Theodor Nöldeke
Mandaean Grammar / Mandäische Grammatik

August Dillman and Carl Bezold
Ethiopic Grammar

William W. Goodwin
A Greek Grammar

William W. Goodwin
Syntax of the Moods and Tenses of the Greek Verb

Ernest D. Burton
Syntax of the Moods and Tenses in New Testament Greek

J. B. Smith
Greek-English Concordance to the New Testament

Ethiopic Grammar

Second Edition

August Dillmann

Revised by

Carl Bezold

Translated by

James A. Crichton

ETHIOPIC GRAMMAR
Second Edition
Ancient Language Resources

ISBN: 1-59244-145-9

The Library of Congress has cataloged an earlier edition of this book as follows:

Dillmann, August (1823–1894)
[Grammatik der äthiopischen sprache. English]
Ethiopic grammar / by August Dillmann. 2nd edition enl. and improved (1899) by Carl Bezold. Translated by James A. Crichton.
London: Williams & Norgate, 1907
xxx, 581 [1] p. ix fold tab. 24 cm.
1. Ethiopic language—Grammar. I. Title. II. Bezold, Carl, 1859–1922. III. Crichton, James A., tr.

PJ9021 .D52 1907 42040768

Manufactured in the U.S.A.

Series Foreword

The study of languages forms the foundation of any study of ancient societies. While we are dependent upon archaeology to unearth pottery, tools, buildings, and graves, it is through reading the documentary evidence that we learn the nuances of each culture—from receipts and letters to myths and legends. And the access to those documents comes only through the basic work of deciphering scripts, mastering vocabulary, conjugating verbs, and untangling syntax.

Ancient Language Resources brings together some of the most significant reference works for the study of ancient languages, includeing grammars, dictionaries, and related materials. While most of the volumes will be reprints of classic works, we also intend to include new publications. The linguistic circle is widely drawn, encompassing Egyptian, Sumerian, Akkadian, Ugaritic, Phoenician, Hattic, Hittite (Nesite), Hurrian, Hebrew, Aramaic, Syriac, Ethiopic, Arabic, Greek, Coptic, Latin, Mandaean, Armenian, and Gothic. It is the hope of the publishers that this will continue to encourage study of the ancient languages and keep the work of groundbreaking scholars accessible.

—K. C. Hanson
Series Editor

Foreword

August Dillman (1823–94) was born at Illingen, Württemberg, and educated at the seminary in Schönthal (1836–40), and then at the University of Tübingen, where he was a student of Heinrich Ewald. He was an assistant pastor at Sersheim, Württemberg (1845–46), but his passion was for the study of Semitic languages. He traveled to Paris, London, and Oxford, studying Ethiopic and cataloging manuscripts in the British Library and the Bodleian Library. He died in Berlin on July 4, 1894.

Dillmann is considered the father of modern Ethiopic studies. He became a renowned Semitist, producing catalogs of Ethiopic manuscripts, an edition of the Bible in Ethiopic, the Ethiopic edition of *1 Enoch,* an Ethiopic lexicon, and a Ethiopic reader (chrestomathy). He taught at the universities of Tübingen, Kiel, Giessen, and Berlin. In 1875–76 Dillmann was the Rektor of the University of Berlin, and in 1881 he was the President of the International Congress of Orientalists.

The select bibliography that follows will hopefully aid the reader to find additional resources for the study of Ethiopic.

—K. C. Hanson

Select Bibliography

Châine, Marius. *Grammaire éthiopienne.* Rev. ed. Beyrouth: Catholique, 1938.

Dillmann, August. *Ascensio Isaiae, Aethiopice et Latine: Cum prolegomenis, adnotationibus criticis et exegeticis, additis versionum latinarum reliquiis.* Leipzig: Brockhaus, 1877.

———. *Biblia Veteris Testamenti Aethiopica.* 5 vols. Leipzig: Vogel, 1853–61.

———. *Das Buch Henoch übersetzt und erklärt.* Leipzig: Vogel, 1853.

———. *Chrestomathia Aethiopica.* Leipzig: Vogel, 1866. Reprint Darmstadt: Wissenschaftliche Buchgesellschaft, 1974.

———. *Codices Aethiopici.* 2 vols. Oxford: Academic, 1848–51.

———. *Lexicon Linguae Aethiopicae.* Leipzig: Weigel, 1865. Reprint New York: Ungar, 1955.

———. *Liber Henoch, Aethiopice: Ad quinque codicum fidem editus, cum variis lectionibus.* Leipzig: Vogel, 1851.

———. *Liber Jubilaeorum: Versione Graeca deperdita nunc nonnisi in Geez lingua conservatus nuper ex Abyssinia in Europam allatus.* Killae: Van Maack, 1859.

Hammerschmidt, Ernst. *Anthologia Aethiopica.* Leipzig: Hinrichs, 1893. Reprint Hildesheim: Olms, 1988.

Knibb, Michael A. *Translating the Bible: The Ethiopic Version of the Old Testament.* Schweich Lectures 1995. Oxford: Oxford University Press, 1999.

Lambdin, Thomas O. *Introduction to Classical Ethiopic (Ge'ez).* Harvard Semitic Studies 24. Missoula, Mont.: Scholars, 1978.

Leslau, Wolf. *Comparative Dictionary of Ge'ez (Classical Ethiopic): Ge'ez-English / English-Ge'ez with an Index of the Semitic Roots.* Wiesbaden: Harrassowitz, 1987.

———. *Concise Dictionary of Ge'ez (Classical Ethiopic).* Wiesbaden: Harrassowitz, 1988.

Ludolf, Hiob. *Grammatica Aethiopica.* Edited by Burchardt Brentjes and Karl Gallus. Wissenschaftliche Beiträge. Halle: Martin-Luther-Universität Halle-Wittenberg, 1986.

Mercer, Samuel A. B. *Ethiopian Grammar with Chrestomathy and Glossary.* Rev. ed. New York: Ungar, 1961.

Miles, John R. *Retroversion and Text Criticism: The Predictability of Syntax in an Ancient Translation from Greek to Ethiopic.* Septuagint and Cognate Studies Series 17. Chico, Calif.: Scholars Press, 1985.

Praetorius, Franz. *Äthiopische Grammatik: Mit Paradigmen, Litteratur, Chrestomathie und Glossar.* Porta Linguarum Orientalium 7. Leipzig: Reuther, 1886.

Schneider, R. *L'expression des complements de verbe et de nom et la place de l'adjectif épithète en guèze.* Paris: Champion, 1959.

Tropper, Josef. *Altäthiopisch: Grammatik des Ge'ez mit Übungstexten und Glossar.* Elementa Linguarum Orientis 2. Münster: Ugarit-Verlag, 2002.

Weninger, Stefan. *Ge'ez: Classical Ethiopic.* Languages of the World: Materials 1. Munich: Lincom Europa, 1993.

———. *Das Verbalstem des Altäthiopischen: Eine Untersuchung seiner Verwendung und Funktion unter Berücksichtigung des Interferenzproblems.* Wiesbaden: Harrassowitz, 2001.

TRANSLATOR'S PREFATORY NOTE.

The renewed interest taken in Semitic studies in general within these recent years, and in particular the continued issue from the Press of numerous and important Ethiopic texts,—encourage the hope that an English edition of the leading Ethiopic Grammar may prove not wholly unwelcome to English-speaking students at the present time. Few competent judges will challenge the claim of DILLMANN'S '*Grammar*' to be thus described. No doubt a long time has elapsed since its first publication, and much investigation has been applied to the language during the interval; but it may be questioned whether any of the essential principles laid down in DILLMANN'S work have been affected by these labours, otherwise than by way of confirmation, or whether any facts of really fundamental grammatical importance have been added to our knowledge. Accordingly, although some useful smaller Grammars now exist,—notably the excellent manual published in 1886 by PROF. PRAETORIUS—, the serious student of Ethiopic must still have recourse to DILLMANN'S work, particularly in the form given to it in the second edition (of 1899) by PROF. BEZOLD. It is from that edition that the present translation has been rendered.

It is not contended, in the light of recent research, that DILLMANN was invariably happy in his frequent excursions into the fascinating but treacherous field of Comparative Semitic; but even when his conjectural etymologies seem farthest astray, they are always stimulating and ingenious. It has been thought right, however, in this connection, to append here and there a cautionary footnote, when the author appears to give play too freely to his imagination. Farther, DILLMANN'S criticisms of the results obtained by his great predecessor LUDOLF are often severe, seldom generous, and occasionally unfair and even inaccurate. Several instances are pointed out in the footnotes. But, with all due deduction made for such blemishes, DILLMANN'S work remains a monument —second only to his '*Lexicon*',—of his genius, industry and special erudition. It may be relied on as a safe guide through the mazes of a difficult speech; and as an institutional work, the foremost in its department, it is entitled to a high rank among the leading Semitic Grammars.

Little or no alteration has been made on the text in the course of translation. I have ventured only to cite a few additional examples, in the Syntax, from some of the more recently published Ethiopic works, inserting them either tacitly in the text itself, or avowedly in the footnotes. The somewhat meagre Table of Contents, given in the German edition, has been considerably expanded; and the details have been applied marginally, in their proper places, throughout the book. A few additions have been made in the first of the appended Tables of Forms; and an Index of Passages has been drawn up and placed at the end of the volume. As far as possible, the supporting-passages have been re-verified. In particular the quotations adduced from the important text of *Henoch*, as edited by DILLMANN, have been compared with the corresponding passages in FLEMMING'S more recent and more accurate edition; and the differences, when of any importance, have been pointed out in footnotes (1). This course was considered preferable to applying in the body of the work the improved readings presented in FLEMMING'S edition, or the suggestions made by DUENSING in his careful discussion of FLEMMING'S *Henoch*, contributed to the "Gelehrte Anzeigen", 1903, No. 8 (Göttingen).

It would be difficult to exaggerate my indebtedness to the distinguished scholar who prepared the last German edition, PROF. BEZOLD of Heidelberg. From the first he took a lively interest in the version. It was submitted to him in manuscript, and his suggestions were attended to. He had the great kindness also to incorporate, at that time, numerous illustrative passages

(1) Just as these lines go to the Press, another edition of the text of *Henoch*, by PROF. CHARLES, is announced as immediately forthcoming. DR. CHARLES has already done excellent work in this field,—witness his elaborate translation and commentary: '*The Book of Enoch*', Oxford 1893. I am sorry to have missed seeing his edition of the text, in time to compare, in the following pages, as occasion might arise and grammatical interest demand, the readings of this new edition with FLEMMING'S readings.

from his admirable edition of the very important text of *Kebra Nagast*, then passing through the Press, and to enrich the version farther by adding many most useful philological and bibliographical footnotes. I have also to express here my sincere gratitude for the unfailing courtesy and patience with which he lent his invaluable assistance in the reading of the final proof-sheets. PROF. BEZOLD's direct contributions are enclosed in square brackets, both in the text and in the footnotes,—with the exception that I am responsible for a few bracketed words of a purely explanatory nature, which occur here and there in the text. My own footnotes are marked by square brackets enclosing the letters 'TR'.

I have also to thank the staff of the DRUGULIN house for the successful accomplishment of their difficult task in printing this edition.

James A. Crichton.

PREFACE TO THE FIRST EDITION.

A fresh treatment of Ethiopic Grammar had for a long time been urgently required; and, so far as known to me, none of the older qualified scholars seemed disposed to supply the want. In these circumstances I readily responded to an invitation addressed to me by the publishing firm in the summer of 1855, to undertake this business, — one quite as laborious as remunerative. I was aware indeed that, if only a larger number of texts had been thoroughly investigated and settled, and greater progress had been made with the deciphering of the Himyaric monuments, many details would have allowed of more certain and complete recognition and acceptance. Seeing however that the accomplishment of these tasks lay still in the distant future, I did not think it wise to wait for it; and, even as it was, a rich field, ripe for cutting and gathering in, already lay before me.

The terms of my arrangement with the publisher restricted, to some extent, the time available for work, and also the compass of the volume. Still, I have endeavoured to satisfy, as far as possible within the prescribed limits, those requirements of a grammatical work which are insisted on by our advanced philology. The material of the language has been thoroughly gone over afresh, in all its parts and on every side; and many new observations, of which LUDOLF had no presentiment, have been the result, as every single section of the book will show. In explaining the phenomena of the language and duly ranking them in its system, I was still more completely left to my own enquiries, as foregoing labours in this department have been much more scanty. Many things here are, of course, matter of grammatical theory previously adopted, so that others, who profess a different theory will attempt a different explanation. Many things, — in the views given of Pronunciation and Accent for instance, — must perhaps always remain uncertain and obscure, because the historical information, which alone could decide, is wanting. Many things too had to be set down without being fully demonstrated, because space was not obtainable for their proper discussion. In the references mentioned, it is but desirable that other scholars should now speak out, and take up the discussion of these more difficult and obscure questions. Science, — to the service of which alone this book is devoted, would be a gainer. But every one who peruses my book will be convinced, I trust, that Ethiopic grammar, which has been neglected so long, sheds quite as much light on the grammars of the other Semitic languages as it receives from them.

Perhaps some justification is required for the great length at which, in the Phonology, I have sought to authenticate by examples the Sound-transitions between Ethiopic roots and those of the other Semitic tongues. I know from experience the perplexing effect, which is produced upon one who approaches Ethiopic from the side of the other Semitic languages, caused by a host of expressions and roots; and therefore I wished to clear the way for a more thorough insight, by discussing a number of etymologies, and by analysing the Sound-changes upon which this phenomenon rests. Much here is, of course, merely matter of conjecture and must long remain so, — in fact until dialectic phonetic interchange is more strictly investigated by Semitic philologists, and traced back to sure principles. However, even the danger of falling into error here and there in detail, did not prevent me from tackling the matter.

In the Syntax I was obliged to compress my work, seeing that the space allowed was already more than exhausted. Accordingly it was only what was peculiar and remarkable in Ethiopic that I was able to treat with any thoroughness; while I could merely touch upon what had become familiar from the other Semitic languages. In the arrangement of the Syntax I have adhered almost entirely to the order adopted in EWALD's '*Hebrew Grammar*', which seemed to be the most accurate and suitable. Altogether this part of the work, for which LUDOLF did almost nothing, claims to be no more than a first draught, which still awaits much filling in by means of farther studies. A few paragraphs I would gladly have altered, if the manuscript had not by that time left my hands. Then too, the Sections turned out somewhat unequal in extent; but, on account of the constant references backwards and forwards, it had become exceedingly difficult to make any alteration in this respect.

The supporting-passages I have taken, as far as possible, from the Bible in print, and in this I have founded upon PLATT's edition of the New Testament, LUDOLF's of the Psalms, LAURENCE's of 4 Esra, and my own edition of the Octateuch and the Book of Henoch. Quotations are occasionally made from Manuscript sources in the case of the other Biblical Books, as well as in the case of the Book of Jubilees, (*Kufālē*), Vita Adami, (*Gadla Adām*), Liturgies, Organon, Hymnologies of the British Bible Society, Abyssinian Chronicles and Ṣalōta Reqēt.

It is hoped that every foreigner will kindly excuse, and every German approve of, my having written the book in German: to write a Grammar in Latin is restricting and troublesome, and to read it is pain.

It seemed to me unnecessary in itself to add an Index of Words and Subjects, and it was besides precluded by my having already exceeded the limits allowed the book.

Kiel, 15th April, 1857.

The Author.

PREFACE TO THE SECOND EDITION.

The highly honouring proposal was made to me on the part of the Publishing firm, at the suggestion of PROF. NÖLDEKE, and with the sanction of the Author's representatives, to prepare a second edition of the present work. A wish which had been cherished for many years by the Author, who has been removed from us, was thereby to be fulfilled. PROF. DILLMANN had gathered together a large number of notes in his own interleaved copy of the Grammar with a view to a revised edition, and had continued the process till shortly before his death. A foundation was thus laid for the present edition, which, at the express desire of the representatives, takes, upon the whole, the form of a reproduction of the original work, with the author's numerous additions and relatively few emendations.

In consequence of the restriction thus laid upon me in the work of revisal, the original character of the book has been absolutely preserved. But another consequence of course was, that it became impossible for the new editor to undertake any thorough-going alterations in individual passages. PROF. DILLMANN himself, if it had been permitted him, would doubtless have undertaken a much more vigorous recasting or regular revision of the book. Beyond trifling alterations of expression, and the tacit correction of manifest errors of the Press, I have merely rectified certain mistakes,— proved by facts to be such,—and which DILLMANN would at this time of day have acknowledged. The entire responsibility, as well as the entire merit, accordingly remains with the Author, even in this second edition. My contributions—in the way of correction of the original work and addition of a few notices of the literature of the subject—are marked by square brackets.

I thought I might venture upon greater liberty in the use made of the Author's Manuscript additions. In particular, the lengthy and frequently recurring extracts from later writings, — which DILLMANN had entered in his copy, manifestly for his own readier guidance, — have been replaced by mere references to the works concerned: other material too, especially all that seemed to lie beyond the scope of an Ethiopic grammar, has been left out of account. On the other hand I considered that I was acting in the spirit of the Author in endeavouring to extend, support and adjust the lists of examples, often very briefly stated by him, and in many cases consisting of a single Ethiopic word, — a labour which was facilitated, and in many cases in fact made possible, only through DILLMANN's '*Lexicon Linguae Ethiopicae*'. Occasionally, instead of a long series of supporting-passages I have given a direct reference to the '*Lexicon*'.

The now antiquated second Table of the first edition, with the "older Forms of Ethiopic writing", has been set aside for various reasons.

A few additions, marked "NÖLDEKE", originated in the course of reading the proof-sheets, which PROF. NÖLDEKE revised at my request on account of the extensions of the new edition springing out of DILLMANN's copy. Of course the distinguished scholar just named does not thereby incur any responsibility for my performance. But, beyond an honest endeavour to restore as well as I could the work of the much revered dead, it was *his* lively interest in this work and *his* continual assistance with head and hand, which alone gave me the needful courage to undertake the task and to conduct it to its close. For this service I hope he will kindly accept here my heartfelt thanks.

Lugano, 25th April, 1899.

C. Bezold.

NOTE ON THE ENGLISH EDITION.

It is with great pleasure that I avail myself of the opportunity, here afforded me, of expressing my thorough approval of Dr. Crichton's translation of Dillmann's work, which will form a worthy companion-volume to his recent edition of Prof. Nöldeke's '*Syriac Grammar*'. The clear and idiomatic English, into which Dillmann's rather difficult German has been rendered, testifies once more to Dr. Crichton's ability and skill in such translation, as well as to the minute and conscientious accuracy, combined with sound scholarship, with which he has undertaken and brought to a successful completion his laborious task. I venture to hope and believe that Dillmann's book will henceforth appeal with effect to a still wider circle of readers, and increase yet farther the interest taken in Ethiopic Grammar among English-speaking students of Semitic.

Heidelberg, November 1906.

C. Bezold.

CONTENTS.

INTRODUCTION.

GENERAL REMARKS ON THE ETHIOPIC LANGUAGE.

PART FIRST. ORTHOGRAPHY AND PHONOLOGY.

I. ORTHOGRAPHY.

Vowel Denotation.

II. PHONOLOGY.

I. THE SOUNDS (OR LETTERS) OF THE LANGUAGE.

1. VOWELS.

2. CONSONANTS.

II. MEETING OF LETTERS IN THE SYLLABLE AND IN THE WORD.

General Rules of the Syllable.

CHANGES OF LETTERS CONSEQUENT ON THE GENERAL RULES OF THE SYLLABLE, OR ON THEIR MEETING WITH OTHER LETTERS.

1. VOWELS.

(A) INFLUENCE OF THE STRUCTURE OF THE SYLLABLE AND THE WORD ON THE VOWELS.

(B) MEETING OF VOWELS.

(C) MEETING OF VOWELS AND CONSONANTS, AND THEIR INTERCHANGES.

(α) *Influence of Aspirates on the Vowels.*

(β) *The Vowels I and U and the Semivowels.*

2. CONSONANTS.

III. THE WORD AND THE TONE OF THE WORD.

PART SECOND. MORPHOLOGY.

A. ROOTS:—THEIR CLASSES AND THEIR FORMS.

B. FORMATION OF WORDS.

FORMATION OF VERBS.

I. STEM-FORMATION OF VERBS.

1. STEM-FORMATION OF TRI-RADICAL ROOTS.

2. STEM-FORMATION OF MULTILITERAL ROOTS.

II. FORMATION OF TENSES AND MOODS.

III. FORMATION OF PERSONS, GENDERS AND NUMBERS.

FORMATION OF NOUNS.

A. FORMATION OF NOUNS—IN THE NARROWER SENSE OF THE TERM.

I. STEM-FORMATION OF NOUNS.

1. SIMPLE NOMINAL STEMS.

2. NOMINAL STEMS FORMED BY DOUBLING OF RADICALS, OR FROM DERIVED VERBAL STEMS AND MULTILITERAL ROOTS.

3. NOMINAL STEMS OF OUTER FORMATION.

(*a*) *Forms reached by means of Prefixes.*

(*b*) *Forms reached by means of Affixes.*

PARTICIPLES AND INFINITIVES.

II. FORMATION OF GENDERS AND NUMBERS.

1. GENDERS OF NOMINAL STEMS.

2. NUMBERS OF NOMINAL STEMS.

(*a*) *Outer Formation of the Plural.*

(*b*) *Inner Formation of the Plural.*

III. FORMATION OF CASES.

B. PRONOUNS AND NUMERALS.

I. PRONOUNS.

II. PRONOMINALS.

III. NUMERALS.

FORMATION OF WORDS OF RELATION.

I. ADVERBS.

1. ADVERBS DERIVED FROM PRONOMINAL ROOTS.

2. ADVERBS DERIVED FROM CONCEPTIONAL WORDS.

II. PREPOSITIONS.

III. CONJUNCTIONS.

PART THIRD. SYNTAX.

A. LEADING WORD-GROUPS OF THE SENTENCE.

I. PERIPHRASIS OF THE ARTICLE.

II. GOVERNMENT OF THE VERB.

1. NOUNS AND PRONOUNS IN SUBORDINATION TO THE VERB.

2. VERB IN SUBORDINATION TO THE VERB.

III. COMBINATION OF NOUNS WITH ONE ANOTHER.

1. SUBORDINATION OF NOUNS.

(a) The Genitive Relation.

(b) Subordination through the Accusative or through Prepositions.

2. CO-ORDINATION OF NOUNS.

B. STRUCTURE OF THE SIMPLE SENTENCE.

C. SPECIAL KINDS OF SENTENCES.

1. NEGATIVE, INTERROGATIVE, AND EXCLAMATORY SENTENCES.

2. CONNECTED SENTENCES.

(*a*) *Copulative Clauses.*

(*b*) *Attributive Relative Clauses.*

(*c*) *Conjunctional Relative Clauses.*

3. RECIPROCAL SENTENCES AND WORDS.

(a) *Conditional Sentences.*

(b) *Correlated Clauses and Words.*

TABLES.

INTRODUCTION.

GENERAL REMARKS ON THE ETHIOPIC LANGUAGE.

§ 1. The beginnings of the great Abyssinian kingdom stretch back to pretty early times, which cannot now be more exactly determined. It emerged into the light of history immediately upon its conversion to Christianity in the third century, and with increasing clearness on to the seventh; and from that time forward, all through the Middle Ages and up to the commencement of the seventeenth century, it occupied an important position in the midst of the bordering populations of Africa and Arabia. In that kingdom once flourished the language commonly called *Ethiopic*, and it is to the description of that language that the present work is devoted. Originally one only of the manifold dialects into which the Arabic-African branch of the Semitic tongue split up, though one of the noblest among them, it gained, through the tribe by which it was spoken, the position of being the leading speech in the kingdom, starting as it did from their country of Tigrē and its chief town Axum, and keeping pace with the development of the kingdom, while the modes of speech native to other tribes in the land lived on alongside of it merely as vulgar dialects. Farther, by means of the numerous writings, chiefly of Christian contents, which were speedily composed in it, it became bound up in the most intimate manner with the life of the Church and the whole culture of the people. In this position it maintained itself, as long as the centre of gravity of the kingdom remained in Tigrē and Axum. It is true that when the South-Western provinces grew into importance, and the seat of government was transferred to the district south of Takazzē toward Lake Ṣānā, another dialect,

Sketch of the History of the Language.

the Amharic, came into fashion as the ordinary speech of the court and of the officials of the country; but Ethiopic even then continued to retain its full importance as the literary language, in which all books and even official documents were written; and the three centuries of this period may be regarded indeed as the age of the second bloom of the Ethiopic speech. It was only when the Galla tribes pressed into the country after the close of the sixteenth century, and thus shook and loosened the entire kingdom, that the language received its deathblow. The kingdom was broken up; the several parts were dissevered from the whole; civilisation yielded to a rapid recrudescence of barbarism; Christianity was pressed hard and partly supplanted by Islam, and in itself it degenerated into the merest caricature of a Christian faith. Along with the power, culture and literature of these lands the venerable speech died out also. To be sure it has remained the sacred language and the ecclesiastical language up to the present day; and, as late even as last century, books, especially the annals of the country, were still composed in it; but it was understood by the educated priests only and perhaps by a few of the nobles, and even such men preferred to write in Amharic. Now-a-days even among the priests, only a few probably are to be found who possess some scanty acquaintance with the Ethiopic tongue ([1]).

The dialects of the several tribes and provinces,—most of them being no doubt of Semitic origin, but containing a strong admixture of elements from the adjoining African tongues—are now flourishing there in motley variety and rank luxuriance. The most widely extended among them is the Amharic ([2]), which in

([1]) For Ethiopic Bibliography *cf.*: G. Fumagalli, '*Bibliografia Etiopica. Catalogo descrittivo e ragionato degli scritti pubblicati dalla invenzione della stampa fino a tutto il* 1891 *intorno alla Etiopia e regioni limitrofe*', Milano 1893; [and L. Goldschmidt, '*Bibliotheca Aethiopica, vollstaendiges verzeichnis und ausfuehrliche beschreibung saemmtlicher Aethiopischer druckwerke*', Leipzig 1893, as well as the "Litteratura Aethiopica" in Praetorius' '*Aethiopische Grammatik*', Berlin 1886, p. 21 *sqq.*; and C. Conti Rossini's '*Note per la storia letteraria abissina*': *Rendiconti della R. Accademia dei Lincei, Classe di scienze morali, storiche e filologiche*, Vol. VIII (Roma 1900), p. 197 *sqq.*].

([2]) Europeans have been made better acquainted with this language through Isenberg's '*Dictionary of the Amharic Language*', London 1841, and '*Grammar of the Amharic Language*', London 1842. [V. now also Praetorius, '*Die Amharische Sprache*', Halle 1879; Guidi, '*Grammatica elementare della*

manifold forms is spoken, or at least understood, in Shoa and in all the district lying between Takazzē and Abāwī. On the other hand the language spoken in the Tigrē country has retained the nearest resemblance to Ethiopic ([1]).

The name, *Ethiopic Language*, which the old national speech of Abyssinia commonly bears among us now, is derived from the classical denomination given to the inhabitants of these regions, and has been taken over from the Greek by the Abyssinians themselves. Accordingly they called their kingdom **ኢትዮጵያ**, and the national tongue **ልሳነ ፡ ኢትዮጵያ**. The original native appellation for the people, however, and farther for their speech, is **ግዕዝ**, literally "*roaming*", then as a national designation, in the sense of "*the Roamers*", "*the Free*"; and thus comes **ልሳነ ፡ ግዕዝ** "*the tongue of the Free*" ([2]). Its Name.

§ 2. In origin and essence Ethiopic is a pure Semitic speech, transplanted by people who migrated from Yemen to Abyssinia. In its sounds and laws of sounds, in its roots, inflectional expedients and word-forms, in all that is reckoned the structure and essence of a language, it bears throughout a genuine and uncorrupted Semitic stamp ([3]). All its roots may be pointed out as recurring in the other Semitic languages, especially in Arabic, although often diverging greatly in form, or preserved merely in a fragmentary condition. From the indigenous languages of these African regions only a very few names of plants and animals have been taken; while the names of the months,—which Ludolf imagined to have come from the same stock,—appear to be of decidedly Semitic origin. True, the Geʿez people learned a few stray things, about matters so external as writing, from the Greeks, with whom the Abyssinians had dealings in times even before Christ, and with whom they continued in uninterrupted intercourse Origin and Character.

---

lingua Amariña', Roma 1889; D'Abbadie, '*Dictionnaire de la langue Amariñña*', Paris 1881 and Guidi, '*Vocabolario amarico-italiano*', Roma 1901.]

([1]) [*Cf.* E. Littmann, '*Die Pronomina im Tigre*': *Zeitschr. f. Assyriologie* XII, pp. 188*sqq.*; 291*sqq.*; '*Das Verbum der Tigresprache*', *ibid.* XIII, p. 133*sqq.*, XIV, p. 1*sqq.*; and Nöldeke, '*Die semitischen Sprachen*', 2nd ed. Leipzig 1899, p. 71*sq.*]

([2]) V. Ludolfi '*Historia Aethiopica*', lib. I, cap. 1, 4, & cap. 15, 3.

([3]) Praetorius tries to point out Hamitic elements in the Ethiopic Lexicon: ZDMG XLIII, p. 317*sqq.*

up to the Mohammedan conquest of Egypt. From the Greeks also they borrowed several names and several terms of art, which passed into the flesh and blood of the language. In a similar way a number of pure Aramaic and Arabic words were adopted into it through intercourse with the Arabs, Jews and Aramaeans. But the entire sum of these contributions does not exceed the ordinary proportion of borrowed words which prevails in other languages maintained otherwise in purity. Ethiopic, from its very start, was protected against such a considerable infusion of foreign elements as we see in Syriac, by the superior richness of its vocabulary, and by the long-continued activity of the faculty of formation possessed by the language, which enabled it to produce equivalent Ethiopic expressions for notions of every kind, however abstract they might be. On the other hand the language kept itself at the same time, as regarded its structure, quite free from Greek influences. Even its Syntax, which in its flexibility, variety and marvellous faculty for co-ordinating and subordinating long phrases in one whole, so remarkably resembles Greek syntax, proves on closer investigation to be founded merely upon a very rich development, and skilful handling, of original Semitic grammatical expedients and formative tendencies. It must, of course, be granted that this peculiar leaning in the Ethiopic language to grandiose periods and bold arrangements of words was confirmed by the familiarity of Abyssinian authors with Greek(1) works, and was thereby stimulated to a more manifold development of its several tendencies.

Close Affinities with Arabic:— Resemblances and Differences.

§ 3. Of Semitic languages Arabic is the one with which Ethiopic has the most numerous and close affinities (2). Nothing else could have been expected, when regard is had to the derivation of the Abyssinian Semites from Southern Arabia, and to the active intercourse which they long maintained with it. This relationship is at once and clearly betrayed by marks like the following:—in the alphabetical system—the division of the old Semitic

(1) V., however, Praetorius, '*Grammatik der Tigriñasprache*', Halle 1871, p. 2, *Rem.*

(2) V., on the other hand, Haupt, '*J. Am. Or. Soc.*', Vol. XIII, p. CCLII *sqq.*, according to whose opinion Ethiopic, of all the Semitic languages, stands nearest to Assyrian.

ח and צ each into two separate sounds; in the structure of words and inflections—the frequent endings in a short vowel, the greater multiplicity of conjugational forms in the Verb, and the fuller development of Quadriliteral and Multiliteral roots,—the Inner Plural or Collective formation in the Noun, the regular distinguishing of the Accusative, as also of the Indicative and Subjunctive in the Imperfect, the capability of attaching two Pronominal suffixes to one verb, and a host of other scattered and subordinate phenomena; in the vocabulary—an unmistakeable array of roots which are elsewhere developed or preserved in Arabic only, and not in the more northerly Semitic languages.

And yet Ethiopic is far from being a mere dialect of Arabic, especially if we understand by that the ordinary Literary or Middle Arabic. In fact the vocabularies of the two present a very peculiar contrast, in respect that Ethiopic usually employs altogether different words and roots from Arabic, for the expression of precisely those notions and objects which are most frequently met with in common life (1), while *vice versâ* the words and roots, usual in Arabic in such cases, are found in Ethiopic in scattered traces only. Then the most of the Prepositions and Conjunctions are quite different in the two, with the exception of a few which are common to all the Semitic tongues. In the structure of its syllables Ethiopic has not developed the richness in Vowels which characterises Arabic, or else it has lost it again: in this respect it comes nearer to Hebrew. As regards its roots, it has, in opposition to all the other Semitic languages, very strongly-marked phonetic changes and transpositions, and it occupies quite a peculiar and unique position in the Semitic family through the evolution of the *u*-containing Gutturals and Palatals. Ethiopic never attained to the copious wealth of Forms possessed by Arabic, although it is certain that it had a greater number of forms in earlier times. In particular, Diminutives and Augmen-

(1) Compare the words for:—*God*, *Man* (Homo), *Man*, *Woman*, *Body*, *Sight*, *Earth*, *Land*, *Town*, *King*, *Animal*, *Sun*, *Moon*, *Day*, *Mountain*, *Valley*, *good*, *bad*, *big*, *little*, *much*, *rich*, *poor*, *remaining*; farther for:—*to go*, *to reach*, *to turn back*, *to follow*, *to send*, *to forsake*, *to fall*, *to sit down*, *to dwell*, *to flee*, *to carry*, *to will*, *to call*, *to command*, *to write*, *to seek*, *to finish*, *to find*, *to repeat*, *to conquer*, *to say*, *to tell*, *to act*, *to rejoice*, *to love*, *to burn*, *to build* &c.

tatives are altogether wanting, as well as the Emphatic state ([1]). It farther took a different course from Arabic in the formation of the Imperfect, as well as in Case-formation—with the exception of the Accusative. In the sensitiveness of its vowels to the utterance of a guttural ([2]) it ranges itself with Hebrew rather than with Arabic. It has gone farther than the rest of the Semitic languages in evolving strong roots out of weak ones; and it has developed the formation of the Conjugations in certain directions with more consistency than Arabic itself. And in various other things ([3]) it has kept to a more antique stage than the rest of the Semitic tongues. Ethiopic has no Article, but it has preserved an originality and a fulness in the department of the Pronouns, unmatched by its sister languages. Then it has a host of pronominal particles, of which not a trace is now left in Arabic, while in the perfecting of Enclitics it has followed out an original Semitic bent with a thoroughness which is found nowhere else. In framing Sentences and Periods it has brought into many-sided use expedients and devices, which have long been given up in Arabic, but are still hinted at in Hebrew as belonging to the ancient Semitic speech. As regards its treatment of the Gender of Nouns, it seems to transfer us quite to the original condition of the language, when the settlement of Gender was still in process, and all as yet was fluctuating; nor has it gained any fixity on this point, even in its latest stages. And finally, we come upon many expressions in the vocabulary, which have disappeared from Arabic, at least in the meaning concerned, although they belonged to the original Semitic common-stock ([4]).

([1]) According to D. H. Müller, '*Epigraphische Denkmäler aus Abessinien*', Vienna 1894, p. 72 = '*Denkschriften d. k. Akad. d. Wiss., phil.-hist. Classe*' XLIII, III—these conditions are to be explained by the influence of the Hamitic tongues upon Ethiopic.

([2]) *Cf.* König, '*Neue Studien über Schrift, Aussprache und allgemeine Formenlehre des Aethiopischen*', Leipzig 1877, p. 137.

([3]) König classes along with these (*ibid.* p. 87 *sq.*) the Imperfect-form **ይነግር**, the endings **ከ**, **ኪ**, **ኩ** in the Verb, and the Feminine formation of Adjectives like **ሐዲስ**, **ሐዳስ**; v. *infra* §§ 92, 129, 135.

([4]) **እሳት** (אֵשׁ), **ዕፅ** (עֵץ), **እብን** (אֶבֶן), **ወርኅ** (יֶרַח) (تأريخ), **ምት** (מְתִים), **ረሲዕ** ([illegible]) (רָשָׁע), **ምጥቀት** (מֶתֶק), **ትማልም** (תְּמוֹל), **መንሱት**

All this leads to the conclusion that Ethiopic, after its separation from the Northern Semitic, pursued a common course with Arabic for some time longer, but parted company with it at a pretty early date and at a time in fact when Arabic had not yet attained to its present luxuriance in forms, nor yet to its strictly regular, inflexible, stiff monotony. Ethiopic in this way saved a good deal of the old Semitic, which Arabic suffered to decay, and it also developed a portion of it in a wholly different manner from Arabic. The most of its force, however, subsequent to its severance from the rest of the Semitic languages, was applied to the elaboration of a multiplicity in the methods of conjoining and arranging words in a sentence,—answering to the multiplicity existing in the possible modes of thought and discourse,—and to the development of the pronominal section of the roots which specially conveys the more subtle relations and conditions of thought.

§ 4. In contrast, however, with the antique character of Ethiopic—in various respects truly remarkable,—stand a large number of decidedly later modes of formation and expression, in which we see it coinciding with languages that have reached an advanced stage of development, like Aramaic. In this reference we attach no particular importance to the softening of the pronunciation of one or two Semitic sounds, such as Gutturals and Sibilants, inasmuch as that process appears to have predominated only in the course of the Middle Ages, and is a phenomenon illustrated contemporaneously in other Semitic dialects, though it has gone farthest in Amharic. But our statement is borne out by the fact that Ethiopic has given up, or replaced by external formations, many old forms and inner formations, which once it must have had, as well as by the fact that, alongside of the old forms and formations which it retains, it has admitted several new and more external ones, mainly with the view of attaining thereby to a greater freedom in the structure of its periods. It has entirely given up the Dual both in Verb Development of the Language.

(מַסָּה), ወግር (יָגַר), እስኪት (אֶשֶׁךְ), ዐመፃ (חָמַם), ሰከበ (שָׁכַב), ኀየለ (חַיִל), ነሥአ (נָשָׂא), ከሀለ (כָּהֵל,יָכֹל), ወፅአ (יָצָא), አልመደ (לָמֵד), ሰፈረ (סָפַר), ነገፈ (נָגַף), ወረወ (יָרָה), አውሰበ (הוֹשִׁיב) (وثب), ጠቅዐ (תָּקַע), ፈረየ (פָּרָה) (فرى), ጠየቀ (דַּיֵּק) (ذاق), and several others.

and Noun, just like Aramaic. Towards the formation of Nouns and Inner Plurals it has manifestly at one time possessed a greater number of forms, but owing to a certain economy, abundantly noticeable too in other matters, it has put many of them aside as being unnecessary. Even in the Verb this frugality is shown, so that only a few verbs make use of more than four Conjugations (Stems), while the most of them do not use even so many. A special Passive voice is no longer met with; and its place is supplied by the Reflexive, just as in Syriac. The Active Participle, in the simple Conjugation (Stem) at least, has almost disappeared: in the derived conjugations it is more frequently formed to be sure, but still not regularly, and it is very often lengthened by an external Adjective-ending. Upon the whole the place of the Participle is taken either by Conjunctional Periphrasis or by some other grammatical device. The simple Adjective-formation has greatly decayed. On the other hand the formation of words by external addition through prefixes and suffixes, and the formation of derived Substantives and Adjectives, have gained ground. Ethiopic, as we know it, has the capacity of forming Adjectives from all possible Nouns by means of added terminations, of deriving many Abstracts by means of endings, and of advancing Collectives to be Nouns of bulk by means of external plural-endings. Even from Nouns that had been formed by means of external increase, it derives new Verbs, still preserving the additions found in the Nominal formation, and it has allowed the external formation strongly to affect the Infinitive also. To express the Genitive relation it has developed, alongside of the old Construct state, the indication given by an external Genitive sign, just like Aramaic. The roundabout expression of the Genitive and Accusative relations by means of a pronoun appended to the governing word, followed by a preposition having reference thereto,—is quite as often met with in Ethiopic as in Syriac, and at the same time it serves in most cases to compensate for the Article. The use of a pronoun affixed to the verb, with a dative signification, has become very common. Then along with the early Semitic form and method of conjoining words in the sentence, ample occupation has been found for Prepositions and Conjunctions in this endeavour. And, —to come back once more to the sounds of the language,— the disappearance of the short *i* and *u*, and the dissolving of all the short vowels, except *ă*, into the most undefined and characterless of all the vowels, viz. the short *ĕ*, constitute a phenomenon not indeed original, but still very ancient, in the Ethiopic speech.

Consequently much that is old and much that is new lie here together, sometimes strangely mingled: Things which in other languages are allotted to different stages of growth or to different dialects are met with in Ethiopic side by side. We may therefore conclude that Ethiopic, as it presents itself to us in its literature, has a long period of development behind it, and that the people who once spoke it attained in early times to a high degree of culture. Moreover the people who produced such an admirable and majestic style of sentence with the implements of Semitic speech must have been endowed with great intellectual genius and logical gifts.

Changes in its Phonetic System and Vocabulary.

§ 5. It would be a highly desirable advantage for us of course, to be better acquainted with the language during the time when it was thus coming into being, and to be able to follow it up throughout its various stages of development. But just as in most other languages, so also in this, such an advantage is denied us. The most ancient of the larger monuments of Ethiopic which we have, viz. the two long Axumite inscriptions, made known by E. RÜPPELL (1)—barely reach back to the end of the 5th century of our era. Certainly other shorter inscriptions from Axum and other places exist, and have been to some extent noticed already in books of travel (2), being of still older date than those first-mentioned,—to judge from the form of their letters: they are, however, both too short and too inaccurately copied to enable us to deduce much from them. Lastly, the Minao-Sabaic monuments, which in quite recent times were discovered in great quantities, exhibit to us a language that, in spite of the agreement in alphabetical character, diverges greatly from Ethiopic, and furnish us

(1) In the Supplement to his '*Travels*' printed 1838—40; v. notice of the work in ZDMG VII, p. 338 *sqq*. [V. also D. H. MÜLLER, '*Epigraphische Denkmäler aus Abessinien*'.]

(2) V. the Travels of SALT AND LORD VALENTIA: One of the Inscriptions mentioned there has been republished in ISENBERG's '*Dictionary of the Amh. Lang.*, p. 209. [V. also C. CONTI ROSSINI, '*L'iscrizione dell' obelisco presso Matarà: Rendiconti della R. Accad. dei Lincei* Vol. V (Roma 1896) p. 250 *sqq*.]

with a proof that the last-named language parted company in very early times with its sister languages of Southern Arabia. Thus it comes that we have not the means of acquainting ourselves with the condition of the Abyssinian national speech in times anterior to the conversion of the country to the Christian faith. And it is only from stray internal evidence, as for instance from the occasional appearance still, with the Noun, of the Suffix Pronoun of the 1st Pers. Sing. *i*, instead of a later *(e)ya*,—from the retention of *ĕ* (אִי) in a few Interrogative Particles, or the Negative *ĕn* (אִין),—and such other things,—that we are able to conclude that Ethiopic in its earliest period of development had a much closer affinity with Hebrew than appears in the later form of the language. For this very reason we need not wonder that the deciphering of the Minao-Sabaic inscriptions yielded many remarkable analogies between that dialect and Hebrew.

Altogether Ethiopic appears at the beginning of its last thousand years of existence as already a full-grown language, which experienced only a few alterations as time went on. The principal changes which it underwent during that period concern on the one hand its phonetic system, particularly in the pronunciation of its vowels, and on the other its vocabulary, and the continuance in use, or the falling out of use, exhibited by one or two Word-forms. In the first reference we hold that not earlier than during that period can the softening of the pronunciation of many Consonants have become so marked and so general,—that many peculiarities in the relation of Gutturals to Vowels are of comparatively late origin,—and that many words and forms have exchanged a fuller and more original Vowel-pronunciation for one more faint and faded. We cannot, it is true, obtain proof for what has been advanced, from a comparison of the Inscriptions with the later literary language, because these inscriptions have themselves only defective and occasionally fluctuating vowel-signs (¹) (§ 12 *sq.*); but the most ancient Manuscripts which we possess, dating from the 13th and 14th centuries onwards, place in our hands evidence of every kind to support those propositions; and we may infer that if we ever came upon Manuscripts belonging

(¹) [This view, however, is not confirmed by the accurate copies which we now possess: The Axumite Inscriptions are fully vocalised.]

to any of the six or seven earlier centuries, such evidence would flow in upon us still more copiously. The details of these questions will be explained farther on, in the Grammar itself.

As regards the other point, all truly careful investigation of old Texts, up to the oldest, and their various readings, proves that many forms and words, and meanings of single words, though in use in earlier days, fell into disuse as time went on, and were replaced by new ones,—also and specially, that Arabic words, which were rarely employed in the language of literature, but were quite intelligible to the people, streamed in again more abundantly in the days of lively intercourse with Arabic-speaking populations and tribes, or through the medium of books translated from Arabic (1).

Ethiopic Literature. Modern Investigations.

§ 6. The language was cultivated for literary purposes mainly in the service of religion and of the Church. The large majority of the extant writings are of ecclesiastical character. These had their basis in the versions of the Books of the Old and New Testaments, in the widest acceptation of the word, which versions were followed forthwith by the translation, or even the independent elaboration, of a series of theological and liturgical works. Beyond question all native authors, in their methods of thought and statement, were dependent more or less on Scripture models. After the Mohammedan conquest of Egypt, and following the cultivation of an Arabic Christian literature, it was in their turn these Arabic models by which Ethiopic authors let themselves be swayed. The language at that time found varied application in setting forth historical, legal, chronological and mathematical material. Many original works of the most diverse kinds were produced in the latest period of prosperity enjoyed

(1) In neither of these points referred to has much been done hitherto for the investigation of Ethiopic. Ludolf paid no attention whatever to such historical examination of the language, and represented many things which are ancient and divergent as being mere copyists' errors. So too Thomas Pell Platt, in the edition of the N. T. which he prepared for the English Bible Society (London 1830) [reprinted at Leipzig 1899], disregarded this point of view. As for myself I have devoted special attention to this matter in my editions of Texts, as the Apparatus Criticus found in them will show, but I must express the wish that others who edit Texts would do the same thing.

by the speech and the nation, namely from 1300 to 1600 A. D., among which incontestably the most important are the great native Chronicles. Mohammedan Magic-books also, and writings on Astrology and Medicine, gained entrance among the people about the time when barbarism and darkness crept over them. Poetry was always cherished by the Ethiopians with special predilection, but almost exclusively in the service of religion, so far as we yet know. The great Service Hymn-books of the seventh and following centuries are fine poetical productions, but constructed very decidedly on the model of the Psalms. Later on, Sacred Poetry degenerates into an innumerable quantity of *Encomia* of Saints—men and women,—and proportionately sinks in intrinsic value. Unfortunately this department of Ethiopic literature has hitherto been very little enquired into; yet this much we can even now see,—that an artistic Metric had never been developed in it; the farthest that was reached in the evolution of orderly form was the articulating of verse in symmetrical strophes, accompanied with rhyme,—for the matter of that often enough very imperfect.

The Ethiopic language has never had native grammarians, as far as yet known; and this circumstance sufficiently explains why one or two phenomena in it,—like, for instance, the Conjugational-formation (Stem) and Imperfect-formation of several derived Conjugations (Stems), or the treatment of the Gender of Nouns—, continued to the last so fluctuating and irregular.

Attempts at Ethiopic-Amharic Dictionaries were made in abundance, it is true, about the time the speech was dying out, but they are all very crude, and do not occupy themselves with the grammatical part of the language.

In Europe people began to interest themselves in Ethiopic, in the 16th century. Besides the Abyssinian TESFA-ZION and his associates, who published the N. T. at Rome in 1548,—and to some extent even before him,—it was JOHN POTKEN of Cologne, MARIANUS VICTORIUS of Reate, JO. SCALIGER, TH. PETRAEUS and J. G. NISSELIUS, JAC. WEMMERS at ANTWERP, and lastly EDMUND CASTELL, who rendered meritorious services to Ethiopic in various degrees, partly by printing some of the shorter Texts, and partly by grammatical and lexical endeavours (1). A more comprehensive

(1) *Cf.* also: '*Chaldaeae seu Aethiopicae linguae Institutiones: nunquam*

and exact acquaintance with the tongue we owe first, however, to the immortal services of JOB LUDOLF(1), who published the *first* edition of his '*Grammatica Aethiopica*', 4to, in 1661, and the *second* edition, folio, in 1702, the latter being still useful. A second and indispensable help was added in his '*Lexicon Aethiopico-Latinum*', the second edition of which, folio, was printed at Frankfort-on-the-Maine in 1699. Inasmuch as LUDOLF in his labours had the advantage of being tutored by a born Ethiopian,—GREGORY,—at a time when Ethiopic was still tolerably well understood in Abyssinia, we must take his facts as the groundwork for all which relates to Pronunciation. It deserves to be kept in view, however, that the facts referred to, justify conclusions merely for the pronunciation of Ethiopic common in later times, and are not to be relied upon throughout. In every other point the labours of LUDOLF have long outlived their sufficiency. Judged from the present position of philology they can no longer be regarded as satisfactory in any single part. During the 150 years that have elapsed since LUDOLF's day, the furtherance of our knowledge of Ethiopic has been almost wholly neglected both in Germany and in the rest of Europe. At the most a few printed texts have been revised or simply re-issued, and an occasional reference to Ethiopic has been made here and there in Hebrew Grammars and Dictionaries(2). In 1825 H. HUPFELD gave(3) a certain impulse

antea a Latinis visae, opus utile ac eruditum. Item,—Omnium Aethiopiae regum qui ab inundato terrarum orbe usque ad nostra tempora imperarunt Libellus: hactenus tam Graecis quam Latinis ignoratus, nuper ex Aethiopica translatus lingua'. And at the end: '*Impressit omnia quae in hoc libro continentur, ex primatum licentia* VALERIUS DORICUS BRIXIEN, *opera* ANGELI DE OLDRADIS. *Romae. Anno natali Christi M.D.L.II.* 4o. [For the first printed text of the Psalms (in 1513), and of the N. T. *v.* also GUIDI, '*La prima stampa del Nuovo Testamento in Etiopico fatta in Roma nel* 1548—1549', in Vol. IX of the *Archivio della R. Società Romana di Storia patria*, Rome 1886.]

(1) [*Cf.* J. FLEMMING, '*Hiob Ludolf: Ein Beitrag zur Geschichte der orientalischen Philologie*' in *Beiträge zur Assyriologie*, Vol. I, 1890, p. 537 *sqq.* and Vol. II, 1894, p. 63 *sqq.*]

(2) The '*Grammatica Aethiopica conscripta*' *a* JO. PHIL. HARTMANNO, Frankfort a. M. 1707, 4to is a poor epitome of LUDOLF's work; nor has learning been advanced by J. G. HASSE's '*Handbuch der arabischen und äthiopischen Sprache*', Jena 1793.

(3) In a paper written in early youth '*Exercitationes Aethiopicae*'

to the resumption of grammatical labours in the field of our language, without, however, this start having been followed up either by himself or others. Some valuable contributions to Ethiopic phonology have been furnished by H. TUCH (1); and many excellent hints on isolated phenomena in the Ethiopic language are found in the latest edition of EWALD's '*Ausführliches Lehrbuch der hebräischen Sprache*' (2).

Lips. 1825, 4⁰. The chief merit of this paper lies in pointing out the true distinction between the first and the second Conjugations (Stems) of the Verb, which LUDOLF had entirely mistaken. As to what HUPFELD has advanced about the Ethiopic pronouns in his treatise '*Semitische Demonstrativbildung*' in the 2nd vol. of the *Zeitschr. f. d. K. d. Morg.*, it appears to me in many respects untenable. DRECHSLER's work '*De Aethiopicae linguae conjugationibus*', Lipsiae 1825, has complicated rather than amended LUDOLF's theory of Stem-formation: the sole value it possesses belongs to its collection of supporting-passages for a series of verbal forms.

(1) I. '*Commentatio de Aethiopicae linguae sonorum proprietatibus quibusdam*', Lips. 1854; II. '*De Aethiopicae linguae sonorum sibilantium natura et usu*', Lips. 1854.

(2) [V. now, particularly A. DILLMANN's '*Lexicon linguae Aethiopicae cum indice Latino*', Lips. 1865, as well as F. PRAETORIUS' *Aethiopische Grammatik mit Paradigmen, Litteratur, Chrestomathie und Glossar*' = '*Porta linguarum Orientalium*'.—inchoavit J. H. PETERMANN, *continuavit* HERM. L. STRACK,—Pars VII, Leipzig 1886.]

PART FIRST.

ORTHOGRAPHY AND PHONOLOGY.

As the Ethiopic alphabetic Character differs completely in form and in kind from that of the other known Semitic tongues, the subject itself invites us to begin with a description of that Character.

I. ORTHOGRAPHY.

§ 7. The Ethiopic Character has been fashioned, by a series of more or less important alterations, from the Minao-Sabaic character, or one resembling it, and together they represent the Southern branch of the alphabetical systems, into which the original Semitic alphabet was very early divided. The opinion of earlier scholars, that the Ethiopic Character was of Greek origin (1), must now be regarded as completely set aside. The characters of the Abyssinian Inscriptions are either identical with the Minao-Sabaic, or so like them that there can be no manner of doubt about their derivation (2). The changes which the Minao-Sabaic

Minao-Sabaic Origin of the Alphabetic Characters.

(1) V. on this point Hupfeld, *Exercitationes Aeth.* p. 1–4 and Kopp, '*Bilder und Schriften der Vorzeit*'. Ludolf too inclined to this view, but still he thought that the 'inventor' had had an eye also on the Samaritan alphabet, therein showing a correct apprehension of the Semitic origin of this Character (*Hist.* IV, 1. *Comment.* p. 60, 555).

(2) As to the literature, *cf.* E. König, '*Neue Studien über Schrift, Aussprache, und allgemeine Formenlehre des Aethiopischen, aus den Quellen geschöpft, comparativ und physiologisch erläutert*'. Leipzig 1877 [in what follows, quoted as "König"]. Farther, Schlottmann in Riehm's HWB p. 1420*sqq.*'; Derenbourg, '*Journ. as.*' VII, 19, p. 375*sqq.*; Frdr. Müller, '*Ueber den Ursprung der himjarisch-äthiopischen Schrift*', Vienna 1869 [and D. H. Müller,

form of writing has undergone in Abyssinia are manifold, and will be farther described by-and-by; but they are not so marked as to prevent us from recognising without difficulty the ancient Minao-Sabaic characters in the ordinary Ethiopic ones, independently even of the intervention of the Ethiopic Inscriptions (*cf.* Table I). The character, like the speech itself, and even more decidedly, has kept to a very antique stage. Both in print, and as a rule in Manuscripts, it is inscribed with large, firmly impressed strokes; and the older the manuscripts, the more pronounced is this feature.

Number of the Consonants.

§ 8. I. Like all the other Semitic forms of writing, the Ethiopic is originally consonantal. The number and the order of these consonants are not the same, however, in this language as in the others. Farther, the names given them are here and there peculiar.

(1) In *Number* the Ethiopic Consonants are *six-and-twenty*, — four more than in the Northern Semitic tongues. Two of these four are accounted for by dividing, in two cases, a sound that once was single into two modes of pronunciation. The strong Guttural ח was divided, just as among the Arabs, into the two sounds ሐ (ح), and ኀ (خ); and in the same way the sibilant צ was divided into ጸ (ص) and ፀ (ض). Other divisions, peculiar to the Arabs, of sounds originally one into two, viz. ת into ت and ث, ד into د and ذ, and ט into ط and ظ, are unknown to the Ethiopians, though perhaps the Minao-Sabaeans had them. On the other hand the Abyssinians possess two additional sounds, which were not admitted into Arabic, viz,— a hard, peculiarly-formed Labial (§ 28) ጰ = *p*; and one that answers more to the usual *p*,—that is ፐ, mostly employed in foreign words. Besides these 26 characters, Amharic letters appear, it is true, in Ethiopic books, when foreign words

---

'*Epigraphische Denkmäler aus Abessinien*', p. 69; M. Lidzbarski, '*Ephemeris für semitische Epigraphik*' I, p. 109*sqq.*, II, p. 23*sqq.*; and Praetorius, ZDMG LVIII (1904), p. 715*sqq.*]. On the earlier theory of the connection of the Ethiopic alphabet with the *Indian*, cf. Salt, '*Voyage to Abyssinia*' (1814), p. 415; Lepsius, '*Zwei sprachvergleichende Abhandlungen*' (1836), p. 76*sq.* and Deeke, ZDMG XXXI, p. 598; on the opposite side, Dowson, '*J. Roy. As. Soc.*' XIII (1881), pt. 1.—Completely astray is the account given in J. Bird's '*Sur l'origine de l'alphabet Himiarite et de l'alphabet Éthiopien*' in '*Nouvelles annales des voyages*', Paris 1845, Vol. II, p. 196*sqq.*

or native proper names from the various Abyssinian dialects have to be written with greater exactness, but these do not concern us here (¹).

§ 9. (2) The *Names* of these alphabetical characters and sounds are essentially the same as among the other Semites, and have manifestly been taken over along with the alphabet (²). Some of them have been so far altered as to conform to the Ethiopic expression or word in use, without the original sense of the Name being affected; a few others remain only in a corrupt form and without any clear meaning. In particular, *Alf*, *Bēt*, *Geml*, *Kāf*, *ʿAin* directly coincide with the old names: *Qāf* is to be understood for *Qōf*, according to § 18; *Tait* and *Ṣadai* rest upon the resolution of the diphthong *ē* into *ai*: *Reʾes* is the ordinary Ethiopic word for "head", *Māi*, for "water": the old name *Yod* was not available, because the Ethiopic word for "hand" was rather **እዴ·**, and it was accordingly replaced suitably by *Yaman* "right hand": for a like reason *Nun* "fish", which word is not in use in Ethiopic, has been exchanged for a word of like meaning *Nahās* "serpent"; in this way in the last two cases the starting sounds *y* and *n* have been properly preserved. But when the Ethiopians exchanged *Pē* "mouth" for *Af* which is their word for "mouth", then the general rule,—according to which the commencing sound in the name must be the same as the sound of the character,—was set at nought, and a clear proof was given at the same time that the Ethiopic name is not the original one. For *Waw* and *Taw* the Ethiopians, in accordance with § 38, say *Wawe*, *Tawe*. For *Ḥēt* they prefer to use an Arabic word, but of the same meaning, *Ḥauṭ* (حَوْط), and for its sister-sound they have created a new name of like meaning, *Ḫarm* (חֵרֶם حَرْم) "hedge" (³). On the other hand *Zai*,

Names of the Consonants.

(¹) [For the benefit of students, however, these letters have been added on Table I. TR.]

(²) On the names of the Ethiopic Consonants among the Abyssinians of to-day, consisting each of an Ethiopic word, which starts with the sound designated, *e. g.* **ነ ነሖእ· ገ ገብረ· ዐ ዐሐዩ** *cf.* PRAETORIUS, '*Amhar. Spr.*' § 1*b* and ZDMG XLI. p. 687. [*Cf.* farther, on the names of the Ethiopic Letters, NÖLDEKE, '*Die semitischen Buchstabennamen*' in '*Beitr. z. Semit. Sprachwissenschaft*', Strassburg 1904, p. 131*sqq.* TR.]

(³) [NÖLDEKE ('*Beitr. z. semit. Sprachw.*' p. 133) rejects this explanation

Dent (v. GESENIUS, '*Thes.*' p. 727, and *infra* § 32) and still more strongly *Lawe*, properly *Law*,—seem to have been corrupted from *Zain*(1), *Dalt* and *Lamed* respectively: These three names have no longer any meaning in Ethiopic. *Hōi* is just as obscure a name as *Hē*, with which it appears to be identical. The most obscure names, however, continue to be *Šaut* and *Sāt* instead of *Shin* and *Samech:* the most probable explanation is that they are imitations of the outward form of the names *Ḥaut* and *Bēt*, to the characters of which their own present a resemblance. *Ṣappā*(2) (originally *Ḍappā*) I compare with ضَبَّة "a bolt", which is quite appropriate to the ancient form of the character. *Pait* is a name formed in imitation of *Ṭait*, next to which it stands in the Alphabet; and *Pa* is the Greek *Pi*: Moreover, the name of the last-mentioned character was once given with a slight sibilation,—*Psa*.

Order of the Ethiopic Alphabet. § 10. (3) Of more importance, however, than its divergence from the Northern-Semitic Alphabet in the Names of the Consonants, is the divergence of the Ethiopic alphabet in the *Order* in which they stand. The Hebrew order of the characters is, as we know, very ancient; but we do not know how ancient the Ethiopic order may be, nor even whether the Minao-Sabaeans had the same order. We are not justified in contending right off that the Hebrew order is the original, and the Ethiopic the derived one. It may, on the other hand, with some reason be thought that during the times which followed the invention and spread of the Alphabet different orders of the letters came into vogue, being definitely arranged in different ways in different regions. And in fact, on closer investigation of the order of the Ethiopic Alphabet, one peculiarity in it appears to yield the inference that that order may well be very ancient, and other orders compared with it be decided innovations (3). The Northern-Semitic alphabet, as is well

---

of the name *Ḥarm*, remarking that حَرْم begins with ح and not with خ, and does not mean "hedge". He says the name rather suggests a connection with ኀርመት "a small stroke". TR.]

(1) Although it should be noticed that the Greeks have no nasal sound either, in the name of their letter ζῆτα (v. HUPF. p. 2).

(2) Certainly not an imitation of *Kappa*, as GESENIUS in 'ERSCH *und* GRUBER's *Encyclopädie*' would have it.

(3) *Cf.* BÖHMER, ZDMG XVI, p. 579.

known, falls according to the *Atbash* (1) into two series of 11 letters each (2). In exactly the same way the Ethiopic alphabet, after the new sounds ጰ and ፐ have been withdrawn, divides into twice 12 letters, *Hōi* to *Nahās* and *Alf* to *Af*. The number 12 results from the circumstance that in each of these 2 rows a new, Arabic-Ethiopic sound is inserted, ኀ in the first, and ፀ in the second. The remarkable fact then reveals itself at once that the second Ethiopic row corresponds essentially to the first Hebrew one, and the first Ethiopic to the second Hebrew; and in this we find an indication (3) that in very ancient times the Alphabet might commence with either row.

Within the two rows, however, the succession of the individual letters with the Ethiopians differs widely from the Hebrew arrangement. Doubtless this is partly the result of innovation, but partly it may be of ancient origin. Generally speaking we find again in the Ethiopic Alphabet the same principles of arrangement which regulated the Hebrew one, and which operated also in giving form to the Alphabet of Arabic. In their case, as well as here, considerations turned in part upon the nature of the sounds, in part upon the form and similarity of the characters and names. (1) The similarity of the characters,—which was still more striking in the oldest script,—brought about the juxtaposition of ወ and ዐ. የ and ደ, አ and ከ, and finally of ኀ and ነ, ጰ and ጸ. (2) This juxtaposing of ወ and ዐ had as a consequence the shifting of ሀ into the first row; and this last letter, as the guttural corresponding to *Alf*, was placed at the beginning of the first row, just as አ begins the second. Then again this proceed-

(1) [*Atbash*, of course, is the name of that cipher-system, in which,—for the word or words which have to be disguised—, the first letter of the Hebrew Alphabet is used for the last one, the second for the second last, and so on. Thus we use א for ת, ב for ש and *vice versâ*,—whence the name *Atbash* or *Athbash*. TR.]

(2) V. HITZIG, '*Die Erfindung des Alphabets*', 1840, p. 12 *sq.*—Neither HITZIG, nor any other scholars who have written on this subject, have attempted to explain the order of the Ethiopic Alphabet. [NÖLDEKE, *l. c.* p. 131, N. 1, expresses himself in favour of the view that the Ethiopic order is a derived one.]

(3) Another indication might be found in the Latin expression *elementa*, according to A. F. WOLF's interpretation (ל מ נ). [*Cf.* also ZIMMERN, ZDMG L, p. 669 and N. 3.]

ing occasioned the shifting of ሐ into the first row, and of ጸ into the second, through which arrangement the juxtaposition of the Gutturals in one and the same row was secured. On the other hand ፈ may have changed place with በ, only when it became necessary to attach ፐ to the Ethiopic alphabet, and then ፈ was finally placed at the end of the second row immediately before ፐ. (3) When men had still a clear consciousness of the twofold division of the alphabet, the two Southern-Semitic sounds ኀ and ፀ were added, one to each row, and in fact at the end of each row. In consequence, the letter ጸ came to stand immediately before its sister-sound at the end; and, in accordance with the first of the points of view which are being noticed here, ነ was moved on to ኀ and in fact placed after it, to separate ኀ from አ. (4) Then a regard to the similarity of the sounds operated as a last regulative point of view. People wanted to have similar sounds as close together as possible, and only separated them in the several instances by one letter of a different nature, in order that two which were similar might not directly clash together. In this way ሐ is brought up to ሀ, but is separated from it by ለ; ሰ to ሠ but separated by ረ; ደ to ጠ, separated by ገ; while ጸ and ፀ at one time did not resemble each other in sound so closely as they came to do later. Thus the *first* row,—originally beginning with ለ and ending with ተ,—contains the Liquids ለ መ ነ and ረ, together with the two Sibilants ሰ and ሠ, along with the three Gutturals ሀ ሐ ኀ and the three Mutes ቀ በ ተ (በ in place of original ፈ); and the entire series begins with a guttural corresponding to the *Alf*. This row gives the most clear indications of purposeful arrangement. In the *second* row, as compared with the corresponding Hebrew one, still more violent transpositions are to be noticed. It is only አ ወ ዘ የ which present any likeness to the Hebrew succession. In ገ ጠ ጰ, however, we again meet with three Mutes placed together, and in ጠ ጰ ጸ ፀ with four Explosives.

I have not up till now met with any deviation from the order developed here(¹); yet it is to be noted that POTKEN inter-

(¹) An Ethiopic alphabet is met with in the MS. Add. 16240 of the British Museum; *cf.* DILLMANN, '*Catalogus codicum manuscriptorum Orientalium qui in Museo Britannico asservantur*'; *pars tertia*, Londini 1847, p. 58, No. LXXI.

changed the positions of the 5th and 7th letters ሠ and ሰ,—an alteration which, provided it rest upon a historic basis, might easily be proved to be the better arrangement.

§ 11. II. With regard to *the Form* of the Ethiopic script, it has already been mentioned that all the letters have been fashioned out of forms presented by the Minao-Sabaic; only the character ፐ appears, like its sound, to have been derived from Ψ (or Π?). The letter ኀ was at one time very like ሀ and seems even to have sprung from it in Minao-Sabaic just by a slight alteration. For *Zai* the Abyssinians took the Minao-Sabaic character for *Dsal*. The origin of the character ጰ is still obscure: it might be nearest the mark to recognise in it a new formation from በ or ፈ (in its old form). **Form of the Script. Direction of Writing.**

By and by, however, there occurred with the Abyssinians an important alteration in the old mode of writing,—*for it gradually became the custom to write from left to right.* Among the Minao-Sabaeans the writing as a rule ran from right to left, just as it did among the rest of the Semites, with the exception of the Babylonian-Assyrians; sometimes too the writing was βουστροφηδόν. A few of the older Ethiopic Inscriptions still indicate that the direction from right to left was at one time known also among the Abyssinians; but evidently the example of the Greek mode of writing, which was familiar to the Abyssinians even in pre-Christian times, and especially in Christian times, helped to bring about the gradual establishment of the direction from left to right (1). The practice of writing towards the right had gained prevalence even in the age of RÜPPELL's pair of long Inscriptions; and in books it is met with exclusively.

This gradual change in direction seems to have had no ulterior effect on the form of the characters themselves; the most of them suited either direction. The characters ገ ኘ ከ lend themselves even more readily to the new direction of writing than to the old; only ፈ, instead of its original curve from right to left, took

(1) The common view, that the direction of Ethiopic writing to the right is a pure innovation of the Greek missionaries, cannot be maintained. If the opposite manner of writing had been the only one known and allowed before the Greeks brought their influence to bear, then it would be inconceivable how and why this complete reversal of the old method had been arrived at.

the opposite curve. On the other hand in still early times, when writing came into more frequent use, a different position with respect to the ground-line was assigned to several of the characters, in order to give them a more pleasing and symmetrical appearance(¹), viz., to ለ, መ, ሠ, ተ, ደ, ፈ; farther, the character for ሐ was reversed. Moreover, the essential and distinguishing lines of a few of the letters were brought more distinctly into prominence (as, for instance, with የ and ቀ), while in other cases unessential lines were given up (ኀ and ፈ); and finally all were set at equal height. While sharp corners predominate in almost all the letters of the Minao-Sabaic and ancient Ethiopic script, the natural result of much writing and of consequent efforts to write with greater rapidity was to round these corners off. In this way what took two, three, or more strokes of the pen in old times could be completed in one stroke (as in ሀ ሐ መ ሠ ቀ በ አ ከ ዐ የ ደ ገ ጠ ጸ ፀ): It is only in characters which have broken lines that the sharper angles remain (ነ ኀ), and in ለ and ሰ, because the rounding off of these might have led to their being mistaken for በ and ከ. Even in RÜPPELL's Inscriptions we find this rounding off of the strokes carried out to some extent, although the angular style would have been easier on stone.

Scarcely a start had been made towards binding individual letters into groups of letters. In RÜPPELL's Inscription II, 38, such a group appears to be met with(²); and in Manuscripts too, in the case of the Ethiopic name for God, we come upon the *crasis* of ግ and ዘ into ግዘ, and upon the group ቆ for ቀም, and upon ገየ for ገዘየ &c. But such interlacing is extremely rare and is evidently meant withal for abbreviation (*cf. infra* § 15 N. 2; and § 16 *ad fin.*). Then the peculiar mode of writing the vowels must have set itself against the prevalence of this device (§ 13 *sqq.*). It has thus remained a rule almost without exception, coming down from the most ancient times,—that the several letters of a word be placed beside one another, but independently and without attachment, just as in other old modes of writing.

(¹) The notion of HUPFELD (p. 2),—that the shape of the letters was affected by the Abyssinian style of housebuilding,—is more ingenious than sound. It can have no application in the case of ቀ ሠ መ ዐ የ ደ ገ ፀ.

(²) [This assumption is not confirmed by BENT's accurate copy.]

So much the more it became necessary to separate the several words from one another in some way, if confusion was not to arise. In the Minao-Sabaic. and in the more ancient Ethiopic writing, a perpendicular stroke (|), which is constantly employed in RÜPPELL's Inscriptions, had come into use as a word-divider. This stroke was transformed later on into two points standing the one above the other (፡), which bore the name ነቍጥ "points" among the Ethiopians; they are quite regularly and indeed without exception placed after every complete word([1]). And this method of separating the words,—which prevents all coalescing of different words,—has also made it possible to break up a word at the end of a line when there is no more room, and put the rest of it into the next line. The introduction of the so-called *literae dilatabiles* has therefore become superfluous([2]).

VOWEL DENOTATION.

Vowel Denotation incorporated with Consonantal Script.

§ 12. III. This mode of writing, inherited by the Ethiopians and farther developed in the way pointed out, was originally consonantal, like all the other Semitic systems except the Babylonian-Assyrian. The vowels in Semitic word-formation are exceedingly changeable and shifting; the consonants are the firm, unalterable portion of the word. It was therefore a subtle conception, suited to the genius of the Semitic tongue that, provided the firm and, so to speak, visible and corporeal portion of the word were written, the spiritual and mobile portion might remain without outward sign.

Meanwhile it is well-known that none of the Semitic modes of writing adhered to this their first and simplest stage. In consequence of the want of any vowel-marking, obscurity in many cases supervened, and an endeavour was made at a second stage

([1]) [In the more recent printing of Ethiopic these points (፡) are kept strictly to the function of *separating* one Ethiopic word from another. For instance they are not usually employed now after an Ethiopic word which stands alone, nor even after the last word of an Ethiopic group. TR.]

([2]) On the Abyssinian method of writing the vowels, v. now also HALÉVY, '*Journ. as.*' VIII, 6, pp. 248*sqq.*, 273 and D. H. MÜLLER, '*Epigr. Denkm.*', p. 69*sqq.*

of development to remedy this defect by employing the semivowels (and finer gutturals) as vowel signs for certain long vowels and diphthongs. Then at a third and last stage all vowels were marked by placing various points and strokes above or below the line. Among the Ethiopians also this advance from defectiveness to greater clearness in the writing was gradually effected; but in their case all that concerns this matter was evolved in a quite independent and quite peculiar manner; and the final result was a most complete and accurate system of vowel-marking, which differs entirely from the other Semitic systems, and in some measure resembles more the Indian system.

It is true that the employment of the semivowel characters to make up for long *ī* and *ū*, or for diphthongs compounded of *i* or *u*, was not unfamiliar to the Southern-Semitic tribes; but, compared with the Northern-Semitic systems, the usage was less common. It was only diphthongs that were with comparative regularity written by means of *w* and *y*, while these letters were not usually employed to indicate *ū* or *ī* except at the end of a word(1). Such is the case in the Minao-Sabaic Inscriptions, as well as in the two or three words of the oldest Ethiopic Inscriptions which one can read from existing copies. No proof has yet been given that the finer Gutturals ever came to be used in the South as Vowel signs; and such a use is peculiarly improbable in Ethiopic.

The Ethiopians appear never to have advanced to any more frequent employment of ወ and የ to denote *ū* and *ī*. In the Inscriptions of Rüppell,—which indeed have many other vowel signs,—we nowhere find them used with this object, not even in cases where *ī* and *ū* belong to the root; ኢ is written አ; ዮም, የመ; ሞአ, መአ; ዘሞቱ, ዘመቱ, and so on(2). Only, Diphthongs proper were continually written with a ወ or a የ: and even after the introduction of the new Vowel signs, this style of writing them

(1) Already pointed out by Ewald in Höfer's '*Zeitschrift für die Wissenschaft der Sprache*' I, p. 302, and by Osiander, ZDMG X, p. 35*sq.*

(2) [The recent copies of these Inscriptions show, however, that they carry out thoroughly the ordinary vocalisation; *cf.* above p. 10, N. (1).]— If in I, 1 and II, 2 ብእስየ is met with for the later ብእሲ, that has no bearing upon vowel writing; it merely shows that the construct state of ብእሲ had at one time a fuller sound.

continued in vigorous use, but yet in such fashion that ው and ዩ were with greater accuracy set down instead of the more general ወ and የ.

In all other cases, however, the Ethiopians entirely abandoned this path, pointed out to them by the rest of the Semites,— a path which, however thoroughly followed up, would never have brought them to their goal,— and they struck out another path which rewarded their efforts far better, and gave a notable proof of their genius. Starting from the fundamental conception of Semitic writing,—that the written consonant is a body in which inheres unseen a soul, a vowel, by which alone it becomes audible—, they set to work to indicate the kind of vowel present in the particular consonantal character, by attaching to it small strokes or rings. This device was appropriate and sufficient, and being governed by very exact rules it brought about the development of the original consonantal script into a highly perfected syllabary, which for completeness and effectiveness leaves little to be desired. There are short Ethiopic inscriptions in which no trace of this new mode of denoting the vowels can be detected. In the Inscriptions of Rüppell it makes its appearance already, half-formed (1). Its beginnings must therefore be referred to no later a date than about the fifth century of our era and may go even farther back. Foreign influences are not to be thought of in this matter (2): the invention of the system was the work of the Abyssinian people.

(1) [*Cf.*, however, above, p. 10, N. (1); and p. 24, N. (2).]

(2) De Sacy entertained the singular idea that the Greek vowel-signs somehow served as a model. Then the Syriac new vocalisation-system cannot have any relevance in this matter, seeing that not only is it quite different in its nature but also was just beginning itself to be formed at that remote time. W. Jones, Kopp, and Lepsius ventured a guess at Indian influence, and the last-named would also have derived from the same source the right-hand direction of the writing; but the Indian vowel-writing resembles the Ethiopic only in taking in the short *ă*, while in every other respect it is formed quite differently. Nor can I agree with Weber in what he advances about India borrowing the principle of the Ethiopic mode of denoting the vowels, in his essay "*Ueber den semitischen Ursprung des indischen Alphabets*" (in '*Indische Studien*'). [Perhaps however, Dillmann's complete exclusion of the *possibility* of foreign influence in this matter has not been altogether justified, even by this Note.]

Short ă assumed as present in Consonantal Ground-form.

§ 13. *This new method of denoting the Vowels was carried out in detail as follows.* The ground-vowel, that is to say short *ă*, predominates in Ethiopic just as it does in ancient languages generally. It is to be pronounced in every case except where some other vowel is expressly indicated, and accordingly it needs no special sign. The ground-form of a consonant is conceived as containing the vowel *ă*, and therefore it has always to be pronounced with *ă*, exactly as in the Sanskrit mode of writing.

Discussion of the Indication of Short Vowels other than ă, and of the Absence of a Vowel.

All the more on this ground, however, it became necessary to give some indication of every other vowel, as well as of the absence of a vowel from a consonant. The vowels, other than *ă*, which are found in Ethiopic speech, are the long vowels *ā*, *ī*, *ū*, *ē*, *ō*, and the short *ĕ* which originally inclined sometimes rather to *ĭ*, and sometimes to *ŭ* (v. § 17). Of these the five long vowels were esteemed so important and essential that it appeared necessary to indicate each of them by a special sign. On the other hand the short vowel *ĕ* appeared to stand beneath *ă* in value and in weight, and to be undeserving of a mark of its own. And so, both in cases where *ĕ*, and in cases where no vowel at all had to be given, one sign indicated that here *ă* was not to be used; but whether *ĕ*, or no vowel at all *was* to be used,—had to be determined by the reader's own knowledge. This system, fashioned by and for those who were familiar with the language, might well suffice for Abyssinian readers; and doubtless only a few cases would present any difficulty to them as to the proper reading. But foreigners, who are not masters of the language, and who are just proceeding to acquire it from this very writing, find here no small defect. It is well known how inconvenient in Hebrew writing is the coincidence of the sign for the absence of a vowel and the sign for the weakest vowel-sound, in the *Sh^eva*(1). The same inconvenience is met with in Ethiopic writing. But take along with this the following:—It is impossible that *ĭ* and *ŭ* should originally have been wanting in any language; and thus we are easily led to suppose that the Abyssinians, like others,

---

(1) [This weakest and most rapid vowel-sound, often called by the Germans "*Vocalanstoss*" and corresponding generally to the Hebrew *Sh^eva mobile*, has been spoken of by Bickell as "a *volatilized* Vowel": *cf.* Wright, '*Lectures on the Comp. Gramm. of the Semitic Languages*', Cambridge 1890. It might perhaps be designated '*the fugitive vowel*'. TR.]

distinguished the use of *ĭ* and *ŭ*, in pronunciation at all events though not in writing, while in writing they threw together in one sign the absence of a vowel and these vowels, as being along with *ă* the more trifling ones. But if that had been the case, the Ethiopic mode of writing would have had the farther inconvenience of obliterating the distinction in pronunciation which has been referred to, and we moderns would be faced with the grievous difficulty, in the absence of farther information, of being no longer able to say in the several cases, whether *ĭ* or *ŭ* or *ĕ* was the vowel used in speech. Meanwhile the following is worth consideration: If, when this system of vowel-writing was formed, the distinction of *ŭ* (*ŏ*) and *ĭ* (*ĕ*) had been still as full of life, and as important for the sense and meaning of a word, as perhaps it was in Arabic or even in Hebrew, then it would be inconceivable that this distinction could have been left unindicated in writing. But the case is otherwise if the then existing speech, *i. e.* the Old Ethiopic, had already ceased to make use of this finer discrimination of the short vowels in word-formation and inflection; for then it was not a matter of essential importance, whether one said *ĭ* or *ŭ*. Of course in these circumstances there was no longer any need to attend to the distinction of these short vowels in pronunciation; and the way was clear for the gradual blending of all the short vowels into one indeterminate *ĕ*, which sometimes leant rather to *i*, sometimes to *u*, sometimes to *a*. We do not know how far this decay in the pronunciation of the short vowels had advanced, but assuredly it spread more and more in later times; and in the 16th and 17th centuries the short vowel was very generally rendered as a colourless *ĕ*.

§ 14. In the actual designation of vowels, six different cases had to be distinguished. **Forms of the Consonants to indicate the Presence of the *five* Long Vowels severally.**

(a) The sign for *ā* consists in propping the letter with a small perpendicular stroke, which is meant to give support and continuance, as it were, to the *ă* contained in the letter(1). This prop is usually applied to the right side of the letter (by way of distinction from *o*). (1) If the letter is closed above, and runs out below into two or three unconnected limbs, the prop is attached

(1) *Cf.* the fact that in the Dēvanāgari system long *ā*,—a double *mora* sa it were,—is expressed by adding the stroke ा. A somewhat remoter resemblance is presented by the Greek sign for the acute accent.

to the right limb with the effect of lengthening the same; but, in order to prevent the letter from stretching over the base-line, it is made smaller in size, and so presents the appearance not of having the right limb lengthened, but of having the left limb or limbs shortened (1), thus ላ ሓ ሳ ባ ኣ ካ ዛ ዳ ጣ ጻ ጳ. (2) If the letter has only one foot, this ought properly to be lengthened; but to avoid passing over the base-line, this prolongation turns off at a right angle towards the left (by way of distinction from $\bar{\imath}$). ቃ ታ ኃ ያ ጋ ፓ (2). (3) If the letter is rounded underneath, then it is propped underneath on the right side ሃ ማ ሣ ዓ ፃ; only ወ has the prop in the centre ዋ. (4) Of the two letters which have a horizontal line below, one—ፈ forms its sign for long $\bar{a}$ by assuming a more upright position and by lengthening its middle stroke, ፋ, while the other, ረ, breaks off its horizontal line in an upward direction and attaches the prop to this ራ. (5) Finally, ነ lets the lower portion of its broken line stand for prop, and completes itself by assuming a new line above, ና.

(b) The sign for $\bar{u}$, or for $\bar{\imath}$, consists in a horizontal stroke applied to the right side of the letter, which may be considered as indicating a divergence in the pronunciation,—a turning aside from the straight, open a-sound. The distinction between the signs for $\bar{u}$ and for $\bar{\imath}$ is made patent by applying the stroke to the lower end of the letter to denote $\bar{\imath}$, and to the centre of it to denote $\bar{u}$ (3). (1) The sign for $\bar{u}$ is in all cases attachable without farther difficulty: Only, in the case of ረ the lower line again has to be broken off, but this time in a downward direction, so that the vowel-line, as distinguished from that lower line, may readily catch the eye ሩ (4): In exactly the same way ፉ must be understood. (2) The sign for $\bar{\imath}$ is also of easy attachment to most of the letters: only, in the case of ሂ ሚ ሢ ዊ ዒ ፂ, the ground-forms of which are rounded below, the attachment is effected by means of a small auxiliary line. With ረ and ፈ the divergence in the pronunciation is signified by the turning upwards of the lower line;

(1) As LUDOLF, in fact, incorrectly supposed was the case.

(2) The hook, attached thereto is not an essential part of the letter or sign, but is a mere flourish both here and in other similar cases.

(3) And yet the reverse proceeding would be more natural, for u is the deeper sound, and i the higher.

(4) Very deserving of notice, however, is Ł = $r\bar{u}$ in the Inscriptions.

and with የ, the ī-sign is applied,—perhaps to obviate confusion with ዩ,—by means of an auxiliary line in the centre of the letter, ዪ.

(c) The sign for ē is a development of the ī-sign. The horizontal line, which represents ī, is bent upwards and back into the letter, thus forming a small ring (1), to represent ē = a + i = i + a (§ 40). The mode of attachment is exactly the same as with the stroke for ī; only, in ሬ and ፌ it is simpler than in that case (2).

(d) The sign for ō is twofold. According to one conception ō was an *Ablaut* of ā, and so was at first marked like ā; but a distinction was speedily introduced, according to which in the case of ō the prop was attached to the left side (ሖ ሶ ቦ ኆ ኮ ዎ ዖ ዞ ዶ ጦ ጶ ጾ ፆ), or in the middle (ሞ ሦ); with ፐ the same is to be signified by slanting the foot, ፖ. According to another conception, however, which we meet with even as early as in the Inscriptions, ō, on account of its origin from u and w, has come to be denoted by a small ring applied to the upper part of the letter,—a sort of small ወ, (ሆ ሮ ቆ ቶ ኞ ኖ ፎ); with ሎ it is attached to the centre (though, in the Inscriptions, to the top (3)). But in the case of የ, to avoid attaching two rings together, a simple stroke put at the head (a kind of higher-placed ā-sign) appeared to be sufficient (ዮ); and similarly it seemed enough in the case of ገ to place a stroke perpendicularly on the upper line, which stroke, it may be, was originally meant to carry the small circle (ጎ). Manifestly writers at one time wavered between these two methods of designating ō; but the first seems to have gained the upper hand, and it was only in cases where it could not well be applied that the second method obtained a firm footing.

(e) The signs for short vowels other than ă, and for the want of a vowel meet in a single sign (4), as has already been mentioned. **Forms indicating the Pres-**

(1) This ring might also be explained as an abbreviated የ = የ, particularly as the ring more than once denotes ī in the Inscriptions.

(2) Laurence's Isaiah-Manuscript frequently gives ዐ° as well as ዔ, *e. g.* capp. 22, 20; 27, 4; 37, 35.

(3) [In the earliest MSS., and down to the 15th century, the characteristic form of *lo* is ሎ: *cf.* W. Wright, '*Catalogue of the Ethiopic Manuscripts in the British Museum*', London 1877, p. X.]

(4) The view that this sign signified at first the weakest vowel-sound, and only in the second line the absence of a vowel—is defended by König, p. 58.

ence of a Short Vowel other than ă, or Absence of a Vowel.

This also, like the sign for ō, varies with different letters and has sprung from different conceptions,—a circumstance which is the less to be wondered at here, seeing that the sign has a different value in different cases. In one division of the letters we find an upright line in the letter either broken, or bent in, whether above or below (ህ ል ር ኅ ክ ግ ጥ ፍ ፕ). or set in a sloping position (ስ),—by which devices the complete breaking off of the direct pronunciation, or, in other words, the virtual absence of the vowel, is probably indicated. With other letters, however, a sign, like the one for ū and ī,—that is, a horizontal stroke by the side of the letter—has become established. The one sign must originally have had a like signification with the other, and certainly had been meant to indicate a divergence—a bending away—from the *a*-sound. By way of distinction from the signs for ū and ī, however. it was, as a rule, attached to the left side of the letter, either at the top or in the middle (ሕ ቅ ት ን እ ዝ, ም ብ), but in other cases to the right at the top of the letter (ው ድ ጽ ጵ); with ዕ, ፅ and ሥ it was transformed into a perpendicular line, to save space; and in the case of ይ it was drawn right under the letter. The alphabet was shared between these two methods of designation; and the grounds which led to the one method being adopted in the case of one letter, and the other method in the case of another, were to some extent merely fortuitous, for with ብ, for instance, the same marking might have been looked for as with ክ. But after the vocalisation had become established, the meaning was quite the same, although the sign used might have sprung from the one or the other conception.

In this way seven permanent forms were gradually evolved for every one of the 26 letters, out of very irregular and fluctuating beginnings. In the alphabetic summary the Abyssinians themselves have brought these forms, of seven different kinds, into a definite succession, as is set forth in Table I. Correctly enough they put in the first position the ground-form which is to be pronounced with ă and which they called ግዕዝ *i. e.* the *nature* or *plan* of the rest, from which they were developed. The remaining six forms take their names from their order, ካዕብ *Second* (Form), ሣልስ *Third* &c. The order which in this way they have arranged has, to be sure, little to recommend it. It seems particularly inappropriate to put the form, which indicates ĕ or the want of a vowel, in the sixth place and before the *ō*-form. But perhaps the sixth and seventh forms were assigned their places at the end on historical grounds, because in fact it was known that both these forms were of composite growth, being each of them derived from diverse principles of designation, and that they were the last of all to be reduced to fixed rule.

§ 15. (f) But alongside of these seven forms, possessed by each of the 26 letters, there grew up farther in the case of 4 of the letters 5 new forms for each. As will be explained farther on (§ 26), a special mode of pronunciation was developed with the letters ኀ ቀ ከ ገ, according to which, when they have to be pronounced with an *a*- or an *i*-*e*-sound, a *u* in certain cases thrusts itself between the consonant and the leading vowel. For this *u*-containing pronunciation of the gutturals the perfection of the system demanded special signs. These were developed out of the ordinary designation of the *u* (*i. e.* by a horizontal stroke placed at the side) by attaching in a special way to the *u*-stroke the sign for the leading vowel. To indicate *uĕ* a perpendicular stroke is placed upon the *u*-sign (ቈ ኈ ኰ ጐ); for *uī* the *ī*-sign is rather attached beneath, the perpendicular stroke reaching over the horizontal line (ቊ ኊ ኲ ጒ); when compounded with the signs for *ā* and *ē* on the other hand the *u*-stroke is shifted to the foot of the letter (ቋ *quā*, ቌ *quē* &c.); to indicate *uă*, the *u*-sign is closed at its end into a ring (ቍ &c.) (1).

Development of the *U*-containing Letters, and their several Forms.

In a later age the *uă*-sign, originally contrived for these four letters, was now and again appended in the signification of *wā* to other letters, namely to በ ተ ለ መ ሰ ረ ፈ; and ቧ, for example, was written for ብዋ, &c. (2). In this way a new kind of grouping of letters is produced, by compressing two written characters into one (*cf. supra* § 11).

The difference of these vowel-signs from one another in their seven respective forms is patent and clear with most of the letters;

(1) For ኲ, ጒ &c. ኵ, ጕ is often written in manuscripts, *e. g.* መኵንንት [and *uī* seems to be written for *uĕ* in certain instances in MS. P (14th century) of the *Kebra Nag.*; v. *ibid.*, *Introd.* p. XV and Note 1].

(2) V. the signs originating in this way in MS. 16240 of the British Museum, referred to above, p. 20, Note (1), and in Isenberg's '*Grammar of the Amharic Language*', p. 4.

but one or two forms become very like each other through the attachment of certain of the vowel signs, and so may easily be mistaken in reading and in writing, viz:—ሩ and ሬ. ሪ and ሬ, ር and ሮ, ኍ and ኊ, ው and ዉ. ዩ ዮ ዪ, ዱ ዶ ዲ, ፉ and ፋ, ፊ and ፍ, ም and ሞ, ሰ and ሰ(1), በ and ገ. ኦ and ኑ, ዋ and ዎ(2). This comparatively early development of a complete vowel-system, which was soon adopted generally in books, gives a great advantage to Ethiopic, as compared with other Semitic languages and modes of writing(3), and greatly facilitates the acquisition of the language from the writing, as well as the comprehension of the books themselves. At the same time we must keep in view that not even with the Abyssinians did such a system of Vowel-writing come into existence all at once, fully and symmetrically formed, but that it was perfected only in the course of a considerable length of time. This may farther be proved by manifold errors in the vocalisation of a number of words, especially of proper names which have been established and handed down in the Texts of the Bible from ancient times(4). Such errors can be explained only on the supposition that in the case of several words the vowel-marking was either entirely wanting, or was somewhat fluctuating and irregular in the use made of the various signs.

Interpunctuation-marks Numerical Signs.

§ 16. Apart from consonantal characters and vowel-marks the Abyssinians did not farther develop any special written signs. The distinction between the aspirated (or assibilated) and the unaspirated pronunciation of certain Mutes seems to have been unknown to them. Nor do they ever indicate the doubling of a consonant by any special mark,— although, like the most of

---

(1) [*E. g.* in the very old Cod. Aeth. 32 of the Bibliothèque Nationale; *v.* Hackspill in *Zeitschr. für Assyr.*, Vol. XI, p. 368, N. 1.]

(2) ጂ for ጇ is met with in d'Abb. 55 in Hez. 1, 26; 10, 1; M. Faus (MS. XI, last page ሰናጂ); Herma መሃጂል.—Ancient and peculiar vowel signs are exhibited by the Cod. Laur. of the Twelve Minor Prophets, in the Bodleian Library. [*Cf.* Dillmann, '*Catalogus codicum manuscriptorum Bibliothecae Bodleianae Oxoniensis*', *Pars* VII, Oxonii 1848, p. 10*sq.*, No. VIII.]

(3) [But the same, of course, must be said of the Babylonian-Assyrian writing, inasmuch as the signs for simple syllables are recognised as being used in this way.]

(4) In my own editions of Bible Texts I have drawn attention to such ancient errors in many passages.

the other Semites, they write every double consonant once only, except when the two sounds are separated by a vowel. There is therefore a slight defect in their writing in this respect: it is only from the rules of formation or from tradition, that we can determine when a letter must be pronounced as a double one, and these aids do not always suffice.

The sign of the close of a sentence is ። [called by the Ethiopians ነጥብ "drop" or "point", or—together with ፤, ፨ and ።=።—ምዕራፍ "pause" or "sign of pause"],—a doubling of the ordinary word-divider (v. § 11). When this sign has to serve at the same time as a section-mark, it is generally amplified into ፨ or doubled as ።=።, after which a new line is frequently commenced. Smaller marks of division are not employed, as a rule; ፤, however, serves this purpose; in enumerations ፤ is very frequently placed between the several words (*e. g.* Henoch 10, 20; 15, 11). In later manuscripts ፤ ። ፨ are oftener employed, but mostly in the wrong place through the ignorance of copyists.

The Abyssinians borrowed their *Numerical Signs* from the Greeks. Whether they ever possessed any of their own,—in particular whether they used their own letters as numerical signs,—we do not know. The Greek signs appear already in the Inscriptions; but an attempt was made, wherever possible, so to fashion the foreign sign that it should come to resemble the character for some Ethiopic letter or syllable: thus ፻ was formed so as to resemble the sign of *šā*, ፱ the sign of *ḥā*, ፫ the ancient sign of *rū* &c. In this way the ciphers given in Table I were finally evolved. In order that they might be more easily recognised as numerical signs, and might not be mistaken for letters of the alphabet, a small horizontal stroke was applied to them both above and below. In the manuscripts the separating points are usually omitted after ciphers, and ፭ and ፬, as well as ፮ and ፯ are frequently interchanged(1).

(1) For ፲ "10" D'ABB. 55 has the sign ፲ዐ Jer. 48, 1. 2. 8. In like manner ፲ዐወ፪ is met with for ፲ወ፪ MS. Jul. M. a. IX. 14 (*Genzat*), foll. 30, 110; MS. Berol. PETERM. II, Nachtr. XXVIII (*Gadla Abbā Garimā*), foll. 39, 61, 63, 64 &c. [An exceptional way of expressing "100" is ፺፲ in *Kebra Nag.* 141 a 18.] On the *Minao-Sabaic* numerical signs *cf.* ZDMG XXVI, p. 748 *sqq.* and '*Journal as.*' VII, 1, p. 511 *sqq.*

The Abyssinians have no *Abbreviation-marks*. In Texts in which a word is repeated very often, it is of course frequently shortened, but this shortening consists merely in giving no more than the initial letter or the two opening letters of the word and then adding the word-divider, *e. g.* ቀ፡ for ቅዱስ. Standing abbreviations are not met with (but *cf.* § 11). እስራኤል is written ፳ኤል in many manuscripts, as if it had been a compound of ዕሥራ *twenty* and ኤል. In like manner numerals, even when they do not appear in their pure ground-form, although they are frequently written in ciphers, have yet one syllable,—a suffix, it may be, of the ground-form,—attached in letters, *e. g.* ፪ሆሙ *i. e.* ክልኤሆሙ. In *Genzat* fol. 13 (Cod. Tub. M. a. IX. 14) we read for 'Hallelujah' occurring thrice: ሃሌ ፡ ሉያ ፡ ˈሌ ፡ ሉያ ፡ ˈሌያ ። *cf. ibid.* foll. 20, 36, 37 &c.(1).

II. PHONOLOGY.

I. THE SOUNDS (OR LETTERS) OF THE LANGUAGE.

1. VOWELS.

Preliminary Observations. Short Vowels other than *ă*.

§ 17. When a glance is cast over the stock of vowels in the Ethiopic language, as it is exhibited in the system of vowel writing, consisting of short vowels *ă ĕ*, of long ones *ā ī ū* and of mixed sounds *ē ō*, the attention is arrested by a peculiar phenomenon, viz. that *i* and *u*, which next to *a* are the two chief vowels in all ancient tongues, are wanting in their shorter forms, though represented in their respective long forms, while a sound of the second rank, *ĕ*, comes forward to take the place of such shorter forms. This cannot possibly be original. The pure sounds *ŭ* and *ĭ* must once have existed in the speech; and the circumstance that both of them gave place to the more general and indeterminate

---

(1) [In Cod. Mon. 11 the Divine name is frequently abbreviated: እግዚአብሔ or እግዚአብ or እግዚአ or እግዚ or እግ; it is in that case mostly written with red ink and without the final points (:); so too, ክርስቶ. አ ·፨· for አሜን is met with in *Kebra Nag.* 113, Note 14; 159, Note 18; 164, Note 26. ሎ ፡ or ሎዲ ፡ for ለዶቅያ *Laodicea*, and ዓ ፡ for ዐረበዊ is found in Brit. Mus. Or. 2263, fol. 6.]

sound *ĕ*, may be regarded as a sign of the early inroads of decay on the vowel-pronunciation. We have, it is true, no express information to guide us as to the age of this decay. But we have already (p. 26 *sq.*) concluded from the nature of the vowel-writing, which has no distinctive sign for *ŭ* or *ĭ*, that even in the time of the formation of that system of writing, the practice of distinguishing *ŭ* and *ĭ* can no longer have exhibited much life, though it might still perhaps be said to exist. The same inference may be drawn from other indications. Nowhere in the language is a different meaning of the word or form bound up with a different pronunciation of the vowel of the sixth class. On the other hand we come upon cases in which an originally short *i* or *u* was prolonged into a long *ī* or *ū*, to preserve the sound, because it was of importance for the meaning. Forms too, in which the *u* is most essential in all Semitic tongues, like the Passive or the Imperfect of the first Conjugation (Stem) and its Infinitive, have even in the oldest Ethiopic known to us either been completely given up, or have made way for new forms in which the missing sound of short *u* has had its place supplied by other sounds and devices. All this seems to justify the conclusion that even in very early times not merely was the short *i* already pronounced like *e*, but also,—which is still more remarkable,—the short *u* was on the point of fairly disappearing, and was altered into *ü* or *ʋ* wherever it could not be lengthened with the help of the tone, and even farther into *ĕ* (1), so that in the end the two sounds lost themselves in the indeterminate *ĕ*. It may be that in some words this *ĕ* was once spoken rather like an *i*, and in others rather like a *u* (2), but this distinction can no longer have been of importance, and at last it was quite given up. But there is at least one remnant of the original short *u* which has been preserved in many cases, namely after the four *u*-containing consonants, so that *e. g.* קָרְבָּן still has the sound of **ቍርባን** *querbān* in Ethiopic (v. on this point § 26).

The Ground-vowel, Short *ă*

§ 18. (1) The fundamental vowel *a* has still a great predominance in Ethiopic, and is very largely employed in word-formation both as a short and as a long vowel. The *short ă* was cer-

(1) Compare *e. g.* Hebr. אַתֶּם or כֶּם from *attúm*, *kúm*.

(2) *Cf.* **እስቁፍ** = أُسْقُف.

tainly spoken at one time with a pure and unmixed sound, and in most cases must have been preserved in all the greater purity for the reason that otherwise it would have been confused with the other two short vowels, and a leading means of formation would thus have been lost to the language. It occurs with great frequency in distinction from *ĕ* to convey a special signification of a word (*cf. e. g.* ገብር "servant" and ግብር "business"). At the same time it shows a tendency even at an early period to take the duller sound of the less pure *ĕ* (1)—less frequently in an open syllable, as for instance, with ሰገም and ሰገም "barley", but more frequently when it is attracted by two syllable-closing consonants,—so that in forms like ረምሕ "spear", *ă* is often changed into *ĕ* ርምሕ (v. § 105). This transition into *ĕ* became specially active under the influence of gutturals (§ 45). Besides, *a* is thickened into *ē* when it is lengthened to make up for the doubling of a consonant (§ 56 *ad fin.*). Then too it often stands in foreign words for η, ε, *e. g.* ኢየሱስ Ἰησοῦς. Again, the softening of the pronunciation of *ă* increased considerably in the course of the Middle Ages: In Ludolf's time it was generally pronounced *ä* (2), except when it formed a diphthong with a following ው, or had to be spoken after one of the five Gutturals or ረ or ቀ, ጠ, ጸ, ጰ (3), in which case it was kept purer through the guttural (ሀ *ha*, not *hä*). Fortunately this decay did not make its way into the writing; and therefore wherever *a* is written, it is better that we pronounce it *a*.

Long *ā*. The *long ā*, on the other hand, continued even in popular speech to retain the pure sound of *a*. The fact that in many foreign words *ā* stands for η, ε, *e. g.* ሊቤርዮስ *Liberius*, should not lead us to infer that *ā* was pronounced like *ē*, but rather that the less pure *ē*-sound was often replaced in Ethiopic by the purer sound of *ā* (4). Very often *ā* springs out of *ă* by Tone-lengthening and by the influence of a following guttural without a vowel (§ 46) or by the contraction of *ă* + *ă* (§ 39); but still more fre-

(1) *Cf.* the like phenomenon in other Semitic languages, *e. g.* in Assyrian: Zimmern, '*Zeitschr. f. Assyr.*' V, p. 396. V. also König, p. 59.

(2) "*Sonus hujus vocalis tam obscurus est, ut parum a murmure absit, haud aliter ac si quis obscure loquens infantes terrere velit*".—Ludolf.

(3) *Cf.* Trumpp, ZDMG XXVIII [in what follows quoted as Trumpp], p. 519.

(4) V., on the other hand, König, p. 62.

quently it is original, and sustains the sense and meaning of a definite word-form (*e. g.* አሕዛብ "nations", from ሕዝብ "nation"). Farther it often stands, as in Arabic, for the mixed sound ō, particularly in several words of early Semitic, like ቃል קוֹל (1), ዳር דּוֹר, ዓለም עוֹלָם (v. *infra* § 105)(2); so also in foreign words ማር ܡܳܪ, ሃይማኖት ܗܰܝܡܳܢܽܘܬܳܐ. Of native word-formations in Ethiopic the form of the 3rd Conjugation (Stem) must be referred to here, ጋብአ for ጐብአ compared with ጉባኤ "congregation", and of a few Quadriliterals, *e. g.* ማሰነ for ሞሰነ, in the Participle Passive ሙሱን.

Short, indeterminate ĕ.

§ 19. (2) The *short, indeterminate* ĕ is of very frequent occurrence. It makes its appearance as the shortest and most colourless of vowels:—(1) where a vowel or a slight vocal effort (*Vocalanstoss*, or *Sh*e*va mobile*) must be resorted to in order to facilitate pronunciation, *e. g.* ይገብር, እምነ; (2) in the sinking of the fore- and after-tone, before or after a long-toned vowel, *e. g.* ጽባሕ "morning", ምሥዋዕ "altar", ትንሣኤ "resurrection", ኃጥእ "sinner", ቈናጽል "foxes". As being the short form for ū and ī, it springs out of these vowels, when they are shortened, *e. g.* ገቡር "made", in the Femin. ገብርት, መይጥ *mayyet* (and *mait*) for መዩጥ, and it is employed in word-formation in all cases in which ĭ, ŭ or tone-lengthened ē, ō are found in the kindred tongues: አምነ "he believed" أَمِنَ, ከብረ "he was honoured" كَبِرَ, ያገብር يُكْتِبُ, ይበርክ يُقَاتِلُ, ይነግር يَكْتُبُ יִכְתֹּב, አንትሙ "you" أَنْتُمْ, ሕግ "law" חֹק(3), እዝን "ear" אֹזֶן, ልብስ "clothing" لِبْسٌ(4).

In several forms ĕ is softened out of ă (§ 18); more rarely it is shortened from an original ē:—እፎ "how?" אֵיפֹה, እንብየ "I may not" אֵין בִּי.

In foreign words it may stand for all short vowels, and even, —after shortening has occurred—, for long vowels of every kind: μυστήριον ምሥጢር, σινδών ሰንዱን, Μανασσῆ ምናሴ and መናሴ,

(1) [Better to regard ቃል as = Assyrian *qālu*, but קוֹל as = قَوْلٌ = Assyrian *qūlu*.]

(2) *Cf.* König, p. 67.

(3) [But v. *infra* (§ 25), where a preferable derivation by Nöldeke is referred to.]

(4) On a like weakening of *a* into *i* in the dialect of the *Banū Tamīm* v. Rödiger, ZDMG XIV, p. 488; *cf.* Fleischer, '*Beitr.*' St. 2. pp. 275, 317; Stade, '*Morgenl. Forsch.*' p. 212 [and Huber, '*Meisir*', p. 18*sq.*].

Βενιαμίν ብንያሚ, σπόγγος ስፍንግ, Χωθάρ ክቱር, Θεόδωρος ቴዎድሮስ, *Lucia* ልክያ, Βααλίμ both በዓልም and በዓሊም &c.

It would seem that the pronunciation of this vowel resembled for the most part our fugitive or obscure *ĕ*, but sometimes it rather approximated an *i*, sometimes an *o* (1). The older grammarians are not quite agreed about its pronunciation. Potken represents it by *ŏ*,—which, however, must be wrong, according to the evidence of Ludolf's tutor: Wemmers taught that the sound was very short, fluctuating between *ĕ* and *ŏ*: Ludolf rendered it by *y* in the first edition of his grammar, and by *ε* and *e* in the second—as did Marianus Victorius before him. It is very remarkable that after short *i* and *u* had quite disappeared at a very early stage, the same sounds appeared again from another quarter, as the pronunciation encountered farther change in the lapse of time. In point of fact when ው and ይ constituted a syllable by themselves at the beginning of a word, they were pronounced *u* and *i* by the later Abyssinians (2),—thus, for instance, ውሉድ *ulūd*, ይገብር *igáber*. This pronunciation is now generally diffused, and seems to have come into vogue in comparatively early times (3); but still it cannot be original (4), and indeed it was always given up again whenever a somewhat closely connected preposition or conjunction was prefixed to the word, *e. g.* ለውሉድ, ለይቁም (5). We shall accordingly transcribe ው and ይ in all cases by *we* and *ye*. At the end also of a word, according to Trumpp, p. 519 *sq.* ው and ይ are pronounced *u* and *i*, when *ā* precedes them, or when *ū* stands before ይ, or when *ĕ* precedes them, which *ĕ* then must take the tone. When ው follows a consonant without a vowel, it is spoken like *u*. Also in the middle of a word ው and ይ, preceded

(1) In MS. Berol., Cod. B, Peterm. II. Nachtr. 55 ቀዑይ is generally written ጡዑይ, manifestly on account of the ጠ.

(2) Ludolf, '*Gramm.*' Lib. I, 5,—just as the Hebrews render וּ "and", here and there by אוּ, and the Syrians *Yūdh* in the beginning of a word, by *ī*. The Abyssinians, however, do not appear to be consistent in their pronunciation of these half-vowels: *cf.* Trumpp, p. 520.

(3) I conclude this from the fact that even in more ancient manuscripts a negative is here and there wrongly inserted before the 3rd pers. m. of the Imperf. (*e. g.* ኢይገብር for ይገብር),—an error which can be explained only on the supposition that ይ was pronounced *i*.

(4) Haupt, '*Beitr. z. Ass.*' I, p. 17, is of another opinion.

(5) Where they neither said *la-ulūd* nor *laulūd*.

by *e*, are pronounced *e-u*, *e-i*, in which cases however *e* has the tone, only when this is fundamental in the form. With a foregoing *a*, ው and ይ regularly form the diphthongs *au* and *ai*.

§ 20. (3) The *long vowels ī, ū* mainly appear (1) in forms from roots, of which one of the radicals is a vowel; (2) in the Pronoun and in Formative syllables of pronominal origin; (3) in various Inner Nominal forms, mostly tone-lengthened out of an original short vowel: **ገቢር**, **ኀጺን**, **ልሂቅ**, **ኀጢአት**, **ገቡር**, **አሕቁል** among others. *ī* and *ū*

Farther *ī* appears occasionally instead of a short *i* founded in the form, only for the purpose of preserving the *i*-sound in greater purity, *e. g.* **መሃፒል** "a fuller" (for **መሃፕል**), **መስጊድ** "house of prayer" مَسْجِد, for the rest a foreign word. In some few cases it is thinned down from fuller sounds *ē*, *ā*, *e. g.* **ኢ** "not", from אַיִן, אֵי, **ሚ** "what?" from מָה, מֶה; but regularly it proceeds, in processes of formation, from *ē* as the more simple sound, where *ē* is shortened, *e. g.* **ጊጉይ** "guilty" from **ጌገየ**, **ፂዋዌ** "captivity" from **ፄወወ**. Where *ī* is shortened, it becomes *ĕ* (§ 19). In many words it is shaded off into the somewhat longer *ē* (§ 21). It is met with frequently in foreign words, not merely for long and short *i*, but also for *υ*, **ቢሶስ** "Byssus", **ኪርያቅ** Κυρίακος; for *η* (in so far as this *i* was pronounced) **ቲጉን** *τήγανον*, **ምሥጢር** *μυστήριον*, and even for the diphthongs *αι* and *οι*, as a result of fusing these diphthongs into one sound, **ኢትዮጵያ** Αἰθιοπία, **ኪሮግርልዮስ** *χοιρογρύλλιος* [1].

The vowel *ū* is already fairly in course of transition to *ō* (§ 21). In formative processes it makes its appearance, where an original *ō*, or an *ā* that has arisen out of *ō* (§ 18), is shortened:— **ቱስሕት** "mingling" from **ቶስሐ**, **ኑኅቤ** "cohabitation" from **ኖኅበ**. Where *ū* is shortened, it passes over into *ĕ* (§ 19). In foreign words it corresponds to *υ*, as well as to *u*, *ū*, *e. g.* **ሁሶጲ** (and **ህሶጲ**) *ὕσσωπος*.

Besides, *ī* and *ū* are hardened into their semi-vowels ይ and ው (§ 40).

§ 21. *The vowels ē, ō* are in their origin mixed sounds, *ē* and *ō*. sprung from *ai* and *au* by fusing the diphthong into a single sound. Their origin is still very clear in Ethiopic, for in by far

[1] *Cf.* König, p. 64 *sqq.*

the greatest number of cases they arise here from the blending of an *i* or a *u* with an *a* to which it becomes joined (§ 39*sq.*); and, having this origin, they are susceptible of being analysed back into their constituent parts, and of passing thus into *ay* and *aw* (*av*) (1). Less frequently they arise from the lengthening of shorter vowels or from *i* and *u* by thickening and lengthening.

In particular *ĕ* may be lengthened into *ē* through the influence of a following soft Guttural, ይሬኢ for ይርእይ, ይቤሉ for ይብህሉ (§ 46); and, without any sufficient grounds of this nature, *ē* arises from *ĕ* through the mere dwelling upon the pronunciation, *e. g.* ምጻቄ (Sir. 27, 20) for ምጻቍ δορκάς, ሐቌ "hip" for ሐቍ. In other cases *ē* is thickened out of *ă* or *ā*; thus from *ă*, and at the same time to take the place of doubling in the Imperfect of the Intensive conjugation (stem), ይፌጽም *yefēṣem* for *yefáṣṣem* (§ 95, 2), and from *ā* in a few cases, ጽሌ "table" alongside of ጽላ, ሰሜን "South" תֵּימָן. In several words *ē* has become established in place of an *ī* fundamental to the form, as being a somewhat fuller sound, *e. g.* ዳቤር and ዳቢር דְּבִיר, ኅጢላ and ኅጤላ "nothingness", ባቄላ "bean" بَاقِلَا (2). In foreign words it corresponds most frequently to ε, η and ει (3): ቴዎሎጎስ θεολόγος. ሌጌዎን λεγεών, ሚካኤል Μιχαήλ, ጵስጥቄስ πιστικῆς, ዴብላታ Δεβλαθά, ሴዴቅያስ Σεδεκίας; and sometimes to υ, ቤሬል Βήρυλλος, ሜሮን μύρον, and to αι, ሐጌ Ἀγγαῖος.

The sound *ō* is produced with great regularity, in certain forms, out of *ū* by compression; thus in the Feminine endings *ōt* and *ō* from *ūt* and *ū* (*e. g.* ገብሮ, ገቢሮት, ጸለሎ, መለኮት &c.), probably also in ውእቶሙ and in the Suffix pronoun ሆሙ; farther, very commonly in words of foreign formation: ሃይማኖት ܗܝܡܢܘܬܐ, ታቦት "ark" تَابُوة, እቶን "oven" אַתּוּן أَتُّون, ሶከር "sugar" سُكَّر, ዘይቶን "olive-plantation" زَيْتُون, ሲኦል "realm of the dead" שְׁאוֹל ܫܝܘܠ, ጎሮኔ "coffin" ܓܘܪܢܐ, ጸላዕ "rock" صُلَّع or صُلَّاع. In foreign words it stands for ο and ω; the Greek termination ιος

(1) [Just as the Guṇa sounds are resolved in Sanskrit. TR.]

(2) It is a different thing when copyists confound *ē* and *ī*,—an occurrence which is very common.

(3) *Cf.* König, p. 68, who assumes for ει, however, the pronunciation *ī*, and then the compression of the *ī* into *ē*.

accordingly sounds ዮ፡ስ; or it corresponds to *ου* ሮቤል Ῥουβήλ, መርቆሬዎስ "*Mercurius*", or to *υ* ቆጵሮስ Κύπρος, or to *αυ* ኖትያዊ *ναύτης*.

When *ō* and *ē* are shortened, they pass into *u* and *i* (§ 20).

§ 22. All these vowels, once they appear in a word, are as a rule held firmly and tenaciously, and accompany the word without change throughout all its farther forms and augmentations. No trace is met with here of the manifold alterations of sound exhibited by the Hebrew of the Masora as a result of altered conditions in the Tone. In the matter of tenacity and constancy in the vowels of a word Ethiopic ranges itself rather with Arabic. Pronunciation of fugitive *ĕ*.

Whether Ethiopic possesses, besides its seven vowels, additional fugitive vowels as they are called, half-vowels, or vowel-touches (*Vocalanstösse*), is a question, which may easily enough be put. But it is a question difficult to answer, partly because too little is known about the mode of pronunciation of words in ancient times, and partly because the question—what is a half-vowel?,—and—what is a short vowel?—is not so easily answered. It is well known that Arabic has a short vowel in all those cases in which Hebrew has merely a *Sh^e^ra* (*Vocalanstoss*). Other languages less rich in vowels, such as the Aramaic, tolerate groups of consonants also, and give utterance to a fugitive vowel-effort, only where incompatible consonants meet together. Upon the whole, Ethiopic is something like Hebrew in vowel resources: and indeed in its short indeterminate *ĕ* in cases like ክረምት, ፍሬ, ግበር, አስተግብሬ it possesses a sound quite resembling the Hebrew *Sh^e^va mobile*; and this shortest and most fugitive kind of *ĕ* may always be compared with the *Sh^e^va*. Other cases, in which an entirely fugitive vowel of this kind has to be resorted to in order to help the pronunciation, will be described farther on. That the *ĕ* was no longer pronounced here like a vowel, but rather like a mere half-vowel, seems to be evidenced by the fact that in the cases named, wherever it was applied just on account of the nature of the coinciding consonants, the later pronunciation fell into the way of wholly suppressing any intermediary sound,—as in *krämt* (v. on this point § 34). Now between the complete disappearance of the vowel in this position and the utterance of a full vowel, such as we have in Arabic, there must certainly intervene as an intermediate stage the uttering of what was a half-vowel and nothing more. This question, however, is not important for the phonology or the morphology. It will be enough to notice *when* we should pronounce an *ĕ* as a sound quite short and fugitive, as cases occur.

2. CONSONANTS.

Preliminary Observations.

§ 23. The consonants found in Ethiopic have already been indicated in a general way in the account that has been given of the characters. With the exception of the dull *p̣*-sound, they are the same with those which constitute the stock of the Northern-Semitic Alphabet, increased by two new Arabic letters. It might seem from this that as regards the consonants of the language there has not been much of a special nature developed in the Abyssinian abodes of the Semites. And yet a comparison of Ethiopic roots with those of the rest of the Semitic languages reveals that while Ethiopic has often retained softer and more slender sounds, or developed them out of harder ones, it exhibits much more frequently harder and duller sounds, in place of the softer sounds of the other tongues. Such preference for rougher sounds is specially declared in the transcription of foreign words. Of still more importance is the fact that Ethiopic has created several types of rougher sounds peculiar to itself. One example is presented in the dull *p̣* **ጰ**, which in one or two roots, and also in foreign words takes the place of an original *b* or *p*. Farther, the Abyssinians have transformed into rough gurgling sounds the four Semitic gutturals **ኀ ገ ከ ቀ** in a way peculiar to them, by fetching them more deeply from the throat, and joining with them an obscure *u*-sound, which in that very process loses its vowel character and stiffens into the consonantal sound. This rougher pronunciation of the four gutturals has, to be sure, in no respect become general, in the sense of supplanting their usual pronunciation: on the contrary, the latter has kept its ground in by far the greater number of roots; but the rougher pronunciation is nevertheless very widely extended. While, however, these phenomena reveal an impulse in the language towards the development of rougher sounds, such as well befits the mountainous nature of the country, another series, on the other hand, of peculiarities in the pronunciation of the consonants indicates a certain struggle to simplify the multiplicity of sounds,—(a feature we found also in the vowel-system)—accompanied with an appearance of effeminacy and degeneracy. We find in fact that the three hardest of the five Gutturals (Aspirate-) had their pronunciation gradually softened: **ዐ** became like **አ**, **ኀ** like **ሐ**, and the last two together like **ሀ**. So too we find that among the Sibilants **ሠ** came to be like **ሰ** (*š* like *s*), and **ፀ** *ḍ* like **ጸ** (1) *ṣ*. Thus the Abyssinians first gave up **ኀ** and **ፀ**,—sounds which had been developed in Arabia and been brought with them from that country,—just as they had in much earlier times given up the lisping transitional letters ث ذ ظ. As regards the Sibilants in particular it comes about that Ethiopic prefers decided Mutes, and, still more strongly, decided Sibilants to the transitional letters, and it is precisely on that account that **ፀ** reverted to **ጸ**. Among the Gutturals Ethiopic could bring about again the coincidence of **ኀ** and **ሐ** all the more readily, after it had contrived the rougher **ኈ** out of **ኀ** (خ). The giving up of *š* for *s* shows the same striving after simplification. On the other hand the gradual weakening of **ዐ** into **አ** and of **ሐ** and **ኀ** into **ሀ** is a decidedly enfeebling process as well; and as the language had formerly made abundant use of these letters in its formation, the process led to many inconveniences, and can only have become general about the time the speech died out. It is so much the more remarkable, when we see Ethiopic striving, at other points, after the rougher sounds; but yet, along with the simplifying endeavours which have been mentioned, it finds an analogy in the phonetic development of other and even non-Semitic languages. In fact a certain easy-going pronunciation, which gives up whatever causes any trouble, and keeps only the absolutely necessary and essential sounds, frequently prevails in popular dialects. In the other Abyssinian dialects, particularly in Amharic, all these phenomena are displayed, and even in a much more decided fashion.

With these preliminary observations we proceed to describe the various Consonants, their phonetic value, their significance and their mutual interchange. We group them together according

---

(1) According to Haupt's statement (*'Zeitschrift f. Assyr.'* II, p. 264), the Abyssinians pronounce **ፀ** as a Fricative (*ts*), while **ጸ** is a Fricative with a firm break. [Trumpp is also of this opinion: v. Trumpp p. 578. tr.]

to the organs of speech by which they are produced, and also according to the peculiarities which they exhibit in practice.

Gutturals (Aspirate-).

§ 24. (1) Of *Gutturals* (*Aspirate-*) there are in all, five, አ ዐ ሀ ሐ ኀ. Of these አ and ሀ are the oldest[1] and the simplest sounds, and are present in other languages as well as in the Semitic: ዐ and ሐ are of comparatively later origin: ኀ is the youngest of all. አ is properly just that gentle breathing which must precede every vowel when uttered separately, and must really follow also a long final vowel,—answering thus to the *Spiritus lenis* of the Greeks. ሀ, having more strength and body in it, is our *h*,—the Greek *Spiritus asper*. ዐ is connected with አ as a breathing of similar character, which of necessity requires a vowel before or after it, to become audible; but it is harder than አ and is formed by a firmer compression of the throat-orifice. With ሀ are associated, first, ሐ, corresponding to ح, like a stronger *h* (*ḥ*) uttered more deeply from the throat, and next, ኀ, خ[2], produced by friction of the upper part of the throat, and therefore inclining rather to *k*, *ch* or *kh* (*ḫ*). አ and ሀ are the weakest and softest Gutturals: in certain circumstances they may completely coalesce with a vowel immediately preceding them (*cf. infra* § 47).

The (Aspirate-) Gutturals represent a double step-ladder of stronger and weaker breathings, one end of which borders, with አ and ሀ, upon the vowels, and the other, with ዐ and ኀ, upon the consonants, and first upon the Palatal-Gutturals. This intermediate position of theirs between the vowels and the consonants explains also their wide extension in the Semitic languages. They make their appearance with considerable frequency in root-formation, when roots, of which one of the radicals is a vowel, endeavour to acquire a third consonantal sound. In that case the weaker sounds, which were in the root at first, are condensed into the harder breathings, mainly through the influence of the other two radicals. In fact this is particularly clear in Ethiopic roots; and those which contain Gutturals are accordingly exchangeable

---

(1) Ewald, '*Ausf. Lehrbuch der hebr. Sprache*', 6th ed. p. 74.

(2) Ludolf has noticed that ኀ corresponds to خ.—Now-a-days ሀ ሐ ኀ are spoken just like *h*; v. Trumpp p. 518.

with those in which vowels appear in the corresponding positions (1). On the other hand these breathings are also found originating from firmer consonants, especially from the Palatal-Gutturals and Mutes, by such consonants giving up their firm consonantal element and retaining only the breathing as the remains of it. Thus አ often stands in Ethiopic as first radical in place of *Kāf*: አቤር "old woman" alongside of كَبِير, while the pronunciation ከብረ in Ethiopic bears rather a spiritual (figurative) sense, አረገ "to be old", beside كَرِج, አለደ "to gather", with كَلَّدَ كَلَزَ; farther in several Ethiopic words ሐ, ኀ are very commonly exchanged for ከ, *e. g.* ሐወሰ and ከወሰ "to stir", ረስሐ and ረኰሰ "to be unclean", ናሕንሐ and ነክነከ "to shake", ዝክር and ዝኁር "monument", ሰሊኖት and ሰሊከ "cassia"; ተከዚ "river" belongs to ውሕዘ, ሐረሠ "to lie in"—to ከርሠ, ሐሰወ "to tell a lie"—to כזב كَذَب (خاس). More rarely ሐ or ኀ corresponds to a *Geml*: ሐመደ "snow"—to جَمَد (in contrast with which ሐመድ "ashes" belongs to خَمَد), ማኅበብት "vat, pit"—to גֵּב, جُبّ, ሕንብርት "navel" to بُجْرَة, ሕንብርብሬ "scab"—to גרב, جَرِب. Still more frequent is the substitution of the rougher gutturals for *Qāf*, *e. g.* ኀጸረ "to be short" קצר قَصُر (حصر), ሐፈሠ "to rake up" קבץ, קפץ (but ح in Arabic also), ጽሕም "beard" זָקָן, ዓምዓም "swamp" قَمْقَام, ዐጠነ "to fumigate with incense" קטר, עתר, قتر, عطر. On the other hand the simplification of a sibilant into a mere guttural breathing is not so common in Ethiopic, though perhaps ሖረ "to go", may be ranged with the Arabic سار (2), and ረትዐ "to be straight" with رَتَزَ (3); the language in other cases prefers to keep by ጸ and ጠ, even where other tongues admit ע in place of them. Farther, the Gutturals are subject also to active interchange with one another, just as in the rest of the Semitic tongues; and upon the whole it is impossible to fail to notice that here the harder letters

(1) It is universally recognised that the harder sounds of an original form pass into the softer, and *vice versâ*, under the influence of a softer or a harder consonant in the root, *e. g.* ሐዘበ alongside of ሐሰበ (influenced by the በ).

(2) Ewald, p. 74.

(3) *Vice versâ*, ፀረፈ "to revile" is probably related to חָרַף.

seek to dislodge the softer. It is true that Ethiopic in many cases retains አ and ሀ even where they pass into harder sounds in other languages; as, for instance, አበል "limb" into هبر (هبل), አፋኪያ "ring" into הֶפֶךְ, أفك; ፈርሀ "to fear", فرخ; ደሀለ "to withdraw" דָּחַל, دحل; just as farther it has no ሀ in the formative syllables of the Causatives, but an አ; yet the harder letter more frequently appears for the soft one of other languages, *e. g.*: ሀጕለ "to full", أبل and وبل; ሀገር "town", probably for אכר (1); ዐጸድ "a court", اصد and وصد, and so in several roots that begin with ዐ (§ 70 *ad fin.*); ኀየል "stag", אַיָּל, أيّل; ሐሠም "guilt", אָשָׁם, أثام (حشم); ረበሐ "to make gain by usury", רְבָא, ربح; and ነድአ "to drive" appears also in harder form as ነድሐ; ግሕሠ "to retire", جهش; ለሐኰ "to be troubled", لهف; ሐጕለ "to perish", הָלַךְ, هلك; ሳሕበበ "to grow mouldy", شهب; ቀኀወ "to be jealous", جهى, كهى; አሥኀርት "new-moons", شهر, ܣܗܪܐ (שַׁחַר, سكر). In a number of instances also ዐ answers to a ח of other languages:—ዐመፃ "injustice", חָמָס; ዘወዐ "to meditate", שִׂיחַ; ሠሥዐ "to be insatiable" (شسع) belongs in the last resort to the root יָשַׁח, وحش. On the other hand Ethiopic frequently has ሐ or ኀ for ע of the other tongues: ርኅበ "to be hungry", רָעֵב, رغب; ጸበኀ "to dip in", צָבַע, טָבַע, صَبَغَ; ጽሕድ "cedar", صعد; ጸንሐ "to be on the watch", نغز; በጦሐ "to scarify", بضع; መልታሕት "cheek, jaw", מַלְתָּעוֹת, لثغ. Both modes of exchange show that different languages altered in different ways the softer gutturals into the harder. The keenness with which the stronger sounds in Ethiopic for some time sought to dislodge the weaker ones, may best be gathered from the fact that in this tongue ዐ, ኀ and ሐ have pushed their way even into several pronominal particles (§ 62, 1 b), while in the other tongues this department at least has been kept free from them. Even the Greek *Spiritus lenis* and *Spiritus asper* are expressed not merely by አ and ሀ (እስራኤል, አልፋ, ሄሮድያኖስ, እሌኒ, ኢላርያ, ሄሬኔዎስ), but also by ዐ, ኀ and ሐ,—so that, in names of Hebrew origin, Ethiopic in several cases again coin-

(1) Ewald p. 347.

cides with the Hebrew pronunciation (ዕብራዊ, ሐናንያ, ሔዋን, ኄሬኔ "Irene") (1).

Of course even when the language was endeavouring to develop harder gutturals, the softening of the harder ones was not impossible, although it was of comparatively rare occurrence: thus, for instance **አዘዘ** "to command, to rule" seems to have been formed at a very early time from **ዐዘዘ** "to be strong" עַז, عَزَّ, by the gradual smoothing down of the **ዐ** into **አ** in the more frequently used sense of "to command". But in a later age, when the language had long been fully formed, a tendency in the pronunciation of the gutturals—the very reverse of what had hitherto prevailed, and arising from causes which are not yet properly cleared up—gained a very notable predominance (§ 23). The hard sounds were gradually softened; **ኀ** was reduced to the level of **ሐ**, and both together to that of **ሀ**, and **ዐ** to that of **አ** (2); and the entire way that had been traversed hitherto was retraced, until the starting-point was reached, at which the Semitic tongue had nothing but **አ** and **ሀ**. It is possible that, besides the influence of Amharic, the frequent intercourse, which took place with populations speaking non-Semitic languages, helped forward this smoothing process in the hard sounds. The retrogression took effect at first in pronunciation only, and not in written character; but gradually the deterioration invaded the written character also; and then, in many cases, **አ** and **ዐ** on the one hand, **ሐ** and **ኀ** on the other, and less frequently **ሐ**, **ኀ** and **ሀ**—came to be exchanged for one another without the slightest distinction. The latest manuscripts go much farther in this direction than the more ancient ones (3); and yet the deterioration never became so general as to permit the alternative use of the harder or the softer letters at pleasure in every single word. For example, the **አ** of the Causative Conjugations (Stems), or that of the Pronouns **አንተ**, **እሉ**, or that of the roots and words **ነሥአ**, **ሰብእ**, **ብእሲ**, **አምነ**, **ኀጥአ**, **አኀዘ**, **አከየ**, **አከለ** &c., is never written **ዐ** in the better class of manuscripts; nor is the **ዐ** ever written **አ** in **ለዐለ**, **ምዕዐ**, **በልዐ**, **ዐበየ**, **በቍዐ**, **ከዐወ**, **ዐቀበ**, **ዐይን** and so on. **ኀ** and **ሐ** are oftener

---

(1) *Cf.* König, pp. 64, 66.

(2) Just as in Samaritan and Mandaean.

(3) [V. the Introduction to the '*Kebra Nag.*' p. XIV.]

exchanged; but yet in certain words they are more firmly retained, *e. g.* **በዝኀ, ድኀነ, በጽሐ** and so forth. Properly speaking, it is only in the latest manuscripts that we find **ሐ** or **ኀ** written for **ሀ**; and in certain words like **ከሀን, ኀቢል, ከሀለ, ሀለወ** it is not so written, even in them; but, on the contrary **ሀ** is rather frequently employed for **ሐ** or **ኀ** (1). Thus the deterioration in pronunciation could never have become quite universal; and the correct form has often held its ground still more tenaciously in writing. In poems, however, **አ** rhymes with **ዐ**, and **ሀ**, **ሐ** and **ኀ** rhyme with one another.

The firmer Gutturals (Palatal-).

§ 25. 2. (2) *The firmer Gutturals* (*Palatal-*), with which **የ** is also reckoned, come next in order to the Aspirate-Gutturals. Of these there are three, the soft **ገ**,—always pronounced as *g* (hard), never as *dj* (*dzh*)—, the hard **ከ** *k*, and the hollow-sounding **ቀ** *q*. The first two may with equal justice be called *Palatals*, seeing they are formed on the boundary between palate and throat; but the last of the three is decidedly more of a throat-sound or Guttural, being formed by a compression of the throat and a sharp breaking off of the stream of air (*Explosive*) (2) and having a peculiarly Semitic character. In foreign words the Ethiopians employ, as a rule, the hollow-sounding letter for *k*, *e. g.* **ቀኖና, ቄድሮስ, ቈስጠንጢኖስ, ቆሮንቶስ**, and thereby again evidence their inclination for rougher pronunciation. It is only in a minority of cases that they render *k* by **ከ**, as *e. g.* in **ከሚን** *κύμινον*, or by **ኀ** even, as in **ኀንዳኬ** Κανδάκη. They employ **ከ** oftener for χ (3), as if **ከ** had to be more aspirated, in contrast with the pure explosive **ቀ**, *e. g.* **መነኮስ, ሚካኤል, ሲራክ, አስኬማ, ከሚሌዎን** (though here and there also **ኀ**, as in **ስኂን** *σχῖνος*), or for γ, by hardening it after their manner, as in **ከልበኔን** "*galbanum*". So too **ክስ** is found for ξ:—**ስንክሳር** *τὰ συναξάρια*, **አር ቶዶክሳዊ** *ὀρθόδοξος*, **ስጳለክስ** *σπάλαξ*.

In Ethiopic itself the harder letters alternate in a few words with the softer ones: **መሰከ** and **ወሰቀ** "to bend (the bow)", **ሐነከ**

---

(1) The more precise treatment of these questions belongs to the province of the Lexicon. Whoever wants to learn the language, must familiarize himself from the outset with these possible phonetic changes, both in using the Lexicon and in reading what has been written.

(2) Isenberg, '*Gramm. Amh.*' p. 6, and Wallin, ZDMG IX, p. 10 *sqq.*

(3) *Cf.* König, p. 64.

and ሐንቀቀ "to be anxious", ዐረከ and ዐረቀ "to be friendly with",—in which cases ከ appears to be the original letter; ኳኳ and ቋዕ "raven". On the other hand ከ is now and then softened to ገ, *e. g.* in ጽጕ and ሰኰት "street" (שׁוּק, سُوق); and even ቀ is found exchanged for ገ in ገማ = ቃማ "necklace".

Changes still more marked are exhibited, when Ethiopic roots are compared with the corresponding roots of the other languages([1]). Ethiopic has often the harder pronunciation: ቀፍር "capital (of a pillar)", כפר, كفر, غفر; ደቀሰ "to be sleepy", نُكاس; ዕቋን "cream", عَكِّيّ, عُجْوَة; ልሀቀ "to grow up, to become old", כֶּלַח, كهل; ቀተረ "to shut up", קָטַר, כָּתַר, قتر; ሞቀ "to be warm", מוג, מַק, مُوق; or ረኵሰ "to be unclean", رجس and رِكْس; ቈልቈለ "to roll away", גלגל; but at least quite as frequently it preserves the softer pronunciation: in fact ከ for ק, *e. g.* in በከ "emptiness", בוק, בָּקַק, باقٍ; ክሳድ "neck", قَسْوَدّ([2]); ክዕሴ "dung", قَعْس; ለከወ "to become dull (of sight)", لاق; ለከየ "to wrangle", لقع and لقا; ኰሰየ "to bear a surname *or* a by-name", قِرْى; ኵናት as a secondary form of ቀኖት "sting", "point (of a spear)", קָנֶה, قَنَاة; ናእከ "groaning", נָאַק, אָנַח, אָנַק; ዘርከየ "to calumniate", "to be jealous", زرق; also ገ for כ, *e. g.* ሀጕለ "to perish", הָלַךְ, هلك; ነገድ "race", נֶגֶד; ጐድጐደ "to knock", كَدْكَدَ; and ገ for ק, *e. g.* ሕግ "law", חק (but according to Nöldeke = حُجَّة "a proof"); ደግደገ "to be lean", דַּק; ግብጽ "Egypt", قِبْط; ስጕርድ "leek", قِرْط, كُرَّاث; ጽጕ "street", שׁוּק, سُوق.

But the effort made by Ethiopic to reach stronger sounds is clearly revealed in the thickening of the Aspirate-Gutturals of other tongues into these hollow guttural forms. Thus ገ for א in

(1) On the nature and pronunciation of ቀ (ጸ, ጠ) *cf.* Trumpp, p. 518; Haupt, '*Beitr. z. Assyr.*' I, p. 15; Edgar Allen, '*Proc. Am. Or. Soc.*' 1888, p. CVIII*sqq.*; on the relation of ቀ to غ, Praetorius, '*Amh. Gram.*' § 45, *c*; '*Tigriñagramm.*' pp. 18, 100; ZDMG XLI, p. 686; v. also *ibid.* XXXVII, p. 449; and Reinisch, '*Bilinsprache*', p. 12, No. 6.

(2) [But in Assyrian there is an answering word, '*kišādu*'.]

ፀጋም "left hand", شَأْم; for ח in ጸገወ "to be gracious" ('friendly') and ጸገየ "to bloom", زهي; for ח in ገበጥ "colic", حَبَط; ምጕጠይ "ox-goad", חָטַט, خاط; ሰገም and ሰሐም "arrow" (*Gadla Adām*); for ע in ጸግበ "to be satisfied", שָׂבַע, شبع; ሰገኖ "ostrich", صِعْوَنّ; ኀደገ "to abandon", خدع (خدج); ጸጕር "hair", alongside of ሥዕርት(1); and with special frequency for غ:—ሠገረ "to run swiftly", شغر; ዘንገገ "to mock", زَغْزَغ, צָחַק; ጊሜ "cloud", غَيْم; ገመነ "to pollute", غمن; ጌሰ "to be up betimes", غلس; ጌገየ "to sin", غَوَى, עָוָה; ገገጸ "to tremble with terror", غَصَّ &c. In a similar manner ከ for ח in ምኵራብ "temple", مِحْرَاب(2); ከተማ "tip (extremity)", خَاتَم; ከከማት "warm baths", حَمِيمَة; ከንቱ፡ "in vain", חִנָּם; ከለለ "to be giddy", حال, חול. Finally, ቀ for ח in ሠረቀ "to rise (of the stars)", זָרַח, شَرَق; ጣቃ "obscurity", טוּחַ, طَخَاطِخ; for غ in በቅል "mule", بَغْل; ቍንቍኔ "an insect (a moth)", from غَنَّ "to buzz": for ع in መጠቀ "to raise on high", مَتَعَ (مَتَحَ); ነደቀ "to build", נָטַע.

The *U*-containing Gutturals.

§ 26. (3) But as if the rough Guttural-Aspirate ኍ and the hollow Guttural ቀ were still not enough, Ethiopic has increased the roughness both of these two, and of the other two Gutturals ገ and ከ, by pronouncing them with an obscure *u*- or *o*-sound immediately following, and yet in such a way that that sound is not fully formed into a vowel, but is interrupted in its formation and is turned merely into a means of roughening the consonantal sound(3). These letters, like other consonants, must be supplied with a vowel, before they can be spoken: as to the formation of the vowels which come after them, see § 41. We may call them the *U-containing Gutturals*(4). This peculiarly hoarse pronunciation

(1) V. König, p. 65 *sq.*

(2) [But this is a mere *transcript* of the Arabic word, ح being the ordinary, recognised equivalent of ከ, in such transcribed forms.]

(3) The Latin *lingua*, *quaero* &c. exhibit a similar sound, though not so rough.

(4) On the nature and pronunciation of these letters *cf.* Trumpp, p. 520; König, p. 41 *sqq.*; on their origin from the Cushitic, Reinisch, '*Die Bedauye-*

occurs only with the Palatal-Gutturals. ኍ participates in it merely as the strongest of the Guttural-Aspirates, but does not assume it with anything like the frequency that the three other letters do. The cases which exhibit the development of the *u*-containing pronunciation of the gutturals invite a short additional survey, and the following propositions are the result (1).

(1) In the great majority of cases this rougher pronunciation is brought about by a *u*-sound, which at one time was uttered after the guttural in the ground-form of the word, but which forthwith,—either because of having to give place to another vowel in the course of farther alteration of the word, or independently of such cause,—took refuge within the consonant, and clung to it irremovably as a roughening addition. (a) Thus a *u*, *o*, or *w* in foreign words, making itself heard after ኍ, ጕ, ኵ, or ቍ, makes its way into the consonant: ጰንጠቈስጤ *πεντηκοστή*; አናጕንስጢስ *ἀναγνώστης*; ጳጕሜን *ἐπαγομένη*; ኵርያቅ Κυριακός; ጕራን *a proper-name*; ቈስጠንጢኖስ *Constantine*; ቍልዝም قُلْزُم (*Clysma*, town near Mt. Sinai); አንቍራ *Ancyra*, and a host of others. (b) In many Ethiopic words a *u* or *o*, grounded in the form, which has disappeared in the forms of other words unprovided with a guttural, has endeavoured to save itself by making its way into the guttural (§ 17), *e. g.* ቍርባን "offering (gift)" קָרְבָּן; ጕርን "threshing-floor", גֹּרֶן; ጕንድ "stem (of a tree)", גֹּמֶד; ቍስጥ "*costus*" (v. *infra* § 105); በኵር "firstling", בְּכוֹר; እልኵቱ "those" (as well as እልክቱ), from እልኩ; ኵሊት "kidney", كُلْيَة. Frequently too a radical *u* or ው has thus made its way into the guttural that precedes it: እኍ and እኅው "brother"; ሐቌ "hip", حِقْو; ሰርጕ "ornament", from ሰርገወ; ጽጕ "street", from ጸገወ (שׁוּק); ኰኵሕ "a rock" (for ኰሕኵሕ) from כוח, كح "to be hard". Some other words leave it optional to exchange the full *u*-sound for the rougher and shorter *ue*, *e. g.* ይኵን and ኵን for ይኩን and ኩን; አህጕር "cities", and አህጉር; ብቍጽ and ብቈጽ "scraped

---

Sprache' (Vienna 1893), vol. II. p. 26 *sqq.* Maltzan has also heard these sounds in the Mehri; v. ZDMG XXVII, p. 261 *sq.*

(1) Tuch also deals with this subject in the first of the two *Commentationes* cited above, p. 14, Note (1). His results agree for the most part with my own.

together". In other words too,—particularly in those which were originally Passive Participles, but which have gradually become Substantives—, the *u* has been permanently modified in this way: ሐጕር "raisin", for ሐጉር; ነቍጥ "point", for נְקוּד[1] &c. Even when a *u* fell to be made audible in the ground-form, not immediately after the guttural, but after another radical which preceded or followed the guttural, it has been attracted to this last: ሐቍ "cedar-wood", from حَبَق through the softening of the *b* into *w*; ልጕት "abyss", لُجَّة; ቶኰላ "jackal", שׁוּעָל, ثُعَالَة; መቍዐል "marrow", مُكَال, מֹחַ; as well as ልጓም "bridle", from an original لُجَام; ጸቍጾ and ጸኊጾ "cedar", صُعْد. (c) In a similar way this *u* has also invaded verbs and roots. Sometimes, when original roots (middle *u*) received farther development, the *u* found refuge in the guttural: ቈጥዐ "to loathe", קוט; so too ቈጠጠ "to be slender"; ዐቈረ "to wrap up", قار; ፀቈነ "to hedge in", from ضاق, צוק; ቈረረ "to be cold", קור, קָרַר; ሰቈቈ "to covet another's goods", שׁוק; በኊበኊ "to rot", بغا, بَخُو, باخ; ሰኰየ "to go astray", שׁוּג, שָׁגַג, שָׁגָה; ኰነነ "to judge (to establish)", כּוֹנֵן; አእኰተ "to give thanks", كَبَّ and كبت (with softening of the *b* into *w*); ጕሐቈ "to bend, to be distorted", جَوِق, where *u* has made its way into both the gutturals, &c. In other cases the verbs have been derived from nouns which had a *u* in the formation: ለጕመ "to hold in check"; ቈለዘ "to hew off"; ቈሰለ "to receive a wound"; ነቈረ "to be one-eyed" (נָקוּר); ቋረፈ, አመጕጸ, አቈረበ, ኰሰተረ, ጕንደየ, ተርጕመ, መንኰሰ, ተመሥኰዐ, ጓሕለወ &c.; compare also በቍዐ "to be serviceable", with قِفْس.

(2) In a few words and roots *ua* or *ue* is of onomatopoetic character, as in ቋዕ and ኳኳ "raven", "crow"; ጕጓ and ጕጋ [and ጕጓ and ጕጕ *Kebra Nag.*] "bittern"; ቈርነነዓት "frog"; ጕርዔ "throat", "gorge"; አንጐርጐረ "to murmur"; perhaps in ጐሥዐ "*eructavit*", unless rather as derived from جُوش,—and in እንቋዕ "hurrah!".

(1) [Better, however, to regard this word as a *pluralis fractus* = نُقَط.]

(3) In another series of words this roughening seems to have made its appearance because of the guttural having undergone a degree of softening from its original pronunciation, and to make amends, as it were, by a second hardening. Thus ገ appears to have come from ከ in ሀጕለ, ጐድአ, ጐድጐደ; ገ from ዐ in ደጐጸ, ጸጕር; ገ from ቀ in ሰንጐጕ, አንጕዐ; ከ from ቀ in ለሐኰ, ኰሰየ, ኵናት; and ከ from ሐ, ኀ, in ምኵራብ(1), ኵሕሰ. A similar process may be noticed in another guise: thus, for instance, in እጓል, እጐልት &c., the ዕ has first been softened into እ, and the hardness has been subsequently restored by means of the *u*-sound combined with ገ.

(4) By and by, however, this *u*-containing pronunciation proceeded to make its way into many words and roots, simply from a general preference in the language for such sounds, although we are not now in a position to indicate the special motives for its exercise, or, on the other hand, to show how the motives hitherto suggested have by no means brought about the same result in all the cases in which it was apparently possible. But the other phonetic relations of the word seem invariably to be taken into account in this matter. Roots altogether weak seek thereby to gain greater fulness of sound, *e. g.*: ጐየየ "to flee"; ጐጕአ "to hasten" (جاء); and in cases like ኵሕሰ this pronunciation is manifestly easier than ከሕሰ. It is particularly common and in high favour before a ረ (about thirty times in Ethiopic words), but less so before Aspirates. Before ለ it occurs about fifteen times, before ነ about twenty times, before ሰ, ሠ some fifteen times, and before ጸ, ፀ about ten times. Though more rarely, it still does occur before the other letters, with the exception of radical ወ and በ (but yet it is found in the reduplicated conjugation ቡኍቡኆ, while before ፉ it appears only in ኵፉር). It never occurs, however, before any one of the other three gutturals, except of course when the *u*-containing guttural is itself doubled, and the two forms of the doubled letter are separated by a vowel,—in which case the rougher pronunciation is repeated. Farther, this pronunciation seems to have established itself in certain roots in order to distinguish them from others of a wholly different meaning, but which otherwise would have the same sound:—compare ኈልቈ [*var.* ኆልቈ, *Kebra Nag.*] with

(1) [But v. p. 50, Note (2).]

ኈልቀ; ተቈልቈለ with አንቀልቀለ; በቈለ with በቀለ; ሰኰየ with ሰከየ. Finally, when two gutturals (though separated by another letter) occur in one word, the establishment of the *u*-containing pronunciation in the one often brings about the same thing in the other: ኈለቈ, ኍሕቈ; farther ድርኍኍት "door-hinge" (Fem. from ድርኩክ, 'that, in which the door moves backwards and forwards').

It must farther be noticed (1), in conclusion, that many words and roots fluctuate between the *u*-containing and the common pronunciation of the Guttural, or else do not employ the first throughout in every one of their several forms (compare ቈረፀ and ቀረፀ; ቋረፈ and ቀረፈ; and the roots ቈጸረ, ሰቈረ and ዘንጐጐ). Also, words which are in frequent use, like ዝኵቱ, እልኵቱ, endeavour by gradually shaking off that pronunciation to simplify themselves into ዝኩቱ, እልኩቱ.

Dental-Lingual Mutes.

§ 27. (4) *The Dental-Lingual Mutes* ደ, ተ, ጠ. Through the co-operation of the tongue and the teeth, there are formed—besides the Liquids, which we are not just now considering—the soft letter ደ *d*, and the hard letter ተ *t*. Ranked with these, just as ቀ is with the Palatal-Gutturals, we find a hollow, explosive sound ጠ *ṭ*, peculiar to Semitic languages, which is formed through the co-operation of the tongue and the palate, "by bringing the root of the tongue up to the back part of the hard palate" (2). Precisely as ቀ and ከ are employed in the Guttural class for *κ* and *χ* respectively in foreign words, so in this class the Greek *τ* is usually rendered by ጠ, *e.g.* ሄጳዲጤን, ልጥር, ምሥጢር, ሚጥራ, while the Greek *ϑ* or *τϑ* is given by ተ, *e.g.* ሊቶስጥራ, ማቴዎስ, ማትያስ, አትሮንስ, ትስብያዊ (3).

These three letters are pretty sharply distinguished in Ethiopic roots; and ተ and ጠ are but rarely exchanged, as in ነተነ and ነጠነ, ነተዐ and ነጥዐ (4) with somewhat different meanings: so too ተብዐ "to be manly" and ጠብዐ "to be steadfast" (تبع). In the beginning of a word ተ is frequently softened into ደ (§ 73).

---

(1) V. Tuch, '*Comment.*' I, p. 18—22.

(2) *Cf.* Trumpp, p. 518.—On the emphatic consonantal pronunciation in Ethiopic there are various notices and theories, which however do not accord with one another: *cf.* Moore, '*Proc. Am. Or. Soc.*' 1888, p. XXX *sqq.*

(3) [*Cf.* Guidi, '*Le traduzioni degli Evangelii in Arabo e in Etiopico*', Roma, 1888, p. 34, Note.]

(4) [V., however, '*Kebra Nag.*' 39, Note 29.]

When compared however with the other Semitic languages, Ethiopic exhibits several changes in these letters. It has somewhat rarely the softer ደ for ጠ, as in ከደነ "to cover", כָּתַן, כָּתַם, كَتَمَ, كدن (¹); and for ט in ነደቀ "to build", נָטַע; ደመነ "to be obscured", טָמַן, ضَمَنَ; ደብር "mountain" טוּר, טַבּוּר; ደምሰሰ "to quench, to blot out", طمس, دمس; ኅዳጥ "a little", حَطِيط; also ተ for ט in ቀተለ "to kill", קָטַל, قتل (²); ቀታሬ "incense", קְטוֹרָה, قُطَار; ትንንያ "gnats", alongside of طَنّ. More frequently it shows the stronger and harder letters in place of the softer; thus probably ተ for ד in ሐተተ "to investigate", حدّ; perhaps in አስተዓ "gift", alongside of שֹׁחַד; ጠ for ד in መጠነ "to measure", מָדַד, مدّ; ነቁጥ "point" (³), נְקוּד, نُقْط; ጠበቀ "to adhere" (as by glue), דָּבֵק, طبق; ወለጠ "to alter, to exchange", بدل; ዐበጠ "to exact compulsory service of", עָבַד, عبط; ሰጠቀ "to rend" ܣܕܩ; ጠነየ "to make strict enquiry", دنا II; ጥቃ "strictness", ጠንቀቀ "to be strict"; ጠየቀ "to explore carefully", associated with דַּק, دقّ, דַּיֵּק, although ደቀቀ also occurs often, in the meaning, "to be small";—the same letter is used for ת in መጠቀ "to raise on high", متع, متح; ምጥቀት "sweetness", מָתֹק, and مَطْقَة; ሰፈጠ "to mislead, to deceive", beside פָּתָה; ጠቀዐ "to sound" ('to wind the horn'), תָּקַע. In many of these roots Ethiopic possesses the ጠ in common with Arabic, and in opposition to the Northern-Semitic tongues.

Farther ደ often answers to ذ, and ጠ to ظ and ث, *e. g.* in አስተዋደየ "to accuse", أَذِيَ; ጠለመ "to act unfairly, faithlessly", ظلم, ܛܠܡ; ጠሬው "Pleiades", ثُرَيَّا; አጥረየ "to acquire", ثَرَا; ጠቀበ "to sew", ثقب, and ثقف and إِسْكَاب, although these Arabic lisping sounds pass over, in other instances, into full sibilants (§ 30). ጠ corresponds frequently to ض: በጥሐ "to scarify",

(¹) *Cf.* Assyr. *nadānu 'to give'*, נתן (between two *n*'s), Haupt, '*Sum. Fam.-Ges.*', p. 43.

(²) V. Haupt, *l. c.* p. 74.

(³) [*Cf. supra*, p. 52, Note (¹).]

بضع; ሐጠቀ "to gag", צוק, ضاق; ጥርስ and ፅርስ "a molar tooth", ضِرْس; ጠግዐ "to adhere to", ضجع; ጠፈር "vault", ضَفْر.

Finally, in contrast with other languages, a marked substitution of Dental-Lingual Mutes in exchange for the corresponding Sibilants has to be noticed. Thus, they said ድኅከ "to be lame, to limp" for زحك; ድምፅ "whispering", for שֶׁמֶץ; ደፈነ "to hide", "to lay aside", for צָפַן, دفن; farther ተልባ "flax", probably equivalent to شَرْب; ዐራት "bed", עֶרֶשׂ, ܥܪܣܐ, عَرْش; and, to conclude, ጠርኀ "to cry" (along with ጸርኀ), صرا, صرخ, צָרַח; ቀጥቀጠ and ቀጸቀጸ "to grind, to bruise"; ጠቀር "soot", connected with سَقَر and صقر; ጥዕየ "to be in health", صَحَّ = ጽሕወ. On the converse side of this exchange v. § 30.

Labial Mutes.

§ 28. (5) *Labial Mutes* በ, ፈ, ጰ, ፐ. The rest of the Semitic languages have only two Mutes formed with the lips, viz. the soft በ and the hard ፈ. With the Northern-Semites each of the two letters is given, sometimes with an aspirated, sometimes with a hard, unaspirated utterance. The Southern-Semites [and the same is to be said of the Babylonian-Assyrians] know nothing of the distinction observed in such two-fold pronunciation, but give to በ the sound of *b* (or even utter it still more softly, like a *v*), and pronounce ፈ with aspiration, not however as *ph*, but as *f*: indeed to an Arabian mouth at least the pronunciation of a *p* is not possible(1). The Abyssinians, however, have contrived to form this harder, unaspirated sound, that is to say, *p*; but as if they too had been, at least at first, unable to utter a pure *p*, they have done so in a peculiar phonetic fashion. Either the *p* is strongly and suddenly puffed forth by a vigorous effort of the vocal organs,—constituting thus in the class of Labials an emphatic letter *p̣* ጰ(2)—

(1) Wallin p. 23.

(2) The best description of this letter is given by Isenberg, p. 8, where, speaking of ጰ as "*the explosive letter of this class*" he says "*the breath puffs off from between the lips, before the vowel is heard*". V. in this reference Wallin p. 10: "in order to produce such an explosive sound, one vocal organ must be pressed against another to form a closure, and by the sudden opening of the same the air enclosed behind it is expelled to articulate the explosive letter". V. also König, p. 45 *sq.*—Compare the emphatic utterance of פ among certain Jews, '*Journ. as.*' VI, 16, p. 517, and among the Syrians, '*Journ. as.*' VI, 13, p. 476 *sqq.*; Nöldeke, ZDMG XXXIV, p. 572.

corresponding to the emphatic ቀ and ጠ in the two foregoing classes; or else it is given with a slight sibilation—p^s ፐ—as in the Greek ψ. This view of ፐ at any rate seems to follow from the old name *Psa*; but at the same time it must be observed that LUDOLF and ISENBERG expressly denote the pronunciation of ፐ by that of our own *p*(¹): it must accordingly have had the sound of *p* in later times at least. The first of these two letters,—ጰ—, was certainly developed independently of Greek(²), for neither the character nor the name of the letter points to a Greek origin, and it is by no means in foreign words merely that it makes its appearance, but in genuine Ethiopic words and roots. In such words it originates as a rule out of a *b* made hard and hollow in sound:—ዌጰ "to throw, to hit (to shoot)"—belongs to هبّ; ቀለጰ "to catch with the mouth something that has been thrown", to כֶּלֶב (كُلَّاب); ምጕንጰ "a quiver" (*pharetra*), to جَعْبَة; ቆጰን "boot", to قَبْقَاب; ገንጰለ "to pervert, to overturn", to قلب, חָבַל. Yet it may also spring from פ:—ጰንጰወ "to sever the limbs, to break", صنف; ዘጶ زَوْفَى; ኀንጰን καλαβώτης, خَنْفَاء. Of unknown derivation are the names ቀጰጶ "chamaeleon"; እንጰንጶ ('name of a disease'). In certain other words also, *b* seems to have assumed even in early times the form of a harder but less dull *p*-sound; but it was not until a new character for *p* had been introduced by the Greeks, that this harder pronunciation could be expressed in writing: ሀፐለ "to full", أُبل, وبل; and ዲ.ፓ "ambuscade, snare", דִּבָּה, דָּבַב, دبّ. The Greek *π* is now expressed sometimes by በ, sometimes by ፈ, and sometimes by ጰ and ፐ: መፐርጶሊስ, ቀበዶቅያ, በትረ፡ ያርክ,

---

(¹) ISENBERG also calls it *Pa* merely, not *Psa*.

(²) Contrary to LUDOLF. The whole account of these letters given by LUDOLF is unsatisfactory. He thinks that *π* was at first rendered by በ and ፈ, and that later an endeavour was made to domesticate the *p*-sound as ጰ, from which there sprung however a '*novus*' and '*mirabilis sonus*':—that, still later, people learned the correct pronunciation of *π* and added the letter ፐ, and often used it at that day. The words in which ጰ and ፐ appear are mistakenly regarded by him as pure foreign words. The only thing that is true in this representation is, that in later times ፐ is more frequently employed in foreign words; but often enough, even in later times, the other three labials are also used for *p*, especially in the foreign words which were introduced through the intervention of Arabic.

ስፍንግ σπόγγος, አስፉሪዳ σπυρίδα, ቡሊቃርጳስ ሰሪጵዮን and ሰሪፍዮን, ስናፒ σίναπι. On the other hand ፈ is used for φ, but also ጰ and ፐ when a full vowel does not precede: ስጲር σφαῖρα; ሰንፔር σάπφειρος.

The other two letters በ and ፈ frequently exhibit mutual interchange, when we compare Ethiopic with the other tongues. An Ethiopic በ is confronted by a פ in the other languages,—in the following words, for instance: ብቍዕ "to be profitable" فقع; ምብኋህ "bellows", פּוּחַ, נָפַח, فاخ, نفخ; ብዕዛ 'a kind of antelope' (also "a small flute"), فَاغُوس(1); ዐንበዘ "to be drained, exhausted", probably نزف. In ነጠበ "to drop", נָטַף, and ነጠፈ "to filter", both the letters have been kept, though with different meanings. ב corresponds to an Ethiopic ፈ in ገዘፈ "to be compact", جَشِيب, خَشِيب, حَزَب; ሐቀፈ "to embrace", חָבַק, حبك, حاق; ነጽፈ "to become dry", יָצַב, نَصِبَ, نَضَبَ; አዕቀፈ "to cause offence", עָקַב, عقف; ለፈጸ "to knead" (if not "to besmear"), alongside of ለውሰ "to knead", corresponding to لاث and لبز.

But these Mutes border also upon the Semivowel ወ through በ; and, on this ground, changes not unfrequently occur in Ethiopic, just as in other languages, both within the language itself and when faced by other dialects: thus we have the expressions ፀወሰ "to be weak-limbed", and ፀብሰ "to be weak"; ቀንጠበ and ቀንጠወ (קָטַב) "to prick, to perforate". ወ corresponds to a ב, ب in ሐሰወ "to utter lies", כזב, كَذَب; ገለወ "to cover with", جلب; ወልወለ "to be irresolute", بَلْبَل; በ to a و in ቀርነብ "tip, sting", قَرْنُوَة. These exchanges appear also in proper names: ስልፋንዮስ *Sylvanius*; ሊዋርዮስ and ሊበርዮስ *Liberius*.

An exchange of like nature makes its appearance between the Mutes and the Nasal of this class(2): በልሐ "to extricate", ملح; በርኀ "to be bald", מָרַח (*cf.* נִמְרָט); ሐርበደ "to wallow in the

(1) [The meaning of this word is quite uncertain. And it may be proper to say here generally, that not a few of the comparisons, ventured upon by Dillmann in this chapter, are very doubtful, if some of them be not demonstrably erroneous.]

(2) An analogous phenomenon is met with in the Minao-Sabaic dialect; v. ZDMG XXIX, p. 606 *sq.*; XXX, p. 704 *sq.*

mire", حَرْمَد ; ነሀበ "to forge (metals)", نهم ; ነምር "tiger" becomes in Amharic ነብር. Conversely, ዐተመ "to be passionate" answers to عتب ; and ሠምረ "to approve of", "to delight in", goes back in the end to ܫܒܰܪ, شبر (شِمْر).

§ 29. If we glance once more over the three classes of Mutes, we must observe that the distinction between an aspirated (or rather assibilated) and an unaspirated pronunciation no more found admission into Ethiopic than it did into Arabic. We have seen, it is true, that ከ often answers to χ, and ተ to ϑ, and may conjecture accordingly that in foreign words ከ, ተ and perhaps also other hard and soft letters, may have been spoken with an aspiration. But in the case of native words no such inference follows. As regards the hollow-sounding letters on the other hand, it is established that they can never stand for foreign Aspirates, unless the aspiration be falling away at the same time.

No distinction recognised between an Aspirated (or Assibilated) and an Unaspirated pronunciation of Mutes.

Reciprocal exchanges between Mutes of different classes are exceedingly rare, and appear to be confined exclusively to the earliest formative stage of the language. Relatively the most common is the exchange between ቀ or ከ and ፈ; ወሰከ "to add to" is יָסַף (وسق): ተርፈ "to be left over", ترك, תָּרַח; ሐይቅ "shore", حَافَةٌ, خَيْفٌ. A very ancient exchange of ተ and ከ appears in the Pronouns of the 1st and 2nd pers. (§ 65).

§ 30. (6) *The Sibilants*,—five in all,—belong to the class of Dental-Lingual letters. Among them ዘ answers to ደ, as the clear and soft letter (*z* of the French and English); the harder ሰ (the firm *s*) to ተ; ጸ, the emphatic Explosive Sibilant, to ጠ. And these three leading letters, at least, Ethiopic has always carefully distinguished. When comparison is made with Arabic, ዘ is not only ز, but also ذ (as even the character ዘ has come from the Minao-Sabaic character for ذ—§ 11(¹)), unless it is rather ذ that slips back into ደ (§ 27); and ጸ is not merely ص(²), but also takes the place of ظ (with the like limitation, § 27). Alongside of these three letters all the Semites have developed another sister-letter to ሰ, somewhat rougher and more sibilant, namely

Sibilants.

(¹) *Cf.* also Hommel, ZDMG XLVI, p. 536.

(²) [Later, however, when ጸ had become *affricata*, ص was represented by ሰ; *v.* Littmann, '*Zeitschr. f. Assyr.*' XIV, p. 84, Note 1.]

š (שׁ, ش), and this is also met with in Ethiopic as ሠ(1). The Southern-Semites alone produced ض ḍ over and above, by bending back the ص to the Mutes,—which ḍ the Ethiopians likewise took with them to Abyssinia in the form ፀ. So far that letter does not properly belong to this class: For the reason why it has been placed here, v. *infra*.

In Greek words ዘ corresponds oftenest to ζ (ዘሞ, ζωμός, ዘይኑን *Zeno*); ሰ is also used for it, *e. g.* ሰሲማ *Zosima*. ሰ or ሠ answers to *s*, though here and there ጸ or ፀ may be so used, and in that case such letter frequently coincides in a remarkable way, in words of Hebrew origin, with the Hebrew (ጽዮን, ፀበኦት). ጸ is also often employed by the Ethiopians for the Greek τι, *e. g.*: ለንጽ λέντιον; አንጾክያ *Antiochia*: oftener however we find ጥየ and ቲየ, *e. g.*: አንጥያክስ *Antiochus*; እንዲቅትዮን "*indictio*".

Outside of their own class these five letters border on the Mutes of the Dental-Labial Class. The perception of this relationship of theirs has been kept up in Ethiopic in an exceedingly lively way, by such a Mute passing into a Sibilant, when one

---

(1) Ludolf had mistaken the correspondence of ሰ with ס, ܣ, س, and ሠ with שׁ, ܫ, ش, by inverting the relationship; but Hupfeld p. 5, has already drawn attention to the real state of the case, and Tuch in the second of the "*Commentationes*", cited on p. 14, has given farther proof of this. I regard the matter as settled thereby, and merely refer to these two treatises. What chiefly led Ludolf astray was his failure to notice the peculiar shifting of sound which prevailed among the North- and South-Semites between שׂ, س, שׁ, ס, and ش. Often enough, in fact, *š* in Arabic corresponds to the North-Semitic *s*, and *s* to the *š* of the North-Semites: while Ethiopic in these cases generally followed Arabic, *e. g.* שֵׁן, سِنّ, ስን "tooth"; קָדֵשׁ, قدس, ቀደሰ; שָׁמַע, سمع, ሰምዐ; נֶפֶשׁ, نفس, ነፍስ; נשׂא, نشا, ነሥአ; נֶגֶשׂ, النجاشي, ነገሠ; כְּרֵשׂ, كَرِش, ከርሥ and so on (Tuch p. 5). But otherwise, when this process of letter-shifting is not in operation, ሰ generally answers not merely to س but also to ס and שׂ, whence it is clear again that ሰ is not equivalent to שׁ, *e. g.* ኀሰረ, خسر, חָסֵר.—Owing to this mistake, the orthography of the Sibilants, which is followed in Ludolf's Lexicon cannot be accepted as correct without being farther tested: it needs repeatedly to be put right. On the gradation of the Semitic Sibilants in general, *cf.* Haupt, ZDMG XXXIV, p. 759 *sqq.* [and D. H. Müller, '*Verh. VII. Or.-Congr., Semit. Sect.*' p. 229 *sqq.*].

of the former, unattended by a vowel, comes upon one of the latter (§ 54). In roots and words also an interchange of Mutes and Sibilants may often be observed. For the manner in which this was effected in the case of the Demonstr. Pron. v. § 62. It has already been pointed out (§ 27) that Mutes occasionally appear in Ethiopic in place of the Sibilants of other tongues. But the converse is much more frequent. In those cases in which Aramaic has a Mute, Arabic a lisping Mute, and Hebrew a Sibilant, Ethiopic has a Sibilant too([1]), *e. g.* ܬܘܪܐ, ثور, שׁוֹר **ሰር**; ܝܬܒ, وثب, ישׁב, **ወሰበ**; ܕܒܚ, ذبح, זָבַח, **ዘብሐ**; ܕܘܢܒܐ, ذَنَب, זָנָב, **ዘነብ**; ܢܛܪ, نظر, נצר, **ነጸረ**; ܛܥܢ, ظعن, צען = טען, **ጸዐነ**; and in this way for the most part it gives Sibilants for the Arabic lisping Mutes, —namely for ث generally **ሠ**, *e. g.* **ሐሠር** "straw", حُثَارة (خُشَار); **ነሠነሠ** "to sprinkle", نثّا, نزا, נָזָה; also **ሰ**, *e. g.* **ሐረሰ** "to plough", حرث, חָרַשׁ; for ذ either **ዘ**, *e. g.* **ዘሐቀ** "to peel off husk, bark or skin", ذحق, ذحج (for other examples v. *supra*), or **ሰ**, *e. g.*, **ዐስቅ** "something variegated", عذق; **ማሕስእ** "a young male" (sheep, goat &c.), جَذَع, جَذْى, גְּדִי; or **ጸ**, *e. g.* **ዐጽቅ** "bough", عِذْق; **መጽለወ** "to fade", ذبل, ذلّ; and for ظ, **ጸ** (v. *supra*). But farther, in not a few cases, it has the Sibilant even where ordinary Arabic shows no transitional sound, and generally in fact the first and commonest Sibilant **ሰ**, as for instance for ד, in **እስከ** "until" (from עַד § 64); **ሰቈረ** "to pierce through", דָּקַר; **ረስነ** "to glow", ردن (in Derivatives); **ጌሰ** "to be up early", غدا; and for ת, in **ሰሜን** "South", תֵּימָן, تَيْمَن; **ሰኰሰ** "to break off, to end", סכת, سكت, and שָׁקַט, سقط: then, ט or ط often passes into the hollow-sounding sibilant **ጸ** (**ፀ**): **ግብጽ**, قبط "Egypt"; **በጸወ** "to fall asleep", بَطَأ; **ዐጸፈ** "to put on one's cloak", עָטַף, عطف VIII, and in rare instances ד or د, *e. g.* **በጸውዕ** "prodigy", like بدع.

§ 31. But these Sibilants also fluctuate a good deal among themselves; and in no class of letters are exchanges between the individual letters so prevalent as in this([2]). We are still keeping out of sight here the special relation which holds between **ሠ** and

Fluctuation and Interchange of Sibilants

([1]) Tuch p. 8*sqq*.

([2]) In this feature Ethiopic quite resembles Arabic.

ሰ on the one hand, and between ጸ and ፀ on the other (which will be considered farther on), and are attending merely to the three stages ዘ; ሰ, ሠ; ጸ, ፀ. (a) We frequently come upon the softest letter ዘ as an alternative form for ሰ (ሠ) or ጸ, or else taking its place: ሐሰበ "to think, to suppose" and ሐዘበ; ሰበረ "to shatter" and ዘበረ in መንዘበር; መሥመር "a line" and መንዝምር; ምንዝር "beer" and ምስር; for other cases v. § 57; and similarly the root ፀመደ "to bind" (צָמַד, ضمد) appears besides, with a slightly different meaning, as ዘመደ. Cases are more common, in which Ethiopic has only ዘ for the *s* or *ś* of other tongues: *e. g.* for *s* and *š* ዘበጠ "to smite", שֵׁבֶט; ዘወዐ "to meditate", שִׂיחַ; ዘንጎዐ "to tattle", سجع and سهج; ዘብጽ "a skin, hide", سَبَد; ዘፈር "border", شُفْر; ገዝፈ "to be thick", جشب; ጕዝጕዝ "mat", حَشِيَّة; መዝመዘ "to stroke, to rub", מָשַׁשׁ, مش, مث, مزمز; more rarely for *ṣ*: ዘፍሪ "something yellow", صَفْرَا; ቤዝ "Morning-star", related to باض, بَضّ; ሕምዝ "poison", חמץ, حمض, حمز. (b) The medial letter ሰ, ሠ often answers to the softer ז, ذ of the other tongues:—ረሥአ "to grow old", רָזָה, رزأ, رثّ, رذى; ነሥነሠ "to sprinkle", נָזָה, نزا, نثا; ወሰነ "to determine, to fix limits", وزن; ሰሐስሐ "to agitate, to move backwards and forwards", זָחַח, זוּעַ, زَحْزَحَ, زحّ; ሰሰለ "to depart", אָזַל, زال; ሰርም "the flood", agreeing with the Arabic شَرْم, but contrasting with the Hebrew זֶרֶם (*cf.* also the instances given in § 30, where ሰ corresponds to a ذ, د, or ד). But in other cases ሰ or ሠ has been retained where other languages already have צ or ض:—ሠሐቀ "to laugh", ضحك, צָחַק and שָׂחַק; ሐፈሠ "to sweep up", קָפַץ, حفش; ፈሥሐ "to rejoice", פָּצַח, فرس; አስፈር "jaundice", صَفَر (*v.* ዘፍሪ *supra*); ሰፈወ "to hope", צָפָה; ቍስል "wound", قَصَل, [illegible]; አንበስበሰ "to glitter", بَصّ, بصبص; and in other Words within Ethiopic itself it exchanges with ፀ:—ስፍሕ and ፅፍሕ "breadth", صفح, צפח; ርሕሰ "to be moist", and ርሐፀ "to sweat", רָחַץ, رحض, and رشح. (c) But certainly still more common is the appearance in Ethiopic of the hardest letter ጸ or ፀ for softer ones present in other languages. For several cases, in which ጸ answers to ذ and د, *v.* § 30. It corresponds to a ز in words like ጽሕም "beard", זָקָן[?];

ጸገወ and ጸገየ (§ 25), زهى; ላጽቄት "lizard", لَزِيق; ለፌጸ (ለሰ) "to knead", لبز; ነጽሐ "to be pure", نصح, with זַךְ, زكا. Still more frequently it stands overagainst a س or ش:—ደጐጸ "to prick", "to stab", ܕܨ݂ܥ, דָּעַץ, دعس; ጽልዕ "ulcer, wound", سَلْعَة, but زحس; ጸላዕት "rocks", "caverns", סֶלַע, سُلوع and صُلّاع; ጸበተ "to swim", سبح; ጸጕር alongside of ሥዕርት "hair", answering to שֵׂעָר, شعر; ጸግበ "to be satisfied (*satur*)", شبع, שׂבע; ጸውዐ "to summon", שִׁוַּע, صاح; አንፈርዐጸ "to leap", compared with פָּרַע; ጸልአ "to hate", شنأ, שׂנא; በቀጸ "to rake together (the fire)", בִּקֵּשׁ, بحث; ጼነወ "to smell", סַמִּים, شَمَّ [?]. In Ethiopic itself ሰ also appears as an alternative for ጸ in ሰኰት and ጸጕ "street" (שׁוּק) (1); and in § 73 reference is made to an example of even the ሰ of the Causative Conjugations being deadened into ጸ. Similarly too ፀ has often originated from ش and س:—ቈፀረ (ቈጸረ) "to confine, to conspire", קָשַׁר, قصر; ፀጋም "left hand", شأم; ፀመረ "to fasten", סָמַר, سمر; ፄወወ "to take prisoner", שָׁבָה, سبا; ዕፄ "worm", עָשׁ, عُثَّة; ፃፄ "moth", סָס, سُوس; ጕፃጕፅ "a rugged road", جَشّ.

From the survey that has just been made of the multiform phonetic interchange between the letters composing this class, it becomes clear as regards the relation of ሰ to ሠ and of ጸ to ፀ (2), that ሰ and ጸ are the chief letters of the second and third stages. They predominate throughout the language, and ሠ and ፀ appear much less frequently. Where the letter ሠ does make its appearance, it answers generally to a ش or ث; yet even in that case it is often supplanted by the simpler ሰ:—compare ሰርበ "to drink", شرب; ሰቀለ "to weigh", شقل, ثقل, שׁקל; ሰተረ "to rend", שׁתר, شتر; ሴበ "to grow grey", שִׂיב, شاب; and so too ሳሕበበ "to become mouldy", شهب (سهب); ሱዕ "tinder"; شُيُوع; farther ሰይጣን, ቀሳር, ቀሰጠ, ቀስፍ, በሰረ and many others, which either invariably, or nearly so, are written with ሰ. As the speech more

(1) This is more doubtful in ሰምዐ and አሰምአ.

(2) According to König, p. 47, ጸ and ፀ are roughened utterances of what were originally Explosives, *tṣ*, *dẓ*.

and more took this direction, the letter *s* gained such predominance that *š* gradually disappeared, and *s* was used instead(¹). In poetry ሰ and ሠ rhyme together; and when Amharic began to be reduced to writing, consciousness of the original phonetic value of the character ሠ had been lost so completely, that a new character ሸ was invented to express the Amharic *š*. Unfortunately this deteriorated pronunciation had such an effect on the writers of manuscripts, even in the case of the older manuscripts, that ሰ and ሠ were exchanged at the fancy of the scribe, and at the present moment we are in doubt about which is the more correct method of writing certain words, particularly those of comparatively rare occurrence. But yet there were several words, which this capricious confounding of the two letters was never able to affect, either because of ሠ still preserving a somewhat different pronunciation from ሰ, or because of the power of tradition, in the matter of writing, proving too strong for caprice. Roots, like ነሥአ, ሠሀለ, ሢመ, ነገሠ, ከሠተ, ወሥአ and others, are never found written with ሰ in the better class of manuscripts; and conversely, roots, like ለብሰ, ነፍሰ, መሰለ, ማሰነ, ረሰየ, ቀደሰ, ብእሲ, ሰምዐ, ሰመየ, ሰበዐ, ሰደደ and others,—are never written with ሠ. But farther, the Abyssinians soon lost the original pronunciation of ፀ as a mute, as well as of ሠ, and suffered it to revert to the sound of ጸ, out of which it had sprung. Hundreds of years ago ጸ and ፀ had come to have exactly the same pronunciation; and they rhyme together in poetry. Meanwhile we can no longer discover from the appearance of ፀ in the individual words concerned, at what time this reversion of the pronunciation may have commenced. We still meet with a good many roots (v. *supra*), in which Ethiopic has ፀ in place of a simpler sibilant in other tongues; but on the other hand we meet with not a few, in which already ض takes invariably the form of ጸ, *e. g.*, ጸረበ, ضرب; ጸበበ, ضبّ; ጸጠ, ضَوِيطَة; ጸፈነ, ضفن; ጸፍዐ, ضفع. When too ፀ and ጸ gave quite different meanings to several roots, which otherwise had the same sound, the confusion of the two characters in writing was never so marked. It is only in one or two words

(¹) *Cf.* Schrader, '*Monatsber. d. K. Preuss. Akad. d. Wiss. zu Berlin*' 1877, p. 79 *sqq.*, and Haupt, '*Sum. Fam.-Ges.*', p. 68.

that such confusion occurs with any frequency. It is curious to observe how Ethiopic sought gradually to revert to the original condition of the sounds of Semitic speech,—the letters ኀ, ዐ, ሠ and ፀ being undoubtedly of comparatively late origin,—by ceasing, little by little, to distinguish between ኀ and ሐ, ዐ and አ, and ፀ and ጸ.

The Liquid and Softer Letters: Nasals; Linguals; and Semi-vowels.

§ 32. (7) *The Liquid and Softer letters*, viz. the Nasals መ and ን, the Linguals ረ and ለ, and the Semivowels ወ and የ—:

Of the *Nasals* the labial መ is the more definite and therefore the firmer; the dental ን is the more general, and as it borders on the Linguals it exchanges with them. In their mutual relations, however, the one Nasal not infrequently passes over into the other.

It has already been shown (§ 28) how መ exchanges with the labial Mutes. It exchanges in the same way with the Semivowel ወ:—on the one hand instead of መሰከ "to draw the bow", ወሰቀ is also used; on the other, an initial ወ is hardened into መ in መዓር "honey", יַעַר; መዐደ "to counsel", יעץ, وعظ, وعد, IV, יעד; and in the more Amharic መዘነ "to weigh" (Geʿez ወሰነ, § 31), وزن (1). It is not often that the more definite መ arises out of the general Nasal ን:—in ዘመወ "to commit fornication" (another form being ገዜት), זָנָה, زنا, and in ጽሕም "beard", זָקָן[?], ذَقَن, *n* certainly appears in all the other Semitic tongues; in አቀምቈዐ "to till the ground thoroughly", መ seems to have come from *n* under the influence of ጠ. On the other hand with comparative frequency *m* becomes *n* (§ 57).

The other Nasal, ን is more liquid and fugitive. Thus it may disappear entirely, particularly in the end of a word (§ 58), or enter with ease into a short syllable which has the tone, to strengthen it (§ 58), or replace the first sound in any double-consonant whatever (§ 58). It also comes readily out of ም before a dental or lingual Mute, whether in native or in foreign words (§ 57). Thus too it frequently replaces in roots the more definite መ: ተባህነነ "to fail", "to withdraw", بهم IV and V; ጼነወ "to smell", סַמִּים, شَمَّ[?]; ስኑሕ "bald", صَمَحْمَح, שִׁפֵּחַ, but also أَصْلَعُ, أَسْلَحُ; ቀነጸ "to leap", قمص and قلص. On the other hand ን and the liquid lingual ለ pass, dialectically, the one into the other: ረሕነ

(1) More frequently has ወ become መ in Amharic; Isenberg, p. 33.

"to spread (housings) over", رحل; ድኅነ "to get off, to escape", זָחַל, ܙܚܠ, زحل; ሰንሰል "chain", שַׁלְשֶׁלֶת, سِلْسِل; and ጸንጸሊ "a cymbal", צֶלְצְלִים, صلصل (1); conversely ጸልአ "to hate", שָׂנֵא, شنأ (2). The exchange between ነ and ረ does not so readily occur; and when it does occur, it may be regarded as brought about by the intervention of ለ; thus, no doubt, in ዐጠነ "to fumigate", (together with ቀታሪ) from קָטַר, قتر, عِطر, and perhaps in አመዝገነ "to repay", שָׂכַר, شكر and شكم (*cf.* also ተንተነ "to stagger", ترتر), and ዝናም "rain", זֶרֶם (*cf.* also ሰርም); [contrast, however, Assyrian *zanānu, zunnu*].

Of the two *Liquid Linguals* ረ certainly inclines rather to the Aspirate-Gutturals; and although here it does not,—as partly it does in Hebrew,—share at all in the other peculiarities of the Gutturals, yet it often brings about the gurgling *u*-containing pronunciation in the Palatal-Gutturals which precede it (§ 26), in which tendency it is followed by ለ (v. *ibid.*). In their mutual relations, ረ and ለ frequently pass into one another, but only in root-formation. In fact at the end of a word, ለ is a more favourite letter in Ethiopic than ረ, thus—ሠዐለ "to paint" ('to fashion'), صوّر (צוּר, יָצַר), سوّل; በቀለ "to punish", ܒܩܪ, בִּקֹּרֶת; አበል "member", "limb", هبر; ሐለለ "to burn", along with ሐረረ "to be hot", حرّ, חָרַר, غلّ, خلّ; ቈጽል "foliage", خضر and خضل XI (3). In the interior of a word this exchange is found in ሰፎልያ "hammer", from the root פוּר, פָּרַר; ብርስን "lentils", بُلْسُن: the harder ገርገረ is found as a secondary form of *galgala* in Syriac also. ለ shares with ነ in the weakness of being capable

(1) Perhaps also *Dent*, the name of the 19th letter of the Alphabet, from *Dalt*.

(2) On the exchange of *am* and *al* (through the intervention of *an*) in the Arabic of Yemen, v. *Mufaṣṣal*², p. ١٥٣, l. 8; on the modern Arabic popular pronunciation أَمْبَارِح (*embāreḥ*) "yesterday" (for أَلْبَارِح) v. Trumpp, '*Sitzber. d. philos. philol. u. h. Cl. d. k. b. Ak. d. Wiss.*' 1877, Part II, p. 119.

(3) Thus too in foreign words, but mostly following the lead of the Septuagint, ለ exchanges with *r* and *n*, *e.g.*, ሞርጡል for ሞርጡር, ርቤል, ሱራፌል, ኪሩቤል, ቃየል &c.

of a complete disappearance in the end of a word (§ 58), just as it exhibits the faculty also of bringing over to its own sound a foregoing *m* or *n* (§ 54). That *r* besides may pass into *s*— seems to follow from ኄስ "it is better", alongside of ኄር "good", خَيْر: compare also ደምሰሰ, دمس and دمر [1].

Finally, *the two Semivowels* ወ and የ are, along with አ, the softest and most liquid of all the letters, and they are constantly changed for the corresponding vowels (v. *infra* § 49 *sqq.*; *cf.* also on ው and ይ *supra*, p. 38 *sq.*). On the other hand they are much more definitely marked off from one another than in the other Semitic languages, and they maintain themselves tenaciously when they have once taken root,—without ወ, for instance, passing into የ, through the influence of an *i*, or የ into ወ, influenced by a *u*. It has already been shown, how ወ is softened out of other labials, or hardened into them (v. §§ 28 and 32). As first letter of a root, it often corresponds to *n* of other languages (§ 68); but this phenomenon is not to be explained as a softening of *n* into *y* or *w*, but as a variety of the root-form. As a Palatal, የ borders upon ገ and ከ; at least ዱኵቱም "made an orphan" appears to be connected with יָתֹם. Compare also ፀጋም with شأم.

II. MEETING OF LETTERS IN THE SYLLABLE AND IN THE WORD.

GENERAL RULES OF THE SYLLABLE.

§ 33. The two kinds of letters, which have hitherto been exhibited separately, appear in speech only in union with one another. Neither a single vowel nor a single consonant can by itself form a word or constituent part of speech: it is not until they are uttered in combination that words or portions of words are produced. In this combined utterance it is always the vowel which gathers to itself one or several consonants and binds them

Constitution of the Syllable.

---

(1) Ewald, '*Hebr. Spr.*', p. 66, has drawn attention to this fact. Meanwhile, ንእሰ "to be small" has its own connection with ܢܥܣ, نعس, and نوّز. The word ጠማር and ጡማር, طومار is derived from τομάριον.

into one whole. A simple phonetic whole, of this nature, held together by one vowel, constitutes *the Syllable*. Every syllable must have one vowel; but no syllable can have more than one, unless it be two vowels which coalesce in a single vowel-sound or diphthong. One syllable even may by itself have the full force of a word, and thus constitute a word, like ዝ "this", ቃል "word"; and Language has a host of monosyllables. By far the greatest number of words, however, contain several of these simple phonetic groups, one of which farther holds the rest round itself as a centre and bears the Tone of the word. Different languages show different dispositions and capabilities in the nature of these simple phonetic groups, according as they severally admit of a larger or a smaller number of consonants being gathered about the one vowel. Semitic languages, generally, do not tolerate the piling up of consonants in one syllable, for they are rich in vowels. Yet there are degrees of difference among them in this respect. Arabic has developed this Semitic tendency with most thoroughness; the Northern-Semitic languages are less rich in vowels; while Ethiopic, in this matter, as in many others, stands midway between these extremes. In particular it resembles Arabic in allowing a short vowel to stand in an open syllable,—that is, in a syllable which ends in a vowel,—independently of its being supported by the Tone; and on the other hand, like the Northern-Semitic languages, it admits long vowels in closed syllables,—that is, syllables which end with a consonant,—and it even allows a word to conclude with a double consonant. Generally, however, open syllables outnumber closed syllables. Farther, Ethiopic evinces a peculiar leaning to the Northern-Semitic tongues, through its very short *ĕ*-sound, which often takes the place of a full Arabic vowel. The rules of the syllable in detail are as follows (1).

Beginning of the Syllable.

§ 34. (1) *Every syllable must begin with a Consonant.* A vowel can never commence a word or syllable, for according to the Semitic conception of phonetic relations, every vowel, however audible in itself, must at least be preceded by a breathing, more or less vigorous. Accordingly in Ethiopic too, all roots which at first began with a vowel have had their initial vowel turned to the

---

(1) Compare with the following representations König, pp. 54*sqq.*, 92*sq.*, 104, 118, 139*sq.*, and 143*sqq.*

consistency of a consonant. The same thing is shown in foreign words, whenever they have to be transcribed in Ethiopic: **አልፋ** ἄλφα; **ሄሬኔዎስ** *Irenaeos*; **ሐናንያ** Ἀνανίας; **ዕብራዊ** Ἑβραῖος; **ኦቦሊ** or **ወቦሌ** Ex. 30, 13 (*o* being resolved into *au* = *ua* = *wa*) ὄβολος; **ውቅያኖስ** *oceanus*; **ውለምሕሳ** Gen. 28, 19; **ይሁዳ** Ἰουδαία. It was only the later pronunciation that contrived a pure *u* or *i* in the beginning of the word in cases like **ውሉድ**, **ይጉብሩ** (§ 19). So when, according to the other rules of formation, two vowels would come together in the middle of a word and thereby bring two syllables into existence (§ 33) in that form, this is not admitted of, and such a hiatus is avoided by contraction or blending into a double or mixed sound (§ 39), or by the interpolation of a separating letter (§ 41), or by the hardening of a vowel into its semivowel (§ 40); and thus the phonetic conditions are reduced to the rule which has been enunciated. It is the same in foreign words, *e. g. Theodora* is either transcribed **ታኦዶራ** or **ቴዎዶራ**.

No syllable begins originally with a double consonant; and in those cases in which the consonant introducing the vowel of the syllable is preceded by a consonant unprovided naturally with a vowel, this consonant is uttered with the shortest vowel *ĕ*, *e. g.* **ግበር** *g*ᵉ*-bár*. But such *ĕ* is of a fugitive character, being little else than a half-vowel or vowel-touch; and this is one of the cases in which the so-called vowel of the sixth order resembles the Hebrew *sh*ᵉ*va mobile* (§ 22). In the later pronunciation of Ethiopic, however, when the nature of the consonants which came together permitted it,—when, for instance, a liquid followed a mute, or a mute a sibilant,—even that vowel-touch was no longer heard and **ፍኖት** was pronounced *fnōt*; **ብላዕ** *blā*ʿ; **ክረምት** *krámt*; and farther even **ክልኤ** *klē* for *kel-*ʾ*ē* (§ 47)(1): So in foreign words **ስፍንግ** *sfeng* for *seféng*, σπόγγος; **ክርስቶስ** *Chrestós*. Not more than one consonant, however, can be prefixed in this way to the consonant which introduces the vowel of the syllable. When, therefore, by the rules of formation several vowel-less consonants come together before it, an auxiliary vowel must be applied to make it possible to pronounce them. This vowel is generally *ĕ*, no longer so fugitive as in the foregoing case, but a complete short vowel, *e. g.* **ይግበር** *yeg-bar*; **ትእምርት** *te*ʾ*-mért*.

---

(1) Ludolf, '*Gramm.*' I, 5.

Meanwhile foreign words, commencing with three consonants, would often be much disfigured by the insertion of an auxiliary vowel in the group; and in this case a device, current in the other Semitic languages also, was adopted, namely the prefixing of a short vowel introduced by አ, to the whole group, *e. g.*, እስክሬን *esk^e rēn*, *scrinium.* In fact this device for facilitating the pronunciation of vowel-less letters in the beginning of a word is frequently employed, even where only one vowel-less consonant precedes the consonant which introduces the vowel of the syllable. In native words of Ethiopic formation the vowel prefixed is mostly *e*, እምነ "out of, from", from ምነ, מִן; እስመ (1) "for", "because"; እስኩ (in wish or entreaty) "O that!"; እብሬት "vicissitude", from በረየ; እግዚእ "Lord", for ግዚእ; perhaps እልታኅ "under-garment" and እምሔው "ancestor"; (on እንግዳ "foreigner", v. § 137 *ad fin.*). In Ethiopic words of earlier formation the vowel *a* is also used, አጽባዕት "finger", أَصْبَع. In foreign words *ă* appears more frequently than *ĕ*, particularly in those which have reached Abyssinia through the Arabic: እስጢፋኖስ *Stephanus*; አክሊሚንቶስ with the older ቀሌምንጦስ *Clemens*; አትሮንስ *ϑρόνος*; አስኬማ *σχῆμα*; አስፉሪድ *σπυρίδα*; አብሮቅላ *Procla*; አብረክሲስ *πράξεις* (Arab.).

Termination of the Syllable.

§ 35. (2) *The syllable may terminate either in a vowel or a consonant.* If it terminates in a vowel, the vowel may be either long or short: ዝ *zé*; ኅበ *ḫába*; ፌጸመ *fáṣṣama*; ቆመ *qōma*; ሜጡ *mḗṭū*. If it closes with a consonant, the vowel of the syllable may be short, as in ገበርኩ *gabárkū*; ገበርክሙ *gabarkémmū*, or long, whether it has the tone, as is usually the case—አምላክ *amlā́k*; እሙንቱ *emū́ntū* (2); ኖምከ *nṓmka*; ታምልክ *tā́mlek*—or has not the tone, *e. g.* ሜጥክሙ *mēṭkémmū*; ይሚጥውዎ, ይፌጽሞሙ &c.

A syllable may end even in two consonants, but only in the termination of a word. Cases like እንትኩ "that" (*fem.*) are no

(1) In the later pronunciation this እ is again rejected: the pronunciation is *sma*, *sku*, and so too እስከ "till" (which has had a different origin) *ska*, Ludolf I, 5.

(2) [But v. Praetorius, '*Aethiop. Gramm.*', p. 23, where—following Trumpp, p. 548—he puts the tone on the last syllable:—*ĕmūntū́*. tr.]

exceptions, for, even granted that it was pronounced *ént-kū*, and not rather *ént^e^kū*(1), this word must be regarded as a compound of two words, and must be estimated in the same way as **ምንትኑ** "what?"; **መንግሥትኒ** "the kingdom also" &c. It is mainly in feminine Nominal stems formed by the closely attached *t*, that a double consonant occurs in the end of a word. The vowel of such a syllable, owing to its being more compressed by the two closing consonants, must of necessity be short; and thus if it was originally a long vowel, it must be shortened: **ፍጥርት** *feṭért*; **ትምህርት** *temhért*; **ከዋክብት** *kawākebt*; **ጸሀርት** *ṣahárt*; **አሕቅልት** *aḥqélt.* It is only when the first of the two final consonants is a Semi-vowel or an Aspirate-Guttural, that the vowel of the syllable may be long (v. § 36). There are, besides, other cases, in which a word ends in two vowel-less consonants (v. § 38).

CHANGES OF LETTERS CONSEQUENT ON THE GENERAL RULES OF THE SYLLABLE, OR ON THEIR MEETING WITH OTHER LETTERS.

1. VOWELS.

Shortening of Long Vowels. Lengthening of Short Vowels.

§ 36. In Ethiopic, as well as in all other Semitic languages, the vowels are the letters most subject to alteration, as forming the more mobile and subtle division of the sounds of speech. And yet this change among them is far from being carried out here as extensively as in Hebrew (§ 22): it is only in a few directions that a comparatively frequent exchange of vowels prevails.

(A) INFLUENCE OF THE STRUCTURE OF THE SYLLABLE AND THE WORD ON THE VOWELS.

The most important phenomena in this reference are *the Shortening of Long Vowels and the Lengthening of Short Vowels.* It is true that, in accordance with § 35, Ethiopic may admit both long and short vowels in open as well as in closed syllables, and

---

(1) [Trumpp, p. 547, transcribes this word in the form *entekú*; Praetorius, '*Aethiop. Gramm.*' p. 28, follows Trumpp, writing the word thus:— *ĕntĕkú.* tr.]

that too, whether they have or have not the tone, the result being that exchange between long and short vowels is by no means carried so far in this language as it is in others. But still there are several cases in which this change occurs. In a syllable ending in two consonants a long vowel is not admitted (§ 35). Thus when a second vowel-less consonant(1) is appended to an ordinary closed syllable, *ā* must be *shortened* to *ă*, and *ū* and *ī* to *ĕ*. Accordingly ሠያጥ "dealer" forms in the Fem. ሠየጥ (for ሠየጥት § 54)); ሠላሲ, ሰማኒ, in the Fem. ሠለስት, ሰመንት; the very common form ግቡር becomes in the Fem. ግብርት *gebĕrt*; and it is only from ርኩስ "unclean", and the like, that ርኩስት even is read in place of ርኵስት (§ 42)(2); እግዚእ and ልሂቅ in the Fem. have the forms እግዝእት and ልህቅት. A syllable of this kind may retain *ā*, only when the first of the two concluding consonants is an Aspirate: in such a case, if it has a short *a*, the vowel must be lengthened, *e. g.* ነዋኅት, ቈንዛእት (§ 46); but any long vowels, other than *ā*, must be shortened even before Aspirates, *e. g.* ብፁዕ Fem. ብፅዕት; and yet here and there one meets also with እግዚእት and even with ሊቅት (from ሊቅ, inasmuch as ቀ occasionally shares in the peculiarities of the Aspirates). Farther, when the first of the two concluding consonants is a semi-vowel, the long vowel may be retained:—thus not only does one say ሠናይት, ማእከላይት,—for here ይ has the sound of *i*,—but also ሕያውት, እምሔውት, where the ው inclines at least to *u* (§ 39). Apart from the very common case which has been described, the shortening of a long vowel in the formation only occurs regularly, when the tone-less *ī* of the Fem.-persons of the verb is brought into the middle of the word, through the attachment of a suffix. Shortening happens also under the influence of a የ or a ወ, which draws to itself a *y* or a *w* out of a foregoing or following *ī* or *ū*, and leaves the vowel reduced to a short *ĕ* (§ 52); or it may happen in consequence of the emphasis of the word, an *ō*, or an *ā* which has come from *ō*, being in certain cases simplified into *ū*, and an *ē* into *ī* (§ 60). Cases

(1) A short *ĕ* originally ending the Noun (whereon v. § 38) is not taken into account here.

(2) An exception is formed also by ኮዑልት '*Kufāle*', p. 142, l. 3.—On forms like አዘዝክኒ = አዘዝኪ + ኒ v. *infra*, § 151, 4. [As regards ርኩስት, when it does occur, it is probably an instance merely of cacography for ርኵስት in an inferior MS.]

fall to be noticed here also, in which *ū* occasionally becomes *uĕ*, just as ዘኩ and እልኩ *zékū*, *élkū*, with the addition of ቱ, are, by reason of this new load in the end of the word, shortened to ዘኰቱ and እልኰቱ and even to ዘክቱ and እልክቱ (v. § 26).—It is only under the influence of an Aspirate coming after it, that *a short vowel is lengthened* in the formation with a measure of regularity, and even then the rule is restricted to *a* and *e* (§ 46). For other cases, in which short *ă* or *ĕ* becomes *ā*, *ī*, or *ū*, or even *ĕ* becomes *ē*,—see above, §§ 18, 20, 21. Besides, when we make a comparison with other Semitic languages, we are obliged to recognise in the *ā*, *ī*, and *ū* of certain Word-forms, vowels which were originally short, and which, merely through the tone, have been gradually turned into long vowels (v. *infra*).

The *weakening and reducing of vowels* occur occasionally in a few words, in particular in the weakening of *a* into *ĕ* (§ 18), the reduction of *ū* to *ō*, and of *ī* on the one hand and *ā* on the other to *ē* (§ 21), and the simplification of *ō* to *ā* (§ 18). A regular phenomenon in Formation is the reduction of *ă* to *ĕ* before Aspirates (§ 45), as well as the reduction, and at the same time the lengthening, of *ă* into *ē*, the lengthening being by way of compensation for a double consonant (§ 56). **Weakening and reducing of Vowels.**

§ 37. Individual vowels may *fall away*, but only when they meet with other vowels (§ 41). On the other hand this fate is very often experienced by Short *ĕ* as a result of change in the conditions of the syllable. In many forms it is not maintained either by the tone or by a closed syllable, and already sounds very short and little else than a half-vowel; and thus upon due occasion it disappears completely. The following cases fall to be noticed here in detail:—(a) A short *ĕ* in an open syllable without the tone, which is preceded by another open syllable having a long or short vowel, can seldom maintain itself, at least according to the later pronunciation: it brings about the attachment of its own introductory consonant to the preceding syllable and then disappears: thus ይገብሩ (originally *yegaberū*) is given as *yegabrū*; ይጸሕፉ (orig. *yeṣeḥefū*) as *yeṣeḥfū*; ይባርኩ *yebārkū*: ይፌጽሙ *yefēṣmū*; ምድራውያን *medrāwyān*; and so in the semi-passive expression of the verb, instead of original ገብረ *gábera*, ተገብረ *tagábera*, the pronunciation is rather *gábra* and *tagábra*. But the *ĕ* which constitutes the so-called Binding-vowel of the pronom- **Treatment of Short *ĕ*, under change of Syllabic Conditions.**

inal suffixes is retained, whether with or without the tone, even in the later pronunciation, thus: አምላክነ *amlākéna*; ቃልከ *qāleka.* Again, this shorter pronunciation is not employed, if the open syllable which precedes the syllable containing *ĕ* is a particle externally prefixed, such as a preposition or conjunction, *e. g.*:— በስታይ *ba-setāi* (not *bastāi*); ለትቁም *la-teqūm* (not *latqūm*); but it appears in special and permanent compounds, like እግዚአብሔር *egzīabḥēr*, ዝክቱ፡ *zéktū.* (b) A short *ĕ* in a closed syllable, which is preceded by an open syllable, is maintained more firmly,—so that ይገብር, ያመልክ, ነግር are rendered *yegáber*, *yāmálek*, *neger.* It is the same with ደናግል *danāgel* and አዋልድ *awāled*; and only a slovenly pronunciation would give these words as *awāld* and *yāmalk.* But when a formative syllable, beginning with a vowel, is applied to such a closed syllable containing *ĕ*, the final consonant of the latter is taken over to the formative syllable, and the *e*,—left with its introductory consonant,—disappears, while the last-named consonant attaches itself to the foregoing syllable: ይገብሩ, ያመልክ, ነግሪ *negri*; ደናግለ *danāgla* (although at first certainly *danāgela*); ዴገን, ዴግኑ *dēgen*, but *dēgnū.*

Treatment of Short *ĕ* at the end of Nominal Stems.

§ 38. A similar loss of a short and fugitive *ĕ* has been experienced by Ethiopic at the end of Nominal stems. It may be proved pretty clearly, from the formation of individual Nominal stems, singular and plural, as well as from some other indications, leaving in fact no room for doubt, that at one time Ethiopic had the *ground-form* of Nominal stems, as distinguished from the Construct state and the Accusative, *ending in a fugitive ĕ*(1), so that at one time, for instance, ገብር "servant" was pronounced

(1) Just as a noun in Arabic ends in *u* in the Nominative and in *i* in the Genitive. In Ethiopic these two cases had not yet been distinguished. The above theory,—which has been contested by Trumpp, p. 532, but has been supported by König, p. 76*sq.*,—I have endeavoured to establish in my Essay ('Observations on the Grammar of Geʿez and on the ancient History of Abyssinia'): '*Bemerkungen zur Grammatik des Geez und zur alten Geschichte Abessiniens: Sitzber. d. K. Pr. Ak. d. Wiss. zu Berlin*' 1890, p. 3*sqq.* On the Arabic literary language, which knows nothing of nouns ending in a consonant, *cf.* Fleischer, '*Beiträge*', *St.* 2. p. 281*sqq.*; *St.* 5. p. 130*sqq.*, and on the form of the Himyaric local name ظَفَارِ, Wüstenfeld, '*al Bakrī*' *II*, p. 463; '*Jāqūt*' *III*, p. 576; *cf.* Olshausen, '*Monatsber. d. K. Preuss. Ak. d. Wiss. zu Berlin* 1881', p. 690.

gábr[e], and ደናግል *danāgel*[e]. This termination in a vowel must, however, have worn itself off in very early times,—a thing which in the case of most of the Nominal stems might well have happened without increasing the difficulty of pronunciation, particularly when the second-last consonant had a vowel of its own, however short, like ነገድ, ዐረዝ, ደናግል and others. Even when the second-last consonant had no vowel, the vowel-termination of the word would be discarded without difficulty, if the two consonants, thus deprived of vowels, were of such a kind that they could be readily attached to each other,—if, for instance, the last consonant were a Mute or a Sibilant, as in መርግ, ረምስ, ግምድ, ከርሥ, or if the second-last were a soft Aspirate as in ዝእብ &c. In such cases, owing to the new pronunciation, a host of words arose, ending in a double consonant (v. § 35), and given thus, *márg*, *ráms* &c. But in other cases, the loss of final *ĕ* left as a result groups of consonants not so easily attached to each other, like ገብር, ኅፍን, ቈጽል, ዐቅም &c. If, nevertheless, final *ĕ* was given up in such instances, as—according to descriptions of Ethiopic pronunciation—seems to have been the case, then of necessity a fugitive *ĕ* must have been brought in after the second-last consonant,—thus, *gáb*[e]*r*, *ḥéf*[e]*n* (1) &c. There are, however, a number of Nominal forms, in which final *ĕ* did not allow itself to be so easily dislodged, but probably continued to be spoken even in later times. *In the first place*, when a word ended in a *u*-containing guttural, the *ĕ* connected with that *u* was bound to maintain its position more tenaciously: for instance, ኍልቍ, አዕናቍ were certainly not pronounced bare *ḥuélq* and *aʿnāq* (2), but *ḥuélquĕ*, *aʿnáquĕ*, so that in pronunciation alone there is no difference between እኅው and እኍ "brother" (3). *In the second place*, when the concluding consonant of the Nominal forms concerned here is a semivowel, as in በድው, ሥርው, ቃኅው, ሩእይ, አሕርው, ሰዋስው, መኃትው, ወላትው, ገማዕይ, the final *ĕ* must always be

(1) Accordingly words, which originally resembled Arabic words like مَلْك, came rather to resemble Hebrew words after the type of מֶלֶךְ.

(2) If even the single word ዐንጕጕ was pronounced *ánguag*, as Ludolf says; for it is also written ዐንጕግ.

(3) How König (pp. 76, 140) could dispute this position, it is impossible to perceive.

retained, to prevent the resolution of the semivowel into the vowel, thus *báduw*^{e}, *šéruw*^{e}, *qāḥw*^{e}, *rā'y*^{e}, *áḥrew*^{e}, and *sawāsw*^{e}, *maḥātw*^{e}, *walātw*^{e}, *gamā'y*^{e}, for original *sawāsew*^{e} &c., the fugitive *ĕ* of the second-last syllable being given up, and its introductory consonant being attached to the preceding open syllable (v. *supra*). At least **ወ** is always maintained in this way as a semivowel, unless preceded by *ă*. **የ** is less stable; and in certain words and forms,—which will be specially indicated farther on, in the account of Nominal formation,—it passes into *ī*, *e. g.*: **መካልይ** and **መካሊ**; *i. e. makāley*^{e} becomes either *makāly*^{e} or *makāley* = *makālī*, just as, for instance, the form mentioned above, **ራእይ**, may easily be pronounced *rā'i* in place of *rā'y*^{e}. But in other Nominal forms also, like **ሀልው** (from **ሀሉው**), **ሕያው**, **ጠራው**, final *ĕ* is maintained in the very same way, and the transition of the semivowel into a vowel is prevented (v., farther, on this matter § 51 *sq.*; *cf.* also some of the names of the letters discussed in § 9). *Thirdly*, the retention of final *ĕ* is generally necessary, when the last consonant is one of the five Aspirates,—particularly in forms like **ነቅዕ**, **ነቅህ**, **ቀብእ**, **ኰስሕ**, where the aspirate is inaudible without a vowel before or after it, and where the pronunciation *náqe'* &c. is likewise difficult. In such forms the preferable pronunciation is *náq'*^{e}, *náqh*^{e}, *qéb'*^{e}, *kuéśḥ*^{e}, resembling the Accusative **ነቅሀ** and the Feminine **ንቅሀት**. But even forms like **ኃጥእ**, **አባግዕ**,—although the pronunciation *ḫāṭe'*, *abāge'*, has a foundation in the formation,—should rather be pronounced *ḫāṭ'*^{e}, *abāg'*^{e} with retention of the original final sound, by reason of the attractive force of the *ā* upon the consonant which follows it and the consequent complete disappearance of the fugitive *e* which came after that consonant. In fact, in all the Nominal forms ending in Aspirates, in which a vowel, different from *a*, *ā* or *ĕ*, comes immediately before the Aspirate, like **ነዊሕ**, **ግቡእ**, this final *ĕ*, it seems, must be heard, if the Aspirate is not to lose all its force (as in the Amharic pronunciation of Ethiopic):—thus we say *nawīḥ*^{e}, *gebū'*^{e} (¹).

The scanty observations made by the earlier grammarians on the pronunciation of Ethiopic among the natives in their day, are far from being sufficient to enable us to settle all its details with exactness. The leading rules, meanwhile, are the result of

(¹) Just as little can one say in Hebrew שְׁלֵח or שָׁלוּח.

observing the modes of formation and the historical development of the pronunciation in general. The fact that no longer was anything heard of final *ĕ* in the Noun, in those very recent times when the pronunciation of Aspirates and Vowels was in full process of decay, does not justify the conclusion that it never existed; and we shall do well to re-introduce it even, in the course of learning Ethiopic, if we recognise that it has a historical foundation. The entire development of the later pronunciation tended to impoverish, and not to enrich, the language in the matter of vowels, as may be gathered both from §§ 37, 38, and from the similar case noted in § 34.

(B) MEETING OF VOWELS.

§ 39. The general rule, that no syllable can begin with a vowel (§ 34), implies that if two vowels come directly upon one another in the formative process, they cannot stand side by side as two separate sounds: the hiatus thus constituted must be remedied somehow. The means for this purpose at the command of the language are the following. **Contraction and Coalescing.**

(1) *Contraction and Coalescing.* Two vowel-sounds meeting together pass readily, in certain circumstances, into one sound, simple or composite, so that they form only one syllable.

(a) If two like vowels, long or short, come directly upon one another, then the pairs *ī* + *ī*, *ū* + *ū* are not indeed contracted into *ī* and *ū*, but one vowel in such a pair has to be hardened into a semivowel (§ 52): on the other hand the pair *a* + *a* is very frequently and regularly contracted into *ā*, *e. g.* in **ሐቍርያ** + *āt* (Plur.), **ሐቍርያት**; **ዕንዚራ** + *a* (of the Cstr. st.), **ዕንዚራ**; **ገብረ** + *ā* (for *hā* Suff.), **ገብራ**; **ዕሥራ** + *āwī*, **ዕሥራዊ**. Two independent words even, viz. **እመ** "if" and **አከ** "not", blend into **እማእከ**. Similarly, *ē* + *a* and *ō* + *a*,—for example in the Accusative form of Nominal stems ending in *ē* and *ō*,—become *ē* and *ō*, while, in other cases of this kind, *ē* and *ō* are resolved into their component parts, or else are separated from the following dissimilar vowel by a disjoining letter.

(b) When unlike vowels meet together, then if they are such as to be capable of blending into one combined sound, they pass into such a sound. An *i* is in this way easily attached to a foregoing *ā*, *ū* or *ō*, *e. g.* **ያይድዕ** "he shall make known"; **ብካይ** "the weeping"; ብዕራይ "cattle"; ተዓይን "camp"; እኩይ "bad"; ሰኑይ (1) "the second"; ሆይ 'name of a letter of the alphabet'; and yet in this case the combination must continue rather external in character, and *āi* or *āy*, for instance, is not allowed to become *ē* (2). On the other hand *u* is much less easily attached to *ā* or *ē*, and accordingly it is better to render it hard, after both of them, as a semivowel, *āw*, *ēw*:—ያውርድ *yāwred* "(that) he bring down"; ንቃው *neqāw*^{e} "tone"; ጠራው *ṭarāw*^{e} "Pleiades"; ጼው *ṣēw*^{e} "salt"; እምሔው *emḥēw*^{e} "ancestor". Ludolf, it is true, says that in his time ጼው was pronounced *ṣēu* (3), and *Europa* is now written ኤውሮጳ, but no conclusion for the original pronunciation follows therefrom. In more ancient times a *ευ*, for instance in *εὐαγγέλιον*, *Eulogia*, *Eustathius*, was expressed quite differently; and in the formation of certain Nominal stems it is farther shown very clearly how little *āw* can ever be contracted into *āu* and *ō*. On the other hand *ă* + *i* and *ă* + *u* regularly coalesce into *ai* and *au*, or in many cases blend still farther directly into *ē* and *ō*. In this matter too it is characteristic of Ethiopic that it differs from Arabic and approaches Hebrew. The *mixed sound* *ē* or *ō* appears throughout in the Perfect of Triliteral verbs *mediae infirmae*, like ሤመ and ቆመ (unless special phonetic conditions had of necessity to introduce the diphthongal pronunciation, § 94), also in all the forms of those Quadriliteral Verbs which have *i* or *u* as second radical, such as ሴለየ, ቆስሐ,—in Nominal stems from roots *tertiae* ወ and የ, which end in the Feminine *t*,—and in the Suffix pronoun of the 3rd pers. sing. masc. attached to the Accusative of the Noun. The *diphthong*, on the other hand, is maintained most regularly in several forms from roots *primae vocalis*, like አውሀበ, ተውሳከ, አይበሰ &c.,—in the Subjunctive of verbs *tertiae* የ,—and in the plural forms ending in ውት and ይት of Nominal stems, *e. g.* ነዐውት (4), ዐበይት, manifestly because the *a*-sound is of essential importance in these forms (5),—and, lastly, in the interior

(1) These forms, however, ought properly to be given as *bekāy*^{e}, *ekūy*^{e}, *ta'āyen*^{e} or *ta'āyen* (§ 38).

(2) To be sure, the form ሠኔት for ሠናይት is met with.

(3) [*Cf.* Trumpp, p. 519*sq.*]

(4) Yet ኖሎት, ገኖት.

(5) At the same time distinguishing them from the forms of the Feminine Singular.

of the word, in all those forms in which a diphthong *ai* or *au* has sprung from an original *áye* or *áwe* just through briefer pronunciation (§ 37), *e. g.* ይመይጡ, ይቀውሙ. But in all other Nominal formations and in the conjugation of verbs *tertiae infirmae*, and of those which end in *u* in the Subjunctive, as well as in some few individual words, the speech fluctuates between the diphthong and the mixed sound, varying with roots, with the age, with authors, with copyists; and the very same word frequently appears under both modes of pronunciation. A comprehensive survey, however, proves that as time went on, the mixed form of pronunciation steadily gained ground, and only a few departments of the language remained unaffected by it. In foreign words also, *au* and *ai* are generally expressed by *ō* and *ē* (*ī*), although the reverse process is also met with, in the substitution of *au* for the *ō* of the foreign word, as in ዮውጣ ἰῶτα. Besides, the mixed sound *ē* or *ō* may arise not merely from *ai* or *au*, but also and frequently from *ia* or *ua* (v. *infra* § 40). When *i* is preceded by *ĕ*, it can only dissolve into the diphthong *ei*, *e. g.* ሕይወት *ḥeiwat*[1], although this is of rare occurrence. When *u* follows *ĕ*, it must be changed into *w* (v. § 49 *sqq.*).

§ 40. (2) *Hardening of the Vowel into a Semivowel.* This process can take place only with those vowels which have corresponding semivowels, that is with *i* and *u*, or with the mixed vowels *ē* and *ō*, by resolving them into their elements. In the beginning of a word *i* and *u* must always be hardened in this way, seeing that no word can begin with a vowel (§ 34), *e. g.*, ውእቱ፡ (*wĕ-'ĕtū*) for *uetū*; ይእቲ፡ (*yĕ-'ĕtī*) for *ietī*. All roots therefore which originally began with *i* or *u* have been hardened into roots *primae* የ and ወ. And since *u* cannot have the sound of a vowel after *ă* or *ĕ* (§ 39), it must always be hardened, when it closes a syllable after those vowels:—ያውርድ፡ *yăwred*; ይውግዑ *yewgeʿū*. The same thing happens after *ī*, *e. g.* ቲሊው. So too *i* is hardened after *ī*, and *u* after *ū* (v. § 39 and *infra*, § 52). In the interior of a word *ī* und *ū* must become ይ and ው whenever either of them happens to come between two syllables, of which the last begins with a vowel of any kind, though the first may be

Hardening of Vowel into Semivowel.

(1) In Cod. B. of Sirach (Peterm. II, '*Nachtr.*' 55) ሒይወት is from time to time written instead of ሕይወት.

either an open or a closed syllable. Thus before the vowel *ĕ*: ይመይጥ, ይቀውም *yemáyeṭ*, *yeqáwem*, from *yema-i-eṭ*, *yeqa-u-em*; ተዓይን *ta'āyen* (1); ወሓይዝት from ውሒዝ; ሥርው *šérwᵉ* out of *šéru-ᵉ*; before *ă*, *e. g.* ማርየ from ማሪ; ትልወኒ from ትሉ; before *ā*, ይበልያ from ይበሊ; ይዜምዋ from ይዜሙ; ሰማያውያን from ሰማያዊ; before *ī*, ትበልዪ from ትበሊ; መዊት for *ma-ū-īt*; before *ū*, ይበልዩ from ይበሊ; ይዜምዉ from ይዜሙ; before *ō*, ይሬእዮሙ from ይሬኢ; ይትልዎሙ from ይትሉ; before *ē*, *e. g.* ሕሰዌ. This hardening is necessary before all vowels except *ă* (2): On the other hand in particular forms, it is true, *ī* or *ū* before *ă* passes of necessity into *ya* or *wa*. However, in several other forms the *a*-sound may press into these, and thus coalesce with them into a mixed sound, *ia* and *ua* becoming *ai* and *au* and farther *ē* and *ō*. Most regularly the Nominal termination corresponding to the Arabic ـِيَّةٌ is in this way shortened into *ēt* and *ē*, *e. g.* ረድኤት "help"; ምሳሌ "parable" (3); and the Accusative and Construct state of many nouns in *ī* have *ē* instead of *ya*, *e. g.* ብእሲ, ብእሴ. In the same way the binding-letter *ē* between several nouns and the suffix pronouns has come from *ia* (§ 167), *e. g.* ማእከሌነ. In other formations also, *ya* and *wa* are exchanged at pleasure for *ē* and *ō*, thus ቅንየት and ቅኔት "service"; ፍትወት and ፍቶት "desire"; while others again admit of the contracted form only, like ፍኖት "way"; ጸሎት "prayer"; ምሴት "evening" &c.

In like manner the mixed letters *ō* and *ē*, although in certain cases they absorb a following *ă* (§ 39), must as a rule be resolved into *aw* and *ay* before a vowel placed immediately after them, of whatever sort it be, *e. g.* ይሕዮ "(that) he live" (= ይሕየው), ትሕየዊ, ይሕየዉ, ይሕየዋ &c.; ገቦ "side", in plural ገበዋት. On the other hand an *ē*, originating in *ia*, is readily resolved into *ya*, *e. g.* ምሳሌ + *āt*, ምሳልያት.

Meanwhile *ī*, *ū* and *ē* do not necessarily pass into pure *y*, *w* and *ay*, but may keep their place before *y* and *w*:— thus in-

(1) These words may farther of course, by shorter pronunciation, in accordance with § 36, be turned into *yemaiṭ*, *yeqaum*, *ta'āin*.

(2) V., however, *infra* § 49 *sqq.*

(3) This law, accepted also by Schrader, '*De linguae Aethiopicae indole &c.*' (Gott. 1860), p. 11, is disputed by König, p. 112 *sq.*, without my being able to agree with his own explanation. *Cf.* also Praetorius, '*Aethiop. Gramm.*' p. 22.

stead of ገበርክምዎ, ገበርክሙዎ is also met with, from ገበርክሙ; or አወፊዮ Deut. 22, 1. This occurs most frequently and most regularly with nouns in *ē*, when they form an external plural, as in ጽጌ "flower", ጽጌያት; ኵነኔ "judgment", ኵነኔያት, and when to the suffix pronoun ኒ another is attached beginning with a vowel, *e. g.* ሀበኒያ "give her to me", from ሀበኒ and *ā* (= የ): V. farther § 52.—We call this the "Semi-hardening".

In foreign words which contain two vowels, the one immediately following the other, the hiatus is obviated, wherever possible, by a like complete or partial hardening of one of them, as in ማርያም Μαριάμ; ልዲያ *Lydia*; ኢየሱስ Ἰησοῦς; ሌውንትዮስ *Leontius*.

§ 41. (3) *Interpolation of a Separating Consonant.* This means of avoiding the hiatus is upon the whole seldom employed (¹). The readiest method in such a case (as in a similar one, § 34) is to insert an አ or some still stronger Aspirate, *e. g.* ነዓ "behold!" formed from ነ and an appended *ā*; yet an Aspirate as a separating letter is hardly met with except in foreign words, *e. g.* ታኦዶስዮስ *Theodosius*, and even ሰሌሖም Σιλωάμ. In true Ethiopic forms, however, the Aspirate (which in other cases also—§ 48—may pass into a Semivowel) inclines to become at once a Semivowel; and the more indeterminate ው is in greater favour in this usage than the pointed ይ. This insertion of a separating ው (²) is most usual in Inner Plural forms: በሓውርት "lands" from ብሔር; ሊቃውንት "eldership" (³) from ሊቃን. The Adjective-ending *āwī* appears also to have come from *āi* in this way, *e. g.* ቀጸማዊ alongside of ቀጸማይ; and to the particle ነ "behold!" the suffix pronouns are attached partly by means of ወ, *e. g.* ነዋ, partly and still more frequently by means of የ, *e. g.* ነያ, ነዮሙ, § 160. On the other hand, cases like ጽጌ "flower", Pl. ጽጌያት, are to be explained according to § 40. The insertion of a separating Semivowel comes also into use in transcribing foreign words into Ethiopic: ቴዎድሬ *Theodora*, a secondary form of ታኦድሬ; ቴዎሎግና "Theology", a secondary form of ቴሎግና or ቶሎግና &c. (⁴).

Interpolation of Separating Consonant.

(¹) *Cf.* König, p. 126 *sqq.*

(²) *Cf.* Ewald, '*Gramm. Arab.*' § 50, and '*Hebr. Sprachlehre*' § 28, *d.*

(³) [V. § 140, *a*, where it is explained that this word,—properly a plural, meaning 'seniors',—has become a collective form, which is used as an official denomination. tr.]

(⁴) König differs from me, p. 129. — d'Abbadie, '*Catal. rais.*', p. 127;

Displacing of one Vowel by another.

(4) *The displacing of one vowel by another* also occurs but rarely. Naturally this can only affect short vowels. The fugitive ĕ at the end of Nouns disappears before the Binding-vowel ĕ or ī of the suffix pronoun, *e. g.* ገብር, ገብርየ, ሥርው, ሥርውከ. In the Subjunctive formation of roots *mediae vocalis* an ĕ or ă is absorbed by ū and ī, *e. g.* ይቁም for *yeqūem* or *yeqūam;* ይሚጥ for *yemīeṭ:* for other similar cases v. § 49 *ad fin.*, § 51 and § 53. Also, in the accusative of the Noun, *e. g.* in ወርቀ, ă before the suffix pronoun የ (§ 154) is dislodged by ĕ (ī): ወርቄየ *warqéya.* For several other cases, in which *u*, *w* or *i*, *y* disappear completely, v. § 52. In the transcription of foreign words into Ethiopic, the absorption of one of two vowels which come directly together is of more frequent occurrence: for examples v. *supra*, and in § 20.

Meeting of the *u* of *U*-Containing Gutturals with certain Vowels.

§ 42. *The meeting of the u of u-containing Gutturals with certain vowels* deserves special notice. This *u*, in fact, by becoming hardened into a kind of consonant, may easily permit of an unlike vowel being heard after it, without its own proper character being thereby impaired: the principal vowel may be heard in *quă, quĕ, quī, quā,* or *quē,* clearly distinguished from the *u*-sound. Whenever then, in the course of framing words and forms, one of the five named vowels should properly appear after a *u*-containing Guttural, this may take place without farther difficulty; and these vowels are treated in such a case with the very same regularity as if they followed the ordinary consonants. Thus we form, for instance, ኈለቈ "he has numbered"; ኈለቋ "they have numbered" (Fem.); ትኄልቊ፡ "thou numberest" (Fem.); ይኄልቊ "he numbers"; ኊልቈ "enumeration". At the same time it is evident that such a guttural can never be completely mute, but a fugitive ĕ must always be heard after it, to make its own *u*-sound audible, even in cases where the corresponding forms of ordinary roots have a vowel-less consonant. This ĕ is found both in the end of the word, *e. g.* in ይኄልቊ *yeḫuēleque* (of the form ይፌጽም *yefēṣem*), —as well as in the Noun § 38—, and in the interior of the word, as in ደጕር *déguer;* ሐጕል *ḥáguel;* ኰኵሕ *kuákueḥ.* Only in a few words is the *u*-sound readily given up completely in such a

---

'*Géographie*' I, p. 12 (*Préface*), shows how at this day in Abyssinia ው and ይ are pronounced between two vowels, in words like ዳዩር, ጊዮርጊስ, ሰራዊ.

case: ዝክቱ and እልክቱ (§ 26); ዐንጐጕ and ዐንጕግ "lizard"(1). On the other hand whenever such *u*-containing gutturals have to take up a *ū* or an *ō*, the *u*-sound of the guttural regularly coalesces with this *ū* or *ō*, so that *ḫualaqu-ū*, *ḫualaqu-ōmū* are given as ኈለቁ, ኈለቆሙ, and from ጐጕእ we have ጕጕእ, after the form ግቡር &c. As soon, however, as such a *ū* falls to be hardened into a semivowel, by reason of the application of affixes beginning with a vowel, the *u*-containing pronunciation of the guttural reappears, *e. g.* ኈለቁ with the pron. suff. becomes ኈለቍዎሙ *ḫualaquewōmū*.

Still, the vowels of these *u*-containing gutturals are always somewhat heavier and weightier than the corresponding vowels of simple consonants. This explains why, in such words, originally short vowels are readily lengthened, so that, for instance, the verb ነቈረ "to be one-eyed" is even met with in one case written ነቋረ. Farther, *ū* approaches *uĕ* pretty closely, and *ō*, *uă*; and therefore an original *uĕ* or *uă* passes easily into *ū* or *ō*, *e. g.* ቍሱል into ቈሱል; ርኵስት into ርኩስት; ሰኰት "street" into ሰኮት; ተሰቈቍዎ into ተሰቆቍዎ; ኈለቈ into ኆለቈ(2). In like manner original *ū* or *ō* passes into *uĕ* or *uă*, *e. g.* ኩን "be (thou)" into ኵን &c. (§ 26); አስቆረረ into አስቈረረ &c. In the more accurate manuscripts an interchange of this nature is not observable.

(C) MEETING OF VOWELS AND CONSONANTS AND THEIR INTERCHANGES.

(α) INFLUENCE OF ASPIRATES ON THE VOWELS.

§ 43. Among the Consonants, the Aspirates and Semivowels stand nearest the Vowels; and this relationship of theirs to the Vowels brings about manifold vowel-changes. Close relation of Vowels and Aspirates.

The Aspirates stand in a peculiarly close relation to the vowels, from the circumstance that on the one hand the vowel, —generally *a*—, always involves a breathing, which is distinctly audible even when the vowel begins or ends a word independently, and that on the other hand the breathing cannot be heard, except it have a vowel before or after it. This reciprocal relation of vow-

(1) In the case of other words, this often rests upon errors of copyists.

(2) [Thus throughout in the old *Cod.* P of the *Kebra Nag.*; v. the Glossary.]

els and aspirates settles their power to effect changes in one another. In languages rich in vowels, like Arabic, or poor in vowels like Syriac, such an influence has asserted itself less decidedly, but in Ethiopic and in Hebrew it has become most thoroughgoing and multifarious. Besides, certain phenomena, which are met with in Hebrew in the case of the softer and weaker aspirates only, have become comparatively common in Ethiopic,—even with gutturals which were formerly stronger—, in consequence of the gradual softening which at an early date crept into the pronunciation of the harder aspirates (§ 24).

Aspirate must have a Vowel directly next it.

(1) *The Aspirate must always have a Vowel directly next it, whether before or after it.* Accordingly, neither in the beginning of a word, when an Aspirate makes its appearance merely as a consonant prefixed to a full syllable, nor in the termination of the Noun, when a guttural follows a vowel-less consonant, could the shorter pronunciation described in §§ 34 and 38 occur; but on the contrary ሐጼ or ኅጸር had always to be pronounced *ḥeṣē*, *ḫeṣár*, and ነቅዕ "a fountain" and the like, *náqʿe*. Even with Nominal stems which end in aspirates, it is better to retain a final *ĕ* there too, when any other vowel than *a*, *ā* or *ĕ* immediately precedes the Aspirate, as has been already pointed out (§ 38). On the other hand, in the middle of a word an Aspirate standing by itself in an open syllable with short *ĕ*, if it is preceded by an open syllable with a short vowel(1), surrenders its *ĕ*-sound quite as readily as other consonants, in the case described in § 37 *ad fin.*, and attaches itself to the foregoing syllable, *e. g.* ይውሕዙ *ye-weḥ-zū* from ይውሕዝ *ye-wé-ḥez*; while it seems better, after long vowels, with the exception of *ā*, to preserve the Aspirate with *ĕ* as an independent syllable, *e. g.* ይጼዕረኒ *ye-ṣē-ʿe-ranī*. Since farther an Aspirate, particularly አ or ዐ, at least with certain vowels, is of easier utterance before a vowel than after it, the vowel in one or two cases seems to be shifted from its position before the Aspirate and placed after it. This appears to be most obligatory, when an open syllable is followed by a closed one ending in አ or ዐ and to be pronounced with short *e*, *e. g.* ይገብእ properly *ye-gá-beʾ*, but certainly better pronounced *yegáb-ʾe*; so with ይሰምዕ; on the other hand, to be sure, ሀ, ሐ and ኀ admit more readily of an *ĕ* coming before them even in this case,

(1) This vowel, in accordance with § 45, is *ĕ*.

as in ይነጽሕ, ይፈርሁ. Nominal stems, like ቈናዝእ, ጸዋልዕ, ደዋርሁ &c. are, independently of this, to be pronounced by preference *quanāz-'e* &c. according to § 38. But whether also in cases like ይኑኅ the pronunciation should be *yenūḫ* only, and not rather *yenūeḫ*, we must leave undecided, through lack of information on the point; but perhaps it should be noticed, that in several formations of this class the pronunciation with *ū* is avoided, and the one with *ā* is substituted: ይማኅ— § 53.

Preference of Aspirates for the *a*-sound.

§ 44. (2) *Aspirates have a marked preference for the a-sound*(1). This preference, however, is made good by them in two quite opposite ways:—they either bring about an *a*-sound next them instead of a different one founded in the form, or else, if for other reasons they cannot bring about such an *a*-sound, they drive off the *a* of a foregoing open syllable, just to avoid being attracted by it. The first case does not occur so often; the second is more common.

(a) An *a*-sound appears most generally before the Aspirates, when an Aspirate, which has to be pronounced with *a*, is preceded by another consonant as a prefixed syllable and therefore one properly to be spoken with short *ĕ*; in this case *ă* takes its place in the prefix also, in room of *ĕ*. Thus we say መሐር, መሐሪ &c. instead of ምሐር, ምሐሪ; ሠሐቅ "laughter" for ሥሐቅ (even መዐት for ምዐት "wrath", although ዐ is properly to be given as a double consonant); አሐውር for እሐውር; የዐቅብ for ይዐቅብ; and, in this way, the personal prefixes of the Imperfect or the Subjunctive of Verbs, which have an Aspirate as first radical, have always *a* instead of *ĕ* (if the Aspirate has *ă*); but when ኢ „not" is placed before the Personal prefix ይ, the ይ may more easily hold its ground instead of የ, because the sound, *yĕ*, is supported by the foregoing *ī*, *e. g.* ኢይዐቅብ and ኢየዐቅብ. However, the rule which is enunciated here about replacing *ĕ* by *ă* came into full prevalence only at a comparatively recent date. In the older manuscripts and the impressions which follow them, forms(2) like ምሐር, ይሐውሩ, ይእምን &c. are still very common, while it is always possible that even in earlier times an *a*-sound was given in speech, although

(1) *Cf.* König, p. 148 *sqq.*

(2) And just because these occur most frequently in the oldest records, they can by no means be regarded,—with Ludolf, II, 7, 7,—as copyists' errors.

not in writing(1). But if the Aspirate has a different vowel from *ă*, a syllable prefixed to it keeps its *ĕ*, *e. g.* ይኄይስ, ጽዓቂ, ምሒር &c. The preference of the Aspirate for *ă* instead of *ĕ* is shown in a different way in the formation of the Subjunctive in Stem I, from roots which have an Aspirate as middle or final radical (§ 92). It is only in rare instances that under the influence of an Aspirate a foregoing vowel, stronger than *ĕ*, passes into *a* or *ā*,—as when one gives for example the word in frequent use for "day", in the form መዐልት, rather than ሞዐልት, its original pronunciation. In a similar manner this influence is shown in the Subj. of several roots *mediae vocalis*, and we say therefore ይማእ, ይበእ, as contrasted with ይኑም, ይቁም &c.; and on account of the Aspirate we also say ነዋኅ "high", instead of ነዊኅ. Occasionally too an original *ă*,—which is softened into *ĕ* in similar words when unprovided with an Aspirate,—is retained on account of the Aspirate, *e. g.* ሁብት "gift" (§ 106) in contrast with ጥንት, and ጸሀርት "pot" a side-form to ጽህርት.

Reduction of *ă* of open Syllable preceding Aspirate to *ĕ* in certain cases.

§ 45. (b) When an Aspirate has a different vowel from *ă* or *ā*,—then *ă*, occurring in an open syllable immediately preceding it, is almost invariably reduced to *ĕ*, because the Aspirate would become strongly attracted to the foregoing *a*, and be obliged to surrender to it a part of its force (v. *infra* § 46 *sq.*)(2). By reducing the *a* to *ĕ*, however, the language obviates this attraction and thereby secures the distinct pronunciation of the Aspirate. Reduction of *a* to *ĕ* is most binding, when the Aspirate following has itself an *ĕ*; but even when it has a different vowel, such reduction almost invariably takes place. Thus from roots *mediae gutturalis* Nouns of the type ገቢር are formed like ልሂቅ "old"; ርሒብ "broad" (but Fem. ረሓብ); and of the type ገቡር, like እሑድ "Sunday"; also Infinitives, of the type ገቢር, ገቢሮት &c., like ድኂን „to escape safe"; ምሒሮት "to pity"; ተምሂር "to be taught" &c.; and even the Imperfect, of the type ይገብር, ያገብር &c., from such roots always takes, in the very same way, the form ይምሕር *ye-mé-ḥer*; ይምሕል *ye-mé-ḥel;* ያምሕር *yā-mé-ḥer;* ይክዑ-

(1) Compare the relation between a Hebrew *Sh*^{e}*va simplex* and ***compositum.***

(2) *Cf.* König, p. 135 *sq.*, who has noticed also a few rare exceptions (p. 136).

yek-'ū for *ye-ke-'ū* (§ 37), instead of ይከዑ or ይከዕዉ; and only when the Aspirate has to be uttered as a double letter, can *a* be retained, *e. g.* in ይመሀር, Subjunctive from ይሜሀር, although even for such a Subjunctive one prefers to say ይምሕር *ye-mĕḥher*. Even in the forms of the Perfect of these roots, of the type ገብረ and ተገብረ—which originally had the sound *gábera, tagábera*, but later became *gábra, tagábra* according to § 37—the *a* of the first radical must necessarily be softened into *ĕ*, partly because the second radical at one time formed a syllable of its own, and partly to prevent the lengthening of the *a* following the first radical into *ā* (by § 46), thus ውሕደ, ርእየ (for ወሕደ, ረእየ); and ተግሕሠ, ተርእየ (for ተገሕሠ and ተረእየ). In the same way ንሕነ "we" is given, instead of the original ነሕነ, to avoid the obligation of saying ናሕነ according to § 46. Roots with an Aspirate as third radical, in all forms in which the second radical should be given with *ă* as an open syllable, turn this *ă* into *ĕ*,—thus, in the Perfect of all the Stems:—ነሥአ, ሰብሐ *sabbeḥa*, ባልሐ, አንሥአ, ተፈሥሐ &c. It is the same with the Subjunctive, Imperative and Imperfect of certain Stems, like ይንሥኡ (for ይንሠኡ); ንሥኢ (for ንሠኢ); ትትነሥኢ (for ትትነሠኢ) &c., and in Nominal forms of the type መገብረ and አገብረ, *e. g.* መንጽሒ "purifier"; መንቅሂ and አንቅሂ "awakener". The *ĕ* of the second radical, which has originated in this way, may however completely disappear, according to § 37, if an open syllable precedes, so that the pronunciation seems to be ነሥአ *náš'a*, ትትነሥኢ *tetnaš'ī*, ንሥኢ *neš'ī*(1).

§ 46. (3) *An Aspirate may lengthen a Vowel which precedes it in the same syllable*, by giving up to the vowel some portion of its own breathing, weakening itself however in the process. In Hebrew, where the same phenomenon occurs(2), it is only the softer Aspirates which exercise this influence; but in Ethiopic the five Aspirates all do so in an equal degree, for even

Lengthening of Vowel preceding Aspirate in the same Syllable.

(1) Hupfeld, it is true, is of opinion, p. 12, that ሰምዐ and መጽአ were pronounced *samā* and *maṣā*, and even አስተበውሐ *astabawa*, with entire suppression of the Aspirate; but this is refuted by the written language, for such forms as መጻ and መጻአ are never met with in writing. Speaking generally, Hupfeld's entire account of the relation of Aspirates and Vowels is a mistaken one, because it starts from the erroneous assumption that the Amharic pronunciation of these letters approaches the original.

(2) Ewald, '*Hebr. Sprachl.*' § 54 *sq.*

the three harder ones became softer and softer as time went on (v. § 24)([1]).

(a) This influence becomes operative most regularly when the vowel of the syllable is *ă*, both in those cases in which the Aspirate closes the syllable, as in ይምጻእ for ይምጸእ; እትፌሣሕ for እትፌሥሕ; አማሕፀነ for አመሕፀነ; ሰማዕኩ for ሰመዕኩ; በቋዕኩ for በቈዕኩ; ባኈብኈ for በኈብኈ; ማእከል for መእከል, and in those cases in which this Aspirate is followed by another consonant either originally vowel-less or which has become so, as a result of later pronunciation, as in መጥባሕት "knife"; ጠፍላሕት "piece of money"; ጸላእት "enemies"; ሳእር "a (skin) bottle"; ሣሕቅ "mockery"([2]). Words in which this lengthening of the *ă* is sometimes avoided are very few in number, such as ገሀህ "full moon"; አኅዝ "pledge"; ጐሕለወ "to be crafty", which occurs oftener than ጓሕለወ. But still it should be noticed, that in the oldest manuscripts and printed works this rule was only in rare cases consistently observed, and መእከል, ይምጸእ and so forth, for instance, were at one time written just as often or even oftener,—from which we may perhaps rightly conclude that this phonetic rule was not developed until later times. They went a good deal farther in Amharic, and in such cases completely suppressed the Aspirate, whether hard or soft, *e. g.* ላም "bull", instead of the Ethiopic ላህም ([3]).

Of course this rule is not to be applied in the combining of words. For example, we can never say ባእከይ for በእከይ *ba-'e-káye* "through wickedness". And farther, the short አ of the Causative Stems and of the Collective forms of the Noun is treated in exactly the same way, and as a mere external attachment, *e. g.* አዕረፈ "he rested"; አኅለቀ "he made an end of"; አሕዛብ "nations"; አሕቅልት "fields";—for which forms we never find ኣዕረፈ &c.;

([1]) *Cf.* König, p. 131 *sq.*

([2]) The pronunciation of those words which end in Fem. *t* presents no kind of difficulty in this case; and even the others, like ሣሕቅ, may easily be pronounced as monosyllables, if the hard Aspirate is given with a soft utterance: but if the older pronunciation of the Aspirate is adhered to, they must be given like *šāḥ-qᵉ*.

([3]) The examples cited by König, p. 132 *sq.* to support the contention that even a Guttural, which is not without a vowel, may lengthen foregoing *ă*, rest upon corrupt readings from Herm. and 4. Ezra.

but other Nominal prefixes, like መ and ተ when set before Aspirates, certainly follow the general rule. In the same way the lengthening of the *a* is better to remain in abeyance before double Aspirates, *e. g.* መሀሮት *mahherōt.* In Reflexive Stems of the type ተገብረ it occasionally happens, it is true, that the first radical has its *a* lengthened before the Aspirate which has become vowel-less, *e. g.* ተኄሕለ; but, as a rule, both in this case and in others in which it is desired to avoid lengthening the *ă*, this *ă* is rather softened into *ĕ*, just as in ተግሕሠ instead of ተገሕሠ, § 45.

But now if a vowel-less Aspirate, which has brought about the lengthening of the *ă* of its syllable, assumes a vowel in the process of formation and inflection, and is thus separated from its original syllable, then the *ă* ceases to be lengthened, and it is, if possible, softened into *ĕ*, *e. g.* ይምጻእ፡ "(that) he come", but ይምጽኡ "they shall come" for ይምጻኡ. Only, in the Subjunctive and Imperative of certain roots I. or II. *infirmae*, the long *ā* is retained even in inflection, because it serves at the same time to compensate for a radical which has been thrown out, *e. g.* in ይባእ, ይባኡ; ባእ, ባእ &c. (§ 53). It is retained in the same way, as belonging to the stem, all through the inflection of nouns of the types ኀጣእ "want", የዋህ "meekness" (§ 143 *sq.*).

(*b*) But even when the vowel of the syllable is *ĕ*, it may be lengthened by a vowel-less Aspirate coming after it. In several words in very frequent use, this lengthening of the *ĕ* into *ē* has been given expression to in writing, even from remote times. The feeble root ርእየ "to see" invariably forms the Imperfect ይሬኢ, by the original ይርእይ (for ይረእይ, by § 45) *ye-ré-'ĕ-i* becoming *ye-rĕ'-ī*= *ye-rē-'ī*, because the *i* drives off the *ĕ* preceding it, and እ influences the foregoing syllable. In a manner quite analogous ይሬዒ(1) is met with, from the root ርዕየ "to herd (a flock)", § 92. In the same way ይቤሉ "they said" was produced from ይብህሉ *ye-béh-lū*, through the lengthening of the *ĕ* and the elimination of the Aspirate in accordance with § 47. In other cases, it is true, this lengthening of the *ĕ* under the influence of the Aspirate is not expressed in written form, but yet it is evident that it must be adopted in pronunciation; for words like ርእየ, though perhaps spoken once like רְאִיָּה, were

(1) A like form, ይሴኢኑ from ስእነ "to be unable"—is cited by Ludolf in '*Lex.*', col. 172.

at a later time certainly contracted always into *ré'ya* or *rē'ya*; and the case is similar with ውእቱ; ይእዜ; ትስብእት *tes-bē't*; ትፍርህት *tefrēht.* Farther, the corresponding groups of letters containing harder Aspirates were in later times assuredly uttered in the same way constantly, *e. g.* አፍርኆት, ትፍሥሕት *afrēḫt, tefšēḥt*; thus too ምዕር፡ *mēʿr* for *mēʿr^e*; ግዕዝ፡ *gēʿz*:—so that one may appropriately transcribe these words, as *meer, geez*(1). Even in cases like ይምሕር for ይመሕር (§ 45); ምሕርከ; ተትሕትከ (§ 102), it is matter of question whether they were not in later times given in speech in a contracted form, as *yemēḥr, mēḥrka, tatēḥtka,* instead of *yeméḥer, meḥérka, tateḥétka.*

Occasional Disappearance of Aspirates.

§ 47. 4. *An Aspirate may disappear altogether, after it has given up its force to a Vowel.* This took place with considerable regularity in several cases, at the end of a word which terminated in an Aspirate, preceded by *ā* lengthened by the Aspirate, as in ሞፃ "parting-gift" for ሞፃእ; ድምድማ(ሕ) "hair of the head"; ጽላ(ዕ) "table (of stone)" &c.; but with other words it occurs in but a few manuscripts. In the middle of the word the suppression of the Aspirate usually occurs, when certain inflectional syllables, or other additions, come before or after it. Quite regularly does this happen in the Imperfect and Subjunctive formations of Verbal Stems commencing with አ, አን, አስተ,—by the personal prefixes ይ, ት, እ, ን before the አ becoming first of all የ, ተ, አ, ነ (§ 44), and then coalescing with the following *a* of አ into ያ, ታ, ኣ, ና, while the Aspirate is thrown out(2); but in other forms from such stems the Aspirate is discharged without leaving a trace, as in መጥመቂ(3); መስተሣህል, ምስትጉብእ. Similarly the *h* of the Suffix Pronouns ሁ, ሃ, ሆሙ, ሆን is often thrown out, § 151. Other instances of throwing out an Aspirate are more accidental and rare, but even in these instances, as well as in those just mentioned, it is chiefly

(1) For farther conjectures v. HAUPT, '*The Assyrian E—vowel*' in '*Amer. Journ. of Philol.*', Vol. VIII, p. 281.

(2) On the other hand, forms like ኣአምር "I know"; እእመን "I am to believe" are not farther contracted: እኀዝ, *Cant.* 7,9, Ps. 17,41 is merely a bad reading for እእኀዝ.

(3) [That is to say, the Participle, or Participial Noun, which is formed from መ and አጥመቀ (II, 1 of ጠመቀ) becomes መጥምቅ or መጥመቂ, the initial አ of the Conjugational form disappearing. TR.]

አ and ሀ which exhibit this fugitive tendency. When the ኦ of the Vocative is appended to a noun, the Aspirate is given up:—እግዚኦ from እግዚእ + ኦ; ብእሲቶ, from ብእሲት + ኦ, § 142. ይክል *yekel* is always said and written for ይክሀል *yekéhel*; ይብል *yebel* for ይብሀል *yebéhel*; ይበል *yebal* for ይብሀል; በል *bal* for ብሀል; አበለ for አብሀለ, and so on (v. also ይቤሉ § 46):—ልሂቅ "presbyter" is usually contracted into ሊቅ; and ማሪ "seer" came from መርኢ. Probably too ስርናይ "wheat" came from ስዕርናይ ("hairy", *cf.* שְׂעֹרָה)(1).

The later pronunciation however, and also the corresponding manuscripts, carry this process farther. A word like ክልኤ was even pronounced *klē*; and በእንተ and ዘእንበለ, although compounded of two words each, had the *a* and እ thrown out and were pronounced *bérta* and *zénbala*: also መላክ is found here and there for መልአክ "messenger", and አርስት for አርእስት "heads"(2). The older times knew nothing as yet of these corruptions of speech and writing. But even in older manuscripts, when in any word an Aspirate, with *ā* or *ă* in an open syllable, follows a closed syllable, the *a*-sound is displaced and set before the Aspirate, *e. g.* ኢጋዕዚ for አግዓዚ. This occurs most frequently in Numerals, among which, particularly in later manuscripts, ሰበዕቱ፡ and ተሳዕቱ፡ are often met with for original ሰብዐቱ፡ and ተስዐቱ፡, § 158. In these cases too the tendency is again indicated, to make the Aspirate dwindle away more and more(3).

Aspirates and the Word-Tone.

§ 48. 5. A final peculiarity of the Aspirates is this, that *they commonly draw the Word-Tone to themselves, when they are given with -a- following them*(4). This phenomenon is explained by the fact that an Aspirate communicates a share of its own force to the vowel *a* which is the most nearly related to it, and thus makes the vowel stronger (§ 46). Thus the Reflexive and Causative-Reflexive Stems, which otherwise take the tone on the third-last syllable, are—when they belong to roots *mediae gutturalis*—pronounced by preference as follows:—ተአኀዘ *ta-'āḥáza*; አስተምሐረ *astamḥára*; አስተርአየ *astar'áya*. Farther, forms like ሥርዐት

(1) On the other hand, the እ is kept on in እማእኮ=እመ+አኮ, § 39.

(2) [*Cf.* also spellings like ዐሪየ = አርአየ, and አስመ = አስምዐ *Kebra Nag.* p. XVII.]

(3) *Cf.* also Platt, '*The Ethiopic Didascalia*' (London 1834), p. 17, 3, Note.

(4) *Cf.* König, p. 140 *sq.*

are not pronounced *šér'at* in the usual paroxytone fashion, but *šer'át*(1). In consequence of this more emphatic pronunciation of *a* after an Aspirate, later scribes began to write long *ā* in such cases, although it had absolutely no foundation in the formation, *e. g.* ተለዓለ; ተመርዓወ; የዓርግ; and, *vice versâ*, a long *ā*, founded in the form, was occasionally written as a short *ă*, as people had become accustomed to pronounce even short *a* long, when it came after an Aspirate; *cf. e. g.* አእምር for ኣእምር. This led at last to confusion in the manuscripts, by long *ā* and short *ă*—especially when accompanying አ and ዐ—being rendered entirely at pleasure either by ኣ, ዐ or by አ, ዓ(2). A farther deterioration in the mode of writing, in another but similar case, appeared later in less accurate manuscripts: the Personal Prefixes of the Imperfect (and Subjunctive), which in the Causative Stems are ያ, ታ, ኣ, ና, are written የ, ተ, አ, ነ by later scribes, when the first radical is an Aspirate, because they clearly thought that an *ă* before an Aspirate is somewhat prolonged, without any farther notification being required, and that there is accordingly no difference in pronunciation between ያዐርፍ and የዐርፍ.

አ passing into a Semivowel. 6. The softest Aspirate አ passes into a Semivowel in certain cases. This takes place more frequently in Arabic and Syriac; but in Ethiopic the phenomenon,—apart from certain root-formations,—is limited to a single case: When ኢ "not" is prefixed to a 1st pers. sing. Imperf. or Subjunct., or to a Causative or Reflexive Stem beginning with አ, the አ passes regularly into የ, except with verbs *primae gutturalis* in the Imperfect of the First Stem:(3)—ኢይገብር=ኢእገብር; ኢያእምር=ኢኣእምር; አ coming after ኢ always becomes ያ then, by the fading Aspirate lengthening the vowel:—ኢያግበረ = ኢአግበረ; ኢያንጦልዐ = ኢአንጦልዐ; በኢያእምሮ = በኢአእምሮ(4). In some rare cases this phonetic transmutation occasions obscurity. For the rest *cf.* § 41.

---

(1) Ludolf, '*Gramm.*' I, 7.

(2) This shifting-about takes place most frequently in the case of the አ of the 1st pers. of the Imperf. and Subjunct. of the Causative Stems. In certain MSS. ኣ is almost always read in this case.

(3) *Cf.* König, p. 125 *sq.*

(4) It is but very rarely indeed that original አ or ኣ is retained after ኢ, as *e. g.* in ኢአትረፈ Numb. 21,35; ኢእሁብ Deut. 2,5,19; ኢእትገሐስ Deut. 2, 27.

On the *Doubling of Aspirates* v. § 56.

Of the other consonants only ቀ and ረ share, now and again, in the peculiarities of the Aspirates, *e. g.* in the matter of their predilection for the *a*-sound, § 105 *sq.*, and in other respects (*cf.* § 96 on ጠቀ)(¹).

(β) THE VOWELS *I* AND *U* AND THE SEMIVOWELS.

Hardening of *i* and *u*, as 1st Radicals, into Semivowels.

§ 49. It has already been pointed out (§ 40) that the Vowels *i* and *u* (and also *ai*, *au*, *ē* and *ō*) are often hardened into their corresponding Semivowels, when they meet with other vowels. The general rules, which were then laid down as governing the appearance of such hardening, must however undergo various limitations and special modifications, according to the immediate peculiarities of the several kinds of roots. Besides, special phonetic changes make their appearance, when an *i* meets with *i* or *y*, or a *u* with *u* or *w*. And lastly, *u* at least or *w* is liable in certain cases to be removed altogether(²).

1. *Hardening of i and u into Semivowels.* (a) All roots, which at one time commenced with *i* or *u*, must of necessity, according to §§ 34 and 40, have hardened these vowels into *y* and *w*. They are therefore pronounced in the ground-form as roots with initial የ and ወ, and this pronunciation is maintained whenever a vowel has to be uttered after the first radical, *e. g.* የድዐ; የብስ; ይቡስ; ወለደ; ውሉድ(³). As soon, however, as these letters come into the interior of a word and terminate syllables, in consequence of formative prefixes being placed before them, they seek to resume their vowel-character. If in that case *a* precedes them, they form with it a diphthong (§ 39) which is written *a*ይ, *a*ው:—አውለደ *aulada*; አይድዐ; ተውላጥ "barter"; ተውኔት "a game"; መውለዲት "midwife"; አውጹብ "(ear-) rings"; and although this diphthong does not indeed pass into a mixed sound in the formation of the Verb, it does so quite usually in Nominal Stems of the types ቆማኅ

(¹) *Cf.* also König, pp. 134 *sq.* and 151.

(²) *Cf.* König, p. 108 *sqq.*

(³) It has been pointed out already (§ 19) that in later times ይ and ው, when they had to be pronounced with *ĕ* in open syllable, were again given directly as *i* and *u*;—thus, *ibūs*, *ulūd*.

"antiphone"; ሞሰርት "a saw", and now and then in Participial forms like ሞረስ "heir" (alongside of መውለዲት, given above). After *ā*, *i* may easily have a vowel-sound, *e. g.* ያይድዕ *yāide'*, but *u* must be hardened, *e. g.* ያውሥእ *yāwše'*. After the short, dissimilar *ĕ*, *u* may become a Semivowel, if it closes the syllable, *e. g.* ይውግዑ፡ *yewge'ū* (not *yūge'ū*), but yet *ew* is not in favour, and as a rule it is simplified in Verbal formation by throwing out the *u* (*w*), § 53. In Nominal formation, on the other hand, the *u* generally pushes out a foregoing *ĕ*; and in this way forms are continually appearing, like ሙላድ, ሙሐዝ;—more rarely we have ምውዓል alongside of ሙዓል before the Aspirate; also ትውክልት and ቱክልት(1); ትውልድ and ቱልድ. *Ī* after *ĕ* is, in this case, of necessity contracted into *ī*.

Vowel-Pronunciation of *i* and *u* as 2nd Radicals.

§ 50. (b) Roots, which have *i* or *u* as second radical, cling most tenaciously to the vowel-pronunciation,—so closely, in fact, that even when according to general phonetic rules hardening ought to ensue, they often throw out the vowel that follows *i* or *u*, in preference to hardening the *i* or *u*. But of course it is only the short vowels *ă*, *ĕ* which can be dislodged in this way, and these only when they are less essential to the formation. Thus in the Perfect of the Simple Stem and Stems derived from it, the *ă* or *ĕ*, which should appear after the second radical, is removed, *e. g.* in ሞተ for *ma-ue-ta*; ሜጠ for *ma-ia-ṭa* or *ma-ie-ṭa*(2). It is the same with the Subjunctive and Imperative of these Stems, *e. g.* ይሙት for *yem-u^e^t* or *yem-u^a^t*; ይሚጥ for *yem-i^e^ṭ* or *yem-i^a^ṭ* (but in these cases *ua* is sometimes contracted into the single sound *ō*, by § 40:—ይሖር "(that) he go", v. § 93); and it is only when the third radical also is a vowel (Semivowel) that the second must of necessity be hardened into a Semivowel, thus—ይወየ; ረወየ (*cf.* § 94 *ad fin.*); ይርወይ *yerwai*; ሐይወ *ḥaiwa* (for *ḥay^e^wa*); ይሕየው. In like manner, when a short vowel comes into the formation after the first radical, the words from these roots preserve the vowel-pronunciation of the second radical (1) by making it coalesce with a foregoing *a* into a diphthong or a mixed vowel, *e. g.*, of

(1) Manifestly both pronunciations, *tew* and *tū*, are possible here; for, had they always said *tū*, it would have been always written in that way.

(2) That the diphthong must always in these cases pass into the mixed sound (*ō* or *ē*) is taught by § 39.

the type ገብር,—ሞት "death"; ሤጥ "price"; or ሐይቅ "shore"; ዐውድ "circuit", "circle" (and often in this way as a diphthong after an Aspirate, seeing that *a* has a somewhat stronger sound after the Aspirate § 48), and (2) by removing a foregoing *ĕ*, unless it is essential to the formation, *e. g.* ቂም "revenge" (type-ግብር); ኑኅ "length"; ሂይት "robbery"; ሑረት "course". On the other hand we necessarily say, in formations from roots which are at the same time *tertiae infirmae* ሕይወት *ḥéiwat;* ጥውየት *ṭéwyat* (rarely ሒወት &c.); v. *supra.* But even these roots must permit the hardening of their vowel-radical in the following cases:—1st, when the second radical is doubled:—ጸውዐ *ṣáwweʿa;* ኀየለ *ḥáyyala;* ጕየ *guáyya;* መፈውስ *mafáwwes;* 2nd, when it is followed by a long vowel, or even by a short one, provided it is essential to the formation:—ዕወር "blindness"; ሀየል "stag"; ንዋም "sleep"; አብያጽ "companions", from ቢጽ; ምዩጥ "turned"; መዊት "to die" (Inf.)—(On *ī* after *i*, and *ū* after *u*, v. § 52); 3rd, when the radical in question comes to stand between two vowels, of which the first is a long one, *e. g.* ተራወጸ; ተካየደ; ሣውዕ "sacrificer"; መጻውር "carrying-poles"; ተዓይን (properly *taʿāyen*, but according to § 40 *taʿāin*), or between two vowels, of which the first is indeed a short one, but of which the second is essential to the form and therefore irremovable:—ይመውት; ይመይጥ properly *yemá-wet, yemá-yeṭ*, but according to § 40 *ye-maut, yemaiṭ* (yet never ይሞት(1); ይሚጥ); 4th, when it is followed by two vowel-less consonants, seeing that by § 35 *sq.* no long vowel can stand in a doubly closed syllable,—thus ትዕይንት *teʿ-yént*; ትዝውፍት *tez-wéft*; አስይፍት "swords" (and yet we have አኪስት as well as አክይስት, because Sibilant and Mute are very closely attached to one another).

§ 51. (c) Ethiopic roots which from the first have had *i* or *u* as their last radical, exhibit a marked tendency towards hardened pronunciation: they farther hold tenaciously to their termination, and do not readily allow it to glide into other vowels. For this reason, roots ending in *i* and *u* are very carefully discriminated from one another, and do not pass into one another in the course of formation, as happens in other languages. The vowel-pronunciation of the last radical, in forms from such roots, appears only when that radical has no vowel after it or at most a short and

Hardening *i* and *u* as 3rd Radicals.

(1) [V., however, *Kebra Nag.* 84 b 7 (እሞት).]

easily removable *ĕ*, and no long vowel before it (§ 40); but yet there is this exception,—that *i* is given with a vowel-sound even after long *ā* (§ 39). This rule is everywhere applied in the formation and inflection of the Verb, thus ተለወ; ርእየ; ረሰየ; but ተለውከ *taláuka*, and ተሎከ; ርኢከ; ረሰይከ *rassáika*. A foregoing short *ĕ* generally coalesces with *ŭ* and *ĭ*, thus ይተሉ; ይሬሲ (rarely ይተልው; ይሬስይ; *cf.* ትዘምው Lev. 20,6; ያኀትው Ex. 27,20; ያኅትው Ex. 27,21—otherwise in 38,13—(1); also ፄውው v. *infra* § 99, I). Farther, in Nominal formation this rule holds good always, when the noun does not end in *i* or *u*, *e. g.* in ልቡና "understanding"(2) and ዕሪና "equality", of the type ግቡርና; ትንቢት "prophecy"; ትሥጉት "incarnation", of the type ትግብርት; መክሪት "spade"; መንሱት "temptation", of the type መግብርት; ነዐውት *naʿáut*, "hunters"; ኀለይት *ḫaláit*, "singers"; መርዔት "herd"; መስኮት "window", of the type መግበርት; and so throughout in all Feminines which are formed by a closely attached, vowel-less ት, *e. g.* ሕፂት "a girl betrothed"—*sponsa*, ዕሉት "apostate" *f.*, from ሕፁይ and ዕልው (§ 36); መፍሪት "fruitful" *f.*, from መፍርይ. When the Noun, however, ends with the last radical, different nouns follow different courses, according as they retain or give up the fugitive *ĕ*, in which (§ 38) the pure Nominal stem once terminated. In such formations final *u* may have a vowel-sound only after *ă*, by forming with the latter either a diphthong or a mixed sound:—መፀው "Spring"; ሥረው "roots"; አበው "fathers"; ህበ "dew"; ገበ "side" (of the body): ማዕጾ "lock of a door": in all other cases the terminal *ĕ* is retained, and the vowel *u* is hardened into *w*:—ሕያው *ḥeyāw*^{e}; ምክዓው *mekʿāw*^{e}; ተሊው *talīw*^{e}; ሥርው *šérw*^{e}; በድው *bádw*^{e}; መኃትው *maḫātw*^{e}, for *maḫātew*^{e} (§ 37); መደልው *madállew*^{e}; መጸግው *maṣággew*^{e}; መትልው *mátlew*^{e}; now and then too *u* is thrown off when it comes after long *ā* (§ 53). On the other hand, *i* has a leaning to the vowel-pronunciation, and maintains itself as *i* after long *ā* and *ū* (§ 39):—ሐጋይ; ብካይ; ጥሬይ; ምርዓይ; ብሉይ (3). It forms with *ă* a diphthong, or a mixed vowel: ዕበይ; ጸጌ; ለሬ; መሥቄ; and as a rule it forms, with foregoing *ĕ*, long *ī*, *e. g.* መፍርይ, መሠርይ,—probably not

(1) [*Cf.* also *Kebra Nag.*, p. XVII.]

(2) Yet here too *ew* is tolerated, *e. g.* ስርግውና "adornment", *cf.* § 49.

(3) Although here too *belūy*^{e}, *bekāy*^{e} &c. may be given.

*mafrey*ᵉ and *mašarrey*ᵉ, but *máfrī* and *mašárrī*, since we find these forms quite as often written መፍሪ and መሠሪ; so also ባሕርዩ "pearl" = ባሕሪ *bāḥrī* or *bāḥreye.* Thus in the Noun, *i* is necessarily hardened into ዩ and *ĕ* added to it, only when it is preceded by a vowel-less consonant, as in ራእዩ *rā'ye*, of the type ገብር; and it may be given at pleasure as a vowel or as *ye*, when the introductory consonant of the syllable should properly have a short *ĕ*, while the preceding syllable ends in a long vowel, *e. g.* መካልዩ "talents", either *makāly*ᵉ (§ 37) or *makālī*, as it may be even written መካሊ. It is the same with መስተዋድዩ "accuser", and መስተዋኒ "actor"; and in like manner ላሕዩ "beautiful" is to be pronounced *lāḥy*ᵉ or *lāḥī*(¹).

Both in the Verb and Noun however, *u* and *i* must invariably be hardened, whenever any firmer vowel than the fugitive *ĕ* has to be uttered after them (§ 40). If in Ludolf's time words like ፊነው, ዕፀው were spoken as *fánnaua*, *eṣaua*, we are not at liberty to regard that pronunciation as original or deserving of imitation.

§ 52. 2. *If a formative vowel ī or ū meets with a radical ī or ū*, it never coalesces originally into one sound (*ī* or *ū*), but the radical *ī* or *ū* must be hardened into ዩ or ው, whether before or after the formative vowel(²):—*yī* and *wū*, when produced in this way, generally remain unchanged, *e. g.* ዩተልዉ, ተበልዪ, ኀላዪ, ፆርዉ. But roots *mediae infirmae*, which in other respects also have peculiar phonetic conditions (§ 50), aim at a shorter pronunciation in such cases, by shortening the long vowel and doubling the semivowel instead (making *yī* = *yĭĭ* = *yyi*, *and wū* = *wŭŭ* = *wwu*), so that the result, in accordance with § 19, is *yyĕ* or *wwĕ*(³). Consequently, Infinitives and Adjectives of the type ገቢር from roots *middle i* may, it is true, run like ሠዪም "to place", መዪጥ "to turn", ቀዪሕ "red"—and these forms are still found in abundance in the older manuscripts(⁴),—but usually they are written ሠይም, መይጥ, ቀይሕ. These forms then are first of all to be pronounced *šayyem*, *mayyeṭ*, *qayyeḥ*; but they may be farther

Radical *ī* or *ū* meeting with Formative Vowel *ī* or *ū*.

(¹) *Cf.* with these deductions the somewhat diverging ones in König, p. 111 *sqq.*

(²) Otherwise with König, p. 152 *sqq.*

(³) *Cf.* Ewald, '*Gramm. Arab.*' §§ 387, 108.

(⁴) [*Cf.* also መዪቅ, *Kebra Nag.* p. XVII, *sub* 6.]

simplified into *šaim*, *maiṭ*, *qaiḥ* (1). In the same way Passive Participles of the type ግቡር, from roots *middle u*, are very often met with, having the pronunciation ምዉት *mewūt*; ድዉይ *dewūy* (*dewūy*[e]), and so in the Pl. ምዉታን &c.; but ምውት and ርውጽ are found instead, particularly in later manuscripts, the pronunciation being first *méwwet*, but afterwards, in abbreviated form, *mewwt* and *mūt*, with the plural both ምውታን *mewwetān* and ሙታን *mūtān*. And yet it should be noticed that in the Singular certainly the style ሙት, ሩጽ does not occur, and even in the Plural it is rare. On the other hand the forms ድዉይ, ርዉይ are preferred, from roots whose third radical also is weak; but in the Plural we have ዱያን (as well as ድዉያን) from *dewweyān*. But when the group *īy* or *ūw* is produced by the meeting of these sounds, it can be tolerated only when its elements are shared between two syllables, as *e. g.* in ነቢያት (along with which we have ነብያት) "prophets". Besides, these sounds — which are somewhat difficult to utter — are simplified by *ī* and *ū* being partly hardened, whereby *īy* and *ūw* become *eyy* and *eww* (2) (§ 19). *Īy* alone has kept its place, and that too in but one single type, viz. in Adjectives of the form ገቢር, as if the formative sound *ī* had been of greater importance for them. It is thus that words like ዐቢይ, ነቢይ &c. originated,—which were certainly spoken at one time, like *ʿabīy*[e], *nabīy*[e]. In later times, however, when the fugitive *ĕ* was given up, *ʿabīy, nabīy* were contracted directly into *ʿabī, nabī*. Thus too we have the Fem. ነቢይት *nabīt*; and although in most cases the ይ is still constantly written, yet, in one or two detached words of this form, used rather in a Substantive sense, it is regularly thrown out, as in ሐቢ "security" (*legal term*); and ጠሊ "goat"; ነቢይት is written also ነቢት.—Thus *ī* and *ī* finally coalesced into *ī*,—a phenomenon, which does not otherwise readily occur. In the other formations, however, the facilitated style prevailed completely. Accordingly, the Passive Participles of roots with final *u* (with a few deviations in detached manuscripts) run thus:—ርኅው *reḫéww*[e], ልብው *lebéww*[e] (3); Plur.

(1) Like مَيْت from مَيِّت for مَوِيت.

(2) *Cf.* Ewald, '*Gramm. Arab.*' § 108.

(3) We never find ርኁ and ልቡ given for these; and therefore Hupfeld is wrong in teaching, p. 16, that they were spoken as *reḫū* and *lebū*. And farther, the pronunciation ሀልው as *helluw* &c., recommended by Ludolf

ርኅዋን, ሌብዋን *reḫewwān* &c.; Fem. sing. ርኑት, ሌቡት for *reḫéwwt* &c. (§ 51). In the same way forms are still met with, here and there, for the Infinitive of the type ገቢር from roots ending in *i*, like ርኢይ,—which is to be read *re'īy*[e]; but these are to be regarded as entirely obsolete. The usual form certainly is given in በላይ, ሰትይ, ርእይ (never በሊ, ሰቲ, ርኢ), which words are accordingly to be pronounced *baléyy*[e], *satéyy*[e], *re'éyy*[e]. At the same time, of course, the pronunciation may become more contracted in special cases, *e. g. rē'yy*[e] for *re'éyy*[e]; and በላዮሙ *baleyyōmū*, ሰትዮሙ *sateyyōmū*, may become, at least when carelessly employed, *balyōmū, satyōmū*. The same aversion to the sounds *īy* and *ūw*, even when they are shared between two syllables, is indicated in some other phenomena, quite outside of the formations from roots with a vowel as middle or last radical. The connecting vowel *ī* of the Construct state usually passes into *ĕ* before the suffix pronoun የ (v. § 153 *sq.*). Forms are still no doubt met with, like አምላኪየ *amlākīya*, but, as a rule, they run like አምላከየ *amlākeya* (1). Even ረዳኢ "helper" may, with the suff. የ, become ረዳእየ *radā'eya*. For the same reason, forms like ገበርክሙዋ, የሀቡክሙዋ are doubtless possible (§ 40 *ad fin.*); but even in these cases the complete hardening of the *ū* is more common than the semi-hardening, thus ገበርክምዋ &c.

§ 53. 3. *Rejection of a u (and an i)* (2). Of the two Semivowels in Ethiopic, *w* ranks as the more indeterminate, and at the same time as the one which stands nearest the softest Aspirate አ. And just as it may for this reason (§ 41) be interpolated to separate two colliding vowels, especially when the first is an *a*-sound, so on the other hand, a radical *w*, hardened out of *u*, may at need give way to an *a*- or *e*-sound. This happens most frequently when *u* at the end of a syllable after *ĕ* or *ā* would have to be hardened into *w* and to form the group of sounds, *ĕw, āw*, which is so little in favour. In the Subjunctive of the Simple Stem from roots with initial *u*, the group ይው, ትው &c., is thus, as a rule, Rejection of *u* (and *i*)

is certainly inaccurate, for otherwise it would be impossible to understand, why people did not keep to the original way of writing it, viz ሀሉው. According to TRUMPP, p. 534, it is pronounced *heléu* (= original *heléw*). In the end of a word the doubling is no longer heard.

(1) But v. König, p. 153 [and *cf. Kebra Nag.*, p. XVI, *sub* 2.]

(2) *Cf.* with what follows, KÖNIG, p. 105 *sqq.*

simplified into ይ, ት &c. (although it has kept itself unchanged in isolated cases of Verbs, *e. g.* ይውኃእ), thus ይረድ from ወረደ; ይድቅ from ወድቀ. While according to § 49 *ew* may easily become *ū* in Nominal formations, the *ĕ* of the Personal prefixes is in this case held to be so essential in the Verb that a *u*-sound is never admitted; and whereas in Hebrew,—where יֵלֵד likewise stands for יִוְלֵד,—the *w* which falls away is at least replaced by a long vowel, it falls away in Ethiopic just as in Arabic without leaving a trace, so that even in the Imperative and in the Nominal forms derived from the Imperf. (Subj.) the root makes its appearance, deprived of its first letter. In the very same way in Nominal stems from roots with ወ as last radical, if they have long *ā* before the last radical, the *u*, hardened into *w* is frequently rejected(1), in order to avoid the by no means favoured group, *āw*. In words with an Adjective meaning, like ጸዕዳ or ጸዐዳ "white", Pl. ጸዓድው, this course is rarely followed, but it is common in Abstracts, the most of which do not admit a plural, *e. g.* ሥጋ "flesh"; ፍና "way"; ጸጋ "favour" &c. (§ 107), and it is almost constant in the type ተስፋ "hope"; ታእኃ (and ተእኃ) "relationship"; ተድላ "pleasure" &c. (§ 111), though on the other hand we have ተእኃዎሙ Esth. 9, 22, as well as ተእኃሆሙ. In like manner it is sometimes thrown out before the closely attached *t* of the Fem., though not quite without compensation, *e. g.* ዐውያት "lamentation" (√ዐውየወ); መርዓት "bride" (√ረዐወ); ሐማት "mother-in-law" &c. (§ 128)(2). More rarely it may happen that in the beginning of a syllable which is preceded by one that is closed, *u* is thrown out before an *a* or *ā*, which for any reason may be irremovable(3). Thus from roots *mediae* ወ, instead of the heavy-sounding Causative Stem አሞተ, a simpler one is formed with lighter sounds, like አቀመ for አቀወመ; አጠቀ from ጦቀ(4), particularly from those roots which have an Aspirate as third radical, *e. g.* አንኀ for አኑኀ(5) (§ 45), for አንወኀ (v. farther on this point § 96). In this case also the *u* or *w* disap-

(1) Just as in the Arabic سَمَآء.

(2) It is a totally different case from this, when in the much used archaic words አብ, ዕፅ &c. the last radical disappears; *cf.* § 105, *a. f.*

(3) As often happens in Arabic, Ewald, '*Gr. Arab.*' § 109, and in Hebrew, Ewald, § 35, *a.*

(4) *Cf.* König, p. 116.

(5) [Which itself is still met with: v. *Kebra Nag.*, p. XXVIII *a.*]

pears without leaving a trace;—yet *cf.* § 96, 1. In Nominal formation this is rare; yet an example is found in ሐሰት "lie" from ሐሰወ, for ሐሰወት[1]. A few roots *mediae* ወ, which have an Aspirate as third radical, transform ō in the Subjunctive into ā and thus give up the vowel-radical; but this ā continues then at least without change (§ 46):—ይብእ, ይማእ for ይቡእ, ይሙእ (v. § 93). A like process is shown in cases like ቃል፡ "word" for ቆል[2], in accordance with § 18.

I or y is much more stable than u or w. The most important case, in which radical ī disappears, or rather unites with another ī, has been already described (§ 52. p. 98), *e. g.* ጠሊ. Otherwise the rejection of *i* or *y* occurs very seldom indeed[3]. ዐሥራት "the tenth part" seems to have come from ዐሥራይት, like ዐውያት from ዐውያውት. We meet with ብዕራ "cattle" for ብዕራይ, for the sake of the rhyme[4]. ሥንት "urine" (√ ሢኒ), seems to have come from a Masculine form ሢን, of which the ī had to be shortened into ĕ, by § 36, in the doubly closed syllable.

The interchange of w and y, which is so common in other Semitic tongues, is exceedingly rare in Ethiopic. True, there are, it seems, many roots originally commencing with *i*, which have passed into roots having an initial ወ (§ 68); but after the roots had once been thoroughly formed, those which had *u* and those which had *i* as the first, second, third, or fourth radical, remained sharply distinguished thenceforth, and passed no more into one another in the course of formation. Accordingly, cases like the plural መራዕይ from መርዓት for መርዓውት are few and far between[5].

It has already been explained (§ 48), that the Aspirate ኣ, occurring after an ī, passes occasionally into የ.

1. CONSONANTS.

Doubling of Consonant as Result of Assimilation.

§ 54. The Consonants form the more stable, unchangeable part of the sounds of the language. In general they maintain, all through the process of Word-formation, the appearance and

(1) Oftener in Arabic, Ewald, '*Gr. Arab.*' § 410.

(2) *Cf.* Ewald, '*Gr. Arab.*' §§ 73 and 387. [Better to regard ቃል = قَال = Assyr. *qālu* and ቆል = قَوْل = Assyr. *qūlu*, as has been already pointed out *supra*, p. 37, Note (1).]

(3) *Cf.* König, p. 107.

(4) Ludolf, '*Lex. Aeth.*', col. 247.

(5) *Cf.* also König, p. 107.

order attaching to them when handed over in the fully formed root. The only thorough-going alteration, which the radicals are subjected to in formative processes, is their Doubling,—one of the leading formative devices in the field of Semitic speech. Meanwhile, and apart from this, groups of sounds may be produced by the formative process, which are somewhat difficult to utter, and which therefore almost necessarily involve transitions of sound among the Consonants. Farther, in certain phonetic conditions, individual consonants, especially the softer ones, may gradually become enfeebled, and either disappear entirely or be turned into vowels. And just as consonants may in certain circumstances pass into vowels, so vowels again may avail themselves of the help of consonants, and add to their own strength by bringing them into the word.

1. The Doubling of a Consonant is sometimes given in the root itself, inasmuch as the language possesses a number of roots in which one of the letters is pronounced as a doubled letter: —a more precise account of this phenomenon falls to be given in discoursing of roots. Sometimes again, doubling serves as an expedient in word-formation: an account of this is also deferred to a subsequent part of the work. Finally, Doubling of a Consonant is sometimes produced by another Consonant becoming assimilated to it, and this is the case which calls for detailed description here.

(*a*) When in any word then Consonants meet together, which in consequence of this encounter are difficult to utter, one of the devices employed by the language to introduce an easier pronunciation is the transferring of one of the two letters to the other, or *the doubling of one Consonant, as a result of the other being made to resemble it* (*Assimilation*). Such assimilation of two letters occurs frequently in the formation of roots. In particular the softer letters, *e. g.* Aspirates or Liquids, readily pass over to a stronger consonant, *e. g.* መበለ *mabbala* "to wield power", from ሙበዐለ; ሰሰለ "to withdraw" *sassala*, from ሰሌሰለ &c. (v. *infra* § 71)([1]). Otherwise, this phenomenon is limited to a few

([1]) Just like መበ፟ለ, Praetorius, '*Beitr. z. Assyr.*' I, p. 30 *sqq.* would also understand ዐመ፟ፀ, ዐረ፟የ, ተከ፟ዘ. In the words ኄጠ, ቢጸ, ሒኪ, ሤጠ, ጼነወ, ጼሐ he sees (*ibid.* p. 28 *sqq.*) a compensatory lengthening, for the disappearance of a doubling produced by the assimilation of ኦ, ዐ &c.

definite cases. When two Consonants come upon one another, without being separated by a vowel, the one passes over to the other in certain cases. 1. When, in the course of conjugation(1), the Guttural ገ or ቀ as radical meets with the ከ of the personal-ending, the latter passes over to the foregoing radical(2): ዐረገ *ʿarágga*, for ዐረግከ; ጸሀቁ *ṣehéqqū*, for ጸሀቅኩ. If, however, the preceding Guttural belongs to the *u*-containing class (§ 26), assimilation is not in favour, just because a kind of vowel then separates the two letters, *e. g.* ለሐኰኩ; ዘንጐጕኩ; ኀለቍክሙ. Only now and then does assimilation take place, *e. g.* ለሐኮ, for ለሐኰከ; ተኀለቈ, for ተኀለቍኩ Ps. 87,4. 2. The ት of the formative syllables of the Feminine and of the Reflexive Stem is assimilated to the radical ጠ and ደ:—ይደሎ *yeddalō*, for ይትደሎ; ይጠመቁ, for ይትጠመቁ; ሠየጥ, for ሠየጥት; ቀሕድ, for ቀሕድት; መወልድ, for መወልድት; ትውልድ, for ትውልድት; ቈገድ, for ቈገድት. It is only in the words(3) አሐቲ "one" (*f.*), for አሐድቲ, and ወለት "daughter", for ወለድት(4), that the radical has given way to the formative letter (just as in אַחַת for אַחַדְתְּ). Inasmuch, however, as the Dental Mutes and the Sibilants belong to the same organ of speech, it is not at all remarkable that the combination of letters *ts, ds* &c., which is regarded as inadmissible in other languages, should be made easier of pronunciation by the Mute passing over to the Sibilant(5). Accordingly ት or ድ before a Sibilant passes over to the latter; and in fact the ት of the Reflexive Stem regularly does so, with every Sibilant: እሠወጥ, for እትሠወጥ; ይሴፌው, for ይትሴፌው; ይዜከር, for ይትዜከር; ይጸሐፍ, for ይትጸሐፍ; ትፀመድ, for ትትፀመድ. ድ passes into ስ in ስሱ, for ስድሱ and in ስሳ for ስድሳ, although both letters belong to the root. Apart from these cases the transition of one consonant to another is exceedingly rare. A Nasal has been

(1) This case rarely appears anywhere else. It is true that the same thing apparently is met with in appending a Suffix Pron. of the 2nd pers. to a Noun which ends in a Guttural, but in point of fact the two letters in that case are always kept from touching, by means of the binding-vowel, and no assimilation is possible. On similar appearances in the appending of enclitic particles to the Verb, v. *infra*, §§ 169 and 152.

(2) *Cf.* König, p. 97 *sq.*

(3) ውስተ seems not to be derived from ውስጥት, but from ውስጥ, by ጥ becoming ተ. [*Cf.* however, Assyr. *ištu* (*ultu*).]

(4) V. König, p. 97.

(5) Other languages evade the difficulty by the transposition *st, sd.*

assimilated to an *l* in እላ "but", "however", from እም (እመ, إِنْ) and ላ (لَا, לֹא) (¹).

Doubling of Consonant, to make up for shortening preceding Vowel.

§ 55. (*b*) The device of shortening a long vowel and restoring the length by doubling the following Consonant, is very rarely made use of, except in the case described in § 52. It appears, however, in ከሙ *kémmū* (Suff. Pron. of the 2nd pers. pl.), the first vowel of which was originally long,—although it answers to كُمْ in Arabic,—and accordingly the doubling of the *m* would seem to have been introduced to strengthen the short vowel in the open syllable. On the other hand in እሉ *éllū* "these", እለ *élla* "who", "which" (*pl.*), the doubling appears to have a different origin (v. § 146).

Doubled Consonant always written in Single Form.

(*c*) Whatever may have been the origin of the doubling of any Consonant, the doubled Consonant in Ethiopic is written only in single form. And the script has adhered so faithfully to this principle, that whenever two identical consonants meet together, without a separating vowel between them, whether in forming or in compounding words, only one consonant is written down, *e. g.* ይቴሐት, for ይትቴሐት; ስእነ, for ስእንነ; አስመኩ, for አስመክኩ; ምውት, for ምውትት; አቅስት, for አቅስትት; እምታ, for እም፡ምታ; ታማስኑ, for ታማስንኑ; ዋሕድ, *fem.* of ዋሕድ for ዋሕድት; even ወውዓ, for ወውውዓ; (on the other hand አምላክከ *amlākeka*; ጸወንነ *ṣawanéna; ይነድዱ yenadedū* &c.)(²). Even in foreign words there is no deviation from this mode of writing, *e. g.* ልዳ *Lydda*; ረቢ "Rabbi"; ስማኮስ *Symmachus*. Variations occur only in those cases in which the consonant itself varies from a pronunciation which employs a vowel, to one which discards it. In particular there are cases (§ 37) in which a consonant that should otherwise be uttered with a fugitive *ĕ* in an open syllable, and which follows an open syllable, gives up its *ĕ* without difficulty, and, having thus become vowel-less, attaches itself to the preceding syllable. If such consonant is the first element of a consonantal double-letter,—which is often the case in formations from roots *med. gem.*,—both

---

(¹) [But see Note to § 168, 6.]. The cases of this sort which have been collected by KÖNIG, p. 98, with the exception of እብሔሩ for እምብሔሩ in the RÜPPELL Inscriptions 1, 28; 2, 51 (cf. D. H. MÜLLER, ZDMG XXX, p. 704 [and '*Epigr. Denkm.*', p. 52]), are doubtful. [V. however *Kebra Nag.*, p. XVII, *sub* 10:—እቤተ=እምቤተ and ኀቤተ=ኀበ፡ቤተ.]

(²) *Cf.* KÖNIG, p. 94 *sqq.*

modes of writing are allowable. It is true that ኄዩ and ተሰዩ are usually written for ኄይዩ and ተሰይዩ, seeing that here the vowelless pronunciation of the middle letter has thoroughly penetrated the form, and so too with ተምዐ *tamé-ʿa*, for ተምዕዐ; but the other mode of writing occurs also. In the very same way ይኔዲ., ያኀበ, ኀሢ, ኀሥም &c. are frequently written for ይኔድዲ., ያኀብበ, ኀሥሢ, ኀሥሥም. Now seeing that no written sign has at any time been contrived (§ 16) to indicate this doubling, it is only from knowledge of the Word-form itself that we can tell when a Consonant has to be read as a double one; and this constitutes a sensible defect in Ethiopic writing, for the beginner in the language. It is still worse that we should in this way be destitute of any ancient external evidence (1) as to those cases in which a consonant is to be uttered as a double one, and that we should therefore be left without guidance, if not in regard to individual types, at all events in regard to individual words, which may belong to the one type or the other.

Giving up the Doubling.

§ 56. (*d*) *Giving up the Doubling.* 1. The doubling of a Consonant is audible only when it is followed by a vowel: It cannot be heard at the end of words which do not conclude with a vowel. Originally, it is true, there were no words in Ethiopic which ended with a consonant requiring to be doubled and yet unprovided with a following vowel, for the Nominal stems, which alone are concerned here, ended at one time in *ĕ*, so that ልብ, *e. g.*, was pronounced *lébb^e* (§ 38). But this *ĕ* was given up at an early stage, and then of course cases emerged in abundance, in which a concluding double letter could only make itself heard as a single one, *e. g.* ልብ *léb*; ሕግ *ḥeg*,—although in such words the double letter was at once heard, as soon as it was followed by a vowel, as in ልበ *lebba*, ሕግከ *ḥéggeka*.

2. In the middle of a word the doubling, particularly of Semivowels and Aspirates, may in certain circumstances more easily

(1) The later pronunciation, as it was heard by LUDOLF, is by no means invariably the correct one. LUDOLF also propounded several decidedly erroneous views on this point, seemingly founded on his peculiar grammatical opinions, as will be farther proved.—According to TRUMPP, p. 522, N. 1, the doubling of Consonants (with the exception of the Aspirates) is still heard to some extent in Geʿez in the middle of a word, but is invariably given up at the end of it. *Cf.* also KÖNIG, p. 117 *sq*.

disappear. On the Semivowels (1) *cf. supra*, p. 97 *sq.*, § 52: cases like **መይጥ** *maiṭ*, properly *mayyeṭ*, belong to this section, as well as **ሙታን**, for **ምውታን** *meww^etān*. In other cases we have the same thing; for instance **የሐውጹ** (from **የሐውጹ**) *yaḥawweṣū* may no doubt become, when somewhat carelessly pronounced, *yaḥawṣū*, *yaḥauṣū*. Gutturals too occasionally cast away the embarrassing doubling. Thus it comes about, that an *á* which has the tone, and which comes before a doubled Aspirate followed by short *ĕ* in a closed syllable, as in **ይመህር** *yemáhher* "(that) he teach", is thickened into *e*, as in **ይምህር**,—an indication that the doubling is no longer clearly heard (§ 45),—and that this *yeméhher* is farther reduced to *yeméhr* (§ 46). Farther, a certain dislike to the doubling of Aspirates can alone explain why some verbs, having a middle Aspirate, should in the Causative of the Intensive Stem,—in all those forms in which a doubling of the second radical would have to be audible (Perf., Subj., Imperf., Inf.),—have recourse to the Causative of the Simple Stem, *e. g.* **አትሐተ**; **አሌዐለ**, as well as **አለዐለ** (cf. § 96). In the same way a still larger number of verbs *middle Aspirate* prefer to adopt, in the Perfect (and to some extent in the Infinitive) of the Reflexive Stem, the form **ተትሕተ**, *tateḥta*, instead of the form **ተተሐተ**, that is to say, the form of Reflexive 1, in preference to that of Reflexive 2;—or at least they admit of both forms side by side (v. § 97). But we cannot follow up this question of the doubling of Aspirates farther than these few hints, seeing that the means of gaining acquaintance with the old pronunciation are wanting.

Occasional Compensation for Loss of the Doubling.

3. In the cases mentioned hitherto, the doubling disappears without any compensation for its loss, but in other cases it is made up for in one way or other. There is the case,—isolated, so far as yet known,—of the doubling of a radical (in a double-lettered root) being thrown back on the first radical, in the word **ተምዐ**, **ተማዕከ** for **ተምዕዐ**, **ተመዓዕከ** &c. (§ 97). Of almost equally rare occurrence is the device of compensating for the doubling, by lengthening the preceding vowel (2), *e. g.* **ሚያኔ** "delusion", for **ምያኔ** *meyyānē*; **ዲጋ** "ambush", דִּבָּה; **ተባረዘ**=تَبَرَّزَ; and in foreign words, *e. g.*

(1) *Cf.* Ewald, '*Hebr. Spr.*', § 64 *a.*

(2) Common in Hebrew and still more frequent in Syriac. *Cf.* also König, p. 416. [It will perhaps be wise to receive with a measure of caution the instances which follow in this paragraph, as some of them seem rather forced and doubtful. tr.]

መርቄሎስ *Marcellus* (1). Oftener the first element of a double letter is softened into a Semivowel, which then coalesces with a foregoing *a* into a mixed vowel, as happens in several Multiliteral roots (v. § 78). Only, in the Imperfects of all the Intensive Stems, in consequence of lengthening the immediately preceding vowel *ă* into *ā*, the doubling of the middle radical is regularly given up, and in compensation an *i*-sound is blended with the *ā*, *e. g.* ይፌጽም *yefēṣem*, from ይፈጽም *yefáṣṣem* (§ 95). A third method of replacing the doubling, and one of very frequent occurrence, consists in interpolating a Liquid: *cf.* § 72.

Exchange of Consonants. Transposition.

§ 57. 2. To facilitate the pronunciation of difficult letter-groups, there are still other expedients at the command of the language, besides the Assimilation of two Consonants,—in particular, (1) exchanging them for others, and (2) transposing them.

Exchanging one Consonant for another is, upon the whole, of rare occurrence (2). A ዝ, meeting directly with ት may easily assume the sound of ስ, and in fact,—although it is retained, as a rule, *e. g.* in ወሓይዝት "rivers",—it has passed into ስ in several words in very common use. This is the case invariably in ኅብስት "bread", for ኅብዝት, and sometimes in አጋእስት "lords", for—or as a companion-form to—አጋእዝት. Probably also a ጥ has been weakened into ት after ስ in the common word ውስት (3). ም, when it meets directly with Labial Mutes, frequently passes into the Dental Nasal:—እንበይነ "because of", for እምበይነ; እንበለ "except", for እምበለ (although one always says እምብሔር, እምብርት (4) &c.); ለንጳስ *λαμπάς*, ለንጴኔ *λαμπήνη*; ምንባሬ *Μαμβρῆ*, Gen. 14, 24; 18, 1; and a like result happens more than once when it comes upon a Dental Mute: ጕንድ "stem", from גֹּמֶד; ስንዳሌ *σεμίδαλις*; and so too, no doubt, in መንታ "twins", for መምታ from תְּאֹם (5). In Ethiopic *the transposition of Consonants* does not appear in Word-formation, for *ts* does not become *st*, but *ss*,—v. § 54 (6). But certainly Ethiopic roots, when compared

(1) Verbs, like ሰረረ, በረከ, I do not regard as Intensive Stems (in the way of בֵּרֵךְ), but rank them rather with Stem 3.

(2) *Cf.* König, p. 100 *sq.* (3) [But *cf. supra*, p. 103, Note (3).]

(4) [V. however *supra*, p. 104, Note (1).]

(5) አስጳዳጦስ for *ἀσπάλαθος* is explained by the Greek uncial writing (Λ having been read as Δ).

(6) *Cf.*, however, አምርሕት and አምሕርት; አፍርኅት and አፍኅርት;

with the corresponding ones in the related tongues, present many examples of the transposition of letters, *e. g.* **መትከፍት** "shoulder", for **መከተፍት** (כָּתֵף); **አርመስመሰ**, for **አምረስመሰ** from **መርሰሰ**, מָשַׁשׁ; **መጥቀዐ**, from مَقْطَع; **አንገለገ** (= **አንገልለገ**) for **አንገልገለ**; **ለዐለ** *lá-ʿa-la*, for **ዐልዐለ**; **ሐቀፈ** חבק, حبك; **ጸገበ**, שׂבע, شبع. In particular it is the more liquid letters and the Aspirates, which tend in Ethiopic root-formation to glide from one position to another:—Examples for **ል**:—**ሠሀለ**, סלח, سهل; **ጸሐል**, צַלַּחַת; **ወለጠ**, بدل; **ሐቅል**, חֵלֶק, חֲקַל, حَقْل; **ለምጸ**, ملس and ملص:—for **ር**:—**ወረድ** "breadth", אדר; **ሕንብርብሬ**, קֶרֶב, جَرَب; **ፈኀረ**, فرع (فهر):—for **ን**:—**ሐነጸ**, حصن, חסן;—for Aspirates besides:—**ሰንአ**, שְׁאָן, عل; **ናእክ**, "lead", אֲנָךְ, انك; **ናእክ** "groaning", אֲנָק, נְאָק; **ፈሐቀ**, הָפַךְ, افك; **ለሰሐ**, لحس; **ሐሰለ**, سحل. In one or two roots all the letters are shifted together:—**ምሕረ**, רחם, رحم (¹); **ልሀቀ**, כֶּלַח, كهل; perhaps too in **እግር** "foot", from **ልግር** (²), רֶגֶל, رِجْل; **መርግ**, رِجَام. For details in these cases reference may be made to the Lexicon.

Inter-polation or Rejection of individual Consonants.

§ 58. 3. *Interpolation, or Rejection, of individual Consonants, and Softening of Consonants into Vowels.* In the first place a short vowel with the tone, in an open syllable, may be strengthened by the insertion of a Nasal: thus **ዝንቱ** *zéntū*, "this", stands for **ዝቱ**; **ሀየንተ** *heyánta*, "instead of", for **ሀየተ**, which still appears along with it; **ኵለንታ**; for **ኵለታ**; **እንበ** for **አበ**; **ሰንበልት**, **ሰንቢል**, along with **ሰብል** (König, p. 102); **ድንቀት** "chance", for **ድቀት**; *cf.* also **መንጠንጢን** "petty", from √**መጠነ**; **ልኵትንት** *lekuetént*,

ማዕበል and **ሙብዐል**; **መቋዕልት** and **መቋልዕት**; **ተምክዖት** for **ተምእኮት**; and **ትምክእት** for **ትምእክት**; **ርሕስት** and **ርስሕት**; **መስእርት** for **ማእስርት**; **ትዕውርት** for **ትውዕርት**; **ትውዝፍት** for **ትዝውፍት**; **አግልዕት** and **አግዕልት**; **እግዚእ** and **አጋእዝት**; **ይትመሀቱ** for **ይትመትሁ** '*Gadla Adām*' (ed. Trumpp), p. 79, l. 24.—.On the question whether the prefix of the Causative-Reflexive,—**አስተ** has been transposed from **አተሰ**, v. § 83.

(¹) But v. Praetorius, '*Beitr. z. Ass.*', I, p. 21.—*Cf.* Arab. رَطْل, from Greek λίτρα.

(²) Ewald, '*Hebr. Spr.*' p. 91; Schrader, '*De Indole*', p. 24; König, p. 144.

λήκυθος; መንገን, μηχανή (1). But just as a short vowel may in such a case be strengthened also by doubling the following consonant (§ 55) (2), so may a Nasal in turn make its way into a word to compensate for giving up the doubling of the consonant (§ 56). This phenomenon, which is quite usual in Aramaic as is well known, is shown in Ethiopic, just as in Arabic (3),—mainly however in root-formation, though in this case, of very common occurrence,—by a ን coming in after the first radical, probably to replace the doubling of the second radical (for examples v. § 72). In the word ምዙኅ Deut. 32,15, we have, alongside of this original form, the variation ምንዙኅ. Of foreign words there may be compared, *e. g.* ሰንፔር σάπφειρος. With less frequency a ር is interpolated for a like purpose in root-formation: ግርላዎስ *Gallus*; ጠርቤንስስ: *Tabennesis* (cf. *infra* § 72) (4). In Syriac and Arabic this practice is more common.

The rejection of a Consonant without any compensation is similarly infrequent in Ethiopic (5). The Nasal ን is the letter most liable to be so treated, *e. g.* ዕንዕዩ for ዕንዕንዩ before the Semi-vowel, or as a final letter after a long vowel, as in the numerals from 20 to 90 (§ 158) and in the Pronominal terminations (*e. g.* § 146). An entire syllable, viz. ነ, (ን along with its vowel), is thrown off from እምነ "from", when it has to be closely attached to the Noun. And just like ን, the Liquid ል is constantly rejected after a long vowel in a word which is in very frequent use, viz. ይቤ "he said", for ይብሀል (cf. *supra*, § 46) (6). The Fem. ት disappears, just as in Aramaic, in the terminations *ō*, *ē* (for *ōt*, *ēt*), § 120 *sq.* On the rejection of Aspirates and Semi-vowels *cf.* §§ 47 and 53. Occasionally too, in forms where several radicals are repeated, a letter is left out for brevity's sake.

The softening of any one of the firmer letters into a vowel is still less common, and has mostly been handed down in very ancient words, like ኮከብ "star", from ኩብኩብ. *Cf.* also § 28, on ብ. **Softening of Consonants into Vowels.**

(1) In Amharic, *e. g.* አንድ "one", for አድ from አሐድ.

(2) *Cf.* Ewald, '*Hebr. Spr.*', § 9 *sq.*

(3) Ewald, '*Gr. Arab.*', §§ 163, 191.

(4) *Cf.* also König, p. 103.

(5) *Cf.* König, pp. 101, 103.

(6) *Cf.* also Gesenius, '*Thesaurus*', p. 600.

III. THE WORD AND THE TONE OF THE WORD.

The Tone of the Word, and its Adjustment.

§ 59. The word, consisting of several syllables, has a unity impressed upon it by means of the Tone, which brings one syllable into prominence as the one which dominates the whole. The pronunciation of the other syllables is then accommodated to this leading syllable, as regards length or shortness, height or depth of note, and even, in certain circumstances, choice of vowels for these syllables. Although the influence of the Tone upon the vocalisation of the word by no means displays itself in forms so manifold in Ethiopic, as, for instance, in Hebrew, it nevertheless asserts itself now and then, and therefore it calls for a short description here.

1. It is true that the method of fixing the tone of the word (1),—in a dead language which has left no grammatical description belonging to the time when it was a living tongue, and which did not employ in its written character any tone-marking (2),—can no longer be exactly determined in detail; but the general principles of the process may be gathered, partly from the rules of word-formation, and partly from later accounts of the accentuation (3), and from a comparison of Ethiopic with Arabic and Amharic. According to these principles the Tone is not bound to any special syllable, as it is in Hebrew, in such manner that it should fall, as a rule say, on the last syllable, or possibly on the penult; but on the contrary in any polysyllable,—so far as mere possibility goes,—it may rest on any one of the last three syllables, and occasionally may lie, it would seem, still farther back, *e. g.* **ባረከተ** *bárakata*; **ባረከተከ** *bárakàtaka*. The adjustment of the tone is regulated by wholly different points of view. In the first place it depends upon the kind of syllables and their vowels. Syllables having long vowels,—or (which is the same thing as a matter of prosody) closed

---

(1) *Cf.* now specially, on this subject, the frequently quoted treatise of Trumpp, '*Ueber den Accent im Aethiopischen*', ZDMG XXVIII, p. 515 *sqq.*: v. also König, p. 154 *sqq.*—On the marked fluctuation of the tone in present-day Abyssinian, *e. g.* in Tigriña, v. Praetorius ZDMG XLI, p. 688 [and in Tigre, Littmann, '*Zeitschr. f. Assyr.*' XIII, p. 140 *sqq.*].

(2) The signs written over the several words in Ethiopic Hymnologies are certainly not Tone-marks, but musical signs, apparently formed in imitation of Greek notes of Music.

(3) Ludolf, '*Gramm.*' I, 7.

syllables having short vowels,—naturally assert themselves in the word, and necessarily attract the tone, in opposition to open syllables with short vowels, *e. g.* ኅጳጥ *ḥedā́ṭ*; ነገርነ *nagárna*. The second fundamental rule, which, besides, is connected with the formative history of words, is this,—that final short vowels, belonging invariably to the form, and final and simply closed syllables which have short vowels, and which have originated from the rejection of a final vowel in pronunciation (*e. g.* ሀገር *hágar*, for *hágar*[e]), do not take the tone; while final long vowels also surrender the tone to the penult, when the penult has a long vowel (thus, of course ይበሊ *yebalī́*; ይትፈኖ *yetfannṓ*; ነገሩ *nagarū́*; but ይቤሉ *yebḗlū*; ሞቱ *mṓtū*; ይሚጡ *yemī́ṭū*; ይሬእዩ *yerḗ'yū*; ይሴፎ *yesḗfō*; ፈጣሪ *faṭā́rī*; ምድራዊ *medrā́wī* &c.). Evidently in most cases the tone avoids the last syllable. Much oftener it rests on the third last syllable, but oftenest on the second last. For the rest, the accentuation of a word is regulated by the nature of its formation, because it is only from this that we can see what vowels and syllables are the most important in the word, what formative additions are attached bearing the tone, and what ones have given up their tone,—why, for instance, ግበር "act", (Imper.) is pronounced *gebár*, but ሀገር: "city", *hágar*; why መሳፍንት "princes" should be *masā́fent*, but ፍጥርት „created" (fem.) *feṭért*; ውእቱ "he", *wḗtū*, and ገብሩ "they acted", *gabrú*, &c.(¹). Accordingly, instead of reckoning up a series of rules on accentuation at this stage, it will be more advisable to give the accentuation of the several forms when we come to describe them. Still, reference may be again made here to § 48, according to which the Aspirates exercise a peculiar influence on the tone.

Ethiopic has a large number of small monosyllabic words, which are too weak to take a position for themselves in the sentence. They are therefore attached to stronger words as prefixes or suffixes; but, like the enclitics of other tongues, they are then unaccented, or only so far accented as to make them discernible to the ear as loosely connected appendages, which do not belong properly to the word. They cause no alteration in the main accent-

(¹) [Without going into particulars it may be said here generally that TRUMPP and KÖNIG are probably safer guides than DILLMANN in the pronunciation of Ethiopic, when the last-named differs from the first two, as he frequently does. TR.]

uation of the word; and yet, according to Ludolf, in words which end in a long vowel, the tone must necessarily fall upon this long vowel before an appended particle, even though it did not rest on this vowel in the word when standing alone: መኑ *mánū*, but መኑመ *manū́ma*; ዮጊ *yṓgī*, but ዮጊኬ *yōgī́kē*. ዝ "this (*m.*)" and ዛ "this (*f.*)" differ from these attached particles, for though they are mostly attached, in writing, to the word which follows them, they still retain their own independent tone.

Nothing is known in Ethiopic of any special pronunciation of a word at the end of a sentence or at the end of a clause of a sentence, and nothing, accordingly, of any influence being exerted by the accent of the sentence upon the accent of a word (*Pause*). Ludolf expressly notices that the Abyssinians modulate their voices very little in reading.

Vocalisation of the Word, as influenced by the Tone.

§ 60. 2. The vocalisation of a word mainly depends, of course, not on phonetic conditions, but on the sense and signification of its own form,—so far as different significations cling to different vowels, as will be shown farther on. And yet phonetic conditions exercise an influence too; for the sense of the form is usually sustained in any word by one vowel only, or by two at most; the selection of the rest depends upon phonetic conditions, and that selection is made in such fashion that the several syllables in the word all sound harmoniously together, and the toneless syllables subordinate themselves to the tone-bearing ones according to their situation with respect to the latter. As regards, first of all, the long vowels, they appear, with some few exceptions, to be essential in Ethiopic to the signification in the forms concerned. The short vowels, *ă* and *ĕ*,—and particularly *ă*,—seem possessed, it is true, of the same property, in the case of many forms, but they are often mere auxiliary vowels, employed to facilitate the pronunciation of consonants which are not supported by the formative vowel or vowels. Of the two, *ĕ* is the more unimportant, indefinite and colourless; *ă* is more important and significant, and accordingly, as a mere auxiliary vowel, it is employed specially in the Noun. Farther it appears that when once *ă* or *ĕ* has established itself in a form, the other syllables readily echo [1] the vowel concerned; thus,

---

[1] For another example of a foregoing vowel recurring in the next syllable as an echo, v. § 26, 4.

both in the Perfect of Verbs and in Quadriliteral and Multiliteral Nouns the *ă* often runs through several syllables:—**ነጐድጓድ**, **ነቀልቃል**, **ደገደግ**; or *ĕ* in **ቈንጽል**, **ድልቅልቅ**, **ድንብዝል**. To precede *ū*, *ĕ* is preferred, **ግቡር**, **እስትጉቡእ**, and *ă* to precede *ī*, **ጠቢብ**. But if a long *ā*, as the weightiest of all the vowels, has newly made its way into the stem, the syllable before or after it must as far as possible be shortened and obscured, and so it is not *ă* that appears in it, but *ĕ*: **ዕሩቅ**, **ሕንባል**, **ምሕዋር**, **ትርጋፅ**, **ምሳሌ**, **ኃጥእ**, **መዓትም**, **ሰናስል**, **መማክርት**. In certain cases, in fact, before such an *ā*, even an *ā*, *ō* or *ē* must be eased down into a *ū* or *ī* at least:—**ጉባኤ**, **ፂዋዌ**. The same rule holds also, when a tone-bearing *ā*, or a formative syllable with *ā*, is attached to the stem as the main syllable of the word: **ፍሥሓ**, **ርሥእን**, **ብዙርና**. Even a mere strongly accented *á*, which is pressing newly into the stem as the bearer of the signification, calls for an obscured *ĕ* either before or after it:—**ይገብር**, **እዘን**, **እበን**. On the other hand an *ĕ* is now and again obliged, through the influence of the tone, to pass into *ă*. Invariably is this the case when, in the Perfect of the type **ገብረ** and **ተገብረ**, the tone falls upon the syllable which begins with the second radical; for although **ገብርከ** *gabérka* is capable of pronunciation, the *ĕ* is yet regarded as too weak here to be retained in the main syllable emphasised by the tone, and therefore it is preferred to replace it by the stronger *á*. In the same way the long *ī* of a tone-bearing syllable,—which is becoming a doubly closed syllable from being a singly closed one, so that its *ī* is necessarily shortened by § 35 *sq.*—does not always pass into *ĕ*, but sometimes into *á*, as perhaps in **ሰንቢል**, **ሰንበልት**; although in similar cases an *é*, shortened out of *ū*, is regarded as regular, like **ፍጥርት**, out of **ፍጡር**(1).

(1) For an account of these conditions, differing from the above, v. König, p. 121 *sqq.*

PART SECOND.

MORPHOLOGY.

A. ROOTS:—THEIR CLASSES, AND THEIR FORMS.

§ 61. Roots are the material out of which Language fashions Words. To explain the mode of their origin and their significations in detail, is the province of the Lexicon. Grammar takes these as given, but it is bound to furnish a survey of the different classes of roots and their forms, because the mode of formation of the words, which have sprung from the roots, is determined by the form of the roots. In accordance with their signification, Roots fall into three classes of very unequal extent.

Inter-jections.

1. The lowest stage of roots is formed by those *Interjections*, which are not derived from Pronouns or Conceptional Roots, but which burst forth as a direct expression of feeling, and are, as it were, the animal utterances of Man. They are mostly short and unbending; and in their case the distinction between root, and formation from the root, falls away. There are, however, only a very few of them in any language. The most common of these ejaculations is ኦ: "O!" (1), employed to express emotion, and particularly wonder, *e. g.* ኦዘመንክር "O what a marvellous thing!": It is therefore often used in accosting any one in the Vocative, § 142, ኦገብር "O man!" It seems also to be involved in ኦሆ "Oh! certainly", v. § 62. As ejaculations of distress and pain there appear:—ኣ (2), in combination with ኦ: as ኦኣ ὢ ὢ Numb. 24,23;

(1) أَوْ; آ, آ; הָהּ, הֶ.

(2) آ; הֶאָח.

አሀ (1) "Ah!"; ዩ and ዮ (2) "Alas!". In more frequent use is ወይ (3) "woe!", always with a following ለ of the dative, *e. g.* ወይ ፡ ሊተ "woe's me!"; and, with like meaning, the longer form አሌ (4), also with a following dative; finally ሰይል or ሴል, with a following Suff. Pron., "ah! alas!" (for these last three v. *infra*, § 199). A secondary form ወይል to ወይ, or አሌል to አሌ, is not necessary to be assumed (§ 167); and yet, just as in Arabic وَيْلٌ has been formed out of وَيْ, so too in Ethiopic a noun ወይሌ "howling", "lamentation", has sprung from ወይ and the ለ which invariably follows it. Besides, we meet with አኄ "come!" (Ex. 4,19; var ነዓ), በሐ, በሖ, በሑ. with a following Suff. Pron., as a particle of salutation, —Arab. بَخْ, بَخٍ; and ጸጥ as a call to silence.

§ 62. 2. The *Pronominal Roots* are one stage higher. They are no longer confined to the field of sensation, but belong to that of the understanding. They do not, however, themselves denote the objects of conception and thought, but only point out these objects in space and time (Indicating-words); and starting from this they are employed, farther, to denote all possible conditions of thought. They constitute quite as important a part of the language as the Conceptional Roots. If the latter contain the material of the language, the type is furnished by the former; and nearly all the formative additions to words, and the majority of the particles which serve to express the relations of clauses in a sentence, are of pronominal origin. Ethiopic has developed this portion of the language, precisely, in a very rich and manifold way, and has preserved much that has been lost in the other Semitic tongues. Pronominal Roots.- Demonstratives.

(1) Of these Pronominal roots, the most widely extended and most variously employed are the *Demonstratives*, in the narrower sense of the term (*Demonstrativa*). In this class we distinguish four orders of roots.

(*a*) The primordial Demonstrative *ta* (5) has been softened into *da*; and then, through transformation of the Mute into the

(1) V. Ludolf, '*Comm. Hist. Aeth.*', p. 41.

(2) V. Ludolf, '*Lex. Aeth.*', col. 484; Arabic يَا in a different meaning.

(3) وَا, وَيْ, وَيْحِ; ܘܳܐ, ܘܳܝ; אוֹי.

(4) אַלְלַי. (5) तत्, स.

Sibilant, the two farther modes of expression *sa* and *za* have been evolved. All the four are represented in Ethiopic. The elementary *ta*, besides appearing in the Feminine termination ት (1), is still preserved in the Personal particles ቱ (2) and ቲ "the" (*m.* & *f.*), though only in compounds, *e. g.* ውእቱ, ይእቲ, ዝንቱ, ዛቲ, ሎቱ, ላቲ, እሙንቱ—, as well as in the Interrogative አይቴ "where?". The softer form of pronunciation *da*, which has become predominant in Aramaic, can only be supported in Ethiopic by the preposition ዲበ "upon" (§ 165). Having passed into the harder Sibilant(3), it has, under the guise of ሰ, produced a series of particles of relation and of exclamation, namely, ሰ δέ, እስመ "for" (conj.), ሶበ "when", ሶ and እስኩ "pray, do—!" (Gr. δή, Lat. *quaeso*). Just as in Hebrew and Arabic, it has become predominant, under the form of the soft sibilation, for the usual Demonstr. Pron. ዝ "this", and for the Relative Pron. ዘ "who" (§ 64), as well as in the particles ዝየ „here", ማእዜ "when?", ይእዜ "now", and perhaps also in ጊዜ "point of time", "hour".

(*b*) The root ተ, or ደ, has become ሀ, through a farther subtilising of the Mute into a mere breathing(4). As such, having been shortened out of the ቱ which has been fashioned into a Personal Pron. (§ 65), it makes its appearance in the Suff. Pron. ሁ, ሃ, ሆሙ, ሆን; elsewhere, only in Adverbial formation, in particular in ሃ as a mark of the Accusative; ሁ as an interrogative; ሂ "away to" (§ 160); ሂ τε, "also"; ሀየ "there"; ሀየንተ "in place of"; doubtless also in አሆ "oh! certainly" (properly, "oh! quite so"; *cf.* § 61). And, remarkably enough (§ 24), this aspirate ሀ is hardened, in Ethiopic, even into ሐ and ኀ in ኀበ "with" and "where" (§ 161)(5), and ከሐ "away yonder", ከሐከ "yonder"; and into ዐ perhaps, in ነዓ "behold!" (but v. § 41).

(*c*) Like the Mute and and Sibilant Dentals, the two Liquids *n* and *l* also serve to form Demonstrative Pronouns, with either a preceding or a succeeding vowel, as *na*, *an*(6), *la*, *al*, and they are

---

(1) [V. on this subject C. Brockelmann, '*Die Femininendung T im Semitischen*' (Breslau 1903).]

(2) *Cf.* Trumpp, p. 546, N. 2: [V. also Bezold, '*Die grosse Dariusinschrift*', p. 25 *sqq.*; Barth, ZDMG, XLVI, p. 685 *sqq.*, and LIX, p. 161 *sq.*; Fischer, *ibid.* p. 443 *sqq.*]

(3) *Cf.* שֵׁם.

(4) *Cf.* هو, הָא.

(5) [*Cf.*, however, Praetorius, ZDMG, LVII, p. 272].

(6) These two are also extensively used in Sanskrit.

still frequently employed in the Ethiopic language. The *first branch*, and first of all in the form ነ, is employed in Semitic generally, and accordingly in Ethiopic too, mainly to form delicate circumstantial particles which express relations either sensible or intellectual(1). From it proceed on the one hand the words for "behold!"(2) ናሁ, ነዋ, ነየ, (§ 160) and for "come now!"(3) ነዐ, and on the other hand a few enclitic particles, which closely resemble in form and meaning those which come from the root ሀ, namely ኑ as an interrogative, ኔ "away to" (§ 160), ነ "away to" (§ 160), and ኒ "also" ("again"). In the form አን, modified into እን, this branch serves partly to form Personal pronouns, in the Feminines of Demonstrative and Relative pronouns, እንትኩ, and እንታክቲ "that" (*f.*), እንተ "who" (*f.*) (§ 64), and as the first element in the Pronouns of the 1st and 2nd Persons (§ 65), and partly to form various particles, like እን "there!" "see!" (in እንክሙ, ኢንቋዕ, እንከ, እንጋ); እንተ "with respect to"; እንዘ "while", "since". As a Demonstrative it seems originally to refer, in opposition to *ta* and *ha*, to the more distant object, and thus to signify "that"; and, seeing that it points away from what is at hand and existing, words which express negation(4) could at the same time be derived from it. Like the Hebrew אֵין, אַיִן in fine, the Ethiopic እን "not", in compounds like እንዳዒ "perhaps" (§ 163) and እንበየ "I may not", is also traceable to this root; and the usual Ethiopic word for "not", ኢ (*cf.* Assyr. [illegible] *ai*) has been shortened out of a form like אַיִן.

The second branch also, *la*, *al*(5), had originally the faculty of pointing to the more remote object, although it has not preserved this more definite meaning in all its formations. In Ethiopic ለ still occurs with a personal meaning, particularly in the reduplicated form ለሊ "he, he", "even he", "he himself", "self", § 150(6); and አል in the same way is found in the compound አልኩ, አልክቱ "those"; while *al* and *la* together, compounded into *alla*, appear in

(1) *Cf.* Trumpp, '*Sitzber. d. philos.-philol. Cl. d. bayer. Akad. zu München vom 5. Mai*, 1877', Part 2, p. 117 *sqq*.

(2) הֵן, הִנֵּה; إِنَّ. (3) נָא; نَّ; ـَنَّ.

(4) Like न "not", अन्य "other".

(5) أَلْ; הַ־, אֵלֶּה, הָלְאָה; ܗܳܠܶܝܢ; هَلُمَّ.

(6) *Cf.* Trumpp, p. 550, N. 2 (contrary to Praetorius, ZDMG XXVII, p. 639).

the plural stem,—running through all Semitic tongues,—of the Demonstrative Pronoun እሉ, እላ "these", as well as of the Relative Pronoun እለ "who, which". And just as from the branch *an*, so too from the branch *la*, *al*, negatives are derived, especially አል (1) "not", in አልቦ "there is not", and ላ(2) "not", in አላ "but"(3).

(*d*) As the original meaning of the roots formed with *l* and *n* has gradually become weak, the new Demonstrative root ክ has been fashioned, to indicate that which is more remote. In the form *ka* it is contained in the adverbs ከሐ "away yonder", ከሐከ "yonder". To form Personal Demonstratives it is appended, under the form ኩ, to other Demonstrative roots, in order to bestow upon them the faculty of pointing to that which is more remote: ዝኩ "that" (*m.*), እንትኩ "that" (*f.*), እልኩ "those". This Demonstrative root can hardly be regarded as one which has sprung from the Interrogative Relative root (§ 63), but it seems (4), like the ከ of the 2nd pers. (§ 65), to have come from original *ta*, *twa*.

For a last Demonstrative v. finally § 65, treating of the Personal Pronouns.

Interrogatives. § 63. (2) *Interrogatives* may of course spring from Demonstrative roots like ሁ and ኑ, through the influence of the tone (§ 62). But as the influence of the tone does not suffice for the formation of all Interrogatives, languages have produced special Interrogative Roots.

(*a*) In Semitic, and accordingly in Ethiopic, the most usual Interrogative root is *ma* (probably hardened out of *wa*) (5). In this short form it is still retained (though no longer invariably interrogative in signification, but brought down sometimes to the level of indefiniteness and relativity), in the attached particle መ (§ 162), as second member of compounds, in ሚመ "*utrum?*" (and ወሚመ "an?"), ከመ "nearly"(6), ከመ "as"(7), and as first member in ማእዜ "when?"(8). In order to turn *ma* into a Personal Interrogative, it was compounded with the Demonstrative stem *na*: መኑ "what (is)

(1) אַל. (2) לא; لَا; ܠܐ.

(3) [*Cf.* however, § 168, 6, Note].

(4) *Cf.* ذَالِكَ, ذَاكَ; דָּךְ, דֵּךְ, אֵלֵּךְ.

(5) As the remains of original *kwa* क quis? (v. Ewald, '*Hebr. Spr.*', § 104).

(6) כַּמָּה.

(7) כְּמוֹ; كَمَا. (8) מָתַי; مَتَى; ܐܡܬܝ.

he?", "who?"(1), — whence also the neuter ምንት "what?". A neuter and adverbial form ሚ "what?" "how!" appears to be a corruption of a form like مَا, מָה, מֶה, — no longer retained in Ethiopic. A few other particles also, of a relative meaning, have been derived from this መ (v. § 64).

(*b*) The second of the most usual Interrogative roots is አይ (2), probably a weakened form of original *kai* (كَيْفَ). It is used in Ethiopic, just as in Arabic, as an interrogative adjective, in the sense ποῖος, *qualis*, "of what sort?". Either in the short form *ĕ* or in the complete form *ai*, it is prefixed to several Demonstrative particles and even to one Conceptional root, to impart interrogative force to them: አይቴ፡ "where?", እፎ "how?"(3), እስፍንቱ፡ "how much?" "how many?".

(*c*) Both of these Interrogative roots in common use point to an original root *kwa, kai*. And there actually appear to be some remains of it, even in Ethiopic, in the interjection እንቋዕ "well now!", properly: — "see what!", where the *k* has at the same time passed into the strongest guttural. But in other cases, just as in the other Semitic languages, the Interrogative root, even in this original form, has assumed a Relative meaning throughout.

§ 64 (3) As in other languages, the *Relative Pronouns* are derived from the Demonstratives and Interrogatives. Relative Pronouns.

(*a*) The ordinary Relative Pronouns are taken from Demonstrative roots, viz. ዘ "who, which" (*m.*); እንተ "who, which" (*f.*); እለ "who, which" (*pl.*), as well as the conjunctions ዘ "that", "in order that"; እንዘ "while" ("seeing that"), and the prepositions እንተ "with regard to"; በእንተ "because of". Also, under the form ሶ this demonstrative root is employed with a Relative sense in ሶበ "when" (with appended በ, while ሶ perhaps corresponds to ذَا, إِذَا).

(*b*) From the Interrogative root *ma* there came, with the help of a prefixed aspirate (4), — the conjunctions አመ "when"; እመ "if"(5); and a form shortened from the last, እም ἄν, in the apodosis of a Conditional sentence (§ 170); and with a prefixed demonstrative ሰ, in accordance with § 34, እስመ (for ስመ "that which"), "while",

(1) מָן; ܡܢ; مَنُو. (2) אֵי, אַיִן, אַיֵּה; ܐܝܢܐ, ܐܝܟܐ; أَيّ, أَيْنَ, أَيْشَ &c.
(3) אֵיפֹה. (4) Somewhat the same as in אֲשֶׁר.
(5) אִם; on its derivation *cf.* Ewald, p. 225, Rem. 1.

"because", "for". From the Interrogative root *kwa* (§ 63, *c*) an impersonal Relative stem has originated, through simplification into *ka*, in the sense "that" (properly:—"what")(1): It occurs in the compounds እስከ(2) "until", "as far as"; እንከ "therefore", "*itaque*" (properly: "see that", "seeing that", "from that circumstance"). But this stem is mainly employed in processes of *Comparison*, with the meaning "as", "like"(3), first in ከመ "nearly" ("like what")(4); ከመ (*Prep.* and *Conj.*) "like", "just as"(5); farther,—when compounded with Demonstratives,—in ኬ "therefore", "now" (probably shortened from כֵּן=כְּהֵן)(6), and in ከ "thus" (from *kāhū*, "like it"), no longer in use alone, it is true (like כֹּה, כָּא; كَهْ), but probably preserved still in አከ "in nowise", "not"(7). ኮ(8) seems to have arisen, by sound-transition, out of ከ in the interrogative እፎ "how?". The same *kō*, subdued into *kū*, seems to me to be involved also in እስኩ (§ 62) which is made use of in appeals (for ስኩ, § 34) "*τοίνυν*", "*quaeso*", "pray do!" (properly:—"since indeed"). The letter *k* might, however, be farther softened into *g*, and thus we can explain እንጋ "well now!" as being another form of እንከ (properly:—"see what!"),—perhaps also ጊዜ "moment", "hour", "time", if this is at all of pronominal origin (for ከ + ይእዜ), and perhaps the quite obscure የውጊ "perhaps", "that . . . not", "lest". For the remains of another Relative *ia*, v. § 65.

Personal Pronouns. § 65. (4) The purely Personal Pronouns of the three Persons, "I, Thou, He"—are, as the strongest Pronouns in the Ethiopic tongue, thoroughly compounded. The special root for the *Third Person* is of a purely vowel-character, viz. *u* or *i*, but not *a*. Although, at one time, even *a* possessed demonstrative force, as is still clearly shown in Sanskrit, it yet looked to that which was more remote, while on the other hand *u* or *i* looked to that which was nearer and more intimate (9). In Ethiopic at least, *u* or *i* was employed whenever a demonstrative root had to be developed into a form with a personal reference (*cf.* ቱ, ቲ, ኩ, ኑ). Even to

(1) *Cf.* Hebr. כִּי, Ewald, p. 230. (2) እስ = עַד, by § 30.

(3) V. Ewald, § 105, *b*. (4) *Cf.* כִּמְעַט.

(5) كَمَا; כַּאֲשֶׁר. (6) *Cf.* also حِينَ.

(7) So that አ, perhaps shortened from አን (§ 62) or አል, is possessed of negative force of and by itself. *Cf.* Trumpp, p. 559, N. 1.

(8) Ewald, p. 232. (9) Ewald, § 103, *a*.

denote any person other than *I* or *Thou*, *u* or *i* was at one time quite sufficient; and so, with the help of a final *ĕ*, the Ethiopic *u*ᵉ, *i*ᵉ emerged, *i. e.* ውእ and ይእ (§ 40)(¹). Both of these stems ውእ and ይእ, however, were judged by the Ethiopians to be too weak, and they were accordingly strengthened by the annexation of the demonstrative root ቱ፡ or ቲ፡(²). When farther the distinction between *u* and *i* had become established in the language, so that *u* stood for the Masculine, and *i* for the Feminine(³), there emerged the Pronouns ውእቱ፡ "he" and ይእቲ፡ "she"(⁴). Both are substantives originally, but in the course of time they have come to be employed also as adjectives, like הוּא &c., and are thereby brought down to the position of mere personal demonstratives. ይእ was even made use of to form an adverb in ይእዜ "at present". The *Second Person* አንተ is a compound of the root *tu* or *twa* for "thou", and the demonstrative *an*(⁵); but in certain types *ta*, which is a curtailed form of *twa*, is exchanged for ከ (§ 29), as in all Semitic languages. The *First Person* is certainly very much curtailed in Ethiopic, and takes the form አነ; but both the plural ንሕነ, and the ኩ which still appears as the verbal termination for the first pers., show that *ana* has been shortened from *anōku* or *anōki*,—still preserved in Hebrew,— a compound of the demonstrative *an* and *ōki* = "I".

Finally from the *ku*, *ka* or *ki*, which appears in the 1ˢᵗ and 2ⁿᵈ Persons, and occurs also as a more general Demonstrative in

---

(¹) In the same way as ዝ *zé*, "this".

(²) This root is the basis of הוּא; ܗܘ; هُوَ; and, in Ethiopic itself, of ሁ, ሃ ሆሙ, and ሆን.

(³) [*Cf.* Barth, ZDMG XLVI, p. 685 *sq.*]

(⁴) Seeing that ቱ፡ and ቲ፡ are still preserved complete everywhere else in Ethiopic, I cannot accept the explanation that ውእ and ይእ, *u*ᵉ and *i*ᵉ are weakened forms of *hu*ᵉ and *hi*ᵉ, and these again of *tu*ᵉ and *ti*ᵉ. That there were original pronouns *u* and *i* is clearly enough discernible still from the declension of असौ and अयम् and the Latin *is*, from Zend and Lettish, as well as from the Guṇa forms एन, एष *αὐτός*, and also from the Relatives य and व derived from these demonstratives (*e. g.* in वत्, एव &c.). In Semitic also there is a Relative *ia*, derived from that *i*, of which a trace is still preserved in Ethiopic in the Binding-vowel of the Construct State, and in the Adjective-ending *ī*; and it is not clear why this *ia* must be only a shortened form of *tia*.

(⁵) Ewald, p. 234.

accordance with § 62, *d*, an Abstract *kiyāt* came into being, shortened into ኪያ "*Selbstheit*", which with the help of appended suffixes serves to express the notion of "self" (v. § 150) (1), and corresponds to the Arabic إِيَّا and the Hebrew אוֹת (2). For another word to signify the notion of "even he", or "he himself" v. § 62 (3).

Conceptional Roots.— General Description. § 66. 3. The third and highest stage of roots is formed by the *Conceptional Roots* (*i. e.* Roots conveying an *idea*, *conception* or *notion*—'*Begriffswurzeln*'). They are the designations expressed in sounds of all the *simple ideas* which have been gathered by the mind of a people from the experience lying within the circle of their contemplation, and which have been developed by their mental activity. They are exceedingly manifold and numerous, but still they are capable of survey, and are not inexhaustible. Inasmuch, however, as no simple idea or notion is ever entertained, in actual thinking or in actual resulting speech, in a pure form, but each in a certain relation of thought,—there are no pure Conceptional Roots in actual speech, but only words which have been formed out of these roots. The root, which constitutes the hidden foundation of a number—which may be large—of words derived from it, is obtained from the actually existing words, only by the scientific process of Abstraction. The tracing back of words to roots in this way results in the announcement,—as the *first* fundamental law common to the whole family of the Semitic languages,—that *the majority of the vowels, and particularly all the short vowels, belong invariably to the formation and not to the root, and that the root thus consists of firmer letters only.* With this announcement is associated another,—as a *second* law quite as universally binding,—that *every Conceptional Root comprises at least three firm letters*(4).

(1) *Cf.* Trumpp, p. 549, N. 1 (contrary to Praetorius, ZDMG XXVII, p. 640).

(2) Ewald, § 105, *sq*; Nöldeke, '*Mand. Gramm.*', p. 390, N. 2; '*Syr. Gramm.*' English ed., p. 226, N. 1; Lagarde, '*Mitteilungen*', I, p. 226; Haupt, '*Beitr. z. Ass.*', I, p. 20.

(3) On the Semitic Pronouns in general *cf.* O. Vogel, '*Die Bildung des persönlichen Fürworts im Semitischen*', 1866; Ch. Eneberg, '*De pronominibus Arabicis dissertatio etymologica*', Helsingforsiae, I, 1872, II, 1874; and H. Almkvist, '*Den semitiska språkstammens pronomen*', Upsala, 1875.

(4) On Biliteral nouns v. D. H. Müller, '*Actes du VIme Cong. d. Orient.*', II, 1, p. 415 *sqq.*; and on the other side, Barth, ZDMG XLI, p. 608 *sqq.*

No root has fewer letters than three, but a root may have more than three. There are Quadriliteral and Multiliteral Roots, but these are recognised without difficulty as later formations, which have been derived from simpler roots. Even within the sphere of these Multiliterals the law of Triliterality has had the effect of reducing many of them again to the form of Triliterals. And it may be remarked generally, that it is in the oldest Semitic languages that the law of Triliterality has exercised the most absolute sway, while in those languages in which the root-forming tendency continued in activity for a longer time,—and Ethiopic is one of them,—roots were more and more elaborated into Quadriliterals, whereas roots with more than four letters are not at all common. Accordingly even in Ethiopic the root usually consists of *three constant letters* (*Radicals*). Consonants or long vowels rank as firm or constant letters, but, for a special reason to be explained farther on (§ 67 *sq.*), the vowels *i* and *u* are the only ones which occur as Radicals. The majority of roots are purely consonantal. Those roots only, which have a vowel as their second letter, like *mūt*, are capable of easy pronunciation. Scarcely any of the rest could be pronounced, for want of the necessary vowels. The usual practice therefore is to exhibit the root under the guise of one of the simplest existing word-forms possessed by the language, viz.—the 3rd pers. sing. masc. Perf. of the simple stem; and we shall adopt this practice throughout, writing *nagara*, for instance, instead of *ngr*, and so on(1).

Now according as a root consists of three (or more) Consonants, or on the other hand has in any position a long vowel instead of a consonant, there arise different kinds of roots; and inasmuch as the general rules for the formation of words from the root undergo special limitations and alterations according to the special kind of the root, the different possible kinds of roots must now be settled and described. The kind and order of the consonants, of which roots are composed, are in general completely free and unrestrained; for, as Semitic languages are generally rich in vowels, and the majority of words have at least two vowels, there may be found

(1) Ludolf has frequently exhibited roots *mediae vocalis* in the guise of the Infinitive, like መዊት; but there is no satisfactory reason for adopting that method in Ethiopic. In this case also we shall write ሞተ.

in a root, without detriment to the forms derivable from it, consonants standing together, which could not be pronounced together as one phonetic group without great difficulty. But yet even here the formative history of roots to some extent, and to some extent regard to convenience of pronunciation and to euphony, have imposed certain limitations upon the general freedom. We are speaking here only of roots made up of three radicals, as Multiliterals follow special rules of their own. The appearance of one and the same consonant twice in the root is allowable, and even common, in the position of second and third radicals. Cases in which the first and second radicals are identical, are, it is true, of more frequent occurrence in Ethiopic than in other Semitic tongues, but all such roots are secondary formations and are recognisable as forms shortened from quadriliterals, v. § 71. Roots too, which have the first and third radicals alike, *e. g.* **ወረወ**, are few in number, and have received this appearance only by a process of transformation from other roots, as in **ነተነ** and **ነጠነ**, from *natala*; **ሰኰሰ**, from *sakata*; **ተሐተ**, from *tūḥ*; **ለዐለ**, from *ʿal*; **ገለገ**, from *gal*, &c.; and, in particular, those roots *med. voc.* which have also the same consonant in the first and third places (1), are mostly replaced in Ethiopic by other roots, and are now represented only by a few Nominal stems, like **ኮከ** and **ዓዒ**. Farther there is no admission within the root for two different Aspirates (with the exception of the softest one, **አ**, which is allowed to accompany other aspirates within roots, and may even stand immediately before or after **ሐ** or **ኀ**, though not immediately before or after any other, *e. g.* **ሀድአ**, **ሐሥአ**, **አምኀ**, **አይሕአ**, **አኀረ**, **አኀዘ** &c.), nor readily for two different Palatal-Gutturals (still we have **ጕሕቈ** and **ቃግስት**), Labial Mutes, or Dental-Lingual Mutes (2). Different Sibilants, however, are admitted in the same root, and even side by side (*e. g.* **ሥበረ**, **ሰዘረ**, **ሰዘየ**, **ገሠጸ**). Also **ለረ**, **ነለ**, **ጠከ**, **ጸከ**, **ከጸ**, **ከጠ**, **ተቀ** (3) are considered difficult of pronunciation, and therefore are for the most part avoided as combinations. Alongside of **ቀ**, **ዐ** is

(1) A still more common occurrence in other Semitic languages, Ewald § 118, *a*.

(2) In **ኅዳፕ**, **ዳ** is no more than a softer form of **ጠ**; **ድንቱት** is a formation from **ዶነነ**; **ተቅዳ** seems to be foreign (تَقْدَة); on **ዶብተሬ** v. § 73.

(3) On this depend *e. g.* **መጠቀ**, **ሰጠቀ**, **ጠቅዐ**, **ጠቀበ**.

placed in preference to አ (ዐቀመ, and ዐቄረ), and ጸ in preference to ሰ or ሠ(1). ተ or ጠ is in rare cases met with before ሰ (*e. g.* ተስዐ and ጠሰየ). Many of the transpositions of letters described above (§§ 24—32) may be traced back to these and similar rules.

Tri-radical Roots:— Strong Roots. § 67. 1. *Tri-radical Roots which are composed of three Consonants*, are those which best answer to the Semitic root-forming tendency. Many of them may have existed in their tri-consonantal form in primeval times, even before the days when the Semitic linguistic family separated itself from a primeval language; but the most of them have assuredly arisen, by a re-casting process, out of longer or shorter original-roots, and by the hardening of such radical elements as originally had a vowel-character. **Weak Roots.** Alongside of these, however, appear a large number of other roots, which have not yet attained this perfect root-form, or have degenerated from a perfect condition to a less perfect one: These constitute the *Imperfect and Weak Roots*.

Roots *med. gem.* (*a*) A whole series exists of roots possessing only two Consonants, which are to be conceived as originally associated about a short vowel, (say *ă*, the one which comes readiest to hand), like *nab*. In order to bring these roots up to the proportion set by the fundamental Semitic law (§ 66), the language has either repeated both of them, and thus elaborated them into Quadriliterals, like *gâsgasa* (*cf.* § 71), or it has only doubled the second letter, and developed them into Triliterals, like *nababa*. With EWALD we then call them *Double-lettered Roots* (more exactly:— *Roots with the second letter doubled*), Lat.—*radices mediae geminatae*(2).

Many of these roots are common to Ethiopic and the other Semitic languages. Others of them are peculiar to it,—the short original roots on which they are founded having been developed into Triliterals by the other languages in a different way, *e. g.* መነነ, مَنّ, מאן, مطل, מנע, منع. A few of these roots in Ethiopic are only recent formations, of a denominative character, like ሐገገ, ጸጕጕ, ቀነነ.

---

(1) Hence ቈዐረ, በቍጸ (בִּקֵּשׁ, קָשַׁר), though, to be sure, we have ቀሠረ.

(2) According to A. MÜLLER, ZDMG XXXIII, p. 698 *sqq.* (*cf.* NÖLDEKE, *ibid.* XLVI, p. 776) both these roots and roots *mediae w* had originally two radicals, and in the course of their inflection the Consonant became strengthened in the case of the former class, and the Vowel in the case of the latter.

These roots maintain their amplified triliteral form throughout the whole formation, and they follow absolutely the course taken by forms from strong roots, and at no point abandon the double letter, although, according to § 56, there may be cases in which the doubling is inaudible in pronunciation. Only, one trace of their origin is still shown in the fact that, when the first of the repeated letters is separated from the second merely by a fugitive *ĕ*, the *ĕ* is readily given up by these roots, and the letters approach each other, without however ceasing on that account to be uttered as a doubled sound,—as has been described in detail in § 55. In some rare cases the doubling is transferred from the second radical to the first, or it disappears entirely (v. § 56).

Roots *med. inf.* (*b*) We come upon a second kind of Imperfect roots in *Roots with a Vowel-centre*(¹), (or *Vowel-centred Roots*), *i. e.* such as have for their second radical a long vowel,—more precisely a *ū* or an *ī* (*radices mediae infirmae*). Long *ā* does not occur as a second radical; for although originally there were roots with middle *ā*, they were bound, in the process of word-formation, to call in the help of some firmer letter, in fact an Aspirate, and they appear to have passed chiefly into roots with a middle Aspirate or with a middle *ī* or *ū*. On the other hand, roots with *ī* or *ū* as second radical abound. It is true that they also, like roots which have the second letter doubled, may be developed into the form of strong roots, by hardening their middle vowel into a Semivowel, but yet this is not always done, where it might have been expected in obedience to other formative and phonetic rules: fidelity to their origin is shown by their preservation of the vowel-pronunciation of the middle letter, wherever that is possible, as has been already described in § 50. Of these roots there are nearly as many with middle *ī* as with middle *ū*. Each of these vowels is tenaciously retained throughout the whole formation, in the root in which it has once been established; and almost no instance can be observed of the *ū* passing into *ī*, or the *ī* into *ū*. Farther, it is but seldom that both forms, with *ī* and with *ū*, have been brought into being to express the same meaning or a similar one (like **ሐወጸ** and **ሐየጸ**, **ሮጸ** and **ረየፀ**, **ኀረ** and **ገየረ**): frequently an entirely

(¹) V. on the other hand König, p. 108.

different meaning is attached to the form with *ū*, from that which belongs to the *ī*-form (*e. g.* **ሢጠ** and **ሦጠ**, **ከነ** and **ኬነ**). Roots *med. voc.* are closely allied in origin with roots *med. gem.*, as is shown in particular by comparing the two kinds of roots in the various Semitic languages. It often happens that what one language has developed into a root *med. voc.* appears in another as a root *med. gem.*, and *vice versâ*; *cf. e. g.* **ኬዴ**=كَدَّ, **ጼሐ**=صَحَّ. But within Ethiopic itself the two kinds are kept strictly separate from one another: they do not pass over to one another in the process of formation, as they do for instance in Hebrew. It is farther a comparatively rare thing, to find both kinds of roots formed to express the same idea or a similar idea, as in **ሀከከ** and **ሆከ**.

§ 68. (*c*) The third kind of weak roots may be called *Vowel-sided roots*, being such as have a vowel for their first or third radical (*radices primae* **ወ** *et* **የ**, and *radices tertiae infirmae*). They fall naturally into two subordinate classes: **Vowel-sided Roots:**

(*α*) *Roots beginning with a Vowel.* There are no roots with *a* for their first sound. Seeing that no word can begin with a vowel, such roots would have to introduce the *a* by means of a Breathing (§ 34); and we may conceive that (as in the similar case, § 67, *b*) many roots, originally beginning with *a*, were consolidated into roots having an Aspirate for the first radical. Roots, on the other hand, which begin with *i* or *u* (although they too are bound,—whenever a word, formed from them starts clear with the first ra-radical,—to harden that radical into the corresponding semivowel) reproduce the vowel readily as first radical when a prefix is applied, and thereby prove their origin (v. § 49). According to the analogy of roots *med. inf.* and *tert. inf.*, it might have been expected that about as many roots would begin with *u* as with *i*, but the fact is otherwise. If Northern-Semitic transformed almost all roots which begin with *u* into such as begin with *i*, Ethiopic, on the contrary,—in this, resembling Arabic,—has preserved the original *i* in a very few roots only, and then for quite special reasons. The root **የድዐ** "to know" retains *i* to distinguish it from **ወድአ**, which is wholly different in meaning; in **የብሰ**, **የበበ**, **የውህ** the transition from *i* to *u* was prevented by the phonetic character of the second radical (a Labial); while **ዮም** and **የማን** are very old Semitic words. All other roots beginning with *i*, if such did **Vowel-beginning Roots.**

exist at first, have been replaced, partly by roots beginning with *u*, partly by vowel-centred and vowel-ending roots, and partly by still others. On the other hand, roots beginning with *u* have been formed in great abundance. The two classes of roots, moreover, have been kept separate throughout the entire formative process, without at any time passing into one another. But sometimes, though rarely, an exchange takes place between roots with initial *u* and those which have a middle *u*: thus we say **ምራቅ** "spittle", probably formed from **ሮቀ**, not from the ordinary **ወረቀ** (1) (§ 116); and **ወሀበ** has in the Imperfect **ይሁብ** (§ 93): Conversely there appears **ሙባእ** "entrance", from **ወብአ** instead of **ቦአ**, § 115. Comparison, however, with the other Semitic languages shows that they often have roots *med. inf.*, *tert. inf.* or *med. gem.*, corresponding to Ethiopic roots beginning with *u*, or else that these languages have still stronger letters in place of *u*, like *n* and *b*, *e. g.* **ወለጠ**, بدل; **ወቀየ**, نما, نجا, יקע; **ወግዐ**, نجع. Others appear to be recent formations of a denominative character, like **ወከፈ**, from כַּף; and **ወፈረ**, from פַּר.

Vowel-ending Roots.

(*β*) *Roots ending in a Vowel.* Those roots, which originally perhaps had *a* for last radical, have in most cases hardened it into an Aspirate. Roots, on the other hand, which end originally in *i* and *u*, although they have a very decided leaning to the stronger form of expression, *i. e.* to the hardening of their vowel into a semivowel,—a much more decided leaning to it, in fact, than have the corresponding roots in the kindred tongues—, permit often enough the vowel-form to re-appear in suitable cases; for details on this point v. § 51. Roots which end in *i* are, however, more common than those in *u*. With some few exceptions in Nominal formation, these roots remain strictly separate from one another. It is but seldom that radical forms of both kinds are evolved in the language, to express the same meaning, like **ረስየ** and **ረሰወ**, **ዘረወ** and **ዘረየ**. In other cases, when both forms were developed out of an original root, the significations were more or less strongly differentiated, *e. g.* **ጸገወ** "to be gracious", and **ጸገየ** "to bloom"; **ጸለወ** "to listen", and **ጸለየ** "to pray" (properly: "to incline" the ear, body or knee); **ሐለወ** "to watch", and **ሐለየ** "to think" (*cf.* बुध्). Of all the kinds of weak roots this is the one in greatest favour

(1) [V., however, Dillmann, '*Lex.*', col. 898].

in Ethiopic. It appears very frequently for the Vowel-centred and Double-lettered (*med. infir.* & *med. gem.*) roots of the other tongues. In some rare instances it is interchangeable, in Ethiopic itself, with roots *med. gem.*, as in **አረረ** and **አረየ** with somewhat different meanings. Certainly the predominant sense borne by the whole of this class of roots is a transitive one; and accordingly, when new roots are to be derived from short nominal stems, the class is of use to express the doing, exercising, owning, &c. of that which is signified by the Noun, *e. g.* **ለበወ**, from **ልብ**; **ገጸወ** from **ገጽ**; **ጠበወ** from **ጡብ**.

§ 69. (*d*) More than one weak radical may be found in one and the same root. Such roots are styled *Doubly Weak*. The most numerously represented among them in Ethiopic are those which are at once 'Vowel-beginning' and 'Vowel-ending', and have only the central radical a Consonant. Such as begin with *u* and end with *i* are of no uncommon occurrence, *e. g.* **ወድየ**, **ውዕየ**. Only one root is known as yet, having *u* both at the beginning and at the end, viz. **ወረወ**; and not a single one is known, beginning with *i* and at the same time ending with *i* or with *u*. In the process of formation each of these two weak letters follows its own peculiar mode. Roots which have both a Vowel-centre and a Vowel-ending are fewer in number. They may have the same sound in the second and third place, just like roots *med. gem.* (**ሀየየ**, **ዐየየ**, **ጕየየ**), or they may have different sounds there, like **ሐየወ** on the one hand, and **ረወየ**, **ደወየ**, **ጠወየ**, **ሰወየ** on the other; but invariably, in the formative process, the second sound—a Vowel—must be hardened into a Semivowel (§ 50), while the third is treated as in the vowel-ending roots. The remaining possible combinations,—namely, the case of both first and second radicals being of a vowel-character, as in **ወውዐ**, **የውሀ**, and the case of the first radical being of such vowel-character, while the second and third are identical consonants, as in **የበበ**, **ወደደ**, **ወከከ**—present no peculiar features to affect the formative process, seeing that they occur only in stems and derivative forms in which a vowel-pronunciation either cannot be developed at all, or only in conformity with rules which hold good even in other cases.

Doubly Weak Roots.

There are no other Weak roots. Roots which begin with **ነ** are all treated throughout as strong roots. And for the rest, it is only the largely employed root **ብህለ** which has anything peculiar about it, its peculiarity being that in one of its forms it gives up the final **ለ**, § 58. But roots which have an Aspirate in the first, second or third place, pursue a course of their own in the formative process, so far as the rules stated in §§ 43—47 are put in force with them. And if such roots, containing Aspirates, belong at the same time to one or other of the classes of Weak Roots, very peculiar forms of course may sometimes arise.

Certain Strong Ethiopic Roots compared with corresponding but Weak Roots in kindred Languages.

§ 70. Even these various classes of Weak roots, still existing in the language, furnish manifold information as to the nature of the most ancient root-construction. But besides, roots which have been fashioned into strong roots in Ethiopic, when compared with corresponding roots in the kindred tongues, discover in multifarious ways the manner of their origin. This is best illustrated in the case of roots, which contain an Aspirate by § 67 *sq.*:—Roots with Aspirates are very often changed in the different Semitic languages into Vowel-beginning, Vowel-centred or Vowel-ending roots, as well as into Double-lettered roots. Thus, for instance, **ሀጕለ** compares with أبل and وبل ; and in Ethiopic itself **ሀድአ** and **ወድአ** are connected. Of roots with Middle Aspirate there may, *e. g.*, be compared:—**ከሀለ**, כָּהֵל, כול; **ጸሀቀ**, شاح; **ግዕዘ**, جاز; **ጸዐቀ**, צוק, ضاق; **ንሁብ**, نوب (and *vice versâ*, *e. g.* **በየጸ**, بعض); **ምዕር**, مَرَّة (معر); **ምዕዝ**, مزّ. Ethiopic roots, which have an Aspirate for their final radical, often correspond to Vowel-ending or Vowel-centred roots in the other tongues, such as—**ሐሥአ**, חָשָׁה, خشع; **ነፅኀ**, נָצָה, نضا; **ቈጥዐ**, קוט; **ፈግዐ**, فاج: For the converse relation compare *e. g.* **በቀወ**, בָּקַע, بقع, بقّ; **ሀከየ**, هكع. The process of forming roots by placing **ነ** before an original root exhibits little vigour in Ethiopic. Nearly all Ethiopic roots, which have initial **ነ**, have been formed in the same way in the other tongues [1]; but many which are formed with *n* in the kindred tongues exhibit a different form in Ethiopic (*cf. e. g.* **ቀየመ**, נקם, نقم). Frequently Ethiopic has **መ** instead of it, *e. g.* in **መከሐ**, نجح and كهى; **መጠወ**, نطا III, عطا IV. Farther **ነ**, as third radical in proper Ethiopic roots,

---

(1) Contrary to Praetorius, '*Beitr. z. Assyr.*', I. p. 36 *sq.*, who would compare Ethiopic Roots beginning with **ወ**, with Roots *primae Nūn* of the kindred tongues (**ወጽሐ**=نضح; **አውሥአ**=اِنْشَأ, נָשָׂא; **ወፈረ**=نفر).

appears to have been lately added, *e. g.* **መጠነ**, מָדַד, مَدّ; **ዐቈነ**, ضاق, צוק, (not سجن, סָגַר). Several Triliteral roots are, properly, shortened Causative stems from Weak roots, formed by prefixing **አ**, which may then be hardened into **ዐ** under the influence of the succeeding radical, *e. g.* **አጠቀ**, from ضاق; **አኰተ**, كبت, كبّ (in the sense:—"to crook", "to bend"); **አዘበ**, זוב, ܕܘܒ, زاب; **ዐቀመ**, קום, قام; **ዐቈረ**, قار V, VII; **ዐረፈ**, הִרְפָּה, رفا; or by prefixing **ሰ** (§ 73):—**ሰዘረ**, from זֶרֶת; **ሰፈጠ**, פִּתָּה; **ሰፈነ**, פָּנִים; or by appending **ተ**, as is done still more frequently in Quadriliteral roots (§ 73):—**ጸበተ** and **ጸበየ** (Hen. 89, 6) "to swim"; **በሐተ** "to have plenary power", from **በውሐ**; **ዐገተ**, عاج, عاك; **ከሠተ** "to disclose", from כָּסָה "to cover". On Triliteral roots which are shortened out of Multiliterals, v. *infra*, p. 132 *sq.*

§ 71. 2. Along with the Triliterals a large number of *Multiliteral Roots* have been formed, which, viewed in the light of historical grammar, are to be estimated very differently. According to their origin we distinguish three leading classes. *Multiliteral Roots: (a) Originating in repetition of Individual Rads., or of the Whole Root.*

(*a*) Many Multiliteral roots originate in *repetition of individual radicals, or of the whole root* according to a formative expedient common to the Semitic tongues, which still displays marked activity throughout the whole process of Word-formation (§ 74 *sqq.*). Accordingly the discussion of all the roots belonging to this class might be deferred, till we come to deal with Stem-formation; and of the forms which have arisen through stronger repetition of the radicals, those at least whose simpler root-form is still retained in the language—had best be relegated to that stage of our subject. But the greater number of these stronger formations appear no longer in their simpler aspect, but are only found in this lengthened form; and on the other hand the ordinary Tri-radical roots do not admit at all of stem-formations effected by such stronger repetition of the radicals, or only very seldom indeed (and mostly in Nominal Stems). It seems advisable therefore to follow the example of the Arab Grammarians and join such lengthened forms to the Multiliteral Roots.

(*α*) A large number of those formations arose out of Biliteral roots as yet undeveloped, or out of weak Triliterals, by *repetition of the whole root* or of its two chief letters. By this device the inner movement or repetition of the conception itself was expressed in a highly picturesque fashion; and so this root-form appears with special frequency for those notions which involve 'movement, mingling, custom, repetition, separation, gradual formation, or steadfast continuance, doubleness, multiplicity, or superfluity of parts or of acts'. Accordingly it is used in conveying the ideas of 'tottering and wavering, trembling and rolling, going backwards and forwards' (**ሳሕስሐ**, **ቀልቀለ**, **ናሕንሐ**, **ነክነከ**, **ተንተነ**, **ወልወለ**, **ፀንፀነ**, **ለጽለጸ**, **ኰርኰረ**, **ቈልቈለ**, **ገርገረ**, **ሰውሰወ**); of the 'trembling, glittering movement of light' (**ለውለወ**, **በስበሰ**, **ዋኅውኅ** Hen. 108, 13, 14); of the 'murmuring sound caused by repeated notes' (**ባሕብሐ**, **ጐርጐረ**, —*cf.* also **ዕንዕያ**, § 58); of 'dropping, welling forth, gushing, sprinkling' (**ነፍነፈ**, **ጠልጠለ**, **ፈልፈለ**, **ሳዕስዐ**, **ነሥነሠ**); of 'knocking, whipping, striking' (**ጐድጐደ**, **ጠብጠበ**, **ጸንጸለ**); of 'stroking, shaving' (**መዝመዘ**, **ገስገሰ**); of 'severing, emptying, crushing, dispersing' (**ለይለየ**, **በርበረ**, **ቀጥቀጠ**, **ቀጽቀጸ**, **ፈርፈረ**, **ዘርዘረ**); of 'growth', of 'superfluity', of 'nourishing', and—*vice versâ*,—of 'wasting away', of 'putrefying' (**ለምለመ**, **ፈድፈደ**, **ዘኀዘኀ**, **ሰይሰየ**, **ደግደገ**, **ቈንቈነ**, **ብኍብኍ**); of 'checking, holding back' (**ጋህግሀ**, **ከልከለ** alongside of **ከልአ**, **ቀይቀየ**); of 'making ready' (**ጣእጥአ**): also for 'conditions and habits of soul and body' (like **ገይገየ** "to sin", **ራህርሀ** "to be tender, soft"). Besides those which are enumerated here, there is a farther series of doubled roots retained only in Nominal stems, which are dealt with in § 112. Similar doubled roots in Arabic also correspond to a very considerable number of these roots. In the rest of the Semitic languages there are weak roots which answer to others of them, *e. g.* **መዝመዘ**, مثّ and مشّ; **ራህርሀ**, רַךְ; **ነፍነፈ**, נוּף; **ጸፍጸፈ**, צוּף; **ገይገየ**, עוה, غوى &c.

Meanwhile many an original doubled root in Ethiopic has been restored to the standard of triliterality by shortening; and thus have arisen several triliteral roots, formed in quite a peculiar way. In particular, by assimilating the second radical of a doubled root to the third a number of Tri-radical roots have been produced, of which the first and second letters are identical: the second, however, is invariably doubled, so that these roots in outward appearance resemble an Intensive stem. These are: **ሠሥዐ** (from **ሠዕሥዐ**, ישח and ישע) "to be insatiable"; **ሰሰለ** (אָזַל, زال) "to withdraw"; **ቀቀየ** "to be avaricious" (side-form of **ቀይቀየ**); **መምዐ** "to be timid"; **ደደቀ** "*accidit*" (from **ወደቀ** "to fall"); **ወውዐ** "to raise a shout" (وَعْوَعَ, وَعَى); ገገጸ "to be in anxiety"; ጕጕኦ "to hasten", "to be eager" (جَاجَا, أَجَّا). On the same process of Root-formation depend also Nominal stems, like ኮኵሕ, ሰሰን, ደደክ and others. More rarely, original doubled roots were shortened into Triliterals by transposing and contracting individual letters (as in ለዐለ = ለዕዐለ = ዐሌዐለ; ገለገ = ገሌለገ = ገሌገለ), or by discarding the last letter (as in ከለከ = ከሌከለ; ለውሌ = لَوْلَوْ).

(β) Many Multiliteral Roots have been developed from Triradical roots already fully formed; by *repetition of the last radical or of the last two radicals*. Both modes of formation are employed also in the derivation of Intensive stems from still existing Triliterals (*cf. infra*, § 77). In this place we have to discuss those roots only, which do not occur in any other form than as Multiliterals. By reduplication of the last two letters, there have been formed ደለቅለቀ "to be shaken" (probably denominative); አጽደሌደለ "to gleam"; and ዐውየወ "to utter lamentations", an abbreviated form of ዐወይወየ (عوى)(1). More numerous than these Quinqueliterals are those Quadriliteral roots, which have been formed from Triliterals by repeating the last radical; and, just like the stronger reduplication of the entire root, this weaker repetition of merely the last radical is employed chiefly to express those ideas which involve the gradual progressiveness or the duration, continuation or constancy of the individual acts, or the vehemence and thoroughness of the action, or ideas which convey some inherent disposition. To this class belong ከውለለ "to become giddy" (חוּל); ጠብለለ "to roll up" (טָבַל); ሰውጠጠ "to fall into perplexity *or* terror" (سلط, *cf.* ሠጠየ); በሕረረ "to be terrified" (בָּהַל or بَكَر); ሐንቀቀ "to be in anxiety" (אָנַק, חָנַק); ሳሕበበ "to be mouldy" (شهب, שׁיב, ሰየበ); ፈርዘዘ "to burst" (of a bud); ፈርገገ "to heal" (of a wound,—properly "to break up" فرج); ጠውለለ "to be flabby", "to hang loose"; ዘሀለለ "to play tricks"; ሐብቀቀ "to bedaub one's self"; ማህለለ "to deal mildly, *or* graciously with any one" (مهل); በሀነነ "to withdraw", "to escape"; ደምሰሰ "to abolish", "to destroy"

(1) But this root in the end goes back to ወይ "woe!" (§ 61); and ዐ, from አ, is Causative: [indeed አውየወ still occurs:—*Kebra Nag.* 54 a 18; 67 b 23; 131 a 16 *sq.*]

(دَمَس); ምርዱድ "obstinate", from the √መርደደ; and, besides, the roots of various Nominal stems, v. § 112. Specially remarkable are the roots ሉኈሰሰ "to whisper softly" (ለሐሰ, לַחַשׁ), and ከሞሰሰ "to be somewhat serious" (from كَمُوس), because they have continued to keep the long vowel of the noun, from which they sprung.

M. R.: (b) Originating in Interpolation of Firm Letter after 1st Rad.

§ 72. (*b*) While, however, the whole of this first class of Multiliteral Roots is due to an original and general formative tendency in Semitic languages, and while the only thing peculiar in this matter to Ethiopic perhaps consists in its scarcely ever retaining, or its never having developed, the triliteral forms alongside of such longer forms,—the occurrence or the predominance of the second class is, on the other hand, a mark of decline in the formative powers of the language. In this second class we rank those Multiliteral Roots, which have arisen from the *interpolation of one of the firmer letters after the first radical.* The interpolation of the mixed vowel *ē* or *ō* is less remarkable, as it may be considered a variety of the formation of the third Verbal Stem (§ 78). It occurs very seldom indeed in Ethiopic(1). Farther it very seldom happens that an Aspirate is inserted after the first radical, as it is in (አ)ንሕሥየ "to overlook", "to forget" (נָשָׁה, نَسِىَ). A Liquid is very frequently interpolated, partly to give the root greater fulness of sound (§ 58), partly to make up for that doubling of the second radical which is called for by the formation (§ 56, *in fin.*). So far, the most of these forms might be dealt with at a later stage, in discussing word-formation; but, to facilitate a general survey, it seems better to set them together here. Generally it is the *Nasal* ን, which amplifies a Triliteral root into a Quadriliteral. This ን occurs most frequently before Labials(2):—ሰንበት, שַׁבָּת; ቍንፍዝ, קִפּוֹד; ዐንበሳ "lion" (عَنْبَس, from عبس); ግንፋል "brick" ([illegible]); ሰንቢል, שִׁבֹּלֶת; ሕንባል "camel's saddle"; ሕንብርት "navel"; ሕንብርብሬ "scab" (§ 57); ከንባል "crisping-pin" (كبل); ከንፈር "lip"; ሕንባብ "berry"; ሐንፈጠ "to scratch"; ገንጸለ "to turn upside down"; often too before Palatal-Guttural Mutes:—ሐንገዝ "eye-brows"; ድንግል "virgin"; ሐንከሰ "to be lame"; ጠንቀቀ

(1) Oftener in Syriac: Hoffmann, '*Syr. Gramm.*', p. 186.
(2) *Cf.* König, p. 99.

"to be exact"; ዘንግዐ "to talk at random"; ዘንጐጐ "to mock"; ደንቀወ "to be deaf, or hard of hearing" ([illegible]); ዐንገዐ "to lie on the side" (whence ምዕንጋዕ along with ምዕጋዕ): rather less frequently before Aspirates and Sibilants, and before ተ and ጠ: ጽንሐሕ "whole burnt-offering" (صحّ, وزّ); ሰንአለ, from ሰአለ; ቈንዛእ "ringlet" (قُنْزُعَة); መዐንሰብ "soothsayer" (חשב); ፈንጸጸ 'a disease'; መንዘዘ "to revile" (مطّ, مظّ); ኀንጸጸ "to pick out grains"; ቀንጠዌ "gnawing hunger" (קֶטֶב); ቀንጠበ "to pierce" (קטב); and probably in አንተለ "to be impatient". This nasal has in one instance passed into መ before ጠ (1): ሰምጥዐ "to put the field in good order"; and in ጽርንዕት "scab" (צָרַעַת) it has slipped in after the Liquid *r*. *R* is found instead of *n*, but only in a few words (2):— መርሰሰ "to feel for, to grope" (משש); ሐርበደ "to wallow in the mire" (حَرْمَد); ፈርፀጸ "to leap" (فَرْشَح, פִּרְעֵשׁ); ሐርገጽ "crocodile". Several of the words and roots enumerated here exhibit also a like form in Syriac or in Arabic (3).

§ 73. (*c*) The last class of Multiliteral Roots,—an exceedingly numerous one,—is *derived from Triliteral Roots and Words by the external application, before or after them, of formative letters*, and in fact in manifold fashion. Several have been formed at first merely as *derived Verbal Stems* from the tri-radical root; but in process of time and on various grounds they ceased to be recognised as derivatives and came to be treated in the language as independent roots. A prefix ሰ,—more fully አሰ, which at one time was employed in the formation of Causative stems (§ 79),—may still be clearly recognised both in certain triliteral roots (§ 70 *ad fin.*), and in certain multiliterals;—partly in Nominal stems, like ሰረገላ "cart" (תִּרְגֵּל, רֶגֶל) [?]; ሰንቡእ "lungs" (נָפַּח); ሰፈሌያ "hammer" (פָּרַר); መስከረም 'name of a month' ("beginning of winter *or* of the year");—partly in Verbal Roots, such as ሰርገወ "to adorn" (*cf.* certain roots in the other Semitic tongues, which begin with *rag* and *raq*); ሰንቀወ "to play the harp", and several others, v. § 85 *ad fin.* In ጸምላጥ "blear-eyed", and ጸብረቀ "to diffuse

M. R.: (c) Derived from Triliteral Roots and Words, by External Application of Formative Letter.

(1) V. also Hoffmann, '*Syr. Gr.*' p. 186.

(2) *Cf.* Ewald, '*Gr. Ar.*' § 191; Hoffmann, cited *supra*.

(3) The origin of the roots ዐንበዘ, ዐንዘረ, ዕንቍራ, ኀንፈጸ is still obscure or doubtful; yet v. next Note.

light", "to scintillate", the ሰ has even been thickened into the sound of ጸ (1). An original ተ, serving to form Reflexives, has been softened into ደ, thus becoming unrecognisable, in ደጎብያ "locusts" (גּוֹבַי); ድርግሐ and ደርግሐ "rag" (ܪܘܩܥܐ, رُقْعَة); ደረክኖ and ደርክኖ "purple" (אַרְגָּמָן, ܐܪܓܘܢܐ, أُرْجُوَان) [from Assyr. *argamannu*]; and ደክተመ "to become an orphan", "to be bereaved" (יתם, ܝܬܡ, يَتِم). By means of the reflexive prefix ተን (§ 87) there have been formed the root ተንበለ "to act as intercessor for any one" (from ብህለ), and the word ተንከተም "bridge" ('covering over of the river', כָּתַם).

A series of Multiliteral Roots of another sort came to be formed from triliteral roots, or rather words, by means of an appended *ē*, *ō*, *i* or *u*, through which also Tri-radical roots ending in a vowel are derived from Nominal stems (§ 68, *ad fin.*). This formative vowel-suffix, when it was a new-comer, and not a fundamental part of the Nominal stem, must originally have had the power of forming Transitives and Causatives. It is therefore of service in the derivation of new roots which have the sense of 'doing or exercising' what is expressed in the ground-root or ground-word. This formation has become a very favourite one in Ethiopic (even in a greater degree than in Syriac)(2). To this class belong:— ሐብለየ "to acquire by trickery" (ሕብል); ዘርከየ "to calumniate" (زرق and زرك); ደርበየ "to shoot"; ገርዐየ "to stab in the throat", "to slaughter"; ጐንደየ "to delay" (ጕንድ); ጸምሀየ "to wither", "to dry up"; አርወየ "to become brutalised" (but also አረወ); ጸሀየየ, from መጽሂት, and ጸሕየየ "to clear of weeds"; perhaps also ሰክተየ and ዘጋደየ. Still more common are those roots which have been formed with ወ:—ሰንአወ (ስንእ); ወልተወ (ወልታ); ወርዘወ (ወሬዛ); ደንቀወ (§ 72); ባሕተወ (ባሕቲት); ኈሕለወ (ጕሕሉት); ጸልሐወ (ጽልሑት); ኄረወ (ኂሩት); ኬነወ (ኪን); ዜነወ (related to אֹזֶן); ኖለወ (נהל, نهل); ጸመወ; ቤዘወ (باز, باص); ቃዐደወ ("to be devout" ܨܡܕ); ጸዐደወ; ጸንጸወ (3). In many cases the form *aya* or *awa* is

---

(1) Similarly an አ of the Causative Stem may have been hardened into ዐ (v. § 70) in ዐንበዘ and ዐንዘረ, if these actually belong, as I imagine they do, to نزف and צנר (כנר); and into ኀ in ኀንፈጸ, if this may be compared with נפץ. The ተ in ቶስሐ "to mix (fluids)" is probably causative also; v. HOFFMANN, p. 187; EWALD, '*Hebr. Spr.*', § 122, *a*.

(2) HOFFMANN, p. 186; and EWALD, '*Hebr. Spr.*' § 125, *b*.

(3) In the existence of several roots of this kind, PRAETORIUS,—'*Beitr.*

already suggested by the termination of the fundamental word: *cf. e. g.* ጕርዐየ, from ጕርዔ; ኅሕለወ, from ጕሕሉት. More rarely an Aspirate (instead of $\bar{e}$ or $\bar{o}$) serves the same purpose, as in መርግሀ "to throw stones", from መርግ; አይሕአ, from አይሕ; ጠውልዐ (טוּל, طال).

While we may see, in the series which has just been dealt with, the Ethiopic offshoots of an original Semitic formative-impulse, which once exercised a powerful influence even in the development of triliteral roots,—*a third series*, which is now to be described, *depends*, on the other hand, *upon an after-formation belonging to the later period of the language*. In the course of time it became usual in Ethiopic to derive,—from Nominal stems which had been fashioned by formative additions of a consonantal character,—new Verbal roots, which continued to retain these formative additions, and which thus had of necessity to be Multiliteral. This recent style of formation is relatively more common in Ethiopic than in Arabic(¹). Such roots are most frequently formed from Nominal stems having መ prefixed, like መዝበረ "to lie in ruins"; ማህረከ "to make booty of". Of some 30 of these forms (²), the following, which have been fashioned from simpler roots beginning with a vowel, are specially to be remarked: ማሰነ "to decay", from أَسَنَ, وَسِنَ, יָשֵׁן; ሞቅሐ "to take prisoner", from وقح, وكح, יכח; ሞጥሐ "to veil". More rarely, Consonantal formative suffixes of the Nominal stems are retained; in particular ነ, in (አ)ሠልጠነ, from ሥልጣን (*cf.* تسلطن); and perhaps in ዴገነ "to persecute"; oftener ተ, as in ሐብረተ "to polish"; (ተ)መትሐተ "to appear as a phantom" (G. Ad.); ጸልመተ; መጽወተ; ኮሰተ; ጋህረተ and (አ)መሰረተ "to found" (from መሰረት, from the root ሰረረ, so that both መ and ተ are formative letters here). And sometimes this ተ appears even to have penetrated, from its position as a final letter, into the original

z. Ass.' I, p. 31 *sqq.*,—is disposed to find a proof "that Ethiopic at one time, like Hebrew and Arabic in the case of roots *med. gem.*, knew of the attachment, by means of $\bar{o}$ or *au.* of inflectional endings which begin with a consonant".

(¹) Ewald, '*Gr. Ar.*' § 191.

(²) I have not enumerated all these forms in this place, seeing that for the most part they may easily be found in the dictionary under the letter መ.

root itself, as in ሐርትመ "to be ill off" (from ሐረመ, *cf.* مَكْرُوم); ገፍትአ "to destroy utterly" (كَفَأَ); perhaps also in ኰሰተረ ([1]).

Through the same energy of the later formative processes, verbs were derived from foreign words, like መንኰሰ from *μοναχός*; መንገነ from *μηχανή* [= *μάγγανον*]; ፈልሰፈ from *φιλόσοφος* &c.

Besides the various classes of Multiliteral roots which have been described hitherto, there are other individual roots, of obscure or rare formation, *e. g.* ዘልገሰ:—for those, in particular, which have been developed into Nominal stems, v. *infra*, § 112. The general result is, that Multiliteral roots are very fully represented indeed in Ethiopic.—They may be estimated approximately as amounting to a sixth or a seventh part of the entire number of roots in the language.

B. FORMATION OF WORDS.

Methods followed generally in Word-Formation. Division of Words into:—1. Verbs; 2. Nouns; 3. Particles.

§ 74. With the exception of Interjectional roots and certain Pronominal roots, which in their first and original form have acquired the value of small independent Words, all roots must pass through one or more stages of transformation, before they can be used as Words of actual speech. Following the various determined modes and conditions of thought, under which the mind of man can regard a conception, the root must also assume various forms, in order to become a suitable expression of the conception so regarded. The more general of these determined modes are the first to receive the stamp of language, and then the process is applied to those which are more special, and so on, until the very finest distinctions, of which a conception is capable, have expression given to them in speech. The formative expedients which are applied in this process in Semitic languages, and accordingly in Ethiopic, are of *three* sorts. 1. Comparatively small and originally independent particles, mostly of pronominal origin, approach the root or the stem in order to fix and determine the general conception contained in it, by means of their own signification; and

---

([1]) The two following forms are to be regarded as secondary abbreviations from Multiliteral roots:—ነበል "flame", from አንበልበለ (root להב, ለሀበ); and ንኩል "reeling", from አንኮለለ (root ኮለ).

in this proceeding the language displays a sustained endeavour to knit together these external additions as intimately as possible with the root or stem, and cause them to coalesce with it. In a few cases such additions, originally external, make their way into the interior even of the root or stem. 2. This expedient is confronted by another, which sets itself to develope the root from its own resources, by doubling one or more of its radicals. But this device, which became very important in the formation of roots (§§ 67, 71), is of comparatively limited application in the formation of words, and extends only to the stem-formation of Verbs and Nouns. And in the farther stages of formation it is not the radicals, but individual formative vowels, which in an analogous fashion are lengthened and broadened, to give expression to a new determination of the fundamental idea. 3. But the expedient most current in Semitic speech, and which is at the same time the most delicate and intellectual, is Vowel-change within the Root. Even the form of Semitic roots (§ 66) testifies to the commanding prevalence of this means of formation. All vowels, with the exception of those which naturally cling to certain weak roots, are mobile; and,—according to their kind, their shortness or their length, their number, position or relation to each other,—they serve the purposes of the formative process and determine the meaning.—The greater number of actual words, however, have been produced by the co-operation of two or even all the three of the means of formation which have just been described.

The most common and obvious distinction, differentiating root-ideas(1), is the contrast between the Verb and the Noun, or between the word which signifies action and the word which indicates a name. All the words of the language take a position either on the one side or on the other. Roots conveying general notions are for the most part developed into both verbs and nouns, Pronominal roots only into nouns. To nouns, taken in the widest sense, belong also by their origin many Particles and Prepositions, which however, by reason of their frequent use, are here and there much mutilated in form. But just because in Ethiopic the majority of Particles and Prepositions (being those of Pronominal origin)

(1) [*i. e.*,—general notions or conceptions presented by those collocations of letters which we call *Roots*. TR.]

have not yet been formed into true Nouns, and exhibit peculiar formations and laws of formation, they must be treated of specially. We accordingly distinguish between 1. *Verbs*, 2. *Nouns*, 3. *Particles*.

FORMATION OF VERBS.

The stages of formation, which the Verb must pass through, are *three* in number; 1. Stem-formation; 2. Tense- and Mood-formation; 3. Formation of Persons, Genders and Numbers.

I. STEM-FORMATION OF VERBS.

General Description of Verbal Stems.

§ 75. The Root is fashioned into the Verb by means of one definite vowel-pronunciation, and into the Noun by means of another. For example, *tkl* is a Verb, when pronounced ተከለ, and a Noun, when pronounced ተክል (1). The difference between Verbs and Nouns, which have proceeded directly from the root, accordingly consists at first in the vowel-pronunciation alone. A more exact account cannot be given until we come to describe the individual forms themselves, seeing that the vocalisation is different in different formations; yet it may be observed, in general terms, that the verb has shorter and more mobile vowels than the noun. But just as from one root, not merely a single noun but an abundance of them may issue, so too there issues from the same a series of verbs, each of which impresses upon the fundamental notion a new determination. Following the lead of others we call those verbs which have been derived mediately or immediately from the root, *Verbal Stems* (or *Conjugations*). In Ethiopic there are twelve of these; or, if one or two stems are taken into account which are employed only in the case of quadriliteral roots, there are thirteen or fourteen different stems, which may be formed from one root. Of these verbal stems, all those whose meaning did not render it *a priori* impossible, appeared, at one time, under the contrast of an Active and a Passive voice by means of internal vowel change; and to this there was added, in the first or simple stem, the distinction of a semi-passive or intransitive voice. But of this passive form, effected by internal vowel change, such as is exhibited in Hebrew, and in the most consistent fashion in Arabic, Ethiopic preserves no more

(1) On the question of priority relative to Noun and Verb, v. A. MÜLLER ZDMG XLV, p. 237 *sq.*

than a few traces (in the Participle); and it is only the semi-passive form in the first stem (and partly in the reflexive of the simple stem) that is still regularly distinguished in Ethiopic. The proper Passive form, however, is made up for by another device, the reflexive form, just as in Aramaic. On this ground we shall deal with the subject of the distinction between Active and Passive, in connection with the account to be given of Stem-formation. The Stem-formation itself assumes different fashions in Triliteral and Multiliteral roots, which must be dealt with separately.

1. STEM-FORMATION OF TRI-RADICAL ROOTS.

§ 76. Scheme of Stems and their Relations: Scheme of Stems.

	I. Ground-Stems.	II. Causative St.	III. Reflexive St.	IV. Causative-Reflexive Stems.
1. Simple St.	ነገረ ገብረ	1. አግበረ	1. ተገብረ ተዐቀበ	1. አስተርከበ አስተረሐቀ
2. Intensive St.	ፈጸመ	2. አፈጸመ	2. ተፈጸመ	2. አስተጸነሰ
3. Influencing St.	ባረከ	3. አላቀሰ	3. ተከፈለ	3. አስተከፈለ(1).

In conformity with this Scheme we shall continue to denote the several Stems by I, 1; II, 1; II, 2, &c.

I. Ground-Stems. I. Ground-Stems:— 1. The Simple Stem.

1. In the first or *Simple Stem*, which proceeds directly from the root, the Verb is distinguished from the Noun of corresponding

(1) [It is to be observed that Praetorius, '*Aethiop. Gramm.*', p. 36 *sqq.*, formulates a Scheme of Verbal Stems, which differs considerably from the one given here. He enumerates 5 original and independent Ground-Stems, instead of Dillmann's 3, the 3rd and 5th being of a *Paial* and *Paual* type respectively, viz.—ቄተለ and ቆተለ. From the first of these two he easily derives the Imperfect form ይቄትል, which is also used as the Indicative of the Intensive Stem.—rejecting as unsatisfactory D.'s account of the origin of this last Imperfect form. Forms, however, presenting the types ቄተለ and ቆተለ—which P. regards as illustrations or survivals of his 3rd and 5th Stems—D. considers as belonging properly to his own 3rd or Influencing Stem, while in their farther formation they follow the Multiliteral roots (*cf. infra*, § 78). At the same time, Praetorius' analysis of Verbal formation,—which is accepted by several scholars,—deserves most careful consideration, even if it does not itself claim to be conclusive on every point. It may be doubted whether all the difficulties of this portion of Ethiopic Grammar are even yet finally settled. Meanwhile, Dillmann's Scheme may be safely adopted as the *Norm* of the Regular Stems. tr.]

formation, by the circumstance that the leading vowel comes after the second radical. This vowel is *a*, when the verb is of active signification. In later times it took the tone, but hardly at first(¹). The first letter of the root, properly being without a vowel, when it forms a syllable for itself, calls in the help of the readiest vowel, that is to say, the vowel *a* in this case too (§ 60), for its own utterance. Farther the last radical letter is always uttered with *a* in the 3rd pers. sing. Perf., just as in Arabic, even with all Roots *tertiae infirmae* (*cf. infra* § 91). Accordingly this stem in the active form is given as ነገረ *nagára*, "he has spoken". Ethiopic, however, like the other Semitic tongues, makes a difference,—by means of a different vocalisation,—between the Transitive or Active verb of the first stem, and the Intransitive or Semi-Passive verb, which expresses participation, not in pure doing, but either in suffering or in a mere condition. In place of the *a* after the second radical in the Active verb, the Intransitive verb has *ĕ*(²), as in ጎብረ "he was active"; and this vowel finally disappeared altogether, so that it was pronounced *gábra* instead of *gabĕra* (§ 37)(³). Thus the Intransitive pronunciation of the strong verb coincides entirely, in outward form, with the Transitive of Verbs *tert. guttur.*, like ከልአ, according to § 92. This mode of distinguishing Intransitive verbs by means of the pronunciation has remained in full vigour in Ethiopic. All verbs which denote properties, bodily or mental states, emotions, confined activities, are pronounced with *ĕ*, like ርሕበ "to be wide"; ዐቢየ "to be great"; ደከመ "to be tired"; ጸገበ "to be satisfied"; ጸድቀ "to be just"; ነግሠ "to be a king", "to rule"; ርኅበ "to hunger"; ርእየ "to see"; ረወየ "to drink to satiety"; ሐመ "to suffer" (= ሐምመ); ሐጕለ "to perish". It is the same too with those verbs which have a reflexive meaning, like ለብሰ "to clothe one's self", and in rare cases even with those which express free activity but

Transitive and Intransitive Forms.

(¹) *Cf.* Arabic, Amharic and Tigriña (Schreiber § 83). König also correctly observes, p. 161, that the toning of the second syllable was not original. In later times, to be sure, *á* at least appears to have received the tone after the second radical; v. Ludolf, '*Gramm*'. I, 7, and Trumpp, p. 525, who however is himself obliged to allow, that, strictly taken, *nâbàra, ágbàra, bá-ràka*, would have to be accentuated, seeing that "the voice lifts up the first syllable with a certain emphasis."

(²) Instead of the *ŭ* and *ĭ* (*ō, ē*) of the other languages, by §§ 17, 19.

(³) *Cf.* König, p. 81.

associated with effort and toil, like **ለጕመ** "to rein in"; **ሰተረ** "to hew in pieces"; **በቍጸ** "to rake coals of fire together". The greater number of them are not strictly intransitive, but are rather to be compared with the Greek Middle, seeing that they may have Objects. Many of them occur under both forms of expression' like **መስለ** and **መሰለ** "to be like"; **ኅርየ** and **ኅረየ** "to be pleased', and "to elect"; **ጐየ** and **ጐየየ** "to flee"; **ሰክበ** and **ሰከበ** "to lie" and "to lie down"([1]).

Intransitive verbs of the Simple Stem may even stand directly for the Passive of their Causatives, at least where the operative cause is not given, *e. g.* **ውዕየ** ἐνεπρήσθη Josh. 6,24; **ሞቱ፡** "they were put to death" Josh. 8,25; **ኅጸረ** (in Transitive expression) "to become short", also "to be shortened" Matt. 24,22; **ገብአ** ἀποκατεστάθη Matt. 12,13 [and **በርሀ** "to become enlightened" *Kebra Nag.* 112 a 21].

§ 77. 2. *The Intensive Stem.* An intensifying of the idea of the verb, whether it be in indicating more or less frequent repetition, or to signify force, eagerness or completeness in the action, is expressed by repeating the radicals; and, according as one or another or several of them together are repeated, very different forms will be produced by this mode of formation. But although, according to § 71, a very large number of Multiliteral roots have sprung, by means of this formative expedient, from simple original roots now lost to the language, yet in the department of ordinary triliteral roots the majority of the possible repetitions of the root-letters have not been brought into common use. The formation which is relatively of most frequent occurrence is contrived by the repetition of the last two radicals. It expresses in a very picturesque manner the notion of 'backwards and forwards', 'unremittingly', 'again and again', in (**አ**)**ርመስመሰ** (§ 57) "to feel as a blind man does" (*palpavit*), from **መርሰሰ** (מָשַׁשׁ, § 72); (**አ**)**ንጠብጠበ** "to drip" (from **ነጠበ**), and interchanging with it, (**አ**)**ንጸፍጸፈ** "to distil"; (**አ**)**ንበልበለ** "to blaze" (from **ነበለ**); (**አ**)**ስቆቀወ** "to howl" (*cf.* **ሰከየ**); (**አ**)**ርሳሕስሐ** "to utter reproaches" (from **ረስሐ**); **አኅሰርሰረ** "to revile repeatedly" (from **ኅሰረ**); and it serves besides

2. The Intensive Stem.

([1]) It is the same with **ሡርጸ፡ ኍብረ፡ ሡምረ፡ ወድቀ፡ በቍለ፡ ተርፈ፡ ከብረ፡ ዐርበ፡ ፀርፈ፡ ፈርየ፡ ምሕረ፡ ምሕከ፡ ሥሕቀ፡ ስሕጠ፡ ስእለ፡ ውሕጠ፡ ግዕረ፡ ሐጸ፡ ነደ.**

to express variation in the case of words denoting colour:—(አ)ቀያሕይሐ "to gleam red" (ቀይሐ); (አ)ኀመልመለ "to become green" (ኀምል), *cf.* § 110. More rarely the repetition of the final radical occurs with a like meaning, as in § 71, *β*:—በርደደ "to hail" (በረድ፡ "hail"); (አ)ማዕረረ "to sweeten" (መዓር "honey"); ገብሰሰ "to plaster with stucco" (*γύψος*); ገልበበ "to veil" (from ገለበ = ገለወ 'to cover over'). In the formation all the stems which are mentioned here, just like those enumerated in § 71, are treated as Multiliterals.

In place of these more vigorous and violent reduplications, a finer and easier intensifying device has become usual in the language, namely, *the doubling (or strengthening) of the second radical,* effected too in such a way, that this letter is simply repeated without any intervening vowel (¹), as in ነጸረ *náṣṣara* "to view, to consider" (*cf. infra,* § 95 *sqq.*, for a more precise statement regarding the vowel-expression in this and the following stems).

1. This Intensive Stem is a favourite mode of conveying those verbal notions that seek to express 'dealings, practices and usages' which consist in a series or group of individual acts, or which by their nature continue for some time, like ሐለወ "to watch"; ሐለየ "to turn over in one's mind", "to meditate"; ዘመረ "to play" (on a musical instrument); ኈለቈ "to number"; ወደሰ and ሰብሐ "to praise"; ጸውዐ "to call upon"; ገሠጸ "to chastise"; ሐሰወ "to tell lies"; ዘመወ "to commit fornication"; አበሰ "to sin"; ዐመፀ "to act unjustly";—as well as those in which 'force, completeness, rapidity, effort, or promptitude' is made prominent, like ኀየለ "to exert strength"; ወረወ "to throw"; መረደ "to hasten"; ሠገረ "to take quick steps"; ጸዐረ "to feel pain";

(¹) Doubling, effected in such a way that the constituents of the doubled letter are separated by a vowel, is found in this case, it is true, in Amharic, but not in Ethiopic; and wherever such stems occur, they are to be regarded as introduced from Amharic, *e. g.* ይትማገየየጥ Gen. 3, 24, Note. According to Trumpp, p. 522, when the second radical is doubled, the second syllable has always the tone, even when it contains *ĕ*: ረሰየ *rassáya*; ሰብሐ *sabbéḥa*—(but ሀሎ፡ *halló*, because contracted from ሀለወ *halláwa*). On the other hand, in Amharic the first syllable has always the tone; and so the second radical is always doubled in the Perfect, even in Non-Intensive stems: v. Guidi, '*Gramm. elem.*', p. 21, and '*Sulla reduplicazione delle consonanti amariche*' in '*Supplemento period. dell' Archivio glottol. Ital.*' II, 1893, p. 1 *sqq.*; [and '*Zeitschr. f. Assyr.*' VIII, p. 245 *sqq.*]

ተከዘ "to be much grieved"; **ሠፀረ** "to split"; **ደቀቀ** "to pound"; **ጠየቀ** "to consider closely"; **ፈከረ** "to explain" &c.

2. This stem serves directly to express active working and doing, associated with the accessory notion of carefulness and zeal. Accordingly it often comes into touch with the Causative stem, by its being also able to signify the making or doing of something, either in actual production or merely in word or thought, as for instance declaring or regarding a person or thing as being this or that: *cf.* **ሐደፈ** "to lead", "to guide"; **ኰነነ** "to judge"; **ፈጸመ** "to complete"; **መሀረ** "to teach"; **ሐደሰ** "to renew"; **ቀደሰ** "to sanctify" and "to declare holy"; **ኣመረ** "to show" ("to make high, *or* clear"); **ወድአ** "to make an end"; **ለቅሐ** "to lend" ("to cause to be taken"); **ኣዘዘ** "to command" ("to exercise power"). And since in Ethiopic many notions are regarded as belonging to the category of Action, which we are wont to express in our own languages rather as properties or conditions, there emerges an explanation of the employment of the second stem in cases like **ሠነየ** "to be beautiful" ("to acquire form"); **ኣደመ** "to please" ("to content"); **ሐወዘ** "to be agreeable to" ("to delight"); **ሀለወ** "to be", "to become" ("to acquire being"), and many others.

3. Accordingly this stem is frequently employed in the formation of Denominatives ([1]), in the signification of 'bringing about' or 'busying one's self with' that which is expressed by the noun, or of 'possessing and using' it: **ለበወ**, (√ לבּ) "to possess understanding"; **ሠረወ** "to eradicate"; **ከወለ** "to form the rear-guard"; **ዐመደ** "to erect columns"; **መልሐ** "to salt"; **ጸፈረ** "to pare the nails"; **ዐየነ** "to fix the eye upon"; **ገየረ** "to plaster with lime". In particular, verbs are derived in this way from Numerals: **ሠለሰ** "to do something for the third time", "to be the third"; **ረብዐ** "to form four"; **ዐሠረ** "to give the tithe".

While, however, in the other Semitic languages, the first stem has, as a rule, continued to be used side by side with the second, Ethiopic, by virtue of the frugality displayed in the housekeeping of its forms (§ 4), has mostly given up the first stem, in the case of those verbal notions which it has developed in the second. In point of fact there are only a very few roots yielding a first and

---

([1]) Which purpose is also served in some cases by one or two of the stronger Intensive Stems: *cf. supra, e. g.* **ገብሰሰ**, **በርደደ**.

a second stem which are both in use together, such as **መስለ** "to be like", **መሰለ** "to compare"; **ሐጕለ** "to perish", **ሐጐለ** (1) "to ruin" (Gen. 35,4; Numb. 21,29); **ዐሰበ** "to hire"; **ጸንዐ** "to be firm"; **ዐርቀ** "to be naked"; **ወገረ** 1 and 2 "to throw" and "to stone". Besides, in most cases, when both stems are fully formed, there is no longer any essential difference in the meaning, as with **መሀረ** 1 and 2 "to teach"; **ነቀወ** 1 and 2 "to give forth a sound *or* cry"; **ኀለየ** 1 and 2 "to sing"; **ዐሰየ** 1 and 2 "to requite"; **ሔሰ** and **ሐየሰ** "to find fault with"; **ጻዐረ** and **ጸዐረ** "to feel pain" &c.

Farther, the roots which have been described in § 71, *a*, of the form **ሠሥዐ**, are dealt with in their formation as verbs of this second stem, seeing that their second radical has to be given as a double letter. But those roots which have made up for the doubling of the second radical by a **ነ** or **ረ** (§ 72) follow the formation of the Multiliteral Verbs.

3. The Influencing Stem.

§ 78. 3. *The Influencing Stem* is formed by the interpolation of a long tone-bearing(2) *ā* after the first radical, and it corresponds precisely to the Arabic Stem III. It is no longer very common in Ethiopic, but in a number of Verbs it is replaced by III, 3 (v. § 82). Besides, the first and second stems of those verbs which have coined this third stem, are either no longer used at all, or only with the same meaning as the third. Meantime, various traces, particularly in isolated Nominal formations (§§ 111 *a. f.*, and 120), show that the Influencing Stem was once used more extensively; and as it serves at the same time as ground-stem to Stems III, 3 and IV, 3, it must doubtless be dealt with in the Grammar as a special Stem. Two kinds of formative principles seem to have co-operated in its production. In part the doubling of the second radical was replaced by a semivowel, which coalesced with a foregoing *a* into *ō* or *ē*: in part an originally exterior causative form, consisting of the prefix **አ**, was brought within the word, and this **አ** became established as *ā* after the first radical. The Influencing Stem is therefore in the last resort to be regarded, both in origin and meaning, as a variety partly of the Intensive Stem and partly

(1) This form, however, is obsolete, and is always replaced in later times by II, 1.

(2) According to Ludolf, Verbs *mediae gutturalis* form an exception, in which the second syllable has the tone. According to Trumpp, p. 522, the tone always rests on the second syllable.

of the Causative([1]). It is formed most regularly in Arabic, as is well known, and there it is employed as the strongest Active Stem, particularly in cases where the action is to be represented as one which influences another being and challenges him to a counter activity,—a meaning which is obvious enough in Ethiopic also, in I,3 even, but particularly in the derived Stems III, 3 and IV, 3:—But other verbs of this Stem in Ethiopic do not go beyond the meaning of the Intensive, or the ordinary Causative Stem. Verbal Stems too which have a formative *ē* or *ō* after the first radical are properly to be referred to this Stem([2]), thus **ፄወወ** "to take prisoner"; **ጼነወ** "to emit fragrance"; **ቆረረ** and **ዖዘዘ** (in **አስቆረረ** "to abhor" and **አስዖዘዘ** "to make torpid *or* stiff" § 73); but in farther formation these follow the Multiliteral roots. The other stems belonging to this class have all *ā* after the first radical, which in many of them is certainly original, but in others appears to be shaded out of *ō* or *ē*. This *ā*, however, seems to have been pronounced *ō* in an earlier period of the language, just as in Hebrew, for it passes into *ŭ* (§§ 18, 20), when the rules of formation require it to be shortened. The verbs of this stem are: **ላሐወ** "to mourn for" (alongside of **ለሐወ** "to mourn"); **ባረከ** "to bless" (by means of 'bending the knee'); **ዋሐየ** "to visit" (وحى); **ሣቀየ** "to torment" (شَقِى "to be unhappy"); **ባልሐ** "to draw one out", "to rescue"; **ቋፀረ** (along with **ቈፀረ**) "to lay a snare", "to surround with snares"; **ላጸየ** "to crop", "to shave"([3]); (**ሳተፈ** "to make one participate", ܫܘܬܦ); **ሳረረ** "to found"; **ቋረፈ** (with **ቀረፈ**) "to flay", "to lacerate"; **ናፈቀ** "to doubt", "to play the hypocrite" (نافق); **ሳኰየ** "to make for the distance", "to wander about" (conn. with **ሰኰት**), which is also simplified again into the first stem; **ናዘዘ**([4]) "to console"; **ጣግዐ** "to bind fast" (Zech. 14, 13 *var.*); **ከደነ** "to cover" (Gen. 9, 23 *var.*); **ዛወገ** "to be equal"; **ዳደቀ** "to come upon"; **ናሥአ** "to lead away" (Is. 57, 13 *Cod. Laur.*); **ዋረሰ** "to take possession of" (*ibid.*).

([1]) V. Ewald, '*Hebr. Spr.*' § 125, *a*.

([2]) Like the Aramaic *Pauel* and *Paiel*, Hoffmann, p. 186. [*Cf. supra* p. 141, Note ([1]). TR.]

([3]) Unless we are to understand here the root موس or لوص and **የ** according to § 73.

([4]) Although this root seems to be closely connected with أَسَا, آسَى, وَاسَى, and the *a* might thus be otherwise explained.

On the other hand ጻመወ "to endure toil and distress" (derived from ጻማ "distress", by § 73), and ማሰነ "to decay" (§ 73) are multi-literal roots. Besides the verbs named, several other roots were at one time used in Ethiopic in the third stem, *e. g.*, ሐቀፈ "to embrace"; ዓጸፈ "to envelop" (*cf.* the forms in § 120); but in the course of time they were allowed to fall back into the first stem, just as some other forms which did not seem absolutely necessary were given up, particularly in later times.

§ 79. II. Causative Stems.

II. Causative Stems: From the three Ground-Stems which have been mentioned, and leaving their other peculiarities untouched, Ethiopic derives three Causative Stems. It does so by means of one and the same formative device, and in this it develops a certain bent of the language with even more consistency than the other Semitic tongues, including Arabic, which form such a Causative only from the Simple Stem. The device employed consists in prefixing an *ă* to the Ground-Stem, introducing it just as in Arabic and Aramaic by means of the softest breathing አ. The Causative *a* is no longer attended in Ethiopic with the stronger breathing *h*, by which it is introduced in Hebrew (1). But traces are found which prove that in Ethiopic also a stronger prefix was at one time employed to form the Causative, namely ተ (§ 73, Note) (2) and more frequently ሰ (§ 70 *a. f.* and § 73 *a. i.*), which ሰ, in its original form አሰ, is still quite regularly employed to form the Causative Stems IV,1, 2, 3. It is possible that አ, originally ሀ, is just a weakened form of this ሰ or ተ (3). In signification the Stems formed with አ are always Causative, *i. e.* they give expression to the 'causing or occasioning' the performance or realisation by some one of the action or dealing expressed in the Ground-Stem.

1. Causative of the Simple Stem. 1. The *first* Causative Stem, of the form አግበረ (4), belongs to the Simple Ground-Stem. It is true that often enough the Simple Ground-Stem corresponding to II, 1 does not occur in common use, or else that the second only of these Ground-Stems is still retained

(1) ሀይመነ "to believe" is a foreign word:—هَيْمَنَ, ܗܰܝܡܶܢ, [הֶאֱמִין].

(2) ተርጐመ "to interpret" is a foreign word from Aramaic (Hoffmann p. 187). [Aramaic borrowed it from Assyrian, and perhaps Assyrian from Sumerian.]

(3) V. on this point Ewald, '*Hebr. Spr.*' § 122 *a*. *Cf.* König, p. 77 *sq.*

(4) According to Trumpp, p. 522, it is to be accented *agbára*.

along with II,1; but any such lack of the Simple Stem rests merely on the contingencies of speech-usage, and so, even in that case II,1 is to be considered as derived from I,1. If the Simple Stem is a semi-passive verb, the Causative turns it into the corresponding active verb, as in **አምጽአ** "to bring", from **መጽአ** "to come"; **አሐረ** "to cause to go", from **ሐረ** "to go";—or it signifies the causing of something to exist either in word or thought, *e. g.* **አርኵሰ** "to declare and hold as unclean", from **ረኵሰ** "to be unclean". If the Simple Stem is a transitive verb, the Causative turns it into a double transitive, as **አስተየ** "to give one something to drink", from **ሰትየ** "to drink"; **አሥዐለ** "to make one paint something". But not seldom the Causative gives a peculiar and even unexpected turn to the root-idea, *e. g.* **አንበበ** (from **ነበበ** "to speak") "to read" (as it were, 'to make the writing itself speak'); **አንፍኀ** "to sound a wind-instrument" (from **ነፍኀ** "to blow"); **አርብሐ** "to lend money in usury" (from **ረብሐ** "to make gain"); **አክሐደ** (from **ክሕደ** "to deny") "to represent one as a liar"; **አንሥአ** "to take up", "to waken up", (from **ነሥአ** "to take"). It is only in appearance that verbs belonging to this stem have now and then an intransitive meaning;—originally and really there is always a Causative sense lying at the foundation of even such verbs: **አዕረፈ** "to rest", originally "to cause to become drowsy"; **አርመመ** "to be silent", properly "to maintain tranquillity"; **አድነነ** "to bow", properly "to cause a bending". When Stem II,1 occurs along with I,2, the two certainly have often different meanings, as in **መሰለ** "to compare", "to make similar", **አምሰለ** "to declare similar", "to put forth a parable"; **አመረ** "to show", **አእመረ** "to discern", "to know" ('to have something high and clear'); **መከረ** "to form a plan", **አምከረ** "to counsel":—but in other verbs the meanings agree, like **ሐጐለ** and **አሕጐለ** "to ruin"; **ነጸረ** and **አንጸረ** "to glance at" (II,1 properly "to cast a glance"); **ደቀቀ** and **አድቀቀ** "to crush in pieces". More rarely II,1 reverts to the meaning of I,1, *e. g.* **ረድአ** "to help", **አርድአ** "to give help", "to help"; **ለጐመ** and **አልጐመ** "to curb", "to tame". An instance of II,1 as Causative to I,3 is found in **አላሐወ** "to cause to mourn", with **ላሐወ** "to mourn for". Examples of II,1, in cases where none of the three Ground-Stems remains extant, are afforded by **አርኀወ** "to open"; **አውሰበ** "to marry" (יָשַׁב); **አይድዐ** "to inform" (יָדַע); **አውሥአ** "to answer"; **አፍቀረ** "to love"; **አዕረፈ** "to rest". Denominatives also are formed in II,1: **አቍጸለ**

"to put forth leaves", from ቈጽል; አስገለ "to practise divination" (ሰገል); አብዐለ "to celebrate a feast" (በዓል); አምለከ "to reverence God", from አምላክ, and several others.

2. Causative of the Intensive Stem. 2. *The Causative of the Intensive Stem.* This form occurs much less frequently, it is true, than Stem II,1, but still [though of later formation] it is sufficiently well represented in the language. Intensive Stems which seem to have an intransitive meaning, become active in the Causative form, *e. g.* አሠነየ (1) "to beautify"; አኀየለ "to strengthen"; አለበወ "to make intelligent", "to instruct". Others which are already transitive, become doubly transitive, but they also adapt themselves to simpler notions, by means of some new turn:—አፈጸመ "to order the completion of"; አገበረ "to cause one to work at something", "to compel"; አኰነነ "to cause to judge", "to appoint as judge"; አጸብሐ "to order one to pay any tax", "to collect taxes"; አሐለየ "to suggest". In rare cases, Stem II,2 reverts in the end to the meaning of I,2, as in ገመነ "to pollute" and አገመነ "to cause to pollute" and "to pollute"; ዐረየ and አዐረየ "to make equal"; መልዐ and አመልዐ "to set out", "to continue a journey". Stem II,2 occurs occasionally, no doubt, along with Stem II,1, and then, as a rule, it bears a different meaning, like አግበረ "to cause one to carry out", አገበረ "to compel"; አምከረ "to counsel", አመከረ "to test": but there are cases in which the two stems occur together, merely in consequence of a certain indecision in the usage of the language. Roots of the type ሠረዐ (§ 71, *a*) form their Causative in Stem II,2, *e. g.* አጕጕአ "to urge to haste"; አሠረዐ "to satiate" (G. Ad.,—inasmuch as ሠረዐ means first "to be insatiable" and then "to eat much", and so on). This Stem also may be denominative, through the intervention of I,2, *e. g.* አቈረበ "to administer the Communion" from ቍርባን.

3. Causative of the Influencing Stem. 3. *The Causative of the Influencing Stem.* This Causative is of very rare occurrence, as the Ground-Stem itself is but little used. The few verbs which belong to it, so far as yet known, are: አላቀሰ "to condole with any one" (لقس "to be afflicted", لاقس "to bear with patience"); አዋከየ "to illumine something by its own light"; አጣየረ "to foretell"; and as a denominative, አዋሐደ "to unite one thing to another", "to add (in Arithmetic)". But አማሰነ "to destroy", አጻመወ (2) "to cause trouble to one" (by § 78),

(1) According to Trumpp, p. 522,—to be accented *ašannáya.*

(2) According to Trumpp, p. 522,—to be accented *aṣāmáwa.*

and አጣዐወ "to worship idols" (derived from ጣዖት "an idol") belong to the Causatives of Multiliteral roots.

§ 80. III. Reflexive-Passive Stems.

III. Reflexive-Passive Stems: These Stems form the antithesis to the Causative Stems: they convey the action which is expressed in the Ground-Stem, back upon the acting Subject, so that it becomes both Subject and Object at once. But just as in the Indo-European languages the Passive was developed out of the Reflexive, so in Ethiopic also (as in Aramaic and to some extent in Hebrew) the Reflexive came in process of time to serve the farther purpose of a Passive; and this use so completely gained the upper hand in the language, that the other Semitic Passive form, effected by means of internal Vowel-change, almost entirely disappeared. One leading cause of this phenomenon certainly lies in the fact that the short *ŭ* or *ŏ*, to which the inner Passive form specially clung, gradually disappeared from the language. It is only in the Noun (Passive Participle),—in which the Passive *u* or *i* was lengthened into long *ū* or *ī*,—that a remnant of the old Passive formation has been retained. And seeing that in this way the Reflexive served also as a Passive, there was all the more reason in consistency to form such a Reflexive out of all the Ground-Stems. Of the two prefixes, which at one time served to form the Reflexive in Semitic, viz.—*in* (*hin*) and *it* (*hit*), only the latter has continued in use for triliteral roots, while the former is retained merely in the Stem formation of Multiliteral roots. But farther, the prefix *it* (originally no doubt a pronominal element of reflexive meaning) has already been smoothed down in Ethiopic to the simpler ተ throughout (just as in Stems V and VI in Arabic).

1. R.-P. of the Simple Stem 1. *The Reflexive-Passive of the Simple Stem.* This form, in its twofold utterance, ተገብረ and ተዐቀበ (*cf. infra* § 97), corresponds to the Arabic Stem VIII and the Aramaic Ethpeel. The greater number of these Stems are both reflexive and passive, *e. g.* ተከድነ and ተከደነ (1) "to cover one's self" and "to be covered"; but many occur only in the one signification or the other. In this matter everything depends upon the usage of the language and upon the fundamental meaning of the Simple Stem. Thus, for instance, ተክሀለ (from ክሀለ "to be able") and ተሰአነ (from ስአነ

(1) According to Trumpp, p. 523,—to be accented *takádna, takadána.*

"to be unable") can only have a passive sense, "to be possible" and "to be impossible". But when the reflexive signification has been fully formed, the backward reference is not always so direct and immediate by any means as it is in ተለብሰ "to clothe one's self", "to put on", but the Reflexive Stem may also express the 'doing of something for and to one's self', as in ተሰከመ "to take anything upon one's shoulders" (Judges 16, 3); ተወከፈ "to see that something be put in one's own hand", *i. e.* "to take"; ተረድየ "to oppress any one for one's own profit", *i. e.* "to practise usury". The Reflexive may farther signify the exhibiting one's self in this or that character, *e. g.* ተሐበየ "to assume the position of administrator and surety", "to take care of anything"; ተዐደወ "to show one's self to be a transgressor", "to transgress". Often several such meanings unite in the same word, *e. g.* ተአመነ and ተአምነ "to keep one's self in a believing attitude", *i. e.* "to trust"; "to entrust (or unbosom) one's self to any one", *i. e.* "to confess"; finally, "to become a believer"; or ተወርሰ "to take anything to one's self by way of inheritance", but also "to be inherited". Several of these Stems approximate to the Simple Stem in signification, particularly when the latter has an intransitive meaning, *e. g.* ተመልአ "to fill itself", "to become full" = መልአ; ተመይጠ "to turn one's self back" ("to return") = ሜጠ; ግሕሠ and ተግሕሠ "to withdraw". But in many cases the Simple Stem no longer survives by the side of the Reflexive Stem, and the latter serves, like a Deponent, for the first, particularly with words which express emotion, *e. g.* ተምዕዐ "to be angry"; ተሐሥየ "to exult". Even from the examples already adduced it is apparent that many Reflexive conceptions may become transitive by means of a new turn; so too, for instance, ተዐቀበ "to be on one's guard", but also "to observe"; ተቀነየ "to subject one's self", *i. e.* "to serve"; ተልእከ "to submit to be sent", *i. e.* "to perform services for one", "to serve".

Since the Reflexive fills also the place of the Passive, Stem III, 1 may farther serve as Reflexive and Passive to Stem II, 1. Thus ተየድዐ "to be made known" is the Passive of አይድዐ; ተፈቅረ "to be loved", of አፍቀረ; ተአምረ "to be recognised", of አእመረ; ተርኅወ "to open" (*intrans.*) and "to be opened", the Passive of አርኀወ. Farther, ተንሥአ "to arise" is the Reflexive of አንሥአ, and ተነበ means both "to be spoken" (ነበበ) and "to be read"

(አንበበ). More rarely Stem III, 1 is the Passive and Reflexive of Stem I, 2, *e. g.* in ተፈክረ "to be explained", from ፈክረ "to explain"; ተመጥነ "to be measured", together with ተመጠነ III, 2, from መጠነ I, 2. This Stem is also employed as a Denominative, *e. g.* in ተልሀቀ "to become a presbyter", from ልሂቅ; ተበከረ "to be delivered of the first birth", *i. e.* "to give birth for the first time", from በኵር.

§ 81. 2. *The Reflexive-Passive of the Intensive Stem.* This Stem in the form ተፈጸመ *tafassama*, corresponds to the Hebrew Hithpael and to the Arabic Stem V, and is likewise of very common occurrence. As regards meaning, all that has been said about III,1 holds good also for this Stem. Often it has merely a reflexive meaning, *e. g.* ተአመረ "to show one's self"; ተመክሐ "to praise one's self", "to boast"; ተጸንዐ "to harden" (*intrans.*); ተመጠወ "to cause anything to be handed over to one's self", *i. e.* "to accept". Frequently it has only a Passive meaning, like ተመጠነ "to be measured"; ተኈለቈ "to be numbered"; ተሐለየ "to be thought"; but often it has both meanings together, as ተደመረ "to mingle" (*intrans.*) and "to be mingled". It is specially in use with verbs which express emotion: ተሰፈወ(1) "to hope"; ተፈሥሐ "to rejoice"; ተወከለ "to confide"; ተዐገሠ "to exercise patience"; ተቀየመ "to take vengeance"; ተመነየ "to wish", "to long for". Often quite simple conceptions have been re-developed out of it, as in the last-named instances, and farther in ተአዘዘ "to obey" ("to let one's self be commanded"); ተመሀረ "to learn"; ተወነየ "to play"; ተቀበለ "to go to meet"; and sometimes there is not much difference between its meaning and that of the Ground-Stem, as in ተሠርሐ and ሠርሐ "to prosper"; ተነስሐ and ነስሐ "to experience regret"; ዐረየ and ተዐረየ "to be equal". By simplifying the idea, it may even take a transitive sense, as in several of the cases mentioned. In conformity with its origin from I, 2, it has in a very special manner the meaning,—'to be declared something', 'to give one's self out as this or that', *e. g.* in ተሐሰወ "to be convicted of falsehood"; ተቀደሰ "to be sanctified, consecrated *or* declared holy"; ተዐወረ "to show one's self blind to" ("to connive at a matter"); ተዐየረ "to appear as a faultfinder"; ተጸደቀ "to think one's self righteous"; so too ተዐበየ "to magnify one's self" (although

2. R.-P. of the Intensive Stem.

(1) According to Trumpp, p. 523,—to be accented *tasaffáwa*.

ዐበየ I, 2 is not in use). When this Stem is developed alongside of III, 1, the two stems, as a rule, have different significations, *e. g.* ተዘከረ "to remember", ተዘከረ "to be mentioned"; ተጸመነ "to become obscure", ተጸምነ "to be covered"; ተገበረ "to conduct a trade *or* business", ተገብረ "to happen". More rarely the usage fluctuates between the two Stems, both having the same signification, *e. g.* in ተመጥነ and ተመጠነ (v. *supra* and § 97, 2). For several of these Stems the Simple Stems no longer exist, as for ተቀበለ, ተሀየየ, ተወነየ, ተወከለ, ተዐገለ, ተመነየ, ተዐገሠ. This Stem is also denominative in cases by no means rare, as in ተነበየ "to act as prophet", *i. e.* "to foretell"; ተዐየነ "to seek one's self a well", *i. e.* "to encamp"; ተጠየረ "to observe the flight of birds" (طَيَّرَ); ተየሀደ = ተይሀደ "to become a Jew", and several others (1).

3. Reflexive of the Influencing Stem:— Stem of Reciprocity.

§ 82. 3. *The Reflexive of the Influencing Stem.* This Stem, with the form ተከፈለ corresponds to the Arabic Stem VI. It may also, it is true, have a purely Passive meaning, in those verbs namely whose only Ground-Stem in use is I, 3, like ተባልሐ "to be saved"; ተማቀየ "to be tormented"; or it may have a purely Reflexive meaning, as in ተላጸየ (from ላጸየ) "to shave one's self"; ተሳተፈ "to take a share in a thing"; but these cases are only of rare occurrence (2). Almost always the meaning proper to the Ground-Stem inclines to appear in III, 3, *viz.*, 'bringing influence to bear upon another by means of the action expressed in the verb'. It signifies either,—'to set forth the Subject as influencing others',—or, if the action is attributed to more than one,—'to influence one another reciprocally'. It has thus in part come directly into the place of the gradually disappearing Stem I, 3, and in part it serves to denote reciprocal action (*Reciprocity*) (3). It is in very frequent use in both references, and may be derived

(1) The following Stems have made their way into Ethiopic writings from the Amharic (v. Isenberg, '*Grammar*', p. 54, No, XIV):—ተመያየጠ "to turn hither and thither"; ተመላለሰ "to run hither and thither"; ተደማመረ "to mingle with"; ተቃበበለ "to be hospitable".

(2) Cases like ተማሰነ "to be laid waste" (§ 78); ተማረየ "to act the soothsayer", from ማረ, do not belong to this class, as these Stems come from Multiliteral roots:—v. *infra* § 86.

(3) Frequently however, when several individuals are spoken of, phrases like በበይናቲሆሙ, or አሐዱ ፡ ምስለ ፡ ክልኡ, are expressly added.

from all the Ground-Stems, or even from derived Stems. This Stem is specially employed to express the ideas of 'contending, fighting, quarrelling, censuring, disputing (at law)' and such like, as ተቃተለ in the Plural, "to fight with each other", or in the Singular, "to fight with one", taking an Accusative, in which case it is presupposed that the person who is fought with displays a counter-activity; ተቃወመ, ተባአሰ, ተጋደለ, ተፃረረ, ተፃብአ, ተፋትሐ, ተሐየሰ, ተሐመየ, ተላኰየ, ተሐመመ, ተማዐዐ. It is also used to convey the ideas of 'separating, dividing, binding, collecting, cohering'; and some of these verbs may also be used both in the Singular and in the Plural, *e. g.* ተፋለጠ(1) "to separate (*intrans.*) from one another"; ተጋብአ "to assemble themselves together"; ተላጸቀ "to cohere"; ተራከበ "to light upon one another", *i. e.* 1. "to meet one another", 2. "to be together". In the very same way Stem III, 3 is derived from many other conceptions, in this sense of reciprocal action, like ተሰምዐ "to understand ('hear') one another"; ተማከረ "to advise together"; ተማሰለ "to resemble one another"; ተናገረ and ተባሀለ "to parley together"; ተራድአ "to help one another". Accordingly it may quite as readily be formed from intransitive as from transitive ideas, since even intransitive actions may be attributed to more than one individual in their relations to one another, *e. g.* ተዋደቀ "to fall away from one another"; ተራወጸ "to flock together"; ተዋነየ "to sport with one another"; ተባዝኀ "to multiply together"; ተዋረደ "to rush upon one":—just as, *vice versâ*, if it is derived from transitive verbs, it is in no wise necessary that the Subjects of the verb should at the same time be its objects, but the Stem may assume an object for itself, *e. g.* ተካፈለ not "to divide themselves", but "to share something among themselves", ተሣየጠ not "to sell themselves", but "to sell among themselves", "to exercise trade", "to purchase something from one"; ተማሰጠ "to contend together over plunder" or "to plunder together". On the other hand it may have a reflexive sense, for instance, in ተናገፈ "to disengage one's self", (while ተነገፈ has a passive meaning). In several cases, however, the idea of reciprocity retires quite into the background, and then the Stem seems to revert to the meaning of III, 1 or 2; but in these cases also some reference,—at least of a tacit order,—to other persons is included, *e. g.* ተሣሀለ

(1) According to Trumpp, p. 523,--to be accented *tafālāṭa*.

"to show one's self propitious", "to be gracious" to others; **ተሣለቀ** "to mock" at others; **ተላሐየ** "to adorn one's self" for others. Or the reciprocity which is expressed is not absolutely bound to refer to the Subject of the action and some other one, but may concern nearer or more remote objects, *e. g.* **ተፋቀዱ** "to tell off after one another", "to muster"; **ተራገፀ** "to kick with both feet".

This stem too is now and then denominative, *e. g.* in **ተዓፀወ** "to cast lots" (with different rods); **ተቃረነ** "to attack each other with the horns"; **ተጋወረ** "to dwell together in a neighbourly way".

About the time that the language was dying out, people began to make this Stem revert to III,1 or 2 (thus frequently **ተመሐለ** instead of **ተማሐለ** "to conspire", "to enter into a confederacy"; **ተበአሰ** "to fight", for **ተበአሰ** &c.),—a phenomenon which, for the most part, occurs only with roots having the first or the middle radical an aspirate, and therefore is to be explained not according to the analogy of the VIIIth Arabic Stem, which here and there also has the meaning of Stem VI, but according to § 48. In such roots also the converse may be met with, III,3 being written for III,1, *e. g.* **ተዓቀበ** for **ተዐቀበ**:—Care should be taken to avoid being deceived thereby.

IV. Causative-Reflexive Stems:—

§ 83. IV. Causative-Reflexive Stems.

From the Reflexive Stems Causative Stems are again derived, and this new formation is an embellishement peculiar to Ethiopic, to which Arabic alone, in its Stem X, presents an analogy. Ethiopic is, in this case as well as in the case of the Causative Stems II, richer and more thorough-going than Arabic, inasmuch as it derives new Causatives from all the three Reflexive Stems together. This richer evolution of IV,1, 2, & 3 brought about the disappearance of several of the simpler Stems in the case of many roots, because the defining of the conception effected by them appeared to be given still more appropriately by means of the form IV. The formative device for these Stems is the syllable **አስ**, which is prefixed to the **ተ** of the Reflexive. True, it is open to conjecture, that the prefix **አስተ**, characteristic of these Stems of Class IV, should not be analysed into **አስ** and **ተ**, but into **አት** and **ሰ**, **አትሰ** having been turned into **አስተ** (اِسْتَ), in old Semitic fashion. But, apart from the fact that such a transposition of letters is not Ethiopic (§ 57), the meaning of Stems belonging to Class IV tells against this explanation, for nearly all of them are Causatives of the Reflexive, not Reflexives of the Causative. That *as* was at one time actually employed in forming Causatives is seen partly in Ethiopic itself even yet, from the forms **አስየዘዘ** and **አስቆረረ** (§ 73 *ad init.*), and partly from the Amharic, in which **አስ** still forms simple Causatives(¹). And **አስ** thus appears to be the original form for later **ሰ**, exactly as הִתְ, إِتْ is the original form for **ተ**, تَ (²). The new Causative, to be sure, is formed as has been said from all the three Reflexive Stems, but still the form IV,3 is by far the most common, manifestly because the Stems III,1 and 2 modify the root-idea frequently in a less special manner than III,3 does. Accordingly the Causative, which is formed from III, 1 and 2, may be more easily replaced by the simple Causative, than the Causative, which is formed from III, 3. As regards signification, all three Stems express the bringing about of the appearance, or the occurrence, of that which is denoted by the Reflexive,—or they directly express the practising of what the Reflexive describes. A Reflexive must then be always presupposed, although in the ordinary speech such Reflexive has in many cases ceased to exist. Occasionally too the three Stems pass over, the one to the other:—in particular IV,1 may be formed from III,2, in place of, or alongside of IV,2, as, for instance, **አስተፈሥሐ** IV,2 and **አስተፋሥሐ** IV,1 from **ተፈሥሐ** III,2.

(¹) Isenberg, *'Gramm.'* pp. 53 & 54, St. 8 & 9; [Guidi., *'Gramm.'*, p. 21; *'Zeitschr. für Assyr.'* VIII p. 286 *sqq.*]. Also the Saho has *öš* placed after the root to form Causatives, *'Journ. Asiat.'* 1843, Tome 2, p. 116.

(²) Trumpp, p. 523, N. 2 agrees with the above view. On the other hand the explanation of **አስተ** as being derived from **አተ** and **ሰ** is maintained by Osiander, ZDMG XIX, p. 240 *sqq.*; XX, p. 206; Wright, *'Ar. Gr.³'*, p. 46, § 65, rem. [*cf.* *'Lectures on the Compar. Gr.'*, p. 214 *sq.*]; König, p. 79 *sqq.*, and Nöldeke, who, in a private communication of the 10th Feb. 1887, observes that even the Arabic اِسْتَفْعَلَ is used quite preponderatingly in a transitive sense. [In many cases it is directly Causative; *e. g.* اِسْتَخْرَجَ is often quite synonymous with أَخْرَجَ, although the former originally contained a subtle side-meaning. At the most there might be a question whether in **አስተጋብረ** the causal **አ** did not come in besides before the *is*. But this *a* was no doubt called forth through the analogy of the other verbal classes.—Nöldeke.]

Causative-Reflexive Stems 1, & 2.

1. *Causative-Reflexive Stems 1, and 2.* In these Stems the Causative signification is for the most part brought out very clearly and decisively: አስተጋብአ 1. "to take (by force of arms)"—"to cause that a city ተጋብአ surrender itself"; አስተክሐደ 1. "to induce one to fall away from the faith"; አስተፅመደ "to accustom one to serve" (ተፀምደ); አስተብረከ 1. "to make a bending of the knees", not very different from በረከ; አስተሰፈወ 2. "to cause one to cherish hope" (አሰፈወ "to give one to hope"); አስተግሐሠ 1. "to cause to withdraw". And it is merely in appearance that occasionally they have an intransitive and reflexive look, *e. g.* in አስተርአየ(1) 1. "to cause to appear", *i. e.* "to reveal one's self", "to let one's self be seen", "to appear"; አስተርከበ 1. "to make one's self cling to something", *i. e.* "to busy one's self eagerly therewith"; አስተዐገሠ 2. "to exercise patience", not very different from ተዐገሠ "to be patient" ('to allow to happen to one's self'). These Causative-Reflexive Stems are also much used to express lasting sentiments and mental dispositions(2): አስተምሐረ 1. "to be prone to pity"; አስተወከለ 2. "to be trustful", and many others. And since in this way the Causative of Reflexives frequently expresses merely the practising of that which the Reflexive speaks of, the Participle of Stems IV, 1 and 2 may replace directly the participle which is wanting in Stems III, 1 and 2 (§ 114). Among the more common significations of these Stems the two following deserve to be specially noticed: (*a*)—*to hold, or pronounce as something*, *e. g.* አስተንአሰ 1. "to deem too trifling for one's self", or generally, "to deem trifling"; አስተብፅዐ 1. "to pronounce blessed"; አስተአበደ 2. "to despise one as a fool"; አስተኄየሰ 2. "to regard as preferable", "to prefer": (*b*)—*to endeavour to obtain something for one's self or for others*, *e. g.* አስተምሐረ 1. "to implore pity", "to intercede" (for another meaning of this word v. *supra*); አስተስረየ 1. "to entreat pardon"; አስተበውሐ 1. "to crave permission"; አስተብዐለ 1. "to want to enrich one's self"; አስተፍአመ 1. "to beg for a morsel". But in other respects also the Stems of this form are distinguished strongly enough from the simple Active Stems, *e. g.* አስተንፈሰ

---

(1) What justification there may be for the forms አስተርከበ, አስተርእየ, which are sometimes met with in MSS., but which are purposely omitted in my *Lexicon*,—still awaits investigation.

(2) V. on this point the instructive passage 1 Cor. 13,3—7.

1. "to inhale" and "to smell" (but also "to cause to breathe again", "to revive", like አንፈሰ); አስተኀሠሠ 1. "to discover" (ኀሠሠ "to seek"); አስተዐበሰ 1. "to alarm" (አዕበሰ "to weaken"). Occasionally all the other Stems are lost, *e. g.* of አስተአዘበ "to make water".

§ 84. 2. *Causative-Reflexive Stem 3.* Stem IV,3 forms Causatives, generally from the Stem of Reciprocity III,3, whether the latter be still retained in the language or not, *e. g.* አስተፃረረ "to breed mutual enmity", "to make certain persons enemies of one another"; አስተጋብአ "to collect together"; አስተጣበቀ "to glue together"; አስተባረየ "to relieve one", and "to do something, in turn with others"; አስተታለወ "to cause to follow each other in succession"; አስተባዝኀ "to cause anything to multiply from itself"; አስተዋለደ "to render capable of propagation" (so far as more than one are concerned in it); አስተኃለፈ "to make (the hands) pass over each other", "to cross (the hands)". It often conveys merely a tacit reference to others, *e. g.* አስተማዕዐ "to bear a grudge" (towards others); አስተሳረየ "to be forgiving" (to others); አስተቃለለ "to expose to contempt" (from others), አስተሓወዘ "to find *or* to make anything pleasant" (for others and so too for one's self); አስተዋሀበ "to give in restitution"; አስተጻኀረ "to preserve to the last" (where the comparison lies with some other). Farther, just as Stem III,3 (by § 82) expresses also the qualifications "in their order", "gradually", "the whole in its several parts", and such like, so the Causative-Reflexive Stem IV,3 is particularly often employed to denote the 'doing of a thing by a series of efforts', the 'bringing something gradually into being', as well as the ideas of 'restoring, adjusting' &c. This qualification, however, of the idea is brought about merely by the two prefixes አስ and ተ operating together; and the Reflexive Stem III,3 hardly ever appears when Stems IV,3 of such a kind exist, or only appears with a different signification. Examples: አስተዋዕአ "to spend (more and more)"; አስተሓየወ "to bring back to life"; አስተማነየ "to restore"; አስተፈትዐ "to improve", "to reform"; አስተናሥአ "to re-establish" (on the other hand ተናሥአ "to rise against another"); አስተጻለወ "to prepare"; አስተናጽሐ "to purify (in process of time); አስተማወቀ "to warm"; አስተፋጠነ "to quicken"; አስተፃምአ "to discover by hearkening", "to listen for some time". Thus Stem IV,3, as compared with IV,1 and 2, has several significations peculiar to itself, while on the other hand it never conveys, or only seldom (1), the two senses of "holding as being this or that", and "endeavouring to obtain something" (§ 83); but no doubt it is employed, just like the other two Stems, to express permanent sentiments and dispositions, particularly when these involve some reference to others (v. 1 Cor. 13,4 *sqq.*). Accordingly, when the forms IV,1 or 2 and IV,3 are both in use, the meanings are generally distinct from one another, *e. g.* in **አስተሰረየ** and **አስተሳረየ** (v. *supra*); **አስተግብአ** and **አስተጋብአ** (v. *supra*); **አስተቀንአ** "to be envious", so **አስተቃንአ**, yet the latter has also the meaning, "to provoke to mutual jealousy". There is however scarcely any difference between **አስተቀሰመ** and **አስተቃሰመ**, both meaning "to divine from omens". **አስተናኀዐ** "to remove the marrow" is derived from a noun (**አንኆዕ** "marrow"), without the intervention of Stem III,3.

The twelve Stems which have just been described may be derived immediately from triliteral roots, or they may be denominative. But nothing like the full number of twelve Stems are to be found actually derived from any one root. Even in other languages such a case does not occur; and Ethiopic in particular, through its tendency to economise its resources, was in the practice of evolving only one or two of the most necessary Stems from any one root, while it allowed others, which might once have existed, to fall away. The most fully developed Verb in this respect, **ገብረ** (2), has only six Stems in ordinary use. As for other verbs, the more fully developed roots have formed one Stem each in the classes I, II, III and IV, and in addition III,3 as a Reciprocity-Stem. The most of them have generated only one Active Stem, one Reflexive-Passive, and perhaps also III,3 or one Stem of Class IV. It farther results from the survey which we have been engaged in, that roots, which are in use in one of the three Ground-Stems, may easily pass over to a different Ground-Stem under II, III, and IV, *e. g.* from 1 to 2, or from 2 to 1; but when Stem 2 has established itself from any root, it is generally continued through the Classes II, III, and IV.

---

(1) For instance in **አስተረኵሰ**, properly "to pollute", then "to esteem unclean."

(2) Which LUDOLF chose for his Paradigm on that very ground.

2. STEM-FORMATION OF MULTILITERAL ROOTS.

Scheme of Stems.

§ 85. How Quadriliteral and Multiliteral roots generally originate, has been pointed out in §§ 71—73, 77, and 78. These sections show also that roots of five letters are, generally speaking, of rare occurrence, while those of six letters are met with only in isolated cases. The four classes of Stems (I—IV), which are employed in the development of triliteral roots, repeat themselves in the Stem-formation of Multiliterals; but the Intensive Stem 2 falls away completely, and the Influencing Stem 3 also disappears in Classes I and II at least. In certain roots, however, a Reflexive Stem,—formed by the prefix **እን**, and which the triliterals have lost—, has been retained. The Scheme of Stems most in use for Multiliteral roots is accordingly as follows:—

Ground-Stem I.	Causative Stem II.	Reflexive Stems III.
ደንገፀ	**አደንገፀ**	1. **ተመንደበ**
		3. **ተሰናሰለ**

Causative-Reflexive Stems IV.	Second Reflexive Stem V.
1. **አስተሰንአለ**	**አንጐድጐደ**
3. **አስተሰናአወ**	

A few other rarer forms might be added, but it seems unnecessary to enumerate them in the Scheme.

I. Ground-Stem.

I. Of Multiliteral roots it is only the Quadriliteral which occur in the *Ground-Stem* (¹); and the second letter in the ground-form is always without the vowel, *e. g.* **ደንገፀ**. The place of the second letter is often taken by a long vowel, as in **ማሰነ**, **ዶገነ**, **ቆስሐ**. There is no distinction here between transitive and intransitive pronunciation. In meaning, the greatest variety prevails, corresponding to the variety in the genesis of these roots. With reference to the last point the following differences may be observed: **ቀጥቀጠ** "to bruise",—where the whole root is repeated; **ሐንቀቀ** "to be anxious",—where there is repetition of the third radical; **ሐንበበ** "to put forth berries", **ሐርበደ** "to wallow in the mire", **ፄወወ** "to take prisoner",—with insertion of a soft letter after the first radical; **ጐንደየ** "to loiter", **ወርዘወ** "to become a lad",—with a weak letter annexed; **ደንገፀ** "to be perplexed",

(¹) Only **ጸምሀየየ** or **ጸማሕየየ** "to wither" seems to form an exception,—from the Quadriliteral **ጸምሀየ**, the fourth radical being repeated.

ዐንዘረ "to play the harp", ቶስሐ "to mix",—a formative letter being prefixed; ማህረከ "to carry off as booty", ሐብረተ "to make smooth, to polish", ሐርተመ "to be in misery",—as derivatives from Nominal Stems increased externally; መንኰሰ "to become a monk",—as an example of a foreign word. This diverse origin makes no difference in the formation, for which only the appearance of weak letters in these roots has any significance; *cf.* § 99 *sq.*

II. Causative Stem.

II. The *Causative* is formed, as a rule, by prefixing አ, just as with the triliteral root. It turns intransitive conceptions into transitive, and transitive into double-transitive, *e. g.* መርሰሰ "to grope", አመርሰሰ "to cause to grope"; አሩኅርኅ "to soften *or* soothe"; አወልወለ and አወላወለ "to perturb"; አጣእጦአ and አጠእጦአ "to dispose in order". It farther occasionally predicates finer distinctions, as ጼነወ "to be fragrant *or* to exhale" in the sense of 'spreading an odour', አጼነወ "to smell" in the sense of 'inhaling an odour'. The majority, however, of the Causative Stems which occur, are derived from some Nominal Stem (externally increased), for the purpose of expressing the 'causing, doing, or carrying on' that which the Noun speaks of &c., like አመስረተ "to lay a foundation for", "to establish"; አማሕፀነ "to hand over to be protected by any one", "to entrust"; አሠልጠነ "to give full power to"; አሰንበተ "to keep the Sabbath"; አሌለየ "to spend the night"; አመንሰወ "to lead into temptation"; አጣዐወ "to worship idols". *Quinqueliteral* roots also occur in this stem, especially those which originate in the repetition of the last two radicals (§§ 71, 77): አርመስመሰ "to seek by feeling for" ('to wish to discover by feeling'); አድለቅለቀ "to shake"; አርሳሕስሐ and አርሰሐስሐ ('to render turbid') "to convict of a crime"; አሕመልመለ "to grow green"; አቀየሐይሐ and አቀያሕይሐ "to become reddish" (properly,—'to acquire that colour', and accordingly Causative); also አንጠብጠበ "to drip", and አንጸፍጸፈ.[1] "to pour out in drops"; አኀሰርሰረ "to revile repeatedly"; also a few which only repeat the last radical, but, because they are denominative, have a long vowel following the second radical: አልኆሰሰ "to whisper gently"; አክሞሰሰ "to address any one harshly", "to reproach".

As relics of an obsolete Causative formation by means of the

(1) By origin at least, these two belong to this Class. As regards their conjugation, they may quite as well be referred to Stem V.

prefix **አስ** (§§ 79, 83), **አስቆረረ** "to feel horror", "to abhor", and **አስዮዘዘ** "to become cramped *or* benumbed"(¹) are still preserved. On the *o*-sound of these words *cf.* § 78. **አስቆቀወ** "to howl" has only an external resemblance to these forms, provided the derivation conjectured in § 77 is correct, and the word not rather founded on a root **ቀው-ቀወ**.

§ 86. III. Multiliteral roots, like the Triliteral, form their *Passive-Reflexive Stems* by prefixing **ተ**. In meaning some are passive, some reflexive, some both passive and reflexive; and the reference back to the Subject of the verb is sometimes direct and immediate, sometimes indirect, just as with the Reflexives described in § 80:—**ተማሰነ** "to be corrupted", "to be laid waste"; **ተገፍትአ** "to be utterly destroyed"; **ተሞጣሕ** "to cover *or* veil one's self", and Passive; **ተሴሰየ** "to nourish one's self with anything", and "to eat", with Accusative; **ተቤዘወ** "to ransom one's self", and "to ransom for one's self", and "to be ransomed"; **ተጸምሀየ** "to exhibit a dry appearance", *i. e.* "to put on a sour look"; **ተረኀርኀ** "to be appeased"; **ተጣእጥአ** and **ተጠአጥአ** "to be arranged". This Stem occurs often, as it serves at the same time for a Passive form of Quadriliteral roots of Active signification. But it is often enough derived also (like the Causative) immediately from Nominal Stems, *e. g.* **ተመልአከ** "to become a prince"; **ተመርጕዘ** "to lean upon a staff", and in general terms "to lean upon"; **ተአርወየ** "to become brutal", "to be brutalised"; **ተመሥኀወ** "to chew the cud"; **ተፈልሰፈ** "to philosophize". Worthy of notice is the word **ተአንሰረ** "to become like an eagle", because it is derived from a plural **አንስርት** (**ንስር** "eagle"), so that in form it resembles the verb **ተአንሰሰ** "to be brutalised" (from **እንስሳ**). Also noteworthy is the word **ተጳጳሰ** "to become a Metropolitan", because it has retained the two long *ā*'s from its Stem-word **ጳጳስ** πάππας, so that it must rank as a Quinqueliteral verb. No other Quinqueliterals are as yet known. A Sexliteral word appears also in this Stem: **ተአንተልተለ** "to be impatient *and* unwilling", formed according to § 77 from the Quadriliteral root **አንተለ** (§ 72) still in use.

III. Passive-Reflexive Stems.

The *Reciprocal Stem* is formed from some at least of the Multiliteral roots. The long *ā*, which is introduced after the first

(¹) [Probably, however, this **አስ** is a shortened form of **አስተ**, just as in the Amharic Verbs of the form **አስ**.—Nöldeke.]

radical in that formation in Triliteral roots, is consistently established only after the second radical in Quadriliteral roots, since the first and second radicals in such roots are always more closely associated than the others, and together correspond to the first letter of Triliteral roots:—**ተደናጸወ** "to contend enviously with another about anything"; **ተሰናሰለ** "to be linked together"; **ተሰናአወ** "to be in harmony with one another"; **ተሰካተየ** "to conspire together"; **ተወላወለ** "to be at variance with one's own mind", ("to be perturbed in mind"); **ተጠናቀቀ** "to go to work with accurate scrutiny"; **ተዘያነወ** "to announce to one another" (**ዜነወ**); **ተጸአጸአ** "to worship"; **ተዐማመቀ** "to engage too eagerly in"; **ተጐናደየ** "to loiter" (1). In Quinqueliteral roots the long *ā* is introduced only after the third radical, that the most important syllable might not be too near the beginning: **ተሏኊዋሰሰ** "to whisper gently to one another".

IV. Causative-Reflexive Stem.

IV. *The Causative-Reflexive Stem* from these roots occurs very rarely indeed. Since the roots, which are already long enough in themselves must in this case be still farther lengthened by two additional syllables, such a Stem is avoided as far as possible. As yet I know of only four examples of IV, 1: **አስተሰንአለ** "to grant discharge *or* leave of absence" (**ተሰንአለ** "to take discharge *or* leave"); **አስተአርወየ** "to render wild"; **አስተጠአዋአ** "to arrange"; **አስተጠንቀቀ** "to explain exactly",—and the very same number of examples of IV, 3:—**አስተሰናአወ** "to render in accord"; **አስተጐናደየ** (G. Ad.) "to think one had come too late for a thing"; **አስተወላወለ** "to perplex"; **አስተጠናቀቀ** "to rouse to zeal".

V. Second Reflexive Stem.

§ 87. V. Besides these Stems which are formed both from Triliteral and Multiliteral roots, *another Stem originally Reflexive* makes its appearance, formed by prefixing **አን**. In this there may be easily recognised the Hebrew ־הִנְ (2) and the Arabic ־اِنْ St. VII, employed in the formation of Reflexives and Passives, and originally of a somewhat weaker meaning than ־הִתְ and ־اِتْ. The *a*-pronunciation is quite as peculiar to Ethiopic as the like pronunciation of **አስ** (§ 83). In Nouns which are derived from this Stem, this

(1) **ተኃሕለወ** belongs to Stem III, 1: **ተሐበለየ**, which LUDOLF, '*Lex.*' col. 42, adduces, is to be explained by § 48.

(2) *Cf.* EWALD, '*Hebr. Spr.*' § 123, *a*.

an is simplified into *na*, like *as* into *sa*, just as הִתְ־ or اِتْ is always rendered in Ethiopic by ተ. But this Stem can by no means be formed from all Multiliteral roots. The language has confined it almost wholly to the roots described in § 71, and in strictness to reduplicated Stems of such roots, which express movement to and fro of any kind, and also of light and sound (¹), such as **አንጐድጐደ** "to thunder"; **አንሶሰወ** "to walk about"; **አንከለለ** "to be giddy"; **አንገለገ** (*angállaga*) "to band together" (²). Of other roots only four are known up till now, which form this Stem: **አንጸብረቀ** "to sparkle", "to shine through" ('to be clear, *or* transparent'); **አንፈርዐጸ** "to spring", "to dance"; **አንቃዕደወ** "to lift up (the eyes"); **አንጦልዐ** "to stretch", "to spread out"; and these come very close, in meaning at least, to the first-named forms. Several of these Stems indicate a transitive signification as well as a reflexive one: **አንኰርኰረ** "to roll" (*transitive* and *intransitive*); **አንገርገረ** "to wallow *or* revolve" and "to drive round" (*trs.* and *intrs.*); **አንቀልቀለ** "to totter" and "to shake" (*trs.* and *intrs.*); **አንሶሰወ** "to go" and "to move"; **አንሳዕስዐ** "to bubble", "to boil", also in a transitive sense; **አንሶጠጠ** "to frighten", "to be alarmed" (*trs.* & *intrs.*). The following have a transitive signification only: **አንጦልዐ** "to stretch out"; **አንዘፍዘፈ** "to expand (the wings)"; **አንቃዕደወ** "to lift up (the eyes)". Seeing that **አን**, speaking generally, forms weaker Reflexives than ተ,—almost pure Intransitives in fact,—and seeing that all these roots, except **ጌገየ** and **ጐድጐደ**, are used in Stem V only, and that in particular no new Causatives are derived from them, this phenomenon might without difficulty be attributed to a gradual transition from the intransitive to the transitive meaning, and in most cases perhaps this explanation might suffice. A Passive-Reflexive, however, of some of these formations occurs, formed by means of ተ: **ተንጦልዐ** "to be stretched out", "to stretch one's self out"; **ተንኰርኰረ** (according to Ludolf) "to be rolled about" (*cf.* the words beginning with **ተን**, § 73). It seems to follow from this that the instinct of the language conceived the **አ** of **አን** in several of these formations as being **አ** Causative, as if these were new Causative forms from Nominal

(¹) Even Ludolf teaches that this Stem expresses *impetum quendam vel motum reciprocantem.*

(²) The rest are: **ጌገየ, ሳሕስሐ, ሳዕስዐ, ቀልቀለ, በልበለ, በሕብሐ, በስበሰ, ኰርኰረ, ገርገረ, ጐርጐረ, ጠልጠለ, ሶጠጠ, ጦለለ, ዘሀለለ.**

Stems beginning with ን (by § 85, II)(1). Accordingly the process may be thought of as taking the following course: አንኰርኰረ "to roll" (*intrs.*);—ነኰርኳር "rolling"; Causative አንኰርኰረ "to roll" (*trs.*); ተንኰርኰረ "to be rolled". A certain want of clearness in the consciousness of the language is unmistakeable here (2). The formations which are derived from Nominal Stems without the intervention of a Causative (by § 86, III), ተአንገየ, ተአንሰሰ are not to be confounded with Passive Stems like ተንጠልዐ; for here, just as in ተአንሰረ, ተአንተለ, ተዐንበሰ, the አ is treated as a radical.

II. FORMATION OF TENSES AND MOODS.

General Remarks.— Uses of the Perfect.

§ 88. In the formation of Tenses, Ethiopic like the rest of the Semitic languages, proceeds from the twofold, and not from the threefold division of time. To that original stand-point it has always adhered. Every action or event is conceived as presenting itself either in a finished—and thus realised—state, or in an unfinished state (3). In conformity with this contrasted view of things, only two Tenses have been formed, the one,—the *Perfect*,—to express the finished or completed action, the other,—the *Imperfect*,—to express the unfinished or uncompleted action. To this category of the incomplete, however, there belongs not only that which is happening in the Present, as well as that which is only to be realised in the Future,—so that the Ethiopic Imperfect, generally speaking, corresponds at once to the Present and the Future of other languages,—but also that which is merely *thought of* and *willed*, that

---

(1) [That አ did actually come in before the *in* in these Nifʿal forms, appears plain also from the fact, that the Stems under discussion (*cf. supra*) have *for the most part* a transitive, or causative signification. Words, like "to thunder", "to sparkle", are to be explained exactly like ܐܰܪܥܶܡ, ܐܰܒܪܶܩ, הֵאִיר, أَبْرَقَ &c, properly "to produce light" &c. In the positively Reflexive nature of the *in* or *na*,—one inclining to Passive (and in Hebrew and later Arabic actually becoming Passive),—it would be a very singular thing if the transitive signification had introduced itself thus in Ethiopic without farther assistance.—Nöldeke.]

(2) In Amharic all this is met with in quite the same fashion, though more frequently employed than in Ethiopic; *cf.* Isenberg, p. 54 No. XXIV; p. 56 Nos. VII–X; p. 60 No. VII; [and Guidi, '*Zeitschr. f. Assyr.*' VIII, p. 258 and Note 3.]

(3) V. farther on this point Ewald, '*Hebr. Spr.*' § 134.

which *may* or *must* be realised. Accordingly the Imperfect here becomes also the source of the formation of the so-called Moods of the Verb, through which the conditions of will and necessity are expressed. In Ethiopic, just as in the other Semitic languages, moods are formed from the Imperfect only. The Perfect has produced from itself no special moods. Farther, the moods which have been formed from the Imperfect (¹) are only two in number. With these few tense-forms and conditional forms of the Verb, Ethiopic is able to convey the force of all the much more richly developed Tenses and Moods of the Indo-European languages.

1. As regards the two Tenses (²), *the Perfect* serves first of all and most frequently (*a*) to express the *Past*. Every action which the speaker regards as having happened, or as being past, from the point of time of his speaking, he expresses in this tense. It is the tense therefore which is usually employed in narration. If an action has to be marked as concluded in the past (as in the Greek Perfect), the Perfect also must suffice for this. In isolated cases only, where Germans would use *schon* or *bereits* ('already') along with the Perfect, the Ethiopian may also put ወድአ "he has completed" (³) before the Perfect (and, according to § 180, 1 *a* α, without a ወ), *e. g.* ወዳእነ፡ ቀተርነ "we have (already) shut" Luke 11, 7; [ወዳእኩ፡ ርኢኩ "I have seen already" Hen. 106, 13] (⁴). Farther, the language has nothing but the Perfect to represent an action as already past at a certain point of time in the Past

---

(¹) [It is perhaps unfortunate that Dillmann employs the same word—*Imperfect*—, both as a generic term for the *Tense* which is contrasted with the *Perfect*, and as a specific term for the formation which is now regarded as that *Mood* of the Imperfect Tense which is differentiated from the *Subjunctive*. It would have conduced to clearness, if like Praetorius and others he had restricted the term *Imperfect* to the *Tense*, and used the term *Indicative* for the *Mood*. TR.]

(²) On the question whether the Semitic Perfect is only a later developed form, *cf.* Haupt, '*J. Am. Or. Soc.*', Vol. XIII, pp. LIV, LXI *sq.*, and on the force and signification of the Perfect in contradistinction to the Imperfect, the somewhat prolix explanations of Knudtzon, '*Zeitschr. f. Assyr.*' VI, p. 408 *sqq.*, & VII, p. 33 *sqq.*

(³) In like manner قَدْ is always prefixed in Arabic; Ewald, '*Gr. Arab.*' § 199 *sq.* But the usage mentioned is not so common in Ethiopic. Besides, ወድአ may also be placed after the verb, *e. g.* ጸለመ፡ ወድአ John 6, 17.

(⁴) [This is Flemming's reading,—not Dillmann's, who reads merely ወርኢኩ. TR.]

(*Pluperfect*); and it has to be gathered, merely from the context and the sense of the passage, whether one action has taken place before another in the Past, or not. Thus the Perfect may most readily stand for the Pluperfect in accessory sentences, particularly in circumstantial clauses, *e. g.* Gen. 31, 34 (accessory to vs. 33 and 35); **ኮነ፡ ይቤ** "he had said", Gadla Adām 90, 13; or in sentences which are introduced by the relative pronoun, *e. g.* **ወርእየ፡ ኵሎ፡ ዘገብረ** "and he saw all that he had made" Gen. 1,31; **ዘኮነ፡ አቀሞ** "that he had set up" Gadla Ad. 147, 20; **ዘኮነ፡ ይሰመይ፡ መልአከ፡ ሠናይ** "who had been called 'Good Angel'" Hexaemeron (ed. TRUMPP, Munich 1882), 36, 20 *sq.*; or by relative Conjunctions like **ሶበ**, **እምድኅረ**, **እምአመ** (also **እምኮነ፡ ይሰሪ፡ ሎቱ** "then he would have forgiven him" Gadla Ad. 90, 18). (*b*) Comparatively seldom does the Ethiopic Perfect serve to express Present time, and for the most part in the two following cases merely. (1) When a transaction has already begun, starting from the Past, and is continued up to the Present, the Perfect is employed, *e. g.* **በክርስቶስ፡ ተኅድገ፡ ለነ፡ ኃጢአትነ** "our sin is forgiven us for Christ's sake"; and the use of the Perfect is obligatory, when a Future cannot be thought of as taking its place without an alteration in the sense, *e. g.* **ናሁ፡ ቀርበ፡ ዘያገብአኒ** "Lo, he that betrayeth me is at hand" Matt. 26, 46. Certain actions especially, for which we would use the Present, are mostly expressed in the Perfect, because the Ethiopian conceives them as not so much 'a state of being', as 'a mode of doing or becoming', *e. g.* **አእመርኩ** "I know" ('I have learned'); **ርኢኩ** "I see"; **አፍቀረ** "he loves". In particular the verb **ሀለወ**, "to be",—in the sense of "he is there", or "he is present", almost always occurs in the Perfect, where in our tongue we employ the Present. (2) The other case is met with when an action coincides with the very moment of its announcement in present speech. Such an action the Ethiopian regards as completed with the very utterance of the word, and therefore he puts it in the Perfect, *e. g.* **ናሁ፡ ፈኖኩከ** "Lo, I send thee" Judges 6,14; **ናሁ፡ ወሀብኩከ** "Behold I give thee" Gen. 23,11; **ናሁ፡ አማሕፀንኩከ** *ἰδοὺ παρατίθεμαί σοι* Tob. 10, 12 (1). On the other hand general truths, practices, and customs are expressed mostly by the Imperfect, less frequently by the Perfect. (*c*) The Perfect is employed even to express *Future* actions, first of all in conditional clauses

(1) [*Cf. Kebra Nag.*, Introduction, p. XX.]

and relative clauses of equivalent import, when the future action has to be represented as preceding another action, which is placed still farther on in the future,—a case in which other languages with greater accuracy use the *Futurum exactum*:—**ኵሉ፡ ዘረከበኒ፡ ይቀትለኒ** "every one who findeth (shall find) me shall slay me" Gen. 4, 14; Mark 16, 16; Matt. 23, 12; Gen. 40, 14; [*cf.* also Hen. 14, 6 (**ርኢክሙ**); 62, 15 (**ተንሥኡ**)]; (*cf. infra*, § 205). So too by dint of a lively imagination, the speaker may transfer himself to the future in such a fashion that a matter appears to him as already experienced and accomplished:—it is upon such a conception that the *Perfectum propheticum* in Hebrew is based, a usage which occurs often in exactly the same way in Ethiopic, in Biblical and kindred writings, *e. g.* Hen. 48, 8; 99, 1; and in looser diction, *e. g.* **ህየ፡ ሀለው፡ ብካይ** ἐκεῖ ἔσται κλαυθμός Matt. 8, 12, just as we too can say: "thére—is crying out", instead of "thére—shall be crying out". In conditional, desiderative, and similar clauses, the Ethiopic Perfect corresponds also to the Moods of Preterites in other tongues (§ 205).

Uses of the Imperfect.

§ 89. 2. *The Imperfect*, as the means of expressing uncompleted actions, serves (*a*) to denote, above all, the *Future*. The Imperfect is the readiest and (with the exception of the cases noticed in § 88, 1 *c*) the only mode of expressing the Future, whether (1) the Absolute Future, like **ይከውን** "he will be"; **ዘይመጽእ፡ ዓለም** "the future world", or (2) the Relative Future, both (*a*) the Future as regarded from a certain point of time in the past, *e. g.* "he held his peace to see **እመ፡ ይሠርሖ፡ እግዚአብሔር** whether God was to grant him success" Gen. 24, 21, and (*b*) the Future which precedes another future occurrence (*Futurum exactum*), *e. g.* **ኢይትቀተል፡ እስከ፡ እመ፡ ይቀውም፡ ቅድመ፡ ዐውድ** "he shall not be put to death, until he stand ('shall have stood') before the judgment-seat" Josh. 20, 6. But in the latter case the Perfect occurs much more frequently (§ 88). Farther, as the Moods, according to § 90, serve only to express what is contemplated or purposed, the simple Imperfect[1] is employed to signify any doubtful, uncertain or conditioned

(1) [Dillmann seems to regard those modifications of the Imperfect Tense, which are presented in the *Subjunctive* and its offshoot—the *Imperative*, as constituting the two proper *Moods* of the Ethiopic Verb (*cf.* § 90), while his "plain" or "simple" Imperfect (=the Indicative) is suggested as standing outside

Future, *e. g.* "take no thought ዘትበልዑ τί φάγητε" Matt. 6, 25; "settle for me thy wages ዘእሁበከ (¹) which I am to give thee" ('as thou thinkest') Gen. 30, 28; "he set apart a present ዘይወስድ፡ ለዔሳው which he would *or* could send to Esau" Gen. 32, 14. In the same way it is used,—in Conditional clauses,—of any future event which is put merely as possible, *e. g.* Matt. 11, 23 (§ 205). Even the Future of Will may be expressed in the plain Imperfect, particularly when a decided and stringent command has to be given, taking the form "thou wilt do it" in place of "thou shalt do it". For some other finer modifications, however, in the predicating of a matter in the future, the Ethiopic language employs periphrastic forms, contributed to by the auxiliary verb ሀለወ "to be". Whenever a future transaction has to be represented as continuing in the Future, the Perfect ሀሎ or ሀለወ is joined to the Imperfect of the principal verb, somewhat like *amaturus est* in Latin; and the Imperfect, as containing the main determining idea, takes the first place, *e. g.* ይጸሐፍ፡ ሀሎ "there will continue to be recording" Hen. 98, 7; 104, 7; ይትሀጐሉ፡ ሀለዉ "they will perish" ('be perishing') 52, 9; ዘይከውን፡ ሀሎ "what will be in the future" 52, 2. But the principal verb may also follow the auxiliary, *e. g.* እንተ፡ ሀለወት፡ ትትፌጸም፡ ዲበ፡ ምድር፡ በመዋዕሊሁ "which (*f.*) shall be done on the earth in his days" Hen. 106, 18; *cf. ibid.* 99, 2. Naturally too the same periphrasis may have the sense of a Future just impending (*Futurum instans*), *e. g.* ይመጽእ፡ ሀሎ "he is about to come" Hen. 10, 2; ትሰጠም፡ ሀለወት "it (*f.*) is on the point of sinking" 83, 7. Meanwhile, precisely to indicate the last-mentioned variety of modification of the Future, a periphrasis,—made up of ሀለወ and a suffix pronoun (with the force of a Dat.) followed by the Subjunctive of the principal verb,—has become more usual, and is very frequently employed (²), *e. g.* ዘሀለዎ፡ ይምጻእ ὁ μέλλων ἔρχεσθαι Matt. 11, 14; 17,10; ሀለዎ፡ ያግብእዎ "they will (shortly) deliver him up" Matt. 17, 22,

of the sphere of Mood, and as being a mere counter-balance of the Perfect Tense. It would conduce to clearness of nomenclature, as well as to accuracy, to follow Praetorius and other scholars, in holding the General Imperfect Tense as being divided into two *Moods*, viz. (1) the *Indicative* (=Dillmann's Imperfect), and (2) the *Subjunctive*, including the *Imperative* as a sub-form. tr.]

(¹) On the other hand ዘእሁበከ, which might also stand, would mean—"which I am to give" ('as thou hast determined').

(²) The Greek μέλλειν is also expressed in this way.

and similarly in 2, 13; 17, 12; Hen. 104, 5. Still more frequently some definite shade of the Future,—as in the notions of *will, shall, must,*—is expressed by this device, inasmuch as **ሀለወ** with a suffix means "it is incumbent on one to—", *e. g.* **ምንተ፡ ትገብሩ፡ ሀለወክሙ** "what will you do (then)?" Hen. 97,3; 101,2; **ሀለወክሙ፡ ትርአይዎ** "you will be obliged to see him", "you must (then) see him" Hen. 55, 4; 98, 12; Matt. 16, 21; Gen. 15, 13; 18, 19; Ex. 16, 23;—similarly **ኮኑ፡ .... ይስግዱ** "they had to worship" Gadla Ad. 147,18 *sq.* Occasionally the suffix pron. for **ሀለወ** is wanting, as in Hen. 100, 8; and **ሀለወ** stands also, although comparatively seldom, after the Subjunctive, Hen. 104, 5.

(*b*) But, by its very conception, the Imperfect expresses also *that which is coming into being*, that namely which already is in process of becoming, but which is not yet completed. (*α*) It is therefore the most obvious tense, and the one most frequently employed, to indicate the *Present* (*Praesens*), especially when the action of the Present is not one which passes by in one moment, *e. g.*:—"tell John **ዘትሰምዑ፡ ወዘትሬእዩ** what you are (at this very time) hearing and seeing" Matt. 11, 4. And it is so much in common use for Present time, that even the Present Participle is usually expressed periphrastically by this tense: **ዘይዘርእ** "a sower", "sowing" &c. ("who sows" Impf.); or **ርኢክዎ፡ የሐውር** "I see him go" ('going'—'that he is going'—). And where usages, customs, and actions, which are continuous or which are often repeated, are delineated, the Imperfect is always summoned to take the duty first; and it is comparatively seldom that the Perfect is used instead. (*β*) But, just as frequently and usually, *that which was coming into being in the Past* is denoted by this tense, and then it answers quite regularly to the Latin *Imperfectum*. Whenever in narration an action has to be represented as continuing, or as being gradually accomplished, or as being repeated, the Imperfect is used throughout: "the governor was wont to release some one at the feast" **ያለምድ፡ አሐይዎ** Matt. 27, 15; **አኮኑ፡ ይነድድ፡ ልብነ፡ ዘከመ፡ ይነግረነ** οὐχὶ ἡ καρδία ἡμῶν καιομένη ἦν ἐν ἡμῖν, ὡς ἐλάλει ἡμῖν; Luke 24, 32; **ዘልፈ፡ እነብር፡ ምስሌክሙ፡ ወእሜህር** "continually I sat with you and taught" Matt. 26, 55; **እምአሚሃ፡ ይፈቅድ፡ ይርከብ፡ ሣኅተ** "from that time he sought (continually) to find an opportunity" 26, 16; Gen. 27, 41; 25, 21; in the description of the manners of Noah's time, Matt. 24, 38 *sq.*, and similar instances in

Matt. 4,23, and Gen. 2,6. The Imperfect is therefore the tense of circumstantial clauses, in which the accessory circumstances, accompanying the main action, are described, whether they are introduced by **ወ**, **እንዘ**, or in some other way, *e. g.* **እንዘ፡ ይበልዑ፡ ይቤ** "while they ate, he said" Matt. 26,21; **ወውእቱሰ፡ ይነውም** "while he slept" 8,24; Gen. 3,8; **ሀለዉ፡ ዕራቃኒሆሙ፡ ወኢየኀፍሩ** "they were naked and were not ashamed" Gen. 2,25. In smoothly flowing narration also, statements which describe anything of a circumstantial nature appear in the Imperfect, *e. g.* **ወሀለወ፡ ብእሲ፡ ወይነብር፡ ውስተ፡ ደብረ፡ ኤፍሬም፡ ወነሥአ፡ ሎቱ፡ ብእሲተ** Judges 19,1. If, however, duration in past time has to be expressed still more precisely, so as to bring into more distinct prominence the notion of the customary character of an action, or its coincidence with some accessory circumstance or other, then the language has once more at its disposal, for this purpose, the periphrasis constituted by **ሀለወ** or **ኮነ** "to be", followed by the Imperfect of the verb concerned(1):—*e. g.*: **ኮነ፡ ይገብር፡ ግብረ፡ ብርት** "he was wont to fabricate implements of brass" Gen. 4, 22; **ወሀሎ፡ ዮሐንስ፡ ያጠምቅ፡ በገዳም** "John baptised, ('used to baptise') in the wilderness" Mark. 1,4; **ወሎጥሰ፡ ሀሎ፡ ይነብር፡ ወስተ፡ አንቀጽ** "just while Lot was sitting in the gate" Gen. 19,1; 18,22; **ኮንኩ፡ እባርክ፡ ለእግዚእ፡ .... ወናሁ** "I was just praising God ...., when lo (they called me)" Hen. 12, 3; **ኮነ፡ ይትፌማሕ** Gadla Ad. 95,28; **ኮነ፡ ይደሉ** "it was fitting" = "it would have been fitting" Gadla Ad. 90,21; but also **ኮኑ .... ኀደሩ** "*habitabant*" Gadla Ad. 103,9; and even **ነበሩ፡ ይሕንጹ** "they kept on building" Gadla Ad. 164,1 *sqq.* [and **ነበርኩ፡ እጼሊ** "I kept on praying" *Philosophi Abessini* (Littmann) 20,23]. In contrast to the similar periphrasis for the Present in the Future (v. *supra*), **ሀለወ** and **ኮነ** must stand first here. A case, different from those which have hitherto been described, arises when the speaker or narrator transfers himself into past time in so lively a manner that he represents it as passing at that very moment, or as being present to himself and his hearers (*Praesens historicum*). In such a case, actions may be described in the Imperfect, which in less lively narration would necessarily have been expressed in the Perfect. This turn of speech is not very common in Ethiopic; but upon it depends the universal use of **ይቤ** "he said" (literally, "says he") in narration.

(1) Just as in Arabic: Ewald, '*Gr. Arab.*' § 208.

Derivation of the Moods from the Imperfect Tense.

§ 90. From the Imperfect, as the expression of uncompleted action, or of action coming into being, are farther derived the *Moods* (§ 88 *in init.*). Ethiopic has developed only two. In particular, if the action coming into being has to be set forth as one that is willed (whether it is one that is founded in the will of the acting Subject or in the will of another), then this condition is denoted by a special form of the Imperfect, which we shall henceforth call the *Subjunctive.* The Subjunctive stands wherever the expression of purpose, or of will or wish is in question. It stands not only in dependent and subordinate clauses, but also in simple and direct deliverances, and therefore it has at once the force of a Subjunctive and a Jussive. It is accordingly employed in plain command (unless the Imperfect(1) is preferred, by § 89), either with an introductory conjunction, as in ለይኩን፡ ብርሃን "Let there be light!" Gen. 1, 3, or without it, as in ያውስብ "he shall marry" Matt. 22, 24 (for the second person, however, the Imperative is used). Farther it appears as a Cohortative, *e. g.* ንንድቅ "Let us build!" Gen. 11, 4, and in wishing, as in እግዚአብሔር፡ ይዕቀብከ "The Lord preserve thee!" Ps. 120, 4. Even in Interrogative clauses, it makes its appearance, whenever the action is conceived as one which is willed by some one, *e. g.* እኅድግኑ "am I to abandon?" Judges 9, 9; እፎ፡ እግብሮ፡ ለዝንቱ፡ ነገር "how can I act in this way (that you require of me)?" Gen. 39, 9; and so in all other sentences of whatever kind, *e. g.* አእመርነ፡ ከመ፡ ንሰብሖ(2) "we know that we must praise him" Hen. 63, 4, whereas ከመ፡ ንሴብሖ means "that we shall praise him"; or አልቦ፡ ዘይስማዕ፡ ቃሎሙ፡ መኑሂ "there is no one whatever, who is to hear their voice", *i. e.*: 'no man must hear it!' Josh. 6, 10. Quite as frequent or still more frequent employment is found for the Subjunctive in dependent or subordinate clauses, which attach to the main clause the object aimed at or only some purposed result, whether the purposed action (or result) may be *immediately* subordinated to the main action, as in አዘዘ፡ የሀቡ "commanded (he) that they give" Matt. 19, 7, ኅድግ፡ ንርአይ "allow that we see" *i. e.* "let us see", 27, 49; መጽአ፡ ይኅሥሥ "he came to seek" 18, 11; or be subordinated *by means of a relative pronoun*, as in "they sought false witnesses በዘ፡ ይቀትልዎ through

(1) [That is to say,—the Indicative. TR.]

(2) [Flemming's edition reads:—ንሰብሐ. TR.]

whom they might put him to death" 26,59; or *by means of a conjunction*, as in አገበሮሙ፡ ከመ፡ ይዕርጉ "he constrained them to go up into" 14,22 &c. Accordingly it must stand regularly after certain final Conjunctions, particularly after ከመ "in order that", and suchlike, and farther, after those which contain the idea of "before", "not yet" (§ 170), *e. g.* እምቅድመ፡ ይብቊል "before it (*i. e.* 'herb or grass') grew" Gen. 2,5,—because in such clauses lies the meaning that there is something to come about, or to be *determined*, but that it is not yet realised (¹). On all these cases, which are merely indicated here, v. *infra* in the Syntax.

The Imperative is a special ramification of the Subjunctive, and has been developed out of it. Although it may be formed from all verbal stems, it is only used in the second person, and never in a subordinate relation, but only in direct speech by way of command, wish, request &c. It takes the place of the second person of the Subjunctive, so far as the latter is Jussive. But since it admits of absolutely no subordination to any other conception, and can only be set down as an independent summons, it is again replaced by the Subjunctive as soon as the summons is preceded and conditioned by a negative.

General Rules of Formation in the Perfect and Imperfect Tenses.

§ 91. *The formation of these two Tenses and Relations (Perfect and Imperfect) of the Verb* is effected by the co-operation of two formative expedients. The one consists in *the different way of attaching to the Stem the additions which form the Persons of the Verb*. Seeing that a Verbal stem, on entering upon the process of Tense-formation, at the same time brings to view of itself the distinction between the persons, there is actually no Tense-formation without Personal-formation; and thus the Semitic tongue was enabled to make use of Personal-formation as a means also of Tense-formation. The contrast between the Perfect and the Imperfect is in fact given expression to by the contrast presented by the two possible positions of the signs used in indicating the Persons. In forming the Perfect the Personal sign is attached to the end of the stem, so that *e. g.* መልአት means:—"full (is) she"; but in forming the Imperfect it is attached to the beginning of the stem, so that *e. g.* ትመልእ means: "she (is about to be) full". In the latter case the action is represented as something still standing *before* the person, in the former as something already set *behind*

(¹) *Cf.* the like in Arabic: Ewald, '*Gr. Arab.*' § 210.

the person; and by this device the essential difference between the two Tenses is hit off with great subtlety. Along with this formative expedient is associated the second, *viz.*—*Internal Vowel-Change.* This change is very simple in Ethiopic, as it now lies before us:—In all Stems of active signification the characteristic vowel following the second-last radical, if it is ĕ in the Perfect, passes into ă in the Imperfect, and if it is ă in the Perfect, into ĕ in the Imperfect. But in Reflexive Stems, which at the same time serve as Passives, and generally are closely allied to the Passive, this change is either not carried out at all [1], or only to a partial extent. For by another rule which takes effect here, the Passive must take, in the Imperfect, ă in the place where the Active has ĕ. This ă prevails without exception in the Imperfect of the stronger Reflexive Stems; and it was due only to the fact that some had introduced into the Perfect an ĕ instead of ă in the critical position, that there emerged a farther partial change between Perfect and Imperfect. On the other hand the weaker Reflexive Stem V (belonging to the Multiliteral Roots) exhibits the same change as the Active Stems. Both the Tense-forms originally possessed,—in those Persons, to which no formative addition was appended,—a vowel-ending (just as in Arabic), which, following the distinction of the tenses, must have changed between *a* for the Perfect and *e* (*u*) for the Imperfect. Such vowel-ending constituted a farther mark of distinction between the two tenses, and served also to distinguish Moods in the Imperfect Stem, by different pronunciation. But Ethiopic soon gave up entirely the vowel-ending of the Imperfect at least, *i. e.* the *e* (just as it did the termination of the Nominal Stems, § 38), while it regularly [2] preserved the ending *a* in the Perfect. And so by this difference a new contrast is brought about between the two Tenses:—The Perfect has a fuller vowel-expression; the Imperfect ends with the last radical in the forms mentioned.

(1) And just as little in the Arabic Stems V and VI.

(2) It is only in the one Perfect **ሀሎ**, used for **ሀለወ** "to be", and occurring quite as frequently in the latter form, that the ă has been thrown off or has blended into an ō, so that it resembles the form of expression of verbs *tertiae infirmae* with the Syrians. That the distinction in meaning between **ሀሎ** and **ሀለወ**, which Ludolf sets up in his '*Lexicon*', is incorrect, has been already pointed out by Drechsler. [On the slight variation of this final ă in the Abyssinian dialects, v. Nöldeke, "*Beitr. z. sem. Sprachwiss.*", p. 15, Note 2.]

Older Form of Imperfect Tense used as the Subjunctive Mood.— Fuller Form as the pure Imperfect [= the Indicative Mood.]

In the other Semitic languages, if they possess Moods at all, such Moods are formed from the Imperfect, partly by modification of the final vowel and of the personal-endings, and partly by shortening; and in the most ancient times this appears to have been the case also in Ethiopic. But in still early days the final vowels here must have fallen away; and the fuller endings which are still retained in Arabic, must have been greatly curtailed and abbreviated, so that they became incapable of showing by themselves, through farther abbreviation, the distinction of Moods. But now, while Hebrew,—which so far had followed nearly the same course as Ethiopic,—either gave up entirely the distinction of Moods, or expressed it by shortening interior formative-, or radical-vowels, and by cutting off final radical-vowels, Ethiopic took a different path. It kept the old form of the Imperfect, curtailed as it was, for the Subjunctive, and from it fashioned a new and *fuller* form for the Imperfect [or Indicative]. It compensated for the vowels and nasals discarded at the end, by interpolating an *a* in the stem itself after the first radical (and in the case of the Multiliteral verb, after the third-last radical) (1). Thus there arose a new Mood-distinction, and a form of the Imperfect which diverges from the Imperfect-forms of all the other Semitic languages [with the exception of Assyrian]. And, since the Imperfect [or Indicative] thus depends upon a later formation, and the old form is represented rather by the Subjunctive, we must, in discussing this class of forms, start always with the Subjunctive as the Ground-form. The Imperative proceeds from the Subjunctive, with which it is intimately allied in meaning, the Personal sign of the 2nd pers. Subj. being discarded from the beginning of the same. In every other respect the Imperative agrees completely with the Subjunctive: only, in one or two verbs of the First Stem it exhibits farther and more pronounced abbreviations.

In the several roots and stems these general rules of formation are applied in the following manner.

---

(1) Like the method followed in Ethiopic in the inner Feminine formation of one or two Adjectives, where formative vowels, which originally were attached externally, forced their way into the interior of the form (§ 129). On the corresponding forms in Assyrian, v. BARTH, '*Zeitschr. f. Assyr.*' II, p. 383 *sq.*, and HOMMEL, ZDMG XLIV, p. 539. On the like in the Arabic dialect of Zanzibar, v. PRAETORIUS, *ibid* XXXIV, p. 225. *Cf.* also KÖNIG, p. 82; PHILIPPI, '*Beitr. z. Assyr.*' II, p. 383 *sq.*, and REINISCH, '*Die Beḍauye-Sprache*', Vol. III, p. 136 *sqq.*

I. Tense and Mood Formation in—1. Simple Ground-Stem. — Transitive and Intransitive Pronunciation.

§ 92. I. 1. In the simple Ground-Stem of the Tri-radical Root, the Transitive and Intransitive modes of pronunciation are differentiated, in accordance with § 76. In the former the Perfect is given as **ነገረ** (*nagára*) "he spoke"; in the latter, as **ገብረ** (*gábra*) "he was active". In the Subjunctive the characteristic vowel takes up a position after the second radical, the first and third having no vowel. The Personal sign for the 3rd pers., **ይ**, by § 101, unites with the first radical to form a syllable with the help of the vowel *ĕ*. The formative vowel after the second radical is *ĕ* for Transitive verbs, according to § 91 (to which *ĕ* the *i—e*, and *u—o* of other tongues have been reduced), and *ă* for Intransitive. Thus the corresponding Subjunctives are given as **ይንግር** and **ይግበር**, with the accent on the first syllable: *yénger, yégbar*(1). The Imperative has the sound **ንግር** and **ግበር** *negér* (or *néger*?), *gebár*. The Imperfect(2) [or Indicative] anew interpolates an *a* after the first radical, by which proceeding the Personal sign is isolated, and it is then pronounced with a mere vowel-touch (*Sh^e^va*). The new vowel takes the accent, and so greatly dominates the word that an *ă*, in the syllable following it, must be reduced to *ĕ*, thus:—**ይነግር**, **ይገብር** *yenáger, yegáber*. The distinction between a transitive and an intransitive pronunciation accordingly disappears in this case. Meanwhile,—just as in the other Semitic languages,—there are several verbs in Ethiopic which merely in one of the two tense-forms follow either the transitive or the intransitive form(3); while

(1) *Cf.* Trumpp, p. 530; König, p. 158 *sq.*—In Tigraï a short vowel is inserted after the first radical, in the Subjunctive (Praetorius, '*Tigriña*', p. 276 Rem.; Schreiber, '*Manuel de la langue Tigraï*', p. 37), which Nöldeke (GGA 1886, No. 26, p. 1014) regards as original.

(2) [V. Notes to §§ 88, 89, as to Dillmann's nomenclature of the Moods:— to be kept in view in what follows. tr.]

(3) [Dillmann means that there are several Ethiopic verbs which are neither solely transitive in form nor solely intransitive, throughout both the Perfect and the Subjunctive. So far as can be made out from what follows, the different varieties under this relation would be:

1. Tr.	in *Perf.* and	Tr. in *Subj.*	regular
2. Intr.	„	Intr. „	regular
3. Intr.	„	Tr. & Intr. „	
4. Tr. & Intr.	„	Tr. & Intr. „	
5. Tr. & Intr.	„	Intr. „	
6. Intr.	„	Tr. „	
7. Tr.	„	Intr. „	tr.]

on the other hand there are some which fluctuate between the two forms in the Subjunctive, just as according to § 76 several verbs admit of both even in the Perfect. The following verbs fluctuate between the two forms of pronunciation in the Subjunctive:—**ቀርበ** "to draw near", **ይቅረብ** and **ይቅርብ**; **ኀልቀ** "to pass away", **ይኅለቅ** and **ይኅልቅ** (v. Gen. 8, 3); **ዐርገ** "to ascend"; **ፀንሰ** "to be pregnant"; **ጸልመ** "to be dark"; **ደክመ** "to be tired"(1). The verb **ሰክበ** and **ሰከበ** "to lie down" forms both **ይስከብ** and **ይስክብ**; **ፈተወ** and **ፈትወ** "to wish", both **ይፍተው** (**ይፍቶ**) and **ይፍትው** (**ይፍቱ**). On the other hand, of those verbs which shift about in the Perfect between the two forms, some exhibit in the Subjunctive the Intransitive form exclusively, or at all events in the great majority of cases:—**ይምሰል** "may he be like!"; **ይኅበር** "let him be connected!"; **ይስአል** "let him ask!"; **ይፍረይ** "let him be fruitful!". The following have only the Intransitive form in the Perfect, and only the Transitive in the Subjunctive:—**ነግሠ** "to be king", **ይንግሥ**; **ገዝፈ** "to be thick", **ይግዝፍ**; **ነፍጸ** "to make escape", **ይንፍጽ**. Contrast with these the following, which have the Transitive form in the Perfect and the Intransitive in the Subjunctive:—**ረከበ** "to find", **ይርከብ**; **ነበረ** "to sit", **ይንበር**; **ዐቀበ** "to keep"; **ዐቈረ** "to wrap up"; **ዐተበ** "to bless with the sign of the cross"; **ከዐወ** "to pour". The Imperative invariably follows the Subjunctive.

T. and M. Formation of Aspirate Verbs.

(1) Of the *Aspirate Verbs* those which have an Aspirate as their first letter have only this peculiarity, that, by § 44, they furnish the Personal sign of the Imperfect with the vowel *ă* instead of a fugitive *ĕ*: **የዐርግ**, **የኀብር**, **የዐቅብ** &c.(2).

(2) *Those which have an Aspirate as their final letter*, whether they be transitive or intransitive, have all, by § 45, the form in the Perfect **መልአ** "to be full"; **ሠርዐ** "to set in order" (*mál'a, šárʿa*); and likewise, in the Subjunctive, seeing that here the Aspirate by rule requires *ă* before it instead of *ĕ* (§ 44), they have only one form of pronunciation, lengthening this *ă* into *ā*, by § 46: **ይምላእ**, **ይሥራዕ**, **ይብቋዕ**,—Imperative: **ምላእ**, **ሥራዕ**, **ምጻእ**, **ስማዕ**. But

---

(1) [*Cf.* also *Kebra Nag.*, p. XXXI, *sub* **ዐጠነ** and **ዘከረ**.]

(2) On the other hand, after **ኢ** "not", **ይ** appears as a result of retrogressive Assimilation, *e. g.* **ኢይሐድራ** "they (*f.*) do not dwell"; v. König, p. 118 *sqq*.

they exhibit no peculiarity in the Imperfect: ይመልእ, ይሠርዕ, ይበቍዕ.

(3) *Verbs with an Aspirate for their middle letter* run, when transitive, like ለአከ "to send"; ሰሐበ "to draw", but when intransitive, by § 45, like ልህቀ "to grow", ክሕደ "to deny", ንእሰ "to be little": Several vary between the two forms (§ 76). In the Subjunctive these roots also have *ă* instead of *ĕ*, on account of the Aspirate (§ 44),—so that from transitives and intransitives alike we have the formations ይስሐብ, ይክሐድ, ይስዐር, ይምሐር. In the Imperative, however, one says regularly, by § 44, ሰሐብ, ከሐድ, instead of ስሐብ, ክሐድ &c. The Imperfect, by § 45, takes the form ይስሕብ *yeséḥeb*, instead of ይሰሕብ (1); and similarly ይጽሕፍ "he writes"; ይልህቅ "he grows"; ይድኅን "he saves himself"; but ንዋዕል appears, as well as ንውዕል Gen. 33, 14 *var.*

Only a few roots in frequent employment, having weak Aspirates, exhibit peculiar forms here. ርእየ "to see" has the form ይርአይ in the Subj., but, by § 46, it lengthens ይርአይ into ይሬኢ in the Imperf.; and in the same way II, 1 የሬኢ; Imper. ርኢ and ረአይ. It is imitated now and then by ርዕየ "to herd", Imperfect ይሬዒ; but this formation is not founded in the nature of the ዐ; and the better class of manuscripts usually have ይርዒ for it (*cf. infra* § 94). Farther ስእነ "to be unable" might lengthen its *ĕ* in the Imperf., thus ይሴእን, as appears from Ludolf's '*Lex.*', col. 172, although, as a rule, it forms ይስእን; *cf.* Dillmann's '*Lex.*', col. 377. Then the root ብህለ "to say" (little used now in the Perfect) discards its ሀ in the Subj. and Imperf.: accordingly we have the Subj. ይበል (for ይብሀል), and the Imper. በል. In the Imperfect the *ĕ* is at the same time lengthened into *ē*, after the manner of the foregoing instances: thus we get ይቤል (§ 46); and, as ል is cut off in all those Persons, in which it would become the final letter (§ 58), the result is ይቤ. But seeing that this ይቤ is invariably used (§ 89 *ad fin.*) with the force of a Preterite, "he said", the language fashioned a new Imperfect ይብል, for ይብሀል, in the sense—"he says" and "he will say". In like manner although the Subj. of ክህለ "to be able" is given in full ይክሀል, the Imperf.

(1) So that the form,—to judge by the written character,—coincides with the Subjunctive of strong Transitive verbs. In pronunciation it is essentially different from it.

12*

is usually shortened into ይክል (*yekel*); but ይክሀል occurs also, v. I Kings, 26, 25. Roots in which two Aspirates meet together are rare (§ 66): ብሕአ "to become sour"; አኀዘ "to take", "to catch" (1). The latter forms the Subj. ይእኀዝ, Imper. አኀዝ, Imperf. ይእኅዝ. The Subj. የአኀዝ, which Ludolf found in an old manuscript, Ps. 15, 6 and 34, 9 (*cf.* also John 7, 30) and for which he printed የአኅዝ (as Subj. of St. I, 2), may perhaps be explained by ይእ having been spoken at one time like יֶאֱ.

T. and M. Formation of Weak Verbs:— Verbs *med. gem.*

§ 93. Of *roots with doubled final letter* (ע"ע) the Transitive Perfect is pronounced like ኀሠሠ "to seek"; ነበበ "to speak"; and the Intransitive, like ሐመ (*ḥámma*, for ሐምመ *ḥámᵉma*, § 55) "to be ill", "to suffer". Some take both modes of expression:—ነደደ and ነደ "to burn"; ሐጸጸ and ሐጸ "to become small", "to decrease"; ጐየየ and ጐየ "to flee". From these come the Transitive Subjunctives ይኅሥሥ, ይንብብ (ይሕትት, ይስድድ, ይግስስ); — also from ጸበበ "to compress" and "to be narrow", ይጽብብ.—Imper. ኅሥሥ, ንብብ, ስድድ,—but the Intransitive ይንደድ, ይጕየይ (2), ይዕየይ (3); Imper. ንደድ &c. The Imperfect is pronounced ይነድድ *yenáded*, ይነብብ, የኀሥሥ (§ 92).

Verbs *prim. voc.*

Of *Roots beginning with a Vowel*, the only one beginning with *i* which is as yet vouched for in this Stem (Simple Ground-Stem) is የብሰ (*intr.*) "to be dry", Imperf. ይየብስ, Subj. ይይበስ, Imper. ይበስ. But those which begin with *u* are numerous. Transitive and Intransitive forms are found in the Perfect:—*e. g.* ወለደ "to beget", ወገረ "to throw" and "to stone", ወረደ "to descend", ወሰደ "to lead away"; ወድቀ (rarely ወደቀ Numb. 14, 5) "to fall"; with middle Aspirate: ውሕዘ "to flow", ውኅደ "to become few", ውኅጠ (and ወኅጠ) "to gulp down", ወሀበ "to give"; with final Aspirate: ወግአ "to butt", "to push"; ወፅአ "to go out". Only a small number of these preserve the initial *u*-sound in the Subjunctive, hardened into a semi-vowel in the combination ይው (§ 49), whence in transitive form ይውግር (Lev. 24, 16; Deut. 22, 24), ይውርቅ, ይውፍር, ይውቅር, ይውጥን, ይውሩ, ይውቅስ Acts 19, 33;

---

(1) አኀረ has Subj. I, 2 ትእኅር, according to a single reading in Ex. 22, 28, in the sense "to delay"; other MSS. have II, 1.

(2) Also ይጕይዩ Numb. 10, 34.

(3) [For the form ይጽኅን, along with ይጽንን, from ጸነ, ጸነነ "to be inclined" v. *Kebra Nag.* 117 b 12.]

of Aspirate roots: ይውኃእ Hen. 89, 43; ይውኃዕ ("to suck") Hebrews 5,12. In the majority of cases the sound,—ይው, which is not much in favour, is simplified by rejecting the ው (§ 53), and then, when the verbs are transitive, the second syllable is strengthened by assuming *ă* instead of *ĕ*. True, the form ይስድ (*yesĕd*) also occurs, *e. g.* in Gen. 27, 10, Note; Ps. 42, 3; but usually *ă* prevails:—ይለድ (1), ይገር John 8, 7 (as well as the above-mentioned ይውግር), ዩፈር (the *u* being retained in this case after the preformative), ይቀር, ይጠን; just as in the Intransitives ይደቅ, ይረድ. From middle-Aspirate verbs, የሐዝ (§ 44); የዐል Luke 19,5; የኅጥ Ps. 68, 18; የሀብ. From final-Aspirate verbs, ይፃእ. Whenever the first radical has fallen out in the Subjunctive, it ceases also to appear in the Imperative, thus ደቅ, ረድ, ለድ, ሀብ, ፃእ; and from forms like ይሰድ, comes the Imperative ሰድ Ex. 33, 12; Gen. 42, 19 (although now and then ስድ is also found, as well as ይስድ). But even from ይውግር there is derived, by rejecting the first radical, ግር Ex. 1, 22 (—yet we have also ውግር, and ገር from ይገር, v. Notes *ad loc.*): and similarly we say ቅር (from ወቀረ "to hew") Deut. 10, 1, as well as ቀር, ውቅር, and ውቀር Ex. 34, 1, v. Notes (2).

The Imperfect of all these verbs uniformly runs thus: ይወድቅ, ይወልድ, ይወርስ, ይወፅእ, and from Middle-Aspirates, ይውሕዝ, ይውዕል &c. Only, the much employed word ወሀበ, by transposing the *u*-sound in ይውህብ *yewéheb*, invariably takes instead of it the form ይሁብ (3).

Verbs med. inf.

Roots mediae infirmae of both kinds,—*i. e.* both with *i* and *u* as middle radical—, do away with (§ 50) the *ă* or *ĕ* in the *Perfect*, which ought to make itself heard after the second radical, thus obliterating any distinction between a Transitive and an Intransitive form of pronunciation. They invariably blend their vowel-radical with the formative *ă* of the first syllable into a mixed sound: ጾረ "to bear", "to carry"; ሮጸ "to run"; ሖረ "to go"; ሤመ "to set"; ሜጠ "to turn"; ቤተ "to pass the night"; and so too when the

(1) *Cf.* يَلِدُ, יֵלֵד; Philippi, ZDMG XL, p. 653.

(2) Some of the verbs concerned here are not yet supported by examples in all the forms.

(3) In accordance with § 68, this may be regarded as a transition from a Vowel-beginning Root to a Vowel-centred one; but in that case it must be assumed at the same time, that here the old form of the Imperfect, which elsewhere took the meaning of a Subj., continued to be retained.

verb is at the same time *tertiae gutturalis*: ሞአ "to conquer"; በአ "to come"; ጼሐ "to make a way"; ቄሐ "to be red" (1). It is only those, which are at the same time vowel-ending, that take another form, § 94. When Ludolf in his Lexicon cites forms like ተወነ, ኀወሠ, ፀወገ, መየሰ, ረየፀ, ሰየበ, ሰየፈ, ደየነ, he has given them this shape only, because he had not yet met with their more exact expression in the Perfect, in the course of his reading. The forms of the Perfect ገየረ, ፊየተ, ፀወሰ are vouched for, it is true, but they appear to represent Stem I, 2 (2). The *Subjunctive* from roots *mediae ī* takes throughout, by § 50, the form ይሚጥ, ይሢም, ይሂድ, ይዓሊ, ይጠይቅ, ይሒስ Matt. 11, 20; Jude 9:—*Imperative* ሚጥ, ሢም, ጺሕ Is. 40, 2. Roots middle *ū* also nearly all have the form described in § 50:—ይጹር, ይፋጽ, ይዑድ, ይሡዕ, ይኑኅ; Imperative ጹር, ዑድ, ሡዕ. Also, ኮነ "to be" has mostly ይኩን in the Subjunctive, and ኩን in the Imperative; but, according to §§ 26 and 36, these forms may be still farther shortened into ይኵን and ኵን. It is, however, unmistakeable that an intransitive form existed also at one time in the Subjunctive and Imperative, at least in roots *mediae ū*, and that this form caused the intransitive vowel *a*,—which has to be given after the second radical—, to remain still audible (3).—It is most frequently preserved still in ይሖር, ሖር, particularly in older manuscripts, though later ones generally have ይሑር, ሑር: So too with ይጾር and ይጹር (4). It may be met with too in other instances here and there, *e. g.* in ሶቅ = ሱቅ; v. Dillmann's '*Lexicon*'. In roots *mediae ī*, such differentiation of an intransitive form cannot yet be authenticated, even for more ancient times. Finally, the Subjunctive of the two roots በአ "to come" and ሞአ "to conquer" were perhaps at one time also pronounced ይበአ, ይሞአ; but, under the influence of the final Aspirate, *ō* passed over, in accordance with § 44, into an un-

(1) *Cf.* the Arabic *Imāla*; König, p. 67; Barth ZDMG XLIV, p. 698. [The *Imāla*, of course, is the 'deflection' of the *a*-sound towards the *i*-sound; v. Wright's '*Ar. Gramm.*' 3rd ed. I, p. 10 C. tr.]

(2) This cannot be determined with certainty before the relative Imperfect-forms have been found.

(3) It is distinguished from the Transitive form, just as יָבוֹא is from יָקוּם, or يَخَافُ from يَقُولُ.

(4) [V. also *Kebra Nag.* 'Introd.' p. XVII.] V. on the other hand König, p. 151 *sq.*

alterable $\bar{a}$ (§ 46), whence we invariably have ይበእ, ይማእ, and in the Imperative በእ, ማእ[1]. The Imperfect of all these roots, of both kinds, whether transitive or intransitive, is formed precisely as in the strong verb; but the vowel-radical which follows the interpolated (v. § 92) and accented *á* must be hardened into a semivowel, thus: ይከውን, ይጸውር, ይነውኁ, የዐውድ, የሐውር, ይበውእ, ይሠይም, ይቀይሕ, የሀይድ, የሐይስ Rev. 2, 4. (On the pronunciation v. § 50).

Weak Verbs continued:— Verbs *tert. inf.*

§ 94. *Roots tertiae infirmae* of both kinds (with $\bar{\imath}$ and with $\bar{u}$) sound the final *a* in the 3rd pers. Sing. of the *Perfect*, just as all the other roots do, and thus regularly harden their vowel-radical in this position (§§ 51, 68). It is only in one or two instances that an Intransitive form occurs in the Perfect from roots *tertiae* $\bar{u}$, and in these instances the second radical is either an Aspirate, or a vowel or semivowel:—ተለወ "to follow"; ፈተወ, more rarely ፈቶወ "to lust after"; also ከዐወ "to pour out"; ሰሐወ "to extend" (*neut.*); on the other hand ጸሕወ "to awake" (*neut.*); ምህወ "to melt" (*neut.*); and so too the doubly weak root ሐይወ "to live" (originally *ḥáyewa*, more shortly *ḥáiwa*); *cf. infra*. In roots *tertiae* $\bar{\imath}$, however, the distinction between the transitive and the intransitive modes of pronunciation is regularly indicated in forms ሰረየ "to pardon"; ሰመየ "to name"; አበየ "to refuse"; ኀረየ and ኀርየ "to elect"; ፈረየ and ፈርየ "to bear fruit"; ሰትየ "to drink"; ዐበየ "to be big"; በልየ "to grow old"; ርእየ "to see"; ርዕየ "to feed", "to herd"; ንህየ "to recover" (*n.*); ውዕየ "to burn". In the *Subjunctive* the short *ĕ* of the transitive form is dislodged by the third radical, § 51, and therefore we have ይትሉ (for *yetle-ū*); ይእቱ, ይግሉ, ይዕጹ, ይዕዱ, ይዝሩ, ይንቁ Matt. 26, 34; and others;—ይብኪ "to weep"; ይክሪ "to dig"; ይስኪ Deut. 4,42; ይርቂ; ይጥሲ Ex. 32,10; ይሕሊ "to sing"; ይእሪ, ይዕሲ, Ps. 130,4. But the *ă* of the intransitive form, as well as the *ă* of roots middle-Aspirate, retains its position, and forms a diphthong with the radical which follows it; thus constantly with a following $\bar{\imath}$;—ይስረይ; ይስተይ (now and then in the transitive form ይስቲ); ይኅረይ;

[1] If it were only በእ that had this formation, it might also have been accounted for in accordance with § 68, *a* [,—an explanation which might be still retained, if we consider ይማእ to be an analogous formation to ይበእ (v. § 103).]

ይብለይ; ይግነይ (from ገነየ); ይጥዐይ; ይንሀይ; ይርአይ, ይርዐይ:—also with a following $\bar{u}$, in which case, it is true, the diphthong often turns into the mixed letter $\bar{o}$: ይፍቶ Ex. 20,17. After an Aspirate, however, the diphthongal form is more closely adhered to, although it is not invariably retained: ይጽሐው; ይስሐው; ይክዐው. Accordingly the *Imperative* takes, in some cases, the form ትሉ; ዕጹ; ጽሉ; ዕዱ; ዕሢ; ኅሊ; ርቂ; and in others, the form ከዐው (§ 44) and even ቅኖ, Rev. 3,19 (Old Ed.); ግነይ; ብለይ; ስተይ (and in transitive form ስቴ); ሬዐይ, *e. g.* John 21, 15, 16 (¹). But ርእየ "to see", although it has always ይርአይ—never ይርኢ—in the Subjunctive, yet takes the shorter (transitive) form in the Imperative, viz. ርኢ.—The form ሬአይ or even ርአይ, which is read here and there, is not a good reading. In the *Imperfect* the ĕ, which should be uttered after the second radical, is regularly dislodged by the succeeding vowel, thus: ይትሉ, ይፌቱ, ይገሉ, ይዘኑ, ይነቁ "to sound", የዐዱ, የአቱ, ይስቴ, ይፌሪ, ይሰሚ, የኅሪ, የዐቢ, የዐሢ. From roots middle-Aspirate (by § 45): ይክዑ, ይንዑ, ይቅኁ, ይጽሑ; ይጥዒ, ይርዒ (and ይሬዒ, § 92), ይልሒ (Liturg., from ለሐየ); but ርእየ has always ይሬኢ, § 92; and in the Berlin Manuscript of Henoch [Cod. "Q" in Flemming's edition] ይዌዒ always appears for ይውዒ, *e. g.* 93,8. Now though these forms of the Imperfect, from middle-Aspirate roots, coincide with the Subjunctive forms of verbs which are not middle-Aspirate, there still is no possibility of mistaking the one for the other, because the latter forms have always a corresponding Imperfect with *a* in the first syllable, and the former always a Subjunctive with *a* in the second.

Verbs Doubly Weak.

As regards *Doubly Weak Roots* (§ 69), ጐየየ and ዐየየ have been dealt with already in § 93. Of those which are both vowel-beginning and vowel-ending, ወደየ "to put in" forms the Subj. ይደይ; Imper. ደይ, ውዲ, and ውደይ (Herm. p. 81 *b*. l. 7); Imperf. ይወዲ; ውዕየ "to burn" forms the Subj. የዐይ (§ 44); Imperfect ይውዒ (the Imper. is not yet vouched for); and ወሐየ forms ይውሒ (v. Dillmann's '*Lex.*', col. 893). The solitary root which has both middle *i* and final *u*, viz. ሐየወ, exhibits no peculiarities which the foregoing account could not explain; it has the Subj. ይሕዮ and ይሕየው; Imper. ሕዮ and ሕየው; Imperf. የሐዩ. Roots which have both middle *u* and final *i* take a transitive form in the Per-

(¹) [For the occurrence of ዕዕው, ሌብው v. *Kebra Nag.*, Introd., p. XVII.]

fect: ደወየ "to be ill"; ሠወየ "to rub the ears of corn", "to ripen"; ረወየ "to quench one's thirst", Gen. 24, 22; ጠወየ (or ጠዉየ?) "to make windings";—Imperf., ይደዊ, ይሠዊ, ይረዊ, ትጠዊ (2 *sg. m.*, Ps. 17, 29); Subj. (not supported for all of them) ይድወይ.

§ 95 2. *The Intensive Ground-Stem* is given in the *Perfect* with three *a*'s, of which the one that follows the second radical is the essential and determining one, and therefore (according to LUDOLF and TRUMPP) it has the Tone: ፈጸመ *faṣṣáma* "to complete". As the second radical must be doubled, the strong formation always appears, even with the double-lettered (ע״ע or *med. gem.*) and the vowel-centred (*med. voc.*) roots, thus: አዘዘ *azzáza*, "to command"; ሐወዘ *ḥawwáza*, "to be agreeable"; ጠየቀ *ṭayyáqa*, "to investigate strictly" (1); and the same formation, of course, occurs with the other roots:—*e. g.* ወረወ "to throw"; ሐለየ "to think"; ፈነወ "to send". But roots which have an Aspirate for their last letter take, in accordance with § 45, the form ሰብሐ *sabbéḥa* (2), "to give praise to"; ጐጕአ *guagguéa*, "to be in haste", "to be eager"; ጸውዐ *ṣawwéʿa*, "to call"; የውሀ *yawwéha*, "to show clemency". In the formation of the Subjunctive, the Personal Sign is put in an isolated position and is therefore uttered with a Voweltouch (or *She*ᵉ*va*), because the first radical, along with the first half of the second and doubled radical, forms one single unalterable, closed syllable; and, instead of the *a* of the Perfect, there appears in the determining position (*i. e.* after the second radical) in the Subjunctive a toneless *ĕ*, which is suppressed by a closing radical-vowel, thus: ይፈጽም *yefáṣṣem* or, in the case of an initial Aspirate, የሐድስ "to renew" *yaḥáddes*; or, with a final Aspirate, ይሰብሕ, ይጐጕእ. From weak roots we have የአዝዝ, ይኰንን, ይየብብ, ይወልጥ, ይወድስ, ይጸውዕ, የሐውጽ, ይየውህ, ይወውዕ *yewáwweʿ* (Josh. 6, 5): ይጠይቅ *yeṭáyyeq*; ይፈኑ, ይዘሙ, የሀሉ *yahállū*, ይወሩ (from ወረወ); ይጸሊ, ይረሲ, የሐሊ. Imperative-forms are ፈጽም *fáṣṣem*, አዝዝ, ወልጥ, ጸውዕ, የውህ, ወውዕ, ጠይቅ, ፈኑ, ጸሊ, ረሲ. Only, as a result of a shortened and inaccurate pronunciation (§ 56), ይጠይቅ, ጠይቅ and the like may have the sound of *yeṭaiq, ṭaiq*. The middle-Aspirate roots ought

Tense and Mood Formation in— 2. Intensive Ground-Stem.

(1) Thus too ሠየነ, ሐየሰ, so far as they belong to St. I,2; not ሤነ, ሔሰ.

(2) LUDOLF, '*Gramm. Aeth.*' II,2.

properly to have formed a Subjunctive after the type ይመህር *yemáhher*, "(that) he teach"; and, in point of fact, in this case *á* is still retained in a number of instances before the double Aspirate, in old manuscripts and impressions (*e. g.* Deut. 4, 9, 36; 6, 1); but even for this case, the expression which is preferred is, in accordance with § 45, ይምህር *yeméhher*, Imper. ምህር, *e. g.* Ps. 118, 26, 64:— In later pronunciation, in which the Aspirates came to be uttered less and less clearly and distinctly, these forms easily degenerated into *yemêhr*, *mehr*, § 56.

In other respects these two Moods have nothing peculiar in their formation. It must however be kept in mind here, that several roots admit Stem I, 1 and Stem I, 2 in the same meaning; in particular, ወገረ, መሀረ, ጸዐረ, and some others besides, v. § 77, *ad fin.* Meanwhile, to form the *Imperfect* an additional *a* is inserted after the first radical; and the double sound of the radical, which follows the resulting long vowel, becomes inaudible, and is made up for by shading off the *ā* into *ē* (from *ā* + *i*). Accordingly the Imperfect [or Indicative] of this Stem, in all classes of roots, is uniformly produced by establishing an *ē* after the first radical, thus: ይፌጽም *yefēṣem*(1), ይሔድስ, ይሜህር, ይሴብሕ, ይኄንን, ይዬብብ, ይዌልጥ, ይዌውዕ, ይሔውጽ, ይጤይቅ, ይፌኑ, ይኄሉ, ይሜኒ, ይጼሊ, ይሔሊ. This *ē* of the Imperf. is at the same time the surest external mark of all the Intensive Stems.

T. and M. Formation in the Influencing Ground-Stem.

3. In the *Influencing Ground-Stem* the *ā* which contains the force of the Stem bears the Tone throughout, except that when the second radical is an Aspirate, it draws the tone in the Perfect to its own syllable(2), thus: ሣቀየ *šáqaya*; but ላሐወ *lāḥáwa*. The Imperfect [or Indicative] in this Stem is not distinguished from the Subjunctive, because the means employed for this purpose in other forms (§ 91) are not sufficient to produce a special form in this case. The forms concerned therefore run thus: Perf. ባረከ, Imperf. and Subj. ይባርክ, Imper. ባርክ; in the same way: ቋዐረ, ይቋዕር, ቋዕር; with final Aspirate: ባልሐ "to rescue" *báleḥa*,

---

(1) According to Praetorius, '*Beitr. z. Ass.*' I, p. 27, this *yefēṣem* must have arisen out of an original *yefiṣṣim* by a compensatory process of lengthening,—to which the Tigriña ይፍጽም [with an audible doubling of the ጸ] points. [For another explanation of this form, derived from an analogous phenomenon in Assyrian, v. Bezold, '*Zeitschr. f. Assyr.*' XVII, p. 273.]

(2) Ludolf, '*Gr. Aeth.*' I, 7, 3.

ይበልሕ, በልሐ; and from weak roots: ሰረረ, ይሰርር, ሰርር; ቆሐየ, ይቆሒ, ቆሒ; ሣቀየ, ይሣቂ, ሣቂ; ላሐወ, ይላሑ, ላሑ.

§ 96. II. Causative Stems.

II. T. and M Formation in Causative Stems.

1. *In the Causative of the Simple Ground-Stem*, the second radical has *ă* in the Perfect, and so too has the third, in the 3rd pers. sing. masc.: the first, primarily being without a vowel, is attached, by way of closing the syllable, to the formative prefix of the Stem. This closed (first) syllable takes the Tone; and only when the second radical is an Aspirate (with *ă*), does the Tone fall on the second syllable (1). The Causative is formed in the same way, whether from transitive or intransitive roots, thus: **አምሰለ** *ámsala* "to declare alike"; **አፍቀረ** "to love"; **አክሐደ** *akḥáda* "to convict of falsehood". From roots with final Aspirate come:—**አንሥአ** *ánšeʼa* "to raise"; **አብርሀ** "to illuminate". Of all the strong and Aspirate roots, **ብህለ** alone has the singular peculiarity of parting with its Aspirate (§ 47): **አበለ** *abála*, "to cause to say", for **አብህለ**. Besides, it must again be recalled here, that roots with an initial Aspirate do not lengthen their Stem-forming **አ** before the mute Aspirate (§ 46), thus: **አሕረመ**, **አእመረ**. (not **ኣሕረመ**). Of the remaining roots, the double-lettered and the vowel-ending have a thoroughly strong formation in this 3rd pers. sing. masc. of the Perfect: **አንበበ** "to read"; **አጕየየ** "to put to flight"; **አትለወ** "to cause to follow"; **አስተየ** "to give to drink"; **አርአየ** "to show". Specially to be emphasised is **አምዐዐ** *ámʻeʻa* "to provoke". The Vowel-beginning roots blend their first radical with **አ** into a diphthong: **አውለደ** *áulada* "to deliver" (in birth); **አውሥአ** "to answer"; **አይበሰ** "to dry up" (*trans.*); **አይድዐ** "to make known". The Vowel-centred (*med. voc.*) Roots for the most part, even in this Stem, do not admit the *a* after the second radical, and they maintain the shorter pronunciation of I, 1, thereby isolating the **አ** of the Causative Stem, while the tone falls on the long radical vowel, thus: **ሖረ**, **አሖረ** *aḥōra*; **ሮጸ**, **አሮጸ**; **ሔሰ**, **አሔሰ** (along with which, to be sure, **አሕየሰ** occurs); **ኬደ**, **አኬደ**. It is only those which are at the same time Vowel-ending roots, that must of necessity, by § 69, assume the strong formation, just as in I, 1: **አሕየወ** "to enliven", "to vivify"; **አርወየ** "to give to drink";

(1) [Trumpp, p. 522, makes the Tone in these Stems fall on the second syllable throughout, *e. g.* *afqára*. TR.]

አድወየ, **አጥወየ**. And yet there are a few roots *mediae ū*, which also admit of the strong formation: **ዖረ** "to be blind" and **ዖቀ** "to attend to" may indeed form **አዖረ** and **አዖቀ**, but, when broken up because of the Aspirate, they may also form **አዐወረ** (and **አዐረ**), and **አዐወቀ**. From roots unused in St. I, 1 Ludolf brings up **አሥወጠ** "to convey back" and **አንወረ** "to insult", though without supporting-instances. A few roots *mediae ū*, especially those which end in an Aspirate or Labial-Nasal, exhibit quite a peculiar formation,—shortening their ō into ă (originally ā) and thus assuming the appearance of simple triliteral Stems(¹): **ቦአ** "to come", **ኖኀ** "to be long", and the obsolete root **ቦሐ** constantly form **አብአ**, **አንኀ**, **አብሐ** "to permit" (in accordance with § 45), for **አበአ**, **አነኀ**,—which still occurs: Josh. 24, 29 v. Notes [and *Kebra Nag.* 145 *a* 17]—and **አበሐ**; and they are imitated by (§ 48, *ad fin.*) **ጠቀ**, **አጠቀ** "to confine" Josh. 19, 47, though we have also **አጥወቀ**, Hen. 89, 15 (²). In the same way **ቆመ** "to rise up", **ኖመ** "to sleep"—form **አቀመ** and **አነመ**, *e. g.* Judges 16, 14, 19, for which the later manuscripts have **አኖመ**; *cf.* also **አመተ** = **አሞተ**, **አምአ** and **አሞአ**, **አረጹ** = **አሮጹ** 2 Esr. 2, 30 *var.* On **አሠጠ** (for **አሥወጠ** or **አሦጠ**) v. the Imperative (*infra*).

In the Subj. and Impf. of this and the other Causative Stems, the Personal formative-prefix **ይ** blends with the Causative **አ** into **ያ**, § 47 (³); but the **አ** appears again in the Imperative, when the Personal prefix has been thrown off. As regards the vowels, ĕ appears in the Subj. after the second radical, in accordance with § 91, while the first radical is mute, just as in the Perfect, and becomes attached as a closing letter to the prefix-syllable, thus:— **ያፍቅር** *yăfqer*, **ያብቍል** *yăbquel* (from **አብቈለ**); from Aspirate roots:—**ያእምር** *yă'mer*, **ያምሕር** *yămḥer*, **ያንሥእ**, **ያብርህ**; but

(¹) König, p. 116. Perhaps at one time the first radical was pronounced as a double letter, to make up for the ū that had fallen out,—so that these forms would answer to the Hebrew in הֵלִין, הֵנִיחַ.

(²) [Flemming, '*Das Buch Henoch*', Leipzig 1902, in this passage adopts the reading **ወአጠቅዎሙ** instead of the reading which Dillmann selected, **ወአጥወቅዎሙ**. tr.]

(³) According to Praetorius, as cited p. 41 the Tigriña **የቅትል** = יַקְטֵל, ܢܩܛܠ has preserved the more original forms in preference to the Ethiopic and Amharic ones. [Farther v. *supra*, p. 92, Note (²), as to the frequent use of **ኣ** instead of the **ኣ** (resulting from **እአ**) of the 1st pers. Sing. Imperf. Causative. Praetorius draws attention emphatically to this usage ('*Aeth. Gr.*' p. 51). tr.]

from አበለ, ያብል;—from double-lettered roots, ያንብብ, ያእትት; from አምዐዐ, ያምዕዕ *yám'é*;—from vowel-beginning roots, ያይድዕ *yáide'*, *e. g.* Hen. 106,12, ያውልድ *yáwled*(¹), ያውድቅ, ያውሕዝ. In accordance with these we have the Imperative አፍቅር *áfqer*, አእምር, አንሥእ, አንብብ, አይድዕ, አውልድ *áuled*. Vowel-centred and vowel-ending roots do not admit the *ĕ* after the second radical, thus:—ያቢት, Imper. አቢት, from አቤተ; ያጼር, ያዑድ; Imper. አጼር; so too አጢስ, Tobit 6, 16. But those Stems *mediae ū*, which have in the Perfect the short pronunciation አብአ, አቀመ, form the Subj. usually after that type, ያብእ, ያቅም, ያንም, ያብሕ (Josh. 10, 19) (²), and therefore the Imper. አቅም (*e. g.* Josh. 6, 3; Judges 20, 7), አብእ *áb'e* (for *á-be'*, § 43), አንኅ (³). But it should be noticed, as regards the longer or the shorter pronunciation, that the Perfects and the Subjunctives and Imperatives do not always conform to each other by any means, seeing that *e. g.* አቀመ may take the form አቁም in the Imper. (Liturg.), as well as አቅም, and that አንኅ may also take the form ያኑኅ in the Subj. In like manner አየቀ or አዐወቀ may form ያዕቅ or ያዕውቅ, and አሥወጠ (?) may have the Imper. አሥጥ Deut 22, 1. Vowel-ending roots give: ያድሉ *yádlū*, ያብቁ, ያዕዱ; ያስቲ, ያዕቢ, ያርኢ; Imper. አድሉ *ádlū*, አብቁ, አኅሩ; አስቲ, አርኢ. Doubly weak roots yield: ያርዊ, Imper. አርዊ; ያሕዩ, Imper. አሕዩ; ያውዒ, Imper. አውዒ. From these forms the *Imperfect* [or *Indicative*] is quite simply fashioned by inserting the accented vowel *a* after the first radical, except that in roots having a middle Aspirate, *é* appears instead, thus: ያፈቅር *yāfáqer*, ያአምር, ያነሥእ; but ያምሕር *yāméḥer* (kept, by pronunciation, quite distinct from the Subj. ያምሕር *yámḥer*), ያብል *yābel*, ያነብብ, ያምዕዕ *yā-mé-'e*, ያየድዕ, ያወልድ, but ያውሕዝ *yāwéḥez* (overagainst Subj. *yáuḥēz*). The Imperfect is formed in a similar manner from all vowel-centred roots, whether they have the long or the short pronunciation in the Subj.: ያሐውር, ያበውእ, ያበውሕ, ያነውም, ያዐውቅ, ያቀውም, ያጠውቅ (Josh. 19, 47), ያበይት, ያከይድ (properly *yākáyed*, then readily *yākáid*); and from vowel-ending roots:—ያተሉ, ያኅቱ, ያደሉ; ያሰቲ, but ያርኢ (*yāre-'ī*, *i. e. yár-'ī*), ያረዊ, ያወቂ, ያውዒ *yāwe'ī*.

(¹) According to Trumpp, p. 529,—to be pronounced *yáuled*.

(²) Also ያጥቅ, Lev. 25, 46.

(³) *Cf.* Philippi, '*Beitr. z. Ass.*', II, p. 380.

2. *The Causative of the Intensive Stem* is distinguished in form from the Ground-Stem 2, merely by the prefixed formative syllable of the Stem, **አ**. The latter is always isolated, as the first radical forms along with the first half of the double letter an unchangeable, closed syllable. The tone (1) is usually on the third-last syllable; and only when the second radical is an Aspirate, is it on the second-last in the Perfect. Accordingly the Perfect is: **አገበረ** *agábbara*, "to compel"; **አለዐለ** *alá‘ála*, "to lift up" (Judges 7, 20); **አኰነነ**, "to make a judge"; **አመነነ**, "to render contemptible"; **አኀየለ**, "to strengthen"; **አጠየቀ**, "to assure"; **አሠነየ**, "to beautify"; **አለበወ**, "to make intelligent". But from roots with final Aspirate we have forms like **አጸብሐ**, "to cause to pay taxes"; **አጐጕአ**, "to urge to haste"; **አሠሥዐ**, "to satiate"; **አመልዐ**, "to proceed farther". Seeing, however, that this Stem is rather lengthy and polysyllabic in the Perfect, many roots,—particularly those of the Middle-Aspirate class (§ 56),—endeavour to replace it by St. II, 1, at least in the Perfect, and occasionally even in the other formations (*cf.* § 97, 2): thus **አልዐለ** is used in the Perfect in preference to **አለዐለ**, *e. g.* in Gen. 7, 17; 18, 2; **አእመረ** always, instead of **አአመረ**; **አትሐተ** always, instead of **አተሐተ**, "to humiliate", but scarcely **አድመነ**, "to wrap up in clouds" (2), for **አደመነ**. **አዒረየ** frequently occurs in the Perfect instead of **አዐረየ**, "to equalise". The *Subjunctive* has the form **ያገብር** *yāgábber*; **ያኰንን**, **ያጠይቅ**, **ያሠኒ**, **ያለቡ**, and the *Imperative* the form **አገብር** *agábber*, **አኰንን**, **አጠይቅ**, **አሠኒ**, **አለቡ**. But from Middle-Aspirate roots:—Subjunctive **ያልዕል** (properly *yālé‘-‘el*, which closes into *yālé‘‘l*, § 56); *Imper.* **አልዕል** *e. g.* Josh. 8, 18 (3). The *Imperfect* in all cases uniformly runs thus: **ያጌብር** *yāgéber*; **ያሌዕል**, **ያቴሕት**, **ያኴንን**, **ያኄይል**, **ያሤውን**, **ያሤኒ**, **ያሌቡ** &c. Noticeable on account of its

(1) Ludolf, '*Gr. Aeth.*' I, 7. This rule, however, does not agree with the teaching of Ludolf about the Tone in the case of St. I, 2 and III, 2. *Cf.* also *supra*, p. 150, Note 1. [In fact Trumpp, p. 522, keeps the Tone throughout on the second-last syllable. TR.]

(2) As Ludolf has it in his '*Lexicon*' p. 496. Certainly Ludolf himself has incorrectly contrived the forms **አሥወነ** "to cause to foam", **አንስሐ** "to lead to repentance", **አውጠነ** "to cause to begin"; **አጕጕአ** (v. *supra*), for **አሠወነ**, **አነስሐ**, **አወጠነ**, **አጐጕአ**. At least the other form of pronunciation has hitherto remained without support.

(3) In like manner **አትሕት** Eph. 5, 21.

fluctuations between II, 1 and 2, is the word አሥገረ, "to catch in the net", "to net", in respect that, for instance, it forms the Perfect (Matt. 17, 27), and the Subjunctive and Imperative (John 21, 3; 1 Cor. 7, 35; Cant. 2, 18) according to Stem II, 1, but the Imperfect (Mark 1, 16; Luke 5, 10) according to Stem II, 2. Farther አየረ and አየቀ form the Subj. from St. II, 1, but the Imperf. from St. II, 2; and a stricter investigation of the treasures of the language would no doubt furnish instances of similar fluctuations in other roots.

3. *The Causative of the Influencing Stem* is likewise distinguished from its Ground-Stem merely by the Stem formative prefix: —Perf. አላቀሰ *alā́qasa*[1]; Subj. ያላቅስ, John 11, 19; Imper. አላቅስ; Imperf. ያላቅስ, John 11, 31. Weak roots: ያዋኪ Subj. and Imperf.—(and from quadriliteral roots, which follow this Stem: ያጸሙ Mark 5, 35; Luke 8, 49; ያጣዑ Acts 17, 16). In middle-Aspirate roots the tone in the Perfect must rest here also on the second-last syllable: አዋሐደ *awāḥáda*.

§ 97. III. Reflexive Stems.

III. T. and M. Formation in Reflexive Stems.

The Stem formative prefix ተ is in the Perfect placed before the root externally and separately; in the Subjunctive and Imperfect it blends with the Personal formative prefix into the syllable ይት and this ት is, in accordance with § 54, assimilated to a following Sibilant or to a mute dental-lingual. In the tense-formation here the change of vowels (§ 91) is never carried out in St. III, 2 and 3, and but seldom in St. III, 1 (v. *infra*). Farther the distinction between the Imperf. and the Subj. is carried out only in Stem III, 2. In Stem III, 3, it could just as little have made its appearance,—for the reasons given in § 95, 3—, as in Stems I, 3 and II, 3. But even in III, 1, where the Subj. has already *a* after the first radical, the Ethiopic means of forming the Imperfect were insufficient to create a special form. To lengthen the *a* would have transformed the Stem into St. III, 3; the lengthening therefore remained in abeyance, and the Subj. and Imperf. coincide. It might be, of course, that in more ancient times the two forms were at least differentiated by means of the tone, *e. g.* that ይትገበር as Subjunctive, was pronounced *yetgabár*, and as Imperfect, *yetgábar* or *yétgabar*.

---

(1) *Cf. supra*, however, p. 150, Note 2.

1. In the case of the *Reflexive of the Simple Ground-Stem*, seeing that in the Perfect the first radical is originally vowel-less, we might have expected the form ተክደነ, like አክደነ in Caus. St. II, 1. This form, however, is no longer met with, with the exception of ተንሥአ "to raise one's self", "to rise up" (1): and even this exception became possible only through the form having been derived, not from St. I, 1, but directly from St. II, 1, አንሥአ "to lift up"—, overagainst which the Reflexive-Passive of ነሥአ "to take" is invariably given ተነሥአ (2). If it is remembered, that ተ itself is merely an abbreviation of እት or አት (§ 80), and that the oldest form must therefore have been እትክደነ, we have the explanation of the circumstance that this ተ does not, like the Causative አ, combine with the first radical to form one syllable. Out of an original እትከደነ the form ተከደነ arose through abbreviation. ተከደነ, in fact, with the tone upon the chief vowel in the second-last syllable is the first and most obvious form of this Stem in the Perfect. But it has not continued to be the only one. On the contrary, in this Reflexive-Passive Stem, the intransitive or passive vowel *ĕ* (§ 75 *sq.*) has very frequently made good its position, in place of the Active vowel *a*, as in ተገብረ *tagábra* (for *tagábera*); and thereby a change of vowels between the Perfect on the one hand, and the Imperfect and Subjunctive on the other, has been at the same time secured, inasmuch as the *ă* of the Imperfect and Subjunctive answers to the passive *ĕ* of the Perfect. But which of the two forms of pronunciation is to be employed in the several roots, cannot be determined by general rules. It was, after all, nothing but the usage of the language (3) which decided for the one form or the other. In many roots the two forms are freely exchanged for one another. The fundamental difference between the two may possibly at first have been, that ተዐቀበ, for instance, signified "to watch one's self", "to take care", while ተዐቅበ meant "to be

(1) I cannot accept the explanation of this word given by König, p. 148. —According to Nöldeke, GGA 1886, No. 26, p. 1016, ተንሥአ is a denominative, from a Substantive like ትንሣኤ.

(2) [For the employment of ተንሥአ instead of ተነሥአ and *vice versâ*, v. Dillmann's '*Lex.*', col. 637 *sq.*].

(3) This, however, has not yet been investigated with sufficient strictness; and many statements made by Ludolf regarding it, in his Dictionary and his Grammar, stand in need of correction.

watched, *or* cared for"(¹); but in later times this distinction was completely obliterated. However, for brevity's sake, we shall call the pronunciation with *ĕ*, "the passive pronunciation". Accordingly we have in the strong verb the twofold form of the Perfect: ተመሰጠ "to be robbed"; ተገብረ "to happen". From the Middle-Aspirate Verb (§ 45) come, for the most part, forms like ተግሕሠ *tagéḥša* "to withdraw"; ተእኅዘ "to be taken prisoner"; ተክህለ "to be possible"(²); more rarely with *ă*, ተበአሰ (=ተባአሰ) "to fight"; from a verb with a final aspirate the form is always ተመልአ "to become full", ተሰምዐ "to be heard". From double-lettered verbs we have either ተኀሠሠ "to be sought"; or more frequently, with the passive pronunciation, ተነበ "to be read"; ተሰደ "to be banished", in some few instances written ተሰደደ (§ 55); but ተምዕዐ *tamé'a*, "to be angry", may, according to § 56, by throwing back the doubling of the second radical upon the first, be simplified into ተምዐ *tammé'a*, and then into *tám'a*. Vowel-beginning and vowel-ending verbs always have the strong formation in the Perfect: ተየድዐ "to become known"; ተወልደ "to be born"; ተውህበ "to be given"; ተዐደወ "to transgress"; ተወድየ "to be put in"; ተክዕወ "to be poured out"; ተርእየ "to be seen". Vowel-centred roots, when uttered with *a*, have the strong formation; if given with *ĕ*, they reject the *ĕ* (§ 50) and produce a diphthong: ተሀወከ Numb. 22, 3 and ተሀውከ Matt. 2, 3, "to be troubled"; ተሀይደ Hen. 89, 58 "to be robbed"; ተሠይመ "to be settled"; very rarely the diphthong blends into a mixed sound: ተሦዐ "to be sacrificed" (Org.); ተቂአ (?) "to be disgorged".—The Subjunctive and Imperfect are formed from the whole body of the roots 'strongly', and uniformly with the chief vowel *a* after the second radical, and with *ă* as the readiest vowel for the first. Vowel-centred roots must harden their vowel-radical; the vowel-ending ones combine it with the preceding *ă* into a diphthong; and it

(¹) As LUDOLF assumed. But LUDOLF, trusting too much to this assumed law of his, often enough set up a form in his Dictionary like ተዐቅበ, without being able to give an instance of its use, even when he had frequently met with the other form ተዐቀበ in the Perfect (v. DRECHSLER, p. 34).

(²) It is not correct in copyists to lengthen the vowel of the first radical before a mute Aspirate, thus: ተኳሕለ "to paint one's eyes", for ተኰሕለ.

is only roots *tertiae ū* which may farther blend the diphthong into a mixed sound (exactly as in the Ground-stem, § 94), thus: ይትገበር *yétgabar* (1), ይትመሰጥ, ይትአኀዝ, ይሰማዕ (§ 46), ይትኀሠሥ, ይትነበብ, ይትወሀብ, ይትየጻዕ, ይትሀየድ, ይትሀወክ, ይሠዋዕ, ይትዐደው or ይትዐዶ, ይትወደይ, ይትረአይ. Also the Perfect ተንሥአ forms the Imperfect and Subjunctive ይትነሣእ, just like ተነሥአ; and in the same way ተምዕዐ and ተምዐ equally form ይትመዓዕ. The Imperative, because derived from the Subj., likewise exhibits *a* invariably after the second radical: ተገበር, ተአኀዝ, ተፈታሕ, ተሠየም, ተፈተው or ተፈቶ, ተፈደይ, ተረአይ &c. But in the Imperative of ተንሥአ the peculiar pronunciation, imitated from Causative 1, comes back again, ተንሥኢ, "Arise!". So too runs the Imperative of ተምዕዐ, shortened into ተምዕ (Plural also, ተምዕዑ). Farther, Middle-Aspirate roots, which have the Passive pronunciation ተግሕሠ in the Perf., occasionally take the shorter form ተግሐሥ, *tagᵉḥāš*, Numb. 16, 21, 26; 17, 10, instead of the regular ተገሐሥ; (in MS. F this shorter form occurs in the passages named, whereas the other MSS. have ተገሐሥ, a reading which is also met with in Ps. 33, 15 and 36, 28) (2).

2. *The Reflexive of the Intensive Stem*, according to LUDOLF, must in the Perfect have the tone upon the vowel of the second radical; in the other forms it rests upon the vowel of the first. The Perf. has the strong formation in all roots: ተቀደሰ *taqaddása*, "to be sanctified"; ተኰነነ *takuannána*, "to be condemned"; ተወሰከ "to be added to"; ተሰፈወ "to hope"; ተዐረየ "to become equal to one another"; ተዐወረ *taʿawwára*, "to overlook"; ተዐየረ "to reprove". But from roots with final Aspirate, regularly:—ተፈሥሐ "to rejoice"; ተመልሐ "to be salted"; ተየውሀ "to let one's self be pacified". Farther, as the Aspirates, following the later pronunciation, readily grew too nerveless for doubling (§ 56), a phenomenon made its appearance, which became noticeable also in Stem II, 2 (§ 96), viz.—that in the Perfect Middle-Aspirate roots fell back from Stem III, 2 to Stem III, 1. Thus ተመሀረ *tamahhára* first of all becomes *tamahhera*, seeing that a Passive *é*

(1) According to TRUMPP, p. 527, to be accented *yetgábar*.

(2) ተንበበ in the Ethiopic Liturgy (ed. BEZOLD, in SWAINSON's '*Greek Liturgies*', London 1884), p. 384, l. 11—is probably a copyist's error for ተናበበ.

is at least possible instead of *a* (v. *supra* in this § 97), and then *tamehhera* (by § 45), which ultimately drops into *tamêhra*. And so we have **ተመሀረ** and **ተምሀረ** "to learn"; **ተተሐተ** and **ተትሕተ** "to be made humble"; **ተለዐለ** and **ተልዕለ** "to be exalted"; **ተዘሀረ** and **ተዝሀረ** "to be vainglorious"; **ተደኀረ** (*e. g.* Judges 5, 28 F) and **ተድኅረ** "to remain behind", "to loiter"; **ተጽዕነ** "to mount upon"; **ተስእለ** "to enquire about"; **ተጸዐረ** and **ተጽዕረ** "to be tormented"; **ተጸአለ** and **ተጽእለ** "to be reviled"; **ተየሀደ** and **ተይሀደ** "to become a Jew". In the Subj. and Imperative, both these and all other roots have *a* after the second radical as chief vowel, and also *a* after the first. In the Imperfect they have *ē* after the first radical, and dispense with the doubling of the second, thus: **ይትቄደስ**, **ይትቀደስ**, **ተቀደስ** *yetqḗdas, yetqáddas, taqáddas*; **ይትሌዐል**, **ይትለዐል**, **ተለዐል**; **ይትፌሣሕ**, **ይትፈሣሕ**, **ተፈሣሕ**; **ይትዬዋህ**, **ይትየዋህ**, **ተየዋህ**; **ይትዔወር**, **ይትዐወር**, **ተዐወር**; **ይሴፎ** or **ይሴፈው**, **ይሰፎ**, **ተሰፎ** or **ተሰፈው**; **ይትዔረይ**, **ይትዐረይ**, **ተዐረይ** &c.

3. *The Reciprocity-Stem* takes the form in the Perfect **ተፋለጠ** "to separate from one another", with the tone upon *ā*, *tafālaṭa*(¹), but in Middle-Aspirate verbs, with the tone upon the penult, **ተሣሀለ** "to be propitious towards any one", *tašāhála*. From roots with final Aspirate the form has always *ĕ* (in place of *a*) after the second radical: **ተጋብአ** *tagābe'a*, and more shortly *tagāb'a*. In all weak roots this Stem takes a full and strong formation: **ተፃረረ** "to be foes to each other"; **ተማዕዐ** *tamā'e'a* and *tamā''a* "to be angry at one another"; **ተያውሀ** "to flatter one another"; **ተዋሰበ** "to intermarry"; **ተዋሥአ** "to conduct a learned controversy"; **ተራወጸ** "to run together"; **ተካየደ** "to enter into a confederacy"; **ተዋነየ** "to play together"; **ተፋነወ** "to take leave of one another". Farther, in the Subj., Imper. and Imperf. this Stem has *a* after the second radical, while there is no distinction between the Subj. and Imperf., thus:—**ይትፋለጥ**, **ይትጋባእ**, **ይፃረር**, **ይትዋሰብ**, **ይትራወጽ**, **ይትዋነይ**; **ተፋለጥ**, **ተጋባእ** &c.

IV.T. and M. Formation in Causative-Reflexive Stems.

§ 98. IV. The Causative-Reflexive Stems, as active verbs, have the active vowel *a* in the Perfect after the second radical, and, like the other Active Stems, change it into *ĕ* in the Imperfect and Subjunctive. The formative prefix of the Stem **አስተ**, when combined with the personal prefix, becomes **የስተ** (§ 47).

(¹) *Cf.*, however, *supra*, p. 155, Note (¹).

1. The *first* of these Stems has two forms of pronunciation in the Perfect. In the form which is most obvious and usual the first radical, originally without a vowel, is attached to the formative prefix ተ by way of closing the syllable (exactly as in II, 1) (1), thus: አስተንፈሰ "to inhale"; with final Aspirate, አስተግብአ "to take (by force of arms)" Numb. 21, 32; አስተብጽዐ "to pronounce blessed"; and አስተብቍዐ "to make intercession"; from weak roots:— አስተውሐሰ "to borrow" (Ex. 12, 35); አስተርአየ "to appear" and "to reveal"; አስተስረየ "to obtain forgiveness"; from roots with initial Aspirate:—አስታሕቀረ "to treat contemptuously" (Gen. 29,25; Judges 16, 10). The tone in these cases rests on the third-last syllable (2), and in Middle-Aspirate roots on the second-last. But, alongside of this,—the usual pronunciation,—another has also become current, which puts forward the prefix አስተ in a separate fashion, after the manner of the Reflexive Stems, and causes an *ă* to be heard after the first radical. In this case the tone must undoubtedly rest on the second-last syllable; *cf.* Trumpp, p. 524. This form of expression appears oftenest in roots *tertiae gutturalis*, *e. g.* አስተቀንአ "to be envious"; አስተበውሐ "to ask permission", and in roots *primae gutturalis* (3), *e. g.* አስተአበደ "to treat as a fool"; አስተአከየ "to declare bad"; አስተኀሠሠ "to invent"; and here and there too in other roots, *e. g.* in አስተረሐቀ, a collateral form of አስተርሐቀ "to remove". It is noteworthy besides, that from the unused root በውሐ, which assumes the short form አብሐ in St. II, 1 (§ 96), አስተብሐ also is formed in this Stem, as well as አስተበውሐ "to ask permission". But the difference between these two forms of pronunciation is of no importance in the formation of the other tenses and moods. In the Subjunctive the first radical is always attached without a vowel to the formative prefix ተ by way of closing the syllable:—ያስተንፍስ, ያስተብቍዕ, ያስተርክብ, ያስታሕቅር, ያስተስሪ, ያስተርኢ; and accordingly in the Imperative we have አስተርክብ, አስተብቍዕ, አስተምሕር, አስተስሪ, አስተርኢ. In the formation of the Imperfect, *á* (probably also accented here) is inserted after the first radical: ያስተረክብ,

(1) *Cf.* König, p. 148.

(2) V. on the other hand Trumpp, p. 523.

(3) To avoid lengthening the *a* of ተ,—for which reason one says አስተሐቀረ as well as አስታሕቀረ.

ያስተበቍዕ, ያስተኀሥሥ, ያስተሰሪ; in Middle-Aspirate verbs, *á* is thickened into *é*: ያስተምሕር *yāstaméḥer* (overagainst which we have the Subjunctive *yāstámḥer*); ያስተብዕል, ያስተርኢ (*yāstaré'ī*, and therefore in some Manuscripts occasionally written ያስተሬኢ(¹), v. St. I, 1ᵹ.

2. The *Stem*, of this class, *derived from the second Ground-Stem* takes the form in the Perfect, አስተዐገሠ, with the accent on the third-last syllable(²) (v. St. II, 2), thus:—*asta'águgaša*, "to practise patience". It takes the strong formation in all weak roots, *e. g.*—አስተዐበየ "to brag", "to swagger"; አስተሰፈወ "to awaken hope in any one"; አስተኀየሰ "to prefer"; አስተወከለ "to have complete trust"; and in roots *tertiae gutturalis*: አስተፈሥሐ "to rejoice" (*astafáššeḥa*). In the Subjunctive the *á* after the first radical is of course maintained, and the *a* after the second becomes *e*: ያስተዐግሥ *yāsta'ággeš*; ያስተኀይስ, ያስተወክል, ያስተዐቢ, ያስተሰፉ, ያስተፈሥሕ(³); so too with the Imperative:—አስተዐግሥ &c. The Imperfect is formed (as in all the Intensive Stems) by means of *ē* after the first radical, while the doubling is given up: ያስተዔግሥ, ያስተፌሥሕ, ያስተዔቢ, ያስተሴፉ &c.

3. The *Stem*, of this class, *derived from the third Ground-Stem* forms the Perfect አስተማሰለ, with the accent on the third-last syllable(⁴); from roots *tertiae gutturalis*: አስተጋብአ; in like manner አስተማዕዐ. For other examples v. *supra* § 84. The Subjunctive and Imperfect are not distinguished from each other; in both *e* appears instead of *a* after the second radical:—ያስተማስል *yāstamásel*, ያስተጋብእ, ያስተፃርር, ያስተባሪ, ያስተሓዩ, ያስተማዕዕ; and, accordingly in the Imperative: አስተማስል, አስተባሪ &c.

§ 99. *The Multiliteral Verb* follows, generally, the same rules as the Triliteral in forming the Tenses and Moods. In the Multiliteral verb also, the inner vowel-change between the two tenses invariably makes its appearance with the second-last radical. The first two radicals are combined into one syllable, with *a* between them, and they are maintained in this combination, throughout nearly the whole of the farther development of the form: in

Tense and Mood Formation of Multiliteral Verbs:—

(¹) Also ያስተሪኢ Herm. p. 85 *a*, l. 3; *cf.* König, p. 119.

(²) In Middle-Aspirate verbs, on the penult. V. however Trumpp, p. 524.

(³) Once however ያስተጽዕንዎ; v. Dillmann's '*Lex.*', col. 1306.

(⁴) V. however Trumpp, p. 524.

the Imperfect, however, and in Stems III, 3 and IV, 3 this group has to be broken up. Farther, in this group the *a*-Sound is held to be so essential, and a long vowel in the first Stem-syllable so reasonable, that this *a* is not thickened into *e* before a mute Aspirate according to § 45, but is lengthened into *ā* according to § 46. In the domain of the last two radicals, however, the same rules prevail with regard to the treatment of Aspirates, radical Vowels and double radicals, as in the Triliteral verb.

I. In Ground-Stem.

I. *The Ground-Stem* does not distinguish between a transitive and an intransitive form of pronunciation in the *Perfect*. It is always uttered with three *a's* (1), the first syllable either closed, or possessing a long vowel having the Tone (2), thus: **ደንገፀ** *dángaṣa*, "to be terrified"; with an aspirate as second radical:—**ማህረከ** *máhraka*, "to take as booty"; with a similar letter as last radical: **ገፍትአ**, "to destroy"; with an aspirate in the second as well as in the last position: **ብኍብኍ** "to rot"; with doubling of the third radical: **ደምሰሰ** "to extinguish"; with a like doubling when the radical is at the same time weak: **ጻሕየየ** "to clear of weeds"; with a long vowel as second radical: **ማሰነ** "to decay", **ዴገነ** "to persecute", **ቶስሐ** "to mix"; with a vowel as last radical: **ደርበየ** "to shoot", **ሰንቀወ** "to touch the harp"; weak in more than one radical: **ዐውየወ** "to lament aloud", **ፄወወ** "to take prisoner", **ጌገየ** "to sin", **ጼነወ** "to give forth perfume", **ሎለወ** "to inflame.

The Subjunctive is formed by the prefixed Personal signs and by the transition of the *a* which follows the second last radical into *ĕ*: **ይደንግፅ** *yedánges̩*; *primae gutturalis*: **የዐንዝር**; farther examples:—**ይማህርክ**, **ይገፍትእ**, **ይብኍብኍ**, **ይደምስስ**, **ይጻሕዩ**, **ይማስን**, **ይዴግን**, **ይቶስሕ**, **ይደርቢ**, **ይሰንቁ**, **የዐውዩ**, **ይፄዊ** or **ይፄውው**, **ይጌጊ**, **ይጼኑ**, **ይሎሉ**. In accordance with these forms, we have in the *Imperative*: **ደንግፅ**, **ብኍብኍ**, **ደምስስ**, **ዴግን**, **ፄውው** (Judges 5, 12), &c. (3). To form *the Imperfect*, an accented *a* is inserted after the second radical, which brings about the separation into two syllables of the syllable made up of the first two radicals:

(1) [Excepting, of course, the necessary modification of the second *a*, when the last radical is an Aspirate. TR.]

(2) V. however TRUMPP, p. 524.

(3) Irregular are: Subj. **ይምህርክ** Kuf. p. 122, N. 4; p. 160, N. 11; and Imperative **መህርክ** Is. 8, 1, 3 *var.*—and **ይጸሐየይ** from **ጸሐየየ**.

ይደነግፅ *yedanágeṣ*, ይመሀርኽ, ይገፌትእ, ይበኊበኍ, ይደመስስ. ይሰነቁ (Rev. 14, 2), ይደረቢ, የዐወዩ. But those roots which have a long vowel as second radical, like ማሰነ, ዴገነ, ቆስሐ, can have no special form for the Imperfect, because an *a* inserted after that radical blends with such long vowel; and even roots like ጌገየ, ሎለወ are too sluggish to break up their mixed sound; thus we have: ይማስን, ይዴግን, ይቆስሕ, ይጌጊ, ይሎሉ (Jas. 3, 6), ይዒዉ (which do not differ from the Subjunctive forms, v. *supra*). Seldom is it,—and it is not good Ethiopic,—that roots which have a vowel for their final radical omit the proper formation of the Imperfect, as, for instance, in the citation by LUDOLF from a manuscript of the *Organon*: እንተ ፡ ኢትመጽሉ "which does not wither", instead of ትመጸሉ.

II. In exact conformity with the same rules are also formed the tenses and moods of the *Causative Stem* of Quadriliteral roots. II. In Causative Stem.
Perfect: አመንደበ *amándaba* (1) "to bring into difficulty"; አማኅፀነ "to entrust to"; አቀምጠዐ "to put the ground in good order"; አጠእጥአ "to prepare"; አመርሰሰ "to cause to feel after"; አሰርገወ "to adorn"; አጕንደየ "to delay one"; አጌገየ "to cause to sin"; አዴነወ "to smell at"; አጻመወ "to cause trouble"; አርኊርኊ (2) "to appease"; አጸንሕሐ "to sacrifice". *Subjunctive*: ያመንድብ, ያማኅፅን, ያቀምጥዕ, ያጣእጥእ, ያመርስስ, ያሰርጉ, ያጕንዲ, ያጌጊ, ያዴኑ, ያጻሙ, ያራኅርኅ, ያጸንሕሕ, or ያጽነሐንሕ; *Imperative*: አመንድብ, አማኅፅን &c.; *Imperfect*: ያመነድብ, ያሙኅፅን, ያቀመጥዕ, ያጠአጥእ, ያመረስስ, ያሰረጉ, ያጕነዲ, but ያጌጊ, ያዴኑ, ያጻሙ. Quinqueliteral roots combine in one syllable the first radical and the formative prefix of the Stem, and the second and third in one, with *a*: the second-last radical supports the vowel-change. In the Imperfect formation *a* establishes itself after the third radical, and the syllable formed by the second and third is thus resolved into two syllables. Thus: አርመስመሰ *armásmasa*, "to feel about"; አቅያሕይሐ and አቅየሐይሐ "to become reddish"; አንጠብጠበ "to drip"; አምዐርዐረ "to sweeten":—*Subjunctive*: ያርመስምስ, ያቅያሕይሕ, ያማዐርር;—*Imperfect*: ያርመሰምስ *yārmasámes*, ያቅየሐይሕ (Lev. 13, 24; Matt. 16, 2, 3), ያንጠበጥብ, Ps. 71, 6. In the same way አጸምሀየየ, አጽመሀየየ, አጽማሀየየ, or አጸማሀየየ "to render flabby"; አሉኖሰሰ

(1) V. however TRUMPP, p. 524.

(2) [A peculiar form for አራኅርኅ, v. DILLMANN's '*Lex.*' TR.]

"to whisper gently", and the two Causatives, formed by **አስ**, § 85 *ad fin.*; except that here the Subjunctive and Imperfect cannot be distinguished: **ያሎኖስስ**, **ያስቆርር**, **ያስዖዝዝ**, also **ያስቆቁ**.

III. T. and M. Formation in Reflexive Stems of Multiliteral Verbs.

§ 100. III. In the *Reflexive Stem* the second-last radical exhibits no vowel-change between the two tenses, § 97; but, on the other hand, it has become possible in this case to make a difference between the Imperfect and the Subjunctive by inserting, in the former, *a* after the second radical, which is without a vowel in the Subjunctive; and it is only in roots *mediae infirmae* that the Imperf. and the Subj. coincide (just as in Stems I and II). Thus we have in the *Perfect*: **ተመንደበ** *tamándaba*(1); **ተደምሰሰ**, "to be extinguished"; **ተማኅፀነ**, **ተገፍትአ**, **ተጸአጽአ**, "to worship"; **ተመንሰወ** "to be tempted"; **ተጸምሀየ**, **ተማሰነ**, **ተሞጥሐ**, **ተሴሰየ**, **ተቤዘወ** (§ 86):—*Subjunctive*: **ይትመንደብ**, **ይደምሰስ** (Ps. 108, 13), **ይትማኅፀን** (Ps. 120, 7), **ይትገፍታእ**, **ይጸአጸእ**, **ይትመንሰው**, **ይጸምሀይ**, **ይትማሰን**, **ይትሞጣሕ**, **ይሴሰይ**, **ይትቤዘው**: *Imperative*: **ተደምሰስ**, **ተማኅፀን** &c. But in the Imperfect we have:—**ይትመነደብ** *yetmanádab*, **ይደመሰስ**, **ይትሙኀፀን**, **ይትገፌታእ**, **ይጸአጸእ**, **ይትመነሰው**, **ይጸመሀይ**; but **ይትማሰን** &c. just as in the Subj. The Reflexive Stem of Sexliteral roots has hitherto been found in the Perfect only. On the formation of the Perfect of the *Reciprocal Stem*, v. § 86. It deserves special notice, that even the root **ዜነወ** resolves the *ē*, which it preserves through all the forms of Stems I and III,—into *ay*, before the inserted *ā*. Of course the Tone falls upon the long *ā*, to which this Stem owes its form. There is no difference between the *Imperfect* and the *Subjunctive* (*cf.* §§ 95—97), nor is there any change of vowels in the two Tense-formations. Thus:—**ይሰናሰል**, Ex. 26, 3; **ይጠናቀቅ**, Lev. 23, 22; **ይደናጸው**, **ይሰናአው**, **ይሰከተይ**; *Imperative*: **ተሰናአው**, **ተዘያነው** &c.

IV. In Causative-Reflexive Stems.

IV. The *Causative-Reflexive* Stem is, in accordance with § 86, of very rare occurrence. In the Imperf. and Subj. it necessarily exhibits the vowel-change found in all the Active Stems, hence **ያስተሰናኡ**, Jas. 3, 17.

V. In Second Reflexive Stem.

V. The *weaker Reflexive Stem*, which is formed by prefixing **አን** (§ 87), so far shows its kinship with the Active Stems, as to exhibit the usual difference of vocalisation prevailing in those Stems between the two Tense-forms. The Imperfect is distinguished from

(1) But *cf.* TRUMPP. 524.

the Subjunctive just as in the other Stems of the Multiliteral roots. The Personal sign in the Subj. and Imperf. is connected with **አን** just as it is in other cases with **አስ** and **አ**. Whence we have, in the *Perfect*: **አንጐርጐረ** *anguárguara* (1); in the *Subjunctive*: **ያንጐርጕር**; in the *Imperative*: **አንጐርጕር**; and in the *Imperfect*: **ያንጐረጕር**. With Aspirates and Radical vowels; *Perfect*: **አንበሕብሐ**, **አንቃዕደወ**, **አንጦልዐ**, **አንሶሰወ**, **አንጌገየ**; *Subjunctive*: **ያንበሕብሕ**, **ያንቃዕዱ**, **ያንጦልዕ**, **ያንሶሱ**, **ያንጌጊ**; *Imperfect*: **ያንበሐብሕ**, **ያንቀዐዱ**, and the rest just as in the Subjunctive (2).

III. FORMATION OF PERSONS, GENDERS AND NUMBERS.

§ 101. It belongs to the very conception of a verb, as distinguished from a mere predicate, that it not only gives what is predicated, but also,—contained within it or at least indicated by it,—the Person, of whom anything is predicated. Accordingly the Verb furnishes its Tense- and Mood-Stems with Personal signs, as the third step which it takes towards its full development. In order to manage this step, it encroaches upon the domain of the Pronouns, inasmuch as it is just the Personal pronouns which are made use of to express the several Persons. The Personal signs have originated in the combination of the personal pronouns with the verbal Stem. The former in due course coalesced with the latter, but in this closer connection they have undergone abbreviation and occasionally considerable mutilation. The entire apparatus of the distinction of the Persons in Gender and Number, which prevails and lives in the language, in the domain of the Personal Pronouns, is thus reproduced in the Verb. And just as, in accordance with § 148, two Numbers, the Singular and the Plural, are distinguished in the Personal Pronoun, and two Genders, Masculine and Feminine, in the two pronouns of the second and third Person, so are these distinctions repeated in the verb in Ethiopic.

Formation of Persons, Genders and Numbers:— General Remarks.

It has already been pointed out in § 91, that the position which is assumed by the Personal sign with respect to the Verbal

(1) But v. TRUMPP, p. 525.

(2) On the peculiar forms of **አንሳሕስሐ** "to move (*intr.*)" v. DILLMANN's '*Lex.*', col. 327. On the Passive-Reflexives formed with **ተ**, like **ተንጦልዐ**, v. *supra*, p. 165.

Stem, is of essential importance in the formation of the two contrasted Tenses. In the Perfect the Personal signs are attached to the end of the Stem; in the Imperfect and Subjunctive, to the beginning. This different method of attachment, however, has caused the modification of the originally complete pronoun to have another character in the Perfect than it has in the Imperfect; and accordingly the Personal signs actually in use in the language fall into two divisions.

Personal Signs of the Perfect.

1. *The Personal signs of the Perfect*(1). The *Third Person Sing. Masc.* is not distinguished by any special sign. Seeing that all the other persons and genders in both numbers were denoted exactly by terminations, the Personal sign could be dispensed with in this one case, by virtue of the contrast. The Third Person Sing. Fem., on the other hand, has *at*, which serves the same purpose also in Nominal Stems, v. § 126. The Third Person Plural Masc. is denoted by *ū*, and the Third Person Plural Fem. by *ā*. The former is shortened(2) from *ūmū*, *ūm*, *ūn*, the latter from *ōn* (ውእቶን), *ān*.—The sign for the *Second Person* Sing. is in the Masc. ከ, in the Fem. ኪ. The vowel-change between the two genders is the very same as in the full pronoun of the second person (§ 148): the other Semitic languages also retain this change, either complete or in traces. ከ or ኪ itself, however, is nothing else than the second element of the full compound Pronoun አንተ or አንቲ (§ 148), inasmuch as (v. § 65), from the original *twa*, from which ተ sprung, ከ might also come, and has come not only in this case, but also in the Suffix Pronoun of the Second Person in both Numbers in all Semitic languages (3). In the Plural also, Ethiopic transforms the original sound into *k* in the same way: Masc. ክሙ *kĕmmū*; Fem. ክን *kĕn*, answering completely to the second

(1) *Cf.* now with this, in particular, Nöldeke, '*Untersuchungen zur semitischen Grammatik*', ZDMG XXXVIII, p. 407 *sqq.*, [reprinted with numerous additions in '*Beitr. z. sem. Sprachwiss.*', Strassburg 1904:—where v. p. 15 *sqq.*]

(2) As is still more clearly seen in the other Semitic languages.

(3) The difference between Ethiopic and the other Semitic languages is merely this, that the latter put into the difference of the types *ta* and *ka*, the contrast between the pronoun used as Subject and the pronoun used in a subordinate position, while the former—the Ethiopic language—employed the type *ta* for the separate pronoun, and the type *ka* for the pronoun when suffixed.

element in **አንትሙ**, **አንትን**, § 148.—For the *First Person* the sign in the Sing. is **ኩ**, in the Plural **ነ**. The *k* in *kū*, it would appear, is more original than the *t*, which all the other Semitic tongues exhibit (§ 65); and certainly the influence of the Personal sign of the second person has had the effect of making this *k* retain its position here more tenaciously (1). But all the more was the vowel *ū*,—which comes just as readily to hand as *ī* (§ 65),—bound to establish itself for the First Person, lest the First Person and the Second Person Fem. should be confounded together. The **ነ** of the Plural is a remnant of the full Pronoun **ንሕነ**, § 148.

Personal Signs of the Imperfect—[Indicative and Subjunctive].

2. For the *Imperfect* [or *Indicative*] and the *Subjunctive* the Personal signs have to be set before the Theme, in accordance with the original meaning of the grammatical form. But as the signs of the Verbal Stems are also set as prefixes, the Personal signs had to be compressed into the utmost possible brevity, to keep the several verbal forms from being overloaded in their commencement. In Ethiopic, therefore, just as in the other Semitic tongues, the prefixed Personal signs are either very short from the outset, or have been much abbreviated, and consist of one single comparatively strong letter. But as such a letter sufficed merely to denote the different Persons, but not the Genders or Numbers, the needful assistance was obtained from signs of Gender and Number attached farther to the close of the form.—The *Third Person*, first of all in the Sing., has in the beginning of the form **ይ** for the Masculine, and **ት** for the Feminine, and no farther marking in either case at the end of the Theme. The **ት** is assuredly the same mark of the Feminine which appears in the Perfect, and very generally besides in the domain of Nominal Stems (§ 126). But, in the same way, **ይ** is nothing else than the original Pronoun of the Third Person (§ 65), and first denotes merely the Third Person, as contrasted with the other personal signs **ት**, **እ**, **ን**, with-

(1) While the *t* of the Second Persons in the other tongues brought about the transition from *k* to *t* in the First.—Erman, ZÄS XXVII, p. 81, points out the *ku* of the 1st pers. sing. Perf. in Egyptian also. *Cf.* farther Halévy, '*Notes sémitiques*' in the '*Mélanges Renier*' (Paris 1886), p. 447 *sqq.* On كُ instead of تُ of the 1st pers. Sing. in Southern Arabia *cf.* v. Maltzan, ZDMG XXV, p. 197, and Mordtmann, *ibid.* XLIV, p. 191.

out distinction of gender (and so in the (1) Plur.). It is only as contrasted with the Feminine ተ, that it receives a Masculine signification (2). In the Plural there are appended, besides, *ū* for the Masc., and *ā* for the Fem., plainly the same signs of the Plural which are found in the Perfect; and in fact they always yield the mere sounds of *ū* and *ā* in Ethiopic, while, as is well known, the other tongues have continued to preserve, precisely in the Imperfect, their more original and complete form. Seeing that *ā*, by its difference from *ū*, of itself denotes the Fem., the change from ይ to ተ in the prefixed Personal sign is omitted in the Plural; ይ suffices for both genders, as being the general expression for the Third Person. To denote the *Second Person*, the sign ተ is prefixed in the Singular and Plural for both genders, that sign being a shortened form of አንተ, አንትሙ (§ 148). The ተ thus prefixed has to suffice for the indication of the Masc. Sing.; and the inconvenience of having in this way the 2nd pers. Sing. Masc. undistinguished from the 3rd pers. Sing. Fem., which has the very same form, has not been remedied in any way in Ethiopic. But the Fem. Sing., and the Masc. and Fem. Plural are again specially differentiated by appended signs. For the Fem. Sing. this purpose is served by the vowel *ī*, which also indicates the Feminine gender in the separate pronoun of the 2nd pers. Sing.; and to denote the Plural,—seeing that the *Person* has already been designated by a prefix as the Second,—the general signs of the Plural, used also in the Third Person, are made use of, viz. *ū* for the Masc. and *ā* for the Fem.— The *First Person* has the prefix እ in the *Sing.*, being a shortened

(1) In Assyrian, according to Haupt, the type *yaqtulu* for the Fem. occurs much oftener than *taqtulu*: v. ZDMG XXXIV, p. 757.

(2) This use of *i* for the Third Person without distinction of Gender points back to a time for the formation of the Personal signs, when ውእ and ይእ were not yet contrasted with each other as Masc. and Fem., any more than this contrast is shown in ይእዜ "now".—That ይ, יְ, يَ is not merely a modification of *we*, will perhaps now be generally acknowledged (v. Dietrich, '*Abhandl. zur hebr. Gramm.*', 1846, p. 122 *sqq.*; Ewald, '*Hebr. Spr.*', p. 434 Note). That Syriac has *ne* instead, still proves nothing for the softening of *ye* out of *ne*, but only that Syriac had in general at a very early stage lost the demonstrative word ይእ (as follows from the want of *ī* in the formation of the construct state) and that another demonstrative element came to be used in its place (§ 62).

form of አነ "I", and the prefix ን in the *Plural*, a shortened form of ንሕነ "We"; and these two prefixes are severally quite sufficient, as there is no distinction of Genders in the first Person.

§ 102. The attachment of these Personal signs to the Stem of the Tenses and Moods is regulated in part by the vowel character or consonantal character of the first letter of the Personal signs to be appended, and in part by the conditions of accentuation (¹). **Attachment of Personal Signs in the Perfect.**

1. Three of the Personal signs of the *Perfect* have a vowel commencement, viz: *at, ū, ā*; the others begin with a consonant. At one time all were certainly accented, but the majority of them have become tone-less. However, *ū, ā, kémmū, kén*, as a rule, keep their accent, and at the same time generally attract the tone of the word, since the actual word can have only one principal accent. The others have all become tone-less; but those which begin with a consonant, throw their accent no farther back than upon the syllable immediately preceding,—which invariably is either closed, or furnished with a long vowel or a diphthong; and only the vowel-beginning *at*, not forming any closed syllable before it, leaves unchanged throughout in the Perfect Stem the accent possessed by the Stem at first. But even the Personal signs *ū* and *ā*, which usually attract the tone to themselves, give it up to the foregoing syllable, if that syllable has a Stem-long vowel, or an unchangeably long vowel (as in ማሰኑ, ቆሙ). The nature of the attachment of these Personal signs, for the rest, is very simple. Seeing that the last radical in the Perfect-Stem is originally vowel-less (§ 91), the signs which commence with a consonant are appended to it in such a way that a closed syllable precedes them, while those which begin with a vowel are attached so as to draw the preceding third radical into their syllable. If the third radical is a vowel, the consonantal-commencing signs are simply appended to it as a new syllable; but, before the vowel-commencing ones, the vowel of the Stem must be hardened into a semivowel, and joined to the syllable of the Personal signs. These explanations may clear up the inflection of most of the Perfect-Stems; *e. g.* ነገረ· *nagárat, nagárka, nagárkī, nagárkū: nagarú, nagará* (²), *nagar-*

(¹) On the conditions of accentuation *cf.* TRUMPP, p. 525, and KÖNIG, p. 160 *sqq*.

(²) [TRUMPP, p. 525, followed by PRAETORIUS, '*Aethiop. Gramm.*' p. 46, puts the accent on the 2nd last syllable in the 3rd pl.:—*nagárū, nagárā*. TR.]

kémmū, nagarkén, nagárna. Or from **አስተርከበ**, *astárkabat, astarkábka,—astarkabū, astarkabkémmū.* But we must again call attention here to the fact that the four Personal signs of the second Person and the sign of the first Pers. Sing. assimilate their **ከ** to a preceding radical **ገ** or **ቀ**, *e. g.* **ዐረጊ** *ʿarággī*, for **ዐረግኪ**; **ነደቅሙ** *nadaqqémmū*, for **ነደቅክሙ** (§ 54); and that when two **ክ**'s or two **ን**'s meet together in such circumstances, the letter in each case is written once only; **መሐከ** *maḥákka*, **ከደነ** *kadánna*, **ድኅነ**, Gadla Ad. 135, 19; **ኮነ** *kōnna* 1st Plur., *ibid.* 23, 9; 25, 10; Hen. 103, 11; [**አመነ**, *e. g.* Chrest. p. 98, l. 24; *Kebra Nag.*, 90 b 8] (§ 55).

The following peculiar Perfect-Stems deserve special notice:—

(*a*) *Perfects which have the semi-passive vowel ĕ (instead of a) after the second radical,* viz. St. I, 1 in the Intransitive pronunciation, and St. III, 1 in the pronunciation **ተገብረ**,—transform their *ĕ* into the stronger *á* (60)(¹), in all those Persons where it stands in a closed syllable with the accent; thus though we have **ገብረት** and **ተገብሩ**, **ተገብራ**, we have also **ገበርከ** and **ተገበርከ**, and they maintain this *a* also in both forms of the Second Person Plural, where the accent rests on the Personal sign; thus we never have **ገብርክሙ** or **ተገብርክን**, but always **ገበርክሙ**, **ተገበርክን**; and from **ረኵሰ**:—**ረኰስከ**, **ረኰስክሙ**.

(*b*) The *Perfects* of the Stems I, 1; III, 1 & 2 from roots *mediae gutturalis*, in the semi-passive form of pronunciation **ምሕረ**, **ተግዕዘ**, **ተጽእለ**, may retain this *ĕ*-form throughout the whole Conjugation, thus, *e. g.* **ምሕርከ**, **ተግዕዝከ**, **ተጽእልከ** (v. Table III); and, in fact, this must be done by the Perfects of those Simple Stems, which in the Ground-form admit this Intransitive form alone, like **ልህቀ**, for instance. But many admit in the first Stem the *ă*-form of pronunciation as well as the *ĕ*-form (v. § 76 *ad fin.*) and besides, in the case of all of them, both pronunciations are possible in Stems III, 1 & 2 (²). Accordingly one may quite as well say **መሐርከ**, **ተገዐዝከ**, **ተጻአልከ** &c. Different manuscripts vary between the forms very considerably, in the case of such words (³). Such types, however, should in the first place be pronounced *meḥérka, ta-ge-ʿézka* or

(¹) *Cf.* Philippi, '*Beitr. z. Assyr.*' II, p. 378 *sq.*

(²) **ተተሕተ**, however, appears always to keep the *ĕ*-pronunciation.

(³) V., *e. g.*, Gen. 16, 13, Note.

more shortly, *tag-'ézka, ta-ṣe'-'élka,* although it can hardly be doubted that the later Abyssinians, who gave a soft pronunciation to all the Aspirates, like *mēḥra, tagē'za, taṣē'la,* said also *mēḥrka, tagē'zka, taṣe'lka* (v. § 46 *ad f.*).—*Roots tertiae gutturalis,* in all the Perfect-Stems, restore the *a* after the second-last radical, before all the terminations which begin with a consonant, but, in accordance with § 46, it must be lengthened into *ā*: **መልአ**, **መላእከ**; **ነስሐ**, **ነሳሕከ**; **ባልሐ**, **ባላሕከ**; **አግብአ**; **አግባእከ**; **አጸብሐ**, **አጸባሕከ**, **ገፍትአ**, **ገፍታእከ** &c., while, before all terminations which begin with a vowel, they retain the *ĕ* of the second-last radical: **ገፍትአት**, **ገፍትኡ**, **ገፍትአ** &c.

(*c*) *The tri-radical roots mediae geminatae,* in the semi-passive pronunciation of the Perfect of Stems I, 1 and III, 1, take, no doubt, the contracted form **ነዱ**, **ተነቡ**, **ተነብ** before all terminations beginning with a vowel, instead of *nadĕdū, tanabĕbū* &c.; but, before all terminations beginning with a consonant, where *a* must appear instead of *ĕ* (v. *supra*), the two repeated letters are always kept separate by this *a*, thus **ተነበብኩ**, **ተነበብክሙ** &c. **ምዕዐ**, the only Ethiopic root which has the same guttural as second and third radical, is regularly conjugated in the Perfect of St. II, 1, **አምዕዐ**, **አምዓዕከ** &c.; but, in accordance with § 97, it may have in St. III, 1, either the full form **ተምዕዐ**, or the contracted **ተምዐ**. The former is conjugated **ተምዓዕከ**, **ተምዕዑ** &c., but the latter like a Perfect of St. I, 2 of a root *tertiae gutturalis,* thus **ተምዐ**, **ተማዕከ**, **ተምዑ** (¹) &c.

(*d*) *Roots mediae infirmae,* whether they be *tertiae gutturalis* or not, in all the Perfect-Stems which have the mixed-sound pronunciation in the Ground-form, retain this pronunciation throughout all the other Persons, like **ሖረ**, **ሖርከ**; **ቦአ**, **ቦእከ**; **አሞተ**, **አሞትከ**; **አቤተ**, **አቤትከ**; **ኮነ** *kónna,* "we have become" Hen. 103, 11. But when they have hardened their radical vowel into a semivowel in the Ground-form, as in **ጠየቀ**, **አዕወረ**, **ተፈወሰ**, or have a diphthongal pronunciation, as in **ተሐውሰ**, **ተሠይመ**, *taḥausa, tašaima,* they carry the hardened pronunciation right through the whole formation, thus **ጠየቅሙ**, **አዕወርከ**, **ተፈወስከ**, **ተሐወስከ**, **ተሠየምከ**. Verbs, which in Stems II, 1 and IV, 1 have the shortened form

(¹) Thus, according to Ludolf; but **ተምዕዕከ** also appears, *e. g.* Ex. 32, 12.

አቀመ, **አብሐ**, **አስተብሐ**, are conjugated like the Perfects of the Simple Stem: **አቀምከ**, **አባሕከ**, **አስተባሕከ**.

(*e*) *Vowel-ending* tri-radical and multi-radical roots must in all Perfect-Stems (v. *supra*) harden their last radical into a semi-vowel before those terminations which begin with a vowel; but before all those which begin with a consonant they must sound that radical as a vowel. Since farther the second radical has generally *a* in this case, *u* or *i* as third radical combines with this *a* first of all into a diphthong: **ተለውከ**, **ገነይከ**, **በለይከ** from **በልየ**, **ሣቀይከ**, **ተጸሐየይከ**, **ተኀረይከ**, **አስተስረይከ**, **ጌገይከ**, **ፄወውከ**, **ተዘያነውኩ**, **አንሶሰውኩ**, and the diphthong is usually retained. But those roots at least which end in *ū* may modify the diphthong farther into a mixed sound: **ተሎከ**, **ተፌቶኩ**, **ሐዮኩ**, **መጽሎኩ** Gadla Ad. 21, 21; and the verb **ሀለወ** "to be", in particular, very commonly does so; thus we have not only **ሀሎከ**, **ሀሎክሙ**, **ሀሎነ** &c., but even **ሀሎት** instead of **ሀለወት**, inasmuch as one may, in accordance with § 91, say **ሀሎ** for **ሀለወ** itself. Less frequently the mixed sound appears in roots which end in *ī*, as in **ኀሬክሙ**, Josh. 24, 22; Judges 10, 14; and in **ተላጼኩ**, Judges 16, 17; Ex. 29, 17. Multi-literal roots have the mixed sound more frequently than have the Triliteral, because the Stems which are formed out of them are longer and are therefore abbreviated as much as possible.—Triliteral roots *tertiae infirmae*, and which at the same time are *mediae gutturalis* and have an intransitive form of pronunciation, take a peculiar conjugation, like **ርእየ** "to see"; **ርዕየ** "to herd (a flock)"; **ውዕየ** "to burn" (**ንህየ**, **ጥዕየ**, **ምህወ**, **ጽሕወ**). When terminations beginning with a consonant are applied to these verbs, types would arise in the first place, according to what has been said (v. *supra*, under *b*), like *re-'é-ī-ka*, but the *é* is regularly thrust aside by the radical (§ 51), and thus we have *re-'ī-ka*, **ርኢከ** &c.[1] (*v.* Table III). It cannot yet be said with certainty, whether those roots, which end in *u* (**ምህወ**, **ጽሕወ**), likewise follow this formation, seeing that they have not yet been supported by instances in the Persons concerned. It is possible that in these Persons they pass into the *a*-pronunciation (**ጸሐውከ**). Even **ርእየ** in St. III, 1, before terminations which begin with a consonant, falls back into the

---

(1) **ርኢይኩ** Hab. 3,2, 7 Cod Laur.; **ርኢይክዎ** Amos 9,1 Cod Laur.; [**ርእኪ** for **ርኢኪ** *Kebra Nag.* 25, Note 23.]

a-pronunciation, so that although we say ተርእየ, ተርእዩ &c. we have ተሬእይከ &c.—Doubly weak roots like ሐይወ, ረወየ, ጕየ, in accordance with what has been said in § 69, present no special features: ሐየውከ, ረወይከ, ጕየይከ &c.

§ 103. 2. *The attachment of the Personal signs in the Subjunctive and the Imperfect* [*or Indicative*]. As regards, first of all, *the Personal prefixes* ይ, ት, እ, and ን, the manner in which ይ is set before the Stem has already been dealt with in §§ 92—99; and all that has been said of ይ holds good of the other three also. Whenever the following radical has a syllable-vowel of its own,—as in the Imperfects of all Ground-Stems, in the Subj. of St. I, 2, 3 of the Triliteral Verb and of St. I of the Multiliteral, as well as in the Subj. of St. I, 1 of Vowel-centred and Vowel-beginning roots of weak formation—, these prefixes are uttered with a fugitive *ĕ*, and with *a* only when the following radical is a guttural, according to § 44. We have therefore not only የዐርግ, የዐንዝር, but also የሐዝ, የዐል from ውሕዘ, ውዕለ. But when these prefixes form along with the first radical a single (closed) syllable, as in the Subj. I, 1 of most of the Tri-radical Verbs, they are uttered with the full vowel *e*. Farther, in all Reflexive Stems formed by ተ, the Personal prefix closes with this ተ,—which gives up its *a*—, into ይት ([1]), in which proceeding the rules, explained in §§ 54, 55, must be attended to. Finally, the prefixes combine with the አ of the Causative Stems II and IV, as well as of the Reflexive Stem V, into ያ, ታ, አ, ና. *The Personal Suffixes* (which are the same in the Subjunctive, the Imperative, and the Imperfect) consist of mere vowels *ī*, *ū*, *ā*. They draw the tone of the word to themselves throughout, thus: ይገብሩ, ትነግሪ, ይፌጽሙ *yegabrū́*, *tenagrī́*, *yefēṣemā́* ([2]). As vowel-suffixes they attract the final letter of the Stem to their syllable, and when that letter is a vowel, as in roots *tertiae infirmae*, it must be hardened into the corresponding semi-vowel. But although the final letter of the last syllable of the Stem moves forward into the syllable of the termination, and the

Attachment of Personal Signs in the Imperfect—[Indicative and Subjunctive].

([1]) Differing thus from the method followed in Arabic, which here also shows itself richer in vowels.—The shortening of ተ into ት is the less surprising, when according to § 80 this ተ itself must in earlier times have sounded *it* or *et*.

([2]) *Cf.*, however, Trumpp, p. 526 *sqq.*

last-mentioned syllable attracts also the tone to itself, yet the formative or radical vowel of the last syllable of the Stem (which now stands in an open syllable) is kept unaltered, as in ይልብስ, ትልበሲ; ይኑም, ይኑሙ; ይለድ, ትለዲ; ይንግር, ይንግሩ; ይበልሕ, ይበልሑ; ይፌጽም, ትፌጽሚ; ያንግር, ታንግሪ &c. Also, in cases where the formative vowel has been absorbed by a vowel occurring as third radical in the Ground-form, as in ይበኪ, ይትሉ, ይጌጊ, it must again appear, after the radical vowel has been hardened into a semivowel:—ይበክዩ, ይትልዉ, ትጌግዪ. In old manuscripts, however, types are found like ይብኪዩ for ይብክዩ Abb. LV; 4 Esr. 6, 25; [ይበኪዩ &c., v. *Kebra Nag.*, *Introd.* p. XVI;] ይማቂዩ Amos 6, 15 Cod. Laur.; ይሰቲዩ Amos 9, 14 Cod. Laur. (1). In altering the syllabic relations the following has to be noticed: If the last Stem-syllable has the formative vowel *ĕ*, as in ይነግር, or at least if it had it or should have it, as in ይትሉ, and if this last Stem-syllable is preceded by an open syllable with a short vowel,—either with *ă* (ይነግር, ይትሉ), or with *ĕ* (ንግር)—, then this *ă* or *ĕ* attracts to itself the first letter of the last Stem-syllable,—when along with its *ĕ* it is being isolated—, with the result that that letter gives up its *ĕ* and becomes attached to the preceding syllable as a vowelless closing letter(2): ይነግር, ትነግሪ *yenáger*, *tenagrí*; ንግር, ንግሩ *negér*, *negrú*; ያስተረክብ, ያስተረክቡ *yāstarákeb*, *yāstarakbú*(3). Farther, if types like ይመልእ, ይነውም, ይመይጥ, are at least against analogy (§§ 43 and 50) pronounced *yemál-'e*, *yenáum*, *yemáiṭ*, the forms ትመልኢ, ይነውሙ, ይመይጡ are, on the other hand, necessarily pronounced *temal-'í*, *yenaumú*, *yemaiṭú*.

Verbs tertiae gutturalis: In all those cases in which the last Stem-syllable should have the formative vowel *a*, these verbs lengthen it in the Ground-form into *ā*: ይምጻእ, ምጻእ, ይትመላእ, ይትፌማሕ, ይትፈማሕ, ይትጋባእ, ተጋባእ, ይትራኃራኃ &c. But if a Personal termination is applied, and the Aspirate is drawn into the following

---

(1) In DILLMANN's '*Chrest. Aeth.*', p. 147, Str. 3, l. 2 the MS. offers ረስዮ in preference to ረስዩ.

(2) *Cf.*, however, TRUMPP, p. 526 *sqq*.

(3) [Or more shortly:—In Impf. and Imper. forms, of the type *yenágĕr*, *nĕgĕr*, the obscure *ĕ* of the last stem-syllable falls away before the increment of the personal vowel-suffixes *ī*, *ū*, *ā*; *e. g.* ትነግር *tenágĕr* (2 *sg. m.*) becomes ትነግሪ *tenagrī* (2 *sg. f.*). TR.]

syllable, not only is the reason for lengthening the *a* removed, but by § 45 this formative *ă* must pass into *ĕ*, and then the second-last radical which introduces this *ĕ*,—in the special cases which have just been more precisely determined,—loses the *ĕ* entirely and becomes attached, as a vowel-less letter closing the syllable, to a preceding open syllable which has a short vowel, thus: ትምጽአ; ምጽኡ *meṣ-'ú* for *me-ṣe-'ú*:—ይትመልኡ, *yetmal-'ú* for *yetma-le-'ú*: ትትፌሦሒ, ትትፈሦሒ *tetfaššeḥī* &c.(1). Only the few Subjunctives and Imperatives of vowel-beginning or vowel-centred roots of weak formation, which have been described in § 93,—viz. ይፃእ and ፃእ from ወፅአ, and ይባእ, ባእ, ይማእ from ቦአ and ሞአ,—preserve the long *ā* throughout the entire Conjugation, inasmuch as it serves at the same time to compensate for a rejected radical letter (v. Table III). ይባእ, ይማእ and ባእ are formed after the analogy of ይፃእ and ፃእ.

Double-lettered Verbs (ע"ע). If in the Ground-form of these verbs the two like letters are separated merely by the weak vowel *ĕ*, and the first of them is preceded by an open syllable with a short vowel(2), then in the case of forms which are increased by personal terminations (*cf. supra*) the two like letters are brought together, without any separating vowel, and they are in that case generally indicated in writing by one letter only. The assumed conditions in the ground-form are exemplified in ይነብብ, ንብብ, ያንድድ, ያስተኀሥሥ, ይደመስስ, ያመረስስ, but not in ይኰንን, ያኰንን, ኰንን, አኰንን, because in this case the first ን has to be pronounced as a doubled letter. The above forms, when increased by personal endings run thus:—ይነቡ, ንቡ, ያንዱ, ያስተኀሡ, ይደመሱ, ያመረሱ, but also with the letter repeated, as ይነብቡ (v. § 55)(3). The Imperfects and Subjunctives from አምዐዐ and ተምዐዐ—, ያምዕዕ and ይትመዓዕ (§§ 96, 97) cannot yet be all substantiated, but they present nothing in their inflection, which might not be understood from the general rules, *e. g.* ያምዕዑ Numb. 16,30; Deut. 31,20,29;

---

(1) [Or,—Forms like ምጻእ+*ū* pass theoretically through the following changes:—*meṣā'* + *ū*=*meṣă* + ኡ=*meṣĕ* + ኡ=*meṣ* + ኡ=ምጽኡ. TR.]

(2) Cases like ይኅሡ for ይኅሥሡ Cod. Pocock., Ps. 77,9 rest on copyists' errors.—Notice the Subj. ያንበለብል *Fal.* f. 51 ('*Lex.*', col. 1235) from a multiliteral root.

(3) V., on the other hand, König, p. 95.

Hen. 69,1; or ይትመዐዉ John 7,23.—In like manner Imper. ተምዕ (§ 97), ተምዒ, ተምዑ, ተምዓ; or ተምዕዒ, ተምዕዑ, ተምዕዓ.

The Conjugation of Verbs *tertiae infirmae* presents no difficulty, seeing that ī, ū, as well as the diphthongs and mixed sounds *ai*, *au*, ē, ō may be easily resolved into their corresponding semivowels, and that, according to § 52, all the groups of sounds, which occur in these cases, viz. *yī*, *yū*, *yā*, *wī*, *wū*, *wā*, are admitted in the Ethiopic language. The first Imperfect of ብህለ (§ 92), ይቤ, which is employed as an Aorist, forms ይቤ, ትቤ, ትቤሊ, እቤ; ይቤሉ, ይቤላ, ትቤሉ, ትቤላ, ንቤ (1). The second Imperfect ይብል, as well as the Subjunctive ይበል and the Imperative በል, together with the Imperfect of ክህለ, ይክል (§ 92) follow the ordinary rules: ይበሉ, ይብሉ, ይክሉ, በሉ &c.

FORMATION OF NOUNS.

Classes of Nouns; and Methods of Stem-Formation.

§ 104. Overagainst the Verb stands the Noun (*Naming-Word*), both the *Noun*, in the narrower sense of the term, which is derived from roots conveying a notion or conception, and the *Pronoun*, which is derived from demonstrative roots. The formation of Nouns, like that of Verbs, passes through stages three in number: 1. The Nominal Stem is formed from the Root; 2. the Stem is then differentiated by Genders and Numbers; 3. the words thus elaborated assume special forms, or Cases, according to the special relations upon which they enter in the Sentence. This formation, however, in the case of Pronouns, differs in some respects from that of Nouns properly so-called; and farther, amongst Nouns themselves the Numerals have much that is peculiar, and in some points they share too in the peculiarities of Pronouns. Accordingly in the account to be given of Nouns, we distinguish these three classes: 1. *Nouns*, in the narrower sense of the term; 2. *Pronouns*; 3. *Numerals*.

(1) *Cf.* Trumpp, p. 526.

A. FORMATION OF NOUNS—IN THE NARROWER SENSE OF THE TERM.

I. STEM-FORMATION OF NOUNS.

Nouns are divided according to their signification, first of all into Words of Conception, or Conceptional words (*Abstract Nouns*), such as bring forward in the form of a Noun, an idea, an action, or a property purely by itself, like *Belief*, *Killing*, *Quickness*,— and into Words of Statement (*Concrete Nouns*), which state the notion as incorporated in some being or thing, and attached thereto. Concrete Nouns themselves are again divided into Self-dependent words (*Substantives*), which give a name to a person or thing in accordance with a conception or notion perceived by the mind as having been realised in the one or the other, *i. e.*, *Names of persons and of things*, and words which are not Self-dependent (*Adjectives*), but which state a conception as being realisable in a person or thing, and therefore always involve a reference to a person or thing, to which they are ready to be attributed, *i. e. Descriptive* or *Qualifying Words*. These two distinctions between Nouns, in accordance with their meaning, are not in themselves very stable.— An Abstract Noun may, by a slight alteration of the sense, be turned into the name of a thing or a person (as *e. g. Clothing* may first of all mean *the act of clothing*, but afterwards also *the dress*; and in like manner, *First-birth* may come to mean *the first-born*); or it may take the place of a descriptive word (as in: 'God is truth'); and a descriptive word may easily become the name of a person or a thing. Nevertheless, that fundamental distinction must be adhered to in treating of Formation, seeing that for the proper understanding of Stem-formation the main consideration is,—what was the original meaning of a word, and not what is its derived meaning. Special classes of Nouns, besides, are formed by *Infinitives* and *Participles*. They are distinguished from other Nouns by issuing from the Stems of the verb, and not directly from the root. They are accordingly more closely connected with the verb than is any other Noun (*Verbal Nouns*), and they set forth the conception contained in the verb in its Stem-determination(¹),

(¹) But the Participle and the Infinitive in Semitic, as is well-known, accompany the Verb no farther than up to the distinction between the Verbal Stems. They do not share in the Tense distinction.

either as a purely Conceptional word (*Infinitive*), or as a Descriptive or Attributive word (*Participle*). Of each of these two classes there are to be found, in those Semitic tongues which still retain their full wealth of form, as many forms as the Verb has Stems. But Ethiopic has sustained serious loss, at least in the domain of the Participle. It is no longer capable of forming a Participle from every Verb in every one of its Stems; and only from a few Stems of comparatively few verbs has it retained the Participles, as the scattered remains, so to speak, of an earlier stage of formation.— Still, it makes up for the Participle in another way. Infinitives are more regularly formed; but as they constitute a special Class of Nouns, we shall deal with them, only in concluding our survey of Nominal Stem-formation. On the other hand the description of the Participial forms, which are still retained in a dispersed condition, has been embodied in the account to be given of the other Nominal Stems,—for the reason, mainly, that such forms have, to some extent, assumed the meaning of ordinary Adjectives or Substantives.

The means employed in the formation of Nominal Stems have already been enumerated (§ 74), viz.: Inner vowel-change; Inner increase by doubling individual radicals; and Outward increase by attaching formative letters or syllables. And in particular the feminine Nominal ending is made use of, even in carrying out the formation of the Nominal Stem itself and in establishing its meaning, inasmuch as Conceptional words and the stronger Abstract Nouns are readily conceived as being of the feminine gender. The Inner vowel-change is unlimited; but as regards multiplicity in the forms produced thereby, Ethiopic is inferior to Hebrew and Arabic, first of all because it has now only two short vowels. It has not even kept all those forms,—still in use in other tongues—, which it might have done, even with its more slender stock of vowels, but it has been content in this matter, as in others, with what is most necessary and essential, and has allowed whatever else once existed to disappear. Thus in many cases older forms, or common Semitic forms, are now represented merely by a few fragments from ancient times, or by words brought in from a foreign source.

Nouns in the narrower sense of the term (apart from Participles and Infinitives) are derived either from the root (Primitive Nouns), or from other Nouns (Denominative Nouns). Of the latter class Ethiopic has a large number. In particular, conceptional words, words denoting properties, and their relative attributive words, are often derived in this way. Individual Nouns, besides Infinitives and Participles proper, are also formed from derived Verbal Stems, chiefly when the Verbal Stem expresses a simple idea and makes up in this way for a Simple Stem which is wanting.

In reviewing the Stem-formation of Nouns we start from simple and original forms, and advance to Compounds (in which several formative expedients have been co-operating) and to Derivatives.

The simplest and most general method of formation is that which makes use of *Inner vowel-change*; for every Nominal form has definite formative vowels, which convey its meaning. *Inner increase of the radicals* constitutes the second stage of formation; and *External formative devices* furnish the third. In all three stages, however, the vocalisation is of essential importance. Its nature cannot generally be described beforehand; but when compared with the vocalisation of the Verb, the peculiarity of that of the Noun is shown in a preference for longer, weightier and broader vowels (1).

Like the Tenses of the Verb the Nominal Stems in Ethiopic once also ended in Vowels; and this vowel-ending, through the change of vowels happening in it, served at the same time to denote the different relations of the Noun in the Sentence, viz. the Cases (v. § 142 *sqq.*). This vowel-ending, however, without assuming which a series of Nominal forms could not have been accounted for, was, in accordance with § 38, given up at an early stage, at least in the Ground-form of the Nominal Stem.

1. SIMPLE NOMINAL STEMS.

1. First and Simplest Formation: with accented Short Vowel after 1st Radical.

§ 105. 1. *The simplest Nominal formation consists in the establishment of a short but accented vowel after the first radical*: The second radical is vowel-less; and the third, which once had the general vowel-ending of all Nominal Stems, was, later on, given without a vowel (§ 38) (2). This form stands in direct contrast with

(1) On the Tone-relations of the Noun v. Trumpp, p. 531 *sqq.*, and König, p. 154 *sqq.*

(2) *Cf.* Trumpp, p. 532; König, p. 145.—Corresponding forms appear in Hebrew מֶלֶךְ, סֵפֶר, קֹדֶשׁ; Arabic قَتْل, قِتْل, قُتْل, Aramaic ܡܰܠܟ, ܣܶܦܪ, ܩܽܘܕܫ.

the coinage of the root as a Verb (where a vowel follows the *second* radical). It has at first always the force of a pure Conceptional word, like ብትክ "gap", ሀጕል "corruption", ውኅድ "fewness", ወርድ "breadth". But by virtue of farther modification of the meaning (§ 104) these Conceptional words were often employed to designate objects and substances in which the idea becomes realised, so that this form goes on to furnish expressions for names of things, names of persons, plants, animals, and the like, *e. g.* ልብስ ("clothing") "dress", ነፍስ ("breath") "soul", ብርት ("cutting") "brass", ወልድ ("birth") "son", ወርኅ "moon", ከርሥ "belly", ከልብ "dog" &c. Many very old words especially, the roots of which are no longer used at all as Verbs, like ዐይን "eye", are formed in this way. But pure Adjectives are not expressed in this form (1). The vowel which is established in the first part of the form is either *ă* or *ĕ* in Ethiopic. Into this *ĕ* have been taken the *ŭ* (*o*) and *ĭ* (*e*) of the allied languages; but in a few roots beginning with Aspirate-gutturals an original *u* has, in accordance with § 26, endeavoured to save itself by taking refuge in a Guttural or an Aspirate, like ጕርን "threshing-floor" (גֹּרֶן), ጕንድ "Stem" (גֹּמֶד), ኵሕል "dye for the eyes" (كُحْل), ቍስጥ "*costus*" (قُسْط), ቍር "cold" (קֹר), ኵል "totality" (כֹּל) (2). Any essential difference in meaning between words with *a* and words with *e* is, generally speaking, no longer discernible. When this form has been produced in both modes of pronunciation by one and the same root, these modes often have also different significations attached to them, in such a way that in some cases the word which contains *a* has a more active meaning or one more connected with a person,—while that which contains *e* conveys a more passive meaning or one more suggestive of a thing, as ገብር "slave", ግብር "business"; ነግድ "foreigner, ንግድ "journey"; but also with other kinds of difference, as in—: ንእስ "youth", ናእስ

(1) For ይምን, ድኅር, ፀግም never mean *dexter, posterior, laevus,* as Ludolf thinks, but "the right, back, left side"; and ኄር "good" خَيْر is doubtless merely an abbreviated form of خَيِّر and thus belongs originally to a different formation.

(2) Farther ቍርዕ, ቍንጽ, ቍጽል, ቈልሕ; ኵርሀ, ኵስሕ, ኍልቍ; also ቍይጽ "leg".—The view propounded above is also approved of by Trumpp, p. 532, but contested by König wrongly, pp. 45, 52.

"smallness"; ሐብል "rope", ሕብል "cunning"; ፍትሕ "judgment", ፊትሕ "solution". But frequently both forms are used with like meaning, as ርሕብ and ራሕብ "breadth"; ርምሕ and ረምሕ "spear"; ዕርቅ and ዐርቅ "reconciliation"; ቅጽር and ቀጽር "citadel"; ቅንእ and ቀንእ "envy"; ነፍቅ and ንፍቅ "chest", "box"; ቍጽል and ቈጽል "leaf"; ኍልቍ and ኈልቍ "number"; ጸልእ and ጽልእ "hatred"; ዳኅን and ድኅን "well", "weal";—for seeing that on the one hand, *a* may be softened into *e* (§ 18), and that on the other, Aspirates and Aspirate-resembling letters (like ቀ in the examples adduced) have a preference for the *a*-sound, this alternation between *a* and *e* in certain words is easily explained, and there is no need to assume the existence of two original forms. Finally, we must not fail to notice (¹) that several of these words which have *á* are nothing other than somewhat maimed forms of original Participles of the type ጋብር. This is the case possibly with ገብር "slave",—originally "a worker", and ዐርክ "friend" &c. On the pronunciation of these words *cf. supra*, § 38.

A *Middle-Aspirate* exerts no influence on the *é*-formation:—ዝእብ "wolf", ምዕር "a time", ምእት "a hundred"; but in the *á*-formation it lengthens that vowel into *ā* (§ 46):—ጋእዝ "quarrel", ሣሕቅ "mockery".

Roots mediae geminatae in both formations leave their double-letter unresolved (²):—ልብ "heart", ሕግ "law", ሥን "beauty" (سُنَّة), ስን "tooth", ዝቅ "a skin", "bottle" (زِقّ), ድብ "a bear" (دُبّ), ግብ "pit" (جُبّ), ፍት "piece" and "gift" (Judges 19,5; Jas. 1, 17), ምት "husband" (*Pl.* አምታት); ሐጽ "arrow" (חֵץ), ሠቅ שַׂק, ረቅ "leaf of paper", በክ "emptiness", ነድ "flame", ተን "vapour", "smoke" (ثُنَّا), ደቅ "little one", ፀር "enemy", ጠል "dew", ጠፍ "an infant" (טַף) (frequently employed in the Abyssinian Chronicles).

From *Vowel-beginning roots* this formation is always strong: ይምን "right side", የብስ "firm *or* dry land", "continent", ውስጥ "interior", ውኅድ "fewness", ወልድ "son", ወትር "sinew" (יֶתֶר).

In the formation from *roots mediae infirmae* the vowel *é*

(¹) V. Ewald, '*Hebr. Spr.*' § 146, Note.

(²) Accordingly ጥን must also be read for ጥንን in Ludolf's Dictionary col. 562: ቲን "length" might be merely a lengthened form of ትን, but it may also come from a root ቲነ=תנן.

(§ 50) is displaced by the radical vowel, thus:—ሒስ "reproof", ሚን "cunning", ቢጽ "comrade", ቂም "revenge", ኪን "art", ጢስ "smoke" (طَسَّان وَطِيس), ሲሕ "dropsy" (فسّ), ጺእ "filth" (צֵאָה), ኑኅ "length", ፀዑግ "baseness"; ሡዕ "tinder" (شَيُوع)(1). On the other hand, the vowel *á* forms with the radical vowel a diphthong, which is often retained, especially in words from roots *primae* or *tertiae gutturalis*, but which often also blends into a mixed sound:—ሀይድ "plunder", ሰይፍ "sword", ኀይል "power", ሐይቅ "shore", አይኅ "flood", ጸይሕ "street", ወይን "wine", ዐይን "eye" (ዐይግ, ደይን, ዘይት, ገይብ, ሠይእ), ዐውድ "circuit", ዘውግ "pair", ለውሕ "table" ('*tabula*'), ዘውዕ and ዛውዕ "jests", አውል "vapour", ሰውጥ "scourge" (ቀውዕ, ከውር); or ሤጥ "price", ቤት "house", ዴር "cloister" (دَيْر), ሜስ "mead"(2), ኬድ *βάσις* Sap. 13, 18, ሞት "death", ሞቅ "warmth", ቆም "growth", ዮም "today", ዖፍ "bird", ዖም "tree", ጎሕ "dawn" (ሦክ, ሶር, ጎል, ጎር, ጾም, ጾር, ጾጥ, ሮስ). But together with these genuine Ethiopic forms, there occurs also another pronunciation,—one with long *ā*,—particularly in some very old words. This *ā* proves in most cases to have been simplified from *ō* in the Ethiopic and Arabic manner (§ 18)(3): ቃል "word" (*cf. supra*), ዷር "race" (not ዶር), ቃስ "breeches" (*cf.* كَوْث); often under the influence of an Aspirate: ሃፍ "sweat", ላሕ "mourning" (whence ሀሬወ and ለሐወ seem to be derived), ባዕ "span" (بَاع, بَوْع), ዓም "year", ሳዕ "hour" (as well as ሰዓት, سَاعَة, properly "moment", שָׁעָה).—On the other hand ፋል "good omen" appears to be shortened from ፋእል (فَأْل), and ዓው "curvature" from a form like عَوًّا and عَوَّة; finally ዳስ "hut" seems to be originally an Arabic Participle دَاسّ (*cf.* دَسِيعَة), or a lengthened form of ደስ.

Roots tertiae infirmae neither reject their last radical, if we except a few very old words of uncertain derivation, nor introduce the vowel-pronunciation, but on the contrary invariably harden

(1) ስውጥ Cantic. 7, 3 cannot be a Substantive, as LUDOLF assumes, but is a Part. Fem.; ጸውዕ "invitation" is derived from the Intensive Stem of the verb.

(2) Perhaps also ጼው "salt", root צוי or صوى.

(3) V. EWALD, '*Gr. Ar.*' §§ 73, 387.

it into a semivowel, and thus possess a thoroughly strong formation. This formation, however, has its explanation solely in the assumption (§ 38) that at one time all nouns, including these, ended in a short vowel; and it is precisely in words of this formation that such vowels must of necessity be given utterance to, in order to render them pronounceable (1). The forms of this sort, known as yet, are: **ሥርው** *šérwᵉ* "root", **ግጽው** "representation", **እኁው** or **እኍ** "brother", **ጽጕ** "a lane" (= **ጽግው** שׁוק), **ሐቍ** 'an odoriferous wood' (*cf.* حَبَق); **ሳሕው** "extension", **በድው** "wilderness" (بَدْو), **ቃኑው** "emulation", **ራእይ** "face", **ላሕይ** "beauty", **ናህይ** "recreation", "refreshment". Obviously this formation has become very rare; and there is no example of it where the word has the vowel *é* and itself comes from a root ending in *ī* (2). The rarity of such words might occasion astonishment, were it not sufficiently explained by the circumstance, that when the final vowel had been dropped in the later pronunciation, the whole of this formation was allowed to fall out of use, and,—so far as pure conceptional words ought to have been formed in it,—was replaced by another formation (§ 106). Farther, a few very old words appear, which have only two radicals, but which,—sometimes before a Suff. Pron. and in the Pl., sometimes in derivatives,—pass into tri-radical roots with final *u*. They are therefore to be enumerated here, although in stray cases the tri-radical root is only derived from them, and not they from the root: **ዕድ** "man", **ስም** "name", **እድ** "hand", **ዕፅ** "tree", **ጥብ** "female breast", **ስት**, **ሰት** "papyrus", **ደም** "blood" (3), **ገጽ** "face", **አፍ** "mouth", **ሐጽ** "arrow", **አብ** "father", **ሐም** "father-in-law". As regards their formation, it is not indeed certain that all of them have been formed precisely according to the first form here assumed by us; but in their type they resemble mostly those words which belong to the first formation; and since their true genesis, from its extreme antiquity, can no longer be established with certainty, and at all events cannot be classified under any of the modes of formation still in force in the language, we have set them down among Nouns of the simplest form.

An onomatopoetic word of this formation is **ቋዕ** "raven"

(1) V. however TRUMPP, p. 532.

(2) For **ርእይ** is an Infinitive and of quite another origin.

(3) Whence אדם seems to have been derived. [—A doubtful derivation.]

[also ጕጕ, a word of similar meaning *Kebra Nag.*, 122 b 17, *var.*]. The following foreign words too have been altered in accordance with this form, viz.:—ህንድ "India", ጽርእ "Greece", ፍሥሕ "passover", ለንጽ "λέντιον", ተይ or ትይ "brimstone" (*θεῖον*) &c.

Several of these forms, especially of those which have received the signification of common Nouns, passed over to the feminine type, like ኀይመት "tent" (خَيْمَة), ጽግንት "bat", ጽፍንት "wallet", (صَفْنَة), ገነት "garden", ቀንአት "*galbanum*", ሐሞት "bile" (for ሐምወት), ሰከት and ሰኰት "street", "lane", (related to ጽጕ v. *supra*), ኆኅት "door" (خَوْخَة), ኖራ "lime" (نُورَة), and several others ending in *ā* (§ 127).

2. Second Formation:—with accented Short Vowel or Tone-long Vowel after 2nd Radical:—

§ 106. 2. The Second mode of formation consists in *the establishment of an accented short vowel, or a tone-long vowel, after the second radical.* Words of this form are Verbal Nouns. They give evidence at once of this relationship of theirs to the Verb by the position of their formative vowel after the second radical, inasmuch as the Verb has its essential vowel precisely in that place. In meaning they are either conceptional words of an Infinitive type, derived from the old Imperfect, or Descriptive words, derived from the Perfect(1). A subdivision naturally takes place into two classes, according as the words issue from the Imperfect or the Perfect.

Conceptional Words derived as Verbal Nouns from the Imperfect (Subjunctive form):—

(1) *Conceptional (or Abstract) words derived from the Imperfect,*—corresponding to Infinitives and Substantives of an Infinitive form in other Semitic languages. The old Imperfect, *i. e.* the Subjunctive (§ 91), in Ethiopic has for its vowel *é* or *á*, the former for the Transitive Verb, the latter for the Intransitive; and these two vowels must turn up also in the conceptional words derived from it.

With original Transitive *é* after 2nd Radical, but now with Fem.-ending *at*, and Accent on the 1st Syllable.

(*a*) *Conceptional words, however, with an accented é after the second radical* are no longer met with. The *é* proved too weak to keep the tone(2), and so they passed over in a body to *the Feminine form* (§ 104),—as when, *e. g.*, instead of ስብር *sebér*, we have ስብረት (*sébrat*, the accent going to the 1st syllable) "breach", and it was only by this Feminine-ending thus assumed, that they were kept from being confounded with the First Simple formation by

(1) V. on this point Ewald, '*Hebr. Spr.*' § 148, *a*.

(2) Just as it also lost the tone in the Subj., § 92.

means of *é*. This Feminine-ending *at*, less frequently *ā*, (§ 127 *b*) is very common([1]). It is the form in which *Nomina actionis*, in accordance with their meaning, almost invariably appear, such as ሩጸት "running", "career", ርክበት "discovery", ርግዘት "piercing through", or Abstract words of Quality like ስክረት "drunkenness", ርጥበት "dampness"; rarely, Common Nouns like ሕገዘት ('lair') "stall", ምትሀት ('apparition') "spectre", ስቍረት ('excavation') "hole", ቍልፈት ('the being uncircumcised') "foreskin", ሕልቀት ('circle') "ring", ጥውቀት "oppression". When nouns of this type and those of the First formation are both developed from one root, then the former always signify action pure and simple:—ሂደት "plundering" (ሀይድ "plunder"), ልብሰት "putting on clothes" (ልብስ "clothes"), ምልአት "filling up", "being full" (ምልእ "fulness") &c. Such words are also formed from Middle-Aspirate and Final-Aspirate roots, although these have the vowel *a* in the Subj.,— like ስሕተት "error", ብሕአት "fermentation", ውግአት "butting", ጕድአት "striking", "stroke" &c., and in the same way from many intransitive roots. From *roots mediae geminatae* this form always runs like ስጠት *séṭṭat* "rent", "gap", ንደት "fever", ግሰት "touch", ጕየት "flight", ("escape"), ሥረት "flying" (of a bird), ሕመት "blackness", "ink", ፍትት "piece", "fragment", መዐት "anger" (§ 44). *Roots beginning with ū* have often the strong form in such words, even when the Subj. has the weak, as in ውሕዘት "flowing", ውግረት "throwing", "cast", ውግአት "butting", ውዷት "accusation" (v. *infra*), but in most cases they have the weak form:— ልደት "birth", ርደት "descent", ርቀት "spitting", ዕለት ('duration') "day", ድቀት "fall", ፀአት (§ 44) "exit", and analogous to it በአት "entrance" from በእ (§ 68). In cases where the two forms,— strong and weak—, both occur, they have different meanings:— ዕየት "brand-mark", ውዕየት "burning"; ግዘት "anathema", ውግዘት "excommunication". Several others of these words are given with an intimately attached feminine-ending (§ 128):—ጥንት "beginning" (ውጥነት "the commencing"), ቅሥት "strife", ግብት "a

([1]) In Hebrew, forms like עֶזְרָה, חָכְמָה, לֶדֶת &c. correspond, Ewald, '*Hebr. Spr.*' § 150; in Arabic, نُقْطَةٌ &c.—On Tone-relations v. Trumpp, p. 533. —According to König, p. 77, these Feminine forms would belong to Nouns of the First formation.

sudden occurrence", ሕስት "loan", ሀብት "gift", in which the *a* of የሀብ has held its ground, by virtue of the Aspirate.

Forms from *Roots mediae infirmae* exhibit invariably (1), in accordance with § 50, the vowel-pronunciation of the middle radical: ሙተት "dying", ሑረት "going", ቁመት "standing", ዑረት "blindness", ፁገት "baseness"; ሚጠት "turning", ኂጠት "deceit", ሢመት ('installation') "office", ዒለት "emigration", ቂሐት "redness"; and only those roots, which are, besides. *tertiae infirmae*, have forms with a diphthongal pronunciation, like ሕይወት "life", ጥውየት "distortion". On ቤእት v. *supra*.

In the case of *Roots tertiae infirmae* this formation is all the more in use, that the employment of the first, simple formation for these roots has greatly declined (§ 105). In accordance with § 40, the type is either ኅርየት "election", ርእየት "face", "aspect", ስቅየት "irrigation", ዕርየት "equalising", ቅቅየት "avarice", ትልወት "succession", ዕልወት "apostasy", ክዕወት "outpouring", ዝርወት "dispersion", — or ምሴት (as well as ምስየት) "evening", ንዴት "poverty", ዕሤት "recompense", ምኔት ('solitude') "monastery". ፍኖት ('sending') "way"; and in several words the two forms are used indifferently, like ቅንየት and ቅኔት "service", ርምየት and ርሜት "throw", ርቅየት and ርቄት "enchantment", ፍትወት and ፍቶት "lust"; *cf. supra* p. 80. With እ prefixed (§ 34): እብሬት "alternation". A few words which have an Aspirate (§ 44) or ቀ (§ 48) for their initial letter exhibit *a* in the first syllable instead of *ĕ*:—ሕምየት and ሐሜት "calumny", ሀኬት "weariness", ሐሤት "joy", ቀንአት and ቅንአት "ardour" (Numb. 25, 11 Note), ሐቅረት "contempt", ቅፌት and ቀፌት "density", "hardness", ቀቶት "bet". Of a more Arabic character is the form (2) ሐሰት "lie", for ሐስወት from the root ሐሰወ, which, according to Praetorius, '*Beitr. z. Ass.*' I, p. 34, possibly comes from حسّ. *Cf. infra* also § 128.

With Intransitive *á* after 2nd Radical.

§ 107. (*b*) *The formation with an intransitive a* is still retained in a variety of fashions.

(*α*) *The second Radical is pronounced with* (3) *á, the first,*

(1) Ludolf, '*Lex. Aeth.*' col. 564, adduces ጥውመት, but without a passage in support.

(2) Ewald, '*Gr. Arab.*' § 410.

(3) At least originally having the Tone; *cf.* Trumpp, p. 533. In Arabic

with fugitive ĕ. This type is formed only from intransitive or semi-passive verbs and is therefore by no means very common. To it belong words like **ኅጽር** "shortness", **ዕመቅ** "depth", **ቅጠን** "thinness", **ሕሠም** "ugliness"; and from roots *mediae gutturalis* (§ 44): **ሠሐቅ** "laughter", **ጸሐፍ** "census", **ረሐብ** "width", **ክሒድ** "denial", **ረኀብ** "hunger"; from roots *tertiae gutturalis* **ትጋሀ** "vigilance", **ስረሕ** "fatigue", **ኅጣእ** "lack"; in words *mediae geminatae*, the doubled letter is always opened out: **ጥበብ** "wisdom", **ክበብ** "roundness", **ቍጠጥ** "thinness"; *tertiae infirmae*: **እከይ** "vileness", **ዕበይ** "magnitude", or, by the diphthong becoming a mixed sound, **ስተይ** and **ስቴ** "drinking", **ጽጌ** "bloom", **ፍሬ** "fruit" (**ዕፄ**, **ኅሬ**, **ሕጼ**), perhaps also **ሀበ** "copious dew" (of obscure derivation) (¹). Roots with initial *u* usually make the feminine take the place of this form (v. § 106); yet to this form belongs **ረቅ** "spittle" (on the other hand we have **ርቀት** "spitting"), and in like manner **ድድ** "foundation" (probably √ידד) (²). From a root beginning with *i* comes **ይበስ** "aridity", because this *i* is never discarded in the Subj. From roots *mediae infirmae* this form is exceedingly rare (**ዕወር** "blindness"), and is replaced sometimes by the Feminine formation, as with roots just mentioned, and sometimes by the First Simple formation. Words of this formation now and then change it for the First Simple formation, still keeping the same meaning: **ግዘፍ** and **ግዝፍ** "density", **እበድ** and **እብድ** "folly".

(β) *The a may be lengthened into ā* (³). The words concerned are thereby more detached from their affinity to the Verb and are raised from Infinitives into Substantives proper. They are not so much an expression of the action itself as the result rather of the action, and are mostly names of things. Examples: **ተረፍ** "remainder", **ስካር** "drunkenness", **ልማድ** "custom", **ሕፃን** "child", **ዝናም** "rain", **ክታብ** "book" [Arabic loan-word, كتاب], **ስባር**

قِصَر and the like correspond (Ewald, '*Gr. Ar.*' § 240), and in Hebrew the intransitive Infinitives of the First Stem.

(¹) *Cf.* Barth, ZDMG XLII, p. 352 *sq.*

(²) That there is a word **ልድ** = **ወልድ** is not perhaps made clear by Gen. 17, 12, but without doubt it is so by Gen. 17, 23; Jer. 2, 14; Kuf. pp. 54, 59.

(³) [V. now on this formation and its passive meaning Nöldeke, '*Beitr. z. sem. Sprachwiss.*', p. 30 *sqq.*]

"piece", **ጽራብ** "chip"; *mediae gutturalis*: **ሥሐቅ** "mockery"; *tertiae gutturalis*: **ጽባሕ** "morning", **ርባሕ** "gain", **ትፋእ** "*sputum*"; *mediae geminatae*: **ሕማም** "pain", **ንዳድ** "fever", **ሕራር** "heat", **ሥዓዕ** "roughness"; *mediae infirmae*: **ሕዋር** "portico" ("corridor"), **ንዋም** "sleep", **ሕዋስ** "sense", **ዕዋል** "foal", **ስያሕ** "a costly vessel", **ፍያል** "vial", **ቅያእ** "vomit"; *tertiae infirmae*: **ብካይ** "weeping", **ስታይ** "drink", **ሥቃይ** "torment", **ጥዋይ** and **ጠዋይ** "colic", **ንዋይ** "vessel", **ብጻው** "slumber", **ፍታው** "desire", **ንቃው** "tone", and,—by rejecting the **ው** according to § 53,—**ግላ** "covering", **ዕፃ** "lot", **ፍና** "way", **ሥጋ** "flesh" (√ سكا)(1), **ዕዳ** "money-debt", **ፍዳ** "recompense"(1). A word with **እ** prefixed (§ 34) occurs in **እልታኍ** "dress" (√ לתח). Traces of an original *ŭ* in the first syllable are shown in **ጕጻድ** "ring", "clasp", **ኰፋር** "*infula*", **ቍማል** "louse". This formation appears now and then side by side with the First Simple formation: **ክላሕ** and **ክልሕ** "outcry", **እጓል** and **እጕል** "the young" (both of men and lower animals). For one or two Feminine forms of α and β v. § 128.

But these forms may be still farther extended by pronouncing the first syllable with the more definite vowel *a*. This is the most usual method of forming Common Nouns, as well as conceptional words.

(γ) *The type which has ă in both syllables*(2) is to be regarded, sometimes as a farther formation from (α), inasmuch as one or two words still admit both forms indifferently, *e. g.* **ሰገም** and **ስገም** "barley",—sometimes as a development of the First Simple formation(3), with which it alternates still more frequently, *e. g.* **ሠረቅ** and **ሠርቅ** "rising", **ሰምር** and **ሰመር** "productiveness", **በቀል** and **በቅል** "mule", **ተረፍ**, **ተርፍ** and **ትራፍ** "remainder" (**ነገድ** and **ነግድ**, **ዐነግ** and **ዐንግ**, **ዐደል** and **ዐድል**, **ፀቈን** and **ፀቍን**, **ገብጥ** and **ገበጥ** Sir. 34, 20), while even in other languages words of the First formation often correspond to them: **ፈለግ** פֶּלֶג, **ዐረብ** עֲרָב(4). Accordingly it cannot any longer be determined in all cases, which syllable supports the tone: In Ludolf's view it

(1) *Cf.*, however, König, p. 116 *sq.*

(2) In Arabic عَمَل, عَجَب; in Hebrew דָּבָר answers at one and the same time to our forms (β) and (γ).

(3) *Cf.* Ewald, '*Gr. Ar.*' § 240.

(4) V. farther, however, Zimmern, '*Zeitschr. f. Ass.*' V, p. 385.

is always the first; *cf.* however TRUMPP, p. 534. Upon the whole this formation is very common, especially from strong roots: በረድ "hail", ፈረስ "horse", ገመል "camel", በለስ "fig-tree", ዘነብ "tail", ሀገር "city". Words beginning with ዐ are often inaccurately written with ኃ: ኃለስ "spelt", (عَلَس), ኃቀብ and ዐቀብ "ascent" (عَقَبَة). *Tertiae gutturalis*: የዋህ "uprightness", ተላዕ "*pectusculum*", but also ገሀህ "full-moon"; vowel-beginning roots: ወሰን "boundary"; *mediae infirmae*: ሀየል "stag", ደወል "district", ጸወን "castle". (አየር "air" is a foreign word); *tertiae infirmae*: መፀው "Spring", ፈፀው "viper" ([1]); but also with mixed sound: ገቦ "side" (no doubt for ገንቦ: *cf.* גַּב, جَنْب), ፀክ "hip" (perhaps for ፀኰ); from roots with final *i*, always with mixed sound: ለፌ "side", ሰፌ "seam", ደዌ "disease", ኀሌ "song". A *u*-containing guttural as first radical does not occur either here or in (δ).—Feminine forms in this formation are comparatively rare, § 127.

(δ) *The form with long ā in the second syllable and short ă in the first* is not common ([2]): በዓል "festival", ሐሳብ "reckoning", ሰላም "peace", ረዓም "thunder", ፈቃድ "will", ገዳም "field" ([3]). *Mediae geminatae*: ከቡብ "circle"; *mediae infirmae*: ሐዋይ "gloaming"; *tertiae infirmae*: ቀላይ "abyss"; but with the ው rejected, when that is the last of the root (§ 53): ጸጋ "favour", "grace", በዳ "desert" ([4]).

§ 108. 2. *Descriptive Words derived from the Perfect* (Verbal Adjectives and Participles). This family of words, still largely represented in Hebrew and Arabic, has been dying out in Ethiopic, (just as in Aramaic),—with the exception of the form employed for the Part. Pass. A periphrasis, effected by the Imperfect of the Verb, or in some other way, became more and more prevalent as a substitute for the Simple Adjective as well as for the Part. Act.; and the old Adjective-forms were given up.—Others have been retained merely because they have become Substantives. The original vowels of the Perfect are universally lengthened, to distinguish these words, as Nouns, from the Verb; and therefore

Descriptive Words derived as Verbal Adjectives and Participles from the Perfect:

([1]) አፈው, "sweet odours" and "sweet odour", seems to be a Plural.

([2]) In Arabic سَلَامٌ, in Hebrew שָׁלוֹם, כָּבוֹד.

([3]) In the case of roots *tertiae gutturalis* this formation cannot be distinguished from the preceding.

([4]) Otherwise with KÖNIG, p. 117.

the vowels ī and ū as well as ā are separately maintained, seeing that the long vowels ī and ū never lose their identity in *e*, though the short vowels ĭ and ŭ may do so.

With ā in 2nd Syllable. (*a*) *The formation with ā in the second syllable* is now but weakly represented. The first syllable has ĕ in the Adjective proper([1]). These words have to some extent the signification of Participles. The following occur([2]): **ሕያው** "living", **ኅዳጥ** "few" (if not originally "fewness", § 107), **ዝላፍ** (=**ዝሉፍ**) "enduring", **ዕራቅ** "naked" (if not a substantive, *cf.* § 156), **ጥሬይ** (טָרִי) "raw", **ንቃህ** "awaking", **ኅዳግ** "abandoning", **ሙቃሕ**=**ሙቁሕ** "fettered", **ረኃጽ** "tender", "delicate", **ክያድ** "trodden down" Is. 18, 2 *var.*, **ጥሬይ** "possessing" or "possessor" (Hen. 14, 6)([3]). But even these few adjectives, which are still in existence, have a marked leaning towards the Substantive use. They are not generally co-ordinated with a Substantive like pure Adjectives, but are placed in a more independent position, like a Substantive in apposition, and they sometimes subordinate themselves to Nouns in the Construct State, or complete themselves with a Suff.-pronoun.—Some words also which belong to this class, but have become pure Substantives, have been retained as a remnant from more ancient times, like **ሰማይ** ('high') "heavens", **ፀሓይ** ('glittering') "sun", (but often **ፀሐይ**), **ጽጋይ** "artificial flower", perhaps also **ቀላይ** "abyss" (*cf.* § 107 *ad fin.*). Several also of the short words, mentioned in the end of § 105, belong at bottom to this formation.

With ī in 2nd Syllable. (*b*) *The formation with ī in the second syllable* is more frequently employed for simple adjectives than any other: a number of these adjectives have become Substantives. This form comes oftenest from roots with an intransitive meaning([4]). More rarely the words concerned have a purely passive sense, and then the formation coincides with the one with ū([5]). The first radical is given with ă, to distinguish the words as Nouns proper from Participles; but in

---

([1]) In Hebrew, יָשָׁר and קָדוֹשׁ; in Arabic حَسَن، جَبَان، طُوَال.

([2]) For the accentuation *cf.* Trumpp, p. 534.

([3]) **ስናም** is not *gibbosus*, as Ludolf thinks, but "hump" (سَنَام), § 107. [In Hen. 14, 6, Flemming adopts the reading **ጥርያኒሆሙ**, while Dillmann preferred **ጥሬያ**". tr.]

([4]) And then Hebrew adjectives like יָגֵעַ and יָגִיעַ answer to it.

([5]) Like פָּקִיד.

the case of Roots *mediae gutturalis*, with ĕ (§ 45) (1). From strong roots: ሐዲስ "new", ረሲዕ "godless", ቀጢን "thin", ኅጺር "short", ነኪር "foreign", አዲም "red", ጸሊም "black", ገዚፍ "thick", ፈጢን "swift", በሊኅ "sharp"; *mediae gutturalis*: ርሒብ "wide", ልሂቅ "old"; *mediae geminatae*: መሪር "bitter", ቀሊል "light", ዐዚዝ "strong", ጠቢብ "wise" (ረቂቅ, ቄሪር, ጸቢብ, ደቂቅ, § 136, 1, ቄጢጥ); *mediae infirmae*: ነዊኅ "long" (and also, owing to the Aspirate, ነዋኅ, § 44), ቀዩሕ (*e. g.* Gen. 30, 35; and *Kebra Nag.*, 12 b 11) and (§ 52) ቀይሕ "red"; from roots with final ī: ዐቢይ "great"; in the case of roots with final *u* this formation does not occur. Substantives: ቀሲስ "presbyter", ሐዲድ "iron" ('sharp'). አሚር "the first day of the month" ('superior'), ጸሪቅ ('thin') "cake" and "small coin", ጠሊ (§ 52) "goat" (טָלֶה), ልሂቅ and the common contracted form (§ 47) ሊቅ "elder", "old man", ብሒእ "vinegar"; —farther, words originally possessing the force of a Part. Act., or forming an expression for the *Agent* (2): ነቢይ "prophet" ('speaker'), ሐቢ (§ 52) "warranter" "manager", ቀሪም "gleanings", ዐጺር "juice pressed out", ኅጺን "iron" ('cutting'); or words with a passive sense: እኂል "dough" (§ 45), መሲሕ "Christ". The forms which have እ prefixed (§ 34): እግዚእ "Lord" and አክሊል "garland", "crown", إِكْلِيل (כְּלִילָא) come perhaps from Stem II, 1. ስኂን σχῖνος, ከሚን κύμινον (where ከ=κυ) are foreign words.

(*c*) *The formation with ū in the second syllable* is by far the most common, and has still such force in the language that it may be derived from the majority of roots (3). It has first a strictly passive sense, and, when derived from verbs of Active signification, it serves as Passive participle, *e. g.* ጽሑፍ "written". The first radical,—properly vowel-less, is always spoken with ĕ, (with the exception of ዲሙስ "dark"). This comes about, partly in accordance with § 60, partly because this form, as being an expression of the Participle, stands close to the verb (4). It may also be de- With ū in 2nd Syllable.

(1) For the accentuation *cf.* Trumpp, p. 534.

(2) Ewald, '*Hebr. Spr.*' § 149, *e.*

(3) For the accentuation *cf.* Trumpp, p. 534.

(4) It answers completely to the Hebrew *Pāūl.* When Ludolf, '*Gr. Aethiop.*' I, 3, maintains, that the second radical is doubled, he is evidently astray, and is as little to be relied upon as he proves himself otherwise to be in his statements about doubling: For instance, he pronounces ነገረ፡ ይነግር

rived from roots, from which only Nouns are formed, *e. g.* ሥዑር "grassy", ልቡብ "prudent". It is even taken from Derived Stems; and,— as no other type is available, by which to form Passive Participles of such Stems, than that of the Pass. Part. of the Simple Ground-Stem,—it is taken according to that type, except that in the process the Derived Stems renounce their Stem-peculiarities, *e. g.* ፍጹም "complete", "accomplished" (from *fașșáma*), ሥቁይ "tormented" (ሣቀየ), ፍቁር "beloved" (አፍቀረ, *Pass.* ተፈቅረ), እኩት "praised" (from አእኰተ), ፍሡሕ "delighted" (from ተፈሥሐ St. III, 2); but *cf.* § 111. From strong roots, as well as from Aspirate roots, Double-lettered, and Vowel-beginning roots, and from those which have a middle *i* or a final *ī*, this type is similarly formed, —that is to say, strongly and fully: ልሙድ "learned", እሱር "bound", ንሒል "destroyed", ምሉእ "full", ኩኑን "condemned", ንዱይ "impoverished", ምዩጥ "turned away". On the other hand from roots with final *ū*, in accordance with § 52, there emerges always the type ልብው *lebúwe* "skilled in", ዕልው "apostate" &c.; from roots with middle *ū* the type ምዉት *mewūt* "dead" is possible certainly, and frequently occurs still; but in accordance with § 52, especially in later times, it usually passes into ምውት *méwwet*:— ምውቅ "warm", ምውእ "conquered" &c. As is proved already by several of the examples which have been adduced, this type is formed not only from verbs of Active signification, but also from Intransitives; and in fact it is very frequently formed from the latter class of verbs, either with the force of a Participle, or directly as an Adjective: ስኩብ "lying", ሥኑር "flying" ('occupied in flight'), ርውጽ "running", ሀልው "existing", ርቡብ "hovering", ውሩድ "descending" G. Ad. 129, 26, ጽቡእ "engaged in a campaign", ምሉክ "subjected", ጥቡዕ "prepared" (intr. and pass.), ጽዑር "laden", ሕሙም "ill", ሕዙን "sad". It may even, like the Reflex-

naggára, yenágger, while he omits to notice that in forms like ሰታይ, § 110, the second radical *is* doubled. The Intensive forms קְטוֹל, קַטּוֹל, קַטִּיל &c. (Ewald, '*Hebr. Spr.*' § 155, *d* and '*Gr. Ar.*' § 248; Hoffmann, '*Syr. Gramm.*' p. 241; [and Nöldeke, '*Syr. Gr.*' (*English Ed.*) p. 73]) are paralleled in Ethiopic rather by ገባር. The manner of formation of the Part. Pass. in the case of Verbal Stems externally increased, and Multiliteral roots (§ 111), tells decidedly against a doubling of the second radical, as also does the peculiar fashion of this formation in the case of roots *mediae infirmae*.

ive-Passive Stems, gain seemingly active meaning (¹), *e. g.* ጽኑሕ (from ጸንሐ "to expect") not "waited for", but "engaged in waiting for" ('lying-in-wait'), ውኩል "confiding in", ፅሩፍ "given to evil-speaking", "blasphemer", ድኁን "safe and sound", but also "wholesome" (G. Ad.), እኁዝ (²) not only "kept a prisoner", but also "clinging to", *i.e.* "holding something", with Accusative (Hen. 56,1) (³). —In the great scarcity of simple adjectives, it has to supply Adjectives too, such as ምሉእ "full" (and "filling up"), ብዙኅ "much", ፅሩዕ "idle", ጽኑዕ "strong", ጥቡዕ "steadfast", ግሩም "terrible", ይቡስ "arid", ፅቁብ "careful", "heedful", ግፉዕ "violent", ጥዩቅ "sharp-sighted" &c. Substantives of this form are very rare: ትጉህ "watchful" and "watchman", ንጉሥ "king", ፀዱው "adversary" (عَدُوّ), ግዩር "proselyte", ብሩር "silver" ('white'), ብሑእ "leaven", ጽቡር "muddy" and "mud", ጕኑድ (from ጕንድ) "trunk" (of a tree), ውጡን "beginner", "novice". For a few Feminines v. § 128.

3. Third Formation:—with Vowels long from the first.—

§ 109. 3. While the essential vowels in the Second Simple formation (*ā*, *ī*, *ū*) have been lengthened out of originally short vowels, as kindred languages show, *a Third series of Simple forms comes into being, by stronger vowels—or vowels which were long from the first—becoming established in the Stem.* To some extent they may be regarded as new and stronger forms derived from words of the Second series.

With *ā* after 1st Radical (and *ĕ* after 2nd).

(*a*) *By the establishment of a long ā after the first radical,* which is followed by the appearance in the second syllable of the shorter vowel *ĕ* (§ 60), a type of word arises, of a strongly active sense, which signifies *the one who does* (the *Agens*), and which accordingly is employed in the other Semitic languages as Part. Act. of the First verbal Stem. In Ethiopic this form, however, can no longer be derived from every verb. It has almost died out, in fact, and is now represented by a few words only, which are used as Adjectives and Substantives, but not as Participles (⁴). The follow-

---

(¹) *Cf.* Ewald, '*Hebr. Spr.*' § 149, *d*; Hoffmann, '*Syr. Gramm.*' p. 177: Ewald, '*Gr. Arab.*' § 244. [*Cf.* also Nöldeke, '*Syr. Gr.*' (*English Ed.*) p. 223 *sq.* tr.]

(²) Like אֲחֻזֵי Cant. 3, 8.

(³) [Flemming reads here ወይእኅዙ፡ መቅሠፍተ፡ ወመሣግረ instead of Dillmann's ወእኁዛን፡ መሣግረ. tr.]

(⁴) For the accentuation *cf.* Trumpp, p. 535.

ing still occur as Adjectives: ጻድቅ "just", ረትዕ 'straightforward", "upright", ዳኅን "sound and well", ('escaping unhurt'), በቍዕ "useful", ባዕድ "other", "different", ላሕይ "beautiful".—As Substantives: ኃጥእ "sinner", ካህን "priest", ሠውዕ ('sacrificer') "idolatrous priest", ረድእ "helper", ዋርስ "heir", ቃውም "sponsor", "patron", በዕል "lord" and "rich", ላህም "ox" (*cf.* לָהֵם, لَهِم), ማህው "glass", ማይ "water" ('fluid' √ מיי); and doubtless too those words in which (§ 105) a long *ā* has been shortened, like አብድ "foolish", "fool" (¹). This type is quite commonly employed in the formation of Numeral Adjectives, § 159.

With *ū* or *ī* after 2nd Radical (and *a* after 1st). (*b*) In contrast with this form, of active meaning, effected by means of long *ā*, new and stronger forms arise, of conceptional words, by means of a long *ū* or *ī*, derived from the Passive vowel *u* or *i*, which has become established in the second syllable, and which is preceded in the first syllable not by the colourless *ĕ*, but by the more definite vowel *a* (²). This form is also very rare in Ethiopic (³); with *ū* we have: ሐሩር "heat" (different from ሕሩር and ሕረር), ሐጹር "wall", "defensive-work", ደቡብ "North" (region of the ዱብ); with *ī*: ኀሪፍ "the current year" (properly "Autumn", the time in which fruits are 'gathered'), perhaps ገሪፍ "net" (with which one 'sweeps together') and ዳቢር with long *ā*, "the hinder space", "*adytum*", (of the Temple, דְּבִיר); and with an *ē* shaded out of *ī*: ጋኔን "spectre", "evil spirit", and a few Feminine Stems, § 127. But what is most important is, that this form is the one most usually employed in Ethiopic in the derivation of Verbal Abstracts or *Infinitives* from the several Verbal Stems, § 124,—which Infinitives only very seldom indeed are used as Noun-Substantives, like አሚን "belief", ውሒዝ "river".—For one or two Feminines v. § 127. A few Numeral-forms, having *a* inserted in their first syllable, make their appearance as new derivatives from Verbal Adjectives of the type ገቡር (§ 107): v. § 159.

An additional number of words are to be found, apparently of simple formation, which cannot be explained from any of the usual word-types, and either depend upon obsolete formations or

(¹) Also ረውሕ "placid" (v. Ludolf, '*Lex.*'), if the reading is correct.
(²) For the accentuation *cf.* Trumpp, p. 535.
(³) It occurs more frequently in Hebrew, Ewald, '*Hebr. Spr.*' § 153.

upon a corrupt pronunciation of antique words, or words adopted from foreign languages. Examples of foreign words occur in ዓለም "world", "eternity", عَالَم, עוֹלָם; ሮማን "pomegranate", رُمَّان; ሶከር "sugar", سُكَّر; ጸላዕ "rock", صُلَّع or صُلَّاع; ሰሜን "South", تَيْمَن, תֵּימָן; ሲኦል, ܫܝܘܠ, שְׁאֹל; እቶን "oven", أَتُّون, אַתּוּן; ዲባግ, دِيبَاج; ዲናር, دِينَار "*denarius*"; ፊቃር, ܦܩܝܪܐ ('*mitra*'); አሜን, אָמֵן; ቈብዕ ('hood'), قُبَّعَة, ܩܘܒܥܐ; ጣዎስ, طَاوُس, ταώς; ባላቅ and በለቅ "marble", بَلَق.—Words of obscure derivation and formation: ሚሬይ "a costly garment"; ሆባይ "a kind of hawk": ማፀን "chest", ('ark') "shrine", ('reliquary'); ቆበር "darkness"; ቆጸን "shoe"; ፊደል "letter of the Alphabet" (መሬት "earth", "dust of the ground"; ብሔር "land", "country", "the earth") and others.

2. NOMINAL STEMS FORMED BY DOUBLING OF RADICALS, OR FROM DERIVED VERBAL STEMS AND MULTILITERAL ROOTS.

§ 110. 1. *Formations from Simple Tri-radical Roots and Verbal Stems.*

1. From Simple Tri-rad. Verbal Stems: Attributive Words, formed by Doubling 2nd Rad., with tone-bearing ā after 2nd Rad. and a after 1st.

(*a*) *From simple tri-radical Verbal Stems, attributive words are formed by the doubling of the second radical,*—which process here indicates the intensifying of the notion,—but in other respects, in accordance with the adjective-formation described in § 108. The first (closed) syllable invariably has the vowel *a*, the second the tone-bearing main vowel *ā*,—just as in § 108, (*a*) (1). The other vowels, which are generally available for the formation of Adjectives (§ 108), and are also represented in the other Semitic languages(2), are wanting here in Ethiopic (unless it be that among the words cited in § 108 (*b*) & (*c*), a few have been admitted which have their middle radical doubled). To this formation belong, first of all, *Adjectives* which express qualities of a more intimate and firmly inherent nature, or properties possessed in a higher than usual proportion:—From strong roots: ፈራሁ "timorous" ('who is continually and easily frightened'), ረዓድ "anxious" (G. Ad.), ጸጓቅ "longing", ተባዕ "masculine", "manly", በሃም "dumb", በራሕ

(1) *Cf.* Trumpp, p. 536.

(2) Ewald, '*Hebr. Spr.*' § 155, '*Gr. Ar.*' § 248; Hoffmann, '*Syr. Gr.*', p. 241 *sq.* [V. Nöldeke, '*Syr. Gr.*' (*English Ed.*) p. 71 *sqq.* tr.]

"bald", አዳም "pleasant", ገሃድ "manifest";—*Denominatives*: ጸጓር "hairy", ቈላፍ ('having the foreskin') "uncircumcised", ቈጻል "covered with foliage" (Deut. 12,2).—From roots *mediae infirmae*: ኀያል "strong", "active", የዋህ "meek", ሠያብ "grey-headed", ጸያፍ "stammering", ፀዋግ "abominable", "hateful"; *tertiae infirmae*: ለዋው "malignant", ከዋው "energetic", ጠዋይ "distorted", ሀካይ "lazy", ነዳይ "poor", ለሓይ (together with ላሒይ § 109) "beautiful", ሠናይ "beautiful", "good". And farther, this form serves also to express the '*doer*' ('who does anything frequently or continually', —'who does it as his occupation' &c.):—ገባር "workman", ዐሳብ "day-labourer", ፈላስ "neighbour", "foreign resident" ('metic'), ሰታዪ "drinker", ዘማ (§ 53) "whoremonger", "whore"; from እግር "foot" አጋር "pedestrian". The most of the words which have this meaning assume farther the extraneous termination *ī* (§ 117); several have even both forms: ጸራብ and ጸራቢ "carpenter", ሐዳፍ and ሐዳፊ "steersman"; from ሐቅል "field" ሐቃል and ሐቃሊ "a countryman".

Adjectives formed by Reduplication of both the last Rads., with *ī* (or *ā*) in the last Syllable and *a* in the other two.

(*b*) *A still more vigorous reduplication,—that of both the last radicals,—is employed, just as in Verbal Stems* (§ 77), for the derivation of Adjectives from roots which denote colours and savoury things, in order to indicate *resemblance* thereby[1]: The last and main syllable has *ī* (perhaps also *ā*); the other two have *a*, just as in § 108, (*b*)[2]: ጸዐድዒድ "whitish", መዐርዒር (also, in abbreviated form, መዓሪር) "like honey", *i. e.* "sweet", ኀመልሚል "green", አበድቢድ "foolish", ደመንሚን "very gloomy", ሐዘንዚን "mournful", መንጠንጢን "small", ዐጸብጺብ "very hard", ደበርቢር "back-prop" (also "*supinus*", v. Gloss.). The only Feminine forms as yet known are ቀያሕይሕት "reddish" (doubtless from ቀያሕዩሕ § 36), and በራሕርሕት "glittering" (from በራሕሪሕ or በራሕራሕ).

2. From Derived Verbal Stems:—Conceptional Words:—from 2nd Ground-Stem, with *a* after 2nd Rad., and strongly accented Fem.-ending *ā*.

§ 111. 2. *Formations from Derived Verbal Stems.* Several of the Nominal forms described in §§ 105—109 belong to these formations, and at the same time retain the peculiarities of the Stems from which they are produced. Of course the First Simple formation (§ 105) is entirely wanting in such Derivatives; for the one vowel after the first radical would not suffice to sustain these longer Stems. But the forms given in §§ 106—108 may more or less repeat themselves in this Class.

(1) Exactly as in Hebrew: Ewald, '*Hebr. Spr.*' § 157, *c*.

(2) *Cf.* Trumpp, p. 536.

(*a*) *Conceptional words from Derived Stems* exhibit different forms according to the Stems from which they come. (α) *From the Second Ground-Stem* (I, 2) conceptional words of an Infinitive-character are formed by means of *a* after the second radical, and the Feminine-ending *ā* strongly accented([1]), which at the same time generally prevents the lengthening of the foregoing formative *a*. The first syllable,—a closed one,—is also pronounced with *a* ([2]). This form, however, is no longer very common: **መከራ** "temptation", **ቀበላ** "meeting", **ዘለፋ** "correction", **አበሳ** "transgression", **ዐመፃ** "injustice", ('wrongdoing'), **ዐጸበ** "distress" ('a making difficult'), **መዐዛ** "odour"; and in like manner from several roots not in use as Verbs in Stem I. 2: **ሐተታ** "judicial investigation" ('*cognitio*'), **ኀሠሣ** "inquiry", **ነከራ** "wonder", "miracle"; perhaps also some Names of things:—like **ቀጸላ** "crown", "garland", **ከወላ** and **ከዋላ**—[for a form **ኋላ** v. *Kebra Nag.* p. XXX *a*] "rear", "hinder part", **ገደላ** "carcase" ('a stretching out'), **ደመና** "cloud" ('a veiling'). Several others among the Intensive Stems have given up this troublesome formation, and have reverted to the form of *Nomina Actionis* which is described in § 106, but have assumed the heavy feminine-ending *ā*, by way of distinction from the forms taken from the Simple Stem: **ንስሓ** "penitence", **ፍሥሓ** "joy", **ቍጥዓ** "displeasure", **ፍግዓ** "pleasure", **ሕሊዩ** "faculty of thinking", "intellect", **ውውዓ** "clamour", **ጕጕኣ** "zeal", "haste", **ምምዓ** "consternation"; instead of **ምሊሓ** "taste", Deut. 32, 28, the majority of manuscripts have **ምሊሒ**. Quite isolated stand **ጽውዕ** *ṣéwweʿ* "invitation", and **የውሀት** *yáwwehat* "mildness" ([3]). From Causative Stems also, the Abstract-formation with *a* after the second-last radical, and with the feminine-ending *ā*, was no doubt at one time in greater use, but in ordinary Ethiopic it is now retained only in **አርአያ** ('to show') "example", "form" (and perhaps in **አስተዓ** "donation").

([1]) *Cf.* Trumpp, p. 536.

([2]) These forms are paralleled with tolerable exactness by the Aramaic Infinitives of the Pael and other Stems (קַטָּלָא &c.) as well as by Hebrew words like בַּקָּרָה. Ewald § 156, *d*.

([3]) **ጸሎት** "prayer", inherited from older times, is the Arabic صَلَوة; in Ethiopic we say **ጸለየ** "to pray", not **ጸለወ**.

From Reflexive-Passive Stems; with $\bar{a}$ after 2nd Rad., the 1st Syllable being formed by *ta* closed by 1st Rad.

(β) *From Reflexive-Passive Stems* formed by prefixing ተ (1), the *Nomen actionis* was once capable of being formed from the Subjunctive, retaining at the same time the vowels of that mood (2); but this formation has died out. The only forms still known are ተመሀር *tamáhhar* "study", and, from Multiliteral roots in like manner: ተንበል ('mediation') "mediator", ተንከተም ('covering over') "bridge". On the other hand the type with long $\bar{a}$ after the second radical, before which ተ retains its *a* and attracts the first radical to its syllable, is very common, but it is formed only from St. III, 1, to which also St. III, 2 has to be transferred. It is in this fashion that Conceptional words of a Passive sense, which may also be Names of things, are expressed (3): ተዝካር "remembrance", ተግባር "performance" ('work', 'deeds'), ተፍጻም "completion", ተስፋሕ "delay", ተጽራሕ "floor *or* story (of a house)", ተሥላስ "third-floor", ታኅምስ "quintupling", "number five"; *mediae geminatae*: ተጥባብ "astuteness", ተድባብ ('crowning') "pinnacle"; Vowel-beginning: ተውሳክ "addition", ተውላጥ "exchange", ተውዳስ "praising"; *mediae infirmae*: ተምያጥ "alteration", ተምያን "fraud", ተቅዋም ('setting up') "basis", "framework"; from Roots with final *u* we have, it is true, ተብቃው "gaping", "ajar", but as a rule the ው is thrown off (4): ታሕማ "affinity", ታእኆ "fraternity", "relationship", ተስፋ "hope", ተድላ "dignity" τρυφή; from Roots with final *i*, only the feminine form ተውኔት "orgies" (for ተውነይት or ተውናይት) is as yet known. Sometimes the *a* of the first syllable elevates itself (5) into *e*, especially in names of things: ትእዛዝ "command", ትርኣስ "what lies at the head" ("bolster", 1 Sam. 26, 7, 11), ትርጋፅ "what lies about the feet", (and perhaps ትንፋግ "wetness of the ground", "marshy quality of the soil", *uligo*, and ትንታግ "firebrand"), also ትንባል "mediation" (from

(1) According to Praetorius, '*Beitr. z. Ass.*' I, p. 38 *sqq.*, these Nominal types, formed with *t* prefixed, should rather be assigned to the Intensive Stem. *Cf.* also König, p. 81.

(2) Like تَقَبُّل.

(3) [A comparison with similar formations in Assyrian makes it highly probable, however, that these nouns have nothing whatever to do with the Verbal Stems III, 1 or III, 2.]

(4) Like تِلْقَآءَ Ewald, '*Gr. Ar.*' § 280.

(5) *Cf.* König, p. 123.

ተንበለ).—*Nomina actionis* are very seldom formed from other verbal Stems in this way, with long *ā* in the last syllable: from St. IV, 1 comes እስትንፋስ "breathing"; from St. I, 3 (in accordance with § 60) ሱታፍ "participation", or ፋኬብ (Ex. 36, 31) "fastening together"(¹) (with *ē* shaded out of *ā*); but generally such forms from St. I, 3, as well as from I, 2, III, 3 and IV, 3, have in addition an external ending (v. § 120).

In the formations, however, which come from Passive Stems,—as we see in Hebrew and Syriac(²) particularly,—the Passive vowels *ū* and *ī* were also permissible. In Ethiopic it is the Subject of the Passive proceeding, rather than the proceeding itself, which is expressed by this method,—so that this form has much more to do with Qualifying-words: ተብሲል and ትብሲል "what is cooked", "dish" *or* "mess" (Gen. 25, 29—34); ተልሚድ "disciple" (probably a foreign word). But the intimately attached Feminine termination ት is usually associated with it(³), before which, in accordance with § 36, *ī* or *ū* is shortened into *ĕ*. In this way a new class of Abstract Nouns and Names of things is derived. In the first syllable *a* was originally kept up (*e. g.* in ተፍሥሕት Gen. 31, 27 F, ተውልድ Gen. Comm. p. 5, ተግብርት Amos 8, 6 A, ተም ውእት 4 Kings 13, 17, ተውፊት as well as ትውፊት "tradition"), but in later times it was universally thickened into *e*, before the *ĕ* of the second syllable. The form is pretty common, v. for instance ትግብርት "production" (G. Ad., as from ተግቡር "what is produced") *tegbĕrt*(⁴), ትሕርምት "abstinence", ትምህርት "doctrine", ትምልክት "principality", ትፍሥሕት "enjoyment", ትግሕሥት "divergence", ትዕግልት "fraud", ትገዕርት "lamentation", ትስብእት "assumption of human nature", ትዝምድ *tezmĕd* (§ 54) "race", "family"; particularly from Numerals, like ትሥልስት "what is threefold, Trinity" ("tripling"), and others, § 159; Vowel-beginning: ትውክልት and ቱክልት "trust", ትውልድ (§ 54) and ቱልድ (Gen. 15, 2 F) "race" (pronounce *tewlĕd* or *tūlĕd*) (⁵); *mediae in-*

(¹) Quite peculiar is ዋከ "lustre" (from ዋከየ), as well as ላኳ "strife" (ተላኰየ).

(²) V. Ewald, '*Hebr. Spr.*' § 161, *a*; Hoffmann, p. 243. [*Cf.* also Nöldeke '*Syr. Gramm.*' (*English Ed.*) p. 76. tr.]

(³) Somewhat as in תַּלְבֹּשֶׁת, ܬܠܒܘܫܬܐ &c.

(⁴) On the accentuation v. Trumpp, p. 536.

(⁵) Although Ludolf I, 5 tells us to say *tewĕld*.

firmae: ትዕይርት "aspersion", ትግዘውፍት "self-conceit", ትምይንት "wiles", ትዕይንት "camp"; *tertiae infirmae* (in accordanc with § 51): ትንቢት "prophecy", ትርሲት "ornament", ትእሲት "dross", ትዕቢት "pride", ትሥግት "incarnation".

Qualifying or Descriptive Words from Derived Stems; with *ū* after 2nd Rad.

(*b*) *Qualifying* or *Descriptive words* from the derived Stems are upon the whole of rare occurrence:—the majority of Participles and those words which stand for them are derived by means of external prefixes and suffixes (§§ 114 and 117). But the Passive-Participle formation, with *ū* after the second radical (§ 108, *c*), besides its use in the first Stem, is at least admissible in several of the other Active Stems and is very common in the case of St. I. 3 (1). From Stem IV, 1 we meet with እስትርኩብ "absorbed in a matter", and from IV, 3 እስትጉቡእ "gathered together", in which the foregoing *a* of the Perfect Stem is in this manner reduced to *ĕ*, and,—in accordance with §§ 18 and 78,—*ā* to *ū*. Following the last rule St. I, 3 produces ቡሩክ "blessed", ሱሩር "founded", ሱቱፍ "sharing in", ሉጹይ "shaven", ጉቡእ "gathered together", ሕቡር "coloured", ኑፋቅ "unbelieving", "doubting" (but also ሥቁይ, in accordance with § 108 *c*).—ንጹብሩቅ "transparent" (√ ብረቀ, *cf. supra* p. 135 *sq*, and *infra* p. 238) may also be referred to this class.

3. From Multiliteral Roots:— Simple Conceptional Words and Names of Things.—

§ 112. 3. *Multiliteral Roots* are, for the most part, formed into Substantives only, rarely into qualifying words. Farther those Substantives are mostly names of things, seldom conceptional words. The feminine-ending (except the ending *ā*, § 127) is rarely attached to these formations, already rather lengthy. A large number of Multiliteral Nouns have been imported from foreign sources, or else have an origin which remains obscure.

(*a*) *Simple Conceptional words* and *Names of things*, derived from Quadriliteral Roots, are formed for the most part in such a way that each pair of radicals is brought into one syllable. A like process is followed in the case of Quinqueliteral Roots, the first radical being attached by way of prefix in front of the first complete syllable. When a long formative vowel is inserted, it bears the tone; but when only short vowels are used, according to the later pronunciation, the tone falls on the first closed syllable. (*α*) *When both syllables have short ĕ* (2) (so that the word answers

(1) On the accentuation *cf.* TRUMPP, p. 536.

(2) In ኰኵሕ "stone", "rock", the *a* of the first syllable seems to

somewhat to the form ግብር, § 105):—ብድብድ "plague"(1), ንፍንፍ "drizzle", ቍስቍስ "furniture", ቍንጽል "fox", ቍንፍዝ "hedge-hog", ድንግል "virgin", ድስክን τραγέλαφος (Deut. 14,5), ብርስን "lentils", ጽንጕን "mud-heap".—A conceptional word of this form is ውልውል "perturbation". *Quinqueliteral*: ድቍንድቍ "axe", ድልቅልቅ "violent agitation" ('earthquake') "quaking", ድብዕኵል, ደብዕኵል and ድንብዕኵል "den" or "cage".—Foreign word: ድርህም "dirhem". (β) *When both syllables have short ă*: ሐምሐም "gourd", ፀፍፀፍ "pavement", ጕዝጕዝ "carpet", ቀልቀል "precipice", ሐገዘሐገዝ "pool", ዓምዓም "pool" (probably written with long ā, merely in error, § 48), ሰውሰው "ladder", ሠቅሠቅ "network", ቈስቈስ = ቍስቍስ, በርበር "booty", ሰንሰል "chain", ቀልደድ ("eyebrow") "orbit of the eye", ሐንዘር "hog" (Hen. 89,10), ከንበል "hair-comb", ሐንገዝ "eyebrows", ቈንዛእ "lock (of hair)", ከንፈር "lip", ዐንበር "sea-monster", ተንከር "topaz", ቀርነብ "eye-lash", ሐርገጽ "crocodile", ከርከዕ "almond-nut", ሰውተል "javelin", ዐይገን "tub", ("pitcher") (إِيجَانَة), ወይጠል δόρκας, ሃይከል הֵיכָל, [from the Assyrian *ikallu*, Sumerian *e-gal*,] መቍዐል "fat", ከከብ "star". A conceptional word of this type is መርሰስ "feeling", "groping". To this division farther belong, according to § 71:— ሰሰን "lasciviousness", ደደክ "frost", ቀቀብ "scabbard". (γ) *When the last syllable has ā, and the first either ă or ĕ*:—ዐቅራብ "scorpion", ሰግላጥ "a costly garment" (سِجِلَّاطٌ), ሰይጣን (شَيْطَان), "Satan", ቶታን "shoe-tie", ቄቃሕ "flour", ሕንባል "saddle for a camel", ሕንባብ "berry", ክርዳድ "weed" (Matt. 13, 25), ኵርናዕ "elbow", ድንባዝ "beam", ድንጋግ "margin", ግንፋል "brick", ጽንሓሕ "burnt-offering"; ዕጕስታር "absinth", ድምድማ (§ 47) "hair of the head", ቍስቋስ=ቍስቍስ, ክርታስ "*charta*".

When both Syllables have short ĕ.

When both Syllables have short ă.

When the last Syllable has ā, and the first either ă or ĕ.

Words of obscure formation and origin are met with in ባሕ ሩስ "reed-pen", አንጺዋ "mouse", ዶርሆ "cock", ጸናታም "rue", በሊኖን "veil", ቀለምጽጽ "spark".—Foreign words: ምሥጢር μυστήριον, ቀንዲል "*candela*", ፍንዱቅ πανδοχεῖον, ዐንጕግ σαῦρα, عَنْجُوج &c.

occur by way of compensation for an Aspirate (ኰሕኰሕ *cf. supra* p. 153); but *cf.* Praetorius, '*Amh. Spr.*', p. 152.

(1) On the accentuation *cf.* Trumpp, p. 536 *sq.*

Descriptive Words, and Substantives derived from them.

(*b*) *Descriptive (or Qualifying) Words, and Substantives derived from them.* The Quadriliteral Verbal Stem is employed in its readiest dissyllabic pronunciation, viz. with two short *a's*, as a qualifying word; or else,—when it has to be more exactly distinguished as an Adjective,—an *a* establishes itself after the second radical also, and the word becomes a trisyllable(1): **ሰንጐጕ** "firm", "massive", (زَنِيق), **ደግደግ** and **ደገደግ** "lean" (Gen. 41, 4 *sqq.*), **ኰሠኰሥ** "speckled" (Gen. 30, 32—39; 31, 10—12, in later manuscripts **ኰሳኵስ**); **ጐፃጕፅ** "rugged". Or otherwise, the last syllable takes a lengthened *ā*, and the first is then pronounced either with *e* (as in § 108 *a*): **ድክታም** "bereaved of parents" (=**ድክቱም**), or more frequently with *a* (as in § 110, 1 *a*): **ሐንካስ** "lame", **ጸምላጥ** "blear-eyed", **ላእላእ** (Constr. St. **ላእላአ**) "stammering"; and with final *a* discarded (§ 53) **ጸዕዳ** or **ጸዐዳ** "white". **እንስሳ** (discarding the **ው**, § 53) "four-footed animal" ('going on four feet')(2) has become entirely substantive. The most common of these forms is that of the Passive Participle, with *ū* in the last syllable (§§ 108 and 111, *b*), before which the preceding syllables retain the shortest possible vowel: **ልምሉም** "tender", **ሕርቱም** "unfortunate", **ሕብቁቅ** "stained", **ምዝቡር** and **መዝቡር** "destroyed" (**ሕብሩት**, **ምሕፁን**, **ግብሱስ**, **ጕንዱይ**, **ሥእሡእ**, **ፍልሱፍ**), **ውልዉል** "unstable", **ዝንጉግ** "derided" (from **ዘንጐጐ**); from roots with long vowel as second radical (§ 20):—**መሱን** "corrupted" (**ማሰነ**), **መቁሕ** "captive" (**ሞቅሐ**), **ቱሱሕ** "mixed" (**ቶስሐ**), **ጊጉይ** "erring" (**ጌገየ**), **ቂቁይ** "avaricious", **ሊሉይ** "separated"; from roots with *u* as last radical (§ 52): **ውርዝው** "young", **ምንስው** "tempted", **ስንእው** "agreeing" (**ውልትው**, **ምንትው**, **አኅርው**), **ጽዕድው** "bleached", "white"; with *i*:—**ጕዕቱይ** "deluded". This Participle may also be derived from the Reflexive Stem V, sometimes in the form **እንፍርዐጽ** "dancing", **እንጡሉዕ** "veiled", **እንጉግው** "erring", **እንቅዕድው** "devout"; sometimes discarding the initial **እ** (§ 87):—**ንጽብሩቅ** "transparent", **ንቅጥቁጥ** (G. Ad.) "delirious", **ንዝህሉል** and **እንዝህሉል** "dissolute"; and with still more marked abbreviation: **ንኩል** "giddy" (from **አንኮለለ**). Some-

(1) On the accentuation *cf.* Trumpp, p. 537.

(2) [Probably to be compared with סוּס; ܣܘܣܝܐ, סוּסְיָא; and, it may be, with Assyr. *sīsū* (although the *i* there cannot yet be proved to be long); v. Littmann, '*Zeitschr. f. Assyr.*' XIII, p. 155, N. 1.]

times these formations assume the meaning of Substantives:—ፍርፉር "crumb", ሰንቡእ "lung", እንጌጋይ "aberration"; fem. ድርኵኵት "hinge of a door".—The form with ī (v. § 110, b) is preserved in a few Verbals only, which have taken a Substantive colouring:—ለጽሊጽ "the index of a balance", ነፍኒፍ "drizzle", ከንፊፍ "border", ሰንቢል "spikenard" (1), ነዘሀሊል and ነዝሀሊል "dissolute", "a debauchee" (√ዘሀለለ).

Stronger Conceptional Words (*Nomina Actionis*); with *ā* in the last Syllable, and *a* in the preceding one.

(*c*) *Stronger Conceptional Words* (*Nomina Actionis*) *arise from Multiliteral Roots, having long ā in the last syllable* (*cf.* § 111, *a*, *β*) and *a* in the preceding one: ጌጋይ "sin", ሱባሱብ "marriage" (√ישׁב from repeated cohabitation), ሡብሣብ "trellis", "basket-work, *or* lattice-work", ሣእሣእ "eloquence" (ወሥአ), ፃእፃእ "shoots" (ወፅአ,—צֶאֱצָאִים 'descendants'), ጸሕጸሕ "dropping", ክሙሳስ "mild gravity", ኩብኩብ "marriage-feast", ፈድፋድ "excess", ሉኖሳስ "soft whispering", ነጸፍጸፍ and ነጠብጣብ "drops", ሐመልማል "greenness", ገበጥባጥ and ጉበጥባጥ "colic" (*Kuf.*); from one or two Causative Stems (§ 85), discarding አ:—ሰቆሩር "horror", ሰዖዘዝ "spasm", ሰቆቃው "lamentation"; and frequently from Reflexive Stem V, discarding አ:—ነጐድጓድ "thunder", ነኰርኳር "whirlpool", ነጐርጓር "murmuring"; ነፈርዓጽ "wantonness", ነጸብራቅ "brilliance", ነጎጋው "hesitation" (ነሶሳው, ነቀልቃል, ነቀጥቃጥ, ነበልባል, ነኮላል, ነገርጋር, ነዘሀላል); also እንጉጋው "aberration"; more rarely with the pronunciation ንብስባስ "tremulous movement", ንዝሀላል "buffoonery", ንስሕሳሕ "motion"; as also from the Simple Stem: ሲሳይ "food", ሊላይ "separation".

3. NOMINAL STEMS OF OUTER FORMATION.

(*a*) *Forms reached by means of Prefixes.*

With the Prefix ይ.

§ 113. The formation, employed in Verbs and associated with the Imperfect, which is effected by prefixing *ye* or *ya*, was at one time extensively used in Nouns, particularly in Minao-Sabaic, but also in the other Semitic tongues (2). In Ethiopic it has died out entirely, and is now represented by a single word only, handed down from remote antiquity, viz. ይርብሕ or ያርብሕ (*yā* lengthened by the tone, for *ya*) "giant" (root רָבָה, ረብሐ). In the same way

(1) ምስኪን "poor" is a foreign word.

(2) Ewald, '*Hebr. Spr.*' § 162, *a*; '*Gr. Ar.*' § 281. Dietrich, '*Abh. zur hebr. Gramm.*' p. 140 *sqq*.

the formation of Adjectives,—with the force of Intensives and Elatives,—which has come into wide-spread use especially in Arabic([1]), effected by prefixing **አ**, was evidently at one time existent in Ethiopic; but, except for some scanty remains, it has wholly disappeared. The following appear still, viz.([2]):—**አንብዕ** "tear" ('flowing'), **አንጐዕ** "marrow" (properly, 'the best' or 'purest'; *cf.* نِقْى), **አዝዩብ** and **አዜብ** (§ 40) "the South" (أَزْيَبُ), **አዝመር** "purple" (أَسْمَرُ), **አስፌር** (Deut. 28, 22, أَصْفَرُ) ([3]) 'a malady', probably of 'the liver', with which is to be compared **ዘፍሬ** "yellow colour", as a fem. from أَصْفَرُ, and in like manner, perhaps, **ዘቡጺ** "skin" (root سبل), because the plural runs **ዘባድው**. And farther, this form perhaps includes **አንቀጽ** "door" ('being ajar', 'gaping', from نَقَضَ, unless it is rather to be derived from قَضَّ VII "to come by a crack *or* hole"). The words **አስከል** "cluster of grapes" (אֶשְׁכֹּל, إِثْكَال) and **አጽባዕት** "finger" (אֶצְבַּע, أَصْبَع) are very old([4]). **አርዩብ** 'the name of a planet' is a foreign word; **አንቃል** "louse" is merely a dialectic variety of **ቍማል**;—**አርዑት** "yoke" is أُرْعُوَّة([5]). [Also **አስሐትያ**, **አስሐቲያ** "hail", "cold" probably belongs to these formations]([6]).

Forms with **ተ** prefixed are, in accordance with § 111, systematically derived from Reflexive-Passive Stems([7]).

With the Prefix *ma*, in Participles from Derived Active Stems, Part. Act. having *e* in last Syllable and Part. Pass. *a*.

On the other hand the prefix *ma*, largely employed in all Semitic languages, in the sense of "he who" or "that which" (from the Interrogative Root, § 63), is very extensively made use of in Ethiopic also, in the derivation of verbal forms, and especially Participles, together with Adjectives and Substantives which resemble Participles.

1. First of all, this *ma* is employed in the formation of *Participles*, which then are farther made use of (just like those described in § 109, *a*) partly as Adjectives, or oftener as words which indi-

---

([1]) Ewald, '*Gr. Ar.*' § 251 *sq.*

([2]) For the accentuation *cf.* Trumpp, p. 537.

([3]) [For ص = ሰ *cf.* Littmann, '*Zeitschr. f. Assyr.*' XIV p. 84, Note 1.]

([4]) On these *cf.* Ewald, '*Hebr. Spr.*' § 147, *b*.

([5]) *Cf.* Ewald, '*Gr. Ar.*' § 243.

([6]) [*Cf.* Dillmann, '*Lex.*', col. 331.]

([7]) [But v. p. 234, Note ([3]).]

cate Persons. But Participles of this sort, formed with *ma*, are never derived from the Simple Ground-Stem, (the Inner-formation being found sufficient in the case of that Stem, in accordance with § 108 *sq.*) [1], but only from the Derived Stems, and of these again, only from the Active Stems, not from the Reflexive or Passive. The latter, in forming their Participles, avail themselves of the type described in § 117. From the Active Stems themselves an Active Participle only is derived. Such a Participle is still very common, but Passive Participles here are seldom met with. This formation, however, is no longer by any means so vigorous as to make its appearance in the case of every Active verbal Stem. It is only in the case of a few Stems of certain verbs that Verbal forms, reached in this way, have continued to maintain themselves in the language, just like the Participles of the Simple Ground-Stem. As regards the method of formation, the formative prefix is invariably uttered with *a*, thus—*ma*; and this *a* holds such an undisputed sway, that even in foreign words, of Arabic origin, the Arabic مُ is replaced by **መ**,—as in **መሐመድ፡** "Muḥammad", **መስልም** "Muslim", **መዘይን** مُزَيِّن, (by **ም**, however, in **እልምዕትዝላ** (اَلْمُعْتَزِلَة). **መ** is always applied to the beginning of the Stem, exactly like the Causative **አ**; and the latter is put aside, without a trace left, whenever **መ** has to go in front, and then **መ** takes its place. Just as it is with the Subjunctive and Imperfect forms of these Stems, the last syllable in the Active Participle has the vowel *e*, and in the Passive the vowel *a*. And farther, the Adjective-ending *ī* may also be attached to such Participial formations; *cf. infr.* § 118.

§ 114. (*a*) From Stem I, 2 come, for example [2]:—**መዐምፅ** (*maʿámmes*) "he who acts unjustly", **መፈክር** "interpreter", **መረብዕ** "he who makes four persons in the Godhead", **መገሥጽ** "castigator";—*mediae gutturalis*:—**መምህር** (*maméhher*) "teacher" (§ 45); *mediae geminatae*:—**መኰንን** "judge", **መሐልል** "dealer in unguents"; *mediae infirmae*:—**መሰውር** (*masáwwer*) "protector", **መፈውስ** "physician"; *tertiae infirmae*: **መሠርይ** and **መሠሪ** Participial formation with *ma*:— From St. I, 2.

(1) I am not able to admit the objections raised by Praetorius, '*Amh. Spr.*' p. 158: **መንእስ** "young" is actually a Substantive = "something small".

(2) For the accentuation v. Trumpp, p. 537 *sq.*

"magician", መጸግው "he who bestows", መሰጥው "he who accepts" (§ 51). These forms also occur occasionally from roots which are not in use as Verbs in St. I, 2, like መከልኢ "hinderer". A Substantive formed in this way is መጠብቅ "glue" ('causing to adhere'); መሠንይ "the best" (of a thing) is commonly used as a neuter.

From St. I, 3. (*b*) From St. I, 3 come, for example,—መዓትም "quarrelsome", "passionate", (*cf.* عتب III) (¹); መናፍቅ "heretical"; መናዝዝ "consoling"; መጸዕን "horseman" (Deut. 20, 1); መናህይ "comforting"; መበኪ "bewailing" (Matt. 9, 23). In መሃፒል "fuller" the short *e* has been lengthened into *ī*.

From St. II, 1. (*c*) From St. II, 1 this form is pretty common:—መጥምቅ "Baptist"; መድኅን "Redeemer"; መስፍን "prince", "chief"; መርዕድ "terrible" ('causing to tremble'); መሥዕር "grassy", "producing grass"; መብእስ "rugged", "stony ground"; መጽልም "dark", "a dark place", &c.;—*primae gutturalis*: ማእምር "acquainted with";—*mediae geminatae*: መድምም "astounding" ('causing astonishment'); መዕርር "a mischief-maker" ('one who stirs up discord');—*tertiae infirmae*: መድልው "hypocrite" (also መደልው St. I, 2); መጥዕይ "physician" ('healer'); መፍርይ "fruitful", መሱሲ (and መሱስይ) "having the same name". ማሪ "a heathen seer" is a curiously shortened form, from መርኢ (²) (§ 47).

From St. II, 2. (*d*) From St. II, 2 these formations are rare; besides, they coincide in outward form with those which are derived from St. I, 2, *e. g.* መጸብሒ "tax-gatherer"; መለብው "teacher"; መሠንይ "beautifier".

From St. IV, 1, 2, 3. (*e*) The Reflexive Stems do not form this Participle: they may form their participles in another way (§ 117), or may pass into the Causative-Reflexive type and then adopt Participles belonging thereto. But the form is in frequent use from St. IV, 1, 2, 3. From the Perfect-form of St. IV, 1, አስተርሐቀ:—መስተምሕር "he who craves mercy for any one" ('intercessor'); መስተብቍዕ "beseeching urgently"; መስተስርይ "he who implores forgiveness". From the type of the Perfect አስተረሐቀ:—መስተመይጥ "one who is prone to change his mind" (ተመይጠ 'to face about'); መስተኀሥሥ "inventor". From St. IV, 2: መስተዐግሥ "patient";

(¹) V., on the other hand, Praetorius, '*Beitr. z. Ass.*' I, p. 25 *sq.*

(²) [V., however, Dillmann, '*Lex.*', col. 168.]

መስተበቅል "avenger"; መስተዐግል "a fraudulent person"; መስተ ጠይር "augur" (ተጠየረ);—*mediae gutturalis*: መስተጽዕን "horseman", "knight" (ተጽዕነ). From St. IV, 3: መስተሣህል "easy to be entreated"; መስተሳልም "peacemaker"; መስተሐምም "anxious", "troubled about anything"; መስተሳልቅ "mocker" (ተሳለቀ); መስ ተቃይም "vindictive"; መስተዋድይ "accuser" or መስተዋኒ "actor", "player".

From Active Stems of Multiliteral Verbs.

(*f*) This Participle is also formed by the Active Stems of *Multiliteral Roots*. From St. I,—which, in the construction of its syllables, corresponds to a St. I, 2 of the tri-radical roots,—come መቤዝው "one who ransoms", "redeemer"; መተርጕም "interpreter"; መጠንቍል "soothsayer"; መጕንድይ "delaying" (1). From St. II:—መደንግፅ "terror-inspiring"; መማዕልይ "tyrant" (from አማዕለየ, ማዕሌት, ዐለየ); or መስዖዝዝ "who *or* what causes numbness *or* stupor", "stupefying"; መንጎግው "vagabond"; መስቆቅው (2) "one who chants a dirge". Also there occurs from the Weak Reflexive St. V, መንጐርጕር "murmurer".

Along with these pretty common Active Participles, a few cases also are met with,—though it is but rarely,—of *Passive Participles*, which have been formed from Active Stems by vowel change. Of this sort are (3) (belonging to St. II, 1):—ማሕተት "witness" ('one who is interrogated'); ሞረስ "heir" ('appointed heir'); ማእመን "worthy of belief", "veracious", "to be relied upon" (the active form being ማእምን "he who believes", *fidelis*) Deut. 7, 9; Matt. 24, 45; Luke, 19, 17,—for which in other passages ምእመን stands (from an original መእመን, according to § 45); መቃዐን

(1) መጕጕይ "impious", if correct at all, would be a much shortened form of መጌግይ or መጌጊ.

(2) Ludolf: መሰቆቅው.

(3) On the other hand መልአክ "messenger"; ማኅፈር "friend", "client",—are, in their origin, names of things, § 116; and so too must be regarded መማዝእ "masted", originally "the mast" (Judges 6, 28 F. Note), and መቡሒት (Josh. 8, 33) originally "unviolated" (root بَكُتَ 'to be pure'). መማረር "subduer", መማሉብ "fisher" (*v.* Ludolf, '*Lex.*'), and ማዕቀብ (Ex. 22, 8) "depositor" must rest either on incorrect readings, or on a tampering with the original forms መማርር, መማልብ, ማዕቅብ.—The word መቅቲል "murderer" in the *Ṣalōta Reqet* is a Hebrew formation and a foreign word; *cf.* Dillmann's '*Lex.*', col. 441.

"pressed together", "narrow", **መቅዐን** "a narrow pass"; **መጸብሒ** "obliged to pay tribute", "liable in taxes".

Prefix *ma*, in the formation of Names of Things, to express the Place of the Action.

§ 115. 2. The prefix *ma* is farther employed in a non-personal meaning,—to form *names of things*, or to express *something in which* the root-idea makes its appearance; and it is but seldom, and then only by transference of the notion, that such names of things can take a personal meaning. To be more particular, this formation is employed to designate—(1) *that, in which* the action is accomplished, or *the place* of such action; or (2) *that, with which* it is accomplished, or *the implement* suitable for the action; or (3) *that which is made or produced* by and in the action, or *the products* of the action, *objects of every kind*, and *the action itself*. This type is almost always formed from the Simple Stem,—seldom from derived Stems or from Nouns. The prefix *ma* is joined to the first radical, forming with it a single syllable. As for the rest, different pronunciations have become established for the different classes of words thus formed.

(*a*) For the purpose of expressing *the place* in which anything happens,—an *a* which follows the second-last radical, and which was originally short, is lengthened, while the *a* of the formative prefix is reduced, before this *ā*, to *e* (1). This is a very common formation, *e. g.*:—**ምሥራቅ** "the East"; **ምዕራብ** "the West"; **ምሕራም** "temple"; **ምሥዋዕ** "altar"; **ምስማዕ** "hearing-distance", "reach of hearing"; **ምኅፋር** "*pudenda*"; **ምኅማዝ** "oven"; **ምእኃዝ** "confines"; **ምኵናን** "court of justice"; **ምሥያጥ** "market"; **ምብያት** "night-quarters"; **ምሕዋር** "path"; **ምርዓይ** "pasture"; **ምስታይ** "watering-place"; **ምክዓው** "place where anything is poured out" (Lev. 4, 12); **ምጕያይ** "place of refuge". From vowel-commencing roots, generally in accordance with § 49, appear **ሙፃእ** "place of exit" (**ወፅአ**); **ሙክፍ** "receptacle"; **ሙቃም** "court of justice"; **ሙጋር** "a stone's-throw" (**ሙላድ**, **ሙሓዝ**, **ሙፋር**); less frequently —**ምውዓል** "prison" (*lit.* 'place of detention') (and **ሙዓል** Acts, 4,3); **ምውዳስ** "place for praise". Even from roots middle-*u*, by their passing over to the vowel-commencing class in accordance with § 68, we have the forms **ሙባእ** "entrance" (*e. g.* in Hen. 73, 3) (2) as

---

(1) It is thus the same form, which serves to denote implements or tools, in Arabic. On the accentuation *cf.* Trumpp, p. 538.

(2) [Flemming adopts here also the reading **ምብዋኢሁ**. Tr.]

well as ምብዋእ (*e. g.* in Judges 1, 24 and Josh. 13, 5), and ሙሓር "space", "path" (*e. g.* 4 Esr. 13, 46 ed. Laur.), as well as ምሕዋር. But from roots *mediae infirmae* the form መካን "place" is unique in its class, and belongs rather to Arabic (¹).

From St. IV, by reducing *a* to *e* in the other syllables as well as in that of the prefix, we can have such forms as ምስትስሬዩ "place of intercession"; ምስትግባር "market"; ምስትስፋሕ "extension"; ምስትጉባእ "assembly" (ጉ, § 18), or even, in a remarkable way, with the Passive vowel *ū* in the last syllable (²), ምስትጉቡእ Hen. 46, 8; 53, 6 ("assembly" = 'the totality of those assembled'): *cf.* also መስተብቍዕ "intercession". In derivatives from Multiliteral roots,—as the first and second radicals together form only one syllable,—the prefix መ or rather ም is separately attached: ምምሕፃን "place of refuge" (from ማሕፀን); ምኵስታር "rubbish-heap"; ምዕንጋዕ "place where one reposes"; ምውልታው "place of safety". This formation is employed throughout to convey the idea of place (³). ማኅደር is not "an inhabited place", but "provision for inhabitation" ('house', 'tent' &c.) or "dwelling". For the rest v. § 116.

§ 116. (*b*) For the purpose of denoting *implements and vessels, products and materials of every kind, even the action itself pure and simple or the nature and manner of the action*, the Passive vowel *a* or the Active vowel *e*, after the second radical, is in general sufficient without being lengthened, while the formative prefix መ retains its natural pronunciation, with *a* (⁴). The *a*-pronunciation in the second syllable is rather more frequent than the one with *e*. Many words have both. No difference in meaning is caused thereby, but it may be observed that all those words which have only the *e*-pronunciation, may be regarded as Neuter participles with an Active signification (§ 114). Many of these words, in both the modes of pronunciation, have farther assumed the closely attached feminine termination ት:—Others appear both with and without the ት.

To express the Implements or the Products of the Action, or the Action itself:—

(¹) Ewald, '*Gr. Ar.*' § 387.

(²) As if it were a Participial formation.

(³) መስጊድ is a foreign word, مَسْجِد, and the pure Ethiopic word is ምስጋድ.

(⁴) V., however, König, p. 121 *sqq.*

Formation with *a* in 2nd Syllable.

(*a*) *Formation with a in the second syllable.* From strong roots, and roots *med. gem.*: **መልበስ** and **መልበስት** (*málbas* and *málbast*(1)) "clothing"; **መንበር** "throne"; **መንፈቅ** "half"; **መንፈስ** "spirit"; **መጽሐፍ** "book"; **መግበር** "tool"; **መስከብ** '*memb. genitale*'; (*Kuf.*) (2); **መሥለስ** "triplet" (*or* "a third", a species of measure, not thoroughly identified); **መደብ** "ledge", "projection" ($\sqrt{}$**ደበበ**): **መልአክ** ('sending') "messenger", "Angel"; **ማኅፈድ** "tower"; **ማዕከክ** "pelvis".—Oscillating between *a* and *e* are:—**መስቀር** and **መስቅር** "ship" ('that which is hollowed out'); **መንሠግ** and **መንሥግ** "bolt"; **መብሰል** and **መብስል** "kitchen-pot"; **መብረቅ** and **መብርቅ** "lightning"; **መቅሰም** and **መቅስም** "divination"; **ማዕሰብ** and **ማዕስብ** ('abandonment') "widower" and "widow". With and without the Feminine-ending:—**መስፈር** and **መስፈርት** "measure"; **መክደን** and **መክደንት** "covering", "ceiling". With Feminine-ending alone:—**መክፈልት** "portion"; **መቅሠፍት** "infliction"; **መርበብት** "net"; **መልአክት** and **መልእክት** "business" (besides **መልእክት** "letter"). In triple form:—**ማዕመቅ**, **ማዕምቅ**, **ማዕምቅት** "depth"; **ማዕቀፍ**, **ማዕቅፍ**, **ማዕቅፍት** "offence"; **ማእሰር**, **ማእስር**, **ማእሰርት** "tie", "string"; **ማእዘን**, **ማእዝንት**, **ማእዘንት** "corner".—Roots *tertiae gutturalis* do not in general lengthen their *a* before the vowel-less Aspirate (in accordance with § 46), but thicken it into *ĕ*, because a long *ā* would transfer them to the formation described in § 115:—**መልክእ** "image"; **ማሕስዕ** "young of the herd"; **መድቅሕ** "consecration"; **መርድእ** "remedy", "aid"; **መርፍእ** "needle". Only a few lengthen their *a* and then they may reduce the *a* of the first syllable to *e*: **መንዝኅ** and **ምንዛኅ** "sprinkling", "sprinkling-vessel"; **ምስማዕ** "what is heard" (and "hearing-distance"). **መሥዋዕ** in the sense of "sacrifice", usually becomes feminine **መሥዋዕት** or **ምሥዋዕ**, and thereby coincides with **ምሥዋዕ** "altar"(3). If they have to retain *a*, they generally take the feminine termination: **መጥባኅት** "knife" [*cf. Keb. N.* p. XIV]; **መስማዕት** "obedience", &c. —In formations from roots beginning with *u*, the mixed-letter pronunciation always makes its appearance, in accordance with § 49: **ሞገስ** "favour", "grace"; **ሞቀር** "chisel"; **ሞገድ** "flood"; **ሞፍጥ**,

(1) V., however, Trumpp, p. 538.

(2) But **ምስካብ** "couch".

(3) For this reason copyists often confound **ምሥዋዕ** and **መሥዋዕት**; v. for instance Gen. 12, 7, Note.

መፍጥ and **መፈጥ** "chimney"; **ሞሠርት** "saw"; **ሞገርት** "sling": *tertiae gutturalis*: **ሞሣኢ** "antiphone"; **ሞሬእ** "apron"; **ሞፃ**([1]) and **ሞፃእ** (§ 47) "gift to one who is going on a journey"; **ሞጣሕት** "veil". For **ሞዐልት** "day" (Amos 8, 9 A) **መዐልት** (**መዓልት**) (§ 44) is usually given. In formations from Roots *mediae infirmae*, the consonantal pronunciation prevails: **መጽወር** and **መጽወርት** "carrying-pole"; **ማሕየብ** "well-bucket"; **መጽያሕት** "beaten *or* made road". **መጸር** "a litter", "*lectica*", must, however, be noticed (for **መጽወር**, § 40), as distinguished from **መጽወር** "carrying-pole"; noticeable, farther, are **መባእ** "gift" (not derived from **በአ**, but from its St. II, 1 **አብአ**) and **መባሕት** "authority", '*facultas*' (from **አብሐ** from **በሐ**). **መሶብ** "basket" (or 'box for unleavened bread') (*cf.* مِسْأَب) is formed just like **መጸር**. Words from Roots *tertiae infirmae* usually contract *ai* and *au* into *ē* and *ō*:—**መስፌ** "awl"; **ማሕጼ** "axe"; **መሥረይ** and **መሥሬ** "medicine"; **መርኆ** "key"; **ማዕጾ** "lock" (of a door); **መትሎ** "rank". Occasionally, however, the diphthong is retained; for example, in the following formations from Middle-Aspirate and Doubly Weak Roots:—**መርዐይ** "herd" (Matt. 8, 30 *sqq.*); **ሞደይ** "composition"; **መጥወይ** "instrument of torture". Feminine forms take the mixed sound always:—**መርዔት** "herd"; **መጽሔት** "mirror"; **ማሕሌት** "song", "ode", "psalm"; **መስኮት** "window"; **መድሎት** "weight"; **ማኅቶት** "a light" &c.

This form occurs from Multiliteral roots but rarely, as in **መንጦላዕት** "curtain" (from **አንጦልዐ**); **መተርአስ** "whatever is near the head" (as "a pillow") (from **ተርአሰ**, whence also **ትርአስ**, § 111); **ምንባሕባሕት** "waterfall" (also **መንባ**" G. Ad., from **አንባ ሕብሐ**); **መንኮኮት** "axis" (Sir. 36, 5, from **አንኮከወ**); **መነሳንስት** and **መነሰንሳት** "fan" (also "*aspergilla*").—A foreign word of this type is found in **መንገን** "machine" (*μάγγανον*).

(*β*) *Formation with e in the second syllable.* It has been already observed that the most of these words may be regarded as Participles, employed in a non-personal signification:—**መንክር** Formation with *e* in 2nd Syllable.

([1]) In like manner perhaps **መንታ** "double birth", "twins", for **መምታ**, is for **መምታእ** (from **መትአ** = תאם), — whence **መንተወ** is a farther derivation. So too, probably, by throwing off **ው**, we have **መርዓ** "espousals", "wedding"—(Root not **ዐረየ**, but **ረዐወ**, *cf.* רֵעֶה).

"a wonder" *or* "miracle" ('what causes wonder'); **መልሕቅ** "anchor" ('that which enables a ship to cling to something'); **መዕምድ፡** "a tie" *or* "connecting strap"; **መንኅር** "pair of bellows" (also, "a pump"); **መፍቅድ፡** and **መፍቀድ፡** "need" ('that which makes one miss something' *and* 'that which is missed'); **መድምም** "miracle" ('that which causes astonishment'); **መጽብብ** "narrow pass"; **መጽልእ** "what is hated" &c. The Feminine forms of this type are frequently Abstracts: **መልዕልት** "height"; **መብህልት** "contradiction"; **መንግሥት** "kingdom"; **መሥልስት** "third rank".

This formation does not appear to be in use from roots *mediae infirmae*. From roots *tertiae infirmae* it takes the form **መፍትው** "what gives pleasure", "what is wished for *or* is convenient"; **መክረይ** "spade"; **መጽርይ** "crocus"; **መርስ** (instead of **መርሰው**) "harbour". Oftener, however, it is found with the Fem. termination:—**መንሱት** "temptation"; **መድሉት** "price"; **መክሊት** "a talent"; **መክሬት** "spade"; **መቅፀት** "pot". From Multiliterals:—**መሌሊት** "joint", "limb" (**ሌለየ**).

Prefix *ma* reduced to *me* in 1st Syllable, with *ā*, *ă* or *ĕ* in 2nd Syllable.

(*γ*) Alongside of these two leading types of Names of things,—as contrasted with designations of locality—, only a few other forms of words appear which call for separate notice. In the forms of several names of things which take *a* in the final syllable, this *a* has been lengthened, and the *a* of the first syllable has been reduced to *e*, so that these words have the same form as Names of Place: **ምግባር** "mode of acting", "actions"; **ምርካብ** "means of livelihood", "mode of subsistence"; **ምንግላግ** "a band" ('*caterva*'); **ምርኣይ** "the sight" (Deut. 28, 34); **ሙዳይ** "vessel"; **ሙላድ፡** not merely "fatherland", but also "derivation" ([1]); and **ምራቅ** "*sputum*" (for *meruāq*) with *u* thrown out, from **ሮቀ** = **ወረቀ** (§ 68); in the same fashion also **ምሣር** "hatchet". In the case of some others, although they keep *ă* or *ĕ* in the last syllable, *ĕ* takes the place of *ă* in the first:—**ምርጕዝ** "staff"; **ምጽርይ** = **መጽርይ** (v. *supra*); **ምስሐብ** (a conceptional word, of Infinitive form) "the extracting": So too with a few fem. Substantive-Numerals, § 159. Farther, some words, originally Participles, have become Names of things: it is thus with **መከየድ፡** [along with **መከይድ፡**, in *Kebra Nag.*, p. XXX.] "footstool", Part. Pass. of St. I. 2 ('that which is trampled on'): so

([1]) On the other hand **ምድራስ** is a foreign word, מִדְרָשׁ; and **ምንባብ** is "a place for reading":—(a) 'A reading-desk', (b) 'a lesson'.

too with መግረምት "horror"; መቃጥን "hook" (Matt. 17, 27), a Part.(1) from St. I, 3 or II, 3 (አቃጠነ); መንኰራኵር "wheel" ('rolling'), a Part. from St. V of the Multiliteral ኰርኰረ, with tone-lengthened ā. Also, in a few Common Nouns derived from St. I,3, the Stem-peculiarities have been retained: መላጼ "razor" (from ላጸየ); ምጕጠይ (2) "ox-goad" (from ጋጠየ, cf. جَخَّ). An Abstract form from ራብዕ "the fourth" is found in መራብዕት "a square" and "squareness". መዝሙር "psalm" is an Arabic Part. Pass.; in like manner መንዲል "female head-dress" is a foreign word (مَنْدِيل). As to certain peculiar feminine forms v. *infra*, § 127.

(b) Forms reached by means of Affixes.

§ 117. The greater number of those words which have been formed by means of Affixes are derived from other and simpler nouns, whether these are still preserved in the language or not (*Denominative Nouns*). In meaning they are either Relative Descriptive words, or Abstract words, and only very seldom mere Names of things. The Affixes themselves are, it is true, of many forms and fashions, but they are essentially traceable to two sorts of terminations having a pronominal origin. The basis of the most of them is constituted by an Adjective-termination common to Semitic tongues. **Denominative Nouns: 1. Adjective-Formation with termination ī.**

1. We start our description, for the reason given, with the *Adjective-Formation*. The termination of Adjectives is taken from a very ancient Demonstrative root *i* ("he") and the Relative *ia* ("who")(3), § 65, and originally it has the form *īya* or *áya* (= "he, who"). In the other Semitic languages it was abbreviated, sometimes into *ī* (ִי, ِيّ), sometimes into *ai*, *ē* (ـَى, ֵי (4) [Assyrian,—*ai* or, with contraction,—*ū*]): In Ethiopic it attained a triple form, as *ī*, *āi*, and—with an intervening letter separating

(1) If it be not an Inner Plural.

(2) Unless it stands for ምጕጠይ.

(3) The propriety of comparing this termination with the Relative Pron. is shown by the fact, that in Ethiopic another Relative Pron. with the force of a Genitive sign is placed before Substantives to form Relative Adjectives: ዘመንፈስ "who (is) of the "spirit"="spiritual".

(4) Ewald, '*Hebr. Spr.*', § 164, *c*.

these vowels (§ 41)—*āwī*. The last two forms have pretty much the same meaning and are occasionally exchanged for one another in the same word; but it is seldom that *ī* on the one hand, and *āi*, *āwī* on the other are interchanged.—Each has its own application.

(*a*) The termination *ī* is chiefly employed to form Nouns denoting the *Agent*, from simpler nouns connected with persons. It is comparatively seldom in use for the derivation of simple Adjectives.

With ī attached to Nouns of the Type gabbār or from any of the Derived Stems.

(*α*) Especially is it attached to those Nouns of the type ገባር *gabbār*, which denote the Agent (§ 110, *a*), and in that case its chief use is to distinguish a Substantive which indicates an Agent from a mere elative Adjective, *e. g.*:—ሐራሲ "husbandman"; ነጋሢ "king"; ወላዲ "procreator"; ረዋጺ "runner"; ነዓዊ "hunter"; ሐሳዊ "liar"; ረአዪ "seer"; ሰያፊ "sword-bearer". But several words of this type have also a purely Adjective-meaning: መሐሪ "merciful"; በቋዒ "useful"; ነባቢ λογικός; ሐማሚ "sickly", "surly"; የዋሂ "gentle"; ዐያሊ "astray" (G. Ad.), &c. The Ending itself in these formations is always accentuated, according to Trumpp, (p. 539): *ḥarrāsī́*.

While, however, the simple type, without any Ending, is formed only from the doubled Stem, that which is compounded with the Adjective-ending may be formed from any of the derived Stems, and then it takes the place of Participles, or is exchanged for them without any essential difference in meaning. Just as in the Adjective-formation (§ 108, *a* and § 110, *a*), the second-last Radical has always *ā* (with the tone); in other respects the pronunciation of the Perfect-Stem is maintained with *a*. From St. I,3: ናዛዚ "comforter"; ናፋቂ "unbelieving"; ሣራሪ founder(1). From St. II, 1: አሥጋሪ "fisher"; አግባኢ "traitor"; አብሳሪ "bringing a glad message"; አንባቢ "reader"; አጥራቂ ἀπεσπασμένος (Lev. 22, 24, Root طرق); አባኢ "he who introduces" (from አብአ, from ቦአ) &c. But from Roots *tertiae gutturalis*, as *ā* is not merely lengthened, but also, in accordance with § 45, dulled into *e*, we have አንቃሂ(2) "awakener"; አብዛኂ(2) "multiplier" (*abzeḫī́*), and from St. II,2: አሰሳሊ "he who removes *or* expels".

(1) ኖናፊ is peculiar, if correct at all.
(2) According to Ludolf's '*Lex.*'.

From the Reflexive Stems III this formation comes all the more frequently, that they do not form any Participles with **መ** prefixed. Examples,—from III,1: **ተሐዋሲ** "that which stirs"; **ተሠያሚ** "set up", "brought forward".—From III,2: **ተፈናዊ** "sent"; **ተዐጋሢ** "patient"; **ተጠያሪ** "augur"; **ተአዛዚ** "obedient"; **ተዐጋሊ** "robber".—From III,3: **ተሳላቂ** "mocker"; **ተዋናዩ** "player" ('actor'); **ተዋራሲ** "co-heir". From Stems IV, 1, 3: **አስተብቍዒ** "intercessor"; **አስተርጓሚ** "interpreter"; **አስተጋብኢ** (because *tertiae gutturalis*) "convener".

From *Multiliteral Roots*: St. I: **ማሳኒ** "perishable"; **ብሕታዊ** "solitary"; **ጠንቃቂ** "inquirer"; **ቶሳሒ** "one who mixes"; **ቤዛዊ** "redeemer"; **ኖላዊ** "shepherd"; **በርባሪ** "robber"; **ደምሳሲ** "destroyer"; **ዘርካዩ** "calumniator" (1):—St. II: **አማሳኒ** "spoiler"; **አጽንሐሒ** "one who brings a burnt-offering".

With ī attached to Participles formed by means of ma, turning them into Nomina Agentis.

§ 118. (*β*) In like manner *this ī is frequently attached to Participles,—formed by means of* **መ**,—to raise them to be *Nomina Agentis* (2). It has the tone. This formation occurs most frequently in the case of Participles of St. II, 1, in which at the same time the *e* of the last syllable of the original Participle passes into *a*. This *a* is but seldom lengthened into *ā*,—and that in the case of Middle-Aspirate roots (§ 48): **መቅለሊ** "one who facilitates"; **መቍሰሊ** "one who wounds"; **መምለኪ** "one who fears God"; **ማሕጐሊ** "destroyer"; **መፍቀሪ** "lover"; **ማሕየዊ** "life-giver"; **መድኅኒ** "saviour" (=**መድኅን**), and many others;—**መብዕሊ** "who makes rich"; **መስሐቲ** "who leads astray" (along with the form **መስሕት**) (3). But *e* remains unaltered in Derivatives from roots *tertiae gutturalis*: **መብርሂ** "enlightener"; **መንሥኢ** "one who arouses"; **መንጽሒ** "purifier"; **መፍትሒ** "opener" &c. We have, however, **መርዳኢ** "assistant". In most of the cases in which this outer formation occurs, the simple form of the Participle is no longer in use.

---

(1) On the other hand **ፄዋዊ** "taken captive" (in Passive sense), from **ፄዋ** and *āwī*, belongs to § 119 (Ex. 12, 29).

(2) The doubts entertained by Praetorius, ZDMG XLI, p. 689 (*cf.* also König, p. 124 *sq.*), appear to me to be without foundation.

(3) **መንስቲ**, **መዝላፊ** perhaps rest only on copyist's errors; **መድላዊ** might have taken that form of pronunciation by way of assimilation to the Adjective-Ending *āwī*.

From the other Stems the outer formation occurs with rather less frequency.—The original pronunciation of the Part. remains unchanged. St. I, 2: መፈውሲ (=መፈውስ) "physician"; St. I, 3: መሳብዒ "exorcist" (Hen. 8, 3); መበልሒ "liberator"; መናዝዚ "comforter"; St. IV, 1: መስተፍሥሒ and 2: መስተፈሥሒ "one who bestows gladness", "comforter"; 3: መስተጋብኢ "one who assembles" (=አስተጋብኢ). From Multiliteral roots St. II: መጣእ ጥኢ "one who prepares food"; መጣዕዊ (and in shortened form መጥዕዊ) "worshipper of idols".

With *ī* attached to Proper Names and a few Personal Words and Names of Things.

(*γ*) *ī* is frequently used, to derive Relative Adjectives from Proper names. In the case of Names ending in a vowel, the *ī* is generally hardened into *y* (v. numerous examples in Numb. 26).—More rarely this *ī* is employed for the purpose of deriving *Adjectives or Nom. ag. from Substantives*: መዝበሪ "destroyer" (from መዝበር); ተፍጻሚ "the last" (ተፍጻም); አረሚ ('Aramaic') "heathenish"; ዐረቢ "Arabic", "Arab"; ባሕሪ and ባሕርይ "pearl" ('sprung from the sea'). It is not seldom attached,—superfluously, to all appearance,—to certain Personal words and Names of things, of the masculine gender: ብእሲ "man" ('bold', 'warlike'); አባዊ "Nile river or flood" (أَبَاب)(1); ከይሲ "serpent" ('cunning', كاس)(2); ተከዚ "river" (√ውሕዘ) [?]; ዐንበሪ "sea-monster"=ዐን በር; ዐረቢ "West" (Ex. 26, 20, 35; Josh. 5, 10); ጸንጸሊ "cymbal" ('tinkling'); አፍራሲ "rider", "horseman". Probably ሐርጌ "ram" (Hen. 89, 43) had also at first the form ሐርጊ, and properly ሐርጌ is the form of the constr. state or the accus. Farther ቍልዔ "a youth", "servant", "boy" is perhaps to be judged of in the same fashion. Feminine Stems take *ē* instead (from *iyah*, ـِيَّة § 40): አንቄ "hawk" as well as አንቄት; ጕርዔ "throat" (v. also § 127, *c*); or *ēt* (ـِيَّة): ላጽቄት *μυγάλη* (*cf.* لَزِيق)(3); ዘርቤት "carpet" (زِرْبِيَّة); more rarely *īt*: ኡባለሊት "stinging nettle".

§ 119. (*b*) The stronger ending *ắwī*(4) serves the purpose of

(1) [A name generally given to the 'Abyssinian Nile', v. '*Lex*'. TR.]

(2) [In '*Lex.*' Dillmann prefers the meaning 'twisting', and chooses the etymon كاس (mid. و, not mid. ى). Others think the word might be of old African origin. TR.]

(3) [*Cf.* also Dillmann's '*Lex.*', col. 64. TR.]

(4) According to Trumpp, p. 539, to be accentuated as *ắwī*.—As to the origin *cf.* König, p. 130.

Adjective-Formation; with termination *āwī*, in the derivation, from Substantives and Adjectives, of New Adjectives and Words indicating Persons.

deriving new Adjectives, and words indicating persons, from Substantives (and Adjectives). It is true that in Ethiopic, Adjectives may with almost greater ease be indicated periphrastically by means of the Genitive relation of Substantives; and, in ordinary prose at least, this periphrastic indication of an Adjective is more in use than the express Adjective-formation. The faculty, however, of deriving new Adjectives by means of that ending has remained active in the language. It is always possible to frame such an adjective from any and every word; and, in poetic and learned diction, it has often been practised. In such cases the interior vowels of the fundamental word remain unchanged, and the termination has a merely external attachment (contrived,—for fundamental words which end in a vowel—, in accordance with the rules described in § 39 *sqq.*). In this way relative Adjectives may be formed even from Plural forms, Foreign words and Proper Names. For example,—**ምድራዊ** "earthly" (**ምድር**); **ባሕራዊ** "pertaining to the sea"; **ዓለማዊ** "worldly"; **ሕዝባዊ** "layman"; **ፈረሳዊ** "horseman", "knight"; **ፈያታዊ** (from **ፈያት**) "robber"; **ገባራዊ** "workman" (*nom. unitat.* from *coll.* **ገባር**); **ፀራዊ** "hostile" (from **ፀር**); even from **አብ** "father", a feminine form **አበዊት** "ancestress" (G. Ad.); from **ሥጋ**, **ሥጋዊ** "fleshly"; from **ዐንበሳ**, **ዐንበሳዊ** "lion-like"; **እንስሳዊ** "animal" *adj.* (**እንስሳ**); **መርዓዊ** "*sponsus*", *i. e.* "bridegroom" (from **መርዓ**). From Nominal Stems increased externally: **መስቀላዊ** "relating to the cross" (**መስቀል**); **መንፈሳዊ** "spiritual"; **ሰንበታዊ** "Sabbatical"; **አእምሮታዊ** "scientific" (from Inf. **አእምሮት**); **ድንግልናዊ** "maidenly" (from **ድንግልና** "maidenhood"). From Plural forms; **አብያታዊ** "domestic"; **ረዐይታዊ** "gigantic"; **ክርስቲያናዊ** "Christian" *adj.* From Foreign words and Proper Names: **መነከሳዊ** "monastic"; **አይሁዳዊ** "Jewish"; **ዕብራዊ** "Hebrew"; **ወንጌላዊ** "Evangelist"; even **እግዚአብሔራዊ** "relating to God"; **እጓለ፡ እመሕያዊ** (1) "human"; **ዘለዓለማዊ** ,'eternal". Farther, this termination may be applied to Adjectives:

(1) [**እጓል** means "progeny", and **እመሕያው** or **እመ፡ ሕያው** means "mother of a living one", *i. e.* "mother of the living".—Accordingly **እጓለ፡ እመሕያው** signifies literally "progeny of the mother of the living", that is "the human race", "*homines*". From this compound substantive, the adjective, given in the text, is formed by attaching *āwī* to the second member. TR.]

ቅዱሳዊ "relating to what is holy"; ብፁዓዊ "appertaining to the blessed"; to the Interrogative እይ (§ 63):—እያዊ and እያይ ('of what kind') "like", "equal"; also to words which are only used as Adverbs or Prepositions: አፍኣዊ "external" (አፍአ); ላዕላዊ "upper"; ታሕታዊ(1) "lower". A foreign word of this kind is met with in ኖትያዊ "sailor", "shipman", *ναύτης*.

Shorter Ending *ai*, alternating with *āwī*, at least in Numeral Adjectives.

The shorter ending āi alternates at pleasure with *āwī*, at least in Numeral Adjectives (§ 159), but otherwise it is retained only in a few words:—ታሕታይ and ታሕታዊ; ላዕላይ and ላዕላዊ; ተባዕታይ and ተባዕታዊ "masculine"; እያይ and እያዊ; ደኃራይ and ደኃራዊ "the last"; ፈያታይ alongside of ፈያታዊ "robber"; ፀራይ as well as ፀራዊ "hostile"; አረጋይ as well as አረጋዊ "old": Also, ሥርናይ "corn" (§ 47, from ሥዕርና 'covering with hair'); ቀሠፋይ "Holiest of all" (Ex. 26,33), properly 'the (place) which is devoted to the service of God' (*cf.* [illegible]).

Somewhat irregular forms are exhibited by:—ጽጋይ "flowery" (from ጽጌ); ጕሕላዊ "treacherous" (from ጕሕሉት); ኰነናዊ "judicial" (from ኵነኔ); (እቤራዊ and) አቤራዊ (from እቤር) "old".

2. Abstract Nouns formed from Words with these Adj.-Endings, by appending Fem.-Sign: as *īt*, sometimes as *ít*.—

§ 120. 2. By attaching the sign of the Feminine to these Adjective-Endings, a number of *Endings* are produced *which are used to indicate Abstract Nouns.*

(*a*) In very rare cases the termination *yā́* has this meaning in the formation of Collectives (v. § 140). Somewhat more frequently the termination *ī́t*(2) is employed to form Abstracts or Collectives, chiefly from verbals in *ī*: ነፋጺት "the portion which has escaped (disaster)" or "remnant" from ነፋጺ)(3); ኀላፊት "people travelling *or* passing by"; in the same way ነጋዲት (*e. g.* Judges 19,17); ፀብኢት "army"; ሀገሪት "townspeople" (Col. 3,11): Farther ደኃሪት "end"; ቀዳሚት "beginning" (Matt, 12,45); ውሳጢት "what is inward"; ባሕቲት "solitude"; መድኅኒት "redemption", "salvation" (from መድኅኒ "Redeemer", "Saviour"); ረዳኢት "help"; በዋኢት "a crowd of people entering"; ታሕጻጺት "diminution", "waning" (Hen. 78,15); ብርሃናዊት "luminous nature" (from ብርሃናዊ

(1) At one time they also used the form ላዕልይ instead, (Judges 1,36 Note) and ታሕትይ Josh. 11,16 (*cf.* 16,3; 18,13) with the simpler ending *ī* ـِىّ.

(2) *Cf.* the same ending in the *Mehri*: v. Maltzan, ZDMG XXVII, p. 282 [and A. Jahn, '*Gramm. d. Mehri-Spr.*', Vienna 1905, p. 55 *sqq.*].

(3) Like פְּלֵיטָה from פָּלִיט.

G. Ad. 15, 16). Even without the interposition of an Adjective in *ī*, Abstracts are derived from simpler Nominal Stems by appending the termination *ī́t*: ንስቲት "a small quantity"; ጽምሚት and ጽሚት "secrecy"; ድኅሪት (1) "the being turned back"; እፎያዊት ("quality") كَيْفِيَّة (2); ግንጽሊት "perversion"; ቍልቍሊት "steepness"; እስኪት "testicles" (אֶשֶׁךְ, √אשך) (3). This termination is often used to derive (from Numerals) Substantives and Adjectives which express multiplicity, v. § 159. But just as in the other Semitic languages, so also in Ethiopic the termination *ū́t* (4) may take the place of this *ī́t*, and with the same force; yet it is only in a few words that this ending continues to be represented:—ኂሩት "goodness" (from ኄር); ጕሕሉት "fraud"; ጽልሑት "artifice", "cunning" (اِصْطِلَاحَة); ውርዙት "youth (√برز) (5).

Oftener as *ét* or *ē*; Abstracts in *ét*; Conceptional Words in *ē* from Verbal Stems.

(*b*) More frequently, however, these terminations are shaded with the *a*-sound. Just as the ordinary Adjective-Endings took the form of *āi* and *āwī* instead of *ī*,—so too, in the formation of Abstract Nouns, the feminine ending, *ét*,—or, with vowel-close, *ē*,—is employed instead of *ī́t*.

(*α*) Some few Abstract Nouns are still derived from simpler words, by means of the ending *ét*, from *iat* = *ait* (6): ረድኤት "help"; በቍዔት "advantage" (from ረድአ, በቍዐ); ተፍጻሜት "consummation", "end" (from ተፍጻም); ዕብሬት "fruit", "succession" (with prep. Gen. 12, 13, *propter*) from a lost word like עֲבוּר (7); and ዕብሬት "sterility" from ዕቡር "unfruitful". The place of an Infinitive, derived straight from አእኰት (II, 1 of አኰተ), is supplied by አኰቴት "thanksgiving" (for አእኰቴት).

(1) [Generally used in the Acc. adverbially, ድኅሪተ "backwards", "again". TR.]

(2) [*Cf.* also ܐܝܟܢܝܘܬܐ, *ποιότης*, *qualitas*. TR.]

(3) Not √ሰከየ, as this does not mean—"to indicate" (Gesenius).

(4) V. Ewald, '*Hebr. Spr.*' § 165, *b*.

(5) ኄረወ, ጐሕለወ, ጸልሐወ and ወርዘወ are only derivatives of these, § 73.

(6) V. on the other hand König, p. 113.

(7) [A different derivation is given in the '*Lexicon*', col. 507, where እብሬት or ዕብሬት, meaning "succession", is said to be made up of ብሬት (from በረየ) and prosthetic እ. TR.]

(*β*) More usual, however, is the shorter, vowel-ending termination *ē*, by means of which Infinitive-like conceptional words are derived from the several Verbal Stems. This formation is at once an inner and an outer one. Into the interior of the form the lengthened *ā*,—which is made use of in the formation of Abstracts (§§ 107, *β* and 111 *a*, *β*),—makes its way: it takes the accent (TRUMPP, p. 540), while the *a* of the preceding syllable must be reduced to *ĕ*, and *ā* (in St. I, 3) to *ū* (1). Externally the toneless *ē* attaches itself to this form. The formation occurs oftenest as a derivative from St. I, 2 & 3 of the tri-radical verb, and St. I of the Multiliteral, but only very rarely from St. I, 1 (**ክዋኔ** "existence"; **ምዋኤ** "song of triumph"). From St. I, 2 come, *e. g.* **ሕዳሴ** "renewal" (*ḥeddásē*); **ፍጻሜ** "completion"; **ምሳሌ** "comparison", "parable"; **ሥላሴ** "Trinity"; **እማሬ** "demonstration"; **ውዳሴ** "praise"; **ይባቤ** "jubilation"; **ውፋዬ** "yielding up"; **ሐሳዌ** "untruth". So too:—**ሕማሜ** "affliction" (St. I, 2 replacing here Stem **አሕመመ**); **አኰቴ** "thanksgiving" (**አእኰተ**); **ሥጣዌ** "answer" (**ተሠጥወ**). Peculiar forms present themselves in **ኵነኔ** (*kuennané*) "judgment"; **ኀበኔ** as well as **ኅበኔ** "skirt of a garment"; **ሕመሜ** "affliction"; **ጽንፌ** "end" (2), in which long *ā* has not made its way within the word,—and **ሚያኔ** "deception" (from **መየነ**), in which long *ī* takes the place of the doubling of the second radical. From St. I, 3: **ጉባኤ** "assembly"; **ኩፋሌ** "partition"; **ቡራኬ** "blessing"; **ሑያጼ** "observation" (*Kuf.*) (3). Several roots, which are no longer used as verbs in St. I, 3, have this formation,—in part from St. III, 3 and IV, 3, like **ሩካቤ** with **ተራከበ**, and **ኑባሬ** "institution" with **አስተናበረ**. From **ሳብዕ** "the seventh" **ሱባዔ** "week" ('the seven') has been derived. This form is exceedingly rare from Reflexive Stems, the formations noticed in § 111 proving sufficient for these: **ትስበኤ** as well as **ትስብኤ** "human nature", "incarnation" = **ትስብእት**; **ትንሣኤ** "resurrection". On the other hand it is very common from Multiliteral roots:—St. I:—**ልምላሜ** "freshness"; **ድንጋሌ** "maidenly bearing"; **ብንኵኔ** "putrefaction"; **ፍልሳፌ** "philosophy"; **ምንሳዌ** "temptation"; **ውርዛዌ** "youth"; **ፂዋዌ** "imprison-

(1) But v. KÖNIG, p. 124.

(2) *Cf.* LUDOLF's '*Lex.*' s. v.

(3) **ዑፃዌ**, **ኑፋቄ**, **ኑታጌ**, **ቡዓዴ**, **ሱላሜ**, **ሱታፌ**, **ሡራሬ**, **ኑዛዜ**, **ሩካቤ**, **ኁባሬ**, **ሉዓሌ**, **ሑቃፌ**, **ሡራሔ**, **ሑጻጼ**, **ዑቃቤ**, **ዑጻፌ**.

ment", "captivity" (ፄወወ); ሙ·ቃሔ "taking captive" (ሞቅሐ) &c.:— St. V: እንጦላዔ "veiling".—A foreign word of this type is met with in ስንጻሌ σεμίδαλις. But even from simpler Stems Conceptional words (and Names of things) may be derived by means of the termination ē, as well as by the termination ēt (v. supra): ወይሌ "howling" (from ወይል § 61); ሕንጼ as well as ሕንጻ "a building"; ናዐዌ "hunting"(1); ሐንብርብሬ "scab"; እንጻንጼ 'name of a disease'; perhaps also ዕድሜ "set time"; ቍንቍኔ "woodworms" ('humming'), and some of the words mentioned in § 127, c.

Forms, chiefly Infinitives, in accented ōt, and ō.

§ 121. (c) Just as ēt is formed from īt by the admixture of an a-sound, so is ōt,—or as a vowel-ending—ō, from ūt. (α) The accented termination ōt (Trumpp, p. 540),—the Hebr.-Aramaic ūt—, has been extensively employed in the formation of the Infinitive (v. § 125), but otherwise it is found only in a few words, some of them foreign. Formations of native origin are: መለኮት "Godhead" (from አምላክ); ምልኮት "property"; ጽላሎት "shadow" (cf. ጽላሌ); ጥብዮት σύνταξις ('daily task', from ጥቡዕ, Ex. 5); ጸ.አት "filth" (G. Ad., from ጼአ); ፂ.ዖት "low grounds", "meadows" (cf. وَضِعَة). The following are foreign words: ሃይማኖት "faith", ܗܝܡܢܘܬܐ; ሰሊ.ኖት "Cassia" (سَلِيخَة); አሶት "healing" (ܐܣܝܘܬܐ); ታቦት "ark" (تَابُوت) (2).

(β) *The similarly accented termination ō* is likewise employed very frequently in the formation of the *Infinitive* (v. § 125). Outside of this use it is chiefly of service in the derivation of *Names of the products of artistic skill* (from Substantives of the type ገቡር):— ሥብኮ "casting"; ቅፍሎ "what is overlaid with metal"; ብስሎ "cooked food"; እንሞ "web"; ውቅሮ "hewn work"; ዝብጦ "tin-work"; ግልፎ "carved work"; ጥብሶ "roast meat"; ጥወዮ "turnery"; ፍሕቆ "turned work"; ፍትሎ "net-work"; ርፍአ "tailor's work"; ዕፍሮ "basket-ware"; ቍጽሮ "net-work", "fringes"; ውጽቦ "nose- and ear-ornaments"; ድርጎ "assignment"; ግዝሮ "circumcision" (3).

(1) The older mode of writing it,—ነዐዌ e. g. Lev. 17, 13 F. H—speaks against the conjecture that ናዐዌ stands for ንዓዌ.

(2) Of unknown derivation are አኮት "small locust" (cf. غَوْغَاء), ጻፀት and ጻዖት 'a stinging insect', ሐለስትዮት "baboon".

(3) Perhaps also እንቁቅ·ኖ "egg", as a result or consequence of cackling, if እንቆቅኅ (cf. قَعْقَع) really means "to cackle". [A startling view! tr.]

In other applications this ending appears only in rare cases:— **ጸልበ** "cross"; **ቀድሑ** "well-bucket"; **ከበሮ** "drum", ('timbrel', Ex. 15, 20) (كَبَر); **ከረበ** "basket" ('basket-, *or* mat-work', كرب); **ጸለሎ** "soot"; **ደረከኖ** and **ደርከኖ** "hyacinth-colour"; **መሰንቆ** 'a musical instrument' (*κιθάρα*, [*cf. Kebra Nag.* p. XXV.] Plur. **መሰንቆታት** Rev. 14, 2) ([1]); **ትክቶ** "the condition of having monthly courses" (from **ትክት** "*mulier menstruata*", probably for **ትክእት** √ تكأ VIII and √ تكأ, 'reclining'; 'sitting'; to elucidate the notion *cf.* Gen. 31, 35); **ከበሎ** and **ከንበሎ** "hook *or* ring" (on a sandal); **ክባሶ** and **ክብሶ** "hair-net" ([2]).

Nouns of Circumstance and Condition, in Tone-bearing *ắt*.

(*d*) The *tone-bearing termination ắt*,—which is applied to Nouns of simpler form, to express notions of circumstance or condition,—has come into being, sometimes from *ōt* by a change of vowels, sometimes from the simple Feminine-ending *at* by the process of lengthening the vowel:—**ልህቃት** "old age", "seniority" (=**ልህቅና**) from **ልሂቅ**; **ነእሳት** "youth", "minority" (Gen. 43, 33) from **ንኡስ** or **ንእስ**; **ቅድሳት** "sanctuary", "holiness" from **ቅዱስ**; **ኅድጋት** "state of divorcement" from **ኅዱግ**; **ስርያት** "the condition of one who has obtained **ስርየት**, *i. e.* 'remission of sins'"; **ቅንያት** "slavery", *i. e.* "the state of **ቅኔ** ('servitude')"; **ምርዓት** "wantonness"; **ጽድቃት** ([3]) "benevolence",—in which **ጽድቅ** ('probity' *or* 'piety') is shown. This *ā*t is occasionally substituted for *at*, *e. g.* in **ስብሓት** "glory", alongside of **ስብሐት**; **ሐብላት** "plaited-work" (Judges 8, 26; Ex. 35, 22, Note) along with **ሐብለት**; and *at* itself is sufficient for the derivation of Abstracts from simpler Nominal Stems:—**ሰብአት** "humanity" from **ሰብእ**; **ምስኪነት** "poverty" from **ምስኪን**. In **ብስራት** "glad tidings" (בְּשׂוֹרָה), *ā* seems to be only

([1]) [Where *φωνὴν . . . κιθαρῳδῶν κιθαριζόντων ἐν ταῖς κιθάραις αὐτῶν* is translated **ቃለ ፡ መሰናቁት ፡ ሰበ ፡ ይሰንቅዉ ፡ በመሰንቆታቲሆሙ**. TR.]

([2]) The following are of obscure derivation: **ፍሕሶ** 'name of a flower'; **ሰገኖ** "ostrich" (*cf.* صِعْوَن); **ዐውሎ** "tempest"; **ዶርሆ** "domestic fowl"; **ገበ** "side" (*cf.* DILLMANN's '*Lex.*' *et supra*) and **ቀፎ** "basket": but the *u* in **ምዕኖ** "mire" seems to belong to the root; *cf.* عَنِيَّة.

([3]) [But in '*Lex.*', col. 1312, DILLMANN represents **ጽድቃት** '*eleemosynae*' as a *plural* of **ጽድቅ**. TR.]

lengthened by the tone([1]). Similarly, simple Feminines of the Passive Participle may also take the meaning of Abstracts, v. § 128.

Abstract Forms in *án* or *ón* and *ná*.

§ 122. (*e*) But besides these terminations, which in the last resort all depend upon the Adjective-ending *ī*, Ethiopic has an additional Abstract ending, also accented, viz. *án* or *ná*, which is manifestly of pronominal origin, v. § 62([2]). As may be perceived from the other Semitic tongues, this termination—*an*—at one time produced Adjectives, and it was only in lengthening it to *ān* or *ōn* that it came to be employed farther in the formation of Abstracts issuing from such Adjectives. Only a few traces have been retained in Ethiopic of the application of this ending in the formation of Adjectives, but examples are pretty common of its use in the production of Abstracts. As has been already pointed out (§ 62), the demonstrative word concerned was capable at first of being pronounced both as *an* and *na*. Ethiopic,—in this again richer than the other Semitic tongues—, has developed and preserved both pronunciations even in the formation of Nouns, with a slight idiomatic variation of meaning, the *nā*-form of pronunciation being the more common one.

(*α*) The termination *án* is commonly applied to Nominal Stems of the First simple form; and by means of this doubled,—inner and outer—, formation, *stronger conceptional* or *notional words* are derived: **ርሥእን** (*reśʾán*) "old age" from **ርሥእ**; **ልህቃን** "seniority" (G. Ad.); **ብርሃን** "brightness", "light"; **ሥልጣን** "authority"; **ቍርባን** "oblation"; **ሕልያን** "bribe"; **ድርሳን** "dissertation"; **ጽልአን** "hatred"; **ኪዳን** "covenant"([3]). The only instance, still retained, of the employment of this termination

([1]) It may be that **ዐሥራት** "the tenth, *or* tithe" is formed in the same way, or else it stands for **ዐሥራይት**, like **ዐውያት** "loud lament", for **ዐውያውት**. On **እሳት** and **ትካት** v. § 128. *Cf.* also König, p. 116 *sq.*

([2]) *Cf.* Ewald, '*Hebr. Spr.*' § 163, *b.*

([3]) Farther: **ዕርቃን**, **ምዕዳን**, **ፍርቃን**, **ፍልጣን**, **ብዕዓን**, **ግዕዛን**; also **ቅጥራን** "tar" (قِطْرَان); but **ልሳን** "tongue" is a very old word of a different formation (לָשׁוֹן, لِسَان, [Assyr. *lišānu*]); and **ሰይጣን** "Satan" (شَيْطَان, שָׂטָן) is a foreign word.—For the formation of these types *cf.* also König, p. 123 *sq.*

in the formation of words indicating persons, is met with in the foreign word ትርጕማን "interpreter". Sometimes *ōn* takes the place of *ān*, as in ዘይቶን "oliveyard" (زَيْتُون), and ዐሥሮን "decade" (1). In Amharic *ān* usually passes into *ām* (2), which is then used often to form adjectives (*e. g.* ስናም "one who has large teeth").—Even in Ethiopic, traces of this *ām* are come upon: ቀስታም "bow" and "shepherd's crook" (from ቀስት, *cf.* قُسْطَان); and perhaps ጌሰም "the morrow", "to-morrow" (Ex. 32,5; Josh. 3,5; Matt. 6,30) from ጌሰ (غدا).

(*β*) *The termination nā́*, also accented, is in much more frequent use, to derive from Nominal Stems of every kind fresh and final conceptional words, which express sometimes conditions and properties, but especially dignities, offices, age, standing, and so forth, and which answer mostly to our conceptional words in *-ness -hood, -dom, -ship*. Derivatives from Nominal Stems of the First simple form are exhibited, for example, in ርእስና "the princely dignity" (ርእስ); ብኵርና (*bekuernā́*) "right of birth" (በኵር); እርግና "old age" (እርግ); ምልክና "lordship" (مُلْك); ቅድምና "precedence" (ቅድም); ዳኅና and ድኅና "health", "soundness"; ዕርቅና "nakedness"; ግዕዝና "emancipation"; ግግጽና "fear". The *ū* of the Passive Part. has to be shortened into *e* before *nā*—ልዕልና "height" (*le'elnā́*, ልዑል); ርጥብና "dampness", "humidity" (ርጡብ); ስብሕና "magnificence" (ስቡሕ); ቅድስና "holiness"; ጥይቅና "exactness", "accuracy" (ጥዩቅ); ትሕትና "modesty" (ትሑት); ግይርና (*geyernā́*) "position of a foreigner" (ግዩር); ሙስና (*mūsennā́*) "corruption" (from ሙሱን); ፍድፍድና "superabundance" (from ፍድፉድ); ፍልስፍና "philosophy" (from ፍልሱፍ):—*Tertiae infirmae*: ህሉና "essence" (ህልው); ልቡና "understanding"; ሕሊና "faculty of thinking"; ዕሪና "equality" (ዕሩይ); ጥዒና "good health", "soundness"; ዕሙና "solitude". Farther, the fundamental Nominal Stems concerned suffer occasionally still stronger abbreviation before this ending; ሕፃንና and ሕፀና (*ḥeṣannā́*) "childhood" (ሕፃን); ቅስስና and even ቅስና "seniority" (from ቀሲስ); ምስፍና (*mesfennā́*) "leadership", from መስፍን; ምልእክና "princely dignity", from

---

(1) ዐሥሮን ፡ ቃል "*Decalogus*" (Hymnology).

(2) Isenberg, '*Gramm.*' p. 33 [and Guidi, '*Gramm. elem.*' p. 15, Note 1].—*Cf.*, in Hebrew, Ewald, '*Hebr. Spr.*' § 133 *sq.*

መልአክ(¹); **ትንብልና** "intercession", from **ተንበለ**; **ምንኵስና** "monastic life", from **መነኮስ**; **ኂርውና** and **ኄርውና** "goodness", from **ኂሩት**. But in other words the vowels of the ground-word are retained, in a body, unaltered: **ሊቅና** "seniority" (**ሊቅ**); **መሲሕና** "Messiahship"; **ጠቢብና** "philosophy"; **እግዚእና** "dominion". "superiority"; **ዋሕድና** "singularity"; **ስርግውና** "ornament" (**ስርግው**); **ውርዝውና** "youth" (**ውርዝው**); **ድንግልና** "virginity" (**ድንግል**); **ቴዎሎግና** "theology"; **ጥንቅቅና** "complete agreement"; **ዐሪቅይና** "mediatorship"; **እጓለ፡ማውትና** "state of orphanage", "pupillarity"; **ሊቀ ፡ ጳጳስና** "archiepiscopate", "patriarchate"; **ብሉየ፡መዋዕልና** "eternity" ('the antiquity of days'); **ከዊነ፡እምላክና** "the becoming God" (*conversio in Deum*); **ከዊነ፡ሥርጽና** "the condition *or* quality of the Procession" (viz. 'of the Holy Ghost'); **ዘለዓለምና** "eternity". Such words are derived even from Infinitives: **ተከልበትና** "canine nature"; **ትህይድና** "the condition of being robbed" (**ተህይድ**); **ትምስውና** "faint-heartedness"; —and from Plural forms: **አምላክና** "Deity"; **አይሁድና** "Judaism". **ቍልዕውና** "boyhood" from **ቍልዔ** is a formation noteworthy by reason of the type it presents, inasmuch as the ending *ē* is here resolved into *ew* (²).—Instead of *nā, nāt* (with the fem. **ት**) appears in two instances: **ግብርናት** "slavery" (from **ገብር**) and **ርስዕናት** "godlessness" (from **ርስዕ**) Hen. 99,1 (104,9 Note) (³).

No Special form for Diminutives; nor any true Compounds.

Diminutives have no special form in Ethiopic, and have therefore to be described by circumlocution, *e. g.* **በግዕ፡ንኡስ** "a lambkin" (*lit.* 'a little lamb *or* sheep') Hen. 89,48.

Compound words do not occur in the domain of conceptional words. It is true that the constituent parts of some very common Word-Groups and of Proper names are written together as one word, without being separated by points, like **እግዚአብሔር** "the Supreme" (properly: 'Lord of the earth'); **እመሕያው** "mother of the living"; **አባጕንባሕ** "horn-bill" (Deut. 14,18 جُنْبُح *crassus, longus*),—though, on the other hand, **መዓረ፡ግራ** "wax"—(*lit.* 'sweetness of the comb'); **ፐፒሩ፡ለይ** "scarlet"—(*lit.* 'purple *or*

(¹) Sc too **ምዕስብና** from **ማዕሰብ**, and **ምዕቅብና** from **ማዕቀብ**.

(²) The word **ባዝግና** "necklace" is difficult to explain.

(³) According to Halévy, '*Revue crit.*', 1885, No. 13, p. 247 the terminations *-nā, -nāt* must have made their way into Geʿez from the Agau.

scarlet of the berry'); but, inasmuch as the first word shows the regular type of the Construct state, these combinations cannot rank as true Compounds. Yet in stray Multiliteral Nominal Stems, Compound words or Compound roots seem to be met with, *e. g.* in **ድንጕብዕዙል** "wild-beasts' cage", "lasso" and **ሰንሰሬቍ** "silk" (the latter part of which is = سَرَق). Noteworthy also are **ከጕርጽ** "leek" (of which the latter part = قِرْط) and **ዕጕሥታር** "aloe".

PARTICIPLES AND INFINITIVES.

Participles: General Remarks: Comparative Failure of Regular Participial Forms.

§ 123. The foregoing account shows that special types exist in Ethiopic for each separate Verbal Stem, according to which it might form its own *Participle*:—the types namely of the Active and Passive Participles, described in §§ 109, *a* and 108, *c*, for St. I,1; those which are formed by prefixing **መ** (§§ 114 and 118) for St. I,2, 3, II,1—3, IV,1—3 of the Tri-radical roots, and St. I, II, IV and V of the Multiliteral; and those which are described in § 117 for the Reflexive Stems III of Triliteral and Multiliteral verbs, as well as for a few other Stems. Yet we can hardly designate all these types as Participles proper, for they by no means admit of being derived from every verb. It depends always upon the usage of the language whether, in the case of the several verbs, Participle-resembling forms,—and which of them—, have been established and retained. These forms, besides, have in most cases lost the force of a pure Participle, and have become either Adjectives or *Nomina Agentis*. This explains also why so many of them have taken the external termination *ī* (§ 117 *sq*). Besides, special types of the Participle Passive have almost entirely disappeared in all Derived Stems of Active meaning, with the general decay of the inner Passive formation—(yet v. §§ 111, *b*; 114 *ad fin.*):—Such Stems were forced to have recourse to the Simple Stems, when the purpose was to form Participles of Passive meaning (*cf.* §§ 108, 111, *b*; 112, *b*). Even the Participle which occurs the most frequently of all,—viz. the Passive Part. of the Simple Stem—, by no means continues to be formed from every root. This failure in Ethiopic of a regular Participial formation was fomented (1) by the peculiar use of the Infinitive (§ 181), through which the Participle could in many cases be replaced, as for instance in ወሐዊሮሙ፡ ይጥቅዑ "and going, *or* as they go (*lit*: 'in their going'), they shall sound the trumpets" Josh. 6, 8; በጽሐ፡ ወፂኦ "he arrived, after he had come forth" Josh. 10, 9—, and (2) by the rise of a practice of indicating the Participial conception by periphrasis in a finite tense. The defect, inherent in the Semitic Participle, of being attached to no sphere of time, was thus compensated, in the course of striving to be clear, by the language gradually coming to represent the Participle through a periphrasis in the proper tense-forms.

Compensated partly 1.—By the Gerund; 2.—By Periphrasis in a Finite Tense.

The case is quite otherwise with the Ethiopic *Infinitive*. It is regularly formed from all the separate Stems, and in fact not merely in one type but in several. The Infinitive expresses the pure conception of the action of the Verb without distinction of tenses or persons, and to that extent it ranges itself alongside of the Abstract Nominal Stems or Conceptional words; but, on the other hand, it partakes of the Verbal character in respect that it conforms to the Verb throughout all the Stems, and produces as many forms as there are Stems in it, and also in respect that it is capable of having Objects of its own. In consequence of possessing this twofold nature, it inclines, in the different Semitic languages, sometimes to the Noun, sometimes to the Verb,—more to the Noun, in Arabic for instance,—more to the Verb, in Hebrew. In this matter Ethiopic has taken a course of its own by constructing different types for the Infinitive in its different functions. It has Infinitive-forms which possess completely the power and independent character of a Noun. They may enter into all relations in a sentence which are open to a Noun, may become Subject or Object, may subordinate to themselves other Nouns in the Genitive case(1), may have themselves preceded by Prepositions or by other words in the Construct state, may be specially determined by an Adjective (*e. g.* ብዙኅ፡ ዘምዎ(2) Hen. 8, 2), or may even,— like

Infinitives: Distinction between Nominal Infinitive and Verbal Infinitive or Gerund.

(1) They do not so often subordinate to themselves objects in the accusative, after the pattern of their verbs: *e. g.* Gen. 6, 7; Deut. 5, 22.

(2) [FLEMMING, '*Das Buch Henoch*', reads in this passage ወኮነ፡ ርስዓን፡ ዐቢይ፡ ወብዙኅ፡ ወዘመወ—, instead of DILLMANN's reading ወኮነ፡ ርስዐት፡ ዐቢይ፡ ወብዙኅ፡ ዘምዎ—, thus referring the adjective ብዙኅ

the Hebrew Infinitive Absolute or the Arabic *Muṭlaq*(1), — be subordinated in the Accusative to their own Verb by way of special qualification. But from this *Nominal Infinitive*, as we shall henceforth call it, Ethiopic distinguishes, by a special form, the *Verbal Infinitive*, which stands closer to the Verb, and which we, following the Latin terminology, shall call the *Gerund*. Of course, being an Infinitive, it has the form of a Noun, and as such may have an Accusative. It does not, however, take the place of a noun, but that of a verb, and properly it is nothing else than the verb deprived of Tense(2). It occurs only as a special qualification to a finite verb, which contains the principal action of the sentence, and it is subordinated to that verb in the accusative for the purpose of adding a secondary action. As the time of the secondary or accompanying action is determined by the tense of the principal verb, the secondary action is given without any time-form, that is, it is put in the Infinitive. But it is exactly like an ordinary verb in being obliged to enclose within itself the acting Subject, while it is completed after the manner of other Nouns by a Suffix pronoun, which in this case always is to be regarded as a Subject Genitive, *e. g.*: ወሰሚዖ፡ ንጉሥ፡ ደንገፀ "and at his hearing, the king was filled with terror", *i. e.* "when the king heard (it), he was struck with terror"; ይጥቅዑ፡ ሐዊሮሙ "they shall blow the trumpets, in their going", *i. e.* "they shall sound the trumpets as they go". We might call this Infinitive also the Infinitive Absolute, just as in other languages we speak of a Participle Absolute. By means of the formation of this Infinitive, Ethiopic diction has gained a peculiar brevity and grace; but the similar employment of the Infinitive Absolute in Hebrew and of the Infinitive Construct with לְ in cases like וַיֹּאמֶר לֵאמֹר— shows that in this it has merely developed a capability which underlies the Infinitive in other Semitic languages too(3).

---

to the foregoing noun, and reading the last word as a finite verb, 3rd pl. Perf. TR.]

(1)[—the "objective complement, which is called by the Arab grammarians اَلْمَفْعُولُ ٱلْمُطْلَقُ, *the absolute object*", WRIGHT's '*Ar. Gramm.*' 3rd ed. vol. II (Cambridge 1898), p. 54 C. TR.]

(2) In some of the cases cited in EWALD, '*Hebr. Spr.*' § 280, *a*, *b*, it is paralleled by the Infinitive Absolute in Hebrew.

(3) EWALD, '*Hebr. Spr.*' § 280, *d*.

§ 124. A few Abstract forms, of those which have been described already among the Nominal Stems, may be used readily for the Infinitive, at least for the Nominal Infinitive, seeing that it is merely a Conceptional Word or Abstract, derived from the Verb. Several of those Abstract forms, in fact, are ordinary forms of the Infinitive in the other Semitic languages. In particular, the forms, described in § 111, *a*, *α* & *β*, may directly supply the place of an Infinitive, as also may the Feminine formations in § 106. *e. g.* **ሞተት** "to die" (Gen. 35, 18), **በአት** "to enter" (Matt. 19, 24), and several other forms, *e. g.* **ምብጻእ** "to come" (Josh. 13, 5). *Cf.* also: **ግብአትየ** (Luke 10, 35), **ፀአቶሙ** Ex. 5, 20, **ምልክናከ፡ ኵሎ** Sap. 12, 16, **ኅሬርኩ፡ ስእለቶ፡ ለንጉሥ፡ ኀይለ፡ ወሰራዊተ** 2 Esr. 8, 22, **መዋዕለ፡ ዕንሳ፡ ኪያሁ** (F. N.). For the Infinitive proper the language has meanwhile contrived special Abstract-formations, which very seldom indeed have become actual Nouns. At the same time this distinction has been established between the two classes of Infinitives, viz. that the Gerund invariably takes an inner formation only, while the Nominal Infinitive takes outer Abstract-terminations, just as they are used with Nominal Stems.

Certain Abstract forms sometimes employed for the Nominal Infinitive.

1. *The formation of the Gerund* conforms to the type which is described in § 109, *b* (*cf.* therewith § 106). It is contrived by inserting after the second-last radical a long and accented *ī*, which in the last resort is connected with the *ĕ* of the Subjunctive of Transitive verbs.

Formation of the Infinitive Proper:— 1. *The Gerund* in the several Stems.

In St. I, 1 of the Tri-radical verb the first radical,—in accordance with § 109, *b*—, has always the vowel *a*, and the form runs: **መቲር** (*matī́r*)(1) "to cut", **በሊዕ** "to eat", **ኀሊፍ** "to go on", **ኀዲግ** "to abandon", **ቀቲል** "to kill", **ዐቂር** "to bind together". No difference is made between Verbs of transitive and those of intransitive pronunciation. In roots *mediae gutturalis* the *a* of the first radical is always dulled into *ĕ*: **ምሒር** "to pity", **ድኂን** "to escape", **ብሂል** "to say", **ክሂል** "to be able"; **ስኢን** "to be unable", **ስኢል** "to ask", **ግዒር** "to moan", **እኂዝ** "to take", **ግሒሥ** "to turn to". The form from roots *med. gem.* is always resolved: **ነቢብ** "to speak", **ሐቲት** "to search into", **ገሢሥ** "to touch". With

(1) *Cf.* Trumpp, p. 540.—In Tigriña, according to Schreiber, § 88, the Gerund even with Suffixes has always the accent on the first syllable.

roots *primae vocalis* the stronger form is made use of: **ወሊድ** "to give birth to", **ወፂእ** "to go forth", **ወሪቅ** "to spit"; and in those which are in addition *med. guttur.*: **ውሂብ** "to give", **ውሒዝ** "to flow", **ውኂጥ** "to devour". Roots middle *ū* take always the strong form: **ነዊም** "to sleep", **ቀዊም** "to stand", **ሐዊር** "to go", **በዊእ** "to come", **መዊቅ** "to become hot" Job 6, 17. Those with middle *ī* either do the same (in older Manuscripts frequently). *e. g.* **መዪጥ** "to turn", **ገዪስ** "to be up early", or follow, as they more usually do, the type given in § 52: **መይጥ** (*mayêṭ*, *cf.* TRUMPP, p. 540), **ገይስ**, **ሠይም** "to set", **ሀይድ** "to rob", **በይት** "to pass the night", **ሐይው** "to live". Roots final *ū* also take the strong form: **ተሊው** "to follow", **ዐዲው** "to pass over"; those with final *ī* maintain here and there, it is true, the strong form as in **ዐፂይ** "to rot" Acts 12, 23, [**ፈሪይ** "to bear fruit" *Kebra Nag.* 106 a 10], and particularly when, by appending a case-vowel or suffix pronoun, the last radical is drawn to the syllable following;—but usually the type in § 52 is reproduced: **ሰትይ** (*satéyye*) "to drink", [with suff. pron. **ሰቲዮሙ**, *Kebra Nag.* 138 b 2], **በልይ** "to become antiquated", **ሐቅይ** "to gnash the teeth", **ወድይ** "to lay *or* place", **ፈድይ** "to pay back"; so with those roots which are at the same time *med. guttur.*: **ውዕይ** "to burn", **ርእይ** "to see" (with suffix pron. also **ርኢዮ**(¹) Hen. 107, 3 [*cf. Kebra Nag.* p. XVI]); but **ጣዕዮ፡ ነፍስ** Sir. 30, 16; and so with roots which are at the same time *med. gem.*: **ጕይይ** "to flee" Hen. 52, 7.

In St. II, 1 the first radical, as in the Subjunctive, is always bound to the prefixed Stem-sign **አ** in one syllable, with the vowel *a* between; the second has *ī*; and in roots with final *ī* the peculiar formation of St. I, 1 is repeated. Examples:—**አእሚር** "to know", **አእኩት** "to thank", "to give thanks", **አስሒት** "to corrupt" Hen. 19, 2, **አስቲት** "to neglect", Hebr. 2, 3, **አንጺው** "to wither" Ps. 89, 6, **አሕኒጽ**, **አውሢእ**, **አግሪር**, **አቢት**, **አኒኖ**; **አቂም** from **አቀመ**; **አኒም** from **አነመ** &c.

In St. III, 1, after the Personal sign of the Subjunctive has been removed, the Stem-Preformative and the first radical take each the vowel *a*, and the second radical takes *ī*: in other respects the peculiarities of roots middle *ī* and final *ī* (and those of guttural or

(¹) [Instead of **ርኢዮ** FLEMMING reads, in his edition of *Henoch*, in this passage, **ወእርእዮ**. TR.]

aspirate roots) are repeated: **ተመሊእ** "to be fulfilled", **ተዘሪእ** "to be sown", **ተኀፊር** "to be ashamed", **ተመይጦ** "to be turned, converted" Luke 22, 32, but also **ተመዩጠከ** G. Ad. 17, 8 [and **ተመዩጠክሙ** *Kebra Nag.* 120 b 22], **ተፈቲው** "to long for" Numb. 16, 15, **ተመሲው** 2 Pet. 3, 11, **ተገዚም**, **ተገዚር**, **ተመዊእ**, **ተጠሚቅ**, **ተጠሚዕ**, **ተሠሪዎ** Chrest. 72, 1; *mediae gutturalis*: **ተግሒሦ** "to withdraw (*intr.*)", **ተእኂዝ** Sap. 14, 16, [*Kebra Nag.* 135 a 24]; and from **ተምዕዐ**, **ተምዒዕ** "to be angry". In St. IV, 1 the first radical has the same pronunciation as in the Subjunctive: **አስተፍሥሒሕ** "to rejoice", **አስተብሪክ** "to bend the knees". The Infinitive-forms, besides, of Stems II, 1, III, 1 and IV, 1, which upon the whole do not occur so often as those of St. I, 1, are not yet sufficiently well supported.

In like manner the Infinitive of the Intensive Stem has hitherto been but seldom met with in the form I, 2; but it may be easily formed from the Subjunctive, which has always *a* after the first radical, modified into *e* in the case of roots *med. guttur.* It is distinguished from the Infinitive of I, 1 merely by the doubling of the middle radical: **ነጺር** "to perceive", "to behold" 2 Cor. 5, 19, **ፈጺም** "to finish" John 17, 4, **ኰኒን** "to rule over" Esth. 3, 14, l. 4 *Apcr.*; **ምሂር** "to teach". Even from roots middle *ī* it is formed just as in the case of I, 1: **ጠይቅ** "to know exactly" Ps. 21, 18, Jas. 1, 24, [along with **ጠዩቅ**, v. *Kebra Nag.*, p. XVII]. Of still less frequent occurrence is the Infinitive of II, 2, *e. g.* **አዘኪር** "to recall to memory", **አመኪር** "to test" 1 Cor. 11, 28. That of St. III, 2 is more common: **ተደሚር** "to be united" Hen. 19, 1, **ተመኪር** "to be tempted", **ተሠጊው** "to become flesh" *Hymnol. Musei Brit.*, and so too **ተዐሪዝ**, **ተገሢጽ**, **ተዐጊሦ**, **ተደሊው**, **ተገፊዕ**, **ተወኪል**; from roots *med. guttur.*: **ተልዒል** "to be exalted" Ps. 87, 16, **ተምሂር** "to be instructed", **ተጸዒር** "to be tortured", **ተጽዒን** "to ride"(¹). From St. IV, 2, *e. g.*: **አስተኀይሶ** "to prefer" (*Encom.*).

The Infinitive of the Influencing-Stem has not yet been vouched for in St. I, 3 or II, 3, but it could without doubt be formed. From St. III, 3 we have:—**ተጋቢእ** "to be assembled together", **ተላህዮ** "to play", **ተሣይጦ** "to buy" Gen. 43, 2, **ተማ**

(¹) *Cf.* also: **ተሥኢን** Eph. 6, 15; **ተዐዊር** Numb. 5, 6; **ተፈኒው** 2 Pet. 1, 21; **ተሰፊው** Hebr. 11, 1; **ተኰኒን** Hebr. 11, 35; **ተፈሥሒሕ** Ps. 64, 11.

ኪ.ር "to take counsel together" Matt. 27, 7, **ተዋቂ.ሥ** "to contend" Job 35. 2, **ተኬንዎ** for **ተኬኒዎ** "to fabricate with skill" Sap. 13,11: From St. IV, 3: **አስተሓሚ.ም** "to tire one's self out" Luke 15. 8, **አስተዳሊ.ው** "to prepare" Josh. 9, 2 (1).

From Multiliteral Roots: St. I: **ቀጥቂጥ** "to break in pieces", "to crush" Luke 9, 39, **ማሰ.ን** "to perish", **ጐድጒ.ድ** "to knock" Luke 12, 36, **ተርጒ.ም** "to interpret", **ደንጊ.ፅ** "to be terrified", **ገን ጺ.ል** "to distort", **ሞቂ.ሕ** "to put in fetters", **ቶሲ.ሕ** "to mix", (*Gadla Lālibalā*, ed. Perruchon, Paris 1892, p. 39, l. 19), **ጐንድ.ይ** "to linger *or* tarry" Matt. 25, 5, **ፄዊ.ው** "to take captive" Eph. 4, 8; Ps. 67, 19: St. II:—**አመንዲ.ብ** "to reduce to distress", [**አመክዒ.ብ** "to double" *Kebra Nag.* 96 a 3], **አናሕሲ.ይ** (with Suff. Pron.) "to forgive" 2 Cor. 5, 19, **አሰሲ.ል** "to remove" Chrest. 73, 7 [**አፈ.ድፊ.ድ** and **አፈ.ድፍ.ድ** "to add" *Kebra Nag.* 12 b 16 & var.]: St. III:—**ተመንዲ.ብ** "to be brought into distress", **ተመርጒ.ዝ** "to lean upon", **ተቶሲ.ሕ** "to be mixed", **ተሞቂ.ሕ** "to be put in fetters"; **ተገልቢ.ብ** "to be veiled", **ተፄዊ.ው** "to be taken captive", **ተጐናዲ.ይ** "to be deferred", **ተዜያኒ.ው** "to recount to one another" *Gad. Lālib.* 39,12: St. V:—**አንጦሊ.ዕ** "to spread out", **አንቃዕዲ.ው** "to be devout", **አንጠብጢ.ብ** "to drop", **አንገሊ.ግ** "to assemble together", "to keep company with" 1 Cor. 5, 4.

2. The Nominal Infinitive in the several Stems.

§ 125. 2. *The Nominal Infinitive* usually has a special form. It is true that in the Simple Ground-Stem the form described in § 124 serves also for cases in which the Infinitive is used rather as a Noun, and it is employed in that meaning far oftener than the special Nominal Infinitive-form, though that form can be framed from this stem too. But in the remaining Stems the Substantive-use of that first form is exceedingly rare. In all these Stems the Nominal Infinitive much prefers to assume a special form, contrived by means of an outer Abstract-termination. Even St. I, 1 may take a form of the same kind. The termination employed is *ōt*, or in abbreviated guise *ō*, § 121, and it always has the accent (Trumpp, p. 540). The formation itself in St. I, 1 is different from that which prevails in the other Stems.

In St. I, 1 *ōt* is simply attached as an Abstract-termination to the type of the Gerund, *e. g.* from **ሐኒጽ** "to build", **ሐኒጾት**. In the same way:—**ዐቂቦት** "to preserve" Ps. 18, 12, **አሚኖት** "to

(1) Other examples are found in Ex. 18, 16, and Deut. 11, 14.

believe" Matt. 13,58, ረዲኦት "to help" Ps. 21,20, ኅሢሦት "to seek", ነቢቦት "to speak", ወሪዶት "to come down" Hen. 63,10, ሰዊቆት "to support", ተሊዎት "to follow" John 13,36, ገሲሶት, ጠፊሖት, ዘሪዎት, ጸቢኦት, ከሢቶት Gen. 48,10, Rev. 5,3, አሲሮት Matt. 12,29, ዐዊዶት Deut. 2,3, ዘጊቦት Tob. 12,8, ተኪሎት Numb. 7,1, ገቢኦት Deut. 17,16, ኀቢኦት Ex. 2,3, በዊኦት 1 Kings 7,13, Sir. 42,6: *mediae gutturalis*:—ምሂከት "to spare", ክሂሎት "to be able", ስኢኖት "not to be able", አኀዞት "to take", ርእዮት "to see", ርሒቆት "to recoil".—With radical *ī* in the middle:—ገይሶት "to be early up" Ps. 126,3, ከይዶት "to tread" Hen. 4, but also in an abbreviated form ኪዶት G. Ad. 22,11, ሚጦት "to turn" *Org.* With *ī* as final radical: ኅርዮት "to choose", ዐስዮት "to requite". This Nominal Infinitive-form of the first Stem is, however, almost never used except when Suffix pronouns are applied. For seeing that in accordance with § 123 the verbal form with suffix pronoun has the force of a Gerund (*e. g.* in ዐቂበሙ "in their keeping" or "by their keeping", ጣዕዮ Sir. 30,16), the language distinguishes by a special form those cases in which the Infinitive with Suff. pron. is not to have that sense, so that, *e. g.* ዐቂቦቶሙ means "their keeping", *i. e.* either "the fact that they keep", or—"the fact that they are kept". The abbreviated form in *ō* does not belong to Stem I, 1 (1).

The *remaining Stems* of the Triliteral roots and all the Stems of the Multiliterals form their Nominal Infinitive from the Subjunctive (2) by throwing off the personal sign and attaching the Abstract-termination *ōt* or *ō*, the *a* of the second radical being replaced in the Reflexive Stems by *e*; *ī* is very rarely met with after the second radical. Between Forms in *ōt* and in *ō* there is no difference in meaning, but merely a phonetic difference originally. The shortened form of expression—*ō* is employed when there is no special reason calling for the other form, and it is then retained even (3) when the Infinitive enters the Construct state, as in አምልኮ፡ ጣዖት "idolatry" ('the worshipping of an idol'), አእምሮ፡ ተአምራት Sap. 8,8, አእምሮ፡ ፍኖቱ፡ 1 Esr. 2,11, ተጊውዎ፡ አዋልድየ Bar. 4,10. The original and longer form in *ōt* regularly

(1) Yet v. Deut. 15,10 ውሂቦ.
(2) V., however, König, p. 163.
(3) Differing in this from Aramaic.

appears before the Suff. Pron. as in ስእነ፡ አመክሮተከ "he could not tempt thee", and it is also occasionally used besides instead of the shortened form, particularly when it is required to denote clearly the Construct state or the Accusative,—which cannot be distinguished in the other form. Neither of the two forms—*ōt*, *ō*—can be used in the sense of a Gerund.

Stem I, 2: ነጽሮ "to look", አብሶ "to transgress", ነስሖ (*nasseḥō*) "to feel penitent", ኰንኖ "to give judgment", ጠቢብ "to be wise", ወልጦ "to exchange", ወርዎ "to throw", የብቦ "to exult", የውሆ "to be gentle", ጠይቆ "to search closely", ኀልዮ "to reflect upon", ጸልዮ "to pray", ሐስዎ "to lie", ሀልዎ "to be"; but *mediae gutturalis*: ምህሮ "to teach" 1 Cor. 9, 14. With *ōt*: ነጽሮት, ወልጦት, ዘምዎት, ሀልዎት Chrest. 45, 20, ምህሮት (¹) &c.

Stem I, 3: ባርኮ and ባርኮት "to bless", ሣርሮ and ሣርሮት "to found", ላሕዎ and ላሕዎት "to lament".

Causative Stems:—St. II, 1: አፍቅሮ and አፍቅሮት "to love", አስሕቶ "to seduce", አርምሞ "to be tranquil", አእምሮ "to know", አውኅዶ "to make few *or* small", አጥርዮ "to take possession of", አርኅዎ "to open", አርውዮ "to water", አጥፍኦት, አጥዕዮት, አምዕዮ, አርውጾ G. Ad. 116, 11, አሞኦት, አሞቶት, አሕውሶ and አሑሶ Sap. 5, 11, አቢቶ I Kings 3, 3; but አቅሞ and አቅሞት "to place", አንሞ, አንኖ, አብኦ. St. II, 2: አለብዎ and አለብዎት "to instruct", አሐልዮ "to remind", አሰስሎ "to remove", አመክሮ Judith 8, 26, አሠንዮት Chrest. 44, 28, አበይኖት፡ ነዋኃት G. Ad. 23, 8 (²); *mediae gutturalis*: አልዕሎ "to exalt", አትሕቶ "to humiliate". St. II, 3: አላቅሶ and አላቅሶት "to show sympathy".

Reflexive Stems: — St. III, 1: ተለብሶ and ተለብሶት "to dress"; *mediae gutturalis*: ተርኅዎ "to open (*neut.*)"; ተንሥኦ and ተንሥኦት from ተንሥአ "to rise, to be raised"; ተሰዶ, ተሰድዶ and ተሰድዶት "to be expelled"; ተሀይዮ and ተሀይዮት "to neglect"; ተመይጦ Chrest. 44, 28 "to turn (*neut.*)", ተመውኦ, ተመውኦት and ተመዊኦት "to be conquered"; ተቀንዮ "to serve"; ተርእዮ "to appear"; ተሰጥዎ "to answer"; ተወቅሮ and ተወቅሮት "to be hewn"; ተፈልጦ Chrest. 44, 24; G. Ad. 11, 19; 127, 16; ተመርሖ Chrest. 44, 26; ተወርዎት G. Ad. 24, 8; ተጠብቦ Prov. 8, 5; ተደሞ

(¹) V., besides, Deut. 31, 27, Note.

(²) Yet v. አስፍዎት Gal. 3, 8, 18, with transition from II, 2 to II, 1.

G. Ad. 53, 16. St. III, 2: **ተሐድሶ** and **ተሐድሶት** "to be renewed"; **ተአዝዘ** "to obey"; **ተሠግዎ** "to become flesh"; **ተጠይቆ** and **ተጠይቆት** "to make one's self certain"; **ተዐግሦ** and **ተዐግሦት** "to refrain"; **ተፌውሶ**; *mediae gutturalis*: **ተልዕሎ**, **ተትሕቶ**, **ተይህዶ**, **ተምዕዖ** and **ተምዖ**; and in both Stems with roots which are both *primae* and *mediae gutturalis*: **ተአኅዎ** "brotherly bearing". **ተእኅዞት** "to be continued". St. III, 3: **ተናገሮ** and **ተናገሮት** "to converse together"; **ተማህሎ**, **ተቃንአ**; **ተያውሆ**; **ተዛውዖት** Chrest. 45, 26; **ተላህዮት** G. Ad. 123, 12; **ተጓሕልዎት** *ibid*. 136, 28 &c.

Causative-Reflexive Stems. In St. IV, 1 the two modes of pronouncing the Perfect (§ 98) again make their appearance: **አስተብቍዖ** and **አስተብቍዖት**; **አስተርእዮ** and **አስተርእዮት**; **አስተአብዶ**, **አስተአብዶት** and **አስታእብዶ**. St. IV, 2: **አስተዐግሦ** and **አስተዐግሦት**; **አስተኀይሶ** and **አስተኀይሶት**. St. IV, 3: **አስተጋብኦ** and **አስተጋብኦት**; **አስተሓውዞ**; **አስተሓይጾ**; **አስተታልዎ**; **አስተፋቅዶ** Numb. 26, 63; [**አስተጣግዖ** *Kebra Nag*. 50 a 1.].

Multiliteral Roots:—St. I: **ቤዝዎ** and **ቤዝዎት**, **ዐውይዎ** and **ዐውይዎት**, **ቀጥቀጦ** and **ቀጥቀጦት**, **ዘርክዮት**, **ገንጽሎት**; St. II: **አመንድቦ** and **አመንድቦት**, **አማኅብሮ**, **አማስኖ**, **አጻዕድዎ** and **አጻዕድዎት**, **አስቆቅዎ** G. Ad. 137, 22 and **አስቆቅዎት** *ibid*. 108, 12; 135, 19; 137, 21, **አመክንዮ**; **አድለቅልቆ**, **አርመስምሶ**; St. III, 1: **ተመንድቦ** and **ተመንድቦት**, **ተፄውዎ**, **ተአንስሶ**, **ተማሕፅኖ**, **ተራህርሆ**, **ተሰርግዎ**; **ተአንተልትሎ**; St. III, 3: **ተሰናእሎ** and **ተሰናእሎት**, **ተሰናእዎ**, **ተወላውሎ**; [St. IV, 3: **አስተጠናቅቆ** *Kebra Nag*. 55 b 23]; St. V: **አንቀልቀሎ** Chrest. 76, 1 and **አንቀልቀሎት**, **አንሶስዎ** and **አንሶስዎት**, **አንሶጥጦ**, **አንሳሕስሖ**, **አንገርግሮት**, **አንጌግዮ**.

II. FORMATION OF GENDERS AND NUMBERS.

1. GENDERS OF NOMINAL STEMS.

§ 126. Semitic languages have long since given up the distinction between a Personal and a Non-Personal (or Neuter) in objects of perception and representation[1]. Thanks to a lively imagination, the Semites have rather conceived every thing that exists as being alive, and have ranked it under one or other of the contrasted conditions of Masculine and Feminine, natural to every-

The Two Genders: Masculine and Feminine. Signs of the Feminine.

(1) V. Ewald, '*Hebr. Spr.*' § 172, *a*.

thing which exhibits life. Even inanimate objects, facts and ideas are thought of as either masculine or feminine, or both together, just in accordance with the view which the genius of a people has taken of them severally. Like the rest of these languages Ethiopic knows only the two genders. To express what other languages regard as Neuter, the Feminine gender may, it is true, appear in Semitic tongues, inasmuch as that gender is the more feebly personal one, compared with the Masculine [1]:—In fact pure ideas (Abstracts) are usually conceived of as procreative and productive powers, and are therefore expressed in the Feminine form. But on the other hand, there are also many facts (or things) and ideas, which do not impress the mind as being so decidedly weak and feminine as to call for an expressly feminine designation. Their names accordingly remain without any special feminine marking; and seeing that the Masculine gender,—as will immediately be shown,—is similarly unprovided with a special marking, these names, as regards outward form, coincide with entities, concerns and notions, which are decidedly regarded as Masculine. Thus it comes about that both Masculine and Feminine serve to replace the Neuter of other languages. And this is shown not only in the Stem-formation of Substantives, but also when the Neuter of Adjectives or Demonstratives has to be expressed in Ethiopic. For this purpose sometimes the Masculine, sometimes the Feminine is used,—more frequently the former however, and particularly in the class of Demonstratives, and in that of words compounded with Prepositions, *e. g.*:—**ዝውእቱ** "that is", **ከመዝ** "such (a thing)" Matt. 9,33, **ከማሁ** "such" Josh. 11,15, **ዝንቱ** "this" Ps. 41,4; 61,11, **እምድኅረ፡ ዝንቱ** "after this" Josh. 24,30, **ወምስለ፡ ዝኒ፡ ዓዲ** "besides this"; **እሙንቱ** "the same things" Matt. 15,18, **ኵሉ** "all" Josh. 23,14. More rarely the Fem. is found, *e. g.* **ኮነት፡ ዛቲ** "this happened", or the two together: **ወበዝ፡ ባሕቲታ** "and only herein" Gen. 34,22. **ዛ** "this" Ex. 17,14. Even in the case of Adjectives the Masc. is often sufficient:—**ኄር** "the good" (*or* "what is good") Matt. 19,17, **ብዙኅ፡ በዕድ** "much besides" 2 Cor. 11,28, **እኩይ** "evil", "what is evil" Ps. 33,14, **ግሩም** "what is terrible" Ps. 105,22, **ሠናይ** "what is good" Ps. 24,14, **ቀዳሚ** "that which is first" (occurring very frequently). But the Fem. also occurs often:—**ሠናይት** "(any)

---

(1) *Cf.* **ጠባዊት** "suckling".

good thing", "well-being" Josh. 21, 43; Hen. 20, 5, ዛቲ፡ ዕጽብት "this troublesome matter" Ex. 10, 7, ተባዕት፡ ወአንስት "male and female" Gen. 1, 27; Mark 10, 6, እኪት፡ ህየንተ፡ ሠናይ "evil for good" Gen. 44, 4. 6; *cf.* also ስሕክት፡ ብዙኅ "much roughness"—Chr. Hom. 30. When the Neuter comprises much detail, the plural is generally employed, taking usually the Masculine gender with a Pronoun, and the Feminine in case of an Adjective: ዐቢያት "great things", "what is great" Ps. 105, 22, ሐዲሳት "what was new" Hen. 106, 13, (*cf. Gadla 'Aragāwī* 6 a 1: GUIDI, 1895), ዕጹባት "what is astonishing" Gen. 49, 3, ኅቡኣት: "what is secret" Ps. 43, 23, ቅድስተ፡ ቅዱሳን "the holiest of all" Hebr. 9, 3 &c.

As regards *the denotation of the two Genders*, the *Masculine* has no special termination. Its distinctive sign consists merely in the absence of the Feminine termination. The *Feminine* has for sign a termination which is applied to the Stem, and which originally had the sound *at* (1). In Ethiopic, however, just as in the other Semitic languages, this termination has experienced several phonetic changes. On the one hand the *t*-sound is obscured into a mere breathing, under the influence of which the *a* is lengthened into an unalterable *ā*, (only rarely changed into *āt*), the breathing itself disappearing (§ 47) (2). This termination *ā* (3) is not the usual one in Ethiopic, it is true, but still it occurs frequently in the class of Nouns derived from Conceptional Roots, and in the Prepositional class:—In one case it has even penetrated into the Stem (§ 129): In a few cases it is still farther dulled into *ē*. On the other hand, by parting with the *a*, the termination *at* is shortened into *t* alone (4), which attaches itself intimately to the Stem. This termination,—rare in Arabic, more common in Hebrew,—is the ordinary Feminine termination in Ethiopic; and in particular it is employed almost universally in the Feminine form of the Adjective. A farther Feminine termination *ī*, contrasted with the Masculine *ū*, is peculiar to the Pronoun, and will be described along with it.

(1) On the origin of this termination *cf.* EWALD, '*Hebr. Spr.*' § 173, *a*.

(2) But v. PRAETORIUS, '*Amh. Spr.*', p. 167.

(3) Hebr. ָה, Arab. ـَى, Aram. ָא, ـܳܐ; v. however ZDMG XV, p. 145.

(4) Just as in the Verb, v. *supra* p. 203, § 101, 2.

Feminine Endings, and the Mode of their Attachment in the case of 1. Substantives:— Ending *at*.

§ 127. 1. Coming now to points of detail in the use of these terminations and the mode of their attachment to the Stem, we direct attention, in what follows, first to the usage in the case of *Substantives*.

(*a*) *The full, original termination at* is applied chiefly to the Second simple form, described in § 106, *a*, of Conceptional words of an Infinitive type,—although, even in this class, in certain derivatives from roots *primae vocalis*, the pure consonantal termination *t* has asserted itself (ጥንት, ቅሥት, ግብት, ሁብት), side by side with other forms of the type ርደት, ርቀት (¹). Apart from these, the full ending occurs but rarely now, and that chiefly with Stems of the First simple form (§ 105), in which of course the Feminines in question cannot any longer be distinguished in all cases with accuracy from feminine Abstract-forms which have become Names of things (§ 106):—ጽግንት "bat", ጽፍንት "travelling-pouch *or* wallet", and several others enumerated in § 105, *a. f.*; also ሶመት "garlic" (שׁוּם, ثُوم, ܬܘܡܐ); from ዓም (§ 105) ዓመት "year"; similarly ናቀት "female camel" (نَاقَة), እመት "ell", and ዕፀት "shrub" (from ዕፅ "tree") (²). From Stems of the Second simple Abstract-formation (§ 107, *γ*), the Feminine type which,—in contrast to the Predicative words of the same formation (§ 128)—, ends always in the *at* sound, is of very rare occurrence: በረከት "blessing", ተለወት "succession". This termination is also met with in other cases, though but seldom; from the form given in § 108, *b*:—ጸሪቀት "cake" (as well as ጸሪቅ), ወዲፌት "lappet", and an older word ግቢነት "cheese" (גְּבִינָה), shortened into ግብነት; from an Infinitive (§ 109, *b*):—ኀጢአት "sin" (foreign word?, ኀጥአ "to sin" Hen. 20, 6); from a Participle (§ 109, *a*):—ሳሬት (for *sāriat*) "spider" (√זרה, *cf.* ذَرَاع); from several Common nouns formed from roots *med. gem.* by prefixing መ (§ 116, *a*) in Arabic fashion (³):

(¹) *Cf.* Philippi, '*Beitr. z. Ass.*', II, p. 379.—On the accentuation v. Trumpp, p. 540 *sq.*

(²) On ሰብአት "relatives" *cf.* § 121, *d*; ብነት "present" (מְנָת?) and ግትት "basket" (*cf.* حَتِّى) are of obscure origin: ሐኖት "slaughter-house" is حَانَة; ቀኖት "sting" is قَنَاة (קָנֶה): ወቄት οὐγκία, وُقِيَّة, أُوقِيَّة, ܐܘܩܝܐ.

(³) Ewald, '*Gr. Ar.*' § 434.

መጸለት "tent" (مَظَلَّةٌ); መሠረት "foundation" (instead of the strong form መሥረርት); መበለት "widowhood" (*cf.* ذُو بَلَّى). Of Multiliteral and foreign words we meet with, *e. g.*: ጼዳንት "satyr" (صَيْدَانَةٌ), መናረት and መራናት, (מְנוֹרָה) "candlestick".

Ending *ā*.

(*b*) The blunted *Vowel termination ā* is in very frequent use to form Abstracts from derived Stems (§ 111, *a*). These are distinguished, by their heavier termination, from the corresponding forms in *at* coming from the Simple Stem, like ግብረት, ተለወት. The termination *ā* is on rare occasions found with the Abstract-form from the Simple Stem (§ 106 *sq.*), and then mostly it interchanges with *at*: ንትጋ and ንትጋት "lack"; ንፍቃ and ንፍቀት "half"; ሕንጻ and ሕንጸት "the building" and "the process of building"; as well as ጕያ and ጕየት "flight"; ፍታ (Judges 19, 5, Note) "piece" = ፍት; መሐላ "oath". It is employed also now and then to form stronger Abstracts from Nominal Stems of the First simple formation (§ 105): አምኃ "salutation", ማሕላ (as well as መሐላ) "oath", ማውታ "carcase", ለብሓ "formation" (1). But farther in many Predicative words, of various formations and in many Stems, which from conceptional words have become names of persons or things, especially in those which are foreign or of great antiquity,—the Feminine form in *ā* occurs oftener than the one in *at*. From the First simple formation, § 105: ሚዓ "oil of myrrh" (مَيْعَةٌ); ዲጋ "ambush" (דִּבָּה) (2); ተቅዳ "coriander" (تَقْدَةٌ); ዐልዋ "aloe"; ቈላ and ቈላት "valley"; ኆጻ "sand" (ܚܘܨܐ); ኖራ "chalk" (نُورَةٌ); ኮራ "cup" (كُوْرٌ); ጸታ "row" (ܨܒܬܐ, צְבַת); ቃማ and ገማ "necklace" (ܩܡܛܐ); ጼና "perfume"; ዜማ "harmony", "melody"; ጌራ "helmet", "mitre"; ኄላ "date-cluster". With middle *ā* (from *ō*):—ጣቃ "darkness" (√טוח); ናላ "brain" (*cf.* نال and נָהַל); perhaps also ጻማ "toil" (√צום); ሐራ and ሐራ "army" (inasmuch as חֹר, حُرّ means first "freeman" and then doubtless "the warrior" (3) &c. (4). From Stems of the formation given in

(1) On እንግዳ v. § 137, 4, Note.

(2) Of unknown derivation are:—ኵሓ "willow", ግራ "honeycomb", ጕማ "sound" (Sir. 50, 18); on ጽላ v. *supra* p. 90, § 47.

(3) It is a corroboration of this, that ሐራ now and then means "officer".

(4) Foreign words:—ፔሳ and ፒሳ "pitch", የውጣ ἰῶτα, ረዳ "rose", ሩዝ and ሩዝ "rice" (ὄρυζα); ጋጋ "pillory" (גַּג?); Onomatopoetic:—ኳኳ "raven", ጉጋ and ጉጓ [also ጕጕ, ጕኝ and ጕኝ *Kebra Nag.*] "night-jar".

§ 107, γ and others:—**ሐመዳ** "snow" (جَمَد), **ሰቀላ** "tent"; **አነዳ** "skin"; **አገዳ** "withers", "leg"; **ከበሳ** "bracelet"; **ከተማ** "tip", "summit"; **ጸደና** "humble-bee" (صَيْدَن); **ሰንአ** together with **ሰንእ** "peace"; **መሐዛ** "youth", "youngster" (perhaps **ደመና**, **ገደላ**, **ከወላ**, **ቀጸላ**, § 111, *a*); **ሰኰና** "sole of the foot" (derived likely from a Pass. Part. of the √שכן). From Stems with **መ** prefixed, § 116, the termination *ā*,—before which the foregoing *a* must be reduced to *e*,—is found, though very seldom:—**ምህርካ** "booty", **ምህልላ** "supplication", **ምጕንጳ** "quiver" (جَعْبَة)(1); **መድብሬ** or **መድብሬ** "wilderness" seems to be a foreign word (מִדְבָּר). From Stems which have *ī* after the second radical (§ 108), and from Participles (§ 109, *a*) come several Feminines, much disfigured occasionally: **ከኒሳ** "meeting of a congregation" (كَنِيسَة); **ሰሊካ** and **ሰሊክ** "cassia" (سَلِيخَة); **ብዒዛ** "horn-trumpet"; probably also **ወሬዛ** "youth", "a young man" (with *ē* from *ī*; *cf.* also König, p. 117); **ባቄላ** "bean" (*cf.* بَاقِلَّى); **ጕሬፋ** "punishment"; **ኊሂላ** and **ኊሄላ** "refuse", "dirt", "filth" &c. Quite obscure or foreign in origin are **ተኬሳ** "shoulder-blade"; **ሰሊዳ** "table" (σελίδα) &c. This termination is farther in special use in the case of Multiliteral Stems: **ደብተራ** "tent"; **ቀምጠራ** "buckle"; **ደንገላ** and **ደንገላት** "lily" (perhaps:—"virgin-like"); **ሰረገላ** "waggon"; **ፈንጸጸ** 'a bad trouble'; **ድርግሓ** "stuff", "cloth"; **ዕንቈራ** "cells of bees"; **ድጕልማ** or **ድልጕማ** χλιδών (Sir. 21, 21); **ብርሃና** "parchment"; **ዕንዚራ** "lyre"; **አበርበሬ** "nettle"; **አሜከላ** "thorns". The singular word **አንደብሬ** or **አንዳብሬ** (Hebr. 12, 8) νόθος appears to mean properly "that which turns away from itself", "that which abandons its own nature" (דבר, دَبَر), as if it were **አንደበር**, an Adjective derived from St. V; in the same way **እንግድእ** "breast" (from **ጐድአ** "to knock") will be the Fem. of an Adjective formed in accordance with § 112, *b*.

On some Names of plants and Animals, which follow this formation, *cf.* 131.—On **ዘፍራ** and **ዘብዳ** *cf.* § 113 (beginning of section). Words also are met with, ending in *yā* (besides those which are explained in § 140), which are to be conceived as Feminine forms of Adjectives &c. with the ending *ī* (§ 117 *sq.*): **ሰፊልያ**

(1) **ምኅዕና** for **ምኅዕንና** belongs to § 122, β; **ምዝጋና** "reward" is of obscure origin.

"hammer" (as if from ሰፌሬ, √ פרר); ሕብልያ "booty" ('that which is got through ሕብል'); እስሐትያ "rime", "snow", "hail"—from እስሐተ፡ 'ruining'; ምጕህያ "weed"—('that which makes waste, *or* belongs to a waste', from جَهِي); perhaps also ጽንጽያ (for ጽንጽንያ "a buzzing swarm", "a fly" *m.* & *f.*) (1).

(*c*) It is only very seldom that this *ā* takes the duller sound of *ē* (2), which seems to belong chiefly to words of the oldest formation. To this class belong first a few words which have *u* as third radical: ሠርዌ "beam (of wood)" (*cf.* سَارِيَة); አርዌ "beast" (אַרְיֵה); ሰርዌ "army" (*cf.* سَرِيَّة) (3); then perhaps these Names of Plants: ቱልቤ "flax" (also, ዐጌ "linen"?); ከርቤ "myrrh"; ዘጼ 'a kind of tree' ('ebony'?); a few names of animals:—ፃፄ "moth" (סָם, سُوس); ቀጻጼ "chamaeleon"; ነጌ "elephant" (नाग); አንቄ "hawk"; and, besides these, perhaps also ጊሜ "fog, mist" (غَيْم); ከዐሴ "dung" (قَعْس); ግምዔ (4) "pitcher", "can" (Pl. ገማዕይ, like فَتْوَى, فَتَاوِى); ቄሥጤ ("maw") "last stomach of ruminants". *Cf.* also ማእዜ, ጊዜ, ዕድሜ, አይቴ፡ &c. It is true that as regards several of the words named it is not yet certain whether they do not rather belong to § 118, *γ*, or to § 120—end (5).

Ending *ē*.

§ 128. (*d*). The closely attached, consonantal ending ት, before which, in accordance with §§ 35 and 36, a long vowel standing in a closed syllable is regularly shortened, is made use of to form the Feminine, in the greater number of Concrete Nouns which do not take the termination *ā* (§ 127). In Stems of the First simple formation it occurs, it is true, only in rare instances:—ስከትት "foundation", along with ስኩትት (*cf.* ܫܶܬܐܣܬܐ); ሥዕርት "a hair" (*še'ért*) (6); ኆኅት "door" (خَوْخَة); ኵሊት "kidney" (כִּלְיָה, كُلْيَة);

Closely attached and Consonantal Ending ት.

(1) ቱብልያ, ቱብሌ, ቱብላይ (Ex. 28) "mantle", "ephod", seems to be a foreign word (or to be derived from טָפַל?).

(2) Hebr. ה ֵ— Ewald, '*Hebr. Spr.*' §§ 173, *sq.* and 176, *a*; *cf.* also Arab. ـَى.

(3) Perhaps also መግዌ "bunch".

(4) V. Numb. 19, 17.

(5) As to ሐቌ and ምጻኄ v. § 21; ጽሌ "table" is only a phonetic change for ጽላ, *cf.* § 47—beginning.

(6) On the accentuation v. Trumpp, p. 541.

ብንት "daughter" (from בֵּן, بِنْتٌ); እኅት "sister" (from እኍ, أُخْتٌ) (1). From እንስ "man" the Fem. is እንስት "woman"; from በግዕ "sheep", በግዕት; from አድግ "ass", አድግት and እድግት (Matt. 21, 2; Ex. 13, 13; Numb. 22, 21); *cf.* also አውስት "vulture". This termination is more frequent in certain Stems of the Second formation:—From Nominal Stems of the types given in § 107, which have taken concrete meanings, occur Feminines like ክረምት "winter", እጕልት "cow", ግረምት "terror", አጽባዕት "finger", ጸባሕት "tax", ሰማዕት "testimony", ገራህት "field", ተመርት "palm-tree", ፌዐንት "fever", አረፍት "wall", ዐዘቅት "well", በቀልት "palm-tree", ጸበርት "palm-branch", ገሐፍት "basket", ጸሀርት (as well as ጽሀርት) "kitchen-pot", ደሴት "island". In the same way ወለት "daughter" (for ወለድት § 54) is Fem. to a word יָלָד = ወልድ (2). Feminines of lost Masculines of the Second simple formation (§ 107 or 108, *a*) from roots *tertiae infirmae* either lose completely the last radical, like አመት "maid-servant" (أَمَةٌ), or replace it by *ā*, like ሐማት (3) "mother-in-law" (حَمَاةٌ), ሰዓት "hour" (also, in abbreviated form, ሳዕ), ለዓት "hilt" (*cf.* DILLMANN's '*Lex.*' col. 60), or እሳት (4) "fire", ትካት "antiquity" (root تَكَا, v. § 121 under ትክቶ), perhaps also ስላት "joy", "malicious joy".

From Qualifying or Descriptive words (*i. e.* Adjectives, Participles &c.) of the type in § 108, *c* there arose a number of Feminine substantives, (formed in accordance with § 129, *b*, *β*): ልሕኵት "formation", ኅብስት "bread" (§ 57), ቅርፍት "bark", ዕቅፍት "stumbling", ዕቅብት "concubine", ሕብቅቅት ἀκρασία, ኵዕንት "hardship", ንግሥት "queen" (from ንጉሥ), ሕጺት "betrothed" (from ሕፀዩ), ትክት (from ትክእት) "menstruous". Also ነፍስት "body" ('having a soul') (5), ሐውልት "column" ('turned') and ዘብርት "fragment" are to be reckoned as belonging to this division, although they have *a* in the first syllable,—perhaps even ጻፍንት

(1) *Cf.* on the last two examples EWALD, '*Gr. Ar.*' §§ 409, 411.

(2) On ሁብት from **hăbet*, **hăbat* v. KÖNIG, p. 121.

(3) EWALD, '*Gr. Arab.*' § 411.

(4) Like the Hebr. מְנָת, קְצָת EWALD, '*Hebr. Spr.*' § 137, *d.* Otherwise KÖNIG, p. 117.

(5) For it is improbable that ነፍስት is merely a simple Fem. of ነፍስ "soul".

"cake baked under hot ashes" (√ ጸፈነ "to conceal"), supposing *a* to have been lengthened into *ā*. Such forms are now and then turned into Abstract Nouns:— ዝሩት "dispersion", Gen. 11, 9 (from ዝርው 'what is scattered'), ድቡት (in በድቡት, ድቡተ "opportunely"), ሕቢት "administration" ('that which is administered', from ሕቡይ) Numb. 4, 28 & 29. To Masculines of the type given in § 108, *b* the following are to be referred:—ጠሊት "she-goat" (ጠሊ), ነቢይት (Judges 4, 4) and ነቢት "prophetess", እግዚእት and እግዝእት "mistress" (§ 36), ሊቅት "abbess" (§ 36). From Participles of the type § 109, *a*—come: ባዕልት "mistress" (from ባዕል), ሳኒት and ሰኒት "the following day" (from ሳንይ), perhaps also ሠዊት "ear of corn",—and, in a much abbreviated form, ናእት "that which is unleavened" (root ناء); also, from an Adjectival word given in § 110, *a*:—ተባዕት "that which is of the male sex". From ቀልዒ (§ 118, γ) comes ቀልዒት "maid-servant".

Forms with inseparable ት from Stems of Multiliteral Roots are represented by—ድንግልት "virgin" (*f.*) (inasmuch as ድንግል may also mean 'a young man, still pure'), ጽርንዕት "scab", "leprosy", ፍርፍርት "quails", ሕንብርት "navel", ኰስኰስት (= ኰስኰስ) "pitcher", "can"; ቈንዘእት "lock (of hair)" (= ቈንዘእ), ጠፍላሕት "coin", ጸላዕት "rocky ground" (*cf.* ضَلَّع) = ጸላዕ Sir. 22, 1; ጸማዕት "hermit's cell" (صَوْمَعَة); ሰንበልት "spikenard" (ሰንቢል, § 36); ድርኩኩት "hinge of a door" (§ 26,—end), ሌሊት "night" (root ለይለየ, *cf.* ܠܠܝܐ); እምሔውት "ancestress" (from እምሔው, § 36).

It has already been pointed out that Feminine forms from Nominal Stems with ተ or መ prefixed (§§ 111 & 116) take the closely attached ት likewise. A peculiar form is met with in መርዓት "bride", "daughter-in-law" ("*sponsa*", from መርዓ "espousals", § 116); *cf.* König, p. 117.

§ 129. 2. *Adjectives and Participles*, with a few exceptions, take the consonantal ending ት. Certain of them have no distinct form at all for the Feminine; while a third series—and not a very numerous one—of Adjectives exhibit Feminines of inner formation.

2. Feminine of Adjectives and Participles: By Interpolation of *ā* in the Stem.

(*a*) Thus,—to begin with the last-named class,—Adjectives, which have *ī* after the second radical, as described in § 108, *b*, like ሐዲስ "new", have given up the outer formation. The reason for this was that the *ī* which thus preceded the closely attached feminine ት was bound to be shortened into *e* (§ 36). This formation, in point of fact, is still met with in the case of a few words, which are used in a more Substantive meaning:—**ልሂቅ** "a senior", ('a venerable person, either by age or office') *m.*; Fem. **ልህቅት** (Plur. **ልሂቃት**); **እግዝእት** "mistress", "lady", from **እግዚእ** (¹). But as the Feminines of these Adjectives would in this way coincide with those of the type **ግቡር**, another formation came into use, according to which the Feminine ending, which consists of the vowel *ā*, is interpolated in the stem itself(²), and either blends with the *ī* into an *ē*, or,—as is usually the case,—is directly substituted for the *ī*. These Adjectives accordingly take regularly *ā* in the Feminine instead of *ī*: **ሐዲስ**, **ሐዳስ**; **ጠቢብ**, **ጠባብ**; **ዐዚዝ**, **ዐዛዝ**; **ጸቢብ**, **ጸባብ**; **ቀይሕ** (**ቀዩሕ**), **ቀያሕ**; **ዐቢይ**, **ዐባይ**. From roots *mediae gutturalis*, which have in the Masculine the form **ርሒብ** "far", "wide", there is formed, in accordance with § 44 *sq.*, **ረሐብ** (Matt. 7,13), and similarly **ረኃጽ** "pampered" (Deut. 28,56). **የማን** "right hand", **ፀጋም** "left hand", and also **ውፃእ** "a divorced woman" (Lev. 21,14) (³) appear now only in the Feminine. The mixed sound *ē*, from *ā*+*i*, is exhibited by **እቤር** and **አቤር** "old woman" (from a lost masculine **አቢር**=كَبِير) (⁴). The Adjectives mentioned in § 110, *b* are hitherto known only in one gender, either Masc. or Fem.—On the Feminine form of some words,—turned Substantives,—which belong to this formation with *ī* and come from roots with final *ī*, like **ነቢይ**, v. § 128.

(¹) As is the case invariably in Tigriña: SCHREIBER, p. 28.—From **ነኪር** "strange", "foreign", there is still found **ነኪርት** ἀλλοτρία, alongside of **ነክር**: So too **ደቂቅት** as a collateral form to **ደቃቅ**; v. DILLMANN's '*Lex.*' coll. 667, 1099.

(²) V. analogues in the Plural-formation.—Similarly in Tigrē, in Verbs *tertiae gutturalis*, *ū* is interpolated before the third radical in the Imperf., Subj. and Imper.: v. NÖLDEKE, '*W. Zeitschr. f. d. K. d. Morg.*' IV, p. 295 [and LITTMANN, '*Zeitschr. f. Assyr.*' XIV, p. 45.]—This inner formation may also be pointed out in Arabic: *Cf.* TRUMPP, p. 541, N. 1.—Other explanations of this form than the above are given in KÖNIG, p. 87 *sq.*, and in PRAETORIUS, '*Amh. Spr.*', p. 148.—For the accentuation *cf.* TRUMPP *l. c.*

(³) Although the word, which would be **ውፂእ** in the Masc., is formed rather as a Pass. Part., and is therefore pronounced with an *ĕ* after the first radical.

(⁴) **ብሔር** and **መሬት** possibly belong to the same formation.

(*b*) All the other Adjectives and Participles have the outer formation through the ending ት. Outer Formation by the Ending ት.

(*α*) The type given in § 108, *a*, has no longer, it is true, a feminine form, as a rule, because the words concerned are more in use as Substantives; however, see ሕያውት (*e. g.* Ruth 1, 19) from ሕያው "alive". Multiliteral Adjectives of the type ደገደግ, § 112, *b*, take their Feminines from the type ድግዱግ.

(*β*) The type given in § 108, *c*, shortens its *ū* into *é*; and all words of this type without exception follow this formation(1): ስኩብ, ስክብት (*sekébt*)(2); ብፁዕ, ብፅዕት; ዙኑን, ዙንንት, ግዩር, ግይርት (*geyért*); ምዉእ (ምውእ), ምውእት; ርሁሩሀ, ርሀርሀት; ሡሩር, ሡርርት. In some cases it serves the purpose of expressing Abstracts, *e. g.* ፍሡሕት ἱλαρότης. Words from roots with final *ĭ* adopt the vowel-pronunciation of the last radical, suppressing the *é*: — እኩይ, እኪት (*ekīt*); ርዉይ (ርውይ), ርዊት(3); ሉጹይ, ሉጺት ("shaven", 1 Cor. 11, 5); ጽሑዩይ, ጽሑዩት; from roots ending in *ŭ*, either the form ሀልውት, *heléwwet* (from ሀልው *heléwwᵉ*), or, with contraction of the diphthong into *u*: ሀሉት *helūt*; ርጉው, ርጉት; ጽዕድው, ጽዕዱት [ዕድው, ዕዱት *Kebra Nag.* 138 a, 16]. In words which have a *u*-containing Guttural as second-last radical, like ርኩስ "unclean" (from ረኰሰ) the *u*-containing pronunciation re-appears in the Fem.: ርኵስት, which only by a wrong use (§ 42) again passes into ርኩስት (Hen. 5, 4)(4). In words which have ጠ, ደ or ተ as last radical the formative ት blends with the final letter: እቱት, fem. እትት (*etét*); ምውት or ምዊት, fem. ምውት; ሥጉት, ሥጉት; ትሑት, ትሕት; ክቡድ, ክብድ *kebéd* (Deut. 30, 11), &c. (§ 54 *sq.*).

(*γ*) The Feminines of the type § 109, *a*, are regularly formed by appending ት without any vowel-change in addition: ጻድቅ, ጻድቅት; ሬድእ, ሬድእት, ባቍዕ, ባቍዕት; ማልስ, ማልስት; ላሕይ, ላሕይት or ላሒት; but from ዋሕድ, in accordance with § 54, ዋሕድ is again given. አብድ "foolish" has in the Fem. the forms

(1) When Ludolf in his Dictionary adduces not only ንእስት from ንኡስ "little" but also a Fem. ነአስ, the latter is of course to be referred to a Masc. form ንኢስ which has disappeared.

(2) For the accentuation *cf.* Trumpp, p. 541.

(3) [Along with ርውይት Is. 58, 11; v. Dillmann's '*Lex.*', col. 307. tr.]

(4) [Flemming reads in this passage ርኰሳት. tr.]

አብድ, አብድት or እብድ (from እቡድ). ኄር "good" also forms, without any vowel-change, ኄርት.

(δ) In place of the type given in § 110, *a*, from which Feminines are not readily formed, comes the type which is described in § 117, *a*, furnished with the Adjective-ending ī, and to which the feminine termination ት is easily attached. The feminine ሠናይት, however, occurs from ሠናይ and even the contracted form ሠኔት Judges 8, 32; and from ሠያጥ "trader", we have, shortening the ā (§ 36), the feminine form ሠየጥ. The adjectives of this type, mentioned in § 112, *b*, from multiliteral roots, appear in like manner to have no feminine forms: the Feminine of ጸዐዳ is the same as the Masc. (Matt. 5,36). መካን "unfruitful" "barren" (*f.*) would be a masculine form used as a feminine, if the middle radical were really double, as LUDOLF represents: it would in that case have to be regarded perhaps like حَامِل(1); but v. PRAETORIUS, '*Tigriña*' p. 180. On the other hand ወላድ "fruitful" (*f.*), "having children", may be understood in accordance with § 36 (=ወላድት). ዘማ "fornicator *or* whore" is both masculine and feminine.

(ε) Farther, the Participles which are described in § 114 take ት, in so far as they form Feminines at all, and do not as Substantives remain unaltered in the Fem. or pass over to the formation given in § 118(2): መደንግፅት, መምህርት, መስተምሕርት, መስተፍሥሕት, መረብዕት, መጥግስት, መወልት "midwife" (for መወልድት, § 36), and so too መጽዕጥ "a female perfumer". From roots *tertiae i* the Fem. regularly gives the vowel-sound to the last radical,—a pronunciation which may be met with even in the Masc.: መፍሪት, from መፍርይ; መጥዒት, from መጥዕይ; መንሂት, from መንህይ; መሴሲት, from መሰስይ(3). On the other hand, roots *tertiae u* take their Fem. from the type given in § 118, instead of a Fem. of their own form.

(ζ) All words which end in the Adjective-termination ī

---

(1) EWALD, '*Gr. Ar.*' § 298, [where the rule is given: *Adjectiva quae e sensu suo non possunt nisi ad feminas spectare, sine term. manent, ut* حامل "*gravida*" &c. TR.]

(2) For the accentuation *cf.* TRUMPP, p. 542.

(3) [ማሪት is also met with in both genders, v. DILLMANN's '*Lex.*' col. 168.]

(§§ 117—119) simply attach ት in the Fem.: መሐሪ, መሐሪት; መዋቲ, መዋቲት; ኀላዪ, ኀላዪት; መምሰሊ, መምሰሊት; መጥዐዪ, መጥዐዪት; መንፈሳዊ, መንፈሳዊት. ት may also be simply attached to the Adjective-termination *āi* (§ 119 end), *e. g.* ማእከላይት "mediatory" (*f.*), Hen. 76, 6; but most of the Masculines in *āi*, instead of the Fem.-form *āit*, prefer to take their Fem. in *āwīt* or *īt*, *e. g.* አረጋዊ and አረጋይ "old", *Fem.* አረጋዊት and አረጊት. Thus is it, in particular, with the numeral Adjectives in *āi*, like ዳግማይ "the second", *Fem.* ዳግማዊት or ዳግሚት.

A few Substantives avail themselves of an Adjective-termination, by way of analogy, for the purpose of forming Feminines: ዐንበሳ "lion", ዐንበሳዊት "lioness"; ዲያቆን "deacon", ዲያቆናዊት "deaconess".

§ 130. Although Ethiopic is in possession of sufficient resources to enable it to distinguish the feminine gender from the masculine by outward indication, and although a host of independent Nouns have a formation marked by the feminine termination, the presence or the absence of that termination is by no means decisive for the actual gender of a word as employed in the language. Not only are there many expressions or names which the language has regarded as feminine from the very first, without marking them as such by their termination, *e. g.* እም "mother", ድንግል "maiden" &c., but difference in time and locality added its influence to render the outward mark of gender of trifling importance in settling the actual gender assigned in speech. That which was regarded as feminine at the time when its form was put into shape, might at another time be thought of, without difficulty, as masculine. When one conception passed into another,—for example, when the Abstract passed into the Concrete, it was naturally attended by a change in the view taken of the gender. The dialectic variations in the several districts, in which the speech was used, have also to be considered in this connection. Owing to the co-operation of these influences, the treatment of gender fluctuated more notably in Ethiopic than in any other Semitic tongue,—more even than in Hebrew, which most resembles Ethiopic in this particular feature. The great majority of Nouns may be used both as masculine and as feminine, whether they are furnished with feminine terminations or not. It is only a few settled principles that can be discerned for dealing with this aspect of the language; but these are not so settled

The Gender-usage in Ethiopic.

or so binding as to prevent speaker or writer from having abundant freedom in his conception of gender. Still, in those manuscripts which are accessible to us, all being of relatively late origin, an advance may be perceived, from an utter want of system to a comparatively settled system. The older manuscripts show invariably the prevalence of a freer standpoint, while the later ones strive at least to avoid, as far as possible, the capricious alteration of the conception of the gender of a word in the same sentence or section.

We cannot therefore pretend to reduce the Gender-usage in Ethiopic to any certain rules, or to give an exhaustive account of it([1]). The task of determining the gender with exactness must be left to the dictionary, in the case of every individual word. It is only the main principles guiding the treatment of Gender in Ethiopic, which fall to be noticed in this place.

The Gender is distinguished with perfect strictness and regularity only in the case of living beings, possessing that distinction in themselves. All proper names of men, all words which indicate a man or a male agent—, like **ብእሲ**, **ሰብእ**, **ነቢይ**, **ገብር**, **ወልድ**, **መልአክ**, **መስፍን** &c.—are constantly treated as masculine; all names and appellations of women and female agents, as feminine, whether these words have any external mark of gender or not. But even in this class a few nouns are met with, having the gender common,—like **ድንግል**,—in particular those which were at first conceptional words or Abstracts, such as **መርሕ** "leader", *m.* and *f.*, **ማዕሰብ** "widow" and "widower", **ሰማዕት** ('testimony') "witness" *m.* and *f.*, **እንግዳ** ('state of an alien') "foreigner", *m.* and *f.* (Ruth 2, 10), and some which end in *ît*, § 120, *a*. In names of animals the gender is seldom distinguished by any special termination,—in fact, scarcely ever, except in the case of those which are oftenest spoken of, like **በግዕ** and **በግዕት**, **አድግ** and **አድግት**, **ጠሊ** and **ጠሊት** (not always used); sometimes separate words are employed([2]), like **ሰር** "bull", **እጐልት** "cow", **ገመል** and **ናቅት**, **ውዕላ**([3]) and **ወይጠል**; but most names of animals have only one

([1]) V. on this subject Ludolf, '*Gr.*' III, 5.

([2]) [Just as in other Semitic languages; *cf.* Bezold, in H. Osthoff's '*Vom Suppletivwesen der indogermanischen Sprachen*', Heidelberg, 1900, p. 76.]

([3]) [Deut. 14, 5 would, however, lead us to suppose that these two words

single form, such as **ከልብ, ድብ, ፈረስ, ዝእብ, ኀየል**, and are distinguished in gender as masculine or feminine, when that has to be done,—only by the gender being differentiated in the predicate, or in some appositional word([1]). In the case of winged creatures, or those which have their habitation in the water, or in the case of reptiles or crawling animals, even this method of distinguishing the gender is usually given up. Some of their names have a masculine form, some a feminine (**ርግብ, አንቄ, ፈፀው; ፍርፍርት, ጽግንት, ላጽቄት** &c.), but they may be treated as masculine or feminine without any regard to their termination.

As to the other words, it is true that the majority of Abstracts, as well as of Nouns of action, production, kind and manner, and of true Infinitives are already marked as feminine by their form; but a minority of the forms show that these conceptions may also be entertained in the gender readiest to hand, that is to say, the masculine. And this alternative possibility is continued in the actual gender-usage. Any conceptional word which is unprovided with a feminine marking may yet be treated as feminine, and any conceptional word which has a feminine termination may be treated as masculine, or rather as being without gender, so that it coincides with the masculine. the latter having itself no outward mark of gender. Even those words which in their formation have been kept absolutely free from a feminine termination, such as Names of Places (§ 115), may be treated as feminine. A few Infinitives may suffice here as examples: **ውእቱ ፡ ምህሮ** 1 Cor. 9. 14; **ተፋቅሮ ፡ ፍጽምት** 1 John 4, 18; **ብዑድ ፡ ዐቂሶት ፡ ወወሊዶት** *Org.*; **ርትዕት ፡ አሚን** "the true faith" [*lit.* 'right believing' *Inf.*] &c. Words like **ልደት, ድቀት, ስእለት, ፍትወት, ጽልመት** may be treated as masculine or as feminine with equal propriety (though fem. in form); and on the other hand words like **ስም, ኀይል, ሕግ** (though masc. in form) may equally well be treated as feminine. Accordingly Collective Nouns and Nouns of Quantity, as well as Collective Plural-forms (§ 135 *sqq.*) may be used both in the masculine and feminine.

In the department of true substantives and designations of

do not indicate the *male and female of one species of gazelle*, but are *names for two distinct species*. TR.]

([1]) Or by other devices: *cf.* the examples in Hen. 60, 7 & 8; 85, 3. [and *Kebra Nag.* 111 b 20.]

inanimate beings and things, the names of countries, districts, cities, towns are preponderatingly feminine, although ሀገር "city" itself is of common gender; and expressions, even, like ሲዶና ፡ ዐቢይ Josh. 11, 8 are met with (but otherwise in Josh. 11, 2; 19, 28). But the names of the various parts of the body, as well as the names of tools, articles of clothing, dwellings and trees are of common gender(1). Names of rivers and mountains, of roads, wells, stars (yet ፀሐይ may also be feminine), of the powers of the heavens (rain, wind, dew, hail &c.), of metals and weapons—are chiefly masculine. መንፈስ "spirit", "intelligence" is of common gender; but when used of the Holy Spirit, it is always masculine. ነፍስ "soul" is usually feminine; ነፍስት and ሥጋ "body" usually masculine. Victuals also have mostly names in the masc. gender,—even ኅብስት "bread".

2. NUMBERS OF NOMINAL STEMS.

Numbers of Nominal Stems:— Faint Traces of a Dual.

§ 131. Ethiopic, like Syriac, has completely given up the Dual Number. Without doubt it once possessed it, just like the other Semitic tongues; and a trace of it is preserved in the word ክልኤ "two", inasmuch as the final *ē* in that numeral can only be explained as a curtailed and blunted dual-ending (כִּלְאַיִם) (2). Similarly in the *Eth. Bilinguis* l. 3 the Dual 𐩱𐩭𐩥𐩺𐩠 أَخَوَيْهِ is still met with, according to D. H. Müller, '*Epigr. Denkm.*' p. 68. Lastly, the remains of a Dual may be recognised,—according to Praetorius, ZDMG XXXIV, p. 222 & XLVII, p. 395,—in the form እዴ "hand", which appears before suffixes, and in ሐቌ "loins" (3). When the notion of "both" has to be more definitely expressed, the numeral "two" must be called in to assist. After losing the Dual, Ethiopic preserved only the distinction between that which was a single individual and that which consisted of several individuals or formed a mass. This distinction, however, has produced, in other Semitic languages, and particularly in Arabic, four Clas-

(1) ክርሥ "body" is generally feminine.

(2) I venture to make the like conjecture regarding the word ደጐ "door", Plural ደጓት, Deut. 3, 5; 6, 9 (as if coming from ደጕ), and ደጐጐያት. I hold ደጐ to be a contraction for דַּלְתַּי.

(3) *Cf.* also Trumpp ZDMG XXXIV, p. 236. But v. Barth '*Deutsche Ltrzg.*' 1887, Sp. 1303: '*Nominalbildung*' p. 6.

ses of Numbers. When, for instance, the ground-form merely expresses the notion of one individual, like "man", a new form is developed from it which expresses plurality, mass, or collectivity, and there emerges the contrast between *Singular* and *Plural*. But when the ground-form gives expression to a generic or collective notion, like "hair", a form is developed to denote an individual specimen from the mass, and thus we have the contrast between the collective word, and the word designating one of the Class (*Generalis* and *Nomen Unitatis*).

1. Contrast between Class-Word and Word denoting an Individual of the Class (*Generalis* and *Nomen Unitatis*)

1. *The latter contrast*, as conditioning a special mode of formation, is but feebly carried out in Ethiopic. In by far the largest number of names given to collective notions, in which any individual can be specially singled out, the *Generalis* and the *Nomen Unitatis* coincide, although such Names *originally* denoted either the one or the other, but not both. Thus ሰብእ stands for both "man" (*coll.*) and "a man"; ሐራ "an army" and (along with ሐራዊ) "a warrior"; እንስሳ "beasts" and "a beast"; ዖፍ "fowl" and "a bird"; ንህብ "swarm of bees" and "a bee"; ዖም "a wood" and "a tree"; ዕፄ "vermin" and "a worm" &c. Many Collectives, serving in this way also as Nouns denoting individuals, come to take the Plural even,—a proceeding not strictly admissible with merely Collective Nouns. Besides, Ethiopic seems at one time to have had the power of deriving Nouns, denoting single specimens, from Collective Nouns, by means of a special form,—namely the feminine-ending. That, at least, is the only explanation of the remarkable circumstance that several names of plants and animals have feminine terminations(¹). The ending in question is generally *ā*(²): ውዕላ *πύγαργος* (Deut. 14,5), ቍራ *βούβαλος* (*ibid.*), ተኵላ "male hyaena", ብዕዛ 'a horned animal'; ዐንበሳ "lion", አንጺዋ "mouse", ጕዛ "falcon", "hawk", አንበጣ "locust", "grasshopper" (also collective); perhaps also ጣዕዋ "suckling", and ጸቢላ "the (male) young

(¹) The case is very similar in Hebrew, *cf.* Ewald, '*Hebr. Spr.*' § 176, *a*. It is remarkable also that "one" = "a single one" is usually expressed in Ethiopic by the fem. አሐቲ, and that not only when it stands by itself, as in አሐቲ ፡ ሰአልኩ Ps. 26, 7, but also, when it qualifies a Common Noun or Conceptional word, as in አሐቲ ፡ ቃል one word" (*e. g.* Josh. 21, 43; 23, 14), although ቃል as a rule, is masc.

(²) As in the Agau dialects; *cf.* Reinisch, '*Bilinspr.*', p. 89; '*Chamirspr.*' I, p. 101; '*Quaraspr.*' I, p. 89.

of an animal", ሰግላ "fig-tree", ዘግበ "cypress". Though some of these words take their plural from the same form, like ቆሬት, ተኰላት, yet others of them start from the ground-form in the formation of their plural:—ዐናብስት. አናብጥ, አናጹት. In certain other words this *ā* seems to be changed for *ē*, see examples in § 127, *c*. It may be that these feminine forms are due to the poetic view of the individual as being the weaker. and the class or kind as being the stronger notion; but the individual, in accordance with another and more sensible conception of the relation, is sometimes indicated by the relative Adjectival-ending *ī* as being *that which belongs to the class*, as, *e. g.* in ዐንበሪ "a sea-monster", from and along with ዐንበር (§ 118, *γ*). Yet this form is of even less frequent occurrence than the other. The derivation, by means of a special form, of a word denoting an individual, from its class-conception, cannot be followed up in Ethiopic beyond these traces. Ethiopic is more disposed to confuse the Class-word and the Individual-word. Thus words denoting Class-conceptions, which represent a secondary formation derived from individualising-words, are, immediately after their production, again treated as words signifying one of a class, *e. g.* those which are mentioned in § 120, *a*: ኀላፊት (from ኀላፊ "passing by") "what passes by", *i. e.* "people passing by", Mark 15, 29, but on the other hand አሐዱ ፡ ኀላፊት "an individual passing by", Mark 15, 21; in the same way ነጋዲት, Judges 19, 17; the originally collective word እንግዳ "strangers" (§ 137, 5) is regularly used in turn for a single "stranger" (= ነግድ).

2. Contrast between Singular and Plural (*One and More than One*).

2. *The Contrast between the Singular and the Plural*, on the other hand, is quite regularly and commonly maintained. It is true that a good many words express plurality even in the Singular number, and may therefore be connected with a predicate in the Plural,—not merely all those words which are Collectives by their origin, such as names of nations, countries and communities, but even names of single beings like ብእሲ "man" or "men", ፀር "enemy" or "enemies". But when it is called for in the interests of clearness, the most of these can either form their own plural, or make up for it by the plural of another word, like ዕደው for ብእሲ. Actual Singular-Nouns, which are incapable of forming a Plural, like ዘይት "an olive-tree" (Plur. used being ዕፀው ፡ ዘይት), are of rare occurrence; and even regular Class-words or Collective Nouns may take the plural, seeing that they frequently

represent the Individual-, as well as the Class-notion (v. *supra*). On the other hand a large number of other Singular-notions, particularly words indicating bulk, are by their very nature incapable of taking the plur.:— such as, ወርቅ "gold", ሐመዳ "snow", መዓር "honey", እክል "food", ፀምር "wool", ጢስ "smoke", ጽላሎት "shadow". And true Abstracts are just as little capable of the plur., such as ውዕየት "burning", ተፍጻሜት "completion", ፍቅር "love", ጽምእ "thirst", and in particular all Infinitives. But even such words, in the case of some definite development of the conception, become again capable of taking the Plur.; *e. g.* ምድር means "earth", but also "land"; accordingly it takes, in the latter sense, the Plur. አምዳር. In the same way from ብሩር "silver" and ብርት "brass" appear the Plurals ብሩራት "silver pieces" and ብርታት "articles of brass"; and from ጠል "dew" comes the Plur. ጠላት "fat". ጥበብ "wisdom" takes a Plur. with the meaning "arts", and ምሕረት "compassion" does the like, in the sense of "displays of compassion". And, in this way, even Infinitive-forms admit sometimes of the Plural, as ወሓይዝት "rivers", from ውሒዝ "to flow", "flowing" = "river"; and አስተብቍዓታት "suppliant entreaties".

Special Uses of certain Plurals.

But the language on the other hand possesses words which are used either in the Plur. alone, or in the Plur. specially ([1]). The signification of the Plural, which indicates a definite or indefinite number of individuals, carries with it as such the possibility of conceiving that sum of individuals as a united and single notion (v. *infra* § 141), like "tents" = "encampment". This explains how Ethiopic expresses certain ideas in the Plural form, which other languages denote by words in the Singular. Add to this,—that in Semitic tongues the Plural expresses not merely a number of individuals which may be counted, but also the mass, the collectivity, and whatever is the highest and most general form of the contents of the notion. Thus existences and objects, which produce the impression of mass and boundless sublimity, or in which the apex and essence of every individual within a given conception is viewed or thought of, are put in the Plural in Ethiopic, while other languages employ a mere Singular instead. *Pluralia tantum*

([1]) Apart from words, whose Singular cannot, as it happens, be supported from any writings as yet known to us.

are, it is true, very seldom met with. The language is too well worn and too thoroughly developed, not to have a Singular formed and in use as time went on, in the case of the greater number of words, even though they might have been allowed only in the Plural at a more antique stage. But there is a series of words which are used in the Plural as single notions and with the same force as a Singular. The name of "God", **አምላክ** designates him as the *highest of the Lords*, the essence of all lordship, just as the poetical name **አርያም** designates "heaven" as *the highest height*. Farther, names of spaces, which have a perimeter and enclose what is individual, or of things which embrace an abundance of what is individual, or which consist of several remarkable portions, —are frequently used in the Plural, *e. g.* **አርማስ** "raft", **ሬማናት** "boat", **ሬግዛት** "doorposts", **አስሬብ** "waterfall", **አማዑት** "bowels", **ጸሬዲት** "the loins", **ሕፀን** (*pl.*) = **ሕዕን** (*sg.*) (Ex. 4, 6 *sqq.*) "the bosom", **ጐማጕዕ** "a rough road" ('a continuation of rough places'), **መቃብር** "burying-place" and "grave", **መፃምርት** "marriage", "spouse", **በይናት** "between" (literally, 'spaces lying between'), **ዕደዋት** "cross-road" (Mark 11,4), **ጸቃውዕ** "honey dropped from the comb". In the intellectual region:—**ጠባይዕ** "the natural disposition" (as the essence of many several faculties [*lit.* 'impressions']), **አምሳል** "image" (inasmuch as it consists of many bits of likeness), **ተአምር** "a miracle" (because of its many startling phenomena), **አምጣን** "measure, size, sum, duration" (because enclosing within it a mass of individual space-, and time-parts). The same way of looking at things has produced in turn new Plurals out of these Plurals, v. § 141.

The Formation of the Plural is either brought about by terminations, which are attached to the Singular Stem, or this outer formation is replaced by an inner formation, exactly as in Arabic.

(*a*) *Outer Formation of the Plural.*

Masculine Plural Ending in *án*; Fem. in *át*.

§ 132. Ethiopic words form their plural either by means of the Masculine termination *án*, or the Feminine termination *át*, both carrying the accent (Trumpp, p. 542)(1). The former,

(1) The Plural-ending *an* is found also in Assyrian [(v. Delitzsch,

which is paralleled by ـُونَ, ־ִים, ـܝܢ in other tongues, seems to have arisen, in accordance with § 18, out of *ōn*, which at one time might take the place of *ān*. Both terminations have been produced by lengthening the terminations of the Singular, *ĕ* (in Arabic *un*) in the Masculine, and *at* in the Feminine. The termination *ān* is always attached to the final radical of the Stem of the Singular, thus taking the place of its original vowel-ending. The termination *āt*, in the case of a good many words, takes the place of the Feminine-ending *at* of the Singular, but in the majority of cases it is applied externally to the Stem of the Singular, whether that ends in *at* or in some other fashion. It is by no means the case, however, that every word which wants the Fem. termination in the Sing. takes *ān* in the Plur., or that every Fem. Stem has *āt* in the Plur.; for while the form without the Fem. termination is the one which comes most readily to hand in the Singular, and the Fem. termination appears only on special grounds, the reverse is the case in the formation of the Plural. Every Plural, as expressing a number or an assemblage of individuals, is a Collective word, and, in a certain sense, an Abstract. But Abstracts, even in the Singular number, are predominantly conceived of as Fem.; and accordingly it is the Feminine termination which prevails most in the Plural Number, and it is the Masculine which only makes its appearance on special grounds.

1. Personal and Descriptive Words taking Outer Plural Ending *ān*. Detailed Rules and Exceptions (*a*—*g*).

1. Words signifying Persons, and Descriptive words, *i. e.* Adjectives and Participles, are the only ones which take the Masculine termination *ān* in the Plural. But not every word which signifies a Person takes its Plural in *ān*: several have *āt* (§ 133, *a*), and many replace the outer formation by the inner, which is the mode followed even by some Descriptive words. When a Descriptive word admits of the Masculine termination *ān*, it takes at the same time the termination *āt* for the Feminine. Besides, one set form the Fem. Plur. from the Masc. Plur.(1), another form it from the Fem. Sing. Coming to details we must attend to the following:—

(*a*) Words of the type given in § 108, *a*, occur but seldom in the Plural, and have an outer formation: **ሕያው**, **ሕያዋን**; **ዕሩቃን**,

'*Assyr. Gramm.*', § 67)]. In Tigre *ām* is the corresponding termination; *cf.* NÖLDEKE, '*W. Ztschr. f. d. K. d. M.*' IV, p. 299.

(1) [But v. Note to (*b*), *infra*. TR.]

ዕራቃት (ጥራያን Hen. 14, 6) (1); in the same way ሕጻጣን "few" (pl.), and ደገደግ (§ 112, b), ደገደጋን.

(b) Words of the type given in § 108, b, so far as they are pure Adjectives, have usually the Outer formation: ሐዲስ "new", ሐዲሳን, Fem.—from the Sing. ሐዳስ (§ 129, a)—ሐዳሳት; in the same way ጠቢብ, ጠቢባን, ጠባባት. Often, however, they form their Fem. Plur. from the Masc. Plur. (2), so that instead of ዐባ ያት the form ዐቢያት is more frequently found; in the same way ጠቢባት; በሊኃት "sharp" (pl.) (Hen. 10, 5); ደቂቃት and ደቃቃት. Some form an Inner Plur. as well as an Outer: ቀጢን, ቀጢናን and ቀጠንት; ዐቢይ, ዐበይት; ጠቢብ, ጠበብት (§ 138): and so too ኄር "good", ኄራን. Of words of this type which are used rather as Substantives, መሲሕ "Messiah" regularly takes the form መሲ ሓን; ልሂቅ (ሊቅ) "the Primus" and "old" has ልሂቃን, Fem. ልሂ ቃት, or ሊቃን, ሊቃት; ቀሲስ "Presbyter" has the Outer formation ቀሲሳን as well as an Inner form. The remainder have other forms, so far as they have any Plural at all.

(c) Participles of the type given in § 108, c (111, b; 112, b) take, throughout, the Outer formation, and derive their Fem. Plur. not from the Fem. Sing., but from the Masc. Plur. (3): ክሡት "manifest", ክሡታን, ክሡታት; ርኅው "open", ርኅዋን, ርኅዋት (rehewwāt). Participles from roots middle ū frequently assume (in accordance with § 52) the contracted form in the Plur.: ምውት "dead", ሙታን, ሙታት; but also ምውቅ "warm", ምውቃን and ምውቃት, or from a Singular ምዉቅ: ምዉቃን, ምዉቃት. It is but very rarely that these Participles have the inner formation, as in ቅድው "pure", "genuine", Plur. ቀደውት; as also in the word which is always used substantively ንጉሥ "king", Plur. ነገሥት; on the other hand ዕድው "enemy", ዕድዋን. Of Feminines of this type (§ 128) which have come to be used substantively, ዕቅብት "concubine" conforms to the Participles

(1) [Flemming adopts here the variant ጥርያኒሆሙ. tr.]

(2) [Would it not be better to say *Sing.*? Just as one form of the Feminine Plural, viz. ዐባያት, comes from the Feminine Singular ዐባይ, by adding *āt*, so the other form ዐቢያት may be regarded as coming from the Masculine Singular ዐቢይ, by adding the same termination, and in the same way; *cf.* Praetorius, '*Aethiop. Gramm.*' p. 105. tr.]

(3) [V. last Note. tr.]

and takes the Plur. ዕቊባት as well as ዕቊባታት. (On the other hand, ንግሥት "queen", ሐብርት "coloured decoration", and others, form the plural quite externally: ንግሥታት, ሐብርታት).

(*d*) Participles of the type in § 109, *a*, and the like, take mostly the outer formation, when they are used as Adjectives—: ክልኤ, ክልኤን, ክልኤት; ኀጥኣን, ኣብዳን, ዐርክን; ዐርክ "friend" has an inner formation also; ረድእ, በዐል (መርሕ, ላህም) have only an inner formation. On ክህን v. § 133, *a*.

(*e*) Words of the type in § 110, *a* have still an outer formation, when used as Adjectives:—ሠናይ, ሠናያን, ሠናያት, but an inner, when they indicate an Agent, whether they are formed in the sing. with or without the termination *ī*. Multiliteral:—ሐንካስ, ሐንካሳን, but ጸዐዳ and ጸዐዳ with an inner formation.

(*f*) Participles and *Nomina Agentis*, formed with the prefix መ (§ 114) take, in the Plur., *ān* for the Masc. termination, and *āt* for the Fem., *e. g.* መምህራን, መምህራት (1). Some form an Inner Plural, *e. g.* መምክር "counsellor", መማክርት; in the same way መቅርን, መኰንን, መዕርር and others. ማረ "seer" (of common gender) has either ማርያን, or ማርያት (§ 133, *a*), or ማረይት (§ 138).

(*g*) All Adjectives with outer Adjective-terminations take regularly the outer formation (§§ 117—119), while the *ī* is hardened into a semivowel before the terminations(2):—ተዐጋሚ, ተዐጋሥያን, ተዐጋሥያት; መፍቀሪ, መፍቀርያን, መፍቀርያት; አረሚ, አረምያን; መንፈሳዊ, መንፈሳውያን and መንፈሳውያት; so ክርስቲያን "Christians", from a Singular not in use. Some words ending in *i*, of the class described in § 118, *γ*, and some, ending in *āi* (v. § 119), form their Plur. from the termination *āwī*:—ዐረቢ "an Arab", Plur. ዐረባውያን. The words አረጋዊ "an old man", ኖላዊ "shepherd", and ኖትያዊ ναύτης have an inner or feminine formation: አእሩግ (from a lost Sing. አርግ), ኖሎት (for ኖለውት), ኖትያት (§ 133). ፈያታዊ "robber" and አይሁዳዊ "a Jew" are words, denoting an individual, which have been derived from

(1) If, as Ludolf says, መድልው has መደልዋን in the Plur. (Ps. 52,7), as well as መድልዋን (Matt. 6,2), a Singular መደልው is the basis of it, and there is no need to explain መደልዋን by any application of Ewald's rule, as given in '*Gr. Ar.*' § 300.

(2) [V., however, *Kebra Nag.*-Introd., p. XVI.]

Plurals (§ 131), and which form their plur., simply by returning to their respective ground-forms ፊደት and አይሁድ. The most of the substantives enumerated in § 118, γ, have an inner formation. Farther, the words which are dealt with in § 117, *a*, of the type ገብሬ,—some of which are interchangeable with those of the type ገብር (§ 110, *a*), usually take the inner formation. It is only a small number of words of this type, and these mostly used as Adjectives, that have outer terminations, *e. g.* ለባዊ, ለባውያን, ለባውያት. Others admit of both formations, *e. g.* ሐራሲ, ገባሬ, and in the same fashion ጸሐፊ, ጸሐፍት and ጸሐፍያን (G. Ad. 164, 4, 20; 166, 29); while some, like ቀዳሚ "the first", have only the inner formation (*cf.* § 138). Yet even these words may take another special Feminine form with an outer termination, as well as the inner formation which may be used for both Masc. and Fem.: ቀዳምያት; ሐላዪ "singer", Plur. Masc. ሐለይት "singers" (*m.*), Plur. Fem. ሐላይያት "singers" (*f.*).

Other words, besides those enumerated here, take the Masc. Plural-ending *ān*, but only on rare occasions and in the language of poetry, *e. g.* ስርናያን ፡ መንፈስ "spiritual grains of wheat" (ስርናይ, originally an Adjective); or ማኅበር "association", "congregation": ማኅበራን "associates", colleagues". Farther *cf.* § 141, 5.

2. Substantives taking Outer Plural Ending *ăt*:— Certain Masc. Personal Names.

§ 133. 2. The *Feminine termination āt* is taken by all other Substantives,—except the Personal and Descriptive Words mentioned in § 132,—which admit of an outer formation of the Plur. at all, whether they have a Fem. form in the Singular or not. The mode of attachment of this termination is generally very simple: It is of more importance to point out the cases in which this Outer Plural formation generally takes place, and this will be attempted in the following survey.

(*a*) *Masculine Names of Persons* have as a rule, it is true, in accordance with § 132 the masculine termination *ān*, but yet there are several cases in which they must take the fem. termination in the Plural. In particular, (1) *All Proper Names*, masculine and feminine, have the outer formation in the Plur., and in fact the termination *āt*: መቃርስ "Macarius", መቃርሳት; ማርያም "Mary", ማርያማት. (2) *Masculine words indicating Persons*, and which denote an office, business, or position, take the Fem. termination in the Plur., and are to be conceived of as Abstracts of the office or dignity:—a plurality of priests, for example, is always "priesthood" to the Ethiopian (1). Accordingly we have **ካህን**, **ካህናት** "priests"; **ዲያቆን**, **ዲያቆናት**; and so is it with **ጳጳስ**, **ኤጲስ ቆጶስ**, **መነኮስ** "monk", **ቆሞስ** "*comes*". Hence also **ፈላስፋት** "philosophers", **ረበናት** "rabbis" (*e. g.* Matt. 16,21 *sq.*), **ተንበላት** "Khalifs", **ፈርዖናት** "Pharaohs" ('*John Madabb.*' ed. Zotenberg, p. 173). Farther, we have **ነቢይ** "prophet", **ነቢያት**; **ሰማዕታት** "martyrs"; **ሠገራት** "guards", "constables"; **መስተራትዓት** "lictors" (Matt. 27,27); **ሰይጣን** "Satan", **ሰይጣናት** (as well as the inner formation); **ማሪ** "seer", **ማርያት** (as well as **ማርያን** and **ማሪያት**); **ኬንያ** "artificer", **ኬንያት** (together with the inner form); **ገባራት** "workmen"; **ሐዋርያ** "apostle", **ሐዋርያት**; **ኖትያዊ** "shipmaster", **ኖትያት** (from **ኖትያ**); perhaps also **ፈያት** "robbers" (if this does not stand for **ፈያእት** from **ፈያኢ**) (2). This termination may be applied even to the Plur. **ሊቃን** "presbyters", to turn the word into the name of the office: **ሊቃናት** (alongside of **ሊቃውንት** § 140). Sometimes also this ending is attached to words which merely express a property, *e. g.* **ዕራቃቲነ** "naked we" from **ዕራቅ** 2 Cor. 5,3 (*cf.* Hen. 32,6 Note); *cf.* also **አአበዊነ፡ ኅላይያት ፡ ቤተ ፡ ክርስቲያን** "O ye fathers of ours, who are solicitous for the Church" (MS. Berol., *M. Berh.* fol. 12 *b*).

(*b*) A whole series of substantives, which have a Fem. form in the Sing., take the termination *āt* in the Plural:—

Singular Fem. Forms taking *āt* in Plural.

(*α*) Singular-Stems which end in *t*, with the exception of the type **መግበርት** and **መግብርት** (3), form the Plural in *āt*, in which the formation itself proceeds in a different way. The greater number apply the *āt* externally to the *t* of the Sing., like **ዓመት** "year", **ዓመታት** (4); only a minority form the Plur. directly from the Masc. Stem and so put *āt* in the place of the Fem.-ending of

---

(1) *Cf.* the like in Hebr., Ewald § 177, *f.*; in Syr., Hoffmann p. 253; and in Arab., Ewald § 301. In Arab. the fem.-ending for official names is comparatively common in the Sing. (Ewald, '*Gr. Ar.*' § 284,4); in Ethiopic only a few forms of this kind occur in the Sing., with the ending *yā* (ـِيَّةٌ): **ኬንያ** "artificer", **ጕሕልያ** "cheat" (by profession), **ሐዋርያ** "ambassador", "apostle". But this termination *yā* has at other times the force of a plural, v. *infra*, § 140, IV.

(2) [But v. § 132,*g*. Tr.]

(3) The following also are exceptions: **መርዓት**, **ኵናት**, **ሥዕርት**, **ሰኮት**, **እስኪት**, **አመት**, **ወለት**, **ኀብስት**, **ኀጢአት**, and others.

(4) *Cf.* Haupt, '*Sum. Fam.*' p. 73.

the Singular. Thus is it with most words of the type አረፍት "wall" (§ 128 *ad init.*), አረፋት; ዐዘቅት "well", ዐዘቃት (together with ዐዘቅታት); farther, ጸበርት, በቀልት; እጕልት "cow" has እጕላት and እጕላት; ጸሀርት (ጽሀርት) "cauldron", ጸሀራት, ጽሀራት, ጸሀራት (and ጸሀርታት); ክረምት "Winter" (from a Masc. *ክራም), ክራማት (or, with the inner formation አክራም); ደሰት "island", ደሰያት;—ተመርት "palm-tree", on the other hand, forms ተመር ታት. The word ቀኖት "nail" may, besides ቀኖታት, take also the form ቀንዋት (for ቀንዋት); ኰሊት "kidney" has ኰሊያት and ኰል ያት; and ዕሴት "remuneration" has,—not ዕሰያት,—but ዕሴያት (Hen. 105, 1), retaining the *ē* and using only a semi-hardening (§ 40). For the rest, there are only a few additional Feminines which retain this more original form of the Plural: ሕልቀት "ring" takes the form ሕልቀታት as well as ሕለቃት (Ex. 30, 4, from the original Masc. form *ሕለቅ). The much abbreviated word እኅት "sister" forms the Plur. አኃት. There are still a few more words which belong to this class, but the examples of them hitherto found occur only in the Plural: ቅትራት "goads", "spurs"; ወረዋት "javelins"; ራግናት "raft", "cordage of a ship"; ራግዛት "door-posts"; ራኩባት "female camels".

The others apply *āt* externally to the ት of the Singular. But the assumption of a plural-form is mainly confined to concrete Common Nouns, like ልገት "hut", ዕለት "day", ዕፀት "shrub", ምኔት "hermitage" &c. Pure conceptional words appear in the Plur. much more rarely, as ዝብጠታት "strokes" (Hen. 69, 6), ጥም ዐታት (Hen. 8, 1), በረከታት (Hen. 71, 12), ሑረታት (Cant. 7, 2), ሙተታት (G. Ad. 124, 7), ኂሩታት "benefits", ሚጠታት "turnings" &c.—Some words belonging to this class, *e. g.* ኆኅት "door" and ክልስስት "sheaf", take both the inner and the outer formations.

(*β*) On the Fem. Singular-Stems which have a vowel-ending v. *infra*, § 134.

Many Masc. Singular-Stems taking Outer Plural Ending *āt* (α—γ).

§ 134. (*c*) Lastly, *many Masculine Singular-Stems* take this form of the Plural:—

(*α*) It is most largely adopted, — without exception seemingly[1] — by all those *words which have long ā before the final radical*, plainly because the presence of this *ā* already in the Singular-stem is unfavourable to an inner formation involving the

(1) ክሳድ "neck" takes both the outer and the inner formation.

interpolation of another *ă*. Accordingly we find: (1) ቃል, ቃላት; ማይ, ማያት; (2) ሕፃን, "child", ሕፃናት; and in like manner ትሩፍ, ዕጣን, ዝናም, እኁል, ንዋይ, ግናይ (ግኑያት), ሕዋስ, ፍያል, ትንታግ, ሕንባል, ሕንቡብ and many others; (3) በዓል "feast", በዓላት; ፈቃድ, ነፋስ, ሰማይ, ቀላይ (ቀላያት and ቀለያት), ሰይጣን and others; (4) ሥልጣን "dominion", ሥልጣናት; ብርሃን, ቀስታም, ቆባር, ዲናር, ሮማን, ነጐድጓድ and others; (5) ትእዛዝ "command", ትእዛዛት; ተስናን, ተድባብ; (6) almost all Names of places, of the type ምሕራም "temple", ምሕራማት; ምሥዋዕ, መክን, ሙላድ, ሙፃእ &c.; also ምግባር "way of acting", "mode of action", and similar forms. A number of other Stems, which have a long vowel before the final radical, also take this external Plural-form: ሐሪር "silk", ሐሪራት "silk dresses"; ብሩር, ብሩራት; ብሔር "land", ብሔራት (as well as the inner formation); እቤር "old woman", እቤራት and አቤራት; እቶን, ገንዖር, አክሊል, ኢዮቤል, ሆይ and others.

(*β*) *The greater number of Nominal Stems which end in long vowels form the Plur. in āt,* whether these vowels represent Feminine-endings, or have some other origin.

In the case of *those which end in ā*, the termination *āt* blends with that *ā*, *e. g.* ዓሣ "fish", ዓሣት; ሰረገላ "waggon", ደመና "cloud", እንግድአ "breast", ምጕንጻ "quiver", (ዕንዚራ, ባዝግና, ከተማ, ኵሓ, ቶሩ, ተኵላ, ዜና, ኖጻ G. Ad. 5, 1, and others):—Also ሥጋ "body", ሥጋት; ዘማ "whore", ዘማት; ጸጋ χάρις, ጽላ "*tabula*". Even Abstracts in ና:—ኀሊና "faculty of thinking" and ጼና "smell" form the plurals ኀሊናት[1] and ጼናት (G. Ad. 4, 12).

Stems ending in *ē* form the plural by changing it into *yāt*, (lengthened from *yat*), when that *ē* is the Abstract-ending spoken of in § 120 (sprung from *ia* or *iat*):—ምሳሌ "similitude", "parable", ምሳልያት; ምንዳቤ, ምንዳብያት; ሥጋዌ, ሥጋውያት; ስባሔ, ስባሕያት; ውዳሴ, ውዳስያት; ውሳጤ "the interior", ውሳጥያት. On the other hand *ē* undergoes semi-hardening (§ 40) before *āt*, if it has come from *a* and a Radical *ī*, or is of obscure origin: ዕፄ "vermin", ዕፄያት and ዕፀያት; in like manner ጽጌ "flower", ግሔ "rabbit", ፍሬ "fruit", ፍሬያት, ፍረያት and ፍርያት (the last not good); ነጌ "elephant" has ነጌያት (Hen. 86, 4). Farther, ጊዜ "time" has ጊዜ

---

[1] If this is not rather to be explained in accordance with § 122, *β*. ሰቀላ, ሰኰና, ዐንበሳ, ተኬሳ, አንጼዋ, ወልታ, ዙብዳ, ዱብተራ, ጽንጽያ, ጼታ have the Inner Plur.-formation.

ያት; and ደ፡ደ፡ "door" ደ፡ደ፡ያት (*cf. supra*, p. 286 § 131, Note 2); ጊሜ "fog", ጊሜያት; ደዌ "sickness"; ደዌያት; ግምዔ "pitcher", which generally has the inner formation, may take the Plural ግም ዔያት and (from ግምዕ) ግምዓት (Numb. 4, 9 Note) (1).

Words ending in ō which take this Plural are rare. The only such Plurals yet known are ገበዋት from ገቦ "side" (of the body); ቀፈዋት from ቀፎ "basket"; ረበዋት "myriads" (*Sing.* רִבּוֹ); and ግልፈዋት, ግልፋዋት [but also ግልፎዋት, *Kebra Nag.* p. XXXII a], admittedly from a form (§ 121, β) ግልፎ "carved work", —in all of which *o* is resolved into *aw* before *āt* (2).

On those words ending in *i* which do not belong to this section, see § 132.

(γ) A few stray Nominal Stems, of comparatively simple form and ending in a consonant, take the outer formation *āt* in the Plural. The following are the most important and most frequently occurring of these—: እም "mother", እማት; ገጽ "face", ጠል "dew", ዝቅ "skin-bottle", ድብ "bear", ድድ "foundation", ነፍስ "soul", ኀይል "power", ሰርጕ "ornament" ሰርጓት, ማእድ "table", ሣህል "grace" "favour", ጕድብ "axe", ኀብር "incantation" [Hen. 65, 6], ነፍቅ "box", ጽድቅ "alms", ዝኀር "tomb", ድልቅልቅ "an earthquake": Also ጥበብ "wisdom", Plur. ጥበባት "arts"; farther, ሀየል "stag", ሐርገጽ "crocodile", ሰገል "divination", አየር "air", ዘመን "time", ዐንጕጕ "water-lizard", ዓለም "world", ባሕርይ "pearl"; ፊደል "letter of the alphabet" (3). Others admit of the outer formation in *āt*, along with the inner:—ቍስል "wound", ግብር "thing", ሠቅ "sack", ሰምር "productiveness", በቍል "plant", ገመል "camel", ከልብ "dog"; and with differing meanings ነገር, ነገራት "affairs", "things", አንጋር "languages". The Plural-formation in all these stems proceeds without any change of vowels; but ከልብ forms ከለባት (4).

(1) The inner formation is taken by—ሰርዌ, አርዌ, ሐርጌ and ጕርዔ.

(2) ዐውሎ "storm" takes the form ዐውሎታት.—መሰንቆ and ዶርሆ take the inner formation.

(3) ጕብላት, Gen. 30, 38, and ሰደዋት Mark 11, 4 can as yet be supported only in the Plur.

(4) To be explained in accordance with Ewald, '*Gr. Ar.*' § 300. Other views of the point are represented by Zimmern, '*Zeitschr. f. Ass.*' V, p. 385 and Philippi, '*Beitr. z. Ass.*' II, p. 377. [and especially Nöldeke, '*Zeitschr. f. Assyr.*' XVIII, p. 70].

(*d*) *Nominal Stems which have the formative prefix* **መ**, § 116, usually take the inner Plural-formation, either with or without a Fem. termination, but sometimes too they take the outer formation: **መንክር** "miracle", **መንክራት**; in the same way **መድምም**, **መፍቅድ**; **መሥመር** "line", **መሥመራት**; **መዝሙር** "psalm", **መክርይ** "spade", **መንኰራኵር** "wheel" (1): **መቅሠፍት** "castigation", **መቅሠፍታት**; **መቅፀት** "pot", **መቅፀታት**; **ማዕፈርት** "mitre", **ማዕፈርታት**. In others the outer formation appears, as well as the inner: **ማኅፈድ** "tower", **ሞገድ** "flood", **ማኅደር** "dwelling" (**ማኅደራት** Hen. 59, 2), **ማእሰር** "bond", **መልህቅ** "principalship" (**መልሀቃት** *Gad. Lalib.*); **ማሕሌት**, **ማዕጠንት**, **መሥዋዕት**. There are, besides, a few of the Feminine Stems cited towards the end of § 111, *a*,—having **ት** prefixed,—which admit of the outer formation: **ተምኔት** "wish", **ተምኔታት**; **ትእምርት** "mark *or* sign", "miracle", **ትእምርታት**; **ትፍሥሕት** "joy", **ትፍሥሕታት**; **ትውልድ** "race", "family", **ትውልዳት**.—**ትንቢት** "prophecy" forms, in accordance with § 133 *b*, *α*, **ትንብያት**.

On a farther employment of the termination *āt*, v. § 141.

Nominal Stems with Prefix **መ**, which sometimes take the Outer Formation in the Plural.

(*b*). *Inner Formation of the Plural.*

General Account of the Inner Plural or Collective Form.

§ 135. Agreeably to the natural bent of the Semitic languages to replace the Outer formation by Inner vowel-change, an Inner Plural-formation has been also developed from the Outer (2). The lengthening and broadening of the terminal sounds, by means of which the Plural-forms, given in §§ 132—134, have come into being, may be turned into a lengthening and broadening of the inner vowel-utterances of the Stem. Just as happens in forming the Imperfect (§ 91) and the Feminine of certain Descriptive words, *i. e.*, Adjectives and Participles (§ 129), so, in order to construct a Collective word out of the word which denotes one of a class, a long or short *a*, more rarely a *u*, penetrates into the middle of the Stem as a kind of remains of the Feminine Plural termination *āt* or the Masculine *ān* (*ōn*), occasionally dislodging *a*-sounds of the Singular Stem and turning them into prefixes. This formation of new Collective-words by means of inner vowel-change, is therefore only a continuation of the process of Nominal Stem-formation;

(1) *Cf.* also **ምጽናዕ** "firmament", **ምጽንዓት** and **ምጽናዓት**.

(2) V. on the other hand König, p. 86 *sq.*

and since the language regards and treats the new forms not as properly words indicating several individuals, but as abstract Collective words, they are with more propriety denominated *Collective-forms* than Plural-forms. In the multiplicity of these Collective formations Ethiopic approaches Arabic, in which precisely this tendency of the language luxuriates most; but even here it again exhibits its more frugal disposition in the development and use of forms; and inasmuch as it employs only the most important of possible types of this formation, it is well calculated to elucidate the complicated Arabic system. All these Collective words, as falling under the general notion of Abstracts, may be conceived of in Ethiopic as feminine, and they sometimes even have in their formation a feminine ት (1). In the usage of the language, they may —whether with or without a feminine termination—be treated either as masculine or as feminine, just like the ordinary Abstract (§ 130). Farther, in their character of Collective words, they may be regarded either as notions suggestive of unity, and be associated with a Singular in the Predicate and the Apposition,—or as notions suggestive of a number of individuals comprised in them, and accordingly be connected with a Plural in these parts of the sentence. Thus, for example, the expression "those days" may be rendered either by ውእቱ : መዋዕል or by ይእቲ : መዋዕል or እሙንቱ : መዋዕል or እማንቱ : መዋዕል.

The formation of a Collective itself is invariably regulated by the form of the Singular-stem, and accordingly such Collective formation falls into three main divisions:—(1) Forms from triliteral Nominal Stems of the simplest kind; (2) Forms from longer Stems, especially from Stems of tri-radical roots containing a long formative vowel after the first or second radical, from stems with outer additions in the shape of Prefixes or Affixes, and from Stems of Multiliteral roots; (3) Special Forms, standing midway between these two divisions, of certain Descriptive words and *Nomina agentis*.—Several Nominal Stems have a two-fold or threefold Collective formation,—for the most part, however, without any difference in meaning. Alongside of these leading modes of the Collective formation, which are still active in the language as used,

(1) Not *āt*, which would of necessity turn them into words expressing a number of individuals, *i. e.* into Plurals.

there occur in rare instances remains of other formations, still preserved in Arabic, which indicate that at one time Ethiopic also had a greater number of forms, but parted with the use of them, with characteristic frugality. On the accentuation of these Collective-forms in general, *cf.* TRUMPP, p. 542 and KÖNIG, p. 159.

I. Collective Words from Singular-Stems of the Simplest Formation from Tri-radical Roots:—

§ 136. I. *Collective words from Singular-stems of the simplest formation from Tri-radical roots.* To this class belong only Singular-stems without the Feminine termination *at* or *t*; for the Fem. Stems (with the exception of ኣመት, ሥዕርት, ክረምት, ፍኖት, ሰኵት) take the outer form of the Plural (§ 133, *b*) or have other Collective forms. Then, Singular-stems of the types ግበር, ግቡር and ገበር do not appear in this class, because the first of these three types has generally no plural at all or at most only an outer plural, while the other two types, in accordance with § 134, *c*, *α*, confine themselves to the outer Plural form. Accordingly the Singular-stems which fall to be considered here are those after the types ግብር, ገብር, ገበር, as well as a few Stems of the type ጕብር following the type ገብር.

1 Collective form, Type ገበር (*gĕbăr*).

1. *The first and simplest Collective-form*, Type ገበር, comes from Singular-stems of the type ግብር and is produced by establishing short *a* after the second radical, which is vowel-less in the Sing. Judging by the Arabic(1), we might even have this *a* lengthened; as yet, however, *ā* can be supported only in the case of ቈያጽ from ቈይጽ "leg" (Cant. 5, 15; John 19, 31, together with አቈያጽ Ps. 146, 11; Judges 15, 8) and ፍናው, ፍናዌ(2) from ፍኖት "way". For short *a* v. *e. g.* እዝን "ear", እዘን; *mediae geminatae*:—ሕግ "law", ሕገግ; ግብ "pit", ገበብ; *tertiae infirmae*: ሥርው "root", ሥረው. Farther, this formation is specially adopted by these old and much abbreviated words (§ 105 *ad fin.*): አብ "father", እኁ "brother", እድ "hand", አፍ "mouth", ዕድ "man", ዕፅ "tree",—in which *u* appears as third radical: አበው, አኀው (§ 44), እደው, አፈው, ዕደው, ዕፀው. The names of the parts of the body in men and animals frequently have this form of the Plural: ብርክ "knee", እዝን "ear", (ቈይጽ), ሕፅን "bosom", እግር "foot", ክንፍ "wing", ጽፍር "nail", ጥርስ = ፅርስ "molar tooth"; and besides these:

(1) EWALD, '*Gr. Ar.*' § 307.

(2) [If this form is not rather to be compared with Arabic فَعالَى; *cf.* PRAETORIUS, ZDMG LVI, p. 694.]

ሕዝብ, ትልም, እብን, ጽንፍ, ሕብር "colour", ምስል, ቍስል, ኍልቍ, (Plur. ኍለቍ), እኅል, ዕቍር, ግብር, ግድም, ጥንፍ. አፈው "frankincense" may also be a *Plurale tantum*. Yet many of these words admit also of the Plural-type አግብር (v. *infra* No. 2):—ሥርው, ቍይጽ, ትልም, እብን, ብርክ, ክንፍ, እዝን, እግር, ግብ, ጽንፍ, ጽፍር, and ሕዝብ, one plural of which, ሕዘብ signifies "tribes", and the other አሕዛብ "nations":—there is a similar result in the case of ዕፅ, v. *infra*. That this type ግበር was at one time exchangeable for another type فَعِيل or فُعُول cannot be proved. ደቂቅ "sons", which is always employed in a Plural sense and which therefore might easily be regarded as a Plural of ደቅ, is rather a Singular used as a Collective (§ 131, 2), as the mode of attachment of the Suff. Pron. indicates. In the same way ውሉድ "children" appears to be both the Plur. belonging to ወልድ and also a Passive Part. used as a Collective; but yet in certain passages it seems to denote "*son*" in the Singular (Gen. 17,16; 18,10 & 14; Cant. 5,10). In like manner ዕድው (1) "men" (Ps. 138,18) might be conceived as a Collective Singular (instead of the usual ዕድ) (2): So long, however, as such a type of the Singular is not otherwise supported, it may perhaps be permitted to regard ዕድው *ʿedéwwe* as rather a Plural, of the type فُعُول (for ዕዱው, like أُخُوّ "brothers").

2.Collective-form, Type አግበር (*agbā́r*). 2. *A second Collective formation*, and the one in fact which is most frequently found with all Singular-Stems of Simple form, takes *ā* after the second radical, and አ as a Stem-prefix forming one syllable with the first radical, but never lengthened before Aspirates: Type አግበር. This form is adopted first of all by Singular-Stems which contain an *a*-sound, in particular by those which have an *a* after the second radical. Accordingly the prefixed አ may be considered as an *a* of the Singular-Stem which has been thrust out of the stem by the interpolated *ā*. Singular-Stems,

(1) *Cf.* also Ludolf's Note on Ps. 72, 5.

(2) [Dillmann gives a very different account of this word in his '*Lex.*' Under ዕድ he says (*col.* 1011):—"Ps. 54, 27. 138, 18 exhibent ዕድው ፡ ደም ፡ *hostes sanguinolenti*, quamquam primitus sine dubio ዕደው ፡ ደም ፡ legebatur; cfr. etiam Ludolfi annot. ad Ps. 72, 5"; and, again, under ዕድው *adversarius* (*col.* 1012)—"In libris Mss. passim ዕድው ፡ cum ዕደው ፡ *viri* perperam permutatur". tr.]

which contain no *a*, share also in this formation, but only as a series of secondary importance. Very seldom indeed does this form take the Feminine termination ት. The intruding *a* is always long, with the exception of **አዕፀው** "trees" (along with **ዕፀው**)* from **ዕፅ** (and **አፍያት** v. *infra*).

(*a*) This Collective form is the one used almost exclusively in the case of Singular-Stems of the type **ገብር**(1), *e. g.*: **ነገር** "speech", **አንጋር** "languages"; **ዘነብ** "tail", **አዝናብ**; **ደወል** "district", **አድዋል**; and in like manner: **ፈለግ**, **ሐመር**, **መጠን**, **ሰመር**, **ቀለም**, **በለስ**, **በሐኮ**, **ነገድ**, **ከፈር**, **ዐጸድ**, **ዘመን**, **ዘመድ**, **ዘፈር**, **ገመል**, **ጸወን**, **ፈረስ**.

(*b*) It is very common in the case of the Sing.-form **ግብር** (from which, it is true, the Collective forms **አግብርት** and **አግብር** also are often taken, v. *infra*):—**ዐምድ** "column", **አዕማድ**; **ደብር** "mountain", **አድባር**; *mediae geminatae*: **ሠቅ** "sack", **አሥቃቅ**; **ፀር** "enemy", **አፅራር**; *primae vocalis*: **ወርኅ** "month", **አውራኅ**; **ወይን** "wine", **አውያን** "vines"; *mediae infirmae*: **ዖም** "tree", **አዕዋም**; **ዖፍ** "bird", **አዕዋፍ**; **ቤት** "house", **አብያት**. Besides: **ሐብል**, **ሜስ**, **ሠርቅ**, **ሠርግ**, **ሦክ**, **ረምሕ**, **ረድእ**, **ሰርም**, **ሶር**, **ሰውጥ**, **ቀምሕ**, **ቤዝ**, **ኀምል**, **አንፍ፡ ወቅፍ**, **ወትር**, **ወጽብ**, **ዐውድ**, **ዐይግ**, **ዐድል**, **ዘውግ**, **ደይም**, **ገልዕ**, **ጎር**, **ጾም**, **ፈትል**. **አርባብ**(2) "myriads" (from رُبَّة) is a *Plurale tantum*. The plural of **ሣእን** "shoe", **አሥኣን** is also written (§ 47) **አሣእን** (*v.* Gen. 14, 23 Note). The words **ሐቅል** "field", **ሰይፍ** "sword", **ሣእን** "shoe", **በትር** "rod" have, along with this Plural, other forms in addition: **አሕቃል** and **አሕቅልት**; **አስያፍ** and **አስይፍት**; **አሥኣን** and **አሥእን**; **አብታር** (Numb. 17, 17) and **አብትር**.

(*c*) But this Collective-form has also come into use in the case of the Singular-form **ግብር**, and with even greater frequency than No. 1,—a circumstance which is the less remarkable, that many words vary even in the Sing. between the types **ግብር** and **ገብር**. Thus **ልብስ** "garment" takes **አልባስ** in the Plur.; **ምድር** "land", **አምዳር**; **ዕንቍ** "precious stone", **አዕናቍ**; **ምእት** "hundred", **አምኣት**; **ልብ** "heart", **አልባብ**; **ምት** "husband", **አምታት**; **ቢጽ**

(1) Only a few have the Collective-form **አግቡር** (§ 137), and a few again take the outer formation (§ 134, γ).

(2) [Again a retreat from the position taken up in the '*Lex.*', and an acknowledgement that LUDOLF was right. TR.]

"companion", አብያጽ ; እድ "hand", አእዳው, as a side-form to the usual እደው ; ሥርው "root", አሥራው ; ጽሕም "beard", አጽሐም. In the same way (besides those already mentioned under No. 1): ሐልም, ርግብ, ብርዕ, ንህብ, እልፍ, ክፍል, ድርዕ, ጕንድ, ጥን, ጽርሕ, ጽድፍ, ፍሕም; and from a Feminine Singular-Stem ክረምት "winter", አክራም (along with the outer form ክራማት, § 133, *b*, *α*). To this section perhaps belongs also the *Plurale tantum* አንጻር "view".

Very seldom does a Feminine termination occur with this second Collective-form. It is possible (in accordance with § 36) in words from roots *tertiae gutturalis*:—አቅማሕት ἡ ὀπώρα (Rev. 18,14), from ቀምሕ (1). Farther, from ሐጽ "arrow" (√ ሐጸየ; *cf.* חֵץ), አሕጻት: So too from ጥብ "the female breast" (originally *tertiae infirmae*) አጥባት, and from ስም "name", አስማት. From ፈዐው "adder" (*tertiae infirmae*) comes the Plur. አፍዖት (ት being applied to አፍዐው, from አፍዓው) (2). In አመት "maid-servant" and ሰኰት or ሰኮት "street", the fem. ት is treated as belonging to the root, whence አእማት and አስካት or አስኳት (3).

3 Collective-form, Type አግቡር (*agbûr*). § 137. 3. *A third Collective formation*, but one which was already decidedly dying out, contains an accented (Trumpp, p. 542) *û* after the second radical, and,—like No. 2,—አ as a prefix, Type አግቡር (4). This form is adopted by several words indicating per-

(1) But አዕባእት "wars", from ፀብእ,—which Ludolf quotes in his '*Lex.*', col. 606, in accordance with his '*Gramm.*' p. 108,—should be amended into አዕባአት, a doubled Plural. [But yet Platt retains the reading (in Mark. 13,7) which Ludolf quotes, and so does Praetorius in the reprint. tr.] So too, in Judges 8, 26, the word is not አውጻብት, as Ludolf quotes it in the '*Lex.*', but አውጻባት, a doubled Plural.

(2) *Cf.* Praetorius, '*Amh. Spr.*' p. 189.

(3) [A peculiar use of this second formation,—viz. its employment to form the inner plural of singulars representing the Arabic elative أَفْعَل,—is exhibited in a passage of the *Kebra Nag.* (74 b 23 *sq.*): አፍራጽ ፡ በአስዋድ ፡ አሕማር ፡ በአብያድ ፡ አክዳር "precious stones, red ones along with black, and dark-brown with white ones", the respective singulars (أحمر, أسود, أكدر, أبيض) being directly imported from Arabic.]

(4) In Arabic, أَفْعُل,—which in Ethiopic must have the sound of አግብር,—does not correspond so well as does فُعُول: *Cf.* D. H. Müller,

sons, and by those notions which are usually apprehended as Masculine,—which fact perhaps explains the presence of the vowel *ŭ* instead of *ă*:—አድግ "ass", አእዱግ; ሐቅል "field", አሕቁል (as well as አሕቃል and አሕቅልት); ዕጽቅ "bough", አዕጹቅ (غُذُوق); ሐጽር "fence", አሕጹር; ሐረግ "vine-shoot", አሕሩግ; ሀገር "city" and "country", አህጉር (አህጕር); ገመስ 'small copper coin', አግሙስ. Without Singular:—አይሁድ "Jews", አዕኑግ "ear-rings";—and from a lost Singular, አእሩግ "old men" (used as Plur. for አረጋዊ) (¹).

4. *A fourth Collective formation* contains short *e* (at first probably *ŭ*) after the second radical, and likewise አ as a Stem-prefix (²):—Type አግብር. This form is rather less frequent even than the foregoing one, and seems to have been supplanted partly by No. 2, partly by No. 5. The most of the words which adopt it have another Plural-form besides:—ወግር "hill", አውግር (*aúger*); ቈጽል "leaf", አቍጽል (³); በትር "rod", አብትር (and አብታር); ኈስል "sack", አኈስል (and አኈሳል Gen. 42, 25; 43, 22; 44, 1); ንጥር and ነጥር "gleam", አንጥር; ጻሕል "bowl", አጽሕል (and አጽሕልት); በቅል "mule", አብቅል (and አብቅልት); ሣእን "shoe", አሥእን (and አሥኣን). The Plur. አሕርው "swine" (*aḥréwwᵉ*) belongs probably to a lost Sing. ሐርው; in the Sing. the form ሐራውያ is used (Ps. 79, 14; Lev. 11, 7) (⁴), which no doubt is also a Collective.

4. Collective form, Type አግብር (*ágbĕr*).

5. Of much more frequent occurrence, however, and, next to No. 2 of this Class, the form in most general use,—is the form

5. Collective form, Type አግብርት (*agbért*)

ZDMG XXXVII, p. 366. It is remarkable that nearly all words of this form come from roots *primae gutturalis*.

(¹) On አእኑስ *cf.* DILLMANN's '*Lex.*', col. 771.

(²) أَفْعُل answers in Arabic.—On the Accentuation *cf.* TRUMPP p. 542.

(³) Not ቈጻል, as LUDOLF has it in his '*Lex.*'. [What LUDOLF has in his '*Lex.*', (col. 221) under this word ቈጽል, is the following:—"Pl. አቍጽል ፡ Marc. 11, 8, & ቈጻል ፡ Deut. 12, 2". LUDOLF was thus well aware of the pl.-form which is given in the '*Grammar*' here; and as for the other plural form ቈጻል, which he cites, Prof. BEZOLD communicates a conjecture that "most probably LUDOLF's ቈጻል is a misprint for ቍጻል, which actually occurs as plur. in *Kebra Nag.* 93 b 17". TR.]

(⁴) [*Cf.* also Tab. Tab. 59 (Chrest. p. 121) and also TRUMPP, ZDMG XXXIV, p. 236 *sq.*, and CORNILL *ibid.* XXXV, p. 650. Also Cod. Mon. Aeth. 11, fol. 48 v⁰ reads there ወለሐራውያ.]

just dealt with, 4, increased by the Fem. termination ት:—Type አግብርት (1).

(*a*) This form is taken only in a few cases by the Singular-Stem of the type ግብር: ርእስ "head", አርእስት; ንስር "eagle", አንስርት; ዝእብ "wolf", አዝእብት; ንህብ "bee", አንህብት (as well as አንሃብ) (say *ansért* &c.).

(*b*) The form is usually found in connection with the Singular-Stem of type ገብር, or even from ጋብር: ዐይን "eye", አዕይንት; በድን "corpse", አብድንት; ባሕር "sea", አብሕርት. In the same fashion:—ፋእም, ማእስ, በቍል, ተክል, ነምር(2), ነቅዕ, ነትዕ, ከልብ, ዐጽም, ዐጽፍ, ዘርእ, ገልዕ, ገብር, ጸልዕ, ጻኅብ, ፀርቅ, ፀርዕ and ዕርዕ, ፈትል. Also, from ሐቅል "field" (v. No. 3), በቅል "mule" (v. No. 4), ጸሐል "bowl" (v. No. 4), ሰይፍ "sword" (v. No. 2). From ቀስት "bow" comes አቅስት (for አቅስትት), ት being considered as a radical. From unknown Singular-forms:—አምትንት "sinews", አሥህርት "new-moons"; አፍርኅት "the young of birds" (أَفْرِخَة, אֶפְרֹחִים): probably also አውስት "birds of prey" (Hen. 89,10(3); 90,2; 96,2 for አዕውስት from עַיִט, عائث): From ላህም "ox", አል ህምት; ረድእ "helper", አርድእት (as well as አርዳእ); ባዕል "rich", አብዕልት; መርሕ "guide", "leader", አምርሕት; ዐርክ "friend", አዕርክት. Also the word ከይሲ "serpent", may form, from ከይስ, —the ending ī being left out of account (§ 118),—the plural አክ ይስት, and in contracted form አኪስት (Hen. 20,7) (4), while from ከይሲ አክይስት is formed (§ 140). In like manner ዐንበሳ "lion" (§ 131) forms ዐንብስት (from ዐንበስ, without prefixed አ, because ዐ is taken for አ, the formative bent having here proved misleading). ሥዕርት "hair" (5) forms (from ሣዕር) አሥዕርት.

---

(1) Arabic أَفْعِلَة.—On the accentuation v. Trumpp, p. 543.

(2) [The plural of this word is given in '*Lex.*' as አናምርት, but አን ምርት is also given there on Ludolf's authority. tr.]

(3) [Flemming reads in 89,10 አንስርት instead of Dillmann's አው ስት. tr.]

(4) [Flemming reads here አክይስት instead of Dillmann's አኪስት, besides adopting certain other slight variants of form and order. tr.]

(5) As if ሥዕርት were a *nomen unitatis* (§ 131) and ሣዕር or ሥዕር were only derived. But in point of fact ሥዕርት is used quite as readily in a Collective sense, Ps. 39,17, as in an Individual sense, Matt. 5,36.—እንግዳ

§ 138. II. *Collective words from certain longer Singular-Stems of tri-radical roots.* Several Descriptive words of the type given in § 108, *b*, *c*, as well as those Adjectives and *Nomina agentis* which have been formed by doubling the Second radical (§ 117), have a peculiar formation, differing from the Collective-forms of the other longer Singular-Stems. That formation is brought about by the essential vowel of the Singular-Stem after the second radical being superseded by a short *á*, the fem. ት being appended at the same time. To this *a* and ት the force of a Collective Abstract becomes attached. Moreover the transformation which passes over the Ground-Stem is so marked that this Collective-form looks more like a new formation directly out of the root:—Type ገበርት (1).

II. Collective Words from certain longer Singular-Stems,—the Collective-form being of the Type ገበርት (*găbárt.*)

1. This form comes into use most frequently in the case of Singular-Stems of the type ገባሪ. For these it is the only practicable type of a Collective formation, and meanwhile it occurs oftener than the outer Plural-formation (§ 132, *g*). If it is allowable to come to a conclusion as to Ethiopic, from that which is observed in Arabic, then we may assume that, in forming the Collective in these cases, the doubling of the second radical is given up (as in أَكَرَةٌ from أَكَّارٌ), although it has as yet been impossible to prove this from Ethiopic itself; *cf.* Trumpp, p. 543 (2). Examples:—ቀዳሚ "the first", ቀደምት (*qadámt*); ጸሓፊ "writer", "scribe", ጸሐፍት; ሰያፊ "swordbearer", ሰየፍት; ሐላዪ "singer", ሐለይት; ነዓዊ "hunter", ነዐውት (*na'aút*). But in words *tertiae gutturalis* we have:—ሠዋዒ "sacrificer", "priest", ሠዋዕት; and from roots with final ጠ or ደ:—መሣጢ "rapacious", መሰጥ; ዐፃዲ "reaper", ዐፀድ (§ 54). The same formation occurs in the case of ኀላፊ, ኀዳሪ, ነዳኢ, ሰራቂ, ከዳኒ, ወቃሪ, ወጣኒ, ዐቃቢ, ገባኢ, ጸላኢ, ጸራቢ and others. It is also met with, along with the outer formation, in ሐራሲ, መጋቢ, ሰማዒ, ቀታሊ, ቀዳሒ, ወዓሊ, ዐጻዊ, ደኃሪ,

---

"condition of a foreigner" and "foreigner" (from a Sing. ነጊድ) seems to be based upon a corresponding form in Arabic إِفْعِلَاء.

(1) The corresponding form in Arabic is فَعَل or فَعَلَة, Ewald '*Gr. Ar.*' § 312.

(2) V. on the other hand König, p. 95.

ገበሬ· ገኖዊ "priest of false gods"(1) forms ገነውት and, with the mixed sound, ገኖት; so too ኖላዊ "shepherd" (from the original root נהל + *āwī*) takes ኖሎት (for ኖለውት), as if ወ were a part of the root. Compare also ጠንቋሊ "soothsayer", ጠንቈልት. Farther, the name ረዐይት "giants" is no doubt to be derived from a Sing. ረዓዩ, thus originally "shepherds", "shepherd people".

2. A few Descriptive words, having *ī* after the second radical, also adopt this formation (as well as the outer formation, § 132, 1, *b*); ቀጢን "thin", ቀጠንት; ጠቢብ "wise", ጠበብት; ዐቢይ "big", ዐበይት: So too the Substantive ሐቢ "warranter", ሐበይት; in contrast with which, other Substantives of this type have the formation given in § 140. Finally, the much abbreviated word ማሪ "seer" (§ 114, *c*) has ማረይት (as well as ማርያን and ማርያት).

3. Of the Participle-type ገቡር, ቅዱው "pure", "genuine" has this formation, ቀደውት, unless it be really founded upon a Singular ቀዲው. And thus too ነገሥት "kings" might be derived from ንጉሥ, and it would be unnecessary to refer it to the Singular ነጋሢ which has become of rare occurrence in Ethiopic(2).

III. Collective Words from longer Stems of Triliteral and Multiliteral Roots:— Type ገበርር (*găbărĕr*).

§ 139. III. *Collective Words from longer Stems of Triliteral and Multiliteral Roots have but one single type*:—long *á* after the third-last strong Stem-letter; before it a syllable with a short *a*, which only very seldom is reduced to *e* (or in Quinqueliteral Stems two syllables with two short *a*'s), and after it a syllable with a short *e* (§ 60)(3):—Type ገበርር. This type is followed by all Nominal Stems of Multiliteral roots(4); by all Stems of Triradical roots formed by external increase(4); and lastly by several

(1) It is a matter of doubt whether this word is to be derived from the root ገነወ=ገነየ or from ጋኔን, جِنّ + *āwi*=جِنِّيّ.

(2) ማውታ,— which appears frequently in the phrase እጓለ : ማውታ "orphans", and also in another connection in Lev. 11,40, and Deut. 14,21, Note,—is a word *sui generis*. I recognise in this word the Collective form فَعْلَى (Ewald, '*Gr. Ar.*' § 313). ማውታ answers completely to the Arabic مَوْتَى from مَيِّت, so that እጓለ : ማውታ means literally: "children of those who are dead". But ጠሬው "Pleiades" is merely the Ethiopic pronunciation of ثُرَيَّا.

(3) Just as in Arabic, Ewald, '*Gr. Ar.*' § 314.

(4) With the exception of those which take the outer Plural formation.

Nominal Stems of Tri-radical roots which have a long vowel after the second or third radical, inasmuch as by the laws of Sounds, such long vowels are equivalent to strong radicals in phonetic value. Sometimes, in obedience to laws farther to be explained, the Fem. ት is attached, in connection with which the fundamental rule generally holds good, that Nominal Stems which have ት in the Singular, seldom have it in the Plural. On the accentuation *cf.* Trumpp, p. 543 *sq.*

1. Collective-forms from various Nominal Stems of Multiliteral Roots.

1. First then, let us consider *Collective Formations bound to various kinds of Singular types, which proceed from Nominal Stems of Multiliteral Roots*: ሰንሰል "chain", ሰናስል (*sanâsel*); ሰውሰው "ladder", ሰዋስው; ጠብደን "a fur-coat", ጠባድን; ድንግል "virgin", ደናግል; ቊንጽል "fox", ቈናጽል; but ቀንዲል "*candela*", ቀናዲል (the ī being retained). Also from Singulars which are not yet supported by any passage:—ሰዋትል, ተያፍን, ጐማጕዕ. Farther, with ት, from Singulars which do not have a Fem.-ending (especially words denoting persons, and Names of animals) we have:—ሰይጣን "Satan", ሰያጥንት; ተንባል "ambassador", ተናብልት and ተናብል; ዐንበሳ "lion", ዐናብስት; ዐቅራብ "scorpion", ዐቃርብት; ዐንበር "sea-monster", ዐናብርት; ከንፈር "lip", ከናፍርት and ከናፍር; ቀርነብ "eye-lash", ቀራንብት.—*Vice versâ* (ት of the Sing. being thrown off in the Plur.): ቈንዘእት (and ቈንዘእ) "lock of hair", ቈናዝእ: ጸላዕት "rocky district", ጸዋልዕ. Also with ት, from Fem. Singular-forms: ክልስስት "sheaf", ከላስስት; ጠፍላሕት "piece of money" "*drachma*", ጠፋልሕት (as well as ጠፋልሕ); ሰብድዓት "viper", ሰባድዕት [and ሰባድዓት *Kebra Nag.* 127 b 15 *var.*]. If the Singular-Stem has other terminations, *e. g.* ā, ī, they are thrown off in the Collective-form: ደብተራ "tent", ደባትር; ጸንጸሊ (ጽንጸሌ) "cymbal", ጸናጽል.

Farther, Nominal Stems which have come from Multiliteral roots through abbreviation, and have become tri-radical, follow this formation: ኰኵሕ "stone", ከዋክሕ (the Palatal-Guttural being separated from its *u*); ኮከብ "star", ከዋክብት; ዶርሆ "cock" and "hen", ደዋርህ; ኆኅት "door" (√ኅውኅወ), ኀዋኅው; ሌሊት "night" (√ሌለየ), ለያልይ (لَيَالِ); and the foreign word ሰንበት "Sabbath", ሰናብት. ጽንጽያ "fly, or "swarm of flies" (for ጽንጽንያ) retains የ, to compensate, as it were, for the lost ን: ጸናጺት.

2 Collective-forms from Nominal Stems which have Prefixes (*a—c*).

2. *All Nominal Stems formed by means of Prefixes and belonging to Tri-radical Roots*, follow this Collective formation, viz.:—

(*a*) *Nominal Stems having* **አ** *prefixed*, however it may have originated:—**አንብዕ** "tear", **አናብዕ**; **አንበጣ** "locust", **አናብጥ**; **አንቀጽ** "door", **አናቅጽ**: And with Feminine-ending (Names indicating Persons, and Names of Animals):—**እምሔው** "ancestor", **አማሑት** (for **አማሕውት**); **አንጼዋ** "mouse", **አናጹት**; **አምላክ** "God" (although itself a Collective-form, § 136, 2). **አማልክት**. A theological term has been introduced from the Syriac through the Arabic (from ܩܢܘܡܐ, *Ar. Pl.* أَقَانِيم), viz. **አቃኒም** "essence", "substance".

(*b*) *Nominal Stems having* **ት** *as prefix* (rare): **ትእምርት** "sign", **ተአምር**; **ትዕይንት** "camp", **ተዓይን**.

(*c*) *Nominal Stems in great number formed by prefixing* **መ**. *Participles* and *Nomina agentis*, it is true, have mostly the outer Plural formation (§ 132 *f*.), but sometimes also the inner, and indeed (being Personal-words) taking that form with **ት** appended: **መምክር** "counsellor", **መማክርት**; **መስፍን** "prince", **መሳፍንት**; **መቅርን** "trumpeter", **መቃርንት**; **ሞረስ** "joint-heir", **መዋርስት**; **መዕርር** "mischief-maker", **መዓርርት**; **መኰንን** "judge", **መኳንንት**. On the other hand **መትልው** "he who follows", "successor", forms **መታልው** without **ት**. Names of localities also, of the type **ምግባር**,—which mostly take the outer Plural, in accordance with § 134, *c*, *α*,—participate to some extent in this Collective formation: **ምኵራብ** "temple" (مِحْرَاب), **መኳርብት**; **ምዕማድ** "base of a column", **መዓምድ**.

This form rules almost exclusively in the case of the remaining words which are formed by prefixing **መ**, § 116; and then those Singular-stems, which have not the sign of the Feminine, generally take **ት** in the Collective-form, especially Personal-words: **መልአክ** "ambassador", **መላእክት**; **መንፈስ** "spirit", **መናፍስት**; **መርኆ** "key", **መራኁት**; **ሞሣእ** "antiphone", **መዋሥእት**; **መከየድ** "stool", **መካይድ**. On the other hand we meet with **ማሕፀን** "mother's lap", **መሓፅን** (Gen. 49, 25); **ማሕስእ** "a young one" ('lamb *or* kid' &c.), **መሓስእ**; **ማኅደር** "dwelling", **መኃድር**; or with double form: **መብረቅ** "lightning", **መባርቅ** and **መባርቅት**; **መንበር** "throne", **መና**

ክል "nail", &c.[1]. Feminine Singular-stems generally take the Masculine form in the Collective: መሥገርት "net", መሣግር; መልታሕት "jaw", መላትሕ; መዐልት "day", (from ሞዐልት), መዋዕል; መንሱት "temptation", መናስው (*manásewᵉ* or *manásẃᵉ*); መስኮት "window", መሳክው; መድሎት "weight", መዳልው; መክሊት "a talent", መካልይ (*makályᵉ* for *makáleyᵉ*) or መካሊ; መጽሔት "mirror", መጻሕይ; መርዔት "herd"[2], መራዕይ (*maráʿyᵉ* for *maráʿeyᵉ*). Very rarely do they take the Fem. form then, as in መርበብት "net", መራብብት. Oftener they have both forms side by side: መጥባሕት "knife", መጣብሕ and መጣብሕት; and in the same way መንቀዕት, ሞጻሕት. This occurs with special frequency when the Sing. has already both Masc. and fem. forms: መትከፍ and መትከፍት "region of the shoulder", መታክፍ and መታክፍት; in like manner ማዕጸ and ማዕጸት "lock of a door"; መጾወር and መጾወርት "carrying pole" &c.

From Quinqueliteral and longer Stems: መሌሊት "joint", መለያልይ; መሰንቆ "*cithara*", መሰናቅው and መሰናቁት; መንጦላዕት "curtain *or* veil", መንጦዋልዕ and መንጦዋልዕት.

§ 140. 3. *The same formation occurs with many Nominal Stems belonging to tri-radical roots, which have a long vowel after the first or second radical or have a Vowel-termination*, as well as with those Stems which have been produced from Multiliterals by abbreviation. The language, by inserting or attaching semivowels or by employing አ as a Stem-prefix, endeavours in various ways to enlarge these Stems, which generally have too small a number of firm letters to be capable of taking in the three syllables *a-á-e*, the last of which must be a shut syllable. The choice of the means adopted in such a case is usually guided by the form of the Singular.

3. Same Formation occurring with many Nom. Stems of Tri-rad. Roots which have a long Vowel after 1st or 2nd Rad., or have a Vowel-termination (*a—c*).

(*a*) In words which have *ī* or *ē* after the second radical, being originally Infinitives or Descriptive-words, two vowels come into contact, when *ā* is interpolated after the second radical and the *ī* or *ē* passes into *ĕ*. In that case the two vowels are first of all separated by means of the semivowel ይ[3] taken from the *ī* or

(1) መቃትልት "opponent", "enemy", and መናቅዕት "counterpart" are to be conceived as *Pluralia tantum*.

(2) መርዓት "bride" (√ረዐወ) forms መራዕው, but with the ው usually passing into ይ, መራዕይ.

(3) It is the same in Arabic; Ewald, '*Gr. Ar.*' § 317.

ē; and then ው is usually substituted for this ይ in Ethiopic, in accordance with § 41. Thus from ውሒዝ "river" we have still ወሓይዝት; from ኀጢአት "sin", ኀጣይእ (Lev. 16,16 Note; Josh. 24,19); from ጸሪቅት "cake", ጸራይቅ, with ይ, as also in the Arabic word ጠባይዕ "natural disposition" (طَبَائِع from طَبِيعَة).—On the other hand ው has been inserted in all other cases: ኀጢአት takes oftener the form ኀጣውእ; ኀጺን "iron", ኀጻውንት "iron tools"; ቀሲስ "presbyter", ቀሳውስት. In like manner ደቂቅ, has ደቃውቅ(1) and ደቃውቅት ("Minutes" Hexaëm. p. 27, 1 *sqq.*). So too we have ጸቃውዕ "dropped honey" (صَقِيع); በጻውዕ "performing of marvels" (بَدِيع); and በሓውርት from ብሔር "land". But እግዚእ "lord", which possesses a fourth firm letter in its prefixed እ, throws off the ī without leaving a trace of it: አጋእስት (§ 57). Similarly እስኪት "testicle" (§ 120) has አሳክት [according to Ludolf] (and አሰክት Deut. 25, 11). The plural form ዐጻውንት "doorkeeper" also seems to belong to the Sing. ዐጻዊ; *cf.* Dillmann's '*Lex.*', col. 1022.

Words, having *ā* or *ū* after the second radical, follow the same formation. Thus ክሳድ "neck" has the form ክሳውድ (and ክሰውድ), and ቅናት "girdle" has ቅናውት, without even the interpolation of *a* in the first syllable. From ገራህት "field" comes ገራውህ; from ኅብስት "bread", "loaf" (Fem. of ኅብዝ) ኀባውዝ. On the other hand ዐዋር "blind" (עִוֵּר), with the second radical doubled, has the form ዐዋውርት (Matt. 15, 14 old ed.), and አጽባዕት "finger" has አጻብዕ (أَصَابِع). From the Pl. ሊቃን "*seniores*", "principals" comes a new Collective-form ሊቃውንት (as a designation of office).

(*b*). Words which end in *ā* or *āt*, must first of all reduce this termination to *ī* or *ĭy*ᵉ, whether it has come from *āw*, *āwt* or is merely a feminine termination; but in Ethiopic *ew* or *ew*ᵉ is always employed instead and all the more readily, when,—as in several of these words,— a final radical *ū* has fallen out(2). Thus ሰቀላ

---

(1) This is the form also which is adopted by the editor of the Rom. N. T., Tesfa-Zion [as is pointed out by Ludolf in his '*Lex.*' tr.]

(2) The corresponding Arabic formations in this case are فَعَالِي and فَعَالٍ, from فِعْلَى and فَعْلَاءُ. In ፍናዌ "ways" Lev. 26, 22; Deut. 28, 7 & 25;

"tent" has the form ሰቃልው; ሰኰና "sole of the foot", ሰኳንው; ተኬሳ "shoulder-blade", ተከስው; ወሬዛ "young man", with fem.-ending ወራዙት; ወልታ "shield", ወላትው; ዘብዳ "hide", "pelt", ዘበድው; ጸታ "series", ጸዋትው; ጸዕዳ "white", ጸዓድው; ሰሌዳ "page" (of a book, *σελίδα Acc.*), ሰላድው; ገበታ "plate", "platter", ገበትው. From ኵናት "stabbing-weapon", for which ኲናት is also used, come ኰያንው and ኵያንው (*cf. supra* ከሳውድ).

But words which end in a formative *ē* retain *ī* or *yᵉ* in the Collective-form, without changing it into *we*; generally, however, they take the Fem.-ending at the same time: ግምዔ "pitcher" forms ገማዕይ (and ገማዕው) together with ግምዔያት and ግምዓት; while ሰርዌ "army", አርዌ "beast", ሐርጌ "ram", have ሰራዊት, አራዊት, ሐራጊት. So too ጕራዒት "the region of the neck" ("neck") is probably just a Collective form from ጕርዔ (*cf.* צַוָּארִים), and ጸራዒት "the region of the haunches", a Plur. in like manner from a lost Sing. ጽርዔ.

(*c*). Several other Stems take አ as a prefix, in order to possess four firm letters. Thus from ጋኔን "ghost" "demon" comes አጋንንት; from ብዕራይ "draught animals" (בְּעִיר), አባዕር; and from ከይሲ "serpent", አካይስት (as well as አክይስት § 137, 5, *b*), and in like manner አማዑት "bowels", from a lost Sing. (*cf.* مِعًى, أَمْعَآءٌ and מֵעִים). From ጣዕዋ "young of the flock" comes አጣዕዋ, retaining the concluding *ā* ([1]) (Hen. 86, 2). Curiously enough, several tri-radical Stems even, of the simplest formation, take this Collective-form ([2]): ነክዕ "rust in grain", አናኵዕ and አናኲዕ "insects that injure the grain"; በግዕ and በግዕት "sheep", አባግዕት and አባግዕ; ጠሊ and ጠሊት "goat", አጣሊ; ነምር "tiger" (besides አንምርት § 137,5,*b*), አናምርት ([3]). Farther, ወለት "daughter" takes the form አዋልድ.

IV. A much simpler kind of Collective formation, which

Judges 5, 6; 20, 32 (from ፍኖ), a fem.-ending *ē* is attached (ـَى): *Cf.* Ewald, '*Gr. Ar.*' § 319 *sq.*

([1]) *Cf.* Ewald, '*Gr. Ar.*' § 319.

([2]) Just as in the Arabic أَهْلٌ, أَرْضٌ, Ewald, § 318.

([3]) These formations may be regarded as constituting a new Collective form taken from the most obvious Collective form, such as አንክዕ, አብጋዕ &c., just like አማልክት "gods", from አምላክ.

IV. Traces of a Collective Formation, contrived by applying Abstract Terminations proper to Fem. Sing.

however is now recognisable in Ethiopic only by a few remains, is produced by the use of *Abstract terminations proper to the Fem. Sing.* Thus from the professional designation **ኬንያ** "artificer" (§ 133, *a*, Note), the Collective may be formed externally, as **ኬንያት** (v. *supra*), but also with the termination *at* coming into the place of *yā*, as **ኬኒት** and **ኪኒት**. From **ጸፍንት** "cake baked under hot ashes" comes the Collective **ጸፍንታ** (v. Gen. 18, 6, Note). In particular the termination *yā*, *iyā* (§ 120), which has been derived from the relative pronoun, is employed for this purpose (1): **አንስት** "woman" may, like **ብእሲ** "man", be itself used as a Collective; but when the Plural has to be expressed definitely, the forms **አንስቲያ** and **አንስትያ** "women-folk" are used. In like manner we have **አፉኪያ** "rings" (Ex. 35, 10), and **አርማያ** "Heathen" (from **አርማይ** = **አረማዊ**) Rom. 10, 12 (old ed.).

While a Proper name is held to be indeclinable, it may be raised to the Plural in outward form also by prefixing **እለ** = "those of":—**እለ፡ ያርቡሕ** "giants" Gen. 6, 4; 14, 5, although **ያርቡሕ** may be put in the Acc. **ያርቡሐ**, Gen. 10, 8. So too **እለ፡ ሰብዐቱ፡** "the Seven" (Ludolf, '*Lex.*').

(*c*) *Plurals of Plurals.*

Plurals of Plurals.

§ 141. Besides the power of forming the Collectives which have been described, Ethiopic possesses a peculiar aptitude for deriving, from Collectives produced by inner formation, new Plurals by means of outer, and in fact feminine, Plural-endings. Of such aptitude it has made so extensive a use, as to be in this matter unapproached by any other Semitic speech (2). Every Collective, in fine, is capable of being regarded as a single compact notion; and when such a notion has to be marked as presenting itself in multiplex form, a new Plural of the same may readily be fashioned. A language, endowed with such an aptitude, enjoys a peculiar brevity in expression, and is enabled to render in a single word notions which in other tongues stand in need of several words for their description. The possible applications of this faculty are, however, manifold.

1. Several words in the Plural express only one single notion,

(1) *Cf.* Ewald, '*Gr. Ar.*' § 323.

(2) On the Arabic *cf.* Ewald, '*Gr. Ar.*' § 326.

and therefore admit of a new Plural in the sense of a number of these being present. To this class belong the conceptions brought forward in § 131, 2: አምላክ "God", አምሳል "image", አምጣን "measure", አርያም "heaven", አማዑት "bowels", አቅላም "writing-appliances", መቃብር "grave", ተአምር "sign", መዓርግ "ladder" (from ማዕርግ "step") &c.; and accordingly we have the Plurals:— አማልክት "Gods", (*cf. infra* 5), አምሳላት, አምጣናት, አርያማት, አማዕዋት, አቅላማት, መቃብራት (Matt. 27, 52 & 53), ተአምራት, መዓርጋት. So also ዕፀዋት "groves of trees", Deut. 28, 40, 42; and from ዐጸድ "court", አዕጸድ "farm-yards" and አዕጸዳት "several farm-yards" Josh. 16, 7 &c.

2. In particular the Names of rivers, lakes, mountains, roads, localities, circles, doors, instruments, times, months, countries, and nations,—may, with reference to the parts, of which they consist, stand in the first Plural but with the force of an ordinary Sing.; they then easily admit of a second Plur., often where the simple Plur. might have been expected: አፍላግ and አፍላጋት "rivers", አዕያግ and አዕያጋት "lakes" (Lev. 11, 36), አድባር and አድባራት "range of mountains", ፍናው and ፍናዋት "ways", "roads", አዕዋድ and አዕዋዳት "seats at an assembly" ('circles') Matt. 23, 6.—Also አጽዋን and አጽዋናት "fortifications", አውጻብ and አውጻባት "ear-rings", አውቃፍ and አውቃፋት "bracelets", መዓጽው and መዓጽዋት "doors" (inasmuch as a door itself frequently consists of several parts), ጸናጽል and ጸናጽላት "cymbals", መሰናቁት and መሰናቁታት "*citharas*", መኃትው and መኃትዋት "lamps", አዝማን and አዝማናት "times", አውራኅ and አውራኃት "months", አንጋድ and አንጋዳት "tribes", አህጉር and አህጉራት "cities". In many cases in which those second Plurals are employed, the underlying idea is, "in their various kinds", *e. g.* አዝማናት "times", in their various kinds, such as—'seasons of the year, years, months &c.'; አውቃፋት Hen. 8, 1 "rings of every sort", &c.

3. Every Collective may be raised to the second Plural,—with or without the accompaniment of ብዙኅ "much", "many", or ኵሉ "all"—, for the purpose of expressing Multiplicity, Multitude or Universality. Thus:— አልህምታት ፡ ኵሎሙ (¹) "all oxen"

(¹) [Flemming reads in Hen. 87, 4 ወኵሎሙ; in 70, 3 አሕባለ; and መባዕልት in 53, 3. 4. tr.]

(Hen. 87,4), ኵሉ ፡ አሕቃላት "all the districts", Gen. 13,10; ኵሎን ፡ አኀማላት "all herbs together", Mark 4,32; አሥቃቃት "all the coverings of hair", Numb. 4,25; አዕዋፋት "all birds", Gen. 8,19; አጽባኣት "all wars"; አእናፋት "the nostrils of all the people", Numb. 11,20; አንቅዕታት "every fountain" (Hen. 89,3); or አእላፈ ፡ አእላፋት "myriads of myriad-masses" ('hundreds of millions').

4. If the Plural of an idea is already assignable to a single individual, the Plural of that Plural is formed, whenever it falls to be ascribed to several individuals. Thus, for example, a single man has አማዑት "bowels", but several men have አማዕዋት. Hen. 70,3 reads: 'The angels took አሕባላተ (1) "cords"', because each took አሕባለ (although in the corresponding passage 61,1, only አሕባል appears). For the same reason exactly, መባዕላት (1) "tools" appears in Hen. 53,3,4. One "code of laws" is መጽሐፈ ፡ ሕገግ, but "codes of laws" can be expressed by መጻሕፍተ ፡ ሕገጋት. Thus one may say ዘበጻውዕ ('a man of enchantments') "a wonder-worker", "conjuror", but in the Plural እለ ፡ በጻውዓት quite as well as እለ ፡ በጻውዕ.

5. A distinction must be drawn between the cases which have been named, and cases like the following; when, for instance, ሊቃን "principals" and ነገሥት "kings" enter upon a second Plural for the purpose merely of denoting the dignity still more specially, as in ሊቃናት and ሊቃውንት, ነገሥታት; or when external Plural-endings, either masculine or feminine, are annexed to a Collective-form of a Personal-word, simply to distinguish the gender more definitely. Thus if one means to use with more precision the word መዓስብ (from ማዕስብ) *i. e.* "widowers" or "widows", he says መዓስባን "widowers", and መዓስባት "widows"; and so too መዓቅባን "watchmen". The termination *āt* is also appended to አዋልድ "daughters", making አዋልዳት, to indicate the gender more exactly.

The formation of this second Plural is effected regularly by appending the termination *āt* (seldom *ān*), and is therefore an *outer* form; it is only in the case of አምላክ and ሊቃን that the new Plural takes the *inner* form (2). The ending *āt* is also com-

---

(1) [See Note on p. 315. TR.]

(2) Irregular forms, influenced by Amharic are found in መረዋሕት, መረዋውሕት; መጸዋዕት, መጸዋውዕት.

monly applied externally to Collective Stems which end in the Fem. ት:—አልህምት, አልህምታት; but when the Collective Stem ends in *ūt*, the form *wāt* is preferred to *ūtāt*, although the former is not absolutely binding (§ 133, *b*, *α*):—አማዑት, አማዕዋት; መዓጹት, መዓጽዋት (¹).

III. FORMATION OF CASES.

1. The Nominative and Vocative.

§ 142. The various relations, upon which a Noun may enter in the course of a sentence, — commonly called *Cases* —, are represented in Ethiopic, just as in Semitic languages generally, only by a small number of special formations. A noun takes its place in a sentence, either without being dependent,—in other words as Subject,—or as dependent, whether on a Verb as Object, or on another noun as a Genitive. On these three leading positions, assumable by a Noun in the sentence, rest the Cases which are possible in Semitic languages generally, and which in Arabic,—the most perfect of these languages in this respect,—have received the impress of special Forms. These Cases are: the *Nominative*, —which may also be regarded as including a second species of the independent Noun, viz. the Noun when used in address, or the *Vocative*; the *Accusative*; and the *Genitive*. All those farther relations of a Noun in the Sentence, which are indicated in other languages by various other Case-forms, must in the Semitic tongue be either expressed with the help of Prepositions,—in particular the Dative by means of the Preposition ለ (§ 164),—or made up for by a wider application of the relational powers inherent in the Accusative and Genitive. But even these four Cases, which alone are possible in Semitic, have been by no means completely developed in all Semitic languages; and in Ethiopic some of these Cases have received only a partial development (²).

1. The *Nominative*, as the Subject-Case, has by way of antithesis the Accusative as the Object-Case. As Subject-Case it

(¹) A remarkable form is the irregular አኅመልማላት (Ludolf, '*Lex.*' col. 274) which Ludolf derives from ኅመልማል. [V. also, on a few Plur.-Plur. Forms not yet registered in the Lexicon, *Kebra Nag.*, *Introd.* p. XVIII.]

(²) In ZDMG XXXIV, p. 758 Haupt very properly opposes the view put forward by Hommel,—that the original Semitic had a distinction of Cases.

is without relation; while the *Casus obliquus* invariably involves a relation to some word on which it depends. Originally the unrelated Case was not denoted in Semitic languages by any special form(1); but the pure Nominal Stem, affected only by gender and number, was able to take its place in a sentence at once, as independent word, when that was called for. Northern Semitic tongues, at least, have remained at this stage. Arabic, however, has advanced a step. As it denoted the dependent character of the Object by a termination affixed to the Nominal Stem, so it denoted also the circumstance of independence by terminations(2). Ethiopic in this matter rather sides with the Northern Semitic. But at all events it exhibits in the greater number of Nominal Stems a different vowel-ending for the independent Case from that of the Object-Case, and thus in a certain sense shows a Nominative-ending contrasted with the Accusative-ending. In the department of the Pronouns the Personal Pronoun in the independent Case has the ending *ū* = "he", for the masculine gender, and *ī* = "she", for the Feminine. The same thing is found too in several other words, particularly in the Numerals, *e. g.* **አሐዱ** "one" (*m.*), **አሐቲ** "one" (*f.*). Now, seeing that Arabic also takes *u* as the termination of the Nominative of a Noun, and that a like phenomenon presents itself in kindred languages(3), and that farther it is to be assumed, in accordance with phonetic laws (§ 38), that Ethiopic Nominal-Stems also ended at one time in vowels, and that some other vowel-ending must thus have existed wherever the vowel-ending of the Accusative was wanting,—we are brought to the supposition that in Ethiopic also, those Nouns which now end in the third radical, had once a vowel-ending in the independent Case. Various traces,—chiefly in the written character—, indicate that this ending was the short indeterminate *e*(4). The fundamental antithesis between Subject-Case and Object-Case was thus at one time also signified in most instances by contrasted terminations. But Ethiopic seems never to have made any attempt to denote in addition, by means of different vowel-endings, the other contrast which

---

(1) V. Ewald, '*Hebr. Spr.*' § 202, *a*.

(2) Exactly as the relations of the verb are, or were, denoted by the kind of vowels which form the terminations.

(3) V. Ewald, '*Hebr. Spr.*' p. 450, Note 1.

(4) Otherwise Barth, ZDMG XLVI, p. 685.

obtains between Nominative and Genitive: it was Arabic alone that took this forward step. The one termination *e* was charged in Ethiopic with signifying both the Noun in its independent condition and the Noun as depending upon another Noun. In this way any specific meaning in that *e* as a mark of the Nominative was taken from it. Besides, the entire development of vowel-expression tended to render the short *ĕ* more and more fugitive, and in certain circumstances to oust it altogether (§ 37 *sq.*); and therefore, in the end, Ethiopic completely gave up marking the Noun in a merely general way, and as a consequence the Nominative, by any vowel-ending,—while on the other hand it continued regularly to mark the Accusative. It was only in certain cases, viz. those in which the demand was enforced by syllabic structure or by the phonetic character of the last radical, that the *ĕ* of the Nominative-Genitive had to be more tenaciously retained, as has been pointed out in detail in § 38.

And if even the Nominative is not outwardly marked, still less is the *Vocative*, which does not present so direct an antithesis to any Case, as the Nominative does to the Accusative. The Nominal Stem, as a rule, suffices for the Noun in address. And yet Ethiopic from another side has made a start in the independent development of a Vocative. Just as in other languages, the Vocative may here also be indicated outwardly by the apposition of an interjection,—the accented (Trumpp, p. 544) particle ኦ (§ 61), *e. g.* ኦገብር፡ ኄር "(O) Thou good servant!" Luke 19,17; ኦአንስትየ "O my wives!" Gen. 4,23; ኦትውልድ፡ ዕሉት "O perverse generation!" Luke 9,41; ኦአብድ "Thou fool!" Luke 12,20; ኦእገሌ "O So-and-so!". In Ethiopic a farther step has been taken, and አ has been appended to the Noun (¹), and a beginning made of a true Case-form. This kind of Vocative-form may at one time have been more extensively used in the language, but it is now confined to a few words which are frequently employed in the Vocative. The aspirate then regularly falls away from አ (§ 47)(²).

(¹) Just as other Cases, in Semitic and other languages, have originated in the attachment of short words, chiefly from Prepositions or Pronouns.

(²) That the relation of the Construct State is not affected by this form is maintained by Ludolf, '*Gr.*' III,7, appeal being made to Ps. 83,1&4;

Thus we still frequently meet with እግዚአ "Lord!", *e. g.* in Ps. 8,1; Matt. 7,21; እሞ (*Org.*) and እሙ "mother!"; ብእሲቶ "woman!" John 4,21; 20,13 & 15. How largely አ in this combination has parted with any emphatic meaning which it had(1), is evidenced by the fact that now and then a second አ is prefixed to a Vocative which has been formed in this way:— አብእሲቶ "O woman!" John 2,4; Matt. 15,28; *cf.* PRAETORIUS, ZDMG XLVII, p. 388 *sq.*

Besides, it is only the word አብ "father", which possesses a special Vocative አባ (Gen. 27,18; 22,7; Matt. 11,25; Luke 15,18, 21 &c.),—probably an Accusative (as in the Arabic يَا رَجُلًا), since the Accusative of አብ, at least before Suff. Pronouns, has still the form አባ (§ 154)(2). In the large majority of cases, however, even in Ethiopic, the Vocative is expressed by the pure Nominal Stem: ገብር ፡ እኩይ "wicked servant!" Matt. 18,32; 25,26.

2. The Accusative: Usual Marking. When such Marking is not exhibited.

§ 143. 2. *The Accusative.* Of the ancient antithetic markings of the Nominative and the Accusative, Ethiopic has retained and carried on the latter at least. In contrast to the *ĕ* of the Nominative-Genitive, the Accusative was denoted by a final *ă*, both in the department of the Pronouns and in that of the true Nouns. In this respect Ethiopic completely agrees with Arabic. But this *ă*, in certain cases, takes the fuller form ሃ *hā*; and, when everything is duly considered, there cannot remain a doubt that ሃ is the ground-form, of which *ă* is only a truncated remnant. This is an impersonal demonstrative particle (§ 62) with the force of "here" or "there"(3), and in origin it is certainly identical with the Hebrew ָה of direction. It thus indicates primarily direction towards an object,—towards which the action is directed as being its peculiar object: አፍቀረ ፡ ብእሲተ "he loves (in the direction

but in his own edition of the Psalms he has printed, not እግዚአ ፡ ኅያላን, but እግዚእ ፡ ኅያላን. [እግዚአ ፡ ኅያላን, however, appears in the "Book of the Mysteries of Heaven and Earth" (ed. J. PERRUCHON, Paris 1903), p. 9, l. 1; *cf.* also PRAETORIUS, ZDMG LVIII, p. 487.]

(1) [On the farther development of this ending *ō*, *cf.* NÖLDEKE, '*Beitr. z. Semit. Spr.*', p. 72 and Note 3.]

(2) *Cf.*, besides, אַבָּא [and NÖLDEKE, l. c. p. 71.]

(3) Of like meaning are the similarly enclitic ሂ, and the affixes ኔ and ን (§ 160) derived from another demonstrative root; the Amharic Accusative-sign *en* proceeds from ን.

of) a woman". And this explains at once not only the appropriateness of such marking to indicate the subordination of an Object to a transitive verb, but also the peculiar use of the Accusative (in Semitic generally, and therefore in Ethiopic) for relations, which in other languages are expressed by other Cases. The Accusative is employed here, like the Locative in Sanskrit, in space-reference to express continuance in a place or motion towards a place, in time-reference to reply to the question 'When?' or 'How long?', and in fine to indicate any reference whatever in a statement, *e. g.* ተገልበበት ፡ ገጸ "she was veiled,—as to her face" (v. § 174 *sqq.*). These various meanings of the Accusative are fully explained by the fundamental signification of the particle ሃ. The following details regarding the Accusative-formation fall to be noticed.

The original form of the Affix ሃ, which invariably takes the accent (Trumpp, p. 544), still appears in Proper names pretty regularly. To be sure it is not absolutely necessary for a Proper name to take the sign of the Accusative, in order to be turned into that Case, for, precisely as being a Proper Name, it is accounted fixed and indeclinable and never enters upon the Construct State, and is thus enabled to dispense with the sign of the Accusative. Indeed in the majority of cases occurring in existing Manuscripts, the Accusative-marking of Proper Names is wanting, especially when the Accusative is easily recognised as such from the context, *e. g.* Josh. 22,23; 24,4. But when a sign does make its appearance, it is always *hā* (never *a*) ([1]), because it is not so closely knit to the Stem as is the form *a*, but is more externally attached, and also because it does not alter the ground-form of a Name which ends in a vowel. Above all, in the case of Compound Names,—which are very common in Ethiopic—, this more external attachment of the sign is altogether necessary. Thus: ይሁዳሃ "Judah" (*Acc.*) Matt. 1, 2; ዘርአ ፡ ማርያምሃ; እግዚአብሔርሃ; ደብረ ፡ ዘይትሃ. For numerous instances of Proper Names in the Accusative, with and without ሃ, v. Matt. 1, Gen. 4. This ሃ, so applied, denotes farther all the relations which are otherwise expressed by the Accusative, *e. g.* ቤተ ፡ ልሔምሃ "to Bethlehem" Matt. 2, 8; but they may also be conveyed without ሃ, *e. g.* ወበጺሖ ፡ ቅፍርናሆም "and when he came

([6]) [And yet *a* seems to occur in the *Kebra Nag.*, p. 12 (Note 14). where in four MSS. the Acc. of ህንድ "India" is given as ህንደ.]

to Capernaum" Matt. 8, 5. ሃ is frequently met with in poetry, attached to words even which have the ለ of direction prefixed to them: ሰላም ፡ እብል ፡ ለኤርሞላዎስሃ ፡ ቀሲስ (Ludolf, '*Gr.*').—But even in appellative Nouns this ሃ appears, although very rarely, instead of the usual *a*, *e. g.* ጎልሃ "the cave" (Epist. Zar'a-Jacob, in Ludolf's '*Comm.*'); *cf.* also እገሌሃ. Moreover it is still preserved as *ā* (without the breathing) in a few words used adverbially, § 163.

The sign of the Accusative is usually attached to appellative Nouns (Substantives, Adjectives, Infinitives) as an unaccented *ă*(1) (*cf.* Trumpp, p. 544 *sq.*), both in Singular and Plural forms. When the word ends in a consonant, after parting with the *ĕ* of the Nom.-Gen., *a* is simply annexed: ንጉሥ "king", ንጉሠ, Plur. ነገሥተ; so with አበ "father" (Matt. 3, 9; 15, 4); ዕንቍ "precious stone", ዕንቈ; እኁ "brother", እኆ, Gen. 43, 6 & 7, or እኀወ Gen. 24, 29. Words which have *ā* in the last syllable, lengthened by the influence of an Aspirate, retain this *ā* in the Accusative, *e. g.* ኀጣእ "want", Acc. ኀጣአ. But when the Stem ends in a vowel, a distinction has to be made between *ē*, *ō*, *ā* on the one hand and *ī*, *ū* on the other. With *ē*, *ō*, *ā* the Accusative sign does not combine in the form ሃ as might have been expected, but *ă* blends with these vowels into *ē*, *ō*, *ā*, whatever their origin may have been (§ 39). Forms like ዕንዚራ "*cithara*", ጽጌ flower", አርዌ "beast", ሐራ "army", ሀበ "dew", ግልፎ "carved work" are the same in the Accusative as in the Nominative; and possible ambiguities may have to be avoided by a periphrasis of the Accusative with the help of a Suff. Pron. and a following ለ (§ 172). There are no Nominal Stems ending in *ū*. When *ū* does occur, *e. g.* in ኵሉ "all", or in አሐዱ "one" (*m.*), it is of Pronominal origin; and these words accordingly form their Accusative after the manner of Pronouns (§ 157 *sq.*). Of words ending in *ī*, those in which *ī* is a Suffix Pron., like አሐቲ "one (*f.*)", also fall under the rules of the Pronouns (§ 158). But, over and above, there are many other Stems which end in a radical *ī* (*e. g.* መፍሪ "fruitful"), or in a formative *ī* (*e. g.* ጠሊ "goat" for ጠሊይ), or in the Adjective-ending *ī*: It is the rule for these not to harden the *ī* into *y*, but to turn the *i-a* of the Acc. into its equivalent *ē*, in accordance

(1) There is a special reason for the length of the *ā* in the Accusatives of several words, before Suffix Pronouns (§ 154).

with § 40: ብእሲ "man" takes the form ብእሴ; ደብረ ፡ ሠረቃዊ Gen. 10,30; ሐረሳዊ ፡ ብእሴ Gen. 49,15. ጠሊ also forms ጠሌ; and only in cases in which $\bar{\imath}$ alternates still with ey^e (§ 51), as in መፍርይ and መፍሪ, መክልይ and መክሊ, ባሕርይ and ባሕሪ, is the Accusative-form መፍርየ, መክልየ, ባሕርየ the usual one, although the other is not impossible.

Alongside of this, the usual Accusative-form with the majority of Nominal Stems, cases occur, in which the form is abandoned, or is not exhibited. The discussion of these cases properly belongs to the Syntax, but still it seems more to the purpose to bring them together at this stage. 1. When the Accusative-construction is continued through several members of a sentence, it is now and then parted with in the later members, after the Accusative has been indicated in the first member of the series, or in the opening members, *e. g.* Numb. 19,16; Hen. 22,1 (¹),—or in the case of a word which is set in apposition to the Accusative, as in Ex. 31,18(²). 2. When the Accusative is definitely determined by means of a word introduced by ዘ, whether this be a mark of the Genitive, or the Relative, the form of the Accusative-relation may on that account be renounced, *e. g.* Ex. 35,22 (F. H.) አውቃፌ ፡ ወኵሉ ፡ ሰርጉ ፡ ዘወርቅ (for ወኵሎ ፡ ሰርጎ); Numb. 8,8 ይንሥኡ ፡ ላህም ፡ ዘዓመት (for ላህመ); Numb. 19,10 & 21 ይኩን ፡ ሕግ ፡ ዘለዓለም (for ሕገ, *e. g.* Gen. 17,7) (³). This is explained by the Attraction of the Noun, —very common in Ethiopic—, effected by the Relative pronoun; and if ዘ as Genitive-sign exercises the same influence, this is simply the result of the very lively consciousness, possessed by the language, of the original relative-force of the Genitive-sign (⁴). 3. Finally, when Suffix Pronouns are attached to the Accusative, the Accusative-marking, in certain cases, gets lost. The same thing occurs when an Accusative is found in the construct state (§ 144).

(¹) [FLEMMING's reading here has the Acc.-construction throughout. TR.]

(²) On the phrase ዕለት ፡ እምዕለት or እምዕለት ፡ ዕለት v. DILLMANN's '*Lex.*' col. 925; *cf.* also ሀገር ፡ እምሀገር Sir. 36,31.

(³) *Cf.* also *Chrest.* p. 52, line 5; PLATT, *Didasc.* 43,9 &c. (KÖNIG, p. 70); also LUDOLF, '*Gr.*' VI,2, 13.

(⁴) On the other hand it is not to be considered a case in point, that after ከመ "like" or "as", the Acc. can never stand,—a circumstance which LUDOLF found so very remarkable (*e.g.* Ps. 37,21; Cant. 8,6); for ከመ is a Prep. and always stands in the Constr. St. with reference to what follows.

3. The Genitive Relation:— (a) The Construct State.

§ 144. 3. To express the third of the possible relations, viz. the *Genitive relation*, or,—to use more general language—, the relation of subordination of one noun to another, Ethiopic makes use of that device which of old has been the common property of all Semitic tongues,—the so-called *Construct State.* Although this Construct State does correspond in many cases to the Genitive relation of other languages, it is capable of a much wider and more multiform signification. It may indicate every possible form of subordination of one noun to another, denoted in Non-Semitic languages by means of Prepositions or Compounds. But besides the Construct State, Ethiopic makes use of still other expedients, to indicate the Genitive relation, in the narrower sense of the expression.

(a) *The Construct State.* The oldest Semitic has a device for subordinating one Noun to another, which is not unknown even to the Indo-European tongues. It is a kind of combination or apposition of words, in which the more general idea, requiring to be more precisely determined, is placed before a special and determining idea, associating itself therewith and subordinating it. The meaning and force of this condition lie just in the close association of the two words, and in the emphatic accent assumed by the subordinate word as being the determining element, just as if our own words 'Landlord', 'Householder' were written 'Lord-Lánd', 'Holder-Hóuse', meaning 'Lord of the land', 'Holder of the house'. North-Semitic farther shows that by merely uttering the two words more closely together, and at the same time accentuating the last, and thereby of course pronouncing the first as short as possible, this relation is established. But a relative particle may also be inserted between the two words, expressly announcing the relativity which obtains between the two. This is the variety of the Construct State formation which appears in Old Hebrew,—in the so called 'binding vowel' of the Constr. St., and it is this variety which has become the predominating one in Ethiopic. But the particle of relativity is not prefixed to the second (or determining) word, —as in Amharic,—nor affixed thereto,—as in Arabic,—by which latter proceeding the second word would be reduced to an ordinary Genitive, and the necessity perhaps removed for placing the two words together at all. The particle is, on the contrary, attached to the first word,—the word which is to be determined—, and marks it as having a relation to a second and immediately following word, so that the arrangement of the two words, in the order of succession thus marked, continues to be an absolutely necessary one. This particle then, which is appended like a termination to the subordinating word, in the case of such a pair,—that is to say, the Ending of the Construct State—, in Ethiopic is invariably *a*. Now such a termination coincides externally with the termination of the Accusative, but it is self-evident that it cannot be originally identical therewith, as it expresses something entirely different, and is appended, not to what is subordinated, but to what subordinates. Before Pronouns, which are subordinated as Suffixes to a Construct State, this Ending takes the form of *ī* (§ 153) and in several cases the still fuller form of *īa* (§ 150). And when it is farther considered that even in Hebrew an *ī* appears as the binding-vowel of the Constr. St., and that Amharic expresses the Genitive by prefixing the relative particle የ (corresponding to the Ethiopic ዘ),—the inference is unhesitatingly drawn, that the termination *a* is merely an abbreviation of the fuller *ia*, and that *ia* itself means nothing other than "the—of" or "who", "which" and is developed from an original *i*, just as is ዘ from ዝ (§ 65). For example, ኆኅተ፡ ቤት means originally: "doors which—house", "doors relating to—house", "doors of a house" or "house-doors"(¹). But the termination *ia* did not become *ē*,—as it might have done, according to Ethiopic phonetic rules,—for there was no need to establish a long vowel dwelling on the Tone between the two closely united words, but as a rule it was curtailed into the shorter *ă*. In many cases, however, as we shall see, *ē* has been maintained (§ 167), but in those cases it is perhaps of a different origin.

An Ethiopic word then, whether Sing. or Plur., is put in the Constr. St. by attaching to it the unaccented (TRUMPP, p. 544) termination *a*. Accordingly when such a word enters upon the Constr. St., its termination is undistinguishable from that of the Accusative.

(¹) TRUMPP adheres to the above explanation of the termination *a* (pp. 544, N. 1; 557, N. 1): v. on the other hand HALÉVY, '*Journ. as.*' VII, 1, p. 453 *sqq.*; and PRAETORIUS ZDMG XXVI, p. 433; XXVII, p. 643. PRAETORIUS seems to be right in emphasising (*Amh. Spr.*, p. 126) the fact that the Amharic የ cited by us is itself only a weakened form (through ዝ) of ዘ.

e. g. ፈነወ ፡ ጸሐፍተ ፡ ሕዝብ "he sent the learned men of the nation". The rules for attaching it are the same as for the *a* of the Accusative (§ 143). To words ending in a consonant *a* is simply annexed: *e. g.* መንግሥተ ፡ ሰማያት "kingdom of heaven" (from መንግሥት); ጸሐፍተ ፡ ሕዝብ "the learned men of the nation" (from ጸሐፍት); አበ ፡ ደም "avenger of blood" (from አብ "father") (1). It is to be noticed that words ending in an Aspirate and having *ā* in the last syllable retain this *ā* in the Constr. St., as ኀጣእ, ኀጣአ; ላዕላዕ, ላዕላዐ. In the case of words which end in *ā*, *ē*, *ō*, *a* disappears in these vowels: እንስሳ ፡ ገዳም "beasts of the field", ትክቶ ፡ አንስት "course of a woman", ጊዜ ፡ ሣልስ ፡ ሰዓት "time of the third hour". Words in *ū*, like ኵሉ, አሐዱ, do not admit of any Constr. St. at all (§ 157). With words in *ī*, *a* blends with *ī* into *ē*, following the rules given in § 143:—ብእሲ "man" forms ብእሴ; ገብረ, ገብሬ; ሐቤ ፡ ምእት "centurion" (*lit.* 'prefect, ሐቢ, of a hundred') Matt. 8, 5: but መስተስሪ has መስተስርየ, and in like manner ማሪ "seer" has ማርየ. Alongside of these, ማሬ and the like are also possible at least, although on the other hand, in the most ancient times, such a form even as ብእስየ seems to have been in use (2). There is no Constr. St. from Proper names.—On the significations of this Constr. St. relation, see § 184.

Periphrastic Indication of the Genitive by Prefixing Rel. Pron. to Determining Word.

§ 145. (*b*) *Periphrastic indication of the Genitive.* The expression of the Genitive by means of the Constr. St. always demands that the two words,—the word to be determined and the determining one,—be ranked immediately together: no third, extraneous word, as for instance an adjective, can ever come between the two (3); for otherwise the ordered combination, which is the very condition of the Constr. St.-relation, would be destroyed. In this way the language was much hampered in the arrangement of its words. Besides, there are many words, such as Proper names, which do not admit of any Constr. St.; and there are others, like those which end in *ā*, *ē*, *ō*, which present no difference in form whether they are in the Constr. St. or in the Absolute St. Finally, the marking of the Accusative cannot be distinguished from that of the Constr. St., in those cases in which the word to be put in

---

(1) It is not accurate for Ludolf to say that አብ, እኁ, ሐም, አፍ *must* indicate the Constr. St. circuitously by means of Suff. Pron. and ለ.

(2) V. the 'Rüppell Inscriptions', I, 1; II, 2. (3) [V. Note to § 185. tr.]

the Constr. St. enters at the same time upon the Accusative. Accordingly it is not to be wondered at, that this, the oldest method of denoting the Genitive relation, was found insufficient for the language, and that a new method was contrived, conducing to clearness of expression and freedom in the arrangement of words. This new denotation rests, it is true, upon the method of indicating the Genitive relation found in the Ethiopic Construct State. Just as in that case, recourse here is had to a Relative Pronoun to indicate the relativity of the situation. But there is this great difference between the old and the new method, that in the latter there is no necessary apposition of the words, and that accordingly the Relative Pron. is not affixed to the word which has to be determined or limited, but is prefixed to the determining one. The Relative Pron. which is employed for this purpose is not the more ancient የ (1), but the form which in later times became the common one, viz. ዘ (2),—a circumstance which is itself a proof that the whole of this mode of marking is of secondary origin. The force of this Genitive-marking cannot be attended with any doubt: **አክሊል ፡ ዘወርቅ** is "crown-which-gold" or "crown-related to-gold", that is "crown of gold" or "golden crown"; **እግዚእ ፡ ዘቤት** "lord-relative to-house", "lord of the house". The position taken in the sentence by a Genitive formed in this way is completely unfettered. The expression may run **ዘወርቅ ፡ አክሊል** quite as well as **አክሊል ፡ ዘወርቅ**, or **አክሊል ፡ ዐቢይ ፡ ዘወርቅ**. But the vigorous life, which the original relative meaning of this Genitive sign still exhibits in the language, is witnessed to, not only by the proof incidentally brought forward towards the close of § 143, but by the circumstance that this sign may, just like the Relative Pron., assume the distinctions of Gender and Number. True, it is allowed and is by far the most usual practice, to denote the Genitive by **ዘ** merely, even when the Noun on which it depends is feminine or stands in the Plural, *e. g.* **ቤተ ፡ ልሔም ፡ ዘይሁዳ** "Bethlehem in Judah" Matt. 2, 1, or **አበግዕ ፡**

(1) Which is still retained in Amharic for this purpose.

(2) Ethiopic in this usage agrees wholly with Aramaic, which employs דִּי, ܕ for this purpose. HALÉVY farther compares ذُو; v. MORDTMANN, ZDMG XLIV, p. 191 *sq.*—**ዘ** is prefixed to the word, which it has to put in the Genitive, invariably without 'separating points' (§ 147).

ዘተሐጕለ ፡ ዘቤተ ፡ እስራኤል "the lost sheep of the house of Israel" Matt. 15, 24; but when the governing word is feminine, the feminine form እንተ at least may take the place of ዘ, *e. g.* ማርያ ፡ እንተ ፡ ያዕቆብ "*Maria Jacobi*" Matt. 27, 56; ዐይንከ ፡ እንተ ፡ የማን "thine eye of the right side" ("thy right eye") Matt. 5, 29; አንቀጽ ፡ እንተ ፡ እግዚአብሔር "the gate of the Lord" Ps. 117, 19; and when the governing word is in the Plural, the Plural Genitive-sign እለ may be used: አልህምት ፡ እለ ፡ ውእቱ ፡ ዐጸድ "the oxen of that farm" Hen. 89, 5; አድባረ ፡ ቆባራት ፡ እለ ፡ ክረምት "the mountains of the murkinesses of Winter" Hen. 17, 7.

This denotation of the Genitive by means of ዘ has so completely gained the upper hand, that it has pretty much pushed aside another method which is possible, and which is in very frequent use in Hebrew, that namely which employs the preposition ለ (לְ), v. § 186.

On another possible method of indicating the Genitive, by means of a Pron. Suff. with following ለ, v. § 172.

B. PRONOUNS AND NUMERALS.

I. PRONOUNS.

I. Pronouns: —1. Demonstrative Pronouns.

§ 146. Many peculiarities have been admitted and retained in the formation of the persons, numbers, genders and cases of Pronouns, which have never found admittance with Nominal Stems derived from Conceptional roots.

1. *Demonstrative words developed into Personal Demonstratives* (*Pronomina Demonstrativa*).

(*a*) The Demonstrative word, readiest to hand, is ዝ "this" (*m.*), § 62, pronounced *zĕ* with a short, sharp utterance, and always accentuated (Trumpp, p. 546). In its first form (Nom.-Gen.) it ends, like other Nominal Stems, in the short, indeterminate *e*. It forms its Fem. with the feminine ending *ā* (§ 126) ዛ "this" (*f.*), and the Accusative with the usual Accusative-ending *ă* (§ 143): thus the Acc. masc. is ዘ "this" (*acc. m.*), *e. g.* Ex. 20, 1, and the Acc. fem. ዛ "this" (*acc. f.*), *e. g.* Matt. 17, 9. This pronoun is still used pretty often in the Nominative, but not so often in the Accusative. As the particle is a very short one, it usually rests against the preceding or succeeding word, *e. g.* ዝሕዝብ Matt. 15, 8; ኢይትከሀልዝ Matt. 19, 26; ዝንቱ 13, 54; ለዝ 8, 9; ዝሰ 27, 47; ዝኑ

Gen. 43, 29; ምስለዝ ፡ ትውልድ Matt. 12, 41; ዝትውልድ 24, 34; ዛቲ 26, 13; ወዝኮነ 21, 4. Only very seldom is it separated from the following word by ፡ as an independent word, as in Gen. 42, 28.

Precisely on account of its shortness the unsatisfactory form of this word made itself felt in the language even in early times, and it was therefore combined with another demonstrative,—with ተ (§ 62), originally akin to ዝ; and as ተ is attached at the end of the combination, it takes the signs of gender and case. It adopts the vowel *ū* in the Nom. Masc., and in the Fem. *ī* (§ 65) = "he", "she": ቱ "this" (*m.*), ቲ "this" (*f.*) (¹). Instead of this *ū* and *ī*, *ă* appears always in the Accusative of both genders, thus ተ "this" (*acc. m.* & *f.*). The compound in the Fem. is simply ዛቲ "this" (*Nom.*), ዛተ "this" (*Acc.*), *e. g.* Ruth 3, 13. But in the Masc. instead of ዝቱ, ዘተ, the form becomes (§ 58) ዝንቱ *zéntū* (²) (*Nom.*), ዘንተ *zánta* (*Acc.*). Both elements of the compound are inflected. This longer form ዝንቱ, ዛቲ, ዘንተ, ዛተ is much more frequently used than the other.

The plural of ዝ, ዘ is formed from another Demonstrative root, as happens too in the rest of the Semitic tongues, viz. *al*, *la* (§ 62), and in fact by the combination of these two forms,—so that in this way the notion of plurality is conveyed by "*the* (Sing.) + *the* (Sing.)" = "*the* (Plur.)", "these". The rendering in Ethiopic is Masc. እሉ (³), Fem. እላ (*ellū*, *ellā*),—forms which probably have been curtailed from longer forms *ellūm*, *ellōm* and *ellān* (v. *infra*). Both are used with considerable frequency. እሉ in particular is very often used, *e. g.* Matt. 15, 20 & 32; but እላ occurs too, *e. g.* Matt. 5, 19; Ps. 89, 11; Hen. 22, 3; 71, 12. They have been too closely pruned towards the end, to be any longer capable of a special Acc.-form, and they are accordingly used very seldom indeed in the Accusative (*e. g.* እሉ Hen. 37, 3). The Accusative is either indicated by Suffix Pronouns and ለ, or is expressed by means of the Compound form. The Fem. እሎን is met with as well as እላ, *e. g.* *G. Lal.* p. 55, line 20; p. 56, lines 4 & 19; p. 59, line 23.

(¹) I am unable to agree with the explanation of this ቲ given by König, p. 124. [*Cf.* now Brockelmann, ZDMG LVIII, p. 521; Fischer, *ibid.*, p. 871 *sq.*; and Barth ZDMG LIX, p. 161 *sq.*]

(²) This is also Ludolf's accentuation; but see Trumpp, p. 546.

(³) Corresponding most nearly to the Rabbinical אִלּוּ.

Now just as the Singular ዝ, ዘ is generally strengthened by the addition of ቱ፡, so also is the Plural, by the application of ቱ፡ to the original forms, እሉ and እላ:—እሎንቱ፡, more rarely እሉንቱ፡ "these" (*m.*), እላንቱ፡, more rarely እላንቲ፡ "these" (*f.*)(1). It is remarkable in this compound that the second member indicates no distinction either of number or gender, manifestly because, if the element ቱ፡ were also to form a plural (ቶሙ, ቶን, § 148), the Stem would become too long; ቱ፡ in this case on the contrary abides in the Sing., and that with both genders, having the force of a strengthening "there": as it were "these *there*". In the Accusative, inflection does not appear in the elements እሎን, እላን, which have no longer a vowel-ending in which such inflection might become audible, but in the element ቱ፡, which (*ut supra*) passes into ተ: እሎንተ, more rarely እሉንተ "*hos*" (Hen. 93, 2; Matt. 10, 5; 13, 53, in the last passage, accompanying a feminine noun), እላንተ "*has*" (Hen. 82, 1; Ruth 3, 17, *et saepe*).

In signification ዝ, ዝንቱ፡ &c. always refers to what is at hand and well-known; and only when it is repeated, as in ዝንቱ፡ ፡ ለዝ ንቱ፡ "this—to that", can it denote on its second appearance what is at a greater distance. Both Masc. and Fem. may be used impersonally (*i. e.* as neuters); but the Masc. occurs much the more frequently in such a use.

(*b*) In order to form a Demonstrative which should point to what is more distant or unknown, the demonstrative pronoun, just described, was combined with the root *ka*, developed personally into *kū* (§ 62). Such is the origin of the Masc. ዝኩ *zékū*(2) "this there", *i. e.* "that" (*m.*). For the Fem., however, *kū* is not combined with ዘ but with a feminine form እንተ (*ént*) "this" (*f.*), derived from the root *an* (§ 62), making እንትኩ "that" (*f.*) (*e. g.* Hen. 85, 5), not እንትኪ, as ኩ has become rigid and admits of no distinction of gender or number. Even the differentiation of the Accusative is not common with *kū*, and when it does occur *ū* takes refuge in the

(1) እሙንቱ፡, እማንቱ፡ (§ 148) correspond exactly in form. For the rest, እሎን appears to have come from እሎም (*cf.* ውእቶሙ), influenced by the following *t*.

(2) But according to Trumpp, p. 547, *zekú*.—The particle ሰ is sometimes inserted between the two elements: ዝሰኩ; v. Dillmann's '*Lex.*' col. 1057, line 1. [But contrast Praetorius, '*Beitr. z. Assyr.*' I, p. 26.]

guttural, and ኩ becomes ኰ. The Accusative Masculine has accordingly the form ዝኰ (the first member remaining uninflected), Hen. 89, 44, 51; Gen. 27, 17 (Note); and the Accusative Feminine runs እንትኩ, እንትኰ and እንተኩ (Prov. 15, 18). Seeing then that the concluding ኩ has lost to some extent its susceptibility of inflection, this form of the pronoun was still farther combined, taking in, as an additional element, ቱ፡ (v. *supra* under *a*). But instead of ዝኩቱ፡,—which never occurs(1),—a shorter, dissyllabic form was used for the Masc., viz. ዝኲቱ፡ and ዝክቱ፡ (*zékuetū* and *zéktū*) "that" (*m.*), § 36; and instead of እንትኩቲ፡, or in its shorter form እንትክቲ፡, the form እንታክቲ፡ (*entắk*^{e}*tī*) "that" (*f.*) came into use for the Fem.,—contrived by the insertion of a feminine *ā* bearing the accent of the word (Mark 11, 21; 14, 25, *et saepe*). The Accusative is regularly formed also from the strengthened Masc.-form, thus: ዝክተ and ዝኲተ "that" (*m. acc.*), *e. g.* Gen. 27, 16; Lev. 1, 8; Numb. 5, 18 & 25; Josh. 21, 40. እንታክተ as a fem. acc. for "that" has not yet been met with.

As እንተ has no Plural, the Plural for both genders is formed from *ella*; and from the shorter form ዝኩ, እንትኩ the Plural is (*m.* & *f.*) እልኩ, while from the longer ዝኲቱ, እንታክቲ፡ it is (*m.* & *f.*) እልኲቱ፡ or እልክቱ፡: the fem. እላክቱ፡ is also met with, Josh. 4, 11. The እለ in this compound has been deprived of its vowel-ending(2); and the doubling of the ለ has probably been also given up, if we must read *élkuetū*, *élketū* and not rather *ellékuetū*, *elléktū*. On the feminine use of እልኩ and እልክቱ፡ v. for instance Matt. 25, 7, 8, 11; Hen. 9, 8. እልኩ can no longer form an Accusative, but there is taken from እልክቱ፡ the Accusative እልክተ or እልኲተ, *e g.* Ex. 34, 4; Hen. 89, 60. This plural is, besides, often replaced by እሙንቱ፡, እማንቱ፡.

With special reference to the signification of this word, it is to be noted that the forms ዝኩ, እንትኩ &c., because they are used in pointing to the unknown, are employed also in the sense of an indefinite article, like "a", "any", when a speaker is introducing a new subject, known to him but as yet unknown to the hearer, *e. g.* Hen. 89, 29,—or for what is undetermined and yet

---

(1) For the passage cited by König, p. 53, viz. 4 Esr. 11, 25, some farther examination of the Manuscript is recommended.

(2) Like אֵל from אֵלֶּה.

is under a certain degree of limitation, like "the (person) concerned", "the (point) in question", *e. g.* Hen. 72, 3, 5. It is also used in a contemptuous sense, like *iste*, *e. g.* in Gen. 37, 19.

Neither a Demonstrative nor any other Pronoun can enter upon the Construct State. They may, however, appear as Genitives dependent upon words in the Constr. St., *e. g.* ደመ ፡ ዝክቱ፡ Gen. 9, 6 (v. § 184), but they also frequently form their Genitive externally by means of the prefix ዘ.

2. Relative and Interrogative Pronouns. § 147. 2. *Relative and Interrogative Pronouns.*

(*a*) The demonstrative root ዝ serves as *Relative Pronoun* in Ethiopic, without any farther combination([1]), but it differs from the ዝ which means "this", by its being always pronounced with *a*, as ዘ "who" or "which" (*m.*); for the accentuation v. Trumpp, p. 547. The corresponding Fem. does not take the form ዛ (for a reason to be mentioned presently) but እንተ "who", "which" (*f.*), derived from the Stem *an*, which also appears in fem. form as እንቲ in እንቲኩ, § 146, *b*. The Plural of both of these, without distinction of Gender, is እለ (*élla*) "who", "which", derived from the Compound Pron. *el-la*, which is present also in እሉ and እልኩ (§ 146). When it is considered that these three forms end in *a*, and differ as Relatives from the corresponding Demonstrative-forms precisely by this ending, no doubt can remain that this *a* is responsible for the Relative force of these forms. Accordingly, since *a* already exists as an essential element in the Ground-form, no Accusative-form is admitted in these three words. Just as ወርቀ signifies both "gold" in the Accusative and "gold" also in the Acc. and Constr. St. together([2]), so ዘ, እንተ or እለ may be employed directly as an Accusative. These Relatives may take the Genitive by subordinating themselves to some Construct State, as in ብእሲተ ፡ ዘሞተ "the wife of him who is dead", or by having prefixed to them the external mark of the Genitive, ዘ:—ዘዘ "whose" (*m.*), ዘእንተ "whose" (*f.*), ዘእለ "whose" (*pl.*).—But just as in some other Semitic tongues the relative pronoun has become rigid and no longer susceptible

---

([1]) Like ܕ in Aramaic.

([2]) [This is a somewhat obscure statement of the fact that ወርቀ or any ordinary Accusative-form, stands not only for the Accusative, but also for the Construct State, whether that Constr. St. happen to be Nominative, Genitive, or Accusative. tr.]

of the distinctions of Gender and Number, so in Ethiopic the form ዘ may be used not only for the Masc. Sing., but also for the Fem. Sing. and for the Masc. and Fem. Plural; and this use of ዘ, as a general Relative-sign, is almost as common as the differentiation of Gender and Number, *e. g.* አበው፡ ዘተጋብኡ፡ በኒቅያ "the fathers who assembled in Nicaea"; እላንቱ፡ ዘኀርዩ "*hae quas elegerunt*". This is particularly the usage, when the notion, referred to by the Relative Pron., is expressly set forth in the relative sentence itself by means of a Noun or a Suff. Pron. [the Arabic عائد], and when accordingly a general Relative-sign is all that is needed at the beginning of the sentence, *e. g.* ዘሞተት፡ ብእሲት "*quae mortua est femina*", or ዘእምኔሃ "*ex qua*", ዘእምኔሆሙ "*ex quibus*". But of course እንተ and እለ can never be employed as general Relative-signs (¹).

If the impersonal "that which" or "what" has to be expressed, ዘ is usually employed for that purpose, not እንተ, *e. g.* ዘይትሐወስ "that which moves" (Gen. 1, 24); ዘየሐውር "that which goes" (Ps. 8,8). The correlative notion, "he" ("he, who"), is included,—as in all Semitic languages,— in relatives like ዘ, እንተ and እለ, whether these be in the Nom., Gen. or Acc. (v. § 201); but the notion may be farther and specially brought out, if any emphasis attaches to it, by means of ውእቱ or some Dem. pron., *e. g.* in ውእቱ፡ ዘመጽአ "he, to wit, who has come". Farther ዘ may express the notion contained in *quicunque*, "whosoever", *e. g.* Matt. 10,11, 14 (v. § 201), or it is doubled,—at least in the form ዘ (though scarcely in the forms እንተ and እለ), in order to gain this meaning, thus:—ዘዘ "who—who"="whosoever". The short particle ዘ, like ኀ (§ 146), almost always rests against another word,—on rare occasions against a word that precedes it (a preposition), but usually against the word which comes next after it in the Relative sentence which it introduces.

(*b*) *The Interrogative as Substantive* is መኑ (²) "Who?", compounded out of the Interrogative root *ma* (§ 62) and the Demonstrative root *na* (§ 62), which, by means of an appended *ū*,

(¹) In the sentence quoted by Ludolf,—እግዚአብሔር፡ እንተ፡ ታፈቅር፡ ጽድቀ, እንተ does not stand for ዘ as relating to God, but is a Conjunction=እንዘ, thus, "*Deus justitiae amans*".

(²) On the accentuation v. Trumpp, p. 547 *sq.*

has a personal turn given it, in the form of *nū* (like *tū*, *kū*, § 146). It is always used personally and substantively, exactly like our "Who?", *e. g.* እመኑ "From whom?" (Chrest., p. 97, line 11), and it is employed farther as a rigid form, alike for the Fem. Sing. and for the Masc. and Fem. Plur., *e. g.* መኑ ፡ ይእቲ ፡ ዛቲ "Who is this (*f.*)?" (Org.); መኑ ፡ አንትሙ "Who are ye?" (Ex. 10, 8); መኑ ፡ ውእቶሙ ፡ እሉ "Who are these?" (Hen. 40, 8); and only occasionally is it expressly put into the Plur. by prefixing እለ (in accordance with § 140 *ad fin.*): እለ ፡ መኑ ፡ እሙንቱ ፡ አኀውየ "Who are my brethren?" Matt. 12, 48; Hebr. 3, 16. But መኑ, like other pronouns ending in *ū*, may form an Accusative: መነ "Whom?" (*e. g.* Gen. 37, 15; Josh. 24, 15) (1).

This word መኑ, as being the Personal Interrogative, must always be used, but only then, — when enquiry is made after Persons. In the case of things (*masc.* and *fem.*) recourse is had to an Interrogative with an Impersonal or Neuter formation, ምንት "What?", fashioned from the Stem መን (which is also involved in መኑ) with the Fem.-ending ት (2). This ምንት is (like መኑ) found both in the grammatical Plural and the grammatical Fem., *e. g.* ምንትኑ ፡ ዛቲ ፡ አበሳ "What manner of transgression is this?" Josh. 22, 16; ምንት ፡ ውእቱ ፡ እሉ ፡ እሙንቱ (3) "What manner of things are these?" Hen, 52, 3; and it likewise regularly forms an Accusative ምንተ "What?" (*Acc.*).

Both መኑ and ምንት are employed alike in Independent and Dependent Interrogation, *e. g.* Matt. 10, 11; Hen. 12, 1, and both are often strengthened with interrogative particles (§ 198). In a negative sentence, whether it be a direct negative or an interrogative sentence with the force of a negative, both forms

---

(1) In the *Org.* Ludolf even found ሃ (§ 143) combined with መነ: መነሃ ፡ እጼውዕ "Whom shall I call?". *Cf.* also Matt. 27, 21, Roman Ed.; Isaiah 51, 12 *var.*—Notice the change from መነ to መኑ in *Chrest.* p. 104, line 25 *sq.* and p. 105, lines 3, 5.

(2) This ት accordingly represents the neuter gender here, in the department of the Pronouns, where the Fem., when used with reference to persons, has *ī* or *ā* for its sign. On this point and on the connection of ት with the Indo-European Neuter-ending, v. Ewald, '*Hebr. Spr.*' §§ 172, *a* and 173, *a*.

(3) [Flemming reads here እሙንቱ ፡ እሉ, changing the order of the last two words. tr.]

assume the signification of an *Indefinite Pronoun* = "any one who", "anything which" (1); and then with the help of ኢ they indicate the notion of "no one", "nothing",—in which combination the enclitic particle ሂ or ኒ "also" may be applied, and ወ "and" be prefixed over and above, *e. g.* ኢመኑሂ "no man" Ex. 34, 24; Matt. 8, 28; ወኢመነሂ "no one at all" (*acc.*) Matt. 17, 8; ወኢምንትኒ "nothing whatever" Cantic. 4, 7; ወኢምንትሂ Matt. 27, 12; ወኢከመ፡ምንት "and not as anything", *i. e.* "as nothing", Ps. 38, 7; እፎ፡ ይክል፡ መኑሂ "How can any one?" Matt. 12, 29. Both forms may also fall into the Genitive by having a noun placed before them in the Constr. St., or externally by means of ዘ,—ዘመኑ "Whose?"; ዘምንት.

Besides the neuter ምንት another form also makes its appearance, viz. ሚ "What?" (On its origin *cf.* § 63). This particle is often used, it is true, as a mere Interjection or Exclamatory Adverb, "How!" "How much!" (*e. g.* ሚበዝኁ "How many are!" Ps. 3, 1), but still it often also has the force of ምንት "What?", and in that case it is nearly always joined to the succeeding word: ሚሀለወክሙ፡ ትግበሩ "What will ye do (then)?" (v. § 89), Hen. 101, 2; ሚላዕሌነ "What is that to us?" (*lit.* "What upon us?") Matt. 27, 4; John 21, 22; [ሚላዕሌየ "What is that to me?" *Kebra Nag.* 84 b 18;] ሚሊተ፡ ወለከ "What have I to do with thee?" (*lit.* "What to me and to thee?") 1 Kings 17, 18. But upon the whole this ሚ is obsolete.

(*c*) መኑ at least cannot be used directly *as an Adjective*; on the contrary a periphrasis must be employed for that purpose, made up of መኑ and ዘ, *e. g.* "What man is able?" መኑ፡ ውእቱ፡ ሰብእ፡ ዘይክል *i. e.* "Who is the man that is able?". As to the Pronoun ምንት, although such a periphrasis is likewise employed with that interrogative, it may more readily take another noun in apposition (§ 198). But, over and above these, the language has also a special *Interrogative Adjective* (§ 63), አይ (2) "Which?" or "What?" (adj.), "What sort of?", which has been developed into an Adjective out of an old Interrogative particle אֵי, and takes numbers, genders and cases. So much of its original inflexibility,

---

(1) [The indefinite pronoun may also be expressed by ዘ (*cf. supra*) or by አይ (v. end of this §), and occasionally also by ብእሲ (*cf.* § 173).]

(2) For the accentuation v. Trumpp, p. 548.

however, still adheres to it, that it has no special form for the Fem. Sing., nor, so far as known hitherto, for the Masc. Plur.; and as in all probability it is not used with reference to Persons, but is only connected with words descriptive of things and notions, the other possible forms suffice for all cases. Thus the usage in the Singular is በአይ፡ ሥልጣን "By what authority?" Matt. 21,24; በአይ፡ ሰዓት "At what hour?" Matt. 24,42; ለአይ፡ መዋዕል "For what time?" 1 Pet. 1,11; በእንተ፡ አይ፡ ኀጢአት "On account of what sin?" Hen. 21,4; and in the Plural አያት "Which?" (viz. ትእዛዛት) Matt. 19,18. In the Acc. Sing. it takes the regular form አየ, *e. g.* አየኑ፡ ቤተ "What house?" Acts 7,49. Like መኑ and ምንት it is used both in direct and in indirect interrogation, and like these too it is often strengthened by enclitic Interrogative particles, particularly by ኑ (Matt. 22,36; Acts 7,49). On አይ as an *Indefinite Pronoun*=*quicunque, qualiscunque, quilibet, quisquis cf.* DILLMANN's '*Lex.*', col. 795. *sub* (2).

3. Personal Pronouns:— (a) The Third Pers. Pron.

§ 148. 3. *Personal Pronouns* (*Pronomina Personalia*).

(*a*) *The Third Personal Pronoun,* in accordance with § 65, takes the form ውእቱ፡ in the Masculine and ይእቲ፡ in the Feminine, "he", "she"(1). Like the other personal pronouns, it is originally Substantive in character, but it is also used quite generally, just as the Hebrew הוּא(2), as an Adjective in the sense of *αὐτός*, "same" "even the", and also, in contrast with ዝ and ዝንቱ፡ for "that"(3), to indicate what is somewhat remote; or, when united to ዝ or ዝኩ, to express "this very", "that very", *e. g.* Hen. 89,9; 106,16; or when united to ዘ, "who" "even he who", *e. g.* ዘውእቱ፡ "even he who" Matt. 10,4; Hen. 15,4 (*pl.*). Now in so far as ውእቱ፡ is a Substantive Pron., it takes no independent Accusative-form (v. § 149); but as an Adjective it admits of an Accusative, which is contrived, just like that of ዝንቱ፡ and ዛቲ፡, by

(1) For the accentuation v. TRUMPP, p. 548 *sq.*

(2) In Tigre ሒቱ፡, ሒታ &c. have still retained the original ה of הוּא; *cf.* NÖLDEKE, '*W. Zeitschr. f. d. K. d. M.*' IV, p. 294 [and LITTMANN, '*Zeitschr. f. Ass.*' XII, p. 193]. V. also D. H. MÜLLER, ZDMG XXXVII, p. 349 and N. 2; 393, N. 2.—On the ī in the formation of the Fem., v. BARTH, ZDMG XLVI, p. 685 *sqq.*; on the secondary form ይኢቲ፡, v. KÖNIG, p. 119.

(3) Often in particular it takes the place of the Plural of ዝኩ.

changing ቱ፡ or ቲ፡ into ተ, thus:—ውእተ, ይእተ. The word has two forms of the Plural, according as emphasis is put on the first or the second member of the combination. In the first of these cases, ቱ፡ continues unchanged (as in § 146), and only the elements ውእ and ይእ are put in the Plural, which then takes the form እሙንቱ፡ *emúntū* (originally *ŭmûmtū*) in the Masculine, and እማንቱ፡(1) *emántū*(2) in the Feminine, like እሎንቱ፡, እላንቱ፡. If the emphasis rests upon the second element of the Compound, the Plural takes the form of ውእቶሙ for the Masc., and ውእቶን for the Fem. In this case the element ውእ is used without change for both genders, and thus comes to be employed in the Fem. instead of the ይእ of the Singular.—In the Plural ቶሙ (where *ō* seems to have sprung out of *ū* by a farther broadening of the vowel), the final *ū* is to be judged of, just as it is in هُمُ [= Assyr. *šunu*] the side-form of هُمْ. In ቶን (a formation from ቱ፡, not from ቲ፡, and sprung out of *tu-ān*) the final vowel *a*, which is possible according to the Arabic هُنَّ, has never been made use of, or, if so, has fallen away again. The distinction between these two forms of the Plural appears originally to have been that the first was used rather for the Pronoun as an Adjective, and the second for the Pronoun as a Substantive. But later usage has almost wholly obliterated this dis-

(1) When it is considered that the Plurals formed from ቱ፡ are ቶሙ, ቶን; from ሁ, ሆሙ and ሆን; and from እሌ, እሎን and እላን,—the inference drawn here, as well as in § 132, is that one mode of forming the Plural is the lengthening of the Singular-ending combined with a nasal utterance. Accordingly a Plural *ūm* is expected from the Sing. *u*[e] (ውእ), while from *i*[e] (ይእ) no Plur. at all seems to have been formed. This *ūm* was then strengthened by the farther attachment of the Plural-ending *ōm*, *ān*, by which the Gender was denoted at the same time, and the first *ū* was thereupon shortened: whence came *umūm*, *umān*, as in הִמּוֹן, אִנֵּין; ܗܢܘܢ, ܗܢܝܢ. The difference in gender in these Plural terminations is signified by a difference in the vowel,—*ū* marking the Masc., and *ā* the Fem.,—just as in ሁ and ሃ, while *m* is the Nasal corresponding to *ū*, and *n* the corresponding one to *ā*. V., however, Trumpp, p. 548, N. 1, [who gives a very different account of the origin of the Form. tr.]

(2) [Praetorius, '*Aeth. Gr.*'. apparently does not recognise the distinction noted here, for he marks the accents, p. 23 like Trumpp, *ĕmūntū́*, *wĕ.-'ĕtṓmū*, *ĕmāntū́*, *wĕ'ĕtṓn*. tr.]

tinction, and retained only one trace of it, in the preference shown for ውእቶሙ rather than for እሙንቱ, whenever this Pron. represents the copula (§ 194). There is no Accusative attached to either of the two forms of the Plural; when called for, it is usually indicated by a suff. Pron. followed by ለ (1).

(*b*) *The Second Personal Pronoun* has the form አንተ "thou" (§ 65), and although no *ū* makes its appearance in this Masculine form, as might have been expected according to § 146 *sqq.*, manifestly because *ta* itself is just an abbreviation from *twa* ,—yet it is faced in the Feminine by the regular formation in *ī*: አንቲ. The Plural in the Masc. is አንትሙ, in the Fem. አንትን. አን ትሙ is manifestly formed from አንቱ, after the analogy of the Plural ውእቶሙ from ውእቱ, by *tū* becoming *tūm* and, with the addition of *u*, *tūmu*, the *u* of *tū* being finally shortened into *ĕ* (2), as the accent rests upon *án*-(3). With less certainty can it be determined whether the Fem. ትን is formed from ቶ or ቲ, and whether accordingly it was at first *tōn* or *tīn* (*cf.* أَنْتُنَّ and أَنْتُمْ).

The First Pers. Pron.

(*c*) *The First Person* አነ "I" is of common gender. It has arisen, it is true, like the Arabic أَنَا, out of an original אָנֹכִי (§ 65) by casting off the last syllable כִי; but the Suffix Pronoun ኒ (§ 149) (4) shows that at one time a second form אני was known also in Ethiopic. The Plural has the form ንሕነ (*néḥna*), and has come, like نَحْنُ and אֲנַחְנוּ, from אָנֹכִי by repeating the entire Stem *anaḥanaḥ* ("I" + "I" = "We"), and gradually shortening this double form.

Formation of the Accusative and Genitive in the Pers. Prons.

§ 149. *Formation of the Accusative and Genitive in the Personal Pronouns.* The three Persons in these Pronouns, — in Ethiopic just as in the rest of the Semitic languages,—whatever be the gender or number, share in the peculiarity of no longer

---

(1) But *cf. e. g.* Numb. 21,25 [and *Kebra Nag.* 52 b 3.]

(2) According to König, p. 120 this alteration depends upon a kind of Dissimilation.

(3) [But Trumpp says, p. 549: "It has farther to be noticed particularly. about አንትሙ that the Tone does not rest upon አን, as Dillmann thinks, but upon *émmu*". Praetorius, '*Aeth. Gr.*' p. 23 also gives the pronunciation —*ăntémmū.* tr.]

(4) Also the Amharic እኔ.

possessing any independent Accusative-form. They cannot even, like the other Pronouns, be subordinated in their independent form to a Constr. St.(1), nor do they admit of the prefix ዘ by way of Genitive-sign. But in order to meet both cases of subordination,—both that under the Verb, in the Accusative, and that under the Noun, in the Genitive,—forms of the Pronouns specially abbreviated and sometimes greatly altered have been contrived, which are joined to the Verb or Noun by way of attached particles (*enclitica*), and which are therefore usually called *Pronomina Suffixa*. These particles blend so completely with the word to which they adhere, that the entire combination has only one Accent. The same Suffixes are used for both kinds of Subordination; but, in the case of the First Pers. Sing., a somewhat shorter form has been developed for the Genitive-Suffix than for the Suffix of the Accusative,—which is to be explained as being after all merely a result of the different method of attachment in the two cases. These appended forms of the Personal Pronoun are as follows (2):—(1) for the Third Pers. Sing. Masc. ሁ, Fem. ሃ; Plural Masc. ሆሙ (3), Fem. ሆን. They are abbreviations (§ 62) of ቱ፡, ታ, ቶሙ, ቶን, as forming second member in ውእቱ፡, ውእቶሙ &c. To be sure, the form of the independent pronoun in the Fem. Sing. is ይእቲ፡ and not ይእታ, *ī* being more widely used in Ethiopic in general as the corresponding feminine to *ū* in the department of the Pronouns. And yet ዛ, confronting ዝ, and እንታክቲ፡ show that even here *ā* was a possible vowel for the Fem. Pronoun. Besides, after ቱ was reduced to ሀ, *ā* associated itself more readily than *ī* with both forms, through the influence of the Aspirate. In this respect Ethiopic coincides completely with the other Semitic languages. (2) The form for the Second Person Sing. Masc. is ከ, Fem. ኪ; Plural Masc. ክሙ (*kĕmmū*), Fem. ክን (*kĕn*). These forms too are just as clearly abbreviations of አንተ, አንቲ፡, &c., except that, in accordance with §§ 65 and 101, *t* has in each case passed into *k*,—a

Suffix Pronouns.

---

(1) But *cf.* ወእምድኅረ ፡ ውእቱ ፡ ተናስሐ *Phlx.* 164.

(2) For the accentuation v. Trumpp, p. 549.

(3) That ሆሙ may stand for the Sing. ሁ, cannot be proved from Luke 2,4; John 19,27; Acts 1,20,—as is the opinion of Ludolf de Dieu, '*Critica Sacra*', p. 226 on Is. 53,6, and of Gesenius, '*Lehrgeb.*' p. 216,6, and Schlottmann, '*Inschrift Eschmunazars* p. 111.

transition which here came about, all the more readily that the introductory syllable እን had fallen away, and that the retention of ተ (*t*) was no longer called for by the proximity of a dental Nasal. Farther, in ከሙ which invariably has the accent, the long *ū* (*kūmu*), although no longer retained, is yet made up for by the doubling of the *m*, just as in كُنَّ, הֵמָּה &c. (3) The Suff. Pron. of the First Person takes, in the Sing., the form ኒ as a Verbal Suffix, and የ as a Nominal Suff.—In the Plur. the Suffix is ነ for both Verb and Noun. Of these Suff.-forms ኒ is an abbreviation of እኒ—a possible side-form of እነ (§ 148, *c*), while ነ has been shortened from ንሕነ. የ however has been developed in the first place from *ī*,—which still frequently occurs in Ethiopic(¹),—in the same way as يَ from ـِي(²), specially to avoid confounding the Suff. Pron. with the binding-vowel *ī* (§ 153). The *ī* itself is manifestly nothing but an abbreviation of *nī*,—a very ancient abbreviation, however, common to the Semitic tongues, and to be explained in fine by the fact of the Suffixes aiming at a still closer union with the Noun than with the Verb. All the Suffixes thus start with a consonant, although the four forms of the Third Pers. easily part with their Aspirate. The forms ከሙ, ከን, ሆሙ, ሆን are always accentuated: the others have given up their accent, ኒ, ነ, የ, ሁ, ሃ, however, merely transferring it to the immediately preceding binding-vowel, whereas ከ, ኪ leave unchanged the accent of the word to which they are attached(³). A special observation must be farther made, on the *signification* of these Suffixes,—viz. that the Suffixes of the Third Pers. may refer to the Subject of the clause, and may thus have a reflexive meaning. This holds good with the Nominal Suffixes in particular, *e. g.* ሎቱ፡ "for himself", Gen. 5,3; ድኅሬሆሙ "behind them" (*hinter sich*), Gen. 9,23.—It is not so common with the Verbal Suffixes, § 151.

It is in the guise of these Suffix-forms then that the Personal Pronouns are usually appended to Verbs and Nouns, when they have to take the Accusative or the Genitive. (On the manner of

---

(¹) In ሊተ (§ 166), ቢ (§ 167), እንጻኢ (§ 163).

(²) Ewald, '*Gr. Ar.*' § 97.

(³) [But *cf.* on the whole subject of the accentuation of the Suffix Pronouns, Trumpp, p. 549 *sqq.* tr.]

attachment v. § 151 *sqq.*). But seeing that cases may also occur, in which such attachment of the Pronoun is not available, or in which a special emphasis rests upon the Pronoun, which cannot be suitably expressed in the form and position it has as Suff. Pron., the language has fashioned some other special forms by means of which a Personal Pronoun may be placed independently and emphatically in the Accusative and Genitive, and even in the Nominative.

§ 150. *Expression of the Acc., Gen. and Nom. of a Personal Pronoun, on which a special emphasis rests.* **Expression of the Acc., Gen. and Nom of a Pers. Pron. on which a Special Emphasis rests.**

(*a*) When a Personal Pronoun in the *Accusative* possesses special emphasis, by being either tacitly or expressly set over-against another Person, and by having on that ground (§ 196) to be brought into prominence by means of an independent and emphatic position in the sentence, Ethiopic may employ in such a case the expedient of combining a Pronominal Substantive, meaning "self" [*Selbstheit*], with the Genitive Suffixes of the Personal Pronouns, in the sense of "the self of me", *i. e.* "myself" &c. This Substantive is (v. § 65) ኪያ, to which the Suff. Pronouns are applied(1):— **Emphatic Acc.-form of *Pers. Pron.***

		Sing.			*Plural.*
1st Pers.		ኪያየ	1st Pers.		ኪያነ
2nd „	m.	ኪያከ	2nd „	m.	ኪያክሙ
	f.	ኪያኪ		f.	ኪያክን
3rd „	m.	ኪያሁ	3rd „	m.	ኪያሆሙ
	f.	ኪያሃ		f.	ኪያሆን.

This Accusative is in very frequent use, but it is available only when a certain emphasis is associated with the Pronoun: ዘኪያየ ፡ ተወክፈ ፡ ተወክፎ ፡ ለዘፈነወኒ "he who receiveth *me*, receiveth him that sent me" Matt. 10,40; ኪያሁ ፡ ባሕቲቶ ፡ ታምልክ "*him* only shalt thou worship" Matt. 4,10; እፎ ፡ እንከ ፡ ፈድፋደ ፡ ኪያክሙ "how much more then (clothe) *you*" Matt. 6,30; ኪያሃ "even it" (the city Gazer) Josh. 16,10. At the same time an impersonal use may be made of the Third Pers. Sing. Masc.: አኮኑ ፡ አሕዛብኒ ፡ ኪያሁሰ ፡ ይገብሩ "do not even the heathen the very same?" Matt. 5,48. And such a Pronoun may even be more exactly

(1) For the accentuation v. Trumpp, p. 550.

determined by means of a Noun in the Accusative, employed like an Apposition: ኪያሃ ፡ ምድረ "even it, the land", *i. e.* "the land itself" Josh. 12, 6; ኵሎ ፡ ኪያሁ ፡ መጽሐፈ "actually the whole book" Hen. 89, 70. 77; በኪያሆን ፡ መዋዕል ἐν ταῖς ἡμέραις ἐκείναις Judith 4, 6; 6, 15; 8, 1. And in Hen. 67, 11 the pronoun even stands with an Accusative (or Nom.) set in anticipation absolutely(1): ወኪያሁ ፡ ማየ "and as to even it, the water", *i. e.* "and the very water". *Cf.* also ወአልበሶ ፡ አልባሰ ፡ ኪያሁ *Chrest.* p. 29, line 25, and ወአኮ ፡ ኪያከ ፡ ባሕቲትከ G. Ad. 40, 7.

Emphatic Gen.-form of Pers. Pron. (*b*) In order to form an emphatic, or even a merely independent *Genitive* from the Personal Pronoun, the three forms of the Relative-sign, which is also the Genitive-sign, ዘ, እንተ, እለ, are combined in Ethiopic with the Genitive Suffixes of the three Persons, the binding vowel *í-a* (§ 153) being interposed(2).

Sing. m.	ዚአየ	ዚአከ	ዚአኪ	ዚአሁ	ዚአሃ
	ዚአነ	ዚአክሙ	ዚአክን	ዚአሆሙ	ዚአሆን
f.	እንቲአየ·	እንቲአከ	እንቲአኪ	እንቲአሁ	እንቲአሃ
	እንቲአነ·	እንቲአክሙ·	እንቲአክን·	እንቲአሆሙ·	እንቲአሆን
Plur.	እሊአየ	እሊአከ	እሊአኪ	እሊአሁ	እሊአሃ
	እሊአነ	እሊአክሙ	እሊአክን	እሊአሆሙ	እሊአሆን·

In signification these forms have always the force of Possessive Adjectives: ዚአየ, እንቲአየ, እሊአየ mean "mine", [*lit.* 'who *or* which (*m.*, *f. sing.*, or *pl.*)—of my possession'] referring respectively to possessions which belong to the Masc. Sing., the Fem. Sing., & the Plur. But they are never placed simply beside the Noun, like other adjectives (after the fashion of *uxor tua*), but demand always the Constr. St. in front of them, thus: ብእሲተ ፡ እንቲአከ "the wife of thine" *i. e.* "thy wife". When then they have to be dealt with as ordinary adjectives, they must once more be preceded by the Genitive-sign: ብእሲት ፡ ዘእንቲአከ "the wife who is in *or* of thy possession". Thus: በፍትወተ ፡ እንቲአሁ "by his own lust" Jas. 1, 14; በኵሉ ፡ ርኵስ ፡ ዚአሆን "in all their (*f.*) impurity" Hen. 10, 11; 41, 5 & 8; 63, 3; and in Acc.,—ርኢነ ፡ ኮከበ ፡ ዚአሁ "we have seen his star" Matt. 2, 2; 6, 33; or ዐውዱ ፡ ዚአሁ "in that circuit of his", *i. e.* "round about him" Hen. 47, 3. It is only when the noun,—

(1) [*i. e.* by way of *absoluter Vorhalt.*]

(2) For the accentuation v. Trumpp, p. 550. [For the lengthening of the ኣ before the suffix in old Mss., v. *Kebra Nag.*, *Introd.* p. XVI.]

to which these forms refer and by which they regulate their gender and number,—stands already in the Constr. St. (whether because a Suff. Pron. is already appended to it or because another word depends upon it) that they can be set beside the noun freely and simply, *e. g.* በአተ ፡ ክዕበት ፡ እንቲአሁ (for በ″ ፡ ክ″ ፡ በአተ ፡ እ″) "his double cave" Gen. 23, 9; ወዓዲ ፡ ነፍሶሂ ፡ እንቲአሁ (where እንቲአሁ merely emphasises again the ō of ነፍሶ) "and even his own life" Luke 14, 26; አርዳኢከ ፡ እሊአከ "thine own disciples" Luke 5, 33; in the last case the Possessive may be placed first: ለእሊአሁ ፡ አርዳኢሁ "to his own disciples". Farther, the Relat. Pron. may fall away, if the Possessive come first in order: እንቲአሆሙ ፡ ሕይወት (for ዘእ″) Hen. 38, 6. Since in this way then the Possessive is always conceived of as a Substantive to a certain extent, it may easily assume the position of a Predicate: ዚአከ ፡ ይእቲ ፡ መንግሥት "Thine is the kingdom"(1) Matt. 6, 13, or that of a Subject:—ተስእልዎ ፡ እሊአሁ "his (followers) asked him" Mark. 4, 10. In particular, the form that comes first to hand (*masc.*), ዚአየ, ዚአከ &c., has often completely the character of a Neuter: "mine" [*das Meinige*] &c.: እምዚአየ "of mine" John 16, 14; ውስተ ፡ ዚአሁ "unto his own" John 1, 11; or, omitting the Noun, to which it refers: እስመ ፡ ኮነ ፡ መክፈልቶሙ ፡ ለደቂቀ ፡ ይሁዳ ፡ ዐቢየ ፡ እምነ ፡ ዚአሆሙ "for the portion of the children of Judah was larger than what properly belonged to them" Josh. 19, 9, although in such cases the Relative may be prefixed a second time: ይኩንከ ፡ ለከ ፡ ዘዚአከ ἔστω σοι τὰ σά Gen. 33, 9. The inflection of the Relative Pron. which appears in this Possessive as its first element, following the Gender and Number of the Noun to which it refers, is farther attended to in this case with a greater sense of urgency, on account of the independent position of such Possessives, and consequently with a stricter observance of the rules, than in the case dealt with in § 147, *a*.

Emphatic Nom.-form of Pers. Pron.

(*c*) But the *Nominative* also of Personal Pronouns has occasionally to be brought into special prominence, as contrasted with other Persons, *e. g.* "even I", "I myself" &c.; and this case sometimes extends also to Demonstratives: "even this", "this very" &c. To express the idea of "*idem*", "even the", it is often enough, in the case of the Dem. Pron. (§ 148, *a*), to compound it

(1) Properly—: "Something belonging to Thee is the kingdom".

with ውእቱ, ይእቲ &c. But the language may place another special particle beside Demonstrative and Personal Pronouns,—ከመ "nearly", "just", "only" (§ 162), which always stands next after them, and may be applied to any Case, *e. g.*: "from eternity to eternity አንተ ፡ ከመ thou art the same" Ps. 89, 2; 92, 3:— ኪያሁ ፡ ከመ ፡ ቃለ "the very same word" (*acc.*) Matt. 26, 44; ዘንተ ፡ ከመ ፡ ሰማዕኩ "this very thing have I heard" Ps. 61, 11; ገብረ ፡ ከማሁ ፡ ከመ "he did the same thing" Matt. 20, 5.

In order to express the idea of "self" in the case of the three Persons, the particle ለለ "he, he" *i. e.* "he himself" (*cf. supra*, p. 117, § 62, 1, *c*) is, in Ethiopic, compounded with the Genitive Suffixes, by means of the binding-vowel $\bar{\imath}$ (1):—

		Sing.			*Plur.*
1st Pers.		ለሊየ	1st Pers.		ለሊነ
2nd "	m.	ለሊከ	2nd "	m.	ለሊክሙ
	f.	ለሊኪ		f.	ለሊክን
3rd "	m.	ለሊሁ	3rd "	m.	ለሊሆሙ
	f.	ለሊሃ		f.	ለሊሆን.

Instead of ለሊየ, ለሌየ (*laléya*) also may appear, in accordance with § 153, *e. g.* 1 Cor. 4, 3; Ps. 50, 4; Gen. 45, 12 Note; ለሉየ also occurs:—Gen. 45, 12 GC (König, p. 153). This compound is always used as a Nominative. For the Accusative the compound with ኪያ (v. *supra* under *a*) or with ርእስ (v. *infra*) is employed: ሶበ ፡ ኰነነ ፡ ለሊነ ፡ ርእሰነ "if we would judge ourselves" 1 Cor. 11, 31; ለሊሆሙ ፡ ያአምሩ "they themselves know" Acts 22, 19; ዘለሊከ ፡ ሣረርከ "which Thou hast founded" Ps. 8, 4; ለሊሃ ፡ ፍኖቶሙ ፡ ዕቅፍቶሙ "it itself, their path", *i. e.* "their very path is the occasion of their fall" Ps. 48, 13; *cf.* also Josh. 10, 1, 4; 17, 18; 22, 2; 23, 3. And in this signification ለለ is frequently introduced alongside of the independent Personal Pron.:—ውእቱ ፡ ለሊሁ ፡ እግዚአብሔር Josh. 22, 23; ውእቱ ፡ ለሊሁ ፡ ኤዶም ፡ ውእቱ αὐτός ἐστιν Ἐδώμ Gen. 36, 1.

The notion of "self" may be indicated periphrastically, for every case except the Nominative, by means of ርእስ "head" (2)

(1) For the accentuation v. Trumpp, p. 551.

(2) Which has become in Amharic completely a Pronoun of the Third Person, as እርሱ.

with a Suff. Pron. appended. It occurs very frequently: **መኑ ፡ ትሬሲ ፡ ርእሰከ** "whom makest thou thyself?" John 8, 53; Matt. 8, 4; Gen. 19, 17; **ይሣየጡ ፡ ለርእሶሙ ፡ መብልዐ** "(that) they may buy themselves food" Matt. 14, 15; also Hen. 10, 2; Numb. 31, 53; Josh. 11, 14; *Chrest.* p. 24, line 4; p. 43, line 8. This periphrasis is employed, in particular, when the Pronoun is subordinated to a Preposition, *e. g.* **ላዕለ ፡ ርእስክሙ** "against yourselves" Josh. 24, 22. **ርእስ** may refer even to things impersonal in themselves, but thought of as persons (*i. e.* personified): **ጌሠም ፡ ለርእሳ ፡ ትሔሊ** "the morrow will take thought for itself" Matt. 6, 34. The word **ነፍስ** "soul", "life" is less frequently employed to indicate "self", and is only made use of when the same idea may stand for "self" in other languages: **መጠወ ፡ ነፍሶ ፡ ለሞት** "he delivered himself to death" (*Liturg.*); Gen. 19, 17; Josh. 23, 11; G. Ad. 5, 3 *sq.*; 7, 4 (where نَفْس will stand in the original Arabic) &c.

Reflexive use of **ርእስ** and **ነፍስ** with Suff. Pron.

§ 151. *Attachment of the Verbal Suffixes*, viz. to the Perfect, Subjunctive and Imperative. On the Infinitive v. § 155.

Attachment of Verbal Suffixes. Binding-vowel.

The Suffix is attached to the Verb by way of Object, and thus in the Accusative-form of subordination. In by far the greater number of cases also, the Suff. Pron. with the Verb represents the Accusative of the Personal Pronoun. But since, following § 143 and § 174 *sqq.*, the Accusative in Ethiopic admits of a much wider signification and more manifold use than in other tongues, and indicates often the notion "with respect to", the Suff. Pron. is naturally employed in Ethiopic not only for the Accusative, but also for the Dative of the Personal Pron.,—the Dative in fact which in an independent word is throughout denoted by the preposition **ለ** "with respect to", "for". Attempts at a Dative-use of the Suff. Pron. are met with, as is well-known, in other tongues also([1]). In Ethiopic all Intransitive, Reflexive, and Passive Verbs may assume a Suff. Pron. with the force of a Dative: **የአክለነ** "suffices us" Josh. 17, 16; **ይትረኀወክሙ** "it shall be opened unto you" Matt. 7, 7; **ይኄይሰከ** "it is better for thee" Mark 9, 45; **ይትኈለቆ** "is reckoned to him" Rom. 4, 5; **ይበቍለከ** "it shall grow for thee" Gen. 3, 18; **እዌስከከ** "I will give thee more" Tobit 5, 15. In particular **ኮነ** and **ሀለወ** "to be" take this Dative, *e. g.* **እሙንቱ ፡ ፈታሕተ ፡ ይከውኑክሙ** "they shall be to you for judges" Matt. 12, 27;

([1]) Ewald, '*Hebr. Spr.*' § 315, *b*; Hoffmann, '*Gr. Syr.*' p. 315.

ኮነኒ "it has happened to me" Tobit 8, 16. A Suffix of the third person may then take a reflexive meaning (§ 149) ከመ ፡ ትኩኖ ፡ ብእሲቶ (1) "that she may become his wife", (*lit.* 'that she may be to him for his wife') Gen. 28, 9 (2).

To be sure, this Dative use has really its origin in the Accusative use; and accordingly the Suffix is joined to the Verb in the same way in both cases. The same vowel *a*, which is the mark of the Accusative with the Noun (§ 143), is placed here before the Suff. Pron. to denote the Accusative, by way of binding-vowel between Verb and Pronoun (3).

In combination with the binding-vowel the Verbal Suffixes (*cf.* § 149) run as follows:

	1st Person.	*2nd Person.*		*3rd Person.*	
		m.	*f.*	*m.*	*f.*
Sing.	*á-nī.*	*a-ka*;	*a-kī.*	*á-hū*, contr. *ṓ*;	*áhā*, contr. *ā́*.
Plur.	*á-na.*	*a-kémmū*;	*a-kén.*	*a-hṓmū*, „ *ṓmū*;	*a-hṓn*, „ *ṓn* (4).

But this intervening vowel does not appear regularly, except when Suffixes are attached to those personal forms of the Verb which end in a Consonant, and even then not invariably. When such forms end in a vowel, the binding-vowel is often pushed aside by these vowel-endings. The Subjunctive, even in such of its forms as end in a consonant, constantly rejects the binding-vowel before the four Suffixes of the Second Person (5), because short, compact expression is characteristic generally of that Mood, and because the binding-vowel is not retained by the Accent. The Accent, in fact, is always attracted to *kémmū* and *kén*, while *ka* and *kī* have become entirely devoid of accent, and even the binding-vowel, where it does precede them, is unaccented (§ 149). The four Suf-

(1) [This is hardly an instance of reflexive meaning in the Suffix, for the Suffix of the third person here does not refer to the grammatical Subject of the clause. TR.]

(2) [A peculiar use of the Suffix occurs in *Kebra Nag.*, p. 65 b. 3: አፍጠኖ ፡ ሐተታ he 'hurried the questioning with respect to him', *i. e.* "he asked him quickly".]

(3) *Cf.* EWALD, *'Hebr. Spr.'* § 247, *b.* On the other hand v. KÖNIG, p. 141 *sq.*

(4) V. on the other hand TRUMPP, pp. 551, 554 *sq.*

(5) So that *e. g.* ይኩነክሙ Matt. 9, 29 in PLATT's edition is decidedly inaccurate; [the Reprint, however, has the correct reading, ይኩንክሙ.]

fixes of the Third Person are mostly contracted, after ሀ has been thrown out (§ 47), particularly when the Verbal-form ends in a consonant. The following are the detailed rules for attaching these Suffixes to the Verb.

1. All personal forms of the Verb which end in a consonant, with the exception of those of the Subjunctive, have the Suffixes of the First and Second Person attached to them by means of the binding-vowel, those of the Third Person being applied in their contracted form. The Persons of the Subjunctive which end in a consonant have the Suffixes of the Second Pers. appended directly, without any binding vowel; while the Second Pers. sing. masc. of the Imperative does not admit of the Suffixes of the Second Pers. being appended at all. The Second Pers. pl. fem. of the Perfect, as ነገርክን, very seldom appears with Suffixes(¹), and then it transforms its ክን into ከ, acquiring thus the same final sound as the Third Pers. plur. fem.; *cf.* ረሰይክሙ፡ ለውጻሴ፡ ቅድሜኪክን፡ ኢብጹሐ Cyr. a Reg. in Tüb. MS. fol. 25, *b*. At the same time, we do meet with forms like ሐፀንክናሁ, ሐቀፍክናሁ(²). 1. Attachment when Pers. Forms of the Verb end in a Consonant.

2. Of the Persons of the Verb which end in *ă*, ነገረ, ነገርከ, ነገርነ, the First Pers. Plur. Perfect retains its *ă* even before the binding-vowel *a*. The short *ă* blends with the latter into *ā*, and contraction with the binding-vowel is thereby usually prevented, even in the case of the suffixes of the Third Person(³). The Second Pers. Sing. Masc. Perfect,—which is never followed by the Suffixes of the Second Person—, gives up its *ă* before the binding-vowel *á*, regularly in the case of Suffixes of the First Person and 2. When they end in *ă*.

(¹) Examples: Ex. 2, 20 and Cantic. 5, 8 (where Ludolf has introduced an inaccurate correction into the text).

(²) V. Cornill, '*Das Buch der weisen Philosophen*' (Leipzig 1875), p. 51; and *cf.* König, pp. 133, 141; Philippi, ZDMG XXXII, p. 71; and Nöldeke, *ibid.* XXXVIII, p. 417. V. also Praetorius, *ibid.* XLI, p. 690 [and Brockelmann, *ibid.* LIX, p. 831].

(³) I prefer the explanation of the long *ā* given above, to the other explanation, defended also by König, p. 141, according to which we have in this ና merely a return to the original pronunciation of the ን, as it appears in the Arabic نَا. In fact in the *Josippon*, at least in *Cod. Frcf.*, the forms ገበርኖ, ገበርኖሙ, ገበርኖን occur rather more frequently than ገበርናሁ, ገበርናሆሙ and ገበርናሆን; and they occur also in *Sx.* frequently, *e. g.* ሰአልኖ *Sx. Genb.* 28; ረከብና = ረከብናሃ, and ቀበርና = ቀበርናሃ *Sx. Genb.* 28 *Enc.* [*Cf.* also *Kebra Nag.*, *Introd.* p. XVIII.]

Plur. Suffixes of the Third Person, and occasionally and capriciously in the case of Singular Suffixes of the Third Person, the type in the latter case being either ነገርከሁ, ነገርከሃ or ነገርኮ, ነገርካ (1). The Third Person Sing. Masc. Perfect gives up its final *a* before all Suffixes (§ 91), and takes the Suffixes of the Third Person invariably in their contracted form.

3. Attachment when Pers. Forms end in formative-*ū*.

3. In those Persons of the Verb which end in a formative-*ū*, as ነገርኩ, ነገሩ, ነገርክሙ, ይነግሩ, ትነግሩ, ይንግሩ, ትንግሩ, ንግሩ, the binding-vowel *a* is thrust aside by the *ū* before all the Suffixes of the First and Second Person. In such cases *ū* takes over the accent, whenever it must have fallen upon *a*, if that vowel had been retained (*e. g.* in ነገርክሙኒ). Suffixes of the Third Person are always attached in their shorter and vowel-commencing form *ō*, *ā*, *ōmū*, *ōn*, originating in contraction with the binding-vowel, *ū* being at the same time hardened into *w* before these vowels, *e. g.* ነገርዎ, although a mere semi-hardening (§ 40) is often exhibited in this case, particularly in the older manuscripts, *e. g.* ሰሐቡዎ, ገበርኩዎሙ, ገበርክሙዎ (2), ዘአውፃእኩዎ Amos 9,7 (A), አምሰጥክሙዎ Herm. 22 *b*, 19.

4. When they end in Fem. formative-*ī*.

4. The Persons which end in the Fem. formative-*ī*, ነገርኪ, ትነግሪ, ትንግሪ, ንግሪ, do not assume any Suffixes of the Second Person. The Suffixes of the Third Person are attached in that form which begins with a vowel and which originates in contraction with the binding-vowel, the *ī* undergoing sometimes complete hardening, sometimes semi-hardening.—The semi-hardening is of specially frequent occurence in the older manuscripts—: *e. g.* ትልዊዩን Ruth 2,8; ሐፀንዩ and ሐፀኒዩ Ex. 2,9 (Note); ግበርያ and ግበሪያ Gen. 16,6 (Note); [*cf. Kebra Nag.* p. XVIII]; አጽንዒዩ Gen. 21,18 (Note); ትሰምዒዩ *Chrest.* p. 74, line 21 (3). On the other hand the Suffixes of the First Person admit in this case of no binding-vowel or hardening of the *ī* into a semivowel, because doubly-closed syllables would thereby be produced in most cases within

(1) According to Nöldeke, ZDMG XXXVIII, p. 413, N. 1, ነገርከሁ contains an *originally* long *ā*, like the Hebr. אַתָּה overagainst انتَ. König, p. 132 explains the length in ከ by extension before an Aspirate. On the accentuation *cf.* Trumpp, p. 551 *sqq*.

(2) V. Dillmann's ed. of the '*Octateuch*', Comm. p. 5.

(3) According to König, p. 127, this takes place to avoid a hiatus.

the word (like ገበርከየኒ, ትነሥእየኒ); but the Verbal forms concerned weaken their final ī into ĕ (¹),—which then probably receives the accent,—and attach to it ኒ, ና without a binding-vowel. In this way forms are produced in the Perfect like ነሣእክኒ Gen. 30,15; አምሐልክና Cantic. 5,9; ኮንክኒ, which seemingly must be pronounced našā'kénī, amḥalkéna, kōnkénī; while in the Imperfect, the Subjunctive and the Imperative we have forms like ትገብርኒ, ትንሥእኒ Gen. 30,15, ንግርኒ Gen. 24,23, 47; አብእኒ Gen. 38,16; ሀብኒ Gen. 30,14; እመንኒ Gen. 35,17; አስትይኒ (from አስትዩ) Gen. 24,17, 43, 45; [ኩንና, ሀብና, ሰአልኒ *Kebra Nag.*, *Introd.* p. XVIII]. These last forms are probably to be pronounced *tegabréni* &c.

5. In those Persons which end in ā, ነገሩ, ይነግሩ, ትነግሩ, ይንግሩ, ትንግሩ, ንግሩ the binding-vowel *a* blends with the ā into ā. Contraction in the Suffixes of the Third Person is accordingly not permissible. 5. When they end in ā.

§ 152. The various individual forms which are possible in this connection may be explained by these rules. A survey is given in Table VII. One or two cases, however, deserve farther and special mention. Special Cases of the Attachment of Verbal Suffixes.

In attaching the Suffixes to the Subjunctive it may happen, in accordance with § 151, 1, that the first letter of the Suffixes of the Second Person, ከ, is brought into immediate contact with the Radical Palatal-Guttural, ግ, ቅ or ክ. In that case, when ግ or ቅ is concerned, the ከ of the Suffix passes into ግ or ቅ (§ 54): ያርሕቅ "(that) he withdraw thee" Deut. 13,11; እኅድጊ "(that) I should leave thee" Ruth 1,16; ኢይርሐቅ μή ἐκλειπέτωσάν σε Prov. 3,3; ያውድቅ Sir. 12,16; ያዕርግ G. Ad. 43,24. Instead of ክከ, when ክ is the Radical, only one character is written (§ 55): እባርክ "I will bless thee" Gen. 27,7, 10, 25; Ruth 2,4; ይንስክ "(that) he bite thee" *Chrest.* p. 44, line 11. The copyists have in this case often gone astray, and, because they no longer recognised the Suffix, they have set down sometimes the Verbal form without Suffix, *e. g.* ትባርክ for ትባርክ Gen. 27,4 (28,3), and sometimes they have made a Suffix of the Third Pers. Masc. out

(¹) This feminine ī, on being brought into the middle of a word, would seem to have a general tendency towards a more fugitive pronunciation. König, pp. 120, 153 assumes a Dissimilation here. *Cf.* also *supra*, p. 72, § 36.

of a Suffix of the Second Person Masc., *e. g.* **ይበርኮ** for **ይበርከ** Gen. 48, 20 *et saepe*(1).

When a vowel-commencing Suffix, or one which is attached with the binding-vowel *a*, is applied to those Persons of the Imperfect, the Subjunctive and the Imperative of verbs *tertiae gutturalis*, which end directly with the last radical and so have the foregoing *a* lengthened into *ā*, as in **ይምጻእ**, **ምጻእ**, **ይትፌሣሕ**, **ይትፈሣሕ** &c.,—then the same changes emerge, which appear in the conjugation of these verbs in applying to those forms Personal-endings commencing with a vowel (§ 103), thus:—**ይምጻእ**, **ይምጽኣኒ**; **ስማዕ**, **ስምዐኒ**, [**ንሥኣ** '*sume eam*' *Kebra Nag.* 55 b 14]&c.(2). On the other hand, Roots which are also *mediae infirmae* maintain the *ā*, just as they do in the inflection (§ 103):—**ይበእ**, **ይበአኒ**, **ይበአሙ** &c. **ምዕዐ** may also maintain the *ā*, *e. g.* **ኢትትመዓዖ** "be not angry with him" Gen. 44, 18, as well as **ትትመዐዐኒ**; *cf.* König, p. 85.

Roots mediae geminatae may contract the repeated letter, exactly as in the inflection (§ 103), whenever a proper occasion occurs, that is to say when a Suffix, introduced by the binding-vowel *a*, or one commencing with a vowel, is applied to a form ending in a vowel-less radical, *e. g.* **ይነበ** or **ይነብበ**, from **ይነብብ**; **አምዖሙ** or **አምዕዖሙ**, from **አምዕዕ** &c.

Verbal forms from *Roots tertiae infirmae*, which end in *ū* or *ī* as third radical, must harden the *ū* or *ī* before the binding-vowel into *w* or *y*, (exactly as in the inflection before vowel-commencing Personal terminations, § 103)(3), *e. g.* **ይትልዎ** from **ይትሉ**, **ትልወኒ** from **ትሉ**, **ያሐይዎ** from **ያሐዩ**, **አሕይወኒ** from **አሕዩ**, **አለብወኒ** from **አለቡ** (Ps. 118, 34):—but in the Subj. with Suff. of the Second Person we have **እትሉከ** (Matt. 8, 19). Farther we have **ይሬእዮ** from **ይሬኢ**, **ርእየኒ** from **ርኢ**, **ትዕስዮ** from **ትዕሲ**, **አርእዮ** from **አርኢ**. But yet the semi-hardening process is also met with in this connection here and there, *e. g.* **ያዐቢየከ** Gen. 28, 3; Ex. 30, 4; Numb. 12, 11; **እሬሲዮ** Amos 8, 10 (A) *et saepe*.

(1) In G. Ad. 29, 10 Trumpp has restored some of these forms on his own authority.

(2) And yet we have also the reading **ብላዮ** Deut. 12, 18, 22 instead of **ብልዮ** as in Deut. 14, 23; 15, 20. In Sirach 6, 12 some MSS. have **ይትኅብአከ** for **ይትኅብኦከ**.

(3) For the accentuation v. Trumpp, p. 556.

The shortened form ይቤ "he said" (ትቤ, እቤ, ንቤ, § 103) must also make the ል appear again before the Suffixes: ይቤለኒ, ይቤሎ &c.

Like Arabic(¹), Ethiopic has the faculty of appending *two Suffixes* to a Verb at one time. Verbs namely, which may govern two Accusatives (§ 177), may also assume two Suffixes. The rule of precedence with these Suffixes in such a case is this, that the First Person precedes the Second or Third, and stands next to the Verb, while the Second precedes the Third. Examples:—ወሀብኩከሁ Numb. 18,8; አሀብከሃ Gen. 15,7 (*cf.* König, p. 133); የሀይድከሃ Deut. 28,30; የሀብክሙዋ and የሀብክምዋ Josh. 9,22; የሀይድንዮ Luke 9,39; ወሀበንዮ G. A. 109,10; ሀበኒያ Gen. 29,21; አብልዐኒያ Ezek. 3,2; አወፍየኒዮ Gen. 42,37; ሀቡኒያ Gen. 23,9; ወሀበኒዮን Gen. 31,9; ተሀበናሃ G. A. 57,2 [ሀብንዮ "give (*f. Sing.*) it me" *Kebra Nag.* 99 b 23]. We also conclude from these examples, that when the first Suffix ends in *ū* or *ī*, and a Suffix of the Third Person (*ō*, *ā*, *ōmū*, or *ōn*) is added, the *ū* or *ī* may undergo either complete- or semi-hardening(²); still, the latter process is the more usual one (*cf.* König, p. 153 *sq.*), the accent in that case falling upon the second Suffix (*cf.* Trumpp, p. 556). If the first Suffix ends in *a*, the Suffixes of the Third Person are always applied in their original form (*hū*, *hā*, *hōmū*, *hōn*), and the foregoing *a* is generally lengthened into *ā*(³), under the influence of the Aspirate and of the accent which it then takes.

Attachment of Nominal Suffixes. Binding-vowel.

§ 153. *Attachment of the Suffix Pronouns to the Noun.* Pronouns are subordinated to the Noun just as other nouns are (§ 144), that is to say,—in the Genitive relation or possessive sense. Of course, as is pointed out in § 150, Ethiopic is furnished with an expedient for deriving from every Personal Pronoun independent Possessives which it may employ with the force of a Genitive. Their use, however, is almost wholly restricted to cases in which a certain emphasis is laid upon the Genitive, or in which the attachment of a Suffix is impracticable on other grounds,—for instance when a Construct State has to be dealt with. But

---

(¹) Ewald, '*Gr. Ar.*' § 674.

(²) And yet in the very ancient *Cod. Laur.* there occurs, in Zech. 3,1:—
ወአርአየኒሁ ፡ እግዚአብሔር ፡ ለካህን ፡ ዐቢይ.

(³) V., however, Numb. 14, 8; Deut. 6, 23; 9, 6.

when such special cases do not present themselves, every Personal Pronoun, which has to take the Genitive, is even in Ethiopic attached usually to its governing Noun as a Suffix, *e. g.* **መዋዕሊሁ** "the days of him", "his days". The power to subordinate a Pronoun to a Noun in this way—depends upon the process of juxtaposition, just as in the case of a Construct State (§ 144); and wherever Suffixes with the force of a Genitive are appended to a word, it is really a Construct State-relation which is then constituted. Now (§ 144) this relation may be conceived, and in other languages may even be realised, without any outward formative expedient, so that by ranking the two words close together and accentuating them in a certain way the whole force of the relation is embraced already. Accordingly it might be thought that even in Ethiopic the Suffixes would attach themselves closely to the Noun without recourse to any farther contrivance, and give expression to the Genitive relation by thus blending together the two elements into one single word. In actual fact, however, this is not the case. For in Ethiopic, just as the Construct State is invariably formed by means of an Ending, so the Suffix in every instance is attached to the Noun by means of a *Binding-vowel* corresponding to such Ending. But this binding-vowel is no longer retained in all instances with the same fidelity to its original form. In order therefore to understand its essential nature, it is necessary to distinguish the different cases which occur.

1. Attachment of Suffixes to Plural Forms.

1. The Binding-vowel appears in its purest form in the case of the attachment of *Suffixes to the Plural* of the Noun, whether outer or inner Plural. Plural-forms subordinate the Suffix by means of the binding-vowel *ī*, which always carries the Tone, except when the Suffix itself requires it, as in **ክሙ**, **ክን**, **ሆሙ**, **ሆን** (§ 149). This binding-vowel is of such essential importance, that, for the sake of it, even the *a* of the Accusative is given up; and accordingly when an Accusative Plural has to take a Suffix, the sign of the Accusative disappears, and the Accusative relation is recognisable only from the context. In this *ī*, which agrees in a remarkable manner with an ancient ending of the Construct State in Hebrew, we can only discern a Construct State-ending; for seeing that the fuller form *īa* is given in the cases adduced in § 150, *b*, it is probable that both the usual Ethiopic ending of the Construct State, *a*, and the binding-vowel, *ī*, are merely two

different abbreviations of one and the same fundamental form *īa* (§ 144) (¹). This binding-vowel *ī* is reduced to the feebler *é* on phonetic grounds in two cases: (*a*) before the Suffix የ, by *ī* + *ya* becoming *éyya*, or again by *ī* being weakened into *é* before *ya*, producing *éya* (²). Yet this is by no means always the case; in particular, forms with *īya* are often exhibited in older manuscripts, like እደዊየ, አምላኪየ &c.; *cf.* König, p. 153; [and *Kebra Nag.*, *Introd.* p. XVI]. (*b*) Before the Suffix ኪ *ī* may be shortened into *é*, plainly to obviate the necessity of two *ī*-sounds being heard in immediate succession. The Suffixes which are attached to the Plural accordingly take the following forms (*cf.* Trumpp, p. 557):—

	I.	II.		III.	
		m.	f.	m.	f.
Sing.	*é-ya.*	*ī-ka,*	*ī-kī.* / *é-kī.*	*ī-hū,*	*ī-hā.*
Plur.	*ī-na.*	*ī-kémmū,*	*ī-kén.*	*ī-hómū,*	*ī-hón.*

For Examples v. Table IX. The form *īya e. g.* is given in አበዊየ Gen. 32, 10; 47, 9, 30; አምላኪየ Gen. 48, 3; አኀዊየ Judges 8, 19; the form *īki* in አበዊኪ Ps. 44, 18; *ékī*, አልባስኪ Cantic. 4, 11; ከናፍርኪ *ibid.*; Ruth 3, 3 (G). If the Plural-Stem ends in ይ, then the approach of the binding-vowel produces ዪ; but before Suffixes of the third Person ዪ occurs only rarely, as for instance in እክዪሁ (a side-form to እከይሁ), v. Dillmann's '*Lex.*', col. 789; ይ inclines rather to blend with the *ī*-sound into ይ (*cf.* Trumpp, p. 558): መራዕይሁ *marā'-i-hū* = *marā'ihū* (³) Gen. 21, 22; 26, 26; መራዕይሆሙ Gen. 34, 23; ኵሎ ፡ ንዋይሁ (Acc. and Col-

(¹) Trumpp also, p. 557, N. 1, holds *ī* to be the remains of an old Constr. St.; *cf. supra*, p. 325, Note (¹), as also König, p. 142.

(²) There is no express announcement that *y* has to be pronounced double in this case, and the alternative possibility is brought nearer by the shortening of the *ī* before ኪ into *é*.

(³) [It looks more like *marāʿyehū*, as if *īhū* had also been shortened into *e-hū*, and applied to መራዕይ, thus *marāʿyᵉ-ehū*, which easily blends into *marāʿyehū*; but not so obviously does *marāʿyᵉ* and *ihu* blend into *marāʿihū*. However Dillmann thinks መራዕይ should be pronounced as if it were written መራዒ (v. § 51 *sub fin.*). Trumpp's pronunciation of the word is *marā-ʿeihú*. Perhaps too the binding-vowel has disappeared in these cases, v. *infra*. tr.]

lective, v. *infra* § 155) Gen. 32,24; ዕበይሁ (Acc.) Tobit 13,4; and also with Suffixes of the second Person ንዋይኪሙ (for ንዋዩ-ኪሙ) Ex. 10,24; ገማዕይሆን Matt. 25,4; and in Ex. 38,26 there occurs even መጻህይዮን from መጻህይ, the binding-vowel having been hardened into a semivowel and the *h* thrown out (but see *annot.* on the passage). And yet, seeing that every Plural in Ethiopic, particularly the Inner Plurals or Collective forms, may without difficulty be conceived again as a simple Singular notion, it is not much to be wondered at, that Suffixes are frequently applied to Plural forms after the fashion of Singulars; v. *infra* § 155.

2. Attachment of Suffixes to Singular Forms:— To Nominal Stems ending in ā, ē, or ō.

§ 154. 2. When *Suffixes are attached to Singular forms*, the binding-vowel ī is shortened into *e* or is entirely given up. At the same time we must distinguish between Nominal-Stems ending in a vowel and those ending in a consonant.

(*a*) *Nominal-Stems, ending in ā, ē, or ō*,—in whatever way the termination has arisen—, have the Suffixes attached without any binding-vowel, in all the Cases of the Noun, just because the latter vowel is absorbed by the long vowel, *e. g.* ሥራቱ "his glory" Ex. 24,17; ግማኖሙ "their impurity" 2 Esr. 9,11; ተፈልጦሙ "their separation" G. Ad. 11,19; ትክዎን (instead of ትክዎሆን) M. M. f. 192. In ሱታፎ, even the ē of the Nominal form is discarded; *cf.* DILLMANN's '*Lex.*', col. 367 (v. Table IX).

To Nom. Stems ending in a Consonant; (α) when these Stems stand in the Accusative.

(*b*) *Nominal-Stems ending in a Consonant.*

(α) When these Stems stand in the *Accusative*, the Suffixes are appended to them (1) in like manner without any binding-vowel, inasmuch as the ă of the Accusative is too important to be thrust aside, and the binding-vowel is unable to obtain a foothold alongside of it. It is true that *a* and *i* might have been contracted into ē, but such mixed sound did not come into use with the ordinary Noun, and it is exhibited in the case merely of a few Prepositions which have Suffixes attached (§ 167). It is only before the Suff. የ, where the binding-vowel ĭ or ĕ has a support in the *y*, that it is regularly strong enough to dislodge the ă of the Accusative, so that ሕዝበ + Suff. የ runs,—not ሕዝበየ, but ሕዝብየ *ḥezbéya* (2).

(1) For the accentuation *cf.* TRUMPP, p. 556 *sqq.*

(2) Of course the form ሕዝብየ might be explained as coming from an original ሕዝቢ; and thus it might be supposed that the ă of the Accusative was in this case displaced by the Vowel-Suffix ī (§ 149); and in like

Now seeing that the binding-vowel, except in this one case, disappears, the *a* of the Accusative must assume the accent which the binding-vowel would have had to sustain: as *á-na*. But instead of *á-hū*, and *á-hā*, *ṓ* and *ā́* are always given in pronunciation, the Aspirate being suppressed. Thus: ሕዝበኒ, ሕዝቦ, ሕዝባ; but ሕዝበከ, ሕዝበኪ with the accent on the tone-syllable of the Stem; farther ሕዝበክሙ, ሕዝበክን with the accent on the Suffix; and finally, instead of ሕዝበሆሙ, ሕዝበሆን, always the contracted forms ሕዝቦሙ, ሕዝቦን, the Aspirate being rejected. Even before other Suffixes than የ, it happens occasionally that the *a* of the Accusative gives way to a binding-vowel *e*, *e. g.* ሕግከ in the Acc., Numb. 18,3 (F); አምላክከ Lev. 25,36; አምላክክሙ Lev. 25,38; 26,12; 3 Kings 1,14 where the oldest manuscripts have ነገርኪ for ነገረኪ; *cf.* also ርእስኪ Sir. 38,21; አእምሮትከ *Tab. Tab.*(¹) 60 (*Chrest.* p. 122 [where *Cod. Mon. Aeth.* 11, fol. 49 v⁰ reads አእምሮተከ]); ረድኤትከ *Tab. Tab.* 79 (*ibid.* p. 126 [*Codd.* TRUMPP, *Francof.* and *Mon.* 11, fol. 57 v⁰ give ረድኤተከ]); PLATT, '*Didasc.*' p. 5, line 10(²); ሕግከ and ጽድቅከ in Laur. 4 Esr. 10,39 (54); 13,55 (58) and 4 Esr. 8,12; 9,32 (New Ed.), to avoid the disagreeable sound of ገከ, ቀከ; also ሐዘንኪ in 4 Esr. 10,15 (20)(³).

---

manner *eya* with the Plural-forms might be thought derivable from an original *ī*: but የ as occupying the position of the Suffix *ī* appears to be very old, as old forms like ምስሌየ (§ 167) prove; and even before other Suffixes the *ă* of the accusative is thrust aside, in old MSS.

(¹) [*i. e.* ጠቢበ ፡ ጠቢባን or *Sapiens Sapientium.* TR.]

(²) [The reference here is to ጸላእትክሙ "your enemies (acc.)" which PLATT found in his MS. and considered a mistake, as he explains in a note. He restores the *a* in the Text and writes ጸላእተክሙ. Evidently DILLMANN thought the *e* legitimate enough, though not quite common. TR.]

(³) LUDOLF also lays down the rule, that, when a Noun in the Acc. with a Suffix is farther weighted with another attached particle like ኒ, ሂ &c., the *ă* of the Acc. passes into *e*, *e. g.* ተዘከር ፡ ሣህለከ ፡ እግዚእ ፡ ወምሕረትከኒ Ps. 24,6; other instances are Ps. 88,6 (contrasted with v. 2); 71,1; 87,12; 91,2 (contrasted with Ps. 70,20,21). These cases, however, are rather to be explained in accordance with § 143, *ad fin.*, the accusative construction being held in abeyance there, and the first form of the Noun appearing instead of the Acc. [From the numerous instances met with in the *Kebra Nag.* (v. '*Introd.*' p. XVI *sq.*) of this formation of the Acc. in *e* before Suffixes of

(β) When they stand in the Nominative.

(*β*) When the Noun stands in the *Nominative*, the binding-vowel *e* makes its appearance before the Suffixes of the First and Second Person, taking the accent at the same time before የ and ነ, thus: *é-ya*, *é-na*, *e-kémmū*, *e-kén*. But the Suffixes of the Third Person are not given as *e-hū* (1), *e-hā*, *e-hōmū*, *e-hōn*, but as *ū́*, *ā́*, *ṓmū*, *ṓn*, the Aspirate being discarded and the binding-vowel suppressed. For the rest v. Table IX. Words, which end in ግ, ቅ, ክ, ይ, ን, are prevented by the binding-vowel from ever making these letters coalesce with those Suffixes which commence with the same letters or similar ones (*cf.* König, p. 96), thus ጸወንኒ (not ጸወኒ); አምላክከ, ራእይየ Hen. 14, 4; ደቂቅከ Gen. 48, 5; ወርቅክሙ Gen. 43, 12. Words which end in *u*-containing Palatal-Gutturals, like ኊልቍ, ሰርጕ, attach in the Nom. and Acc. the Suffixes of the third Person, after the same manner as other nouns, observing however the principles noticed in § 42: ሰርጎ, ሰርጓ, ሰርጎሙ, ሰርጎን; but in order to preserve the peculiar pronunciation of their last radical they may also adopt the full form *ehū*, *ehā*, *ehōmū*, *ehōn*, *e. g.* ሰርጕሆሙ Numb. 31, 49 (Acc.); ሰርጕሃ Deut. 17, 3. So too words ending in *ai* may take ሁ, ሃ, ሆሙ, ሆን, *e. g.* እከይሆሙ Judges 20, 34, 41 (= እከዮሙ), but this seldom happens.

To Nouns ending in ī.

(*c*) *Nouns which end in ī* do not admit of any binding-vowel in the Nominative, but annex the Suffixes directly, just like other Stems ending in a vowel, and retain the Aspirate in Suffixes of the third Person. But *éyya* or *éya* is occasionally read for *īya*, *e. g.* መድኀኒየ Ps. 18, 16; 68, 17 (from መድኀኒ); 90, 2.—*Cf.* also ረሰይክምዎ፡ ቀታሌየ (*varr.* ቀታሊየ and ቀታሌ፡ ዚአየ) 1 Sam. 22,13; መጋቤሁ Tob. 1, 13 Francof. When such nouns stand in the Accusative, the Accusative-sign *a* may be suppressed between the termination *ī* and the binding-vowel, at least pretty regularly before የ, ሁ, ሃ, ነ, ሆሙ, ሆን, *e. g.* ረዳኢየ Ex. 15, 1; ፈጣሬሃ Matt. 1, 16; ፈጻዪሃ Hen. 6, 3 (2); ፈጣሬነ *Phys.* 5, 12; *Hexaem.* 33, 6 (3). But before Suffixes of the Second Person, the *a* of the Accusative

the Second person, it would appear that this was the regular formation in Geʿez at an early stage of its development.]

(1) An anomalous form occurs in Ex. 36, 12, በሕቊቲሁ.

(2) [Flemming reads here ፈጻዩ. tr.]

(3) Farther Numb. 35, 23; Deut. 4, 42; 21, 1; John 7, 32; Hebr. 11, 7; James 4, 4, 11.

is mostly retained, *e. g.* ጸላኢከ Matt. 5,43; Ex. 23,22; Deut. 32,38; but v. ጸበኢከ Job 13,24; ነበሪከ Sir. 4,4 *var.* In Ex. 23,25, ፈጣሪከ is to be explained in accordance with § 143 *sub fin.*

(*d*) A few short and old words have a somewhat anomalous method of attaching their Suffixes. The four nouns አቡ "father", ሐም "father-in-law", እኍ "brother", አፍ "mouth" restore to view before Suffixes their original termination, namely *ū* in the Ground-form, and *ā*(1) in the Accusative; but for that very reason they reject other binding-vowels: they also adopt the Suffixes of the third Person in their complete form. Accordingly, from the Nominative-form proceed አቡየ (Ps. 26,16), አቡነ, አቡከ (John 8,19), አቡኪ, አቡክሙ, አቡክን (Gen. 31,5), አቡሁ, አቡሃ, አቡሆሙ, አቡሆን; in like manner እኁየ Luke 6,42, እኁከ Matt. 5,24, እኁሁ Gen. 38,29; ሐሙኪ Gen. 38,13, ሐሙሃ 38,25; አፉየ Ps. 16,5, አፉሁ 9,29, አፉሆሙ 5,10, አፉከ Rev. 10,9. In the Accusative these words ought properly to run አባየ, አባከ Eph. 6,2, አባሁ John 6,42, አባሆሙ Mark 1,20; እኃክሙ and እኅዋክሙ Gen. 42,20 (Note), እኅዋሆሙ or እኃሆሙ Ps. 37,21, እኅዋሁ Matt. 5,22; Ps. 48,7; ሐማሁ Ex. 18,26; አፋሁ Matt. 5,2; but they readily give up the Accusative form, and stand in their first form for the Accusative also. Thus there appear as Accusatives አቡሁ *Chrest.* p. 24, line 5,; አቡነ Judges 18,19; አቡሆሙ Gen. 4,21; አቡሃ Deut. 21,13; እኁከ Deut. 25,3. In particular አፍ employs its first or Nominative-form for the Accusative almost without exception: አፉሁ Ps. 68,19; Hen. 106,3; አፉሃ Gen. 4,11 (Note); Hen. 56,8; አፉየ Judges 11,35; አፉከ Judges 11,36; አፉሆሙ Ps. 9,42; Hen. 17,8. The Noun እድ "hand",—although it exhibits ው in the Plural as its third radical, like the words just mentioned,—does not form እዱየ &c., but always takes the form እዴ before Suffixes, thereby indicating an original pronunciation of እዴ, something like יְדֵה, but

To certain Short and Old Words

(1) Which *ā* is taken in exchange for *ū* in the very same way as *ă* is for *ĕ* in the ordinary noun. For the rest, in the case at least of አቡ, a second Acc. occurs even without a Suffix, viz. አባ in Matt. 19,29; *cf.* the Vocative § 142.—With reference to this peculiarity in the words mentioned, compare Arabic, Hebrew and Syriac; Ewald, '*Gr. Ar.*' § 411; '*Hebr. Spr.*' § 256, *a*, and Hoffmann, '*Gr. Syr.*' p. 273 *sq.*—V. also König, p. 108. [*Cf.* farther Nöldeke, '*Syr. Gr.*' (*English Ed.*) p. 91. tr.]

making no distinction between Nominative and Accusative: **እዴዮ**, **እዴከ**, **እዴሁ**([1]), **እዴነ**, **እዴክሙ**, **እዴሆሙ** &c. ([2]).

3. Suffixes often attached to Singular Stems in the Plural fashion, and to Plural Stems in the Singular fashion.

§ 155. 3. Often however in Ethiopic the *Suffixes* are *attached to Singular Stems in the Plural fashion*, and *vice versâ* to *Plural Stems in the Singular fashion*.

(*a*) 1st case, when the Sing. Stems are similar in form or meaning to Plurals

(*a*) Singular-Stems,—by reason of similarity of meaning (that is when they convey the sense of a Collective noun) or still oftener similarity of form,—at times take Suffixes which belong properly to the Plural forms([3]). Especially are Suffixes of the Plural adopted with almost perfect regularity by those Singular-Stems which contain a long *ā* before the last radical or formative letter, both on account of outward resemblance to the Plural type **አምሳል** and because an *ĕ* as a binding-vowel would be too weak, after the long *ā*, to carry the tone. These stems almost invariably fasten the Suffixes to themselves, both in the Nominative and the Accusative, by means of *ī*:—**ቍርባኒሁ** Gen. 4, 4; **ምእላዲሁ** Gen. 1, 9; **ምግባኢኪ** Gen. 3, 16; **ድንጋጊሁ** Josh. 3, 15; 4, 18; **ሙራዲሁ** Josh. 10, 11; **ምሥናኒከ** Ps. 2, 8: **ምሥዋዒሁ** Ps. 42, 4; **ምዕራቢሁ** Hen. 72, 2; **ሙባኢሁ**, **ሙፃኢሁ** Hen. 73, 3; **ልህቃቲሃ** Luke 1, 36. Words also of the type **ሥርዐት** from roots *ultimae gutturalis* have here and there the same forms, in accordance with § 48:—**ስብሐቲከ** Ps. 47, 9; 72, 28 (*cf.* § 121, *d*); **ርሥአቲሁ** Gen. 21, 2; but also **ምግባሩ** Ps. 61, 11; **ምግባሮሙ** Ps. 27, 5; **ቅድሳቲ** Ps. 29, 4; 96, 13 &c. In the very same way words of the Second simple formation, belonging to the type **ክቡድ**, may, from their outward resemblance to the first Collective-form, attach their Suffixes by means of *ī*:—**ክቡዲከ** Ps. 121, 7; **ጥበቢሁ** Ps. 146, 5; **ዕጸቢሁ** 2 Sam. 22, 6 &c.; also **ዐረቢሆሙ** Judith 1, 7. So is it, farther, with words of the type **መግበር** and **መግበርት**, particularly when they are used collectively, *e. g.* **ማኅደሪሆሙ** Ps. 48, 11 &c., and many other Singu-

(1) But **እዲ** is found in *Tab. Tab.* 53, 1; 66, 4 (*Chrest.* pp. 120, 123). For farther explanation *cf.* Philippi, ZDMG XXXII, p. 74; Barth, *ibid.* XLI, p. 637; König, p. 107; *et supra* p. 286 and Note (3).

(2) But when in Hen. 44 and Ex. 34, 13 the MSS have **ምስሌሆሙ** for **ምሰሊሆሙ** "their images", that form has been reached simply through the copyists mistaking the Conceptional word ('image') for the Preposition **ምስለ** ('with') (§ 167). [In Hen. 44, Flemming reads **ምሳሌሆሙ**. tr.]

(3) *Cf.* in Hebrew, Ewald, '*Hebr. Spr.*' § 259, *b*.

lar-forms besides, especially when used collectively, *e. g.* ዓመቲነ Ps. 89, 10, ዓመቲሆሙ Ps. 77, 37.

(*b*) Plural-stems at times adopt suffixes properly belonging to the Singular, inasmuch as any Plural may be conceived of as a notion suggesting unity:—ጻድቃኑ Ps. 31, 14; 33, 16; ላእካኑ Ps. 102, 21; ጸላእቱ Ps. 67, 1; ጸላእቶሙ Ps. 105, 11; ጸላእትከ Ps. 20, 8; አብያቶሙ Hen. 94, 7; አሣእኖ Matt. 3, 11; ኅባዝያኑ Gen. 40, 5; አግብርቶ Gen. 44, 16; መዋዕሎሙ Lev. 7, 36; ጸሐፍቶሙ Matt. 7, 29; አልባሲኪ (Acc.) Ruth 3, 3; አጻብዕቶን "their (*f.*) fingers" M. Berh. *f.* 43 *a*; ምግባራቶ (Acc.) G. Ad. 50, 17; particularly those Plurals which give expression only to a simple Singular-conception, *e. g.* አምላክ "God" or መቃብሮሙ Gen. 47, 30; መቃብርነ Gen. 23, 6.

(*b*) 2nd case, when the Pl. Stems may be conceived of as suggesting Unity.

4. Suffixes are also applied to *the Infinitive*, just as to ordinary nouns. Infinitives which end in *ō* take no suffixes, it is true, in that form (§ 125), for they must revert, before the suffix, to their original form in *ōt*(1); but suffixes are attached to both of the other possible Infinitive forms. The Gerund must always stand in the Accusative (§ 123), and thus it attaches the Suffixes just like other Nouns in the Accusative which have a consonantal ending (§ 154, *b*, α): ወጺአየ Ps. 67, 24; ርእይየ Ps. 72, 3; ገቢረከ Ps. 49, 21; ተመይጦከ Luke 22, 32; ተንሢኦ Matt. 2, 14 &c. The Substantival Infinitives may be used both in the Nominative- and the Accusative-form, and they attach their Suffixes in these cases exactly like other nouns that end in consonants (§ 154, *b*, α, β), *e. g.* አሚኖትከሙ Nomin., አሚኖተከሙ Accus. On Suffixes in the case of Prepositions and other Particles v. *infra*, (§ 167).

4. Suffixes applied to the Infinitive.

§ 156. Lastly, as regards the *signification* of the Suffixes to the Noun, they must in the first place be an expression of the Genitive of the Pronoun (whether Subject-Genitive or Object-Genitive, § 184), because they are related to the Noun as a subordinate element to a Construct State (§ 153). In the large majority of cases this is the position which is actually met with. But just as (§ 184) the Construct State serves at times to determine a word with greater exactness by means of the second element, and may therefore be employed even in those cases in which other

Use of the Suffix in certain cases, equivalent to Apposition

(1) Accordingly አስተፋቅዶሙ, Numb. 26, 63 is not a good form, and Cod. C. gives a better one in አስተፋቅዶቶሙ.

languages make use of the co-ordinate relation or Apposition (¹),— so too the Suffix to a Noun may annex a more exact determination to the Noun concerned. In such a case it would be expressed in our languages as in apposition to the Noun, *e. g.* ዕራቅየ, literally "a naked one of (*or* 'belonging to, *or* associated with a personality') I", *i. e.* "naked I" or "I, naked". In this way, just as the Accusative-, or Verbal-suffix, is also used with a Dative reference (§ 151), a new signification of the Suff. Pron. has likewise branched off from the Genitive-, or Nominal-suffix. In Ethiopic this practice of subordinating in form, as a Genitive-suffix, a Pronoun which is coordinate in meaning, predominates largely in one case: — When a Personal noun, or an adjective expressing the condition of a Person, makes its appearance in free co-ordination, or as a predicate of a Personal Subject or Object in a sentence, it is not placed in the sentence in mere vacancy, but always in a form completed by the Suffix of the Person with which it is co-ordinated: ጐየ ፡ ዕራቁ *lit.* "he fled *a naked one, of a personality he*", *i. e.* "he fled naked" Mark 14, 51; ያውድቁኒ ፡ ዕራቅየ "let them cast me down *(as a) naked (one of a personality I)*", *i. e.* "let them throw me down naked" Ps. 7, 4; ሀለዉ ፡ ዕራቃኒሆሙ "they were naked" Gen. 2, 25; 3, 7 (ዕራቅ, in fact, is used only in this way: v. also Gen. 1, 2 Note; 3, 10; Hen. 32, 6, *et saepe*); ተወልደ ፡ ዕዉሩ "he was born blind" John 9, 1, 13; ሖረ ፡ ትኩዞ "he went away grieved" Mark 10, 22; Ps. 37, 6; ይኄይሰከ ፡ ትባእ ፡ ውስተ ፡ ሕይወት ፡ ሐንካሰከ ፡ ወዕዉሰከ ፡ . . . ወ″ . . . ነቋርከ Matt. 18, 8, 9; አኀዝዎ ፡ ለንጉሦ ፡ ሕያዎ Josh. 8, 23; ንበሪ ፡ ማዕሰብኪ "remain a widow" Gen. 38, 11 (where more exactly it should stand ማዕሰበኪ); ይነብር ፡ ትኩዞ *Chrest.* p. 42, line 20; ተረፉ ፡ ቅውማኒሆሙ G. Ad. 29, 26; v. also ጥራዮ in DILLMANN's '*Lex.*', col. 1221. For other instances of this kind v. *infra* §§ 163, 2; 172, *b*; 189; and in the case of Numeral Adjectives § 191.

II. PRONOMINALS.

§ 157. 1. We find in Ethiopic a few *Compounds of Pronouns and Conceptional words*, which take the place held by Pronominal words in other languages.

(¹) Like פֶּרֶא אָדָם (Gen. 16, 12) in Hebrew, or *the Karma-dhāraya* Compounds in Sanskrit; [v. WILLIAMS' '*Sanskrit Gr.*' p. 281. TR.]

The conception "such" is expressed in Ethiopic, as in other Semitic tongues, by means of the preposition ከመ (§ 165)—which is itself of Pronominal origin—together with the Demonstrative ዝ or ዝንቱ፡ "this": ከመዝ Hen. 25, 7; ከመ ፡ ዝንቱ፡ Gen. 41, 38; or with a Suffix Pron.: ከማየ, ከማሁ &c. (§ 167). In both cases the relative pron. may also be prefixed: ዘከማሁ literally "*who as he is*" *i. e.* "such a—"; ዘከመዝ Matt. 17, 21; ለእለ ፡ ከመዝ "for such" (Dat. pl.) Matt. 19, 14.

II. Pronominals:—1. Compounds of Pronouns and Conceptional Words taking the place held by Pronominals in other Languages.

The idea "so great" is brought out by means of the Constr. St. (generally Accusative too) of መጠን "measure", *e. g.* ሃይማኖት ፡ መጠነ ፡ ኅጠተ ፡ ሰናፔ "faith ('of the size of') as great as a mustard-seed" Matt. 17, 20; ሕለት ፡ ወርቅ ፡ ዘመጠነ ፡ በትር "a golden reed ('of the size of') as large as a rod" Rev. 11, 1; similarly Luke 18, 16; or with ዝ or ዝንቱ፡ appended, *e. g.* መጠነዝ "so great" Jas. 3, 4; በመጠነዝ "for so much" Acts 5, 8; or with the relative pron. prefixed also: ዘመጠነዝ "so great" (*lit.* 'which is according to the measure of this') Matt. 8, 10; 15, 33. In like manner መጠነ, by leaving out the pron., may also signify "how great", "how much" (in a relative sense or in a dependent question): "I will tell you መጠነ ፡ ገብረ ፡ ለነፍስየ (*lit.* 'the measure of what') how much he has done for my soul" Ps. 65, 15; Matt. 27, 13; Ex. 19, 4; in relative sense Gen. 34, 12. In order to convert it into an Interrogative, ሚ "what?" or "how?" (§ 63) is prefixed, which, at least in introducing a direct question, is indispensable: ሚመጠነ ፡ ትሁቡኒ "how much will ye give me?" Matt. 26, 15; ሚመጠነ ፡ መዝርዐ ፡ አግሐ ሥከሙ Matt. 16, 9; 15, 34; Gen. 30, 29; 47, 8; Ps. 118, 84; Hen. 89, 62.—Notice also the peculiar word ስፍን properly: "prominence", "size", which is used only as an Interrogative in the sense of "how much?" "how great?" Originally እስፍንቱ፡, from interrogative እ (§ 63, *b*) and ስፍንቱ፡, means properly, "what is the size of it?" *i. e.* "how much?" (Ludolf, '*Lex.*' p. 188), "how often?" (G. Ad. 45, 6); then, without an interrogative sign, ስፍነ ("measure of", for ስፍነ ፡ ዝ) = "how often?" Matt. 18, 21; and, finally, plain ስፍን "how much *or* many?" in the Nom. (Ludolf, *l. c.*). In this case the interrogative force lies merely in the Tone.

2. Conceptional Words, used only when compounded with Suff. Prons.

2, So too there are several *Conceptional words which are only used when compounded with Suffix pronouns.* These words contain in fact nothing but quite general conceptions of space, measure or existence, and to that extent they stand always in need of a complement. This complement they should in strictness have subordinated to themselves by the Constr. State, just like many other conceptional words,—blank in themslves,—which ordinarily complete their meaning only by means of a second word (§ 185) (1). The words which are now to be described, however, have this peculiarity, that they are never completed by a conceptional word, but always by a Suffix Pronoun and by nothing else (2). The following are of this class.

The old Semitic word **ኵል** "entirety", "totality" still occurs occasionally in independent form, but only as an Adverb (**ኵልሄ** and **ኵለሄ** "everywhere" and "in every direction", § 160). In other positions, however, it must always be completed by a Suffix, by means of which the completing notion is referred to, either beforehand or by way of addition. Then having been combined with its suffix into one word, it is always placed in free apposition beside the conceptional word to which it refers. As a rule, it is compounded with Suffixes of the third Person: **ኵሉ**, **ኵላ**, **ኵሎሙ**, **ኵሎን**; Accusative **ኵሎ** (§ 154, *b*, *α*), **ኵላ**, **ኵሎሙ**, **ኵሎን**. With the Singular-suffixes it signifies "all", "every", "the whole of"; with the Plural suffixes "all the". **ኵሉ** may stand by itself, and then it means "everything", *e. g.* **እግዚእ ፡ ኵሉ** "the Lord of all". However, it is generally connected with other nouns: **ኵሉ ፡ ብእሲ** or **ብእሲ ፡ ኵሉ** "every man" or "all men"; **ኵሎሙ ፡ ነገሥት** "all kings", or **ነ″ ፡ ኵ″**; **ኵላ ፡ ምድር** or **ም″ ፡ ኵ″** "the whole earth"; **ኵሉ ፡ መንፈስ** "all living beings" &c. Properly the suffix should be regulated in gender and number by the conceptional word to which it refers. But often enough the Masc. form **ኵሉ** appears for the Fem. **ኵላ**, even when the reference is to conceptional words of the feminine gender, as in **ኵሉ ፡ መንግሥት** Luke 11, 17; and still more frequently the Singular **ኵሉ** appears in the expression of a Plural notion. Indeed any word may be continued in the Singular (and yet have a Plural force) alongside of **ኵሉ**,—even a word which in other positions never has a Collective meaning—, just because **ኵሉ** itself expresses collectivity:—**ኵሉ ፡ ባሕር** "all seas" or "every sea". Even when the notion "all" (*pl.*) stands entirely alone, **ኵሉ** may

(1) Such words occur in every Semitic language; *cf.* Ewald, '*Hebr. Spr.*' § 209, *c*.

(2) Like יַחְדָּיו, לְבַדּוֹ in Hebrew.

remain in the Singular: "all perished" ኵሉ ፡ ሞተ or ኵሎሙ ፡ ሞቱ. Many instances are also met with, in which ኵሉ is not adjusted to the Case of the word to which it belongs, but continues in its first form,—particularly if it follows the word,—inasmuch as the Case has been already indicated in that leading word and the whole relation between the two is only that of a loose co-ordination.—Then too, this word may adopt all the other suffixes (with the exception of የ), in the meaning "all of us" ("we all"), "all of you" &c; and it must assume these suffixes instead of those of the third Person, whenever the notion "all" (*pl.*) refers to the first or second Person: "we have all gone" ኵልነ ፡ ሖርነ or ሖርነ ፡ ኵልነ; so ኵልክሙ Matt. 23,8; Ps. 2,10; ኵልክን; *Accus.* ኵለነ Ex. 16,3 &c.

From the Feminine form ኵለት sprung ኵለንታ in the sense of "entirety", "totality", by the attachment of the Collective-forming *ā* (§ 140, IV) and the insertion of ን (§ 58). This word in like manner appears only when completed by suffixes, and for the purpose of expressing the notion "whole", in the sense of "in the whole being": ኵለንታየ "I wholly" ('my whole being'); ኵለንታከ "thou wholly" Luke 11,36; ኵለንታሁ "the whole of him" Gen. 25,25; Hen. 72,4(1); ኵለንታሁ ፡ ሥጋከ "the whole of thy body" Matt. 5,30; ኵለንታሃ "all of it (*f.*)" Gen. 13,15; እንተ ፡ ኵለንታሆሙ "in the direction of their entirety", *i. e.* "they in all directions", "they wholly" Rev. 4,8; ኵለንታሃ ፡ ሌሊተ "the whole night" Ex. 14,20.

The word ባሕቲት "solitude" (§ 120, *a*) is always(2) combined with suffixes, to bring out the notion, "alone": ባሕቲትየ "my solitude" *i. e.* "I alone"; ባሕቲትከ "thee (*acc.*) alone" Ps. 50,5; ባሕቲቱ "he alone" Josh. 22,20; ኪያሁ ፡ ባሕቲቶ ፡ ታምልክ Matt. 4,10; 10,42; ባሕቲትክሙ "you (two) alone" Matt. 18,15; ባሕቲቶሙ Matt. 17,1; ባሕቲቶን Gen. 21,28. But still it keeps here and there its Substantive meaning: በባሕቲቶሙ "in their solitude", "when they were alone" Mark 4,10; [*Kebra Nag.* 97 a 11].

The word ከንቱ, besides, (compare: *gratis*, חִנָּם "in vain") as Constr. St. ከንቶ, "emptiness", "nothingness", has always the suffix of the third Person sing. masc. (like ኵሉ) ከንቱ, Acc. ከንቶ to express "a thing of nought", "a vain thing" Ps. 38,8; 2,1. But it is chiefly employed as an adverb, either in the form ከንቶ or com-

---

(1) [Flemming's reading here is ኵሉ. tr.]

(2) *Cf. supra* p. 360, § 156 ዕሩቅ.

bined with በ as በከንቱ፡ (§ 163). On a few other words compounded with the suffixes of the third Person, which occur always as Adverbs, v. *infra*, § 163; *ibid.* also on ገጹ፡ with suffixes.

III. NUMERALS.

III. Numerals:— 1. Cardinal Numbers. § 158. The Numerals in Ethiopic are almost all of them the very same as in the other Semitic languages. As regards therefore their Root-formation, and partly also their Stem-formation, enquirers may at this point be referred to the grammars of these other languages.

1. *Cardinal Numbers* (1). The Numeral for "one", according to its root and its stem, has the form አሐድ፡; and, just as in other languages, it is properly an Adjective. When therefore it is connected with a Feminine conception, it assumes the Feminine termination: አሐት (for አሐድት, § 54). It no longer occurs, however, in these bare forms (2), but, like the demonstrative pronouns, it becomes a Personal Numeral by the attachment of the termination *ū* for the Masculine, and *ī* for the Feminine, so that the actual Numeral for "one" has always the form አሐዱ (*masc.*) or አሐቲ፡ (*fem.*). It takes the Accusative, by changing, like the Pronouns, *ū* or *ī* into *a*: አሐደ, አሐተ. It is quite as incapable of taking the form of a Construct State as the Pronouns (3) are; and accordingly "one of them", and the like, must be expressed as "one from them" አሐዱ ፡ እምኔሆሙ &c.

The Numeral for "two", employed by the rest of the Semitic languages, is indeed found in Ethiopic also, in a few scattered expressions like ሰኑይ "the second day" ('of the week *or* of the month') and ሳኒት "the following day", but it has passed out of use as a Numeral proper. In its stead a fresh Numeral, viz. ክልኤ meaning properly "a pair", and in form a Dual, § 131,—has been derived from the root כלא, ከልአ ("to separate", "to divide", "to hold back from anything", "to hinder"). This numeral has

---

(1) On the *diptosis* of the Cardinal Numbers from "one" to "ten" v. BARTH, ZDMG XLVI, p. 691 *sq.*—For the accentuation v. TRUMPP, p. 558.

(2) A Plural አሐዳት "*uniones*" (*i. e.* Numbers from one to ten,—'units'), v. DILLMANN's '*Lex.*', is met with, Abush. (Abushakeri *opus Chronographicum*), 11.

(3) *Cf.*, however, አሐድን, *var.* አሐደን Mark 10, 37.

points of connection with כִּלְאַיִם and كِلَانِ, كِلْتَانِ. It occurs still, now and then, quite independently, as Subject or Predicate, in the sense of "a pair" or "two", *e. g.* **ክልኤ ፡ ይሄልዉ።** "two shall be" Matt. 24, 40; **ሰይፍ ፡ ዘክልኤ ፡ አፉሁ** "a sword whose edge is two" (*i. e.* 'which has two edges' or "a two-edged sword") Ps. 149, 6; or again it may, in the form of a Construct State, be completed by a Genitive, and then it generally takes suffixes, as in **ክልኤነ**, **ክልኤክሙ**, **ክልኤክን**, **ክልኤሆሙ**, **ክልኤሆን**, to express the notion "both of us", "both of you", "both of them". But it may also,—and this is the usual case,—be connected, by mere apposition, with the idea, of which the two-fold character has to be declared, just like the other Numerals (v. *infra*), *e. g.* **ክልኤ ፡ ደቂቀ** (*Acc.*) Gen. 48, 1. Now as gender cannot be expressed with the form **ክልኤ**, the Feminine termination **ት** (1) was applied, following the analogy of the other Numerals, and to this modified form *ū* for the Masc. and *ī* for the Fem. were added, (exactly as in **አሐዱ**.), whence we have *masc.* **ክልኤቱ**, *fem.* **ክልኤቲ** "two", and an *Acc.* **ክልኤተ** for both *masc.* and *fem.* When the gender has to be distinguished with precision, one of these two forms is made use of; but when the gender is either of no consequence, or is quite obvious from the context, then even **ክልኤ** may be employed. In loose diction we often have **ክልኤቱ**, as the readiest form, even with names of things and notions which by grammatical gender are feminine.

The remaining Numerals from 3 to 10 are as follows:—

CARDINAL NUMBERS.

3—10.

	Masc.	*Fem.* a	*Fem.* b
3.	ሠለስቱ፡	ሠላስ	ሥልስ
4.	አርባዕቱ፡	አርባዕ	ርብዕ
5.	ኀምስቱ፡	ኀምስ	ኃምስ
6.	ስድስቱ፡	ስሱ	ስድስ
7.	ሰብዐቱ፡	ሰብዑ	ስብዕ
8.	ሰመንቱ፡	ሰማኒ	ስምን
9.	ተስዐቱ፡ *or* ትስዐቱ፡	ተስዑ *or* ትስዑ	ትስዕ
10.	ዐሠርቱ፡	ዐሥሩ	ዕሥር.

(1) **ክልኤት** "the being two",—an abstract form.

All these Numerals are originally Substantives. True, in their earliest form and expression they had assuredly no Feminine ending; but at a pretty early stage Abstracts were formed out of them by means of the Feminine termination (in all the Semitic tongues), and this type became the usual one. In still later times, when these words were no longer put in due connection, like Substantives by means of the Constr. St., but like Adjectives by way of apposition, the gender also began to be distinguished in them. The form which was most in use at that time, viz. that which had the Feminine ending, was retained for the first or *Masculine* gender, while the ancient form or a newly fashioned shorter form, without the Fem. ending, was employed for the *Feminine* gender. In this general process of development Ethiopic agrees entirely with the other Semitic languages. But as regards individual forms, the form, contrived by means of **ት**, seldom occurs now in this naked shape, as *e. g.* in **ሰብዐት** Josh. 6, 13, although it could not be avoided in those cases at least in which the Numeral in the Constr. St. had to govern a Genitive, § 191, or to attach Suffixes to itself, *e. g.* **ሠለስቲሆሙ** literally "their 'three'" *i. e.* "the three of them"; **ሰብዐቲሆሙ** "the (aforesaid) seven" Mark 12, 22; **ዐሠርቲሆሙ** 4 Esr. 3, 60. As a rule, these Numbers are no longer connected as Substantives in the Constr. St. with the numbered object, but as Adjectives and by means of apposition, § 191. They are accordingly converted from Abstracts into Attributive words, by the attachment of the Pronominal ending *ū* (1), exactly like **ክልኤቱ፡**; and when they take the Accusative case, they change this *ū* into *a*:—**ሠለስቱ፡**, **ሠለስተ** &c. In fashioning these forms, furnished with a feminine **ት**, a long vowel occurring in the ground-form must be shortened (§ 36):—**ሠለስት** from **ሠላስ**, **ሰመንት** from **ሰማን** or **ሰማኒ**, and hence **ሠለስቱ፡**, **ሰመንቱ፡**. And yet in Judges 3, 8, 14 we meet also with **ሰማንተ** (*Acc.*). The two forms **ሰብዐቱ፡**, **ተስዐቱ፡**,

(1) **ሠለስት** is "the Three" (abstract Subst.), **ሠለስቱ፡** "three" (attributive word). It is true, one is apt to conceive of *ū* as an ordinary Suff. Pron. and to explain **ሠለስቱ፡** according to § 157 as "three of it". But this is a wrong conception; for in that case the Accusative would be bound to have the form **ሠለስቶ**, which is not the case; and, besides, **ክልኤቲ፡** would be inexplicable. Rather is the formation the same as when a Demonstr. Pron. **ቱ፡** "he" with a Personal meaning is formed from the root **ቱ**. *Cf.* also **እስፍንቱ፡** *supra*, p. 360, § 157, 1.

constructed in accordance with § 127, *a*, frequently pass into ሰበ ዐቱ፡, ተሳዐቱ፡ (1) in accordance with § 47, *sub fin.* Then, in the numeral "nine" ትስዐት is made use of quite as much as ተስዐት. For "eight" a form ሰማኒቱ፡ is also met with, 1 Pet. 3, 20; Gen. 46, 22, preserving the *ī*, from ሰማኒ (שְׁמֹנֶה) (2).

The form which is used as a Feminine, but which is Masculine in its type, is constructed from the foregoing form in ት, by throwing off the ት and reducing the word to its original, radical constitution. Two varieties are possible: 1.—Recourse may be had to the obsolete ground-form, for the purpose of re-introducing it into use, whence come ሠላስ, שָׁלוֹשׁ (§ 18 *sub fin.*); አርባዕ, אַרְבַּע; ኀምስ (3), חָמֵשׁ, خَمْس; ስድስ, سِتّ (*cf.* سَادِس); ሰብዕ שֶׁבַע [*Kebra Nag.* p. XVII]; ሰማኒ Josh. 21, 39, Numb. 35, 7, שְׁמֹנֶה, ثَمَانٍ; ተስዕ and ትስዕ, תֵּשַׁע; ዐሥር (4) עֶשֶׂר. 2.—Or an entirely new form may be fashioned, after the manner of Nouns of the First simple formation, as has been noted in the above list, in the second column of Feminine forms. This form, however, is not in very great favour. One or two examples are met with, as in 1 Kings 7; Deut. 3, 11; Ex. 37, 1; Ruth 3, 15; but it is chiefly used to form Numeral Adverbs (§ 159). Of the Fem. Numbers of the First form, those which do not end with a vowel, or do not have a long vowel in the last syllable, usually take *ū*, for the purpose of becoming Attributive words, exactly as the Masc. Numbers do. Thus we have ስሱ (for ስድሱ) *séssū*, ሱብዑ, ተስዑ or ትስዑ (5), ዐሥሩ; probably ኀምሱ may also be formed; ዐሥር also appears as a side-form to ዐሥሩ. For "three", "four", "five", "eight" the forms ሠላስቱ፡, አርባዕቱ፡, ኀምስቱ፡, ሰመንቱ፡ are more generally used in association even with Feminine words, unless when a preference is given to ሠላስ, አርባዕ, ኀምስ, ሰማኒ. But while an Accusative may still be formed for Masc. Numbers ending in ቱ፡, the forms ስሱ, ሱብዑ, ተስዑ

(1) LUDOLF held these forms to be the original ones.

(2) [On the relation between שְׁמֹנֶה, ܬܡܢܝܐ, ثَمَانِي, ሰማኒ *cf.* PHILIPPI, '*Beitr. z. Assyr.*' II, p. 364, Note ***, and PRAETORIUS, ZDMG LVI, p. 695.]

(3) Occasionally written also ኃምስ (§ 48).

(4) Occasionally written also ዓሥር (§ 48).

(5) Josh. 21, 16; 15, 57.

and as a rule also ዐሥሩ (1), have become indeclinable, and even in the Accusative and before Suffixes they retain their *ū* (Numb. 8,2). But no doubt ኀምስ and the entire Second series of the Fem. Numbers may enter upon the Accusative by appending *ă*.

For the Tens, from 20 to 90, a Plural-form should have been expected, according to the analogy of the other Semitic tongues. In fact they appear to have been formed at one time from the original ground-forms of the units by attaching the Masculine Plural-ending *án* (2); but in later times, because they no longer distinguished Cases or Genders, they allowed the Nasal at the end to disappear (§ 58) (3). Accordingly we have:—ሠላሳ 30, አርብዓ 40 (for አርበዓ, § 45), ኀምሳ 50, ስሳ 60 (for ስድሳ), ሰብዓ 70, ሰማንያ 80, ተስዓ 90 (*e. g.* Luke 15, 4, 7; Matt. 18, 12, 13) or ትስዓ (*e. g.* Gen. 17, 17). The form derived from 10, ዕሥራ (never ዐሥራ) serves, not for 100, but for 20,—a special word being used for 100.

The Numeral 100 is ምእት; Constr. St. and Acc. ምእተ; Plur. አምእት (§ 136, 2, *c*). The Semitic word for 1000 እልፍ has in Ethiopic rather the meaning 10,000; Constr. St. and Acc. እልፈ; Plur. አእላፍ; Plur. of Plur. አእላፋት. ምእት and እልፍ are both Substantives originally, but they are usually associated with the object numbered, by mere co-ordination, like all the other Numerals (§ 191). አርባብ and ረበዎት "myriads" are obsolete forms, very seldom used (§§ 136, 2, *b*; 134, *c*, *β*). እልፍ can be used in Ethiopic for the number 1000, only when the notion merely of a great number has to be signified, and exact enumeration is not required: thus *e. g.* in Deut. 33, 17 both *μυριάδες* and *χιλιάδες* are translated by አእላፍ: so too in Dan. 7, 10:—አእላፈ ፡ አእላፋት ፡ ወትእልፌተ ፡ ትእልፌት *χίλιαι χιλιάδες καὶ μύριαι μυριάδες*; *cf.* Hen. 40, 1 (4) [and *Kebra Nag.* 141 b 18]. In more exact numerical expression 1000 must be signified by ዐሠርቱ ፡ ምእት = 10 × 100;

(1) V., however ዐሥሮን, DILLMANN's '*Lex.*', col. 959.

(2) [The corresponding Assyrian forms, however, ending likewise in *ā*, are not in favour of this theory.]

(3) Much as the Personal-ending *ū* in the case of the verb came from an original *ūn*, *ūm*.—For the accentuation v. TRUMPP, p. 558.

(4) [FLEMMING reads here አእላፈ ፡ አእላፍ ፡ ወትእልፌተ ፡ ትእልፌታት. TR.] [For another word for '1000', ሲሕ, v. *Kebra Nag.* p. XVII.]

thus 2000 is ዕሥራ፡ ምእት, 3000 ሠላሳ፡ ምእት and so on. 100,000 is ዐሠርቱ፡ እልፍ, and 1,000,000 ምእት፡ እልፍ.

When numbers have to be compounded by way of addition, the larger number generally comes first, and the smaller one is almost always joined on with ወ. As regards the numbers 11—19, it calls for special notice that like genders and forms are combined in all cases:—ዐሠርቱ፡ ወአሐዱ 11, ዐሠርቱ፡ ወክልኤቱ 12, ዐሠርቱ፡ ወሠለስቱ 13 &c.; or ዐሥሩ፡ ወአሐቲ, ዐሥሩ፡ ወክልኤ (Josh. 21,7, 38), ዐሥሩ፡ ወሠላስ &c.; or ዕሥር፡ ወሥልስ, ዕሥር፡ ወርብዕ &c. When numbers are compounded by way of multiplication, the smaller precedes the larger, and of course without ወ:—ክልኤቱ፡ ምእት 200, ዐሠርቱ፡ ወአሐዱ፡ ምእት 1100, or ዐሥሩ፡ ወአሐቲ፡ ምእት 1100 &c.

§ 159. 2. *Derived Numerals.*

2. Derived Numerals:—Ordinal Numbers.

(*a*) *Numeral Adjectives* or *Ordinals* are derived, in the form of an Act. Part. (§ 109, *a*) which is no longer much used for any other purpose—, from the ground-form, just as in Arabic [and Assyrian], and in fact from the tri-radical root-form, without regard to any firmer vowels, or to any fourth letter attached to the commencement or the end of the root and established in the ground-form; thus ሣልስ, ራብዕ &c. For "the first" an adjective is used which has been formed according to § 117 from the √ቀደመ, namely ቀዳሚ; for "the second" either the word ካልእ "the other",—confined indeed for the most part to cases in which only 'two' are spoken of (*alter*),—or the word ካዕብ, already becoming obsolete, from the √ከዐበ "to be double",—or,—and this is the word most used—, ዳግም (ደገመ I, 2 "to repeat", *cf.* دِجْمَة, دَغَمَ IV, VIII). The Feminine of all these Participial forms is fashioned by appending ት: ካልእት, ዳግምት, ሣልስት &c. But, following a formative tendency which is peculiarly active in the construction of Numerals, and perhaps also because the old Participial form had otherwise gone out of use in the tongue, these Adjectives have acquired new forms, brought about by attaching terminations. The Participial form, in fact, attaches to itself either the long ending *āwī*, Fem. *āwīt* (§ 119, *b*):—ሣልሳዊ, ሣልሳዊት, or the shorter ending *āi*, to which a Fem. *īt* or *āwīt* corresponds, in accordance with § 129, *b*, ζ:—ሣልሳይ, ሣልሲት or ሣልሳዊት. From ዳግም also both these forms are contrived, but not from ካልእ. In very rare instances we have the form ከዐበዊ from ከዕብ. Along with ቀዳሚ we have from ቀዳም the forms ቀዳማዊ and ቀዳማይ, but in the Fem. only ቀዳሚት. Thus:—

ORDINAL NUMBERS.

1–10.

	Masc.			*Fem.*	
	1.	2.	3.	1.	2.
1.	ቀዳሚ	ቀዳማዊ	ቀዳማይ	ቀዳሚት	—
2.	ዳግም	ዳግማዊ	ዳግማይ	ዳግሚት	ዳግማዊት
3.	ሣልስ	ሣልሳዊ	ሣልሳይ	ሣልሲት	ሣልሳዊት
4.	ራብዕ	ራብዓዊ	ራብዓይ	ራብዒት	ራብዓዊት
5.	ኃምስ	ኃምሳዊ	ኃምሳይ	ኃምሲት	ኃምሳዊት
6.	ሳድስ	ሳድሳዊ	ሳድሳይ	ሳድሲት	ሳድሳዊት
7.	ሳብዕ	ሳብዓዊ	ሳብዓይ	ሳብዒት	ሳብዓዊት
8.	ሳምን	ሳምናዊ	ሳምናይ	ሳምኒት	ሳምናዊት
9.	ታስዕ	ታስዓዊ	ታስዓይ	ታስዒት	ታስዓዊት
10.	ዓሥር	ዓሥራዊ	ዓሥራይ	ዓሥሪት	ዓሥራዊት.

The Cardinal Numbers usually appear for the Ordinals also, in the case of the *Tens*, just as in other Semitic languages ("the thirtieth year" = "the year thirty"):—አመ ፡ ሠላሳሁ ፡ ለወርኅ "on the thirtieth of the month",—(*lit.* 'at the time of the thirty of the month') Ludolf, '*Lex.*' col. 333. But yet there occurs, besides, an Adjective-form in *āwī*: 20, ዕሥራዊ; 30, ሠላሳዊ; 40, አርብዓዊ; 50, ኀምሳዊ; 60, ስሳዊ; 70, ሰብዓዊ; 80, ሰማንያዊ; 90, ተስዓዊ. On the other hand no Adjective-forms are derived from ምእት or እልፍ.

Number of the Day of the Week or Month. (*b*) The Ethiopians have peculiar forms for the days of the week and of the month ([1]). From a Pass. Part. of the type ግቡር a Substantive Noun is derived afresh by the interpolation of an *a* after the first radical (so that if ግቡር = قَتُول, then ገቡር is = قَاتُول), with the force of a Substantive like πεντάς, ἑβδομάς &c. (*cf.* § 109, 3, *b*) ([2]). Thus, ሰኑይ—"the second day (of the week *or* of the month)" ([3]); ሠሉስ "the third"; ረቡዕ "the fourth"; ኀሙስ

([1]) *Cf.* Ewald, '*Gr. Ar.*', § 364.

([2]) *Cf.* Ewald, '*Hebr. Spr.*' § 152, *c*.

([3]) Hence too the Fem. ሰኒት, while ሳኒት (*postera dies*) comes from ሳንይ.

"the fifth"; ሰዱስ "the sixth"; ሰቡዕ "the seventh"; ሰሙን "the eighth (day of the month)"; ተሱዕ "the ninth"; ዐሡር "the tenth". The "first" (day) of the week is እሑድ (for አሑድ, on account of the Aspirate ሑ); the "first" of the month ሥርቅ ('summit'); hence the "eleventh" of the month is ዐሡር ፡ ወሠርቅ Numb. 7,72; so ዐሡር ፡ ወረቡዕ Acts 27,27; ዐሡር ፡ ወኃሙስ Lev. 23,6. These forms make no distinction between genders (1), and may be used quite independently without the word "day" being placed beside them: በዐሡር ፡ ወረቡዕ "in 14 days" Hen. 78,6; or else they may, like other numerals, be connected with the object numbered, by way of co-ordination. They are nearly always used, in place of the other numerals, whenever days, months or hours are numbered, *e. g.* ነበረ ፡ ህየ ፡ ሰኑየ ፡ መዋዕለ "he tarried there ('a two-days') two days" John 11,6; ሠሉሰ ፡ ዕለተ ፡ ወሠሉሰ ፡ ሌሊተ "three days and three nights" (*lit.* 'a third day and a third night') Matt. 12,40; 15,32; John 2,19; Luke 13,14; John 20,26; Gen. 7,4, 10; 8,10; 24,55; Ex. 7,25; 20,9; Lev. 15,13; even መዋዕለ ፡ ፫፻ወ፷ወረቡዐ "364 days" Hen. 72,32. In like manner they stand for Numeral Adjectives, when days are enumerated: አመ ፡ ሰሙን ፡ ዕለት "on the eighth day" Luke 1,59; 2,21; but a complementary Suffix of the 3rd pers. sing. Masc. is usually attached in that case (as with ኵሉ &c., § 157):—አመ ፡ ዐሡሩ ፡ ወረቡዑ ፡ ሌሊት Acts 27,27 (Old) (v. also § 191). In rare instances they are employed in enumerating other objects than divisions of Time, Hen. 77,8(2).

(*c*) To express Numerals in the sense of *Manifoldness* (*Multiplicatives*), Passive Participles of the type ግቡር may be used. For since verbs even may be derived from the Numbers 1—10, according to § 77, a Passive Participle may also be formed: ሥሉስ "threefold, triple", "triangular", "triune"; ርቡዕ "fourfold", "quadrangular" &c. For "two" in this application ክዑብ "double" is used. Multiplicatives.

Farther, Substantives of the type ትግብርት (§ 111) and ትግብሬት and still more commonly of the type ምግብርት and ምግብሬት (3), are derived, to express "Multiplicity" and "the Manifold"

(1) And yet we read in Matt. 27,46: ሰዓት ፡ ተሱዐት (ተሱዓት) "the ninth hour".

(2) [Flemming here reads ሰብዑ, the cardinal numeral, instead of Dillmann's ordinal ሰቡዐ (*acc.*). tr.]

(3) Being in fact, first of all, Passive Participles of the type መገሙር

(properly, "the product"). Hence: ትሥልስት "threefold" and "Trinity"; ትርብዕት "fourfold" Luke 19,8; Ex. 21,37; ትኅምስት "five-fold" Ex. 21,37; ትዕሥርት "ten-fold"; ትእልፊት "ten-thousand-fold" = 10.000 (Hen. 21,6; 40,1; 71,8. 13 &c.); or ምሥልስት "threefold"; ምኅምስት "five-fold" Gen. 43,34; ምስብዒት "seven-fold", ምእልፊት "ten-thousand-fold" Ps. 67,18. In the Accusative these Substantives are used adverbially (§ 163): ምሥልስተ "threefold" Deut. 19,3; ትርብዕተ "fourfold"; ምኅምስተ "five-fold"; ምስብዒተ "seven-fold" Ps. 11,7; 78,13; ትዕሥርተ "ten-fold" Is. 6,13.

From the number "two" is formed ክዕበት "the double" ('doubling') and ክዕበተ "twofold" (Adv.), and also from the same root ምክዕቢት "doubling" in the general sense of "multiplying", "multiplied". This last word may be combined with any number, to express "manifoldness": ምእተ ፡ ምክዕቢተ "an hundredfold" Gen. 26,12; Matt. 19,29; Luke 8,8; ክዕበተ ፡ ምክዕቢት "double" Rev. 18,6; ብዙኀ ፡ ምክዕቢተ "manifold" Luke 18,30; ፻ ምክዕቢተ Hen. 91,16; ምክዕቢተ ፡ እልፍ ፡ እምአእላፍ Rev. 9,16 (1):—even ፻ ምክዕቢታተ ፡ ትምህርት Hen. 93,10.

Simpler expressions are met in በሠላሳ "thirtyfold", በምእት "an hundredfold" Mark 4,20.

Abstract Numerals. (*d*) *Abstract Numeral Substantives* are given in ሥላሴ "Trinity"; ኆማሴ "the Five"; ሱባዔ "the Seven", "Week" (§ 120, β), also in ኃኅማስ (§ 111, β).

Numeral Adverbs. (*e*) To express *Numeral Adverbs* in the signification of 'so and so-many-times', the Cardinal number of the second Fem. type (§ 158) is put in the Accusative: ሥልሰ "thrice" Matt. 26,34; Hen. 65,2; ኅምሰ "five times" 2 Cor. 11,24; ስብዐ "seven times" Gen. 4,15: or,—and this may be said to be still more frequent,— that form is left entirely uninflected and is used in that guise as an adverb (§ 163): ስብዕ "seven times" (of very frequent

(§ 116, γ), or names of things, of the type መግብር and መግበር (116, β & α), increased next by the Fem. ending ት or *īt* (§ 120, *a*), before which መ is reduced to ም.

(1) [It is much more likely that ምክዕቢተ occurs here in its *particular* meaning of "double", and not in its general sense of "so-many-fold", for it comes before, instead of after, the other numerals, and it purports to be a translation of δύο μυριάδες μυριάδων. TR.]

occurrence). For "once", **ምዕረ** is employed (مَعِرٍ, مَرَّةً) Mark 14,41; 7,27; Titus 3,10; or **በምዕር**, although the latter properly means "all at once" Cant. 4,9; or **አሐተ** (وَاحِدَةً) Judges 6,39; 16,18.—For "twice", **ክዕበ** Titus 3,10, or **ክዕበተ**, or **ዳግመ**. For higher as well as for lower numbers a periphrasis may also be employed by means of **ጊዜ** ("time", "hour", "turn"): **ሠለስተ ፡ ጊዜ** "thrice"; **አርበዕተ ፡ ምእተ ፡ ጊዜ** "four hundred times"; or **ሠለስተ ፡ ጊዜያተ** "thrice". **ጊዜ** may also be left out, if the meaning is clear from the context: **ሰብዓ ፡ በበ ፡ ስብዕ** "70×7 times" Matt. 18,22; **ሰብዐተ** "seven times" Josh. 6,16. Or **ምክዕቢተ** is used (v. *supra c*).

In answer to the question, 'For which time?' the Ordinal is given, either in the neuter with the preposition **በ**, *e. g.* **በሣልስ** "for the third time" Luke 23,22; **በዳግም** "for the second time" Matt. 18,16 (but also **ክዕበ** Luke 23,20, or **ዳግመ**); **በሳብዕ** Job 5,19; also in the Fem. and Acc., *e. g.* **ራብዕተ** "for the fourth time" Numb. 10,6;—or as a Personal by way of Apposition to the Person to whom the action is ascribed as repeated for such-and-such a number of times, *e. g.* "thou strikest me **ናሁ ፡ ሣልስከ ፡ ዝንቱ፡** for now the third time" Numb. 22,28: v. *infra* § 191.

(*f*) *The part of the whole* (or *Aliquot Fraction*) is usually expressed by **እድ** (יָד) "hand", more rarely by **ክፍል** "division" Hen. 78,4, with the Ordinal number in Masc. or Fem. form:—**ራብዕት ፡ እዴሃ ፡ ለምድር** "the fourth part of the earth"; **ሳብዓይ ፡ እድ** Hen. 73,3; **ሳብዒት ፡ እድ** 73,5; **ኃምስተ ፡ እዴሁ** (Acc.) Lev. 5,16; Gen. 47,24, 26; **ዓሥርተ ፡ እድ** Lev. 6,13. But the Ordinal is often put in the Constr. State:—**ራብዕተ ፡ እድ** "the fourth, as to the part" = "the fourth part", *e. g.* Rev. 6,8; v. also § 191; thus **ዓሥራተ**(1) **፡ እድ** "a tenth part" Gen. 14,20; 28,22; Matt. 23,23. "Two parts" are also given as **ምክዕቢት** Deut. 21,17. *Fractional Numbers* are *e. g.* **፫ ትኅምስት** "three-fifths" Hen. 78,7; **በበ ፡ ፯፯ እድ** "by sevenths" Hen. 74,3. [*Cf.* also Hen. 73,6—8]. Fractional Numbers.

(*g*) To express the idea "so many each" (*Distributives*) in numbers, Ethiopic has no special formation. Repetition of the numeral, first of all, does duty instead, at least in the case of uncompounded numerals: **አሐዱ ፡ አሐዱ**, **አሐቲ ፡ አሐቲ** "*singuli*, Distributives.

(1) V. on this word *supra*, p. 259 Note(1).

singulae" Hen. 72,1, 3; 7,1; 89,59; Gen. 40,5 (1); ክልኤ ፡ ክልኤ Gen. 7,9; 15,2, 3; ሰባዕተ ፡ ሰባዕተ (*acc.*) Gen. 7,2, 3 (2). When this is not practicable, or is regarded as too prolix, the Prefix-Particles በ, ለ, ዘ are employed in a double form, as በበ, ለለ, ዘዘ. Of these forms ዘዘ may be used only when a Genitive relation, or a Relative clause is already present in the case, *e. g.* ነሥአ ፡ ውእቱ ፡ ብእሲ ፡ አዕኑገ ፡ ዘወርቅ ፡ ዘዘ ፡ ሕልቅ ፡ ድልወቱ ፡ ወአውቃፌ ፡ ለእደዊሃ ፡ ዘዘ ፡ ዐሥሩ ፡ ሕልቅ ፡ ድልወቱ "the man took ear-rings of gold, each an ounce in weight, and bracelets for her hands, each ten ounces in weight" Gen. 24,22; *cf.* also Gen. 34,25; 37,7; 43,21. So too, when the prepositions በ and ለ would have been used, even had there been no distributive meaning, the double form of these is obviously the proper form to express the distributive "each": በበ ፡ ዲናር ፡ ለዕለት "for a penny each a-day" Matt. 20,2; Hen. 34,2; ለለ ፡ ፩ "to every one" Matt. 25,15; Hen. 7,1; Judges 11,40 (3). But these last two prepositions, በ and ለ, may also be placed, in the double form, before any other word in the sentence, —be it Subject or Object, or in any other reference,—for the purpose of expressing ἀνὰ, κατά:—ወነሥኡ ፡ በበ ፡ ዲናር "and they received ἀνὰ δηνάριον or a penny each" Matt. 20,9, 10; ወወሀቦሙ ፡ ዐሬዘ ፡ በበ ፡ ክልኤቱ "and he gave them each two vestments" (*literally*: "garments by the pair") Gen. 45,22; ንነሥእ ፡ በበ ፡ ዐሠርቱ ፡ ዕደው ፡ ለለ ፡ ምእት "we will take ('by way of ten

(1) [That አሐዱ ፡ አሐዱ (፩፩) may also be employed in the sense of "some" or "a few" is shown by a passage in '*Le Livre des Mystères du Ciel et de la Terre* (ed. Perruchon), p. 18, l. 14; *cf.* Praetorius, ZDMG LVIII, p. 488.]

(2) Other words too are repeated in like manner to express "*singuli*" ብእሲ ፡ ብእሲ "*viri singuli*", "every man" Judges 8,24; 17,6; ነግሀ ፡ ነግሀ "every morning" Ex. 36,3; 2 Kings 13,4; ኈበ ፡ ኈበ "more and more" 2 Kings 3,1; ከመ ፡ ከመ Ludolf, '*Lex.*' col. 397; ክምረ ፡ ክምረ Ex. 8,10.

(3) In older Manuscripts ለእለ is also met with, instead of ለለ, which is to be judged of in accordance with § 140 *sub fin.*; *e. g.* instead of ለለ ፡ ፩ "to every man", we meet with ለእለ ፡ ፩, whereby ፩ is raised to the Plural, Gen. 42,25 Note, 47, 12 Note, 49,28 Note. We farther come upon the expression "twelve princes ለእለ ፡ (instead of ለለ ፡) ሕዘቢሆሙ for their several tribes" Gen. 25,16, in which the Collective ሕዝ″ "their tribe" is raised by እለ to a new Plural with a distributive force.

men') ten men out of every hundred" Judges 20, 10; ይበሉ ፡ በበ ፡ ፩ "they begin to say one by one" Matt. 26, 22; ዘለለ ፡ ዚአሁ ፡ ሕማሞሙ ('whose maladies were—so to speak—κατ' ἰδίαν') "each of whom had his own special disease" Matt. 4, 24 &c.

Expressions for πρῶτον, δεύτερον, τρίτον.

(*h*) To express the ideas πρῶτον, δεύτερον, τρίτον ("in the first, second *or* third place") we find አሐቲ, ከልኤታ, ሣልስታ Sir. 23, 23 (the Subj. is Fem. gen.).

FORMATION OF WORDS OF RELATION.

Under this title Adverbs, Prepositions and Conjunctions fall to be specially dealt with.

I. ADVERBS.

1. ADVERBS DERIVED FROM PRONOMINAL ROOTS.

§ 160. 1. *Adverbs of Demonstrative meaning.*

1. Adverbs of Demonstrative meaning:—Particles of Demonstrative force.

(*a*) The most general particle in this class had originally the form of ነ, ና (§ 62) "there!" "see there!" as if pointing to an object. It no longer, however, occurs in this short form, but only as a Compound. 1. It may be compounded with the *a* (*hā*) of direction (§ 143), as ነዐ (Ps. 79, 3; Gen. 4, 8 Note; Herm. 82 *a*, 13); ንዐ 4 Esr. 3, 26 (König, p. 136); ንዓ Mark 10, 21 (Rom. ed.); or, usually, ነዓ = "hither", "come", always employed by way of summons or incentive, corresponding to δεῦρο or ἔρχου Matt. 19, 21; 8, 9; 9, 18; 14, 28 and equivalent to "come now!" "up!" *e. g.* Rev. 6, 1 (¹). As it is always used by way of command or summons, it is conjugated just like an Imperative (²),—in particular, taking the 2nd pers. fem. sing., ንዒ (Gen. 19, 32; John 4, 16), as well as the 2nd pers. pl. masc., ንዑ (Matt. 11, 28; 21, 38; Ps. 94, 1; Judges 16, 18), and fem. ንዓ (and ነዓ Matt. 28, 6). A verb usually appears along with it, *e. g.* Gen. 11, 4; yet ነዓ even by itself yields complete sense: ወንዑ ፡ ኀቤየ "and hither to me!" (*i. e.* "come ye to me!") Gen. 45, 18. 2. It may also be compounded with *Suffix Pronouns in the Acc.-subordination* (*i. e.* as Verbal Suffixes).

(¹) *Cf.* also Trumpp, p. 559, and '*Sitzber. d. k. bayer. Ak. d. W.*' 1877, p. 119 *sqq.*

(²) *Cf.* in Hebrew—Ewald, '*Hebr. Spr.*' § 101, *c.*

With the suffix, however, of the 1st pers. sing. the form is not ነኒ but ነየ (doubtless to avoid in this case repetition of the *n*) = "there I am!" *or* "here I am!" *i. e.* "see! I am here!" Matt. 8, 7; Acts 9,10; Hebr. 10,7; Ps. 39,10; or ነየ is even combined with a repetition of the pronoun አነ "I", as in ነየ ፡ አነ Gen. 22, 1, 11; 27, 18. It appears also with the suffix of the 3rd pers. sing. masc. as ናሁ(1) (having the *a* lengthened by the tone and the aspirate) "there he is!" or "there it is!", and, generally, "behold!" *e. g.* Ps. 7, 15; Gen. 19, 8; Matt. 10, 16; 15, 22. The suffixes ሃ, ሆሙ, ሆን it takes, in their truncated form, *ā*, *ōmū*, *ōn*; but then, in accordance with § 41, it lets a separating semivowel be heard between itself and them, thus ነያ "behold her!" John 19, 27; Luke 19, 20; Gen. 12, 19, or ነዋ. Usually however ነዋ has a neuter sense and is thus equivalent to ናሁ "behold!" John 19, 5, 26; Luke 17, 21, 23; Matt. 11, 19; 24, 23, 26; Ps. 51, 6; farther ነዮሙ "behold them!" Mark 3, 32, 34; Acts 5, 25; and ነዮን "behold them (*f.*)!" Gen. 19, 8. It is not in use with the suffixes of the 1st pers. Plur. or 2nd pers. Plur.

Another particle(2), which is used like ነዋ in the sense "there!", is እን (הֵן, הִנֵּה), from the same root as the foregoing, but with the pronunciation *an* (§ 62) or *ĕn*; whence እንክሙ "there! you!" = λαβέτε Matt. 26, 26, also by way of incentive or summons like ነዋ.

There are, besides, several other short enclitic particles of indication, from the same stem. The particle ነ, which hitherto has only been met with as an affix to the preposition and conjunction እስከ "till", expresses direction, እስከነ "as far as—":—እስከነ ፡ ዐረብ "as far as the west" Ps. 49, 2; 112, 3; Malachi 1, 11; እምሰብእ ፡ እስከነ ፡ እንስሳ Ex. 13, 2; እስከነ ፡ ኅበ ፡ ዐጽሙ ፡ መንከስ Judges 15, 14; እስከነ ፡ ርኢክምሙ Hen. 89, 5, 8, 75. It is perhaps merely a shortened form from the fuller ኔ, which still occurs with the Accusative of direction: ውስተ ፡ አሐተኔ "to one place", or (John 11, 52) አሐተኔ alone, "in one", "into one place" (v. Ludolf, '*Lex.*' col. 332)(3). Corresponding in meaning to this ኔ, but formed from another root (§ 62), is ዜ "there", "here", in use still as an

(1) Hence the Amharic ነው "he is".

(2) On the other hand ኣሚ βάδιζε Ex. 4, 19 is scarcely in this class.

(3) In the view of Praetorius, '*Amh. Spr.*' p. 197 this ነ or ኔ is considered to have become the ordinary Accusative-sign in Amharic.

affix to ኵል "universality": ኵሌ "everywhere", but Accusative ኵለ "in every direction"; በኵሌ "everywhere" Ex. 40, 32; እምኵሌ "from every quarter" Mark 1, 45; እምኵለ, with the same meaning, Hen. 28, 2. And just as the form ነ alternated with ኔ, so was it also at one time with the forms ሃ and ሄ, *cf.* §§ 143 and 163.

(*b*) *Independent Adverbs of Place and Time.* To this class belong, in the first place, ህየ (¹), "there", "thither", and ዝየ "here", "hither". These two particles in this form have probably come from ሄ and ዚ (*cf.* what is given under (*a*); *cf.* also *infra* ዚ in ይእዚ). Examples:—ዝየ "here" Matt. 14, 17; 26, 36; "hither" Matt. 8, 29; 14, 18; ህየ "there" Mark 11, 5; "thither" Rom. 15, 24. Both of them are also compounded with prepositions:—በህየ Matt. 13, 42; በዝየ Matt. 17, 4; እምህየ "thence" Matt. 11, 1, also of time Hen. 38, 6; እምዝየ; እስከ ፡ ህየ &c. To point to what is more remote, the language has a derivative from ከ, formed with the ሃ of direction, which is here hardened into ሐ (§ 62), ከሐ and ከሓ "to yonder place" Matt. 26, 36; Numb. 17, 2; or with prepositions: ኀበ ፡ ከሐ "to yonder place" Matt. 17, 20; also በከሐ "in yonder place" Heb. 7, 8; እምከሐ Josh. 8, 22. Besides, from ከሐ "to yonder place" a word for "in yonder place" or "there" may be formed by appending ከ a second time, ከሐከ "there" Luke 17, 21, 23; Matt. 24, 23; Gen. 19, 9; whence በዝየኒ ፡ ወበከሐከኒ "here and there"; also in the sense of *ultra*, *supra*, v. DILLMANN's '*Lex.*', col. 823. ይእዚ is treated as an Adverb of Time, "just now", "now". It is a compound of ይእ (§ 65) and an adverb ዚ (²), which certainly at one time referred to Place, and was merely transferred to Time. It is in very frequent use, compounded also with prepositions: እምይእዚ "from this time forward"; እስከ ፡ ይእዚ "till now". Meanwhile it is employed not merely for the Time which is present to the speaker, but for a present Time in the future or in the past, like the Hebrew עַתָּה, *e. g.* Hen. 38, 4; 50, 5. Other Adverbs of Time must be expressed by periphrasis: "thereafter" እምዝ, እምኔሃ, እምኔሁ (Hen. 83, 10: 89, 19), እምድኅረ ፡ ዝንቱ፡

Independent Adverbs of Place and Time.

(¹) [In older MSS. ሄየ; v. DILLMANN's '*Lex.*' col. 13; *cf.* also *Kebra Nag.*, *Introd.*, p. XVI.]

(²) Formed from the √ዝ, like ሄ and ኔ. With respect to the termination, all three may be compared with the Hebrew אַיֵּה, אֵי, מָתַי.

and the like; "at that time" አሜሃ፡ ይእተ ፡ ጊዜ፡ በውእቱ ፡ መዋዕል &c.

§ 161. 2. *Interrogative Adverbs and Adverbs of Relative Meaning.*

(*a*) *Interrogative Adverbs.*

2. Interrogative Adverbs and Adverbs of Relative meaning:—(*a*) Interrogative Adverbs.

Ethiopic has no introductory particles (1), such as other Semitic tongues have, to mark a sentence generally as an interrogative one, and thus introduce a question in the absence of a more definite interrogative Adverb.—It has only a few short particles, in particular ኑ and ሁ, which are appended to some word in the Interrogative sentence, like, for instance, *ne* in Latin. On the degree of difference between these two, compare § 198. They seem originally to mean "it", in the sense of "it (is the case)" (2); and they have gained their interrogative force through their enclitic position conjoined with the tone:—ተአምኑሁ Matt. 9, 28 "you believe;—(is) *that* (the case)?" = "do ye believe?" አንተኑ ፡ ዘይመጽእ Matt. 11, 3 "thou art he that should come;—(is) *that* (the case)?" *or* "(is it) so?" = "art thou he that should come?" (On the use of these Interrogative particles in certain Conditional Clauses, *e. g.* ሶበሁ ፡ ረሳዕነ ፡ ስመ ፡ ለአምላክነ "if we had forgotten the name of our God" &c. Ps. 43, 22, v. § 205). The particle ኑ is often attached also to fuller and more definite Interrogatives, like ምንት፡ አይቴ፡ እፎ &c. If ኑ comes in contact with the vowelless ን of a Verb, only one ን is written:—ትማስኑ "wilt thou destroy?" Gen. 18, 28; on the other hand, in the case of the Noun we have ዳኅንኑ "is he well?" Gen. 29, 6, because it has to be pronounced *dāḥnᵉnū* (3). For the alternative interrogation, Ethiopic has ወሚመ, literally "and what perhaps?" *i. e.* "or?", compounded of ሚ and መ (§ 63). For the dependent interrogation, እመ is employed, properly "if", and then "whether". On this word *cf.* § 198.

---

(1) Like הֲ, أَ.

(2) One is greatly tempted, of course, to put ኑ in the same class as नु and *ne* and *num.* But as ሁ (from ቱ § 62) is manifestly formed in the very same way, and can mean nothing but "*it*" and, farther, as በ "*it is*" is very often used to introduce a question (§ 198), it is more advisable to explain ኑ in this way too; and all the more, that ኔ, ሄ; ነ, ሃ; ኒ, ሂ correspond to one another throughout, in formation and in meaning.

(3) But v. TRUMPP, p. 559, and *cf.* KÖNIG, p. 96.

Interrogative Adverbs of more definite force are: (1). **አይቴ** "where?" and "whither?" (the latter sense occurring, for example, in Gen. 37, 30 and in Hen. 102, 1), employed both in dependent and in independent interrogation, and formed from the Interrogative **አይ**, which converts Demonstratives into Interrogatives, and **ቴ** "here" (¹); often combined farther with **ኑ**, **አይቴኑ** "where?" "whither?". Combined with prepositions:— **በአይቴ** "where?" (Matt. 2, 4; Judges 20, 3); also "in what way?" Matt. 9, 15; 12, 34; **እምአይቴ** "whence?" Matt. 21, 25; Hen. 41, 5; Gen. 29, 4; **ኀበ ፡ አይቴ** "whither"; **እስከ ፡ አይቴ** "to what point?". **አይቴ** is also used indefinitely in Negative sentences, either with or without **ሂ** or **ኒ** in the sense of "anywhere", 3 Kings 3, 36; 10, 12; 4 Kings 5, 25.—(2). **ማእዜ** "when?", formed from **እዜ**, **ይእዜ** by means of **መ** (§ 63), and often strengthened also by **ኑ**;—**እማእዜ** "how long since" ("*a quo tempore?*"), **እስከ ፡ ማእዜ** "till when?" "how long?" (Ps. 12, 1—3; Josh. 18, 3; Matt. 17, 17); **ለማእዜ** "for what time?" 1 Peter 1, 11. (3). **እፎ** "how?" formed from **እ**(**አይ**), § 63, *b* and **ፎ** "here", "thus", § 64, *b*. It may be strengthened by **ኑ**, and may be compounded with **በ**, **በእፎ** "in what way?" Mark 2, 18, and it is very often used in dependent interrogation, as well as in the exclamation—"What!" Hen. 21, 8. Frequently it exhibits a conception somewhat more distinctly coloured, *e. g.* **ጽልመትከ ፡ እፎ** "how great must *thy* darkness be!" Matt. 6, 23; 1 John 3, 1; **እፎ ፡ ፈድፋደ** "how much more!" Matt. 6, 30; 7, 11; 10, 25. Instead of plain **እፎ**,—**እፎፎ**, **እፉፎ**, **እፈፎ** and **እፈእፎ** are also met with, particularly in Cyrillus Alexandrinus; v. Dillmann's '*Lex.*', col. 807. (4). In Ethiopic one uses for the interrogative "why?" **ምንት** or **ምንትኑ** "what?", *e. g.* Hen. 83, 6; Gen. 40, 7; or more frequently the same word in the Accusative **ምንተ**, **ምንተኑ** Gen. 26, 27; Matt. 7, 3; or **ለምንት** "wherefore?" Ps. 2, 1; or **በእንተ ፡ ምንት** "for what reason?" Matt. 17, 19; while **በምንት** means "in what way?" Ps. 118, 9. Or "why?" may be indicated by means of turns like **ምንት ፡ አሥሐቃ** "what has made her laugh?" *i. e.* "why does she laugh?" Gen. 18, 13; 24, 31; Matt. 20, 6; Judges 18, 8.

(¹) The original form for **ሂ**, allied to **ዚ**, preserved in מָתַי, مَتَى, אַכְתַּי.—Notice **አይቴ** with **እም** following = أَيْنَ in sentences like أَيْنَ هٰذَا مِنْ ذَاكَ "what is this to that?" G. A. 7, 5, 6bis, 7, 8, 9, 14.

(b) Relative Adverbs.

(b) *Relative Adverbs.* For the meaning "where" **ኀበ** is usually employed, formed from **ኀ** (hardened out of **ሀ**, § 62, 1, *b*) and the Preposition **በ**, here set last(1); originally demonstrative "in—there", and the Compound is a Preposition in very frequent use in this sense (§ 165); but it has also become relative: "in—where", "where" and "where to", *e. g.* **ኀበ ፡ ሀሎኩ ፡ አነ ፡ ህየ ፡ ይሄሉ ፡ ዘይትለአከኒ** John 12, 26; Matt. 8, 19, 20; 13, 50; Ps. 83, 3 &c. Farther, in the relative clause which it introduces, **ህየ** may be placed in addition to it, but yet separated from it by a word or two (2):—**ኀበ ፡ ሀለዉ ፡ ህየ** "wherein they were" Hen. 17, 1 (3); Gen. 13, 4; Josh. 22, 19 &c. **ኀበ** is also compounded with prepositions: **በኀበ** "there, where" or simply "where" Matt. 13, 57; Josh. 8, 24; Hen. 12, 1; 33, 2; "wheresoever" Matt. 26, 13; **እንተ ፡ ኀበ** "wheresoever" Hen. 16, 1; **እምኀበ** "whence" Hen. 41, 3; Matt. 12, 44. For "when" **አመ** is used (§ 64, 3, *b*), *e. g.* John 4, 21; **ለአመ** "till" Zeph. 3, 8. Still, **አመ** is employed rather as a Conjunction or a Preposition (v. *infra*). Besides, the mere relative **ዘ**, referring to a fore-mentioned word expressing time, is quite sufficient to express "when" (v. § 202, 3). The conception "how", "as" or "like" is expressed by **ከመ**, but it is always either Preposition or Conjunction.

§ 162. 3. *Negative, Affirmative, Exclamatory, and Restrictive Particles, and some Enclitics of the most general meaning.*

3. Negative, Affirmative, Exclamatory and Restrictive Particles, together with certain Enclitics.

The ordinary particle which serves to *negative* either a single word or an entire clause, is **ኢ**, § 62, *c*. It is always prefixed to some other word, and in fact to that word which has to be negatived first or specially; and in such a combination it occasionally exercises an influence upon an initial **አ** (§ 48, 6) (4). Stronger and more independent negations are conveyed by **አከ** (§ 64, *b*) "in no wise", "not", and by **አልቦ**,—on which last compare §§ 167 and 197,—mostly corresponding in conception to the Hebrew אַיִן and the Arabic لَيْسَ, seeing that it signifies first of all: "it is not", "there is not". It is used also for "no" Matt. 5, 37; 13, 29; Ex. 10, 25 &c. The word **እንብየ**, a compound of **እን** (= אַיִן),

(1) [V., however, PRAETORIUS, ZDMG LVII, p. 272.]

(2) אֲשֶׁר־שָׁם.

(3) [FLEMMING's reading is **ኀበ ፡ እለ ፡ ሀለዉ ፡ ህየ**. TR.]

(4) The accent of the word which is connected with **ኢ**, remains unaffected by it: TRUMPP, p. 559.

§ 62, *c* and ·ብየ "with me" (§ 167), literally "not with me (is it)",— signifies "I am not in the position", "I am not allowed", "I am not able". It is with this word that one declines to accede to a request: Jas. 4, 7; Matt. 21, 29. There is an older form እንቢ (§ 167). *Cf.* also እን·ብከ, እንቢከ and እንቢከሙ.

As an Affirmative we have እወ (¹) "yes", "of course", "certainly" Matt. 5, 37. With እሆ "Oh! yes" consent is announced to a summons, so that it is the contrary expression to እን·ብየ:— Judges 6, 13, 15, 22; Matt. 21, 29, 30; 27, 20; Rom. 3, 26; Jas. 3, 3; 4, 7; 5, 6. As to its origin, v. § 62, *b* (²). To beseech any one, the particle ሰ "now!" "I pray" is made use of, attached as an enclitic to the Imperative: ተመየጥሰ "turn, I pray thee" Ps. 79, 15; አድኅንሰ "save, I beseech thee" (³) Ps. 117, 24. It comes from the demonstrative root ሰ (§ 62, 1, *a*); and, being no doubt originally a mere form of pointing out something "there!", it has thence been used to direct the attention of the person who is entreated, to some object or circumstance. The same meaning is given more emphatically by እስኩ "O now!" (§ 64, *b*) (⁴), of independent force it is true, but yet placed after the Imperative: Acts 22, 27; Gen. 24, 23. For "yes indeed!" "certainly!" "it is so!" ኋ is also used: Isaiah 14, 10; Phlx. 3 (⁵).

An exclamation of joy or mockery is found in እንቋዕ "ha!" (§ 63, *c*) Ps. 34, 24; 39, 21; 69, 4; Job 39, 25.

Of restrictive force is ከመ (§ 64, *b*), regularly put last, which means first "thus", then "like what" (כַּמָּה indef.), and thence 1. "nearly" Gen. 32, 32; Gen. 39, 10 (where it is put first for a special reason); 2. "nothing other than", or "just", "merely": ውስተ ፡ ከርሥ ፡ ከመ "merely into the belly" Mark 7, 19; አኮ ፡ በኅብስት ፡ ከመ "not by bread alone" Matt. 4, 4; 5, 47; 21, 21; Ps. 61, 9. It is therefore specially used with Pronouns, to express the notion of "just" (*idem*), § 150, *c*.

(¹) Probably abbreviated considerably from an older type. I refer it provisionally to إِيْ, إِيهِ, אִיהִי, אִיהוּא.

(²) Yet it might also have sprung from *u-hu*, *hu-hu*, "that it is", "thus it is".

(³) Thus like נָא and the Arabic *Modus Energeticus*.

(⁴) I do not think that this comes from ሰከወ = ሰከየ, as this word does not mean "to beg".

(⁵) [*i. e.* Philexius, *Quaestio* 3. TR.]

The particle መ, always enclitic, and manifestly nothing but an old interrogative for "what?" (§ 63), which appears as second member in ከመ, ሚመ, serves to emphasise the conceptional word to which it is appended([1]). It is commonly used,—(1) with words implying comparison, in order to express "precisely", "quite": Hen. 23, 2—"it does not halt in its course day or night አላ ፡ ከማሁመ but precisely in that way ('in that very fashion') runs on"; ወመንፈስ ፡ ቅዱስ ፡ ከማሁመ ፡ ውእቱ (*Org.*) "and with the Holy Ghost it is the very same"([2]): in both these instances even ከመ might be used instead;—(2) in questions also it appears, appended to the interrogatives, in order to strengthen them, answering to our "then" or "pray": ምንትኑመ "what, pray?" Matt. 11, 8, 9; አይቴኑመ "where then?"; መኑመ ፡ አንተ ፡ እንከ "pray who art thou then?" John 1, 22; Gen. 27, 33; እፎመ "how then?" John 7, 45; Ex. 2, 18; እፎኑመ Rom. 4, 3; ማእዜኑመ Gen. 30, 30;—(3) in certain other cases also, *e. g.* "Abimelech bore it ውስተ ፡ መታክፊሁመ (*lit.* "upon his shoulders, what?") upon his own shoulders" (to bring out the striking feature of the incident) Judges 9, 48 F; ይእቲመ "she herself"; አሐቲመ "the one (*f.*)" (Ludolf, '*Gramm.*'); [ወበትረ ፡ አሮንመ "and Aaron's rod (as well)" *Kebra Nag.* 169 a 4 *sq.*].

Finally there falls to be mentioned here the particle ከ, which is employed whenever the exact words of messages, letters, and, generally speaking, utterances of a third person are quoted in narration, and which is then appended to every single word of such a quotation([3]), however long it may be, the particle invariably retaining its own accent (Trumpp, p. 559 *sq.*), *e. g.* John 1, 19; Numb. 20, 14—20; 21, 21 *sqq.*; 22, 5 *sqq.*; Gen. 32, 5 *sqq.* Note; 38, 25; 45, 9—11; 50, 4, 5; Judges 2, 1—3; 9, 7—20; 11, 12 *sqq.* By certain writers it is appended even to small words like ኪ, ዘ &c., which in other cases are always supported by another word. One may be permitted

---

(1) *Cf.* Assyr. *ma*: [Pognon, '*L'inscription de Bavian*', p. 72 *suiv.* and] Haupt in Schrader's KAT[2], pp. 55, N. 3 and 66.—D. H. Müller, '*Epigr. Denkm.*' p. 67 *sq.*, would regard this መ as being a remnant of 'mimation', exactly like the ም in ትማልም "yesterday".

(2) *Cf.* Assyr. *kīma*, Haupt, '*Keilschriftt.*' p. 195.

(3) Platt has usually omitted it in his edition of the N. T. In my own editions I have generally given it merely with the first and last words of the utterance announced.

to discern in it a faded form of ን "it" or "thus", in the sense of इति "so" (1).

2. ADVERBS DERIVED FROM CONCEPTIONAL WORDS.

§ 163. 1. The greater number of words which are used adverbially are originally nouns; and only a very few spring directly from the verb. Every noun, when subordinated in the Accusative to the verb of a clause, may limit and determine that verb after the fashion of an Adverb (§ 174). Thus the *Accusative* is precisely the proper Case, with which to form Adverbs. And in fact such formation has been brought about with the Adjective, as well as with the Substantive; for, seeing that every Adjective may easily be conceived of as Neuter,—thereby coming to resemble a Substantive in meaning—, it may, when put in the Accusative under such a conception, become an Adverb also. Besides, several Conceptional words continue in use in the language, only in the form of this adverbial Accusative; and it is such words especially which fall to be described in this place.

1. Adverbs of Place and Time (Acc. of Noun); of Kind and Manner (Acc. of Adj.); and Adverbs formed by prefixing Prepositions to Substantives or Adjectives, instead of taking Acc.

Qualifications of Place and Time, or Nouns which are used in the Accusative of Place and of Time, are, *e. g.*, the following words, originally Substantives:—ለፌ "side" (*e. g.* ኢለፌ ፡ ወኢለፌ "neither this way nor that way" Josh. 8, 20; Ex. 2, 12); መልዕልተ "above" and "upward"; ቍልቍሊተ "downward"; ማእከለ "in the midst" (Mark 3, 3); መትሕተ "below"; ከዋለ "behind"; ዐውደ "around"; ማዕዶተ "beyond"; ይምነ "on the right hand"; ፅግመ "on the left hand"; ደቡበ "northward"; ድኅረ "behind" and "afterward" (Matt. 25, 11); ድኅሬተ "backward", "back"; ፍጽመ "in front" (Numb. 1, 53; 32, 17; Deut. 20, 4; Josh. 6, 9; Ps. 45, 5); ውስጠ "in", "within"; ግድመ "awry", "across"; ሌሊተ "by night"; መዐልተ "by day" and "to-day" (Gen. 43, 16, 25); ሰርከ "in the evening"; ቅድመ "in front", "eastward" (Gen. 2, 8), "first", "before" (Matt. 13,30; 17,10); ኅሬፈ "this year" (Luke 13,8); ነግሀ "early in the morning"; ዘልፈ and ወትረ "continually"; ጌሠመ "to-morrow"; and words originally Adjectives:—ልዑለ

(1) [For another explanation of this እ v. Bezold, '*Zeitschr. f. Assyr.*' XV, p. 398.—It also appears to have been employed merely to indicate that the thoughts of another person are being introduced by the speaker or writer; v. *Kebra Nag.*, *Introd.*, p. XX.]

"high", "upward"; ታሕትየ "under" (Josh. 16,3; 18,13, Note); ነዊኀ or ነዋኀ "far", "far away" (Matt. 15,8; Mark 7,6); ርሑቀ "far distant"; ወትረ "entirely" (Heb. 9,4); ዘልፈ "continually" (Ex. 21,6); ክሡተ φανερῶς; ጕንዱየ "a long time", "some time". The following are retained in use only in this adverbial Accusative:—ላዕለ "above" (chiefly as a preposition, v. *infra*); ታሕተ "below", "down" Matt. 4,6 (but chiefly as a preposition).

Qualifications of Size or Measure comprehend the Numeral Adverbs (§ 159, *e*): ከዕበተ and ምክዕቢተ "repeatedly"; ክዑበ "doubly" ('the second time'); ከዕበ and ዳግመ "again"; መጠነ and አምጣነ ('the bigness of—') "as large as"; ሚመጠነ and ሚመጠን "how greatly" (Job 35,5); ፈድፋደ "very", "exceedingly", "specially", "above all" (even as Predicate); ስፍን "how often?"; v. *supra* § 157,1.

Qualifications of Kind and Manner are nearly always formed from Adjectives, *e. g.* መሪረ "bitterly"; ሠናየ (as well as ሠናይ) "finely", "well"; እኩየ "badly", "ill", ጽኑዐ "strongly", "powerfully"; ፍጹመ "perfectly", "entirely"; ዐቢየ "highly"; ጥዩቀ and ጥንቁቀ "exactly"; ጽፉቀ "frequently; ብዙኀ "much", "often"; ኅቡረ "all together", "together"; ድሩገ "at the same time"; ድሙረ "jointly"; ትሑተ "humbly", "modestly"; ጽሩዐ "idly"; ርቱዐ "rightly", and "directly opposite" (Hen. 72,8), "correctly" (*Chrest.* p. 76, line 14); ኅዳጠ "little"; ፍጡነ "quickly", "suddenly"; ድንጉፀ ፡ ወፍጡነ *φρικτῶς καὶ ταχέως* Sap. 6,5; ኀዩለ *κραταιῶς* Sap. 6,8; አዳመ *εὐμενῶς* Sap. 6,16; ንጹሐ *σωφρόνως* Sap. 9,11; ሀልወ "in reality", and many others.—*Cf.* also እመ ፡ ዳኅነ ፡ አቶ ከመ Tob. 5,15. But the following forms, derived from Substantives, are of very frequent occurrence, being mainly retained in use as Adverbs only: ሕቀ "by degrees", "a little"; ስንአ "unanimously"; በከ "in vain" (በክ "emptiness"); መትልወ "in succession", "forthwith"; ንስቲተ "a little", "gradually"; ደርገ "together", "at the same time"; ግብተ "suddenly"; ጽሚተ (ጽምሚተ) "secretly"; and with especial frequency ጥቀ properly "exactly", then commonly "very", "even", farther "precisely", "certainly"; ጥቀ ፡ ኢ "not even" (*ne quidem*) (1).

(1) A remarkable intensive-form is found in Ps. 44,2, viz. ጠበጠበ "most skilfully" ("dexterously"), from an intensive Adjective ጠበጠቡ, derived, in accordance with § 112, b, from the √ጠበበ "to be wise".

But *by means of the preposition* በ (§ 164) the language attains the same object as through the agency of the Accusative. By prefixing this preposition to a Substantive or Adjective, Adverbs of Kind and Manner may be formed: በጽባሕ "in the morning"; በጸጋ "for nothing" (Matt. 10, 8); በፍጻሜ "lastly", "at last"; በጽርእ "in Greek" (Luke 23, 38); በግዕዝ "in Ethiopic"; በሐሰት "falsely" (Matt. 5, 33); በትዕቢት "proudly"; በጽሚት "in secret"; በፈቃድ "voluntarily" (with Suffix); በኵርሀ "by constraint" (*'invito animo'*): በሠናይ "in a friendly way" (Gen. 26, 29); በሕሡም "miserably" (Matt. 21, 41); በንጹሕ "innocently" (Gen. 20, 6); በኅቡእ "in secret"; በዳኅን "in safety" (Gen. 26, 31); በኵሉ &c. In words which convey the notion of "gradually", በ is doubled (*cf.* § 159, *g*): በበ ንስቲት, በበሕቅ. Other Prepositions also are employed to express Adverbial notions, such as: ለዓለም "for ever"; ኀበ ፡ ካልእ ('to another side') "elsewhere"; እምትካት "once" and "long ago" ('from of old'). Thus እም is prefixed, over and above, to ድኅረ "afterward", making እምድኅረ "after that" (Matt. 21, 32).

2. Other forms of Adverbs, being originally Nouns with or without inflection or with Special terminations.

2. A certain number of Adverbial qualifications also are expressed by means of other forms. A Noun may be set in the sentence adverbially, without inflection and otherwise lifeless, in the very form in which it issues from the Stem-forming process; but, save for the Numeral Adverbs (§ 159, *e*), this takes place only in a very few words, which have become entirely or almost entirely obsolete in any other use: ዮም "to-day" ("day"); ትካት "once" ("antiquity") Eph. 5, 8; አማን "truly", "certainly" (¹); ቀዳሚ "in the first place", "at first" (occurring often; but also the Acc. ቀዳሜ, though rarely) (²); *cf.* also ዓም ፡ እምዓም; ዕለት ፡ እምዕለት; ሀገር ፡ እምሀገር. —A few others have a Suff. Pron. appended (like ትካትየ "formerly"), or other terminations originally pronominal. The most common among them is the Neuter *ū* (*hū*) (³) "of it", "thereof": ቀዲሙ ("the first of it") "in the first place", "earlier", "once", "sooner" (very common); ቀዳሚሁ and ቀዳሚየ, v. DILLMANN's *'Lex.'*, col. 463 *sq.*; ላዕሉ ("height of it") "above", Josh. 16, 5; በሕ ቲቱ ("solitude of it" § 157, 2) "only", "alone", "merely", Gen. 2, 6

(¹) Still used as a Predicate, Hen. 82, 7.

(²) On the other hand ቅድም in Matt. 20, 8; 23, 26 is Imperative.

(³) According to BARTH ZDMG XLVI, p. 691, this *ū* is to be regarded as the Nominative of an original Diptote declension.

(generally placed after the qualified word); and still oftener the shorter form ባሕቱ፡ "only", "yet", "however", "but rather" (v. § 168); ታሕቱ፡ "under"; ጽእሙ (the firmness of it", "the truth of it"; same root as in أَدَمْ, أَدِمْ, عَدَمْ) "much more", "however", *e. g.* Ps. 1, 2, 5; Mark 4, 17; 5, 36; Philipp. 2, 12; ከንቱ፡ (§ 157, 2) "in vain", "for nothing" (also በከንቱ፡ and ከንቶ); በሕቁ፡ (properly 'according to the measure of it'; በ is preposition here) "considerably", "greatly", Mark 7, 3; Deut. 9, 21; Josh. 8, 4 &c.; ለዝሉፉ and ለዝላፉ ('for the duration of it') "for ever". In other instances it is *ā* on the contrary that makes its appearance, and not *ū*; but this *ā* is not to be regarded as the Suff. Pron. of the 3rd pers. Sing. fem., but as the *ā*, ሃ, which originally signifies "toward", and which next is made use of in the formation of the Accusative (§ 143): አፍኣ(¹) and አፍአ ('at the mouth') "outside", "without", "beyond", "outward" (and Suff. Prons. may here again be attached, as in አፍአሁ "outside of it", Matt. 23, 25 *sq.*, or even Prepositions prefixed, *e. g.* በአፍአ Gen. 9, 22(²)) and ግሙራ ('toward the complete', 'toward completion') "wholly", "ever", "altogether", "at all", *omnino*, nearly always in clauses of negative import, *e. g.* ግሙራ ፡ ኢተናገረ ፡ ሰብእ "never has a man spoken" John 7, 46; ኢትምሐሉ ፡ ግሙራ "ye shall not swear at all" Matt. 5, 34: also ለግሙራ "for ever and ever". And in the same acceptation in which these words take an *ā*, ዝኩ takes ዚ, and አሐተ, ኔ (§ 160). Of more obscure origin is ትማልም(³) "yesterday", "long ago" (תְּמוֹל). Of quite peculiar character is ዓዲ "yet", "farther", in form manifestly an Adjective, fashioned afresh out of an original ዓድ (עוֹד)(⁴), and thus meaning properly "lasting", and then farther stiffened into an Adverb, just like ቀዳሚ. But, from its original Adjective-signification, it has preserved the peculiarity of assuming personal Suffixes with great frequency, in the mode and the meaning which are explained in § 156, making its appearance in this

(¹) This way of writing the word is still pretty constant in the older manuscripts.

(²) The *ā* in ከዋላ and ከወላ "behind" is probably to be explained differently, as the word in this form appears also as a Subst.

(³) On this word v. Ewald, '*Hebr. Spr.*' p. 91; [and Jensen, '*Zeitschr. f. Assyr.*' XI, p. 352 *sq.*].

(⁴) [V. also Barth, '*Etymol. Studien*', p. 60 & '*Wurzeluntersuchungen*' (Leipzig 1902), p. 34, where ዓዲ is said to have sprung from *ʿād* + *ye.*]

way in the sentence as an independent word in apposition to another: **ዓዲሁ ፡ ሕያው ፡ ውእቱ** "he is yet alive" Gen. 43, 28 (but **ከመ ፡ ዓዲ ፡ ሕያው** in V. 27); 45, 3 (but otherwise in V. 6); **እመ ፡ ዓዲሁ ፡ ሕያው ፡ ዮሴፍ** Gen. 45, 28; **እንዘ ፡ ዓዲሆሙ ፡ ሀለዉ** Judges 19,11; 6,21; farther Gen. 18,12; 44,14; Acts 9,1; Hen. 89,25. Lastly, **ዓዲሁ** ('it continuing') is once more used adverbially for "yet", "still" Matt. 16, 9.

3. Adverbial Notions expressed by Verbs.

3. Many Adverbial notions may be expressed in Semitic, and accordingly in Ethiopic, by means of Verbs,—a subject which will be dealt with in § 180. Somewhat different is the case of a fully inflected Verb being brought,—parenthetically as it were—, into the current of the words which constitute the sentence, so that it presents the appearance of an additional qualification. Thus **አክለ** or **የአክል** "it amounts to", "it suffices for" is very often interpolated in a sentence, sometimes impersonally, sometimes as a personal Verb assuming the due changes of gender and number, —for the purpose of expressing the idea of "nearly", "about": **ወነበሩ ፡ ህየ ፡ የአክል ፡ ዐሠርተ ፡ ዓመተ** "and they remained there about ten years" Ruth 1, 4: "there fell of Israel" **የአክሉ ፡ ፴ብእሲ** "about thirty men" (Nominative) Judges 20, 31; in the same way **አሐዝብ** "I imagine", for "probably", "likely" Gen. 37,10; Ps. 123,2, 3; and **ብቍዐኒ** ("oblige me", "do me the favour") for "pray!" in requests; also **ኅድጎሰ** "let it alone!" or **ኅድጉሰ** "let (*pl.*) alone!" for "not to speak of", "without mentioning", *e. g.* 1 Cor. 6, 3. A Perfect, employed in an Optative clause, in the Arabic fashion (but v. § 199) is met with in **ሓሰ** or more commonly **ሐሰ**(1) "far be it", either set by itself Gen. 18, 25, or followed by **ለ**, *e. g.* **ሐሰ ፡ ሊተ** "be it far from me!" Acts 10, 14; Matt. 16, 22; Josh. 22, 29.—A very old word, which can only be explained now from the Hebrew, is found in **እንዳዒ** "perhaps" (followed by **ለእመ** "whether") John 4, 29; Acts 11, 18; 23, 9; 2 Cor. 11, 3; Rom. 5, 7; compounded of **እን** = אִין (§ 62, *c*) and **ዳዕ**, an old Infinitive from יָדַע, **የድዐ** "to know", with the Suff. Pron. of the 1st pers. Sing. ī, which is obsolete in Ethiopic (§ 149), and thus meaning literally "not my knowing", "I do not know". In this sense it still occurs, 2 Cor. 12, 2, 3 (*cf.* Gal. 4, 11). We can also understand from this

(1) حَاشَ Ewald, '*Gr. Ar.*' I, p. 369.

account of the word, why it should be so often followed by ለእመ "whether".

4. Adverbial Indication of the Language in which anything is spoken or written.

4. Finally, in Foreign words from the Greek, a termination *ιστι* has been taken over, to form Adverbs,—from Adjectives derived from the names of Nations—, which indicate the *language*, in which anything is spoken or written: ሮማይስጢ "Roman" *i. e.* "in Latin", ዕብራይስጢ "in Hebrew" &c. The later writers leave out the *ī*: ሮማይስጥ John 19, 20 (PLATT); ዕብራይስጥ Acts 26, 14; ሶርስጥ "in Syriac". These forms may also have the prefix በ:—በዕብራይስጥ Luke 23, 38; John 19, 20; or they may be preceded by a Construct State: ነገረ ፡ ዕብራይስጢ "the Hebrew language". Acts 21, 40; [ልሳነ፡ዕብራይስጥ '*Chrest.*', p. 17, line 10].

II. PREPOSITIONS.

General Account of Prepositions.

§ 164. Except the two or three Prepositions which have to make up for the Cases wanting in Nouns (§ 142), and which are accordingly in very frequent use and are greatly abbreviated in form, the greater number of Prepositions are derived from Nouns, and are kept true to their original form. A few are words originally Conjunctions, or at least Adverbs derived from Pronominal roots. The number of simple Prepositions in Ethiopic is very large, and the body of Prepositions becomes all the larger that a host of simple Prepositions may be farther combined with others, in order to reach the finer distinctions of relation. Every one of these Prepositions has the power of subordinating to itself a Noun, many even an entire sentence. The nature of the subordination is the same as with every other Noun,—that is to say, it is effected by means of the Construct State relation (§ 144). Every word which is employed as a Preposition stands, to the word dependent upon it, in the relation mentioned, and all of them therefore end in *a* (or *ā*). At the same time it will be shown farther on, that several of them once had a fuller ending, in *ē* (§ 167). Many of them, particularly those which originally indicate relations of Space and Time, must be conceived as simultaneously standing in the Accusative (of Place or Time). As the Preposition is in the Constr. St., it must naturally precede the Noun. Still, Ethiopic has the power of placing a few Prepositions after their regimen, at least when that is the Relative Pronoun (§ 202)(1). Besides, Prepositions may be combined together or be made dependent on one another in manifold ways: በ, ለ, እም, እንተ are those which combine most frequently with other Prepositions. The majority of those words which are in use as Prepositions, are no longer preserved in the language in any other signification; it is only a minority that appear in still other uses. Along with these decided Prepositions, there are words too which are just at a transitional stage, on the way to become decided Prepositions. Several Nouns, which indicate a place or a time, a measure, or other relation, may, on taking the Accusative or the Construct State, supply the place of a Preposition. They are but rarely used, however, in this way, and it is matter of doubt whether they should altogether be counted among the Prepositions.

The Prepositions in most frequent use:—1. በ.

(*a*) *The Prepositions most frequently employed, and most subjected to abbreviation*, and which at the same time are prefixed either invariably, or at least often, to the word depending on them, are the following:—

1. በ(2) (always attached to the following word) "in", but branching out from this original meaning into many other meanings. (*a*) It expresses, first of all, rest and continuance at a place, or in a time or an object: በምድር "in the land"; በዛቲ ፡ ሌሊት "in this night"; በሠረቀ-ቆሙ "in their rising" ("while *or* when they rise"); በስመ ፡ እግዚአብሔር "in the name of God"; ኀለፉ ፡ በፍርሀት ፡ ወበፍሥሓ "they departed, (being) in fear and joy" Matt. 28, 8. On rare occasions it is used with verbs of motion, in the sense of "toward", "to", though rather oftener in the hostile meaning of "against". More frequently it may express mere neighbourhood or contiguity to anything, *e. g.* ተዐቅፈ ፡ በእብን "to stumble against (*or* at) a stone" Matt. 4, 6; 11, 6; or passing through anything, *e. g.* ይገብእ ፡ በ፩ኆኅት "he returns ('in the first') through the first door" Hen. 72, 25. Still more frequently it is associated with certain verbs, which may thus be regarded as representing a figurative entering into, or abiding in, the object concerned, such as ሠምረ ፡ በ

(1) Just as even ኀበ, ሶበ, ዲበ have themselves originated from the appending of በ.

(2) No doubt connected with בֵּין, በይነ;—in use, besides, in all the Semitic languages [except Assyrian].

"to take pleasure in"; **አምነ ፡ በ** "to believe in"; **ተማኅፀነ ፡ በ** "to entrust one's self with", "to open one's heart to" &c.

(*b*) Inasmuch as a single individual, proceeding in the society of others or with a crowd, is, so to speak, *in* the same or *among* the same, **በ** takes also the signification "with", *e. g.* Hen. 1, 4, 9, or "among" (*inter*);—and inasmuch as that which takes place through a certain means, or by the operation of a certain cause, is regarded as contained *in* the same, it may farther signify "with", "by means of", "by reason of", "from" *or* "out of", *e. g.* **አእመረ ፡ በ** (= بِ) 1 John 3, 16 &c.; **በክነፊከ ፡ ክድነኒ** "cover me with ('by means of') thy wings" Ps. 16, 9; **በግዝፈ ፡ ልብ** "from hardness of heart"; **በኵሉ ፡ ዘአበሰ** "on account of every fault" Matt. 19, 3; **በእደ** "in *or* by the hand (of any one)", *i. e.* "by means of him"; **ዘመወ ፡ በ** "to commit fornication with any one" (as the means) Matt. 5, 28; **ሐይወ ፡ በ** "to live by something" Deut. 8, 3; Gen. 27, 40; Matt. 4, 4; and accordingly it is used even of a personal agent (*per*, *a*) Matt. 18, 7; 14, 2 &c. In like manner one says in Ethiopic that something happens "in" this or that way, *e. g.* **በሐሰት** "in falsehood", "falsely" (for other examples, v. § 163, 1), where it answers to our "after", "according to", "—ly", "in": **በሥምረትከ** "in thy good pleasure" Ps. 50, 19; **በአስራብ** "in streams", "like a stream"; **በእግረ ፡ ደቂቅ ፡ ነሐውር** "according to the foot of the children ('as the children are able to walk') we proceed" Gen. 33, 14 &c.; or **በኍልቍ** "in number", "by number" Hen. 89, 60; and then too it is used in reduplicated form with a distributive sense (§ 159, *g*): **በበ ፡ ምድሮሙ** "according to their (several) countries" Gen. 10, 5; **በበዘመዶሙ** "after their several kinds" Gen. 7, 14. Hence it is also found with words conveying comparison, "with", "to", "by", "after", *e. g.* **ትትሜሰል ፡ በድንግል** "thou art to be compared to a virgin", and with words of naming "by" or "after" something, *e. g.* Hen. 72, 36; and particularly to indicate the price "at" or "for", in conceptions of buying, giving, taking, *e. g.* Gen. 30, 16; Hen. 5, 6; or words of punishing "for", *e. g.* **ተቀየመ ፡ በ** "to avenge one's self for (something)". But manifold as are the meanings of this Preposition, they are yet far from being all in frequent use. On the contrary, for the most of these derived meanings the language possesses other words devoted exclusively thereto, which are much more frequently employed. The most usual significations of **በ** are "in", "at", "with" or "by means of" (Instrument), "on" or "after" (Kind and Manner); "at" or "for" (Worth or Value).

2. ለ(1) (always attached to a following word) expresses direction toward something: "to", "toward". (*a*) It may thus take an entirely Locative meaning: ሖረ ፡ ለ "to go to" Hen. 56, 2; ይገብእ ፡ ፀሐይ ፡ ለጽባሕ "the sun returns to the east" Hen. 72, 13, 15; አሐዱ ፡ ለካልኡ ፡ ይኔጽር "one looks to the other" Hen. 41, 7; or in a Temporal sense: በጽሐት ፡ ለተፈጽሞ "it has reached completion" Gen. 6, 16; ለጸቢሐ ፡ እሑድ "toward the dawn of the first day (of the week)" Matt. 28, 1; ለዓለም "for ever"; ለዝላፉ "*in perpetuum*". It farther introduces the object for which an action is set a-going, *e. g.* ይጽምኡ ፡ ለጽድቅ "(and) thirst (3rd *pl.*) after righteousness" Matt. 5, 6; ረስሐ ፡ ለኵነኔ "he is liable to doom" Matt. 5, 21; or with verbs of becoming it introduces that which anything comes "to", *e. g.* ወኮነ ፡ ለመንፈሰ ፡ ሕይወት "and he became a living soul ('soul of life')" Gen. 2, 7. It also points to the 'purpose', *e. g.* "the stars are ለተአምር for signs" Gen. 1, 14, 15; ሠናይ ፡ ለበሊዕ "good to eat" Gen. 2, 9; ይበርቁ ፡ ለበረከት "they flash for a blessing" Hen. 59, 1; Matt. 23, 5; 26, 12. Whence it is farther employed to specify "for whom",—"for whose advantage" anything happens (*Dativus commodi*): ለክሙ "for you" *i. e.* "for your benefit" Hen. 5, 1; "give him this ሊተ ፡ ወለከ for me and thee" Matt. 17, 27; ጸለየ ፡ ለ "to pray for" any one; ሐዘነ ፡ ለ "to mourn for" one; ተበአሰ ፡ ለ "to fight for" one; and, generally, it is the word to express the *Dative*. (*b*) But it also expresses quite commonly "with regard to", *e. g.* ምንት ፡ እንከ ፡ ትፈቅዱ ፡ ሎቱ ፡ ሰማዕተ "what farther need have you of testimony with regard to him?" Matt. 26, 65. It may accordingly indicate any relation, and therefore the Genitive relation, *e. g.* ካልአ ፡ ትእዛዘ ፡ ለብርሃን ፡ ንኡስ "a second (*acc.*) ordinance (namely) of the smaller light" Hen. 73, 1; እግዚእ ፡ ለሰንበት "Lord of the Sabbath" Matt. 12, 8, as well as the Accusative relation, especially with those verbs which in other tongues also may be easily connected with the Dative: ሰብሐ ፡ ለ; ባረከ ፡ ለ; ጸውዐ ፡ ለ &c. "to praise, bless, name (call for) any one"; ፀረፈ ፡ ለ "to speak evil against (any one)" Matt. 12, 31.—*Cf.* also '*Chrest.*', p. 42, line 26; p. 44, line 1. Still, this employment of ለ, to indicate the Genitive and Accusative, has 2. ለ.

(1) Connected with אֶל, إِلَى, as in the rest of the Semitic languages.

continued to be of rather infrequent occurrence in Ethiopic; but so much the oftener does it come about that, when a person or an object has been signified by a Suff. Pron., and this person or object is subsequently and specially mentioned, **ለ** is prefixed to it, in order to establish the reference of the Suffix to the Noun, *e. g.* **ጸውዖ ፡ ለሕዝብ** "he called to it (referring to) the people" = "he called to the people". **ለ** is employed in this way in almost every sentence, seeing that, on special grounds (to be afterwards discussed), this periphrasis of the direct Genitive-, Dative-, and Accusative-subordination, effected by means of a Suff. Pron. and **ለ**, has attained extraordinary predominance. As the most general Preposition **ለ** may take the place of other prepositions in the course of an extended series, *e. g.* **ምስሌክሙ ፡ ወለዘርእክሙ** "with you and with your seed" Gen. 9, 9. Comparatively seldom does it express "conformity" or "suitability", as for instance in **ለመፍቅደ ፡ ዚአሁ** "according to *his* good pleasure", or **ለቅንአቶሙ** "διὰ φθόνον" Matt. 27, 18. Like **በ**, **ለ** also may be reduplicated, with a distributive force (§ 159, *g*), *e. g.* **ሲሳይ ፡ ዘለለ ፡ ዕለት** "daily food" ('which is for every day') Matt. 6, 11; **ለለ ፡ በዓል** "at every feast" Mark 15, 6; also with an adverbial accusative:—**ለለ ፡ ነግሀ ፡ ወሰርከ** *Enc. Synax.*

3. እምነ. 3. The third most important preposition is **እምነ** (1), or in its prefixed form, **እም**, the former being the ground-form, which occurs more frequently than **እም**, particularly in the older manuscripts (2), and which must always re-appear whenever Suffixes come to be attached. The latter is just an abbreviated form of the other,—as **ነ**, coming after **ም**, readily disappeared. **እም** is invariably attached as a prefix to the word which follows it, losing even the **ም** in writing, if that word itself begins with *m* (§ 55): **እምታ** *emmetă*, **እመካን** *emmakăn*, **እሞቱ** *emmōtū*. **እምነ** or **እም** signifies "from", "out of", and is most variously applied. First it is used with reference to Place: **አፍአ ፡ እምሀገር** "away out of the city"; "they gather all the unbelievers **እመንግሥቱ** out of his kingdom" Matt. 13, 41; **እምልብ** "out of the heart" Matt. 12, 34; 18, 34: and also with reference to Time, "since", "from—forward":

(1) V. § 34. It is the Hebr. מִן, in the Constr. St. **ምን** and with **እ** prefixed; and in the last resort it is to be referred to a root מנה "to part". *Cf.* König, p. 144.

(2) [*Cf. e. g.* N. Roupp, '*Zeitschr. f. Assyr.*' XVI, p. 306 *sq.*]

—እምውእቱ ፡ ሰዓት "from that very hour" Matt. 9,22 (*cf.* V. 20); እምዝ ('from this time onward', 'henceforward') "thereafter"; እም ሰሚዐ ፡ ቃሉ "as soon as he heard the word"; እምቀድመ ፡ ዓለም "from the beginning of the world onward" Matt. 24,21; Hen. 41,4. Deserving of notice are cases in which the preposition is associated with adverbial locutions, like እምይእተ ፡ ዕለተ Dan. Ap. 1, 64 (in some manuscripts); እምይእተ ፡ አሚረ 1 Kings 16,13; 30,25. Farther, እምነ is employed to introduce the person or thing, from whom or from which anything is sought, taken, or derived, *e. g.* አስተብቍዐ ፡ እም "to crave (a thing) from (any one)" Hen. 63,1; ሰአለ ፡ እምነ "to make enquiry of (any one)", "to ask of" &c.; also to point to the material, of which a thing is made or from which it has originated, Hen. 26,5; 28,2; and hence it is found with verbs of fulness such as መልአ, ጸግበ and the like. It is used especially to indicate the author, *e. g.* ፀንሰት ፡ እምነ "she conceived by (so-and-so)", *cf.* Gen. 19,36,—and the cause, እምፍርሀቱ "for fear of him" Matt. 28,4; [*Kebra Nag.* 39 b 21]; እምትዕቢት "from pride"; እምፍሥሓሁ "for joy thereat" Matt. 13,44; *cf.* Matt. 14, 26; Ps. 37,8; ኢይትኌለቍ ፡ እምነ ፡ ብዝኁ "(which) cannot be numbered for multitude" Gen. 32,13, *cf.* 48,10; whence እምነ has the meaning "by reason of" in Gen. 27,46. It not unfrequently occurs with a Passive, just like the Latin preposition *a*, Matt. 8,24; 14,24 &c. It is also used to indicate the grounds on which a recognition or judgment proceeds, *e. g.* እምፍሬሆሙ ፡ ታአምርዎሙ "by their fruits ye shall know them" Matt. 7,20; 12,33 (but yet በ also appears in this sense, as in Gen. 15,8); ርእየ ፡ እም "to see *or* understand from *or* by (me)" Judges 7,17; እምቃላቲከ ፡ ትጸድቅ "by thy words thou shalt be justified" Matt. 12,37. Its meaning has more of its original material reference, when a 'withdrawal from' something, a 'separation, parting or sundering' is given expression to, *e. g.* in Matt. 13,49; 21,43, or in የዐርብ ፡ ፀሐይ ፡ እምሰማይ "the sun sets from out the heavens" Hen. 72,5; Gen. 8,2; hence it is used with verbs of 'withholding from' ከልአ ፡ እምነ, or ኢምሀከ ፡ ለወልድከ ፡ እምኔየ "thou hast not kept back thine own son from me" Gen. 22,12; with verbs of fearing, or 'fleeing from anything', or 'guarding against' anything, or of 'concealing from' (Matt. 11,25; Gen. 18,17); and with verbs of defectiveness and of emptiness (like ዐርቀ) (1). The

(1) In the Arabic text of *G. Ad.* عَنْ is often the corresponding Prep.

meaning of 'choosing out of' is associated with that of 'separating from', and so እምን is also the word which indicates comparison between higher and lower, and which is used in the periphrasis for the Comparative and Superlative: ቡርክት ፡ አንቲ ፡ እም አንስት "blessed art thou among women" Luke 1, 28; ዐቢይ ፡ እምን ፡ ዚአሆሙ "greater than theirs" Josh. 19, 9; "the serpent ትጠብብ ፡ እምኵሉ ፡ አርዌ was more subtle than all the beasts" Gen. 3, 1; ("the ark was lifted up እምን ፡ ምድር above the earth" Gen. 7, 17). So too it is invariably employed, when a part of the whole has to be expressed: ክልኤቱ ፡ እምኔክሙ "two of you" Matt. 18, 19; መኑ ፡ እምክልኤሆሙ "which of the two?" Matt. 21, 31; ወቦ ፡ እም አርዳኢሁ "and there was one of his disciples" Matt. 12, 47; ይቤ ፡ ለእምጠቢባን "*dixit uni e sapientibus*" *Fal.*(1), f. 60; and thus it often serves to supply the place of the missing conceptional expression for "a few", "one or two", "several": ነሥአ ፡ እምን ፡ እንስሳ "he took one or two beasts" Gen. 8, 20; 6, 2, 19; 27, 28; 45, 23(2). —Lastly, in Ethiopic one may say "on the side of" (በለፌ, በገቦ), or "from the side of" እምለፌ John 19, 18; Rev. 22, 2; and so እምን often stands as specifying the direction of anything in space:— እምን ፡ አፍአ "outside" Gen. 7, 16; እምውሳጢሁ "inside" Ex. 25, 11; እምድኅር "behind", "from behind" Ex. 14, 27.—On በእምን and ለእምን *cf.* the '*Lexicon*'.

The other more frequently used Prepositions (4—10).

§ 165. (*b*) *The other more frequently used Prepositions* are: 4. ኀበ "with" and "toward"(3), compounded of ኀ and በ, meaning literally "in—there", and also in use relatively as "where" (§ 161, *b*). It is found both with verbs of 'rest' and of 'motion', and signifies "near to", "with" or "to": ቃል ፡ ሀለወ ፡ ኀበ ፡ እግዚአብሔር "the Word was with God" John 1, 1, 2; ኀበ ፡ ሙሐዘ ፡ ማይ "by a stream of water" Ps. 1, 3; ኀበ ፡ መኑ ፡ ነሐውር "to whom shall we go?" John 6, 68; እንተ ፡ ኀቤየ "who (*f.*) is with me" Cant. 1, 9, 15; 2, 2. It is always employed with verbs of 'going', 'coming', 'sending for *or* to' any person or place, and

(1) [*i. e. Mashafa Falasfā*, '*Book of the Philosophers*'. TR.]

(2) [*Cf.* also *Kebra Nag.* 121 b 16: ከመ ፡ ኢትርከቦሙ ፡ እምእንተ ፡ ትመጽእ ፡ መቅሠፍት ፡ ለኃጥአን "so that there may not befall them something of the punishment that overtakes sinners"; and *ibid.* p. 57 (Ethiop. text), *Ann.* 16, እምሰብእ.]

(3) It corresponds in meaning both to إِلَى and عِنْدَ. [On its etymology *cf.* also Praetorius, ZDMG LVII, p. 272.]

'delivering up to' any one, አግብአ ፡ ኀበ Matt. 20, 18. It also expresses in a general way 'direction toward' anything, just like "toward": ነጸረ ፡ ኀበ ፡ ሰማይ "to look toward heaven" Matt. 14, 19; and it is often used by way of an alternative for ለ, *e. g.* ጸርኀ ፡, ጸለየ ፡, ሰአለ ፡, ተማኅፀነ ፡ ኀበ "to cry, pray, or address a request to" any one, "to trust in" any one; and ከፈለ ፡ ኀበ "to distribute to".—It is frequently compounded with ለ, በ, እም; ለኀበ "away to" anything Hen. 56, 5, and in a peculiar use in Ex. 4, 16; በኀበ "with", "among" (*inter*), *e. g.* "ye shall be hated በኀበ ፡ ኵሉ ፡ ሰብእ among all men" Matt. 10, 22; አእመረ ፡ በኀበ "to seek instructions from *or* to be instructed by *or* of" Matt. 14, 8; used particularly to express buying 'at' any one's (= 'from' any one) Gen. 23, 19; and, farther, having the meaning "with reference to", "in comparison with": በኀበ ፡ መዋዕለ ፡ አበዊየ "in comparison with the days of my fathers" Gen. 47, 9. Lastly እምኀበ "from the side of any one", "from" (מֵעִם, מֵאֵת), is very common with verbs of 'borrowing', 'demanding', 'taking', 'learning by enquiry', and 'being given' John 6, 65; Matt. 2, 9, 16; 5, 42; 11, 27; and of frequent occurrence with the Passive, to introduce the author or agent, *e. g.* Matt. 1, 22; 2, 15; 3, 6; 4, 1; 6, 2, being more usually employed in this signification than እም or በ.

5. እስከ "till", "as far as", "up to", from עַד and ከ, properly "till that" (§ 64, *b*), was originally a Conjunction, and then came into use in a more extended form as a Preposition, dislodging the old עַד;—it is still occasionally lengthened by means of ነ (§ 160, *a*) (¹). It is used for Space and Time, and is the only word to express this relation, as ለ rather means "toward": እስከ ፡ አጽናፈ ፡ ምድር "as far as the ends of the earth" Ps. 2, 8; እስከ ፡ ይእዜ "till now" Ps. 70, 18; also እስከ ፡ ፴ጽባሕ "for 30 mornings" Hen. 72, 9; or እስከ ፡ ክልኤ ፡ መዋዕል "within two days" Matt. 26, 2; Gen. 40, 13; and እምተባዕቱ ፡ እስከ ፡ አንስቱ "men and women" Josh. 6, 21; እስከ ፡ ውእተ ፡ አሚረ Dan. 12, 1 (*cf. supra* p. 393, l. 5 *sqq.*). It is often followed by additional Prepositions of Time and Direction: እስከ ፡ ለሞት "until death"; እስከ ፡ ኀበ ፡ ቤተ ፡ ሚከ "up to the house of Micah" Judges 18, 13; እስከ ፡ ቅድመ "as far as in front of", ("up to the front of") Judges 19, 10; እስከ ፡ ለዓለም "to eternity" Hen. 72, 1.—Frequently it passes into the idea of "even", in which

(¹) [Or the old form እስኬ, v. HACKSPILL, '*Zeitschr. f. Assyr.*' XI, p. 128.]

case it is remarkable, that now and then the word which follows it stands in the Accusative, depending on a Verb: እስከ ፡ በግዐ (Accusative) "up to the sheep" Josh. 6, 21, as if it only meant "even".

6. ከመ "as", "like", is similarly a Conjunction of comparison originally (§ 169, כְּ and מָה § 64, *b*), but it is very frequently employed in the Construct St. as a Preposition. It is the same with the compound በከመ ('in which manner, *or* sort') "as", "like"; when used with numerals it also means "nearly" or "about" Matt. 14, 21.

7. ውስተ "in", "into" (ἐν and εἰς), is an Accusative, being at the same time in the Constr. St.,—probably from ውስጥ "interior" (§ 57) (¹). It is a Preposition in very common use, and in meaning corresponds for the most part to the Hebr. אֶל and עַל. Its meaning is "into", *e. g.* ወድቀ ፡ ውስተ ፡ ግብ "he falls into the ditch" Matt. 15, 14; በአ ፡ ውስተ ፡ አፍ፡ "enters into the mouth" Matt. 15,11; or "upon", "on the surface of (anything)", "on", "to" or "at", "with", with verbs of motion and of abiding, like ነበረ ፡ ውስተ ፡ መንበር "to sit upon the chair" (properly: 'to seat one's self upon'); and it is of more common occurrence with verbs of motion than በ. "To ascend to" is ዐርገ ፡ ውስተ Mark 16, 19; Matt. 15, 39; "to bring sacrifices 'to the altar'" ውስተ ፡ ምሥዋዕ; "to wander 'on the earth'" ውስተ ፡ ምድር; "to write 'in a book'" ውስተ ፡ መጽሐፍ; "dampness on the grass" ጊሜ ፡ ውስተ ፡ ሣዕር Deut. 32, 2; "to withdraw to" ተግሕሠ ፡ ውስተ Matt. 15, 21; "to invite to (a feast)" ጸውዐ ፡ ውስተ Matt. 22, 9; "to cast into (anything)" ወደየ ፡ ውስተ Matt. 13, 47 &c. Specially to be noticed are the expressions: "to attach to (anything)" ወሰከ ፡ ውስተ; ደመረ ፡ ውስተ "to join to" Gen. 30, 40; and "to set one over (anything as overseer)" ሠየመ ፡ ውስተ Matt. 25, 21; Gen. 41, 41 (ላዕለ V. 43); also with verbs of making, ረሰየ ፡ ውስተ "to make into (anything)" Ex. 32, 10; Deut. 9, 14. It forms compounds with በ and እም; በውስተ is "within", "in", "with", "among" (*inter*): በውስተ ፡ አህጉር "in the cities" Matt. 11, 20; በውስተ ፡ሞት "in death" Ps. 6, 5; በውስተ ፡ ምሳሓት "at feasts" Matt. 23, 6; በውስቴቶሙ "among them" Matt. 23, 34; the use is peculiar in ንስማዕ ፡ በውስተ ፡ አፉሃ "we will learn it ('in') out of her mouth" Gen. 24, 57;—እም ውስተ is "out of anything" or "down from anything", always with the implied idea that previously the subject was *in* that thing or

(¹) But *cf.* Assyrian *ištu*.

up in that position: ዘይወፅእ ፡ እምውስተ ፡ አፍ፡ "that which proceeds out of the mouth" Matt. 15, 11, 19; ወረደት ፡ እምውስተ ፡ ገመላ "she alighted from her camel" Gen. 24, 64; or ይመትሩ ፡ አዕጹቀ ፡ እምውስተ ፡ ዕፀው Matt. 21, 8; መኑ ፡ እምውስቴትክሙ "what man is there ('from the midst of') among you?" Matt. 12, 11. Notice also the Adverbial combination ውስተ ፡ አሐተኔ (as well as በአሐተኔ) *Sx. Genb.* 18.

8. ላዕለ "upon", "over", "above", Acc. and Constr. St. of ላዕል (¹) "height", is equivalent generally to עַל, and signifies first, "on" an object and "upon" an object, being often exchangeable in this meaning with ውስተ, *e. g.* ላዕለ ፡ ደብር "on the mountain"; ረሐነ ፡ ላዕለ "to spread upon *or* over anything" Matt. 21, 7; አንበረ ፡ ላዕለ "to place *or* lay upon anything" Matt. 12, 18; 19, 15; ተጽዕነ ፡ ላዕለ "to ride upon" (also with በ and ዲበ): farther, ዘርአ ፡ ላዕለ ፡ ብእሲት "to impregnate a woman" Hen. 15, 5; ይምጻእ ፡ ሰላምክሙ ፡ ላዕሌሃ "let your peace come upon it (*i. e.* 'upon the house', —*fem.*)" Matt. 10, 13. Next, it comes to mean "at", "in" or "on", *e. g.* ላዕለ ፡ ባሕር "by the sea" Josh. 16, 3; አልቦ ፡ ሥርወ ፡ ላዕሌሁ "there is no root in him" Matt. 13, 21; or "in addition to", "besides", ኢትንሣእ ፡ ብእሲተ ፡ ላዕሌሆን "thou shalt take no wife besides them" Gen. 31, 50. More figuratively it is used to express 'the duty which is laid *upon* any one': ትፈዲ ፡ ዘላዕሌከ "pay what thou owest" ('that which is laid upon thee'); ሚላዕሌነ "what is that to us?" Matt. 27, 4; [or 'duty *toward* any one': ምንተ ፡ ባቲ ፡ ላዕለ ፡ ወልድ ፡ ለብእሲት ፡ ዘእንበለ ፡ ዘ "what other duty has a woman toward a son but to—?" *Kebra Nag.* 34 a 20 *sq.*] and "to rule over", *e. g.* Matt. 20, 25. Then too it means "to set above any one", to the extent of meaning "to have superior force against him", or again "for him", and thus it occurs very often in the hostile sense "against" with verbs of mocking, fighting against, or doing harm to any one, *e. g.* ተሳለቀ ፡ ላዕለ Matt. 2, 16; 20, 19; አሕሠመ ፡ ላዕለ Gen. 19, 7; አበሰ ፡ ላዕለ Matt. 18, 21; Ps. 3, 1; 12, 3; Matt. 10, 21; ስምዕ ፡ ላዕለ "testimony against any one" Matt. 24, 14; ይቤ ፡ ቃለ ፡ ላዕለ "(whosoever) speaketh a word against" Matt. 12, 32; ኢይኩን ፡ ላዕሌከ ፡ ዝንቱ፡ "this shall not be unto thee" Matt. 16, 22; or in a friendly sense "for", "for the advantage of" አሠነየ ፡ ላዕለ "to do good to any

(¹) [But v., on the other hand, Barth, in '*Orientalische Studien*' (1906), p. 790.]

one"; ይጼሊ ፡ ላዕሌከ "he will pray for thee" Gen. 20, 7; ዘንተ ፡ ጽድቀ ፡ ግበሪ ፡ ላዕሌየ "do me this right" Gen. 20, 13; በእንተ ፡ ፈሪ ሆትየ ፡ ላዕሌክሙ "by reason of my fear for you" G. Ad. 109, 23. ላዕለ also forms compounds with በ and እም. በላዕለ is still more precise than ላዕለ "upon", "over", *e. g.* Ps. 4, 7; "judgment upon any one" በላዕለ Hen. 22, 4; በላዕሉ "over it" Hen. 28, 2; "there was found no unrighteousness በላዕሌየ in me" Ps. 16, 4; Gen. 44, 17; and in particular it is employed for "through", when any one is represented as the instrument, passive or active, of the completion of a transaction:—መንፈስ ፡ ይትናገር ፡ በላዕሌክሙ "the Spirit speaks through you" Matt. 10, 20; ይትወለዱ ፡ ውሉድ (1) ፡ በላዕሌሆን "(that) children be begotten of them" Hen. 15, 5; ዘበላዕሌሁ ፡ ይትሜጠውዎ "through whom they get him" Matt. 26, 24; በላዕለ ፡ ሙሴ "under Moses" ('under his rule') Josh. 20, 2. እምላዕለ is "down from", "away from" (מֵעַל) Hen. 28, 2; Matt. 17, 18; 18, 9; or even much the same as እምኀበ, *e. g.* ንሣእ ፡ እምላዕሌየ "accept from me" Gen. 21, 30.

9. መልዕልተ, the Accusative and Constr. St. of መልዕልት "height", is always found referring to Place—"above", "over", "upon": መልዕልተ ፡ ምድር ('above') "upon the earth" Luke 6, 49; Gen. 7, 24; መልዕልተ ፡ ርእሱ "over his head" Matt. 27, 37; Hen. 32, 2; መልዕልተ ፡ ነፋሳት "above the winds" *Gadla 'Arag.* (Guidi, 1905), p. 5. And,—just as in Hebrew,—"over a thing" has also the meaning "before it", especially in the phrase ቆመ ፡ መልዕልቴሁ "he stood before him" Gen. 18, 2; 22, 9; 24, 43; 41, 1. በመልዕልተ has the same meaning as መልዕልተ.

10. ዲበ "upon", "above", "over", to some extent synonymous with ላዕለ, seems to be compounded of ዲ (§ 62, *a*) and በ (2), and thus would properly mean "at—the". First of all it is found with the same force as ላዕለ; we say "to build upon a rock" ዲበ Matt. 7, 25, 26; ተጽዕነ ፡ ዲበ "to ride upon"; ወድቀ ፡ ዲበ ፡ ኰኵሕ "it fell upon stony ground" Matt. 13, 5; "to settle upon", "to set upon" Matt. 14, 19; 23, 2; "to lay upon" Matt. 23, 4; "power over" Matt. 10, 1; "to place (as lord) over" Hen. 24, 6; ነፍኀ ፡ ዲበ ፡ ገጹ ፡ መንፈሰ ፡ ሕይወት "breathed upon him ('his face') the breath of life". Gen. 2, 7. Next, it is often used in a hostile sense, "against", "in opposition to" Hen. 10, 9; 56, 7; Matt. 24, 7; Acts 23, 5;

---

(1) [Flemming's reading is ውሉዱ, tr.] (2) Like ኀበ, ሰበ.

ፀረፈ ፡ ዲበ "to blaspheme against" Mark 3, 29. Farther, it is employed to introduce the object of an action, particularly with verbs which mean "to rejoice (over)" ተፈሥሐ ፡ ዲበ Hen. 97, 2; "to weep (over)" Hen. 95, 1; "to mourn over" Hen. 12, 6; "to rely upon" Hen. 94, 8; and with verbs of 'adding to' "thereto", "in addition to" ተወሰከ ፡ ዲበ Hen. 82, 11 (1); Numb. 32, 14; ዲበ ፡ ዝኒ "and besides".—በዲበ is interchangeable with ዲበ and is almost as common, *e. g.* Ps. 9, 42; Gen. 6, 12; 24, 18; Job. 16, 14; Hen. 20, 5(1). እምዲበ is "down from" Matt. 14, 29. — A peculiar use is met with in ወሰከ ፡ እምዲበ ፡ ቆሙ ፡ አሐተ ፡ እመተ "to add to his stature one cubit" Matt. 6, 27.

§ 166. 11. መንገለ "towards", "to" (*versus, juxta, erga*) expresses in the most forcible manner 'direction towards anything', and is chiefly used with reference to Space in the sense of "away to", "opposite to", "along": መንገለ ፡ እስጳንያ "towards Spain", "to Spain" Rom. 15, 24; መንገለ ፡ የማን "to *or* on the right hand" Luke 1, 11; መንገለ ፡ ባሕር to the sea", and "by the sea" Matt. 4, 13; 13, 1; Mark 1, 16, and thus always in notices of the direction of a place, and of the cardinal points &c. More rarely it stands, with verbs of 'inclination' and the like, for "towards", in the sense of the Latin *erga*. The word itself is the Accusative and Constr. St. of መንገል "the visible side of anything" (√ نجل, *cf.* نَجْل, נֶגֶד)(2). It is also compounded with other prepositions, as in ለመንገለ "towards", in the sense of direction in space, Gen. 13, 14; and in a metaphorical sense '*erga*' Hebr. 2, 17: or እመንገለ either "in the direction of" (v. on እም, § 164, 3) Gen. 13, 11; or "on the side of", *e. g.* "she is my sister እመንገለ ፡ አቡየ on my father's side" Gen. 20, 12; እመንገለ ፡ ወንጌል "considered from the side of the Gospel", "having regard to the Gospel" Rom. 11, 28;—or it is placed before other Prepositions of Place, as in መንገለ ፡ ድኅረ "to the rear (*or* back) of"; መንገለ ፡ ቅድመ "to the front of" &c. እንተ ፡ መንገለ is very common, v. *infra* No. 19.

Prepositions (Class *b*) continued (11—23).

12. ምስለ "with" (*cum*), the Accusative and Constr. St. of ምስል "likeness", properly signifies "in the likeness of", *i. e.* "like",

(1) [In Hen. 82, 11 Flemming reads ምስሌሆሙ instead of Dillmann's ዲቤ"; and in 20, 5 the former has ዲበ for the latter's በዲበ. Tr.]

(2) [V., however, Praetorius, ZDMG LVII, p. 273, who compares the Southern Arabic מנקל "way".]

and is always used for "with", in order to express 'accompanying' and 'companionship'. It is the ordinary word for this relation ('he [it] *as* he [it], or he *like* him' = 'he *with* him'), *e. g.* ሖረ ፡ ኢየሱስ ፡ ምስለ ፡ አርዳኢሁ "Jesus went with his disciples". It finds frequent employment with words which express reciprocal action: 'to be at peace with', 'to fight with', 'to confer with', *e. g.* ተናገረ ፡ ምስለ Matt. 17,3; next it expresses 'in relation one to another', *e. g.* ኢኀደገ ፡ ምሕረቶ ፡ ምስለ ፡ ሕያዋን "he has not left off his mercy to the living" Ruth 2,20; ወሃይማኖቶሙ ፡ የዐቅቡ ፡ ፩ ምስለ ፡ ካልኡ "and they keep faith one with another" Hen. 41,5; even with verbs of 'separation', ንትራሐቅ ፡ ፩ ምስለ ፡ ካልኡ "we are to be separate the one from the other" Gen. 31,49 (for which እምነ (እም) appears in Gen. 32,17). In conformity with its fundamental meaning it is specially in place with verbs of 'assimilating and equalising', *e. g.* ተመሰልኩ ፡ ምስሌከ "I may be compared with thee"; ይትዔረይ ፡ መዓልት ፡ ምስለ ፡ ሌሊት "the day is the same as the night" Hen. 72,20; and farther with verbs which indicate 'being numbered among *or* regarded as', *e. g.* ተኈለቈ ፡ ምስለ ፡ ኃጥአን Is. 53,12 and Luke 22,37; *cf.* Ps. 87,4; as well as with verbs of 'joining', *e. g.* ዘይትቄሰክ ፡ ምስሌሆሙ "who is joined to them" Hen. 82,20. On rare occasions the preposition is used to indicate that which one has upon him, or carries with him, *e. g.* "they came ምስለ ፡ መጣብሕ ፡ ወዕፀው with swords and staves" Matt. 26,47 (for which in Verse 55 በ appears); or, again, in the sense of the Latin '*penes*' Hen. 9,5.

13. ቅድመ "before" (*ante* and *coram* לִפְנֵי), the Acc. and Constr. St. of ቅድም "front", is used both of Space and Time: ቅድመ ፡ ምሥዋዕ "before the altar" Matt. 5,24; ቅድመ ፡ ዮም "before the present time"; ቅድመ '*coram*' Matt. 25,32; 27,11. በቅድመ "before", is very common in the sense of *ante* and *coram*, Matt. 10,32; 11,10, 26; Ps. 9,26, and "overagainst" Hen. 4(1): also እምቅድመ (מִלִּפְנֵי) "from before", "before", *e. g.* እምቅድመ ፡ አይኅ "before the flood" Matt. 24,38; እምቅድመ ፡ ገጽከ ፡ ይወፅእ ፡ ፍትሕየ "from before thy face shall come forth my sentence" Ps. 16,3; and "by reason of" Hen. 9,10; as well as '*contra*': ዘእምቅድሜሆሙ ፡ ነፋስ '*ventus contrarius*' Matt. 14,24.

---

(1) [Here the reading adopted by FLEMMING is በቅዳሜሃ for DILLMANN's በቅድሜሃ. TR.]

14. ድኅረ "after", "behind",— the opposite of ቅድመ—, the Acc. and Constr. St. of ድኅር "rear", is also used both of Space and Time: ድኅሬሆሙ "back" Ps. 6, 10; ድኅረ ፡ ኵሉ "last of all" Mark 12, 6; ተለወ ፡ ድኅረ "to follow after" Matt. 10, 38. Still more common is እምድኅረ in both meanings, of Time and Space: ሖረ ፡ እምድኅሬሆሙ "he came behind them"; እምድኅረዝ "after this"; እምድኅረ ፡ አይኅ "after the flood" Gen. 9, 20; እምድኅረ ፡ ሕቀ Herm. p. 80; Matt. 21, 32. Still, in these cases እም is pretty often to be understood in its fundamental meaning: ሑር ፡ እምድኅሬየ "get from behind me" Matt. 16, 23. We meet also with በድኅረ Hen. 65, 4; Matt. 15, 23.

15. ማእከለ "in the midst of", "between", "among" (*inter*), the Acc. and Constr. St. of ማእከል "the middle" (properly, 'that which is comprised in something else, *or* contained in it',—from አከለ, Causative of כּוּל); *e. g.* ማእከሌየ ፡ ወማእከሌከ "between me and thee"; ፈነዎሙ ፡ ማእከለ ፡ ተኵላት "he sent them among wolves" Matt. 10, 16; ማእከለ ፡ ባሕር "in the midst of the sea" Matt. 14,24. We have also በማእከለ "in the midst of" Matt. 14,6; and እማእከለ, מִבֵּין Gen. 48, 12.

16. ታሕተ "below", "under" (*sub*), the Acc. and Constr. St. of ታሕት "the ground *or* bottom", *e. g.* ታሕተ ፡ እገሪሁ "under his feet" Ps. 8, 7; Matt. 22, 44; also found compounded with በ and እም.

17. Of the same meaning as the preposition last-mentioned appears መትሕተ "underneath", the Acc. and Constr. St. of መትሕት "the underside", Gen 1, 9; 6, 17; Ps. 17, 40; Hen. 26, 2. Also እመትሕተ, מִתַּחַת Hen. 14, 19 (1).

18. ዐውደ "about", "around" (*circa*), the Acc. and Constr. St. of ዐውድ "circuit", is of common occurrence, *e. g.* Mark 3, 34; Ps. 30, 16.

19. እንተ (2) "—wards", "in the direction of", or "to" &c., is manifestly taken from the Dem. Pron. እንት (§ 146, *fem.* of ዝ). It is quite as manifold in its references as the Accusative is, and it is withal one of the most subtle prepositions in meaning, to be found in Ethiopic. It often serves as a mere periphrasis for the

(1) [Given as እምታሕተ in FLEMMING's 'Henoch'. TR.]

(2) Corresponding in origin,—not in meaning—, to אֵת and عِنْدَ.

Accusative, particularly with verbs of motion: **ኀለፈ ፡ እንተ ፡ ይእቲ ፡ ፍኖት** "went past that way" Matt. 8,28; **ተግሕሠ ፡ እም ህየ ፡ እንተ ፡ በሕቲቱ** "he withdrew from that place into retirement" Matt. 14,13, 23; **ገብኡ ፡ እንተ ፡ ካልእ ፡ ፍኖት** "they returned by another way" Matt. 2,12; **ቦአ ፡ እንተ ፡ አንቀጽ** "he entered ('the door', *i. e.*) through *or* by the door" John 10,1,2; **የዐውድ ፡ እንተ ፡ በድው** "he wandereth through the waste" Matt. 12,43; thus always **ኀለፈ ፡ እንተ** "to pass through" Judges 11,17 *sqq.*; **ሐወጸ ፡ እንተ ፡ መስኮት** "he looked out at the window" ('through the window') Gen. 26,8; [*Kebra Nag.* 54 b 3 *sq.*]; **እንተ ፡ ኆኅት** "through the gate" (interchangeable with **በ**) Hen. 72,6 *sqq.*; **እንተ ፡ የማንየ** "at my right hand"; **እንተ ፡ ውስጣ ፡ ወእንተ ፡ አፍአሃ** "inwardly and outwardly" Gen. 6,14; **እንተ ፡ መንጸር** 'in the direction of that which one is looking at', *i. e.* "forward" Gen. 33,12; **እንተ ፡ ኀበ** "on what side" Judges 1,25. Being a preposition of such general meaning, it is often placed before other prepositions, to determine their signification more exactly by the subordinate idea 'in the direction of': **እንተ ፡ ዲበ ፡ ማይ** "on the water (motion)" Matt. 14,28; **እንተ ፡ መንገለ ፡ ገራውህ** "through the fields" Matt. 12,1; **ኀለፍኩ ፡ እንተ ፡ ዲበ ፡ ባሕር** "I crossed over the sea" Hen. 32,2; **እንተ ፡ ድኅሬሁ** "(came) behind him" Matt. 9,20; Cant. 2,9; **እንተ ፡ ቅድመ** Ex. 34,6; Josh. 8,14 &c.

20. **በእንተ**, a compound of **በ** and **እንተ** No. 19, is properly "in the direction of" or "in regard to". Accordingly it signifies very frequently:—1. "by reason of" (more vigorously and clearly than **በ**), and then, "in payment of" and "for", of price and wages, *e. g.* "I will serve thee seven years **በእንተ ፡ ራሔል** for Rachel" Gen. 29,18; 30,15; and "for", *e. g.* "to beg for any one", "to intercede for":—2. "with regard to", "about", to introduce the subject spoken, thought, or written &c. 'about', *e. g.* "what are we to do with the rest **በእንተ ፡ አንስት** with regard to wives?" Judges 21,7; **ይቤሎሙ ፡ በእንተ ፡ ዮሐንስ** "he spake to them of John" Matt. 17,13; 11,7, 10; 13,10 &c.,—very often occurring in this sense; and thus it is the usual word to indicate the contents, in the headings of books and sections of books.—On **ከመ ፡ እንተ** *cf.* DILLMANN's '*Lex.*', col. 827.

21. **ህየንተ** "instead of", originally **ህየተ** (¹),—formed from

(¹) V. DILLMANN's '*Octat. Aethiop.*', *Comm.* p. 5. The Nasal is interpolated in accordance with § 58.

ሀየ "there" ('in the place') and an ending ት, which supports the sign of the Constr. St.,—is used in the case of 'barter' and 'substitution' (being interchangeable with በእንተ in the former meaning): "they requited me evil ሀየንተ ፡ ሠናይት for good" Ps. 37,21; Gen. 44,4; "he dies ሀየንተ ፡ ሕዝብ for the people" John 11,50; and in the case of succeeding to a kingdom 'in place of' Gen. 36,33 *sqq*.

22. በበይነ and በበይናተ, from በይን (בֵּין) "interval" ('separation') and በ. The Singular-form stands:—1. in a few instances, in the sense of "between" (*inter*), referring to space: እለ ፡ ይትላጸቁ ፡ በበይኖን "which are joined together" Ex. 28,7; ገጾን ፡ ይትናጸሩ ፡ በበይኖን "their faces must look to one another" Ex. 25,20.—2. Inasmuch as that which is between two objects is withal the binding element between them, በበይነ signifies farther "occasioned by", "caused by" (1), "through the influence of", or "by reason of", and it is frequently used with this meaning: Judges 20,10; Mal. 1,2; በበይነዝ "therefore" Ex. 20,11; or "with regard to" (like በእንተ) Judges 21,16.—The Plural-form, which is also written በቤናት, appears only associated with Suffixes, and has always the meaning of "between", "among", with a spatial reference, *e. g.* Ex. 26,3. It is greatly used in regard to anything which a number of persons do or cause "between *or* among themselves", and thus it is specially found with verbs of St. III, 3, *e. g.* Matt. 9,3; 16,7,8; 12,26. We have even መንግሥት ፡ እንተ ፡ ትትናፈቅ ፡ በበይናቲሃ "a kingdom which is divided against itself" Matt. 12,25; and, with a reduplicated በ:—በበ ፡ በይናቲሆሙ Gen. 42,21,28.

Along with በበይነ, appears እንበይነ (for እምበይነ § 57) (2) frequently, in the sense of "for the sake of" and "about" (*de*): እንበይነ ፡ ዝንቱ "for this cause" Mark 1,38; እንበይነ ፡ መኑ ፡ ይብል "of whom he is speaking" John 13,22; (and with the meaning "on account of") Ex. 29,36.—But the use of በበይነ and እንበይነ began generally to decline, and በእንተ came into more frequent use in their stead.

23. እንበለ, and still oftener ዘእንበለ "without", "except", is originally a Conjunction, and is still employed greatly as a Con-

(1) *Cf.* بَيْن *intervallum* and *nexus*; अन्तर "interval", "cause", "occasion".

(2) [According to Jensen, '*Zeitschr. f. Assyr.*' XI, p. 352, እን here is = Assyrian *in(a)*.]

junction. It stands for እምበለ (§ 57) (¹), and is a compound of እም "if" (§ 64, *b*) and בַּל "not", answering to בִּלְעֲדֵי; ዘእንበለ is literally "which-if-not", "if-it-not". It means "without": እንበለ ፡ ኵነኔ "without judgment" (*Lit.*); አርብዓ ፡ እንበለ ፡ አሐቲ "forty, save one" 2 Cor. 11, 24; Judges 20, 15, 17; ዘእንበለ ፡ ምሳሌ "without a parable" Matt. 13, 34; ዘእንበለ ፡ ፍሬ "without fruit" Matt. 13, 22; 15, 38; Hen. 89, 44; "except" Matt. 11, 27; 14, 17, 21; 21, 19.

Words occurring as Prepositions, but less frequently (24—38).

(*c*) *Words occurring as Prepositions, but less frequently*, or those which are just beginning to be used as Prepositions.

24. መቅድመ "before", "in preference to" Hen. 48, 2, the Acc. and Constr. St. of መቅድም "that which is in front".

25. ማዕዶተ "beyond", "along" (from ማዕዶት "a crossing", "a ford" (²)): Hen. 18, 10; Matt. 19, 1; Gen. 41, 3.

26. ፍና "towards" (properly, "way", "direction"),—used both of Time and Place, *e. g.* ፍና ፡ ሰርክ "towards evening" Gen. 3, 8; 8, 11; 19, 1.

27. ጠቃ and ጥቃ "hard by", "close to" (properly, "exactness") Matt. 20, 30; Ex. 24, 4; 29, 12; 15, 27; Josh. 8, 35; also, በጥቃ Ps. 140, 7.

28. ቢጸ "beside" Gen. 30, 40 (from ቢጽ "fellowship").

29. ምእኃዘ "beside", "close to" (from ምእኃዝ "boundary"); also ማእኅዘ Numb. 34, 3; Deut. 11, 30; Josh. 12, 9.

30. ውእደ "along" (connected with יַד, Amhar. ወደ) in the Book of Jubilees; and በውእደ Deut. 32, 51.

31. ተክለ "in place of" (ተክል "place") Ex. 21, 36; Hen. 89, 39; 103, 3.

32. ተውላጠ "for", "in exchange for" (ተውላጥ "exchange"), v. Ludolf, '*Lex.*'.

33. መንጸረ and አንጸረ "over-against" (properly:—"that which one sees before him", "the quarter one is looking to") Josh. 8, 14; Mark 12, 41; 13, 3; Gen. 12, 8.

34. አምሳለ and አርአያ "like", in poetic diction, (properly:—"after the image of").

35. መጠነ, oftener አምጣነ "of the size of", "as large as" (v. § 157, 1).

(¹) [V. Note (²) on preceding page.]

(²) [Also "the region beyond", *regio opposita*, *ripa ulterior* (v. '*Lex.*' & '*Gloss.*'), which seems to come nearer the meaning of the Prep. Tr.]

36. ከወላ and ከዋላ "behind", and አፍአ (አፍአ) "outside of". Finally, we have farther the following remarkable words:

37. በዕብሬት, only used with suffixes, "for the sake of—" (בַּעֲבוּר, "because of"): በዕብሬትከ. Gen. 12,13 (1).

38. አመ, of Pronominal origin (§ 64, *b*), and properly a Conjunction, and Relative Adverb of Time (§ 161, *b*) "when", but also used as a Preposition "at the time of", *e. g.* Judges 14,15,17; Ps. 77,12; Matt. 11,22; 17,23; Hen. 22,4. In old printed books and manuscripts it still occurs often in the form አሚ (*cf.* § 167), which it must always take before Suffixes. It is very frequently found with the Suffix of the 3rd pers. Sing. Fem. ሃ, thus አሚሃ for "at that time" Matt. 2,17; 13,43; Luke 13,1 (§ 160, *b*). Of quite similar origin and meaning is ሶበ (§ 62, 1, *a*), from ሶ (ذا) "there" and በ "in". It is regarded as a Relative at times,—and in those cases it means "when",—but also as a Demonstrative, and then it signifies "at that time". The latter is the fundamental meaning, of which the relative signification is only a development. In olden time it had the termination *ē* (2),—sometimes used absolutely, as in ይእቲ ፡ ሶቤ "in that 'then'", *i. e.* "at that very time" Matt. 7,23, sometimes governing a Genitive; but in later Ethiopic this form is retained only with the Suffix ሃ, ሶቤሃ "at that time", "forthwith", "then", *e. g.* Matt. 12,13 &c. Both አሚሃ and ሶቤሃ are farther compounded with other prepositions: ለሶቤሃ "for the moment" Luke 8,13; እምሶቤሃ "from that time forward", "forthwith" Hen. 85,4; 89,20; እምአሚሃ "thereafter" Matt. 26,16. Probably ጊዜ (3) is also of the same order with these,—according to the conjecture which has been already ventured (§ 64, *b*),—being of like origin, although it has usually the meaning "point of time", "hour", "moment" (*cf.* ይእቲ ፡ ሶቤ). It is used exactly like አመ = "in the time of", with Genitive following, and it may even subordinate an entire sentence in the Genitive relation: ጊዜ ፡ ፈቀድክሙ ('the time of—you will') "whensoever you will" Mark 14,7: and hence it is on the way to become a Conjunction, just as ሶበ is nearly

(1) As to the form በዕብሬትከ ἐπί σοι, Judges 11,23, it is certainly better to regard it as standing for እብሬት from በረየ. [FIELD's LXX (Oxford 1859) gives ἐπὶ σοῦ here. TR.].

(2) [*Cf. Kebra Nag.*, *Introd.* p. XVII.]

(3) ዜ as in ይእዜ, ማእዜ.

always a Conjunction. But just as we say ይእተ ፡ ሶቤ, we also say ውእተ ፡ ጊዜ, ይእተ ፡ ጊዜ "at that time" Matt. 21,2; Ps. 18,14; or ጊዜሃ, በጊዜሃ "forthwith", "at that time", just like አሜሃ, ሶቤሃ Matt. 14,27; 21,3 &c.

On ቤዘ ὑπέρ, ἀντί, περί, and ፍዳ *pro*, ἀντί v. DILLMANN's '*Lex.*', coll. 538, 1380.

Attachment of Suffixes to Prepositions.

§ 167. *Attachment of Suffixes to Prepositions.* Almost all the Prepositions may take the Personal Pronoun as a Suffix, just as, with the Constr. St., they govern Nouns. But the manner of attachment varies greatly, corresponding to the origin and use of the Preposition.

1. The two quite short and exceedingly common Prepositions, በ and ለ, follow a way of their own.

(*a*) ለ attracts the Suffixes of the 2nd Pers. *m.* and *f.*, and the Plural Suffixes of all the Persons, without any binding-vowel, but yet in such a manner that *la* with ሆሙ and ሆን is contracted into ሎሙ and ሎን. The suffix of the 1st Pers. Sing. was appended, in accordance with § 149, in its oldest form *ī*, to ለ, or rather to ል, becoming ሊ. In the same way the Singular Suffixes of the 3rd Pers. with ለ brought about the contracted forms ሎ and ላ (1). But these forms ሊ, ሎ, ላ were erelong considered too short, and were therefore strengthened by a repetition of the attachment of Personal signs,—in the 3rd Person by ቱ and ቲ (as in ውእቱ, ይእቲ), and in the 1st by ተ, which in this case must be explained as standing for ነ of አነ "I" (2). We have therefore (TRUMPP, p. 560):

	1.	2. m.	2. f.	3. m.	3. f.
S.	ሊተ "to me";	ለከ,	ለኪ "to thee";	ሎቱ "to him",	ላቲ "to her";
Pl.	ለነ "to us";	ለክሙ,	ለክን "to you";	ሎሙ "to them",	ሎን "to them".

Instead of ሎን, met with *e. g.* in Matt. 24,19; Hen. 9,8 (3), a form ሎንቱ is found, having ቱ appended (just as in እሎንቱ,

---

(1) לִי, לוֹ, לָהּ.—ሎቲ 4 Esr. 6,62 (KÖNIG, p. 124) is manifestly an error of the Press.

(2) Just as the Personal-ending of the 1st pers. Perf. in Arabic and in the North-Semitic tongues is *tu*, *ti*; *cf.* EWALD, '*Hebr. Spr.*' § 105, *e*; '*Gr. Ar.*' I, p. 285 *sq.*

(3) [FLEMMING's reading of this verse, besides exhibiting other differences, gives ሎንቱ instead of DILLMANN's ሎን. TR.]

እላንቱ:) Ex. 26,4,37; Gen. 31,43, and another form ሎቶን for ሎንቶን, having ቶን appended (as in ውእቶን). Some rather peculiar Suffixes also are taken by ለ when it is compounded with ወይ and አሌ (§ 61, *cf.* Dillmann's '*Lex.*'): besides ወይሊተ "woe's me", one says farther ወይልየ (for ወይሊ; *cf.* ብየ for ቢ); and so too አሌልየ (for አሌሊ) as well as አሌሊተ; and in the 3rd Person ቱ: is sometimes dropped, as in አሌ ፡ ሎ Job 31,3; አሌሎ ፡ ለውእቱ ፡ ብእሲ Matt. 18,7; አሌሎን ፡ ለከናፍረ ፡ ጕሕሉት Ps. 30,21; Matt. 24,19. It is otherwise in the case of ወይለከ, ወይለኪ, አሌ ፡ ለክሙ &c.

(*b*) Suffixes are attached to በ by *a* going back to *e*; only, in the 3rd Person *a* blends with *hū*, *hā* &c. into *ō*, *ā*, *ōmū*, *ōn*, thus (Trumpp, p. 560):

	1.	2. m.	2. f.		3. m.	3. f.
S.	ብየ "in me";	ብከ,	ብኪ "in thee";		ቦ "in him",	ባ "in her";
Pl.	ብነ "in us";	ብክሙ,	ብክን "in you";		ቦሙ "in them",	ቦን "in them".

Yet ቦቱ:, ባቲ: also occur in place of ቦ, ባ (like ሎቱ:, ላቲ:), and ቦንቱ: also, in place of ቦን, as in Josh. 24,31; Matt. 25,16; Numb. 13,28; 14,34; farther ቦቶን just like ሎቶን, as in Numb. 32,17; finally even ቢየ instead of ብየ Sap. 2,13 (A = Abb. 55). Another trace of an original ቢ "in me" has been preserved in እንቢ for the usual እንብየ, § 162. Moreover በ when provided with Suffixes, although it has not yet given up its fundamental meaning, has usually assumed quite peculiar significations, and is with great frequency employed in these. 1. In particular, —inasmuch as (§ 194) the Copula "is" is already involved in ብየ &c., ብየ, ብከ &c. may signify: "it is with me" (1), *i. e.* "I have", "thou hast", "he has", *e. g.* ዘብከ "that which thou hast". Therefore in many cases this form takes the place of our verb "to have", and is (§ 176, *h*) almost always construed with the Accusative, *e. g.* አበ ፡ ብነ "a father have we" Matt. 3,9. 2. The 3rd pers. Sing. Masc. ቦ or ቦቱ: may also signify: "therein (is)", *i. e.* "there is present", "there is *or* there are", corresponding in meaning, completely, to the יֵשׁ of the Hebrews, *e. g.* ቦ ፡ እለ ፡ በጽሑ "there are those who came" "there came some". The word is always imper-

(1) For this use of በ *cf.* passages like Hen. 37,5 ኮኑ ፡ ብየ "they fell to my share".

sonal in that case, and its subject may be mentioned either in the Nominative or the Accusative, v. § 192. To give the negative of **በ** in these two significations, the negative **አል** (אַל), which is now preserved only in this compound, was prefixed to it even in the oldest times (§ 62, *c*), whence[1]:—

	1.	2. m.	2. f.
Sing.	**አልብየ**	**አልብከ**	**አልብኪ**
Plur.	**አልብነ**	**አልብክሙ**	**አልብክን**

	3. m.	3. f.
Sing.	**አልቦ** or **አልቦቱ**	**አልባ** or **አልባቲ**
Plur.	**አልቦሙ**	**አልቦን** or **አልቦንቱ**.

2. Of the other Prepositions, some have continued to exhibit various peculiarities, just because they are of Pronominal origin. The Preposition **እስከ** "till", and **እንተ** (§ 166, No. 19) do not take any Suffixes,—the former, because it is properly a Conjunction and signifies "till that", "until",—and **እንተ**, because the use of it with Suffixes is reserved to indicate the Possessive (§ 150, *b*). On the other hand **በእንተ** "by reason of", "for the sake of" permits the approach of Suffixes, and indeed does so quite in accordance with § 150, *b*[2], thus: **በእንቲአየ**, **በእንቲአሁ** &c. Finally **ከመ** "like", originally a Conjunction too, calls for the appearance always of a long *ā* (from **መ** = מָה) before the Suffixes (כְּמוֹ, כָּמוֹ):—

	1.	2. m.	2. f.	3. m.	3. f.
Sing.	**ከማየ**	**ከማከ**	**ከማኪ**	**ከማሁ**	**ከማሃ**
Plur.	**ከማነ**	**ከማክሙ**	**ከማክን**	**ከማሆሙ**	**ከማሆን**.

ከማሁ farther stands in many cases for "such a one", and as a neuter ("like it") for "such a thing", and for "thus" (§ 157, 1).

3. The majority of the other Prepositions take the ending *ē* before Suffixes instead of *a*. This can only be explained as a trace of the old ending of the Constr. St. in *ia* (§ 144), which has clung more tenaciously to these forms, manifestly because they are

(1) Corresponding in use in manifold ways to لَيْسَ and אֵין.

(2) [—including the lengthening of the **አ** before the suffixes in old Mss.]

all in the Accusative as well, and the old ending of the Constr. St. *ia* has coalesced with the *a* of the Accusative into ē (1). And this *ē* is preserved in a remarkable way with many prepositions, even in cases when they have nothing but an ordinary noun following them (*cf.* DILLMANN's '*Octateuch*', *Apparat. Crit.* p. 5): ኀቤ Josh. 10,4, Note; መንገሌ Numb. 20,19, Note; እምኔ Lev. 20,5 F; እስኬ (2) Gen. 35,20 F; Amos 6,15 (A); 8,12(A); ምዕሬሃ 4 Kings 7,18; ዘእንበሌ Matt. 15,38 (Rom.); ህየቴ Gen. 47,19 F; ህየንቴዝ Gen. 44,33 F; ዲቤ Matt. 14,26,28 (Old); መጠኔ Sap. 12,20 (A); and frequently in the N. T. (Old Ed.) &c.; *cf. supra* § 166, No. 38 አሜ, ሶቤ. This form appears always before Suffixes, *e. g.* from ምስለ "with":—

	1.	2. m.	2. f.	3. m.	3. f.
Sing.	ምስሌየ	ምስሌከ	ምስሌኪ	ምስሌሁ	ምስሌሃ
Plur.	ምስሌነ	ምስሌክሙ	ምስሌክን	ምስሌሆሙ	ምስሌሆን.

It is the same with እምነ, ዲበ, ኀበ, ቅድመ, ድኅረ, ላዕለ, መልዕልተ, መንገለ, ማእከለ, ታሕተ, መትሕተ, ህየንተ, እንበለ. And yet suffixes are also met with, attached without an *ē*, *e g.* እምኖሙ "of them" Ex. 1,7,—particularly to those prepositions which are still used on other occasions as substantives also:— መትሕቱ and መትሕቶ Josh. 7,21, 22, Note; መልዕልቶሙ Gen. 7,20; መልዕልቶ Hen. 89,4; እምታሕታ G. Ad. 49,9; ማእከሎሙ Ps. 54,17; Matt. 18,20; Numb. 17,2; Lev. 26,46.

4. The Preposition ውስተ "in" takes before Suffixes a new Abstract-form ውስቴት "the interior", "inside", and appends the Suffixes to this, like በዕብሬት, thus: ውስቴትከ, ውስቴትክሙ, ውስቴቱ, ውስቴታ, ውስቴቶሙ, ውስቴቶን (3). To the preposition በበይነ the Suffixes are applied as to an ordinary noun: Ex. 26,9;

(1) Thus we can neither compare the binding-vowel of the Plural ־ֵי, which is found with many prepositions before the Suffix in Hebrew, as PHILIPPI, '*Wesen und Urspr. des St. c.*', p. 107, PRAETORIUS, ZDMG XXVII, p. 644, and TRUMPP, p. 560, N. 1—would have us do, nor even the *ē* of ይእዜ, ማእዜ, ጊዜ. —*Cf.* farther BARTH, ZDMG XLII, p. 348 *sqq.* [V. now PRAETORIUS, ZDMG LVI, p. 685 *sqq.*]

(2) [V. *supra* Note, § 165, p. 395.]

(3) The form ውስቴተ in the Constr. St. is met with in RÜPPELL, II,39, [and D. H. MÜLLER, '*Epigr. Denkm.*' p. 45].—On ውስቴት v. now also BARTH, ZDMG XLII, p. 348, N. 6.

36,11; and to its Plural-form **በበይናት**, just as to ordinary plurals, viz., with *ī*: **በበይናቲሆሙ** &c.

5. **ዐውደ** "around", as if it were not yet a full preposition, assumes the Suffixes just like an ordinary noun in the Accusative:—**ዐውድየ** Ps. 30, 16; **ዐውዶ** Mark 3, 34; **ዐውዳ** Josh. 21, 40; **ዐውዶን** Josh. 21, 39; 24, 33 &c.; and it is the same with **ማዕዶተ**, **መንጸረ** &c., or **አምሳለ**, **አንጻረ** (§ 153, 1), **ጥቃ**, **አፍአ**, **ከዋላ** and others (§ 154, 2, *a*).

III. CONJUNCTIONS.

General Account of Conjunctions.

§ 168. Several of those Words of Relation which have been adduced among the Prepositions, are also employed as Conjunctions, being either Prepositions originally, and Conjunctions only in a derived way, or *vice versâ*. In fact, when we consider that a Preposition is always in the Constr. St. relation, and farther that by means of this relation a word may govern an entire clause, whether it be introduced by a relative pronoun or not (*e. g.* **አምጣነ ፡ ሀሎ ፡ መርዓዊ ፡ ምስሌሆሙ** "in the measure [of this] that" —*i. e.* "*so long as* the bridegroom is with them" Mark 2, 19), the possibility of a Preposition passing into a Conjunction becomes clear; and several Conjunctions have been produced in this way. By the side of these, there are others which are originally mere Adverbs, but which have acquired the power, by a slight alteration of the sense or even of the form, of connecting clauses together. The most numerous Conjunctions, however, and the most current, are of pronominal origin, and come usually from a relative pronoun or a demonstrative pronoun used relatively, inasmuch as the relative pronoun is precisely the one which serves to bring words and clauses into relation with one another. Again, among Conjunctions themselves, one very essential distinction consists in this, that some of them hold the clause, which they introduce, in stricter subordination, while others only loosely precede it. Necessarily the former must stand invariably at the head of the sentence, and are either combined with relative pronouns or appear in the Constr. St. The latter are nothing but adverbs, and, therefore, like other adverbial particles, they readily retire behind the first word or words of the sentence, or they may even be attached to one of these in the form of an enclitic. Conjunctions are arranged, in what follows, in accordance with their signification.

1. COPULATIVE, DISJUNCTIVE, ADVERSATIVE, AND RESTRICTIVE CONJUNCTIONS.

1. The simplest Copula is **ወ** "and" (וְ, وَ), always attached to the word which follows. It connects both individual words and clauses, and corresponds frequently to our stronger "also", and not seldom to our "but", inasmuch as that which may be regarded in the one language as a simple continuation or ranking together, is expressed in the other rather as a contrast or opposition. It may even answer to our "or", or "up to", *e. g.* "two *and* three" for "two *or* ('up to') three", Hen. 3. Still, there are special particles, in common use, for "also", "but" and "or". 1. Copulative, Disjunctive, Adversative and Restrictive Conjunctions (1—9).

2. **አው** "or" (أَوْ, אוֹ, ܐܘ(1)) is sometimes disjunctive, sometimes explanatory; but for "or" in the sense of "that is" there is also a periphrasis with **ብሂል** (§ 193), and in like manner there are still other expressions for "or" as '*sive*' (§ 170).

3. For the idea, "also", "even", the peculiar word **ሂ** is made use of, always enclitic like τε and *que*, an adverb of the shortest formation from the root **ሀ**(2) (§ 62), *e. g.* **መጸብሓውያንሂ** "even the publicans" Matt. 5,46; **አንተሂ** "even (or 'also') thou" Matt. 18,33; **እለሂበ** "even those, which he hath" Matt. 13,12. It serves also to link words together, and then it is equivalent to "and", *e. g.* **እሴስየክሙ ፡ ለቤትክሙሂ** "I will nourish you and your house" Gen. 50, 21. Most frequently it occurs in association with **ወ**, **ወ —ሂ** "and also", "farther", "and": **ወእንስሳሂ** "and (also) the beasts" Gen. 1, 26; **ወሶበሂ ፡ ትጼልዩ** "and when ye pray" Matt. 6, 5. In all such cases it connects individual words as well as whole clauses. It is often made use of to turn the interrogatives **መኑ** and **ምንት** into indefinites (§ 147, *b*)(3), but only in clauses which have a negative meaning.

4. A somewhat stronger conjunction than **ሂ** is found in **ኒ**, formed from the root **ን**, just as **ሂ** is from the root **ሀ**(4). It may indeed be translated frequently by "also", but more precisely it

(1) Also = وَإِلَّا فَ G. Ad. p. 110, line 7 and Note 2.

(2) If not rather a weakened form from an interrogative root *kwi*, *ki*.

(3) Like चित् and चन.

(4) —*ni* has also been found in Assyrian; v. HAUPT, '*Der keilinschr. Sintfluthbericht*' (Leipzig 1881), p. 29, [and DELITZSCH, '*Assyr. Gramm.*' § 79, β].

answers to "on his part", "on the other hand", for it is the proper particle to express the correspondence of two or more members, whether words or clauses, in cases where the relation of reciprocity occurs. In Greek we should most readily express it by μέν or δέ: "whatsoever ye would that men should do to you **ግበሩ ፡ ሎሙ ፡ አንትሙኒ** even so do ye to them on your part" Matt. 7, 12; "if ye forgive men their trespasses **የኀድግ ፡ ለከሙኒ ፡ አቡክሙ** your Father will also forgive you", Matt. 6, 14, 15; **በከመ ፡ በሰማይ ፡ ወበምድርኒ** "as in heaven, so also upon earth" Matt. 6, 10. Thus the combination **ወ**—**ኒ** is very often equivalent to δέ, when anything new is added: **ወካህናትኒ** "and the priests again" ('on their part') &c. Josh. 6, 13, 14; 9, 3; *cf.* especially the instructive passage Matt. 13, 37—39: "the sower is the Son of Man; **ወገራህቶኒ** *the field again* is the world; **ወሠናይኒ ፡ ዘርእ** *while the good seed* are the children of the kingdom" &c. When two or more members of a sentence are strung together by **ኒ**, **ወ**—**ኒ**, this arrangement answers to our "as well—as", "both—and": **ወወፅኡ ፡ እሙንቱኒ ፡ ወነገሥቶሙኒ** "and they went out, both themselves and their kings" Josh. 11, 4; or **እምኵሉሂኒ ፡ የዐርግ ፡ ወእምህየኒ ፡ . . . . ጠል** "as on all other sides, so on this side too . . . . . the dew arose" Hen. 28, 2; in the same way **ኒ ፡ ወ**, *e. g.* **ውእቱኒ ፡ ወእለ ፡ ምስሌሁ** "both he and they that were with him" Matt. 12, 3; or **ሂ ፡ ወ**—**ኒ** Gen. 42, 35. **ኒ** is also appended to the interrogative, just like **ሂ** and with the same object; but **መኑ** more readily takes **ሂ**(¹), and **ምንት**, **ኒ**(²).

5. The notion "but", if it has no special emphasis, is regularly expressed by **ሰ**, which likewise appears invariably as an enclitic. It comes from the root **ሰ**(³) (§ 62, 1, *a*), and means in the first place "there". "But" is by no means its fundamental meaning. It is rather attached to a word for the purpose of bringing it emphatically into notice; and thereby peculiar delicacy and brevity are lent to Ethiopic diction. *E. g.*: "Take no thought for the morrow, **እስመ ፡ ጌሠምሰ ፡ ትሔሊ ፡ ለርእሳ** for *the morrow* will take thought for itself" Matt. 6, 34; **እመ ፡ ወልዱሰ ፡ አንተ ፡ ለእግዚአ**

(¹) Because **መኑኒ** would be uneuphonious.

(²) When **ኒ** encounters the final **ን** of a noun, there is usually no contraction (§ 55, *c*), *e. g.* Lev. 25, 22; Deut. 2, 23, 29 (*cf.* § 161, *a*); v., however, Numb. 6, 4.

(³) Quite similar are अथ, तु, δέ.

ብሔር "If thou be (really) the Son of God" Matt. 4,3; Gen. 4,25; Matt. 3,15; 6,9; 21,13; Josh. 23,2; Hen. 15,7 (¹); 16,3 &c. Hence it answers to *μέν*, wherever this particle gives a degree of prominence: **ማእረረሰ ፡ ብዙኅ ፡ ወገባረ ፡ ኅዳጣን** ὁ μὲν θερισμὸς πολύς, οἱ δὲ ἐργάται ὀλίγοι Matt. 9,37; **ቃልሰ ፡ ቃለ ፡ ያዕቆብ ፡ ወእደው ፡ ዘዔሳው** Gen. 27,22; and it stands both for *μέν* and for *δέ*, *e. g.* in John 3,29, 30. On the position of **ሰ** in the sentence, *cf.* **ወእለ ፡ ይኤብሱሰ** Tob. 12,10, where later manuscripts present **ወእለሰ ፡ ይኤብሱ**. In order to produce a specially marked emphasis, it may even be attached to more than one word in the sentence: **እም ዮምሰ ፡ እንከሰ ፡ ያፈቅረኒ** "now from this day he will assuredly love me" Gen. 30,20. When it actually expresses merely our "but" or the Greek particle of continuation or opposition, *δέ*, it is then frequently joined with the additional particle **ወ**, thus **ወ—ሰ**, *e. g.* **ወእመሰ** "but if" (²).

6. Contrast or contrariety is expressed more strongly, and almost always after clauses of negative meaning, by **አላ** "but" (*sondern*), "but rather", formed from **ላ** = لَا (§ 62) and **እም** = **እም** "if" (§ 170) (³). It is used pretty often, and it always stands at the beginning of the clause, *e. g.* "man does not live by bread alone, **አላ ፡ በኵሉ ፡ ቃል** but by every word" Matt. 4,4. It appears in the sense of "if not", *Chrest.* p. 4, line 21; p. 92, line 13. In translations from Arabic it also corresponds to إِلَّا "except", *e. g.* **አላ ፡ እም** "excepting if" ('unless') G. Ad. 148, 1.

7. **እንበለ** and **ዘእንበለ** (§ 166, No. 23) are often used also

(¹) [The appended **ሰ** does not appear in the reading which Flemming adopts here. tr.]

(²) On **ዝሰኩ** (**ዝሰኩ**) v. Dillmann's '*Lex.*', col. 1056 *sq.*, and *cf.* Praetorius, '*Beitr. z. Assyr.*' I, p. 26.

(³) Formed thus like إِلَّا. Nöldeke is of a different opinion. In a letter dated 4th Dec., 1882, he explains **አላ** as ἀλλά, which according to him has pushed its way into Ethiopic, through the Coptic, where it is in full use (*cf.* Stern's '*Gramm.*'). Against any comparison with إِلَّا the same scholar lays stress upon these facts,—that *lā* is not otherwise attested in Geʿez,—that *m* and *n* are not progressively assimilated in Geʿez,—and that the Semitic particles for the idea "if" constantly contain *i* (أَمْ = إِمْ = הַאִם).

in a like meaning, after a negation: Matt. 9,12; 16,23; Mark 7,15; Ps. 43,5.

8. **ባሕቱ** (§ 163, 2), which properly signifies "only", is also frequently employed to express "yet", "but rather", "but". It is, in that case, usually placed after another word, mostly the leading word upon which stress is laid: **አግብኡ ፡ ባሕቱ ፡ ለእግዚአብሔር** "but rather render ye to God" Matt. 5, 33; **ይኩን ፡ ባሕቱ ፡ ነገርክሙ** "rather let your speech be" Matt. 5, 37; 10, 6; **እለ ፡ ኢኮኑ ፡ ባሕቱ ፡ እምኔነ** "but yet who are not of us" 1 John 2, 19. When compounded with **ወ** as **ወባሕቱ**, it expresses "but" (*sondern*): **ወባሕቱ ፡ ዑቁ** "but take heed" Matt. 6, 1; 8, 4; **ወባሕቱ ፡ እብለክሙ** "but I say unto you" Matt. 8,11; **ወባሕቱ ፡ ፍርህዎ** "but fear ye him (who)" &c. Matt, 10,28; and also, separated from **ወ**, **ወእብለክሙ ፡ ባሕቱ** "but I say unto you" Matt. 17, 12; and thus frequently. Farther **ሰ** may be added in the same clause: **ወእመሰ ፡ ኢፈቀደት ፡ ባሕቱ ፡ ይእቲ ፡ ብእሲት** "but if that woman be not willing" Gen. 24, 8; **ወባሕቱ ፡ ለሊሁሰ ፡ ኢየሱስ ፡ ኢያጥመቅ** "but Jesus himself baptised not" John 4, 2.

9. On **ዳእሙ** "rather" (also in the combined form: **ዘእንበለ ፡ ዳእሙ** "but rather" Mark 7, 15) v. § 163, 2.

2. INFERENTIAL, CAUSAL, AND FINAL CONJUNCTIONS.

2. Inferential, Causal and Final Conjunctions (1—10).

§ 169. 1. **ኬ** "now", "thus", denotes an inference. It is always enclitic, and is probably an abbreviated form of כֵּן, § 64, *b*. It is very common, particularly in the N. T., *e. g.*: **ወኵሎንኬ ፡ ትውልድ** "and all the generations therefore are" &c. Matt. 1, 17; **አንሰኬ** "now I indeed" Matt. 3, 11. It is also appended to **አ**, to emphasise astonishment: **አኬመምህራን** "O what teachers!" The *k* of **ኬ** may be assimilated to the vowel-less **ግ** or **ቅ** of a verb: **እኅድጌ** Gen. 33, 15.

2. In like manner **እንከ** is at first inferential, meaning "thus", "now", but afterwards having also the meaning "now then", "forthwith". It is always set after one of the first words in the clause, and is to be derived from **እን** and **ከ** (§ 64, *b*). The word is of very common occurrence, *e. g.* **ለምንት ፡ እንከ ፡ ትትመዐዑኒ** "why then are ye angry with me?" John 7, 23. It is often found along with **ኬ** with a meaning equivalent to "now therefore", *e. g.* **ግበሩኬ ፡ እንከ ፡ ሠናየ ፡ ፍሬ** "now therefore produce good fruits" Matt. 3, 8; 5, 13; 6, 31; 10, 26; 22, 9; or it is strengthened by **ሰ**;—**በእ ፡ እን**

ከሰ ፡ ኅበ ፡ አመትየ "go in therefore unto my maid" Gen. 16, 2; 29, 19, 21; Hen. 16, 4. It may even, when strengthened by other enclitics, introduce the sentence: እንከሰኬ Matt. 19, 6. When it is used with the Perfect or Imperfect, in narrative diction, and in combination with ወ, it indicates "and so"(1): ወአኀዙ ፡ እንከ "and so they began" Hen. 86, 6; 93, 3; ወያጔጕዮሙ ፡ እንከ "and he will ('now') forthwith urge them on" Hen. 62, 10; Ex. 5, 7, 10; 6, 7; 7, 5; or in certain connections it answers to our "again", "more": አሐተ ፡ እንከ ('once again') "once more" Judges 16, 28. On ኢ—እንከ "no longer", *οὐκέτι, μηκέτι* v. the '*Lex.*'

3. A similar compound, but somewhat different in meaning, is found in እንጋ *ἄρα*, which is usually set back in its clause, but which now and then introduces it. It occurs nearly always in questions, deriving from admitted assumptions consequences which may with probability be inferred: "then indeed?" "surely then indeed?" &c.: መኑ ፡ እንጋ ፡ የዐቢ "who then indeed is the greatest?" Matt. 18, 1; እንጋ ፡ አግዓዝያንኑ ፡ እሙንቱ ፡ ውሉዶሙ "are not then their children free?" Matt. 17, 26; or without an interrogative: እንጋ ፡ በጽሐት ፡ ላዕሌክሙ ፡ መንግሥት "then surely the kingdom has come unto you" Matt. 12, 28.—V. also መኑ ፡ እንጋ Matt. 19, 25; ምንተ ፡ እንጋ Matt. 19, 27. A very good example occurs in መኑ ፡ እንጋ ፡ ውእቱ ፡ ዝንቱ "what manner of man truly is this?" (namely 'the man who can do the things which have been done by him',—thus drawing an inference from his deeds) Matt. 8, 27. The shade of meaning, differentiating the word from እንከ, must lie in ጋ.—If እንከ is equivalent to "(there) see, that—" and to "accordingly", "thus", then እንጋ must be "see, indeed!" or "see, what!". This explains such a use of the word as we have in Mark 1, 37: እንጋ ፡ ኵሉ ፡ የኀሥሡከ "all men seek then for thee", where reference is made to a circumstance well-known which might have been taken into consideration even by the person addressed.

4. እስመ (from ሰ and መ, § 64, *b*)(2) is causal, or justificative,

---

(1) Corresponding to the וַ and וְ *consecutivum* of the Hebrews.

(2) [Praetorius compares ስም (إِسْم), '*Beitr. zur Assyr.*' I, p. 378, and R. Kraetzschmar, *ibid.*, p. 442 Note*, the Assyr. *aššu(m)*. Jensen, '*Zeitschr. f. Assyr.*' XI, p. 352 (*l. c. supra*), explains እስመ from **en sema*, comparing **en* with the Assyrian *in(a)*.]

"because", and "for" (1),—almost the only word for this idea, and so in very frequent use. Less frequently like ὅτι it is equivalent to "that" (conj.) (§ 203).

5. The Relative Pronoun, conceived as neuter, ዘ (2), also stands for the conjunction "that" ('so that') and "because" or "since".

6. The usual word for "that" is ከመ (3) ('according to that which', 'like as'), which is also employed as a preposition § 165, 6. It signifies "that", "so that" as well as "in order that"; and in the latter case it must invariably be followed by the Subjunctive. Taken with ኢ it signifies "that—not", "in order that—not", "lest".

7. The preposition ለ (§ 164, 2), which expresses the aim or object, is, like لِ in Arabic, prefixed even to a whole clause, to express a Wish, a Command, or a Purpose. It is employed in independent clauses, and in dependent final-clauses (*cf.* DILLMANN's '*Lex.*' col. 24 and *Hexaem.* 15, 3), and must always be followed by the Subjunctive, which it immediately precedes. Manifestly the whole following clause is dependent upon this ለ in the Constr. St. It should properly be given as ለዘ "for this, that—"; but here, on account of the brevity of utterance in one who is giving a command or expressing a wish, ዘ is never used.

8. እስከ, properly "till that" (also a preposition § 165, 5), is farther "so that", *e. g.* Josh. 23, 5, 13. As, however, the word is already in frequent use as a preposition, it is again compounded with ሶበ, as እስከ፡ሶበ "until when", also "so that", ὥστε, Matt. 8, 24, 28; 13, 2, 54; 15, 31 &c. In the *Hexaemeron* it often corresponds (joined to an Indicative or Subjunctive) to حتّى, *e. g.* 5, 15; 9, 17; v. also G. Ad. 27, 11.

9. እንበለ and ዘእንበለ (§ 166, 23) may also govern an entire clause, in the sense of "except that", "without", "so that not" (*ita ut non*): Matt. 10, 29 &c. (It should properly be given in fulness as እንበለዘ).

10. Finally, the word ዮጊ, which is so exceedingly obscure

(1) Just like כִּי, it combines the two.

(2) Like אֲשֶׁר, שֶׁ, ?, यत्, *quod*.

(3) Like ὡς, ὅπως, यथा, *ut*.—According to NÖLDEKE, GGA 1886, No. 26, p. 1013, ከመ "that" is different from ከመ "as" or "like" which is = كما, and is to be ranked with كَيْما,—as in Tigriña *kĕ* = كَيْ, כִּי, plays a great rôle.

in its origin, belongs to this class. It corresponds often to our "perhaps", and expresses doubt, uncertainty, or bare probability: **በኢያእምሮ ፡ ኮነ ፡ ዮጊ** "peradventure it happened from oversight" Gen. 43, 12; 20, 11; Luke 11, 20. It is employed much more frequently, however, when the uncertainty farther awakens misgiving; and then it answers to the Greek μήποτε, the Hebrew פֶּן and our "lest": **ዮጊ ፡ ይመጽእ ፡ ዘይከብረከ** "lest haply there come some one, who is more honoured than thou" Luke 14, 8; **ዮጊ ፡ አነ ፡ እትሀጐል ፡ ምስሌሃ** "that I perish not with it" Hen. 65, 3; **ወይእዜኒ ፡ ዮጊ ፡ ያሌዕል ፡ እዴሁ** "and now peradventure he will (*i. e.* 'it is to be feared that he will') stretch forth his hand" Gen. 3, 22; **ዮጊ ፡ ትጌጊ** "thou mightest possibly fall into sin" Deut. 4, 19; Gen. 26, 9; Deut. 8, 12—14; Gen. 38, 11. It appears, accordingly, after verbs which express fear or wariness: **እፈርሀ ፡ ዮጊ ፡ ኢትፈቅዱ** "I am afraid you will not be willing" Hen. 6, 3; **ዑቅ ፡ ዮጊ** Rev. 22, 9. Accordingly the word must mean, properly: "it may be, that", or "it is to be feared, that" (¹).

3. CONJUNCTIONS EXPRESSING CONDITIONAL AND TEMPORAL RELATIONS.

§ 170. Ethiopic has to some extent the same words for both these relations, just like other languages. 3. Conjunctions expressing Conditional and Temporal Relations (1—10).

1. From the interrogative and relative **መ** there have been derived, by prefixing an Aspirate (§ 64, *b*), the forms **አመ** and **እመ**, the former a Temporal particle, the latter a Conditional particle, —a distinction which is of a purely phonetic nature, and one which assuredly has been impressed only in process of time (²). **አመ** "when", "at the time that" is not very common, and its place is generally taken by **ሶበ**. When it does appear, it still keeps the full meaning of "at the time when" (*cf.* also § 161, *b*). It takes also the compound forms **እምአመ** "since", *e. g.* Gen. 11, 10 (*et saepe*), and **እስከ ፡ አመ** (v. *infra*). But in **ዘአመ** "when" (*e. g.* superscription

(¹) So that **ጊ** seems to be equivalent to כִּי (§ 64, *b*), but **ዮ** to be a form mutilated beyond recognition from some longer word, perhaps from an Optative of הָיָה, הֱוֵה (?), as if it were יְהִי כִּי (?), or a weakened form of לוּ, لَوْ, so that **ዮጊ** would properly be "if that" (لَوْ أَنَّ). [**ዮጌ**, **ዮጌኬ** *Kebra Nag.* 25 Ann. 26 are hardly correct.]

(²) *Cf.* **አላ** ('if not', 'unless') "but".

of Ps. 3 &c.) አመ is a preposition placed after the relative (§ 164), and thus means properly at "the time (of this) that". እመ "if"[1] is the ordinary conditional particle, and is employed whenever anything is posited as a fact or a possibility. Along with ለ it forms the compound ለእመ ፡ (*lit.* 'towards when', *i. e.*) "in case that", equivalent to እመ "if", *e. g.* Ps. 45, 2; Gen. 15, 5; 18, 24; Matt. 11, 23. In a dependent interrogation both have the meaning, "if" or "whether". "If not", "whether—not" are expressed by the addition of the negative particle: እመ ፡ ኢ or ለእመ ፡ ኢ. "If even" or "although" is እመሂ (ለእመሂ) or ወእመሂ. The repetition of እመኒ or እመሂ signifies that two possibilities are set overagainst each other:—*sive*—*sive*; "it may be that—, or", *e. g.* እመኒ ፡ ሕይወት ፡ ወእመኒ ፡ ሞት 1 Cor. 3, 22; እመሂ ፡ እወ ፡ ወእመሂ ፡ አልቦ Matt. 5, 37. And in certain situations ወእመሂ or ወለእመ may even by itself signify "or": Matt. 12, 25; Hen. 59, 2[2]. But if "or" is meant in the sense of exclusion, *i. e.* as a Disjunctive, then the negative word አከ "not" is combined with እመ to form እመ ፡ አከ or እማእከ; and this combination signifies 1, "or" (*aut*), *e. g.* Luke 2, 24, and when it is repeated, like እማእከ ፡—ወእማእከ or እማእከሰ ፡—እማእከሰ, "either—or" (v. § 206); or 2, "when—not", *i. e.* "otherwise", "else" (*sin minus*): Mark 2, 21; Matt. 6, 1, 24 &c.

2. እም is a form, shortened from እመ, and generally to be found at the head of the apodosis of a Conditional clause which does not state actual fact[3]. It answers to the Greek ἄν[4]. As it has ceased to be a true conditional particle, and has only the function, in its place at the head of the apodosis, of indicating again that the whole sentence must be regarded as merely hypothetical, it is always attached to the beginning of another word (as in እምነስሑ "they would have repented" Matt. 11, 21), and it is for this reason that the *a* of እመ has (generally) fallen away. Farther, እመ is also used in Optative clauses, if the realisation of the wish has to be represented as doubtful or improbable: መኑ ፡ እምከፈለኒ "O that one would give me!"

---

(1) אִם, إِنْ, إِلْ.

(2) [Flemming here reads ወእመ instead of Dillmann's ወለእመ. tr.]

(3) Yet see G. Ad. 54, 25 አልቦ ፡ ዘእምኮን "then would we not have been", and *cf. ibid.* 55, 2.

(4) It is related to እመ just as ἄν is to ἐάν (εἰ ἄν).

3. ሶበ (§§ 62, 1 *a*; 166, No. 38),—properly "in the 'there'", "there",—is chiefly used relatively, like our "since", "as", "when", and is the ordinary Temporal particle. Now and then a farther form ሶቤ (§§ 166, No. 38; 167, 3) is met with in old manuscripts and printed matter, especially if enclitics are attached, *e. g.* ሶቤሰ "when however"; ሶቤሁ "when indeed". In conditional sentences not stating actual fact ሶበ is employed as the conditional particle "if" (1), with እም following in the apodosis. The transition to this meaning is represented by its use in Optative clauses, in which ሶበ was given for "would that sometime!" just as መኑ was for "would that some one!" (§ 199).

4. እንበለ and ዘእንበለ (properly: "if not", "unless", "except", § 166, No. 23; and "without", § 169, 9) are also used as Temporal conjunctions: "when not yet", "before", and are then associated with the Subjunctive (§ 90); so too, more in the sense of a condition, "unless when", "unless", "except", Matt. 19, 9, 11; ዘእን በለ ፡ እመ "excepting if", "except", Matt. 12, 29.

5. እንዘ "while", "whilst" has the same rôle in the department of Conjunctions that እንተ (2) (§ 166, No. 19) has among Prepositions. The prefix እን ("there!", "see!") puts the relative conjunction ዘ "that" in the Accusative as it were,—with the object of bringing the whole clause, which is thus introduced, into subordination to the verb of the principal clause, as an Accusative of limitation, or as a circumstantial clause: "seeing that", "in *or* by this (fact, manner, or circumstance) that". This እንዘ is used very often indeed, to take the place of Participles which are wanting (exactly like the German *indem*), or even with the force of the Gerund (§ 123), and frequently instead of it, when for special reasons it is inconvenient to form or employ the Gerund. It corresponds often to our "although", particularly after negatives or in negative sentences, *e. g.* "he ate nothing costly እንዘ ፡ ባዕል ፡ ውእቱ፡ while yet he ('although he') was rich"; or Matt. 13, 13.

6. እስከ "until that", "until" (also እስከነ § 160), is also used as a Conjunction of Time, but it appears more frequently in the form እስከ ፡ እመ "till when", "until" Matt. 2, 13, 15; also "so long as" Cant. 3, 5; or እስከ ፡ ሶበ "till that", "until" Matt. 2, 9; 5, 18, 26.

(1) It corresponds then to לוּ, لَوْ.

(2) Which itself in turn appears as a Conjunction, though seldom.

7. እምከመ, and more rarely ለእምከመ and ለእመ ፡ ከመ, from እመ and ከመ, stand for "as soon as", Matt. 5, 23; 9, 21 &c.: v. DILLMANN'S '*Lex.*' col. 829, *sq.*

8. Original Prepositions, which are employed as Conjunctions without being followed by any Relative, are met with in እም ድኅረ "after that" (occurring very frequently); and እምቅድመ "before", "ere"; also ቅድመ, the two last-mentioned being joined with the Subjunctive (§ 90). Farther we meet with መጠነ, እም ጣነ and በእምጣነ "as long as", *e. g.* Mark 2, 19; Matt. 9, 15; Gal. 4, 1; Ps. 103, 34 (v. §§ 166, 35; and 157, 1).

9. Compounds of the Relative ዘ are found in እምዘ "from the time that", *i. e.* "after that", Hen. 6, 1; Matt. 20, 8; Gen. 24, 22, and በዘ "while" (= እንዘ), "when", Gen. 24, 36; 40, 15.

10. Besides, various other Prepositions and Substantives may be employed as Conjunctions too, taking then the Constr. St. In these cases ዘ is sometimes added, sometimes omitted: ጊዜ "when", "whenever" (*lit.* "the time of"), Mark 14, 7; ህየንተ ፡ ዘ "instead of" Josh. 24, 20; or ህየንተ ፡ ጻመወ "for the reason that he had toiled"; ተውላጠ ፡ ሴሰይዎ Enc. Mag. 8 "as they had fed him"; በእ ንተ ፡ ዘ "for the reason that", "because", Hen. 13, 2; Gen. 6, 6; Mark 1, 44, "for this,—that" (*pro eo ut*) Gen. 29, 27, and several others.

Prevalence and Force of Prefix- and Affix-Particles in Ethiopic. § 171. A survey of the Adverbs, Prepositions and Conjunctions shows us that Ethiopic contains a large number of small words, which have lost the power of standing alone, and are attached to other and stronger words, either as Prefixes or Affixes. Attachment by way of Prefix is current in the other Semitic languages too. Here it affects ነ and ዘ among the Pronouns. Similarly,—among the Particles,—it affects the very short monosyllables (but those only), which are too feeble to stand alone or to sustain any accent of their own, namely the Prepositions በ, ለ, እም, the Conjunctions ለ, ወ, ዘ, እም, the Negative ኢ; the Interrogative ሚ; and the Interjection አ (1). This last particle, however, may sometimes be appended instead of being prefixed. These particles unite with the word which they begin, in taking one accent for the combination. It is only when they have long vowels

(1) And those particles also which now occur only in compounds: እን, አል, እ &c.

that a kind of independent accent is maintained. But yet, their connection with the word is not so close as to influence the phonetic conditions. The final and the initial letters in the particle and the word, which thus meet together, continue unchanged, except that in certain cases ኢ makes its influence more strongly felt upon the initial sound in the word which follows it (§ 48, 5).

All such particles, however, are treated as prefixes in Ethiopic, only because by their very conception they are bound to stand either at the head of the clause or in front of the word which they introduce[1]. But when the case is otherwise, and a particle appears in its conception to be subordinate, and to be a mere addition to the leading idea, it is characteristic of Ethiopic to place such particle after the word which contains the leading idea, or to append it thereto as an Enclitic (or Affix). Nearly all the more subtle and ingenious particles,—which express with ease and brevity the chief modes and proportions of thought, or merely impart certain shades of meaning to the more definite ideas,—are, in accordance with their subordinate significance, placed last. They do not on that account disappear, or lose anything of the importance which belongs to them; but the current of discourse becomes more easy and accommodating, and the whole more lucid, by the finer or accessory ideas seeking to withdraw themselves, and appearing only as a lightly applied shading of the leading forms in the sentence. We see, it is true, from stray phenomena in the other Semitic languages, that they too possess the faculty of post-positing certain words; but no other Semitic tongue has made so extensive a use of such faculty as the Ethiopic. By applying that principle almost universally, it has made a decided and manifest advance; it has drawn nearer to the Indo-European tongues; and it has gained much for the ease and flexibility of its Syntax. እንከ, እንጋ, ባሕቱ፡ are nearly always made to follow; often also ዳእሙ; and ከመ and እስኩ always. ኒ, ሂ, ኔ, ሄ, ኬ, ሁ, ኑ, መ, ነ, ሰ, አ, ሶ, ሃ are Enclitics only, and እ not unfrequently. But as in other languages, so also in Ethiopic, enclitics are only attached externally, and, as a rule, they cause no change in the phonetic conditions of the word to

---

(1) One or two prepositions, however, are found transgressing the law now stated, by here and there becoming suffixed, at least to Pronouns, just as in the Indo-European tongues.

which they are applied. Nor are the accentual conditions of the word altered by that application, *cf.* Trumpp, p. 559; but v. § 59. It is only a few enclitics that introduce any alterations in the letters. It has already been indicated (§ 142) how the ኦ of the Vocative is applied. Before ሰ; አነ *ána* "I" regularly foregoes its second *a*; and thus we have constantly አንሰ. It very seldom happens, or never, that any other words, having similar phonetic conditions, give up their final *a* before ሰ (1); for if in Deut. 11, 27, 28 በረከትሰ and ወመርገምሰ stand dependent upon a verb (v. 26), this may be explained by § 143 (2). Before አ, in the sense of इति (§ 162), an original *ē* occasionally re-appears instead of a final *a* (§ 167, 3): መንገሌአ Numb. 20, 19 Note; ኀቤአ: Josh. 10, 4 Note; or *a* is lengthened into *ā*: መንገላአ Numb. 20, 19 Note (3); or it is thrown off: እማእከስአ Numb. 20, 18 Note; *cf.* 2 Kings, 2, 5; 4 Kings, 5, 26; 19, 29. In like manner an original final *ē*, which had in later times become *a*, re-appears readily besides, before suffixes and affixed particles, as in ሶበ (§ 170, 3), አመ, መጠነ &c. (§ 167, 3).

These particles, attached to the beginning or the end of a word, may occur not only singly, but by two, three or more at a time, *e. g.* ወለእመሰኬ "and if now"; ወበዘእምሕዝብኒ "and again with him who (is) of the people"; አንሰኬ "now I"; ወኵሎሄኒ "and even everywhere" &c.

---

(1) [*Cf.*, however, ፊድፋድሰ for ፊድፋዲሰ *Kebra Nag.*, *Introd.* p. XXXIV.]

(2) And in this way we must also explain Col. 1, 23 ተሠየምኩ ፡ ዐቀዶ (though Platt gives ዐቀዲ ፡ [retained also in the Reprint]) ወላእክኒ (*cf.* Col. 1, 25: Eph. 3, 7). In ይትፌሦሐኒ ፡ ልብየ Ps. 12, 6, ኒ is certainly to be regarded as a Suff. Pron. (contrary to Ludolf's view).

(3) *Cf.* *ā* in Bilin, Quara, Saho, and 'Afar; Reinisch, '*Wörterb. d. Bilinspr.*' p. 1.

PART THIRD.

SYNTAX.

§ 172. Every Sentence, however simple, must necessarily include (1) a Person or Thing, called the *Subject*, about which something is stated, and (2) that which is stated about it, or,—as it is called,—the *Predicate*. When both these parts are present, we have a complete Sentence; when one or the other is wanting, the Sentence is incomplete. But, starting with these two constituents, a Sentence may extend more and more widely, and to great length, by accumulating other words either about the Subject or about the Predicate or about both,—which words may in their turn surround themselves with still farther words, and so on. All such members of a Sentence, grouping themselves about the one or the other of the two fundamental constituents, must indicate in some way that they belong to the same; and *Syntax*, or the Description of the Sentence, is just an endeavour to point out in detail the modes in which, and the means by which, a fundamental member of a Sentence may become associated with other words and qualifications. Simple Sentences themselves fall, in their turn, into various classes, according to their special meaning. Finally, two Sentences,—each complete in itself, may stand in a certain relation of reciprocity to one another, so that the thought which seeks expression can be fully exhibited only when the two are used together, and not by either of them without the other. Accordingly the Compound Sentence stands contrasted with the Simple Sentence, as a special class. Syntax then deals first of all with the extension of the chief members of the Sentence by means of complementary members, or with the chief Word-Groups of the Sentence.

Subject and Predicate. Periphrasis of the Article: 1. Methods of indicating *Definiteness* in the Noun.

A. LEADING WORD-GROUPS OF THE SENTENCE.

In all kinds of *Word-Groups* we have Nouns occurring; and as the structure of these groups at times assumes a different form, according as the Nouns which appear therein are determined or undetermined, we shall treat first of the methods by which this determination is effected.

I. PERIPHRASIS OF THE ARTICLE.

No special Article has been developed in Ethiopic, any more than in the other Abyssinian tongues([1]) or in Assyrian; and in this way the language has kept to a more antique stage than the other Semitic tongues, with the exceptions noted([2]). Various devices and methods have, naturally, presented themselves, to distinguish between the Noun determined or definite and the Noun in its indeterminate condition. All continues, however, still unsettled, as in the start of a process. None of the pathways pursued has led to the production of a fixed and recognised Article.

1. In many cases there is no need of any addition, to show that a word is determined or definite, because the sense and connection make it obvious who or what is meant, and no doubt can arise. Any conception, or conceptional word, which stands as the sole representative of its class, must, from its very nature, be invariably a determined word, such as **እግዚአብሔር**—**አምላክ** "God"; **ፀሐይ** "the Sun"; **ሞት** "Death"; **ሕይወት** "Life"; **ምሥራቅ** "the East". It is, on the other hand, when these words have to be regarded as undetermined, and as representing one or other of their special classes, that some special appositional expression has to be employed, *e. g.* **ሞት ፡ እኩይ** "an evil death"; **አምላክ ፡ ነኪር** "a strange god". In the very same way, all Proper Names are by their nature determined. Again, in other languages the definite article is frequently employed to refer to something which has been already mentioned, *e. g.* "the man", namely, 'the man who has been spoken of before'. But it is generally quite clear from the current or

([1]) With the exception of *Saho.*

([2]) On the other hand D. H. Müller, '*Epigr. Denkm.*' p. 68 (*cf.* pp. 20, 72) would conclude, from the occurrence of the appended Sabaic Article *ān*, that Ge'ez at one time also possessed the Article, but has since given it up,—a view in which we are unable to concur.

connection of the discourse, when the same Subject is meant which has been mentioned before; and accordingly the referring article may in that case be dispensed with; *e. g.* in Matt. 4, 25 we have: "many people followed him" (**አሕዛብ፡ ብዙኃን**), immediately after which Chap. 5, 1 proceeds with **ወርእዮ፡ አሕዛበ** "and when he saw the people",—without any farther intimation that the word is determined, just because that determination is at once inferred. In other cases, in which languages that possess the Article make use of it, it is all the more superfluous when the complement, by means of which the word having the Article is really determined, stands close beside the word, *e. g.* in **ሕዝበ፡ እስራኤል** "the people of Israel"; **መንግሥተ፡ ሰማያት** "the kingdom of Heaven".

(*a*) But should the sense and the connection be insufficient to prevent any misunderstanding, Ethiopic is able to come to the rescue in various ways. First, by adding the referring Pronoun **ውእቱ**[1]:—*καὶ ἔλαβεν ἀπὸ τῶν λίθων τοῦ τόπου* **ወነሥአ፡ እምውእቱ፡ እብን፡ ዘውእቱ፡ ብሔር** Gen. 28, 11; *καὶ ὑψώθη ὁ ἄνθρωπος* **ወተለዐለ፡ ውእቱ፡ ብእሲ** Gen. 26, 13; *cf.* also Tob. 6, 2, 3, 13; 12, 5; *Chrest.* p. 26, lines 8, 11, 29, *et saepe*; or by **ዝክቱ** when the preceding mention of the word lies somewhat farther back, *e. g.* Gen. 27, 16; Numb. 20, 8 (*cf.* with verse 9); Ruth 4, 1; very frequently by means of **ዝኩ**, *e. g.* Tob. 6, 4, 6, 13; 8, 2, 3; 11, 3, 5, 7; 12, 1; also by means of **ዝ**, Tob. 6, 4; 11, 3; and by **ዝንቱ** Tob. 6, 16; 12, 2. The same purpose is often still better served by appending a Suffix Pron., *e. g.* *καὶ προσῆλθον οἱ μαθηταί* ("the disciples", *i. e.* 'Christ's disciples') **ቀርቡ፡ አርዳኢሁ** Matt. 18, 1; **ክልኤሆሙ፡ አኃው** "the two brethren" Matt. 20, 24 (while **ክልኤቱ፡ አኃው** would be "two brethren", *cf.* Matt. 20, 30); and even *ἐν τῷ ἐνιαυτῷ ἐκείνῳ* **በዓመቲሁ** "in the year thereof" Deut. 14, 28; **እስመ፡ ፈጸምኩ፡ መዋዕሊሁ** *πεπλήρωνται γὰρ αἱ ἡμέραι μου* Gen. 29, 21; **እምነ፡ በለስ፡ አእምሩ፡ አምሳሊሁ** *ἀπὸ τῆς συκῆς μάθετε τὴν παραβολήν* Matt. 24, 32. And this reference by means of a Genitive Suffix is, in certain cases, so fixed and binding, that it is not omitted even though a Demonstrative pron. should accompany the word, *e. g.* **ዘመኑ፡ ዝንቱ፡ መልክዑ፡ ወመጽሐፉ** *τίνος ἡ εἰκὼν αὕτη καὶ ἡ ἐπιγραφή*; Matt. 22, 20.

---

[1] Just as happens so often in Sanskrit: in fact this is the origin of the Article in most languages.

(*b*) The use of the Suff. Pron. to compensate for the Article has spread from such cases, to cases in which a Genitive relation appears unthinkable to us. When a subject, to wit, is introduced into the discourse, and later on is mentioned again by the same name, it takes, in other languages, the Article upon its second appearance. In Ethiopic, however, a Suffix of the third Person is very often attached to it, upon its second appearance, by way of reference to the name as first used, *e. g.* ሐለምኩ ፡ ሕልመ ፡ ወከመዝ ፡ ሕልሙ "I dreamed a dream, and this is ('its dream') the dream" Gen. 37, 9; "they cast him into a pit (ዐዘቅት ፡) ወዐዘቅታሰ ፡ ሐዲስ "but the pit was new" Gen. 37, 24; "I saw there a high throne (መንበረ ፡) ወእመትሕተ ፡ መንበሩ ፡ ዐቢይ and from under the great throne (proceeded) &c." Hen. 14, 18, 19; "ye stood by the base of the mountain (ደብር ፡) ወይነድድ ፡ ደብሩ while the mountain burned" Deut. 4, 11; 9, 15. *Cf.* also Tob. 6, 5, 12; 7, 9; *Chrest.* p. 31, line 2; and notice particularly ካልኡ = ὁ ἄλλος. Cases in which the definite Article is indicated in this remarkable way are by no means rare, *cf. e. g.* farther Deut. 13, 16; Ex. 3, 2; Judges 1, 8; 6, 20 (ሥጋሁ); 17, 2 (ወርቁ); 17, 5 (ብእሲሁ); 19, 16; Ruth 2, 17 (ስገሙ); Mark 2, 22 (ወይኑ and ዝቁ); Hen. 26, 5 (ወኵሉ ፡ ቈላቲሁ (1) "and all the (= those) valleys", referring back to vs. 2—4); [*Kebra Nag.* 97 a 18 (ዕለቱ); 97 b 10 (ጊዜሁ ፡ ወዕለቶ ፡ ወሰዐቶ)] &c. In all these cases the Suffix is to be explained in accordance with § 156: ደብሩ relative to ደብር is "mountain, it" *i. e.* "it, the mountain", thus = ውእቱ ፡ ደብር.

(*c*) A third method of replacing the Article, and in fact the most usual one, is the following: — When there appears in the sentence a determined word, subordinated to a Verb or to a Noun in the Constr. St. (with which last, the Prepositions coincide), a Suffix relating to this word is appended to the governing Verb or Noun, and the relation of this Suffix to the dependent word is indicated by prefixing ለ to the dependent word (§ 164, No. 2); *e. g.* ወሰመዮ ፡ እግዚአብሔር ፡ ለብርሃን ፡ ዕለተ "and God called ('it', referring to 'light') the light, day" Gen. 1, 5; ላዕሌሁ ፡ ለበዕለ ፡ ቤት "against ('him',—referring to 'master of the house') the master of the house" Matt. 20, 11; (ነፍኆ ፡ ላዕለ ፡ ገጹ ፡ ለአዳም "he breathed upon the face of Adam" *Le Livre des Mystères* 16, 3); ቀዳሚሁ ፡ ለጥበብ "the begin-

---

(1) [Flemming reads here ቈላት. tr.]

ning of wisdom": but also **ቦቱ ፡ በነገር** "with it, with the word" = "with the word" G. Ad. 6,17. Yet the same turn is occasionally found even with undetermined nouns, *e. g.* **ርእየ ፡ ለእሐቲ ፡ አመተ** *Chrest.* p. 42, line 14; *cf.* also *ibid.* p. 40, lines 17, 19, and G. Ad. 146, 10.

This form of periphrasis for the definite Article is by far the most usual one; and although doubtless the anticipation of a determined Noun by means of a Suffix relating thereto was introduced merely for the purpose of signifying the definite and known character of the Noun(1), yet the idiom came into such favour and currency(2) that it is employed even in cases where the definiteness of a noun is already sufficiently indicated by means of accompanying demonstratives, or attached suffixes, or in some other fashion. In this respect the usage is exactly the same as in those languages which are in possession of an Article, for they employ it even in cases where it is not absolutely necessary, as in *ὁ πατήρ μου.* Examples: **ጸሐፍ ፡ ሎቱ ፡ ለመልአከ ፡ ቤተ ፡ ክርስቲያን** "write to the leader ('angel') of the church" Rev. 2,1; **ርኢናሁ ፡ ለእግዚእነ** "we have seen our Lord" John 20,25; **ወከመዝ ፡ ትገብሩ ፡ ለይእቲ ፡ ታቦት** "and thus shalt thou make that ark" Gen. 6,15; **ዴግኖቶ ፡ ወእኂዞቶ ፡ ለዝኩ ፡ ጸላኢ** "to pursue and capture that enemy" *Annales Johannis I,* (Guidi, 1903) 33, 2; **ምሕረቱ ፡ ለእግዚአብሔር** "the mercy of God"; **ይጼልሎን ፡ ሠናያተ** *ἀμαυροῖ τὰ καλά* Sap. 4, 12; **ወምክርከ ፡ መኑ ፡ አእመሮ** Sap. 9,17; **ልበ ፡ ዚአሁ ፡ ትፈቅዱ ፡ ታእምርዎ** Judith 8,14. It is safe to say that this anticipation, by means of a relative Suffix, of a noun already determined by some other process, is more usually given than omitted. In a few cases **ለ** which generally serves to indicate the reference is left out, when the construction is self-evident, *e. g.* when the noun is governed in the Accusative: **ሀበኒዮ ፡ እንከሰ ፡ ብእሲትየ** "give me now my wife" Gen. 29,21; **ምድር ፡ ትገሥዮ ፡ ሥጋሁ ፡ ለአቤል** G. Ad. 89, 15; and in the Genitive connection: *Chrest.* p. 14, ll. 10,18; p. 18, ll. 7 & 15.

If more than one determined word be dependent on one Verb or Noun (or Preposition), the Suffix may then be made to correspond with the first of these alone, as in **ወተዘከሮ ፡ እግዚአብሔር ፡ ለኖኅ ፡ ወለኵሉ ፡ አራዊት ፡ ወለኵሉ ፡ እንስሳ** &c. Gen. 8,1;

(1) As appears from the fact that very rarely indeed are undetermined Nouns indicated in this way, that is, by means of an anticipatory suffix; *cf. supra.*

(2) Even more perhaps than in Aramaic.

9, 8; 12, 20; ይባርክ ፡ ለኅሩይ ፡ ወለኅሩያን "he praises the chosen one and the chosen people" Hen. 40, 5; ዐሥራተ ፡ እጼሁ ፡ ለአዛብ ፡ ወለጸናታም ፡ ወለኵሉ ፡ አኅማላት Luke 11, 42; and thus regularly, when the first dependent word is the most important of the series; or the Suffix is made to correspond with the whole body of them, as in ረከቦሙ ፡ ለስምዖን ፡ ወለእንድርያስ "he found Simon and Andrew" Mark 1, 16; Gen. 14, 2; or, finally, the Suffix is made to correspond simply with the nearest Genitive or Accusative; and the plain Genitive- or Accusative-subordination is continued with the others, *e. g.* ወነሥአ ፡ ለሳራ ፡ ብእሲቶ ፡ ወሎጥሃ ፡ ወኵሎ ፡ ንዋዮሙ Gen. 12, 5; 14, 16; 32, 8; ልቡ ፡ ለፈርዖን ፡ ወዘዐበይቱ "the heart of Pharaoh and of his great ones" Ex. 14, 5.

It is, however, by no means necessary that a Suffix of this kind, referring to a determined Noun, named in the sentence, should invariably precede the noun, and the noun invariably come second. On the contrary, when it is demanded by the sense and structure of the sentence, an Accusative or Genitive of this kind may also be placed before the word on which it depends, *e. g.* ወለብእሲትኒ ፡ ይቤላ "and unto the woman in turn he said" Gen. 3, 16 (v. *infra* § 196). Even when the Accusative or Genitive is placed after the Suffix, it does not need to follow it directly, but may be separated from it by several words. It is evident that by means of this circumlocutory substitute for the definite Article with Nouns standing in any sort of subordination, it has been made possible to attain also a greater freedom in Word-arrangement; and this consideration has contributed to the great predominance of such a periphrasis in the language.

2. Methods of indicating *Indefiniteness* in the Noun.

§ 173. 2. As Ethiopic has thus means enough to signify specially the determination of a Noun when required, there was the less demand for a special indication of the undetermined Noun by means of the so-called Indefinite Article. The context, in fact, together with the absence of any note of determination, suffices to show that a word is undetermined: መጽኡ ፡ መሰግላን "there came Magi" Matt. 2, 1; ዘይሬኢ ፡ ብእሲተ "whosoever looketh on a woman" 5, 28 &c. If indefiniteness is not sufficiently shown thereby, it is generally a matter of indifference whether the word in question is regarded as determined or undetermined, as in Matt. 2, 12 ወነገሮሙ ፡ በሕልም "and he told them in a dream *or* in the dream"; and in 2, 13 ናሁ ፡ መልአከ ፡ እግዚአብሔር ፡ አስተርአዮ "behold, an angel *or* the angel of God appeared to him"; and in 19, 21 ለምስ ኪን "to the poor man *or* to a poor man". But in those cases in which the indefinite article of other tongues expresses the notion of "any one", and in the same way with the plural "any", "some", Ethiopic has, to be sure, a mode of its own of denoting this idea. When a human being is meant, "any one" is ብእሲ or ሰብእ *e. g.* Matt. 22, 16; [*Kebra Nag.* 141 a 19]; and fem. ብእሲት, *e. g.* ብእ ሲት ፡ ዕብራዊት "a Hebrew woman": and yet አሐዱ, አሐቲ "one (*m.* & *f.*)" is also used for it, and in fact not only in cases where εἷς stands even in the Greek original text, as in Matt. 8, 19; Gen. 22, 13, but also in other cases, *e. g.* Gen. 38, 2 καὶ εἶδε θυγατέρα ἀνθρώπου Χαναναίου ወርእየ ፡ አሐተ ፡ ወለተ ፡ አሐዱ ፡ ብእሲ ፡ ከናናዊ; *Chrest.* p. 24, ll. 20, 21, 25; p. 25, l. 14; p. 31, l. 1 (ውእቱ ፡ ፩ብእሲ) &c. "One another" too is generally expressed by አሐዱ and ካልኡ with a preposition of some kind before the ከ". With names of things an express indication of indeterminateness is still less necessary; but አሐዱ may also be used in the case of things, *e. g.* Josh. 24, 32, or turns of speech like ዕዳ ፡ ዘከነ "any thing as a debt" Deut. 24, 10. In plural-notions, the mere plural often serves to express "some" or an undefined "several", "many", as in እምድኅረ ፡ መዋዕል "some days *or* several days after" Judges 14, 8; 15, 1. Besides, Ethiopic possesses the following additional means, very frequently adopted, of expressing these notions: (*a*) the employment of the preposition እምነ, which denotes part of a whole (v. § 164, No. 3), *e. g.* እምዕፀብ "some difficulty" Matt. 19, 23; አለ ፡ እምውስተ ፡ ጸሐፍት "certain scribes" 9, 3; ክልኤቱ ፡ እምአርዳኢሁ "two of his disciples" 21, 1; እምነ ፡ ትብሲ ልከ "some of thy pottage" Gen. 25, 30 (for other examples v. § 164, 3):—(*b*) the periphrasis which consists of ቦ: "there is", *or* "there are" (§ 167, 1, *b*) and the relative pronoun following, *e. g.* እመቦ ፡ ዘኀደገ "whosoever putteth away" (*lit.*—"if there is who hath put away") Matt. 19, 9; ቦእለ ፡ በጽሑ "some came" Gen. 14, 3; ቦእለ ፡ ሀለዉ ፡ እምእለ ፡ ይቀውሙ ፡ ዝየ "there be some standing here" (*lit.* "there are who are of those who stand here") Matt. 16, 28; hence ቦዘ፡—ቦዘ፡—ቦዘ (or ቦእለ &c.) "some—, others—others" &c. Matt. 21, 35; 22, 5; 25, 15:—(*c*) the negative for "not any one" or "no one", "no man", "nothing",—either አልቦ ፡ ዘ "there is not one, who", or ኢ with መኑሂ following, or in the neuter ምንትኒ (§ 147, *b*):—"nothing at all" or "no one at all" is also rendered by ኵሉ with a negation.—For any one who is spoken of indefinitely, but definitely thought of, his name being withheld, —in Greek ὁ δεῖνα, and in Hebrew פְּלֹנִי אַלְמֹנִי,—Ethiopic has the expression እገሌ Matt. 26, 18, the formation and derivation of which are still quite obscure.

II. GOVERNMENT OF THE VERB.

1. NOUNS AND PRONOUNS IN SUBORDINATION TO THE VERB.

Accusative of an associated *Nomen* as determining the idea of the Verb. 1—Accusative of Determination.

§ 174. The Verb may govern Nouns in the Accusative, and this form of subordination is the most direct and usual one. When it falls short, recourse is had to prepositions to assist the Verb. There is no third mode by which a Verb can bring a Noun into combination with itself. Even the so-called Adverbs are almost invariably dependent on the Verb as Accusatives or as prepositional forms; and even the comparatively small number of Adverbs which (being of pronominal or other origin) are not formed by means of the Accusative, or by prepositions (§§ 160—163), must yet be thought of as subordinated to the Verb as *quasi*-Accusatives.

(*a*) *The Verbal Object expressed by the Accusative.*

The Accusative in Ethiopic has the most varied functions to fulfil, as has been already indicated (§ 143).

1. It serves to complete the idea of the Verb by means of *some definite limitation.*

(*a*) Adverbial Accusative of Kind and Manner.

(*a*) A Noun (*Nomen*) of some sort, in the Accusative case, may in this way be associated with the verb, to signify the *kind and manner*,—as a general condition,—*of the action* (Adverbial Accusative).

Adjectives in the Accusative describe the kind and manner of the action, as in: በከየ ፡ መሪረ "he wept bitterly ('a bitter *weeping*')" Matt. 26, 75; ዘእንበለ ፡ ይርሐቁ ፡ እምሀገር ፡ ነዋኀ "before they had withdrawn far from the city" Gen. 44, 4; ሠናየ ፡ ተነበየ ፡ ኢሳይያስ "well hath Esaias prophesied" Matt. 15, 7. And in this way Adjectives may form Adverbs, by taking the Accusative § 163). In those cases, however, in which such limiting expression applies to the Subject or Object rather than to the Verb, as, *e. g.*

"he fled naked", or "he took him alive", it must be immediately referred, in Ethiopic, to the Subject or Object, and placed in apposition to it (v. § 189).

And so too may the idea of the Verb be supplemented by Substantives in the Accusative to describe the kind and manner of the Action, by way of special circumstances, although in that case prepositions are employed oftener perhaps than the Accusative: **ግብተ ፡ ይነድፍዎሙ** "suddenly they shoot at them" Ps. 63, 4 (v. also § 163); **ነበረ ፡ ዐውደ** "he sat ('judgment') on the judgment seat" Matt. 27, 19; **ይነብር ፡ ጽሙ ፡ ውስተ ፡ ምግሐሡ ፡ ጽርሑ ፡ ቅስሬ** Judges 3, 24; **ቆሙ ፡ ዲጋ** "they stood (in) ambush" Judges 9, 44; **ሐመ ፡ ፈጸንተ** "he was sick of a fever" *cf.* Luke 4, 38; **ሞተ ፡ ሠናየ ፡ ርሥአ** "he died in a good old age" Gen. 25, 8; **ርኢክዎ ፡ ለእግዚአብሔር ፡ ገጸ ፡ በገጽ** "I have seen God face to face" Gen. 32, 31; Judges 6, 22; **ሕገ ፡ ዘየዐቢ** "by the law ('right') of the greater" *Chrest.* p. 97, l. 21 *sq.*; *cf.* p. 96, l. 16.

In the same way a Substantive-Infinitive may be subordinated to the verb to determine it more definitely: **አጥፍአ ፡ ያጠፍኦሙ** "*delendo delebit eos*" Josh. 17, 13; *cf.* § 181.

(*b*) Accusative of Place and Time.

(*b*) *Determinations* of *Place* and *Time* are combined with the verb in the same way (Accusative of Place and Time), and that both in the case of Verbs of Motion and Verbs of Rest. This use of the Accusative is very common. Thus one says **ወፅአ ፡ ገዳመ** "he went out to the field"; **ወፅአ ፡ ፀብአ** "he went out to war" Judges 3, 10; **አተዉ ፡ ብሔሮሙ** "they returned to their own land" Matt. 2, 12; **ዐርገ ፡ ሀገረ** "he went up to the city" Matt. 21, 18; **እቀድመክሙ ፡ ገሊላ** "I shall go before you into Galilee" Matt. 26, 32; [**በጽሐ ፡ ኢየሩሳሌም** *Revue sémit.* 1906, p. 277, l. 21]; **ቤተ ፡ አቡከ** "in thy father's house" Gen. 24, 23; **ወወደየ ፡ ትርአሲሁ** "and he set (them) for his pillow Gen. 28, 11; **ሤጥዎ ፡ ብሔረ ፡ ግብጽ** "they sold him into the land of Egypt" Gen. 37, 36; Hen. 14, 2; **ሀለወ ፡ ገዳመ** "he was in the field" Gen. 4, 8; Matt. 24, 26; **ምሥራቀ** "eastward" (in answer to the question, 'where?') G. A. 30, 23; **ቆመ ፡ ምድረ** βέβηκε ἐπὶ γῆς Sap. 18, 15 A; *cf.* also **ብሔረ ፡ ሕያዋን** *Tab. Tab.* 12, 2 (*Chrest.* p. 110); **ምድረ ፡ ርስት፡** *Tab. Tab.* 18, 1 (*Chrest.* p. 112). In all these cases prepositions, like **በ**, **ኀበ**, **ውስተ** &c., might also have been employed; and frequently both modes of connection are made use of, side by side, in the same sentence, if several indications of place are mentioned: **የአቱ ፡ ሀገሮ ፡ ወው-**

ስተ ፡ ቤቱ "he goes home to his own city and to his own house" Josh. 20, 6; so too in Gen. 30, 25 and 31, 3; or እትዉ ፡ ውስተ ፡ አብያቲክሙ ፡ ወውስተ ፡ ደወልክሙ ፡ ብሔረ(1) ፡ ዘወሀበክሙ ፡ ሙሴ Josh. 22, 4.

Of *Time*: ማእከለ ፡ ሌሊት "at midnight" Matt 25, 6; አሐተ ፡ ሰዓተ "for one hour" 26, 40; ሌሊተ "to-night" Gen. 19, 5; ቀትረ "at midday" 18, 1; ዓመ "in a year" 18, 10; አሐተ ፡ ዕለተ "(on) one day" *Chrest.* p. 44, l. 16; ጽናሕ ፡ ንስቲተ "wait a little" Hen. 52, 5; ወሐይወ ፡ አዳም ፡ ፪፻ ወ፴ ዓመተ Gen. 5, 3(2); and in Relative clauses: በዕለት ፡ እንተ ፡ ትበልዑ "on the day on which ye shall eat" Gen. 2, 17. Prepositions may be used for this relation also.

(c) Accusative of Measure.

(*c*) In like manner determinations of *Measure* are expressed in the Accusative: ተለዐለ ፡ ዐሠርተ ፡ ወኀምስተ ፡ እመተ "it rose fifteen cubits" Gen. 7, 20; ወእመ ፡ ውሕዱ ፡ እልክቱ ፡ ጻድቃን ፡ ኀምስተ "and if those righteous men are five fewer" Gen. 18, 28; የሐጽጽ ፡ ፶ መዋዕለ "he is too short ('too late') by fifty days" Hen. 74, 14; ክፍልዋ ፡ ለምድር ፡ ሰብዐተ ፡ ክፍለ "divide ye the land into seven parts" Josh. 18, 6; Hen. 77, 3; Gen. 32, 8; ዐበየ ፡ ክፍሉ ፡ ምኍምስተ ፡ ዘእልክቱ "his portion was five times as great as theirs" Gen. 43, 34; ከመ ፡ ኖጻ ፡ እሙንቱ ፡ ብዝኖሙ "they were as the sand in their multitude" Judges 7, 12; እመ ፡ ብክሙ ፡ ሃይማኖተ ፡ መጠነ ፡ ኅጠተ ፡ ስናፔ "if ye have faith as great as a grain of mustard seed" Matt. 17, 20. አክለ "it amounts to", in particular is always associated in this way with the Accusative of the measure: የአክሉ ፡ እልፈ ፡ ወኀምስተ ፡ ምእተ "there were about 10,500" Judges 8, 10; 9, 49.

2. Accusative of Purport or Reference: (a) Emphatic Acc. of Derived Noun, or Noun of Kindred Meaning.

§ 175. 2. A Verb may also be completed by means of an Accusative which gives *its purport or its reference*, in both of which cases the governed Noun is coupled still more closely with the verbal idea (3).

(*a*) Thus a Verb may govern *a Substantive derived from itself*, in order to explain itself by itself, as in ተምዕዐ ፡ መዐተ "he was angry" (*lit.* "he was angry with anger") Judges 2, 14; 9, 30;

(1) Where, to be sure, the Accusative may also be explained by Attraction (§ 201).

(2) [The Ethiopic, as usual, follows the Septuagint here, *διακόσια καὶ τριάκοντα ἔτη*, instead of the Hebrew שְׁלֹשִׁים וּמְאַת שָׁנָה. TR.]

(3) Cases like ይልሕቅ ፡ እከየ "is weaker than it in malice" are rare (v. DILLMANN's '*Lex.*', col. 30).

መሐላ ፡ ንምሐል "let us swear an oath" Hen. 6,4; ሐለምነ ፡ ሕልመ "we have dreamed a dream" Gen. 40, 8; or to give thereby a special emphasis to the idea which belongs to the Verb (a purpose which at other times is served by the Infinitive instead of by a noun, v. § 181, ծ): ጻማ ፡ ጻመውነ "we are wearied out" Hen. 103, 9; ብዕልነ ፡ ብዕለ "we have become rich" Hen. 97, 8; Gen. 2, 17; በኑ ፡ በእሰ ፡ ተባአሰ ፡ ምስለ ፡ እስራኤል "did he fight at all with Israel?" (contrasted with keeping the peace) Judges 11, 25; but chiefly to attach to the Accusative a farther determining factor, *e. g.* an Adjective, by which combination of Substantive and Adjective an Adverbial conception is indicated: ተምዕዐ ፡ መዐተ ፡ ዐቢየ "he was angered exceedingly" Gen. 39, 19; ተፈሥሐ ፡ ፍሥሓ ፡ ዐቢየ "he rejoiced with great joy" Matt. 2, 10; ፈርሁ ፡ ዐቢየ ፡ ፍርሀተ "they feared exceedingly" Mark 4, 41; ወሣቀዮ ፡ ዐቢየ ፡ ሥቃየ ፡ ወእኩየ "and he plagued him with a great and evil plague" Gen. 12, 17; Josh. 10, 10, 20; Gen. 46, 29; 27, 33; Hen. 12, 4; 65, 5; or ተሐሞ ፡ ለርእስከ ፡ ተሐምዎ ፡ ዘዚአየ "perform thou for thyself the kinsman's duty which belongs to me" Ruth 4, 6. Thus too in Relative Clauses: በእንተ ፡ በረከቱ ፡ ዘባረኮ ፡ አቡሁ "because of his blessing wherewith his father had blessed him" Gen. 27, 41; በኵነኔ ፡ ዘኰንንክሙ "with the judgment with which ye judge" Matt. 7, 2. Occasionally also Nouns from other roots, but of kindred meaning, are subordinated in this way: ሰባሕኩ ፡ . . . ስሞ ፡ ለእግዚእ ፡ . . . በረከተ ፡ ወስብሐተ Hen. 39, 9; ቃለ ፡ ጽራኃቲሆሙ ፡ ዕራቃ ፡ ጸርኀት ፡ ምድር Hen. 9, 2. In such cases the preposition በ is frequently used instead of the Accusative: ይትፌሥሑ ፡ በፍሥሓ Hen. 25, 6; ወወውዑ ፡ በዐቢይ ፡ ውውዓ ፡ ወጽኑዕ Josh. 6, 20.

(b) Acc. of Related Noun with Verbs of Plenty and Want &c.

(*b*) In particular, verbs which express *Fulness and Abundance or their opposites* attract in the Accusative the object with which a person or thing is full or empty (although such object may also be introduced by እምነ, in accordance with § 164, No. 3): ይትመልኡ ፡ ጥበበ "they grew full of wisdom" Hen. 48, 1; Ps. 64, 14 (with እምነ Hen. 56, 4; Matt. 22, 10); ፃዕፈ ፡ ጸግቡ "they are full of new wine" Acts 2, 13 (with እም Hen. 63, 10); ኀጣእኩ ፡ ፈውሰ "I was in want of healing" Ps. 37, 7. Thus we say ምድር ፡ እንተ ፡ ትውሕዝ ፡ ሐሊበ ፡ ወመዓረ "a land, which flows with milk and honey" Ex. 33, 3; Josh. 5, 6; ኵለንታሃ ፡ ትትከል ፡ ዕፀወ "it is all planted with trees" Hen. 10, 18.

So also, Verbs of *Clothing oneself* (ተለብሰ, ተዐጽፈ &c.) and of *Overlaying* or *Covering, e. g.* ትቀፍሎ ፡ ወርቀ "thou shalt overlay it with gold" Ex. 25, 11, 28; ትቀብኦ ፡ ፒሳ "thou shalt smear it with pitch" Gen. 6, 14 &c. *Cf.* also ኰሐሎ ፡ ሐሞተ Tobit 11,10.

(c) Accusative of Relation or Limitation.

(*c*) The Accusative assigns to the Verb *the relation which the Verb has to some object;* or else it restricts to some limited part of the object, the relation of the Verb which is already given in a general way in the Subject-Case or Object-Case. In Passive and Semi-passive Verbs, the Subject which is referred to in the action, is given in the Subject-Case (or Nominative); but if,—properly speaking,—it is not the whole Subject, but only a part of it, that is affected by such action, then this part is attached in the form of an explanatory Accusative: ልያ ፡ ትደዊ ፡ አዕይንቲሃ "Leah was tender-eyed (*lit.*—'suffered in her eyes')" Gen. 29, 17; ተመይጡ ፡ ገጸሙ "they turned their faces" ('they turned about as to their faces') Judges 18, 23; ተገልበበት ፡ ገጻ 'she veiled her face' (*lit.* 'she veiled herself as to her face') Gen. 38, 15; 24, 65; ትትከደን ፡ ዕርቃነከ "(that) thou mayest cover thy nakedness" (*lit.* 'cover thyself as to thy nakedness') Rev. 3, 18; ተኀፀብ ፡ ገጸከ "wash thy face" ('thyself as regards thy face') Matt. 6,17; 27, 24; Mark 7, 3; Gen. 43, 31; ወተሀውከ ፡ ዮሴፍ ፡ አማዕዊቲሁ "and Joseph was perturbed in his emotions ('bowels')" Gen. 43, 30; v. also 4 Esr. 9, 39 (Laur. 40). With Active Verbs, the subject to which the action of the verb relates is given in the Object-Case, but the reference may farther be restricted to a portion of the Subject, by means of a second Accusative, and thus be indicated more accurately. This combination is very common in Ethiopic, and contributes a peculiarly delicate turn to the language: ገሰሳ ፡ እዴሃ "he touched her hand"; አኀዛ ፡ እዴሃ "he took her by the hand" Matt. 8, 15; 9, 29; 20, 34 [1]; ይኰርዕዎ ፡ ርእሶ "they smite him on the head" Matt. 27, 30; አዕወርዎሙ ፡ አዕይንቲሆሙ "they blinded their eyes" ('them in their eyes') Gen. 19, 11; ሐቀፎ ፡ ክሳዶ "he took him round the neck" ('embraced him round his neck') Gen. 33, 4; ሐቀፈቶ ፡ ክሳዶ Tobit 11, 8; አጽንዖሙ ፡ ልበሙ "he hardened their heart" ('them in their heart') Josh. 11, 20; ቀረፀቶ ፡ ፯ቈናዝዐ ፡ ርእሶ "she shore off from him the seven locks of his head" ('shore him as to the seven &c.') Judges 16, 19. And even where other languages in

[1] [V., however, *Chrest.* 26, l. 9,—ወአኀዘ ፡ በእዴሁ.]

such positions have only one Object-case, as in ἥψατο τῆς χειρὸς αὐτῆς "he touched her hand", the Ethiopian invariably employs two Accusatives.

§ 176. 3. Finally, the Accusative introduces the Person or Thing affected by the action, *i. e.* the material dealt with, or the *Object*. This is the ordinary use of the Accusative, such as is found also in other languages. Not only may all transitive verbs assume such an Accusative, but also many which originally are semi-passive may do so, by their passing into transitives through a new turn of the conception; just as ገብረ "to be active", for example, is quite usually employed for "to make", "to do", without on that account surrendering its intransitive form (§ 76). In particular, the following verbs take the Accusative, contrary, in some instances, to the usage in our languages.

3. Accusative of the Object Proper, with Verbs of various meaning (*a—h*).

(*a*) *Verbs* of *Saying, Speaking, Narrating, Calling, Commanding* &c. Not only is that which one says rendered in the Accusative; but the person also to whom he speaks (whom he addresses) is introduced in the Accusative just as well as in the Dative (with ለ): ይቤሎ "he said to him"; ይቤሉኒ "they said to me"; and so with the verbs ተናገረ in Matt. 28, 18; Mark 14, 11, *et saepe*; ነበበ in Matt. 25, 36, 39; and አበየ "to refuse (something) to one", taking the Accusative of the Person, Matt. 18, 30, &c. Particularly if the person is expressed merely by a pronoun (Suffix), this Accusative connection is made use of; otherwise ለ is more frequently employed. The verb መሐለ with the Accusative may mean "to swear by (something)"—'to invoke anything by way of oath', Matt. 5, 34, 35; 23, 18, 22; but yet በ may also be used in this case, Matt. 23, 16, 18.

(*b*) Verbs of *Equality, Resemblance* &c., *e. g.* ይመስል ፡ ብእሴ Matt. 7, 24; 13, 24, 31; but yet such verbs also may be connected with ምስለ, ከመ, በ or ለ.

(*c*) For Verbs of *Fulness and Want*, v. *supra*.

(*d*) Verbs of *Ability and Weakness*, and of *Slightness*, in so far as by a new turn of the idea they assume the sense of Overpowering and Surpassing, or the reverse. Thus ከሀለ with the Accusative means "to be able for one", *i. e.* "to master him" Gen. 32, 26; ጸንዐ with the Accusative, "to be too strong for one", "to overcome him" Josh. 17, 13; Mark 1, 7; ኀየለ "to be strong", with Acc. "to vanquish" Matt. 16, 18; Luke 11, 22; Ps. 17, 20: in the same way ተክህለ "to gain power over any one" Matt. 24, 24; ተኀየለ Ps. 37, 12; Gen. 19, 9. This union also is adopted the most readily, when the Accusative is a Personal Pronoun (Suffix). A peculiar delicacy and brevity in the Ethiopic speech, in stating comparisons, depends upon this Accusative-use, inasmuch as in every comparison, the person or thing, with which comparison is made, may when expressed by a Pronoun be attached, as an Accusative Suffix, to any Intransitive or Passive verb,—although on the other hand እምነ must be employed, when it is expressed by a Noun: አብ፡ የዐብየኒ "the Father is greater than I" ('surpasses me in greatness') John 14, 28; የዐብዮ Gen. 48, 19; እለ፡ የአክይዎ "who are more wicked than he" Luke 11, 26; ዘይልህቀክሙ "who is greater than you" Matt. 23, 11; ይሰአነክሙ "is impossible for you" Matt. 17, 20; Gen. 18, 14; እንተ፡ ትሤንያ "who is fairer than she", Judges 15, 2; ይጸብበክሙ "is too narrow for you" Josh. 17, 15; ዘይንእሶ "who is younger than he" Gen. 25, 23; Judges 15, 2; ጸናዕከነ፡ ጥቀ "thou hast become much too powerful for us" Gen. 26, 16; አልቦ፡ ብእሲ፡ ዘይጠብበከ "there is no man who is wiser than thou" Gen. 41, 39; አልቦ፡ ዘእፈደፍደከ "in nothing shall I be greater than thou" Gen. 41, 40; ወይቴሐቶ፡ ሎቱ "and it is lower than the same" Hen. 26, 4 (*cf. infra*, § 187, 3).

(*e*) Verbs of *Coming, Going, Arriving at,* are connected with an Accusative, not only in the sense given above, § 174, 1, *b*, but also with a true Object-Accusative: ሖረ፡ ፍኖቶ "he went his way" Gen. 19, 2; አንሶሰወ with the Accusative of the land = "to go through it" Judges 18, 9; ኀደ with Accusative "to pass through (a land)" Gen. 12, 6; ዐደወ፡ ፈለገ "to cross the river" Gen. 31, 21; ኀለፈ with Accusative "to step aside from anything" "to pass from" Hen. 41, 5; and thus too with Personal Objects, *e. g.* በጽሐ and መጽአ with Accusative "to surprise one", "to overtake him" Matt. 23, 36; Gen. 14, 15; 15, 12; Judges 16, 9; ሖረ with the Accusative of the female "to lie with", "to cover" Ex. 22, 19; Mark 7, 21; ተራከበ "to meet with any one" Matt. 28, 9 &c. In the same way, Verbs of *Following, Pursuing, Getting before, e. g.* ቀደመ with Accusative "to get before any one" Matt. 21, 31; Mark 6, 45; Judges 7, 24 (F).

(*f*) The following Verbs also take an Accusative:—Verbs of *Recollecting and Keeping in mind, e. g,* ዘከረ "to call any one to mind" Matt. 26, 13; of *Pleasing* and *Being agreeable to*, inasmuch as the idea of 'satisfying' is at the root of them, as **አጸመ** (always with the Accusative); **ሐወዘ** Matt. 21, 15; and of *Delighting in* (*Choosing*), like **ሠምረ** Mark 1,11.

(*g*) All those Verbs, which may be referred to the idea of "*dealing with one*", of "*doing something to one*", may govern in the Accusative the object affected by them, *e. g.* **ሠሐቀ** with Accusative, "to laugh one to scorn" Mark 5,40; **ኀፈረ** with Acc. "to be ashamed of one" Mark 8, 38 (or "to be bashful *or* timid in presence of one", 'to fear him' Matt. 21,37); **ክሕደ** with Accusative "to disown *or* deny any one"; **ዐለወ** "to be offended at any one" Matt. 26, 31, 33; **ረሰየ** with the Accusative of the person "to do anything to one", "to deal with him" Matt. 21, 36; **አምነ** "to believe *or* trust any one" Gen. 45, 26: whence, in particular, many Verbs of Stems I, 3 and III, 3, *e. g.* **ላሐወ** "to mourn for any one" Gen. 37, 34; **ተቃተለ** "to fight with one" Judges 1, 5; **ተጋደለ** with the same meaning; **ተቃወመ** and **ተናሥአ** "to rise against one" Ps. 147, 6; **ተዋቀሰ** "to dispute with one" Hen. 1, 9(1); even **ተምዕዐ** "to be angry with any one" Gen. 30, 2; **ተአመነ** "to trust any one" Rom. 15, 14 &c.

(*h*) Finally there belong to this class the forms already mentioned (§ 167, 1, *b*), and still farther to be discussed in a subsequent section (v. § 192, *b*), viz.:—**ቦየ**, **ቦከ**, **ቦ** &c., by which the idea "to have" is indicated,—together with their negatives **አልቦየ** &c. Whenever these words express the idea "to have", they are joined with the Accusative of the object (while, in the sense "there is" or "there exists", they are completed by a Nominative). The only explanation that can be given of the association of the Accusative with these forms also,—is that the derived meaning gradually preponderated over the original one. Thus: **አልቦከ ፡ ክፍለ** "thou hast no part" Josh. 22, 25; **አበ ፡ ቦነ ፡ አብርሃምሃ** "we have Abraham for father" Matt. 3, 9; **እስመ ፡ ቦ ፡ ብዙኀ ፡ ጥሪተ** "for he had great possessions" Matt. 19, 22; **ቦቱ ፡ ውስተ ፡ አፉሃ ፡ ቈጽለ** "she had a leaf in her bill" Gen. 8, 11; **ጋኔነ ፡ አልቦየ** "I have not a devil" John 8, 49. This very favourite idiom may be employed even when the possessing Subject is not only indicated by a substituted pronoun, but also by a Noun (Appellative or

---

(1) [In this passage FLEMMING reads **ወይዘልፍ** instead of DILLMANN's **ወይትዋቀስ**. TR.]

Proper):—In the latter case **በ** receives the Suffix referring to the Noun, and the Noun itself is added, with **ለ** (as in § 172, *c*):—**ወባቲ ፡ ለርብቃ ፡ እኅወ** "and she,—Rebecca—, had a brother" Gen. 24, 29; or **ለ** may even be left out (as in § 172, *c*):—**ወቦሙ ፡ ደቂቀ ፡ ሮቤል ፡ እንስሳ ፡ ብዙኀ** "and the children of Reuben had many cattle" Numb. 32, 1; **ወቦቱ ፡ ላባ ፡ ክልኤ ፡ አዋልደ** "and Laban had two daughters" Gen. 29, 16: or the Noun may stand as *absoluter Vorhalt* (in accordance with § 196):—**ብእሲ ፡ ቦቱ ፡ ክልኤተ ፡ ውሉደ** "a (certain) man had two sons" Matt. 21, 28; and this is specially in place, when the Noun is indefinite, as in the case given here. However it frequently happens that in those cases in which **ቦ** and **አልቦ** imply the notion of "*having*", the Manuscripts nevertheless give the Nominative instead of the more usual Accusative, as in **ኀይል ፡ አልብየ** "I have no strength" ('strength is not in me') Ps. 68, 2; **አፍ ፡ ቦሙ** "they have a mouth" Ps. 113, 13 *sqq*. (Note); **ዘቦሙ ፡ ጥበብ** "who have wisdom" Hen. 5, 8([1]); **አልቦ ፡ ጥንት ፡ መዋዕሉ** "his days have no beginning" *Chrest*. p. 92, line 22 (on the other hand in line 26 we have **ጥንተ**); **አልቦ ፡ አብ ፡ ክርስቶስ** *ibid*. p. 93, line 2 &c. Such deviations may be explained by the supposition that **ቦ** is used in this combination, rather in accordance with its original sense than with its derived signification.

4. Double Accusative (*a*—*g*). Triple Accusative.

§ 177. 4. In the wide-spread use of the Accusative, explained in §§ 174—176, we naturally find that many Verbs may be associated with *a double Accusative*. A transitive Verb for instance may take, besides its nearest Object-Accusative according to § 174 *sqq*., a farther Accusative, of an adverbial or locative nature, as is proved by the examples which are adduced in these sections. Such instances need not be farther discussed at this stage. But there are, besides, many Verbs which govern a double Object-Accusative. Of this sort are (*a*) all Causatives of transitive Verbs, §§ 77, 79 *sqq*.; (*b*) in accordance with § 176 *c*, Verbs of Filling, Satisfying, Depriving; (*c*) following § 175, *b*,—Verbs of Clothing, Covering, Girding, Crowning, Surrounding, Overlaying, Removing, *e. g.* **ከደነ** Hen. 54, 5; **ሰለበ** Matt. 27, 31; Gen. 37, 23; (*d*) Verbs of Giving, Entrusting, Bestowing, Taking, Robbing, in so far as the ideas which they convey are of the same order with (*b*) and (*c*), *e. g.* **ወሀበ** Matt. 20, 8; 21, 23; Gen. 30, 18; **አወፈየ** Gen. 39, 4; **ሄደ**

([1]) [Flemming reads here, however, **ጥበበ**, the *Accusative*. tr.]

Luke 9, 39; 19, 26; ነሥአ Gen. 14, 16 (30, 15); ሰረቀ Gen. 44, 6; መጠወ *Chrest.* p. 96, line 11; (*e*) in accordance with § 176, *g*, Verbs of Hindering, Forbidding, Refusing, *e. g.* ከልአ Prov. 30, 7; አበየ Gen. 24, 41; and of Requiting, and Doing or Dealing with, *e. g.* ፈደየ Ps. 7, 4; ረሰየ Matt. 21, 40; 27, 22; (*f*) in accordance with § 176, *b*, those of Comparing, and with § 176, *a*, those of Naming([1]), Asking, Begging, Teaching, Relating, Addressing, *e. g.* ተስእለ Matt. 21, 24; Mark 4, 10; ሰመየ Gen. 1, 5, 8 and frequently, &c. (*g*) Lastly, many Verbs, which express a Making or a Judging, may take, besides their nearest Object, another also as a Predicative-Accusative, that is,—such an Accusative as would form the predicate to the nearest Object, if that Object were set in an independent sentence as Subject. For example, አምሰላ ፡ ዘማ "he considered her a whore", *i. e.* "he thought that she was a whore" Gen. 38, 15; ኪያክሙ ፡ እለ ፡ ዘእንበለ ፡ ሐዘን ፡ ንሬስየክሙ "we shall make you free from concern" Matt. 28, 14; እገብሮ ፡ ሕዝበ ፡ ዐቢየ "I shall make him a great nation" Gen. 17, 20; እገብሮሙ ፡ መብልዐ "I shall make them into a dish" Gen. 27, 9; እስርዎሙ ፡ ከላስስተ "bind ye them into sheaves" Matt. 13, 30; ንግበሩ ፡ ለዛቲ ፡ ምክር ፡ ግብረ "we will put this plan into execution" Hen. 6, 4; and thus frequently ገብረ with the Acc. of the material (v. DILLMAMN's '*Lex.*' col. 1160); also ንነሥእ ፡ አዋልዲክሙ ፡ ለነ ፡ አንስቲያ "we will take your daughters to us for wives" Gen. 34, 16. Still, in the cases last-named, the second Object, which here gives rather the product or result, may also be introduced by ለ (§ 179)([2]). And indeed with many of the verbs which have been mentioned, the association of a double Accusative is unnecessary, as one of the two Objects may be introduced also by a preposition (*cf. infra*). Farther, it may be observed, that when a verb takes two Objects, one of them is generally 'determined', and it is accordingly subordinated, by means of Suffixes and ለ (§ 172, *c*), provided it is not a mere Pronoun.

([1]) Yet we find here and there, in a less careful style, in Verbs of Naming, expressions also like ይጼውዕዎ ፡ ለነፋስ ፡ ቀዳማዊ ፡ ጽባሓዊ Hen. 77, 1; Gen. 26, 21,—where the Name remains as a Proper Noun in its first form. [In Hen. 77, 1, however, FLEMMING now reads ለጽባሓዊ. TR.]

([2]) Of a different description are cases like the following: ያመውእከ ፡ ለጸላእትከ "he gives to thine enemies the victory over thee" *Chrest.* p. 44, line 1; ያሰትዩ ፡ ለአሕጻሃ ፡ ሕምዘ *ibid.* p. 42, line 15; *cf. infra* p. 445.

A Triple Accusative is also met with,—that is to say, the Double-Accusative just described and an additional Accusative in the sense of a Dative,—*e. g.* in **ዘአርበሕከነ ፡ ኵሎ ፡ ፍጥረተ ፡ ዘዘ ዚአሁ ፡ ፍሬ** *qui fecisti, ut singulae creaturae nobis fructus varios afferant* II Const. Ap. 39.

5. Accusative after Reflexive Verbs, and after the Passives of Verbs which govern two Accusatives.

5. That even Reflexive Verbs (St. III) govern an Accusative, has already been indicated by several examples in § 80 (1); and,—inasmuch as it makes no difference in the subordination of an Object, whether a Verb is used semi-passively and reflexively in St. I, 1 or in St. III (like **መልአ** and **ተመልአ** "to be full" and "to fill oneself", both being joined with an Accusative, or **ለብሰ** and **ተለብሰ** "to put on" and "to clothe oneself"),—this case does not differ essentially from those which have been described in §§ 175, 176. In the very same way a verb, which takes again a simple meaning in the Reflexive Stem, in many cases no longer differs at all, as regards association with an Accusative, from a simple Transitive, as in the case of **መጠወ** "to hand over", **ተመጠወ** "to cause to be handed over to oneself", *i. e.* "to receive", "to take"; **ተልእከ** "to let oneself be sent", *i. e.* "to serve", with the Accusative of the Person, Matt. 25, 44; 27, 55; **ተፀምደ** "to bind oneself to", *i. e.* "to be attached to", "to be a follower of", with an Accusative, Matt. 27, 57; **ተቀበለ** "to go to meet" Gen. 14, 17; **ተአመነ** "to confess" Mark 1, 5; **ተጽዕነ** "to ride", with Accusative, Gen. 49, 17. In fact Reflexive Stems, which have again become Simple in their meaning, may take two Accusatives, *e. g.* **ተስእለ** (v. *supra*, under No. 4).

In like manner all Passives of Verbs which have two Accusatives in the Active, take the Accusative of one of the two Objects of the Active Stem, *e. g.* **ተምህረ** "to be taught" ("to learn") with Accusative of the Object, Luke 1, 4; **ተፈድየ** "to receive something in compensation" with Accusative of the thing, Deut. 15, 2, 3; Ps. 39, 21; **ተዐስየ** with Accusative "to be recompensed for something" Mark 10, 30; **ኵሉ ፡ ተውህበኒ** "all things have been given to me" Matt. 11, 27; **ተከፍለ** with Acc., "to receive something allotted". —For other examples v. Ex. 36,6; Deut. 11,11 [and CORNILL, '*Weise*

---

(1) *Cf.* also, *e. g.* Judith 10, 3 *sq.*: **ተኀፅበት ፡ ሥጋሃ ፡ በማይ ፡ ወተቀብአት ፡ ዕፍረተ ፡ ሥዕርተ ፡ ርእሳ ፡ ወተነፍቀት ፡ ሥዕርታ ፡ . . . ወተሰርገወት ፡ አውቃፊተ.**

Philos.', p. 51]. It is especially binding, in the case of all verbs, which in the Active along with the nearest Object take a Predicate-, or Product-Accusative,—that this Predicate or Product appear also with the Passive, as an Accusative([1]). Thus we have such an Accusative with all verbs which express the idea of "being called anything" or "found, thought, or declared to be anything", or of "being made, chosen, appointed, or designated anything", *e. g.* **ተሰምየ ፡ ንኡሰ** "he is called([2]) the least" Matt. 5, 19; 23, 10; **ድልወ ፡ ዘተረክበ** "who was found worthy"; **ይትኅደግ ፡ ለክሙ ፡ ቤትክሙ ፡ በድወ** "your house is left unto you desolate" Matt. 23, 38; **ተኈለቈ ፡ ሎቱ ፡ ጽድቀ** "it was reckoned to him for righteousness" Gen. 15, 6; **መድኅነ ፡ ተተርጐመ** "it is interpreted (as) Redeemer"; **ሀብተ ፡ ተውህቡ ፡ ለእግዚአብሔር** "they are given to God ('as a') for a gift" Numb. 18, 6; **ተሠየምኩ ፡ ላእከ** "I was appointed a minister" Eph. 3, 7. Only rarely is the Nominative employed in these cases, in place of the Predicate-Accusative, and then in such a way that the Predicate is associated with the Subject as an Apposition: **ተሠይመ ፡ አልዓዛር ፡ ወልዱ ፡ ካህን ፡ ህየንቴሁ** "his son Eleazar was ordained (as) Priest in his stead" Deut. 10, 6.

The employment of the Accusative with these Passives explains also the peculiarity, found both in Ethiopic and Arabic([3]), according to which the Verbs of '*Being*, *Becoming* and *Remaining*' **ሀለወ**, **ኮነ**, **ነበረ** (**ቆመ**) take the Predicate in the Accusative, in respect that the idea of "having been made something" or "being made something" is always present in these verbs,—for instance: **እከውን ፡ ንጹሐ** "I shall be pure" Ps. 17, 26; **ዘኮነ ፡ ወይነ** "that was made wine" John 2, 9; **ኮነ ፡ ነዳፌ** "he became an archer" Gen. 21, 20; **ዘሀለወ ፡ ድልወ** "who is ready" 1 Peter 4, 5; **ምንተ ፡ ኮንኪ** ("what hast thou become?") "what aileth thee?" Gen. 21, 17; **ኩኒ ፡ አእላፈ** "become thousands" Gen. 24, 60; **ይነብር ፡ ክበቡ ፡ በከ** "its circle remains empty" Hen. 78, 14; **ጉቡአነ ፡ ይነብሩ** "they sat assembled together" Hen. 13, 9; **ከመ ፡ ይንበሩ ፡ ጻድቃነ ፡ ወንጹሓነ** "that they remain just and pure" Hen. 69, 11; **ይቀውሙ ፡ ፅሩዓነ** "they stand idle" Matt. 20, 3: In the same way also, **ወፅአ**, *e. g.* **ይወፅእ ፡ እኩየ** *ἀποβαίνει σκληρός* Sir. 30, 8. Connected with this

Accusative after Verbs of Being, Becoming &c.

([1]) Just as in Arabic, Ewald, '*Gr. Ar.*' § 546.

([2]) In verbs of "being called", proper names for the most part are not put in the Accusative, *e. g.* Gen. 17, 5; 11, 9.

([3]) Ewald, '*Gr. Ar.*' § 553 *sqq.*

also is the use of ኮነ with the Accusative, meaning "to serve as something", *e. g.* ወትከውን ፡ ተአምረ "and it shall be for a token" Gen. 9, 13; ወኮኖሙ ፡ ግንፋሎሙ ፡ እብነ "and their bricks served as stone to them" Gen. 11, 3. This is the established rule which is followed in the case of ኮነ, ሀለወ, ነበረ; but in cases where the Predicate may also be regarded as an Apposition, owing to the verbal idea being less vacant than in ኮነ or ሀለወ, (*e. g.* in "why *stand* ye idle?) another form of connection is also possible (§ 189). If indeed a Nominative is often found with ኮነ and ሀለወ [1], when we might have looked rather for an Accusative according to what has been said, then the cause is—either a mere piece of carelessness on the part of a copyist, or a different conception of the sentence: *e. g.* "it was *or* there was light" may be expressed by—"light arose", and then the Ethiopic would be ኮነ ፡ ብርሃን; or *light* may be regarded as a predicate to the impersonal form "it was *or* became", and the Ethiopic would then be ኮነ ፡ ብርሃነ; hence variation in Manuscripts, Gen. 1, 3; Hen. 89, 8. Thus we can say: ኢኮነ ፡ ሠናየ "it is not good" Matt. 15, 26, and ኢኮነ ፡ ሠናይ "it is not a good thing" Gen. 2, 18; ወኮነ ፡ ሕግ ፡ ውስተ ፡ እስራኤል "a custom arose in Israel" Judges 11, 39,—where ሕገ might quite as well have appeared, "it became a custom"; ሀለወ ፡ ድፉነ (instead of ድፉን) "it had been hidden in the ground" Josh. 7, 21, 22; ጻኅንኑ ፡ ሀሎኩ *Chrest.* p. 29, line 13.

6. Suffix Pronoun used as a Secondary Accusative or a Dative of Special Reference.

§ 178. 6. A distinction must be made between all the cases which have been hitherto mentioned, and those in which a *Suff. Pron.* in Ethiopic is attached, *in the sense of a Dative* to Active, Intransitive, Reflexive, or Passive Verbs (§ 151). Such an Accusative expresses, not the nearest object, but the idea of "in relation to", or "for", and thus indicates the same thing which otherwise is expressed by ለ. It has most resemblance to the Accusative in the cases mentioned in § 175, *c*, but it is again distinguished from these by the circumstance that it is only allowable for the Suffix Pronoun. Thus we say አርኅወነ "open unto us" Matt. 25, 11; ወይዌስክዎ "and they shall add to him" Matt. 25, 29; ተርፈኒ "remains for me" Matt. 19, 20; ዘይረትዐከ "what is right to thee" ("what is

(1) That the Predicate cannot stand in the Accusative, when it is introduced by the preposition ከመ follows of course from § 165, No. 6; *e. g.* ኢትኩኑ ፡ ከመ ፡ መድልዋን Matt. 6, 5.

thine opinion") Matt. 22, 17; ይኄይሰከ "it is better for thee" Matt. 5, 29, 30; ኢትከውንክሙ ፡ ሰላም "peace shall not be unto you" Hen. 5,4: *cf.* also ሀለወኒ "it impends over me" in the periphrasis for the *Futurum instans* (§ 89), and ምንትከ (§ 198). Now since this employment of the Suff. Pron. with a Dative sense is in general possible, the periphrasis for the definite Article by means of a Suffix appended to the Verb (§ 172, *c*) may be extended to Nouns which stand in a Dative subordination to the Verb:—ኮኖ ፡ ለኖኅ "there was to Noah" Gen. 7, 6; ወይከውንከ ፡ መብልዐ ፡ ለከ ፡ ወሎሙ "and it shall be for food for thee and for them" Gen. 6, 21 &c. This use of the suffix is most frequent with ኮነ, to express the notion of "being something to one", or "serving as something to one" (1), and the Suffix is but seldom omitted in that case: "that she may become his wife" is always given in Ethiopic as ትኩኖ ፡ ብእሲተ or ትኩኖ ፡ ብእሲቶ, not ትኩን ፡ ብእሲቶ; so too ይኩንከሙ ፡ ላእከ "let him be your minister" Matt. 20, 26; እፎ ፡ እንከ ፡ ይከውኖ ፡ ወልዶ "how then can he be (at the same time) his son?" Matt. 22, 45. In virtue then of a peculiar subtlety in the Ethiopic language, every verb which has for Subject or Object some part of a living being (such as a member of the body, the soul, name, honour, qualities &c.) has a Suff. Pron. appended to it, referring to the Being itself and having a Dative or Accusative force,—for the purpose of signifying that the action proceeds from, or passes over to—not merely the part in question but also the Being itself, *e. g.* ይትፌሣሐኒ ፡ ልብየ "my heart rejoices (in me)" Ps. 12, 6; Judges 19, 6; ገብአ ፡ ልቡ "his mind came back (to him)" Mark 5, 15; Luke 8, 35; ደንገፆሙ ፡ ልቦሙ "their heart was perturbed (within them)" Gen. 42, 28; 45, 26; ሐይዎ ፡ ልቡ "his spirit revived (within him)" Gen. 45, 27; መረረተኒ ፡ ነፍስየ "my soul is embittered (within me)" Ruth 1, 13; ብእሲት ፡ እንተ ፡ ደም ፡ ይውሕዛ "a woman, who had an issue of blood" Matt. 9, 20 (for which the form of expression in other languages would be ደማ ፡ ይውሕዝ); ስምዐኒ ፡ ቃልየ "hear (me) my voice" Gen 27, 43; ሰምዖ ፡ ቃሎ "he hearkened to (him) his voice" Judges 13, 9; መተሮ ፡ እዝኖ "he smote off his ear

(1) [Dillmann seems to mean, both here and throughout this section, that the Dative use of the Verbal Suffix conveys an emphatic reference of the idea which is contained in the verb and its complement, to the personality indicated by the Suffix. tr.]

(from him)" Matt. 26, 51; ወርእያ ፡ ነፍስታ ፡ ለዲና "and he saw (her) the person of Dinah" Gen. 34, 3; ወአእመሮሙ ፡ ኢየሱስ ፡ እከዮሙ "and Jesus recognised them in their wickedness" or "perceived their wickedness (in them)" Matt. 22, 18; ይእስርዎ ፡ እገሪሁ "they shall bind his feet"(1) Matt. 22, 13; *cf.* also ይስምዐነ ፡ ቃለነ Judith 8, 17; አእመረኪ ፡ ሕዝብ ፡ ጥበበኪ 8, 29; ኢይፍራህኪ ፡ ልብኪ 10, 16; in the very same way, for "he called his name so-and-so" the expression is—sometimes, it is true, ሰመዮ ፡ ስሞ ፡ but with more elegance, ሰመዮ ፡ ስሞ ፡ ሴት Gen. 4, 25; 3, 20, Note. The Cases mentioned in § 175, *c* all resemble those which are enumerated here, except that in the former group the Person itself is always the proper Subject or Object, and the Part of it which is dealt with, is always in the Accusative of Reference—, while, *vice versâ*, in the group before us, it is the Part which is always the nearest Subject or Object, and the Person itself is mentioned by way of addition and put in the secondary Accusative.

An explanation has thus been given of the most important uses of the Ethiopic Accusative; but of course it is not a matter of necessity that every verb, which is capable of taking an Accusative, should do so always. Even Active verbs and Double Transitives may often stand in a sentence without any Object. This may happen because the Object, being understood from the connection, is suppressed and is not even represented by a Pronoun, *e. g.* Matt. 21, 2 "there shall ye find a she-ass and an ass's colt, ፍትሑ ፡ ወአምጽኡ ፡ ሊተ loose (them) and bring (them) to me"; ኢትእመኑ "believe (it) not" Matt. 24, 23; Mark 13, 21; Gen. 9, 2;—or, of two Objects, at least one is omitted: "my house is a house of prayer ወአንትሙሰ ፡ ትሬስዩ ፡ በአተ ፡ ሰረቅት but ye make (it) a den of thieves" Matt. 21, 13. The same thing may happen too, because these verbs—which in other languages are often better expressed intransitively—yield, of and by themselves, a satisfactory meaning: ዘያበርህ ፡ ወያውዒ "which enlightens and warms" ('diffuses light and warmth') Hen. 72, 4; ኢወለደት ፡ ሎቱ፡ "she did not bear to him" ('she bare him no children') Gen. 16, 1:—(2); ያጠምቅ "he baptised" (without mentioning any Object) Mark 1, 4; አእመረ "to know" Matt. 27, 65 ("to have knowledge about, *or* to

(1) Which may also be explained according to § 175, *c*.

(2) [*Cf. Kebra Nag.*, 'Introd.' p. XX.]

have skill in"); አንትሙ ፡ አእምሩ "see ye to it" Matt. 27, 24; ፈቲወ ('to wish', 'to desire') "to be willing" Matt. 26, 41 &c.

(b) *Subordination of Nouns and Pronouns by means of Prepositions.*

Subordination of Nouns and Pronouns by means of Prepositions.

§ 179. If a Noun cannot be governed in the Accusative by a Verb, in one or other of the modes described in §§ 174—178, it must be subordinated to the Verb by the aid of a *Preposition*. The Dictionary will point out which Prepositions are possible and usual in the case of the several verbs. A good deal has been brought forward incidentally on this head (v. *supra* § 164 *sqq.*) in treating of Prepositions; but the following observations still fall to be added here.

1. Instead of the more strict subordination in the Accusative, the looser form may appear, effected by ለ, the preposition of most general reference [1]. But upon the whole this has been seldom resorted to, being confined to no more than a few cases. In exemplification of this use of ለ as a mere substitute for the Accusative, we find in Gen. 17, 12 ወለሕፃን ፡ ትገዝሩ (where ትገዝርዎ would have been a more accurate expression) "and the child ye shall circumcise"; farther እለ ፡ ያዐርቡ ፡ ለክበበ ፡ ፀሐይ "who cause the orb of the sun to set" Hen. 18, 4; እስመ ፡ ለትእምርት ፡ ወለአዝማን ፡ . . . . አርአየኒ "for he showed me the signs and the times . . . ." Hen. 75, 3; and ዘኢያውፅአ ፡ ለጽድቁ ፡ ወለርትዑ ፡ እምኔሁ "who hath not withdrawn from him his righteousness and his truth", Gen. 24, 27 [2]; and thus an Accusative-attachment, which has been begun, may be continued in effect by ለ, as in ከመ ፡ ኢትዔምፀነ ፡ ወኢለዘርእየ "that thou wilt injure neither ourselves nor my descendants" Gen. 21, 23. The use of ለ in exchange for the Accusative is more common in the case of all those verbs which contain the idea of "addressing", inasmuch as the 'reference' in such verbs may be always held to be—the 'speaking *to* some one'. Thus not only may such words as "to say", "to relate", "to speak" have ለ associated with them, quite as readily as the Accusative (§ 176, 3, *a*), but also, in particular, words involving such ideas as "to beg", "to ask", and farther "to praise"

(1) Analogous to the procedure in Aramaic.

(2) *Cf. supra*, p. 439, Note (2).

and "to extol" (ባረከ, ሰብሐ &c.), "to call", "to command", "to forbid", "to blame", (*e. g.* ዘለፈ Hen. 13,10), "to reprimand", and so on. But especially does ለ come forward to introduce the *aim* and *purpose*, when a Noun in that signification is subordinated to a Verb. Thus Verbs of Giving govern the person, to whom a thing is given, as much by ለ as through the Accusative (§ 177,4); and the Predicate-Accusative, in particular, (§ 177,4 & 5) may be replaced by the connection through ለ, wherever the notion of a purpose is conceived: ተሣየጡ ፡ ምድረ ፡ ለመቃብር "they bought a field as a burying-ground" Matt. 27,7; Gen. 49,30; ከፈሎሙ ፡ ለሠለስቱ ፡ ሰራዊት "he divided them into three companies" Judges 7,16; ሥጋ ፡ ጽድቅ ፡ አቅም ፡ ለተክለ ፡ ዘርእ "establish the flesh of righteousness as a seed-bearing plant" Hen. 84,6; እገብራ ፡ ለበረከት "I will make it (*f.*) a blessing" Hen. 45,4,5(¹) [*cf. Kebra Nag.* 5a22]; ይትኀረይ ፡ ብእሲ ፡ ለተክለ ፡ ኰነኔ ፡ ጽድቅ "there will be chosen a man to become a plant of the judgment of righteousness" Hen. 93,5. Thus too ኮነ "to serve for something" and "to become something" is associated with ለ as readily as with the Accusative (§ 177,5): ወኮነ ፡ ለመንፈሰ ፡ ሕይወት "and he became a living soul" Gen. 2,7; 20,16; ወይከውን ፡ ለበረከት ፡ ግብር "and the doing . . . shall serve as a blessing" Hen. 10,16; 52,4; ይከውኑክሙ ፡ ለዕቅፍት "they shall become a stumbling-block to you" Judges 2,3. Now and again too, other prepositions of direction are employed instead: እብን ፡ ኮነት ፡ ውስተ ፡ ርእሰ ፡ ማእዝንት "the stone has become the head of the corner" Matt. 21,42; ያገብአከ ፡ ውስተ ፡ ሊቀ ፡ ቀዳሕያን "he will restore thee to the post of cupbearer" Gen. 40,13; or ተወለጠ ፡ ኀበ "to be changed into something (else)" [or with በ, *Kebra Nag.* 133 b 21].

As for the rest, the Dative of other languages is generally expressed by ለ.

2. Several Verbs, which may govern an Accusative, may also introduce their Object by means of Prepositions, but in that case they generally assume a somewhat different meaning; and the subordination of an Object to a Verb by means of a Preposition corresponds often in its effect to the Compound Verbs of the Indo-European languages: ሰምዐ with Accusative means "to hear

---

(¹) [DILLMANN's reading has the ለ—construction in both verses; FLEMMING reads በረከተ in V. 4, and ለበረከት in V. 5, with an identical meaning. TR.]

any one", but with ለ, "to listen to" and "to obey"; ርእየ with በ "to look at anything" Hen. 39,10; ጸውዐ with ለ "to call to any one" Gen. 21,17; ወረቀ ፡ ላዕለ "to spit upon one" Matt. 27,30; ነጸረ ፡ ውስተ "to look towards" Gen. 15,5; ሰትየ with Accusative "to drink anything", but with እምነ "to drink of it" Gen. 9,21 [and with በ "to drink out of anything" Gen. 44,5; *Kebra Nag.* 97 b 1,3]; አኀዘ "to hold", "to keep", but with በ "to take hold of" Gen. 19,16; ነፍኀ "to breathe", but with ዲበ "to breathe upon any one" and "to breathe into *or* inspire any one" Hen. 82,7 &c. Otherwise whenever a Verb attaches its object to itself by a Preposition, that preposition is chosen to suit the meaning of the Verb, *e. g.* አበሰ ፡ ለ "to sin against any one" Judges 10,10; ሐዘነ ፡ ለ "to mourn for any one"; ሰገደ ፡ ለ "to bow down to *or* before any one" Gen. 27,29; 42,6; መልከ ፡ ለ, ነግሠ ፡ ለ "to be king over *or* of any one" Judges 9,8, 22 (and with ላዕለ Judges 9,9); ርዕደ ፡ እምነ, ፈርሀ ፡ እምነ "to tremble, to fear before", "to be afraid of" Gen. 9,2; 32,12; ጐየ ፡ —ተዐቀበ ፡ እምነ "to flee from", "to beware of"; አዕረፈ ፡ እምነ "to rest from" Hen. 53,7; ነጽሐ ፡ እም "to be pure from anything" Hen. 10,22; ተበቀለ ፡ እም "to take vengeance on" Judges 16,28; Hen. 54,6; ጸለየ ፡ ኀበ "to pray to", Gen. 20,17, and similarly ሰአለ ፡ ኀበ Gen. 25,21; አምነ ፡ በ "to believe in"; ሠምረ ፡ በ, ፈተወ ፡ በ "to have a liking for,—a desire for"; ቀንአ ፡ ላዕለ "to be jealous *or* envious of" Gen. 26,14; 30,1 &c. All Verbs too which indicate properties may be compared with other conceptions by means of the comparative word እምነ and a few other Prepositions (v. *infra* § 187).

Finally, an author may occasionally associate a Verb in quite a bold and peculiar fashion with a Preposition, which according to its usual sense does not properly belong to the Verb, as ጸሐፈ with the Accusative of the thing and ላዕለ of the Person, "to record something *on* or *regarding* any one" (*i. e.* "to set to his credit *or* his blame", "to impute") Hen. 10,8; ናዘዘ with እምነ "to console one *from* a thing", *i. e.* "to comfort one about a thing" Gen. 5,29; መልአ ፡ ማይ ፡ ውስተ ፡ ሐመር "the water filled *into* the ship", *i. e.* "the ship became full of water" Mark 4,37; *cf.* Ex. 28,3; ንቀጥቅጦ ፡ እምድረ ፡ ሕያዋን Jer. 11,19; [*cf.* also *Kebra Nag.* 'Glossary', *sub* ተሥእነ, ቀጸበ, ወዕአ, ፈነወ &c.]. But yet these bolder associations are rare, at least in ordinary Ethiopic speech.

Generally speaking, Prepositions are very frequently made

use of in Ethiopic. It is true that the employment of the Accusative in its more ancient significations is still in full activity, and is just as current as in any of the oldest Semitic languages; but side by side with that use, a connection of the words by means of Prepositions is often available; and a certain striving after freedom and variety in word-association is unmistakeably proclaimed even in this department.

2. VERB IN SUBORDINATION TO THE VERB.

1. Second Verb determining (a) Kind and Manner, Circumstances or Time of the action of the First.

§ 180. Just as the Verb may be supplemented by subordinating to it a Noun or Pronoun, so also may it be supplemented by another Verb. In this case, should the supplementary Verb merely appear as a Substantive-Infinitive, and be governed by the principal verb just like any other noun, special discussion of such an instance would be superfluous here. But in point of fact there are several other methods of subordinating one Verb to another, and these must now be explained.

The sense in which one verb governs another is varied in character.

1. The second verb may define *the kind and manner* of the principal verb, *the more detailed circumstances of the action*, and *its time*.

(*a*) *When* an *adverbial determination of Circumstance* has to be joined to the principal Verb (or to the Predicate of the sentence), this is often expressed in Ethiopic by a Verb,—partly because adverbial expressions of this character in a fully formed condition are comparatively few, and partly because such determination of circumstance may have to be more strongly emphasised than is possible with an adverbial expression. In such a case the two verbs may be united together, mainly in the following two ways:—

α) By the two Verbs being set side by side without ወ.

(α) The pair of verbs are set side by side, in the same tense, mood, number and person, not connected however by the usual ወ, but remaining unconnected; and by that arrangement, since there is no Copula coming between them, they are the more closely linked together. In this way are attached, in particular, certain adverbial conceptions of Time and Place, of the most general sense, which precede the principal verb, while completing the idea conveyed in it. Thus, although the sentence "and she bare again" may be expressed with the help of an adverb in Ethiopic also: ወወለ ደት ፡ ዓዲ, *e. g.* in Gen. 29,34, yet, if this "again" has to be emphasised, it is expressed by ደገመ "to repeat": ወደገመት ፡ ወለደት "and again she bare" Gen. 4,2; 29,33; ደገመ ፡ ፈነወ "again he sent", although ወዳግመ ፡ ፈነወ may also occur, Luke 20,11; so too in Judges 20,22; Gen. 25,1. In the same way ወድአ "he has finished" serves to indicate the idea of "already" (v. § 88): እሳት ፡ ወድአት ፡ ነደት "the fire is already kindled" Luke 12,49; ወዳእነ ፡ ግእዝነ "we have already reprehended" Rom. 3,9; Numb. 17,11, 12; 22,29, 33; Matt. 5,28; 11,21; 17,12; and this word may even be placed after the principal verb: ወመስየ፡ ፡ ወድአ ፡ ሰዐት "and the evening hour has already come" Mark 6,35 (¹).—*Cf.* farther ወፅኡ ፡ ተቀበልዎሙ "they went out against them" Judges 1,10; ሑሩ ፡ ተቀበልዎሙ "go ye out to meet them" Josh. 9,9; ተንሥኡ ፡ ንሑር "arise! let us go" Gen. 33,12; 27,19; Josh. 7,13; ንበር ፡ ትትኔበይ ፡ ሎሙ "remain thou prophesying to them" *Chrest.* page 3, line 22 *sq.* &c. In such unions, it is true, the two verbs frequently occur also, joined by means of ወ; but the better manuscripts avoid this.

(3) By the Verb of Principal Action being subordinated in the Acc. of the Inf. to the Verb of Circumstance or Time.

(*β*) Still more frequently the principal verb is subordinated in the Accusative of the Infinitive to those verbs which determine Time or Circumstance; and every verb, whether Active or Passive, may be subordinated in this way, by taking the form of the Substantive-Infinitive. The governing Verb, which contains the adverbial and auxiliary determination, is mostly transitive or causative, but it may also be reflexive-passive; and the Accusative of the Infinitive in the latter case is to be explained in accordance with § 174. Thus: ተገምሩ ፡ ዐዲወ "they had all crossed over" ('they had all been included in the crossing over') Josh. 4,8, 11; ቀደምኩ ፡ ነጊሮተክሙ "I have told you before" Matt. 24,25; 12,29; 17,11; አፍጠንክን ፡ መጺአ (= ፍጡነ ፡ መጻእክን) "ye (*f.*) are come soon" Ex. 2,18; Gen. 18,7; Josh. 4,10; ኅበርክሙ ፡ አሚነ ፡ ምስሌየ "you have believed along with me" Rom. 1,12; ኢ.ይ

(¹) Precisely in the case of ወድአ the tense as a rule agrees with that of the leading verb: both are in the Perfect. But yet, to express a Present, ወድአ is also joined to the Imperfect: ወድአ ፡ ማሕጼ ፡ ውስተ ፡ ጉንድ ፡ ይነብር "already lies the axe beside the stem" Matt. 3,10. It is unnecessary to assume an adverb ወድአ here.

ደግም ፡ እንከ ፡ ሀልዎ ፡ ምስሌክሙ "I will continue to be with you no longer" Josh. 7,12; Gen. 8,12; 38,26; አኅለቁ ፡ ተሴስዮ ፡ እክለ "they had eaten up the corn" Gen. 43,2; Josh. 8,24; 10,20; አሠነየ ፡ ገቢረ "he has done good" Judges 17,13; አቅደመት ፡ አእምሮ "she had informed herself before" Matt. 14,8; 17,25; አፈድፈዱ ፡ ጸሊአቶ "they hated him still more" Gen. 37,8; Matt. 27,23; ሰለጠ ፡ መዊተ "he was already quite dead" John 19,33; አብዝኀት ፡ አብኦ "she brought most" Luke 21,3; ማይ ፡ ያርሕቅ ፡ ቀዊመ "the water stood up afar" Josh. 3,16. An Abstract also may occur instead of the Infinitive, *e. g.* ዘአዘለፈ ፡ ትዕግሥቶ "who is steadfastly patient" Matt. 24,13.

Second Verb expressing (*b*) more exact Determination of Time, Circumstance &c.:- (*α*) By the Gerund.

§ 181. (*b*) If a more exact determination of the Kind and Manner, of the Circumstances or of the Time is attached to a verb, and if it is a determination which can only be expressed by means of a verbal form, then Ethiopic has various devices for expressing it.

(*α*) The auxiliary qualification may be subordinated in the form of the *Gerund* (§ 123). In that case the Infinitive itself takes the Accusative, in accordance with § 174 *sq.*, but only in rare instances does it appear without a suffix, as in ኵሎ ፡ ዓለመ ፡ ፈጸመ ፡ እግዚአብሔር ፡ ገቢረ ፡ ግብሮ "God completed the whole world, carrying out his work" Gen. 2,2. Nearly always, in fact, the Subject which performs the subordinated action,—whether it be at the same time the Subject of the leading proposition or its Object,—is yet more specially expressed by a Suffix Pronoun appended to the Infinitive. Thus determinations of condition are expressed, as in ተዐጊሠከ ፡ አፅምአኒ "hear me patiently" Acts 26,3; ወወፅአ ፡ ተዐጊሦ "and he went out, putting restraint on himself" Gen. 43,31; and even ሀለወ ፡ ነዊሞ "he was 'sleeping'", *i. e.* "he was just then asleep". Still more frequently are thus expressed determinations of Time (and even conditions bordering upon determinations of Time), which may be understood as referring to Past, Present or Future, according to the context, as the Infinitive has no distinction of tenses: ወፈሊሶ ፡ እምህየ ፡ ሖረ ፡ ውስተ ፡ ምኵራብ "and departing thence he betook himself to the Synagogue" Matt. 12,9; ወወሪዶ ፡ እምሐመር ፡ ተቀበሎ ፡ ሶቤሃ ፡ ብእሲ "and on his coming out of the ship there met him then a man" Mark 5,2; ዐርበ ፡ ፀሐይ ፡ በጺሖሙ ፡ ገብአ "the sun went down as they reached Gibeah" Judges 19,14; ዘይበቊል ፡ በዘርኡ ፡ ተዘሪአ "which sprouts by its own seed, when it is sown" Gen. 1, 29; ወሰሚዖ ፡ ሄሮድስ ፡ ደንገፀ "and when Herod heard, he was alarmed" Matt. 2, 3; ሐዊረክሙ ፡ ተሰአሉ "going away, enquire ye" Matt. 2, 8; መጽኡ ፡ ሠኒቆሙ ፡ ወአስተዳሊዎሙ "they came, after they had collected provision for a journey and made their preparations" Josh. 9, 2; እንተ ፡ መሊአ ፡ አዕረጉ "which, when it was full, they drew up" Matt. 13, 48; መኑ ፡ እኩዩ ፡ ከዊኖ ፡ ዘቆመ ፡ ቅድሜሁ Job 9, 4; and so almost on every page of a historical narrative. Even when the Circumstantial or Temporal clause has a Subject of its own, which is not mentioned in the Principal Clause either as Subject or as Object, the Gerund may appear. The Subject is then, — after having been referred to by the Suffix of the Infinitive, — adjoined independently to this Suffix, and in its primary form (not in the Accusative): ወወፂአ ፡ ውእቱ ፡ በኡ ፡ ደቂ "and when he was gone out, his servants came" Judges 3, 24; ወኀሊፎ ፡ ሰብዐቱ ፡ ዓመት ፡ ዘጽጋብ ፡ አኀዘ ፡ ይምጻእ ፡ ሰብዐቱ ፡ ዓመት ፡ ዘረኃብ "and when the seven years of plenty had passed away, the seven years of famine began to come" Gen. 41, 53; ኀሊፎ ፡ መዋዕል ፡ ብዙኃ Job 2, 9; ወተወሊዶ ፡ ኢየሱስ ፡ ናሁ ፡ መሰግላን ፡ በጽሑ "and when Jesus was born, behold there came wise men" Matt. 2, 1; or, with the Infinitive of Impersonal Verbs: ወምሴተ ፡ ከዊኖ ፡ አምጽኡ "and when evening was come, they brought" Matt. 8, 16; 26, 20; ወመስዮ ፡ መጽአ ፡ ብእሲ "and when it was evening, there came a man" Matt. 27, 57.

(β) When the auxiliary qualification sets forth a condition of the Acting Subject of the Principal Verb (a condition which is expressed in other languages by a Participle, co-ordinated with the Subject), it may be expressed by an Imperfect, ranked alongside of the Principal Verb, the Imperfect being the proper tense to describe a condition or circumstance (§ 89). In this case, however, as in similar cases (§ 180, 1, *a*, *α*), the copula ወ must always be left out, in order that by such close connection the subordination of the accessory idea to the principal one may be signified. It is unnecessary in such a case to have the two verbs placed immediately together; several words, according to circumstances, may intervene, *e. g.*: ነበሩ ፡ የዐቅብዎ "they sat down, watching him" Matt. 27, 36; ትሰክብ ፡ ትፈዕን "she is laid down sick of a fever" Matt. 8, 14; ይገንዩ ፡ ዘበሙ ፡ ጥበብ ፡ ኢይደግሙ ፡ አብሶ "those who possess wisdom will humble themselves, no more

(β) By the Imperfect without ወ.

committing sin" Hen. 5, 8; **እመ፡ ኀደግምዎ፡ ትገብኡ፡ ውስተ፡ እሉ፡ አሕዛብ** "if ye forsake him, turning back to those nations" Josh. 23, 12; **ወይነውም፡ ባሕቲቱ፡ ይፈርህ** G. Ad. 93, 19; [**ኢያእትት፡ . . . ይሄሉ** *Kebra Nag.* 114 b 20 *sq.*]. On this usage rests also the periphrasis of the Latin Imperfect through the employment of **ሀለወ** with the Imperfect (§ 89), as in **ሀሎ፡ ያጠምቅ** "he baptised" ('was baptising'). *Cf.* also § 189 *sq.* When, on the other hand, the auxiliary qualification does not exactly express a condition of the Subject, but a continuation rather of the principal action, then it is put in the same Tense as the Principal verb, and is ranked beside it without farther connection: **ወነሥኡ፡ አዋልዲሆሙ፡ አውሰቡ** "and they took their daughters in marriage" (*lit.* 'and they took their daughters,—they married') Judges 3, 6; **መጽአ፡ እቶን፡ ዘይጠይስ፡ ኀለፈ** "and there came a smoking furnace, passing by" &c. Gen. 15, 17; **ወፅአት፡ . . . ኀሠሠት** "she went away, . . . seeking" Hen. 85, 6 (*cf.* § 180, 1, *a*, *α*).

(γ) Qualifying Verb being introduced by Conjunction, such as **እንዘ** &c.

(*γ*) Besides, for the cases mentioned, and for the attachment of every auxiliary qualification which has to be expressed by a Verb,—whether it be a qualification of Kind, Circumstance or Time, Conjunctions are available (§ 189), such as **እንዘ** "while, when", **ሶበ** &c., and these are very frequently used for this purpose.

(δ) When the Qualifying Verb is represented by the Subst.-Inf. of Principal Verb.

(*δ*) A special Case occurs, when a Verb has its own Substantive-Infinitive in the Accusative associated with it by way of supplement (*cf.* § 174),—in which case the particular force of such a mode of expression may differ in character. The repetition of the Verb must either signify the repetition of the action itself, and thus express the gradual, continuous or complete nature of that action: **ወደምስሶ፡ ደምሰስዎሙ** "and destroying they destroyed them" (action gradually becoming complete) Judges 20, 43; **አብዝኆ፡ አበዝኆ** "multiplying I will multiply" ('I will make many and ever more') Gen. 3, 16; 16, 10; or else such repetition is meant to direct forcibly the attention of the hearer to the conception, and lend strong emphasis to the Verb. The latter use of the Infinitive is the more frequent of the two by far: **ሰሚዐ፡ ትሰምዑ፡ ወኢትሌብዉ** "you hear indeed, but you do not understand" Matt. 13, 14; Mark 4, 12; **ባርኮ፡ እባርከከ** "bless thee I will" Gen. 22, 17; **ነጊሠኑ፡ ትነግሥ፡ ላዕሌነ** "shalt thou indeed reign over us?" Gen. 37, 8; **ወቀቲለሰ፡ ኢንቀትለከ** "but kill thee we shall not" Judges 15, 13; **አእምሮ፡ አእምር** "know thou assuredly" Gen. 15, 13; farther,

Gen. 20, 18; 50, 16; Judges 8, 25; [እምሕሎ ፡ እምሕለከ *Kebra Nag.* 166b 13*sq.*], &c. The Infinitive stands at the beginning of such clauses, as these examples show, but it may also be put at the end, particularly when it indicates the continuance of the action: **ከመ ፡ ያምልክዎ ፡ አምልኮ ፡ ለእግዚአብሔር** "that they may ever continue to worship God" Josh. 22, 27; also **ዘከነ ፡ ከዊኖ** "whatever it may be" Ex. 22, 8; Gal. 5, 10; **አንክሩ ፡ አንክሮ** "wonder ye greatly" *Gadla Yārēd* (ed. Conti Rossini, 1904) p. 5, l. 5.

2. Second Verb determining the Contents of the Leading Verb:— (a) In the form of the Acc. of the Subst.-Inf. of Subordinate Verb.; or (β) in the form of a Finite Verb introduced by a Conjunction.

§ 182. 2. The Subordinate Verb may have the force of a Determination of the *Contents* of the leading Verb, or the force of an *Object* thereto, and then it is always to be thought of as in the Objective Case.

(*a*) The most obvious mode of union in this case, is that by which (*α*) the Subordinate Verb takes the form of the Accusative of the Substantive-Infinitive. This mode is allowable and very common, even when the Subordinate Verb has objects depending on it. The Infinitive in that case is either regarded more in the light of a Noun governing its Object by means of the Construct State relation (v. p. 463) or more in the light of a Verb, although there is no necessity that it should take the Gerund-form, governing its Object in the Accusative or by means of Prepositions. First of all, there are certain verbs which convey no sense by themselves, —viz. Auxiliary Verbs, and particularly Verbs of *Being able*, or *Being unable*—, but which connect themselves for the most part with such Infinitives: **ኢይክል ፡ ኀዲገ ፡ አቡሁ** "he cannot leave his father" Gen. 44, 22; **ወነፍሰክሙሰ ፡ ኢይክሉ ፡ ቀቲለ** "but are not able to kill your soul"; **ዘይክል ፡ ነፍሰ ፡ ወሥጋ ፡ ኅቡረ ፡ አሕጕሎ** "who is able to destroy soul and body together" Matt. 10, 28; 9, 15, 28; 7, 18; 5, 14, 36; 3, 9; **ስእንክሙ ፡ ተጊሀ** "could ye not watch?" Matt. 26, 40; **ስእነ ፡ አውፅኦቶ** "could not we cast him out?" Matt. 17, 19; Josh. 17, 12; and farther, other Verbs in which the idea leans to that of *Being able*, like "to know" ('how to do &c.'), "to love" ('to do &c.'), "to be accustomed" ('to do &c.'): **ያለምድ ፡ አሕይዎ ፡ አሐደ** "he was accustomed to grant one person his life" Matt. 27, 15; **ታአምሩ ፡ ሠናየ ፡ ሀብተ ፡ ወሂበ** "ye know how to give good gifts" Matt. 7, 11; 16, 3; **ያፈቅሩ ፡ ቀዊመ ፡ ወጸልዮ** "they love to stand and to pray" Matt. 6, 5; farther, Verbs of *Hindering, Refusing, and Being unwilling*—(in contrast with which, Verbs of *Willing*, as expressing a purpose, have mostly a different manner of connection): ትከልእዎሙ ፡ በዊእ "ye hinder them from entering" Matt. 23,14 (*cf.* § 176,3,*a*); Hen. 63,10; ኢትክልእዎሙ ፡ መጺአ ፡ ኀቤየ "forbid them not to come unto me" Matt. 19,14; Judges 15,1; ራሔል ፡ ተአበ ፡ ተናገዘ። "Rachel refuses to be comforted" Matt. 2,18; አበዩከ ፡ ወሂበ "they refuse to give thee" Gen. 24,41; 37,35; ርእዮቶ ፡ ክሕዱ ἰδεῖν ἀρνοῦνται Sap. 17,10 A. But several other Verbs also,—which in some cases admit of other methods of union,—may join to themselves the Accusative of the Infinitive: ነቢረ ፡ በየማንየ ፡ አኮ ፡ አነ ፡ ዘእሁብ "to sit on my right hand it is not I who grant" Matt. 20, 23; ጠበወ ፡ ተስእሎቶ "ventured (3 *sing.*) to ask him" Matt. 22,46; ረስዑ ፡ ነሢአ ፡ ኅብስተ "they had forgotten to take bread with them" Matt. 16,5; ይጐንዲ ፡ አቲወ "he delayeth to come" Matt. 24,48; ፈርሀ ፡ ሐዊረ ፡ ህየ "he was afraid to go thither" Matt. 2,22; 1,20; Gen. 19,30; ትኀድጉ ፡ ተሊዎቶ ፡ ለእግዚአብሔር "(in that) ye cease to follow the Lord" Josh. 22,16, 18, 29; Gen. 11,6; *cf.* besides, § 180,1, *a*, *β*. It may happen too that the governing Verb is supplemented beforehand by a Suffix referring to the Object of the subordinate Verb,—a practice which again forms a delicate turn in the Ethiopic language, similar to that which is described in § 178: እክሎ ፡ ነሢቶቶ ፡ ለቤተ ፡ እግዚአብሔር "I am able to destroy the house of God" Matt. 26,61; መኑ ፡ ይክሎ ፡ ለዝንቱ ፡ ገቢረ 4 Esr. 2,6. Indeed the governing Verb may even attract completely to itself the Object of the dependent verb, if that Object is merely a pronoun: ስእንዎ ፡ ፈውሶ "they could not heal him" Matt. 17,16 (for ስእኑ ፡ ፈውሶቶ).—The subordinated Infinitive may pass into a finite Verb, as the sentence goes on, and *vice versâ*, *e. g.*: ተመይጦሙ ፡ ለሐዊር ፡ ወጐጕአ ፡ ፈነውዎሙ "turning to go and pursue them more swiftly" Sap. 19,2; ይደልዎሙ ፡ ይትከልአሙ ፡ ብርሃን ፡ ወተሞቅሖ ፡ ውስተ ፡ ጽልመት "they deserve to be shut out from the light and to be cast into the chains of darkness" Sap. 18,4.—In the same way also the Subject-Infinitive may be passed on, *e. g.* 4 Esr. 13,20.

Strangely enough even Impersonal Verbs (§ 192) may be completed by an Infinitive in the Accusative, though other constructions may be employed. Thus in particular ኮነ is often joined to the Accusative of the Infinitive, when it has the meaning of ἔστι, ἔξεστι, "it is possible" or "it is lawful *or* permitted": ዘኢይከውን ፡ ገቢረ "which is not lawful to do" Matt. 12,2; ይከውን ፡

በሰንበት ፡ ገቢረ ፡ ሠናይ "it is lawful to do good on the Sabbath-day" Matt. 12,12; 12,10; Deut. 22,19; ኢይትዐጸብከ ፡ ፈንዎቶ "let it not seem hard to thee (§ 178) to let him go free" Deut. 15,18; እመ ፡ ኢይትከሀል ፡ ዝንቱ ኀሊፈ "if it is not possible that this pass away" Matt. 26,42; ኢኮነ ፡ ሠናየ ፡ ነሢአ ፡ ኅብስተ ፡ ውሉድ ፡ ወወሂበ ፡ ለከለባት "it is not proper to take the children's bread and to give it to the dogs" Matt. 15,26; ይቀልል ፡ በእተ ፡ (§ 124, beginning) ገመል ፡ እንተ ፡ ስቍረተ ፡ መርፍእ ፡ እምባዕል ፡ በዊአ ፡ መንግሥተ ፡ እግዚአብሔር "it is easier for a camel to go through the eye of a needle than for a rich man to enter into the kingdom of God" Matt. 19,24 (*cf.* 9,5); ኮንክሙ ፡ ዐዊዶቶ ፡ ለዝንቱ ፡ ደብር ('there has been for you enough of the compassing of this mountain') "you have compassed this mountain long enough" Deut. 2,3([1]). Such unions are explained most readily by the consideration that in thought the impersonal turn of the Verb is replaced by a personal one (*e. g.* "it is lawful" is thought of as "we may" *or* "one may"). Meanwhile, this construction is not absolutely necessary: the complement may be applied to such verbs in the Subject- or Nominative-case, and then they cease to be impersonal: ሊተ ፡ ይኄይሰኒ ፡ መዊት "it is better for me to die" 1 Cor. 9,15; እሉ ፡ ቀዳሚ ፡ ይኄይስ ፡ ብሂል Hen. 37,3; የዐጽብ ፡ ወሊደ "it becomes hard for her to bring to the birth" Hen. 62,4; አከለክሙ ፡ በሊዐ "it is sufficient for you,—to eat" Hen. 102,9 (*cf.* Hebr. 9,27; 10,31). In the case of Infinitives in *ō* it is impossible to discern which of the two constructions they are following, *e. g.* in አከ ፡ ሠናይ ፡ አውስቦ "then it is not good to marry" Matt. 19,10, inasmuch as አውስቦ may be Nominative as well as Accusative.

On the Accusative with the Infinitive after Verbs of *Saying* and *Perceiving*, v. § 190.

(*β*) When this, the most obvious form of union, is not found practicable, a Conjunction like ከመ, ዘ, እስመ or other similar form, is employed, *e. g.* "he said, *that* &c."; *cf.* § 203.

(*b*) If the verb to be subordinated is related to the principal verb,—rather *as the intended result* or *the aim*—, it takes the following forms.

([1]) An instance in which ሀሎ is first construed with the Subjunctive, and afterwards with the Accusative of the Infinitive, is met with in Sap. 16,28 A.

(*b*) Forms adopted by Second Verb to express intended Result or Aim of Principal Verb:— (α) Subst.-Inf. with ለ prefixed; (β) Subjunctive without Conjunction.

(*α*) The connection may be effected,—though this method is seldom adopted upon the whole,—by means of ለ followed by the Substantive-Infinitive, (v. also § 183), *e. g.*: ዘኢይከውኖ ፡ ለበሊዕ "which was not lawful for him to eat" Matt. 12, 4 (1).

(*β*) Most frequently the Subjunctive is employed, which is subordinated to the principal verb, just like an Accusative, directly, that is, without any Conjunction. It occurs particularly after verbs of *Willing, Wishing, Begging, Commanding, Permitting, Promising* and *Beginning*: አዘዘ ፡ የሀቡ "he commanded (that) they should give" Matt. 19, 7; 27, 64; ይቤ ፡ ይትዐቀቡ "he said ('commanded that') they should beware" Matt. 16, 12; Hen. 69, 14; እመ ፡ ትፈቅድ ፡ ፍጹመ ፡ ትኩን "if thou wilt be perfect" Matt. 19, 21; 12, 46; 14, 5; Josh. 24, 15; Hen. 39, 8; እመ ፡ ፈቀድከ ፡ ይዕበይ &c. *Chrest.* p. 42, line 6; ፈተዉ ፡ ይርአዩ "they have desired to see" Matt. 13, 17; የኀሥሡ ፡ ይትናገሩከ "they seek to speak with thee" Matt. 12, 47; ኅድጉ ፡ ይልሀቁ ፡ ኅቡረ "let them grow together" Matt. 13, 30; 24, 43; 27, 49; ሰአልዎ ፡ ያርእዮሙ "they asked him that he should show them" Matt. 16, 1; አብሐኒ ፡ እንብብ "suffer me to speak" Gen. 18, 32; 31, 7; አስተብቍዕዎ ፡ ይኅልፍ "they besought him that he should depart" Matt. 8, 34; የሀብክን ፡ እግዚአብሔር ፡ ትርከባ ፡ ዕረፍተ "the Lord grant (you) that you may find rest" Ruth 1, 9; አኀዘ ፡ ይስብክ "he began to preach" Matt. 4, 17; አኃዘ ፡ (for አኀዘ ፡) ይሰብሖ ፡ ወይቀድሶ ፡ ወይዘምር ፡ ለእግዚአብሔር "he began to laud, bless and praise God" *Gadla Yārēd*, p. 6, l. 24 *sq.*, and very frequently. The same construction is found also with many other verbs of like signification, *e. g.*: መሀርዎሙ ፡ ይዕቀቡ "teach them to observe" Matt. 28, 20 (with the secondary idea of 'charging'); አልጸቀት ፡ ትሙት "she was at the point of death" ('was about to die') Mark 5, 23; ተበዋሕኩ ፡ እትናገር "I have taken upon me to speak" Gen. 18, 31; also with ክሀለ, *e. g.* in Hen. 14, 21 (2); Hexaëm. 9, 20; and with other words that suggest *Ability*, *e. g.* ወ ኢኮነ ፡ ለሙ ፡ አእምሮ ፡ ይፃኡ ፡ ወኢይዕርጉ Hexaëm. 9, 16 *sq.*; and with Verbs of *Hoping*, *e. g.* ተሰፈወ ፡ ያዕርፍ (var. ያዐርፍ)

---

(1) לבלתי שתות־יין Jer. 35, 14, even with its negation, is rendered in the *Cod. Francof.* by ለኢሰትዮ ፡ ወይን.

(2) [This passage, Hen. 14, 21, exhibits the peculiarity of presenting in the same verse and with the same meaning ክሀለ followed by an Inf. and ክሀለ followed by a Subjunctive. TR.]

Sir. 11, 19.—In the very same way too Impersonal Verbs are connected with the Subj. (v. *supra, a*): **ይኤድመክሙ ፡ ትረስዩ** "it pleases you to do" Josh. 9, 23; **ኢኮነ ፡ ሠናየ ፡ ይንበር ፡ በሕቲቱ** "it is not good that he should be alone" Gen. 2, 18; **ኢይከውነከ ፡ ታውስባ** "it is not permitted thee to take her to wife" Matt. 14, 4; Deut. 22, 29; **ኢይደልወኒ ፡ እድንን** "it befits not me to stoop down" *or* "I am not worthy to stoop down" Mark 1, 7; Matt. 3, 11, 15; **ይኄይሰከ ፡ ትባእ** "it is better for thee to enter" Matt. 18, 8, 9; **አኮ ፡ መፍትው ፡ ይሑሩ** ("it is not necessary that they go away") "they need not depart" Matt. 14, 16; 23, 23; [*Kebra Nag.* 46 b 14]. To this class belongs also **ሀለዎ** with the Subjunctive (§ 89).

(γ) Subjunctive with Conjunction.

(γ) In most of the instances, however, cited under (β), the Subjunctive may also be introduced by the conjunction **ከመ**:— **አስተብቍዕዎ ፡ ከመ ፡ ይልክፉ** "they besought him that they might touch" Matt. 14, 36; **ኢይደግም ፡ ከመ ፡ እፌኑ** "I will not send again" Hen. 10, 22; **ይቤለነ ፡ ከመ ፡ ኢንብላዕ** "he told us that we must not eat" Gen. 3, 3; **መሐለ ፡ ከመ ፡ የሀባ** "he promised with an oath to give her" Matt. 14, 7; **ገሠጾሙ ፡ ከመ ፡ አልቦ ፡ ለዘይንግሩ** "he charged them to tell no man" Matt. 16, 20; v. also § 203. Even after Impersonal Verbs **ከመ** with the Subjunctive may be employed: **ይኄይሰከ ፡ ከመ ፡ ይትሐጐል** "it is better for thee that (one member) perish" Matt. 5, 29, 30; **ኢይትፈቀድ ፡ ከመ ፡ ይትሐጐል** "it is not desired that (one) should perish" Matt. 18, 14; **ኢይደልወኒ ፡ ከመ ፡ አንተ ፡ ትባእ** "it is not befitting me (*i. e.* 'I am not worthy') that thou shouldest come" Matt. 8, 8; **ብዉኅ ፡ ሎቱ ፡ ከመ** with the Subjunctive, "he has power to—" Mark 2, 10. In the same way we have **ኮነ** with **ከመ** and the Subjunctive, Deut. 24, 4. Even **ክህለ** is connected thus, though very rarely: **መኑ ፡ ዘይክል ፡ ከመ ፡ የሐሊ ፡ ሕሊናሁ** "Who is able to think his own thoughts?" Hen. 93, 11.

(δ) Usage with Verbs of Beginning and Ceasing.

(δ) Verbs of *Beginning* and *Ceasing*, which in other languages are joined with a Participle, are very frequently connected in Ethiopic by **እንዘ**, and usually with an Imperfect coming after it: **አኀዙ ፡ እንዘ ፡ ይወግኡ ፡ ፩ ለካልኡ** "they began pushing one another" Hen. 87, 1; 89, 72. The same construction is found with **ወጠነ** Hen. 89, 15 &c.

§ 183. 3. Finally, just as a Verb may have dependent upon it, besides its proximate Object, other Nouns with the force of a Dative or of other relations, so a verb may be approached by a

3. Second Verb as Remote Object, specifying Direction, Purpose or Consequence of Principal Action:— (*a*) In the Infinitive.

second verb, not as a proximate Object, but as a more remote Object, in order to specify the *direction*, the *purpose* or the *consequence* of the principal action. This is particularly the case with Verbs of *Moving*, *Making*, *Giving*, *Constraining*, *and Occasioning*.

(*a*) The Verb, which has to be subordinated, may in these circumstances stand in the *Infinitive*. The idea of Purpose is thereupon given expression to, either by putting the Infinitive in the Accusative of Direction (§ 174): **ዘቦ ፡ እእዛነ ፡ ሰሚዐ ፡ ለይስማዕ** "who hath ears to hear, let him hear" Matt. 11,15; 13,9,43; **ፈርሀ ፡ ቤተ ፡ አቡሁ ፡ በዊአ ፡ መዓልተ** "he was afraid of his father's household, so as not to come by day" (*or* "should he come by day") Judges 6,27; **ኢትትሀከዩ ፡ ሐዊረ ፡ ወበዊአ** "be not ye slothful to depart and to come" Judges 18,9;—or again,—which is more usual—, by introducing the Infinitive through **ለ**:—"they shall show signs **ለአስሕቶ ፡** . . . **ለኅሩያንሂ** so as to lead astray . . . the very elect" Matt. 24, 24; **ይኩኑ ፡ ለአብርሆ** "let them serve to lighten" Gen. 1,15; **በጻሕነ ፡ ለኀዲር** "we came to put up (for the night)" Gen. 43, 21; **እስርዎሙ ፡ ከላስስተ ፡ ለአንድዶቶሙ** "bind them in sheaves, to burn them" Matt. 13,30; **አጽንዐት ፡ ለሐዊር** "she insisted upon going" Ruth 1,18; Gen. 9,11; 18, 2; 37,18: also Gen. 2, 9.

(*b*) In the Subjunctive without Conjunction.

(*b*) But much more frequently still, the Verb which has to be subordinated, is added immediately, in the Subjunctive: **ፈነወ ፡ አግብርተ ፡ ይጸውዑ** "he sent forth servants to call" Matt. 22, 3, 7; Josh. 8,2; **ወለአከኒ ፡ እንግርከ ፡ ዘንተ** "and he commissioned me to tell this to thee" *Gadla Ferē-Mikā'ēl* (ed. Turaieff, 1905), p. 9, l. 3; **መጽአ ፡ ይኅሥሥ** "he came to seek" Matt. 18,11; [**ዘኍለፈ ፡ ይኅሥሥ** "who was travelling about in search of ('to seek')" *Chrest.* p. 93, l. 24]; **ኢይረድ ፡ ይንሣእ** "let him not come down, to take—" Matt. 24,17; **ዐርጉ ፡ ይትቃተልዎሙ** "they went up to fight against them" Josh 22,12; [**ተንሥአ ፡ ይቅትሎሙ** "he rose to kill them" *Kebra Nag.* 64 a 15]; **ዐበጥዎ ፡ ይጹር** "they compelled him to carry—" Matt. 27,32; **ወሀብዎ ፡ ይስተይ** "they gave him to drink" Matt. 27,34; Gen. 3,12; **ኀሬክምዎ ፡ ለእግዚእ ፡ ታምልክዎ** "ye have chosen the Lord, to serve him" Josh. 24,22; **ወእመ ፡ ከነከ ፡ ትቅትለኒ** "and if thou must of necessity slay me"='وان كان لا بد لك من قتلي' G. Ad. 89, 3; **ይሬስዮ ፡ ይትነፋኅ** "it (wine) makes it (the body) become bloated" *Chrest.* p. 41, line 13; **ሰፍሐት ፡ እደዊሃ ፡ ኀበ ፡ እግዚአብሔር ፡ ትኅሥሥ ፡ እምኔሁ** G. Ad. 8,8 *sq.*; specially too in the case of verbs of *Guarding against*: **ዑቁ ፡ ኢትንሥኡ** "beware lest ye take" Josh. 6, 18.

(c) In the Subjunctive with ከመ.

(*c*) **ከመ** with the Subjunctive is also available, however, in this case, and it is occasionally made use of, although the method of connection without **ከመ** is more elegant, *e. g.*: **ፈነወ ፡ አግብርተ ፡ ከመ ፡ ይንሥኡ** "he sent forth servants, to fetch" Matt. 21, 34; **አገበሮሙ ፡ ከመ ፡ ይዕረጉ** "he obliged them to go up" Matt. 14, 22. The difference between the constructions in (*b*) and (*c*) is shown in the following example: **አምጽእ ፡ ሊተ ፡ እብላዕ ፡ ወከመ ፡ ትባርከ ፡ ነፍስየ** "bring (it) me (1) to eat (2) that my soul may bless (thee)" Gen. 27, 4. And,—speaking generally—, the less an indication of purpose is involved in the fundamental idea of the Principal Verb, and the more loosely such purpose is added to it in conception, the more readily is choice made of the looser connection by means of **ከመ**.

4. Second Verb subordinated as Subst.-Inf., with the help of Prepositions.

4. Verbs, just like Nouns, are subordinated to Verbs with the help of *Prepositions*. The Verb to be subordinated must in that case take the form of the Substantive-Infinitive, which is governed by the Preposition, *e. g.* **ነሳሕኩ ፡ በእንተ ፡ ፈጢሮትየ ፡ ኪያሆሙ** "I repent of my having created them" Gen. 6, 7; **ኢያእመረ ፡ በሰኪቦታ ፡ ወበተንሥኦታ** "he perceived not when she lay down nor when she arose" Gen. 19, 33; **አስረሐቶ ፡ በነቢብ ፡ ኵላ ፡ ሌሊተ** "she wearied him with talking the whole night" Judges 16, 16; **ውስተ ፡ ወሊድ** "in giving birth" Gen. 35, 16; **ለመዊት** "to die" ('for dying') Gen. 47, 29 &c. Instead of such a construction, which is not farther distinguished from the subordination of any Noun to a Verb by means of a Preposition (§ 179), the action to be subordinated may also be expressed by a finite tense introduced by the Conjunction which corresponds to the preposition concerned,—as in **ነስሐ ፡ በእንተ ፡ ዘገብሮ ፡ ለሰብእ** "he repented that he had created man" Gen. 6, 6 (*cf. infra* § 203).

III. COMBINATION OF NOUNS WITH ONE ANOTHER.

(*a*) The Genitive Relation:— 1. The Construct State.

§ 184. The only two possible ways of joining individual words together are, in general terms, by Co-ordination and Subordination. Even in the department of Verbs, Co-ordination may take place, but its appearance there (v. the instances cited in §§ 180, 1, *a*, *α* and 181, *β*) is far less common than in the department of Nouns, in which both methods of Word-connection frequently occur.

1. SUBORDINATION OF NOUNS.

The characteristic device for subordinating one Noun to another is,—by § 144,—the Genitive Relation. When this does not suffice, the two Nouns may be referred to one another by the intervention of Prepositions; and with certain classes of Nouns which approximate the Verb, the subordination may be effected even by the Accusative.

(a) *The Genitive Relation.*

1. The first device we meet with, for expressing the Genitive Relation, is the *Status Constructus*, the *Construct State* (§ 144). All Nouns in Ethiopic (Substantives, Adjectives, Infinitives, Numerals) may take the Construct State, with the exception of Pronouns and Proper Names. Other languages may, at least in case of need, admit even of Proper Names in the Constr. State; but Ethiopic has the less need of this, as it possesses other current expedients for indicating the relation of the Genitive. In like manner all kinds of Nouns are capable of becoming dependent upon a Constr. State, *e. g.* ማሕመመ ፡ ወሊድ "the pains of child-birth" Gen. 35, 17; መዋዕለ ፡ ወሊዶታ "the days for her giving birth" Gen. 25, 24; አዋልደ ፡ ውእቱ ፡ ብሔር "the daughters of that land" Gen. 34, 1; ደመ ፡ ዝክቱ "the blood of that (man)" Gen. 9, 6; ወለተ ፡ መኑ ፡ አንቲ "whose daughter art thou?" Gen. 24, 23; አግብርቲሁ "his servants"; even ቀትለ ፡ ቀዲሙ "the battle of the 'at-first'" *i. e.* "the earlier battle" Judges 20, 39; also Relatives: እደ ፡ ዘይትዔገል "the hand of him who oppresses". And the *meaning* which attaches to this relation is just as wide and manifold as the meaning found in the word-compounding process,—in the case of Nouns—, in Indo-European languages.

(a) Relation of Possession. (*a*) It is most frequently employed to express the *Genitive* in the narrower sense, or the relation of Possession, and Being-possessed, as in ንጉሠ ፡ ምድር "the king of the land"; አቡሁ "his father". In such a case, if the word which stands in the Constr. State is the name of a Person or of an Object, the dependent word is always *Genitivus subjectivus*; but if the first word is an Abstract word, the dependent word may be either *Genitivus sub-*

jectivus or *objectivus*: ፍርሀተ ፡ ብእሲ meaus either "the fear of the man",—*i. e.* 'the fear which the man experiences', or "the fear with respect to the man"—*i. e.* 'the fear with which the man is regarded'; እምግርማሁ "for fear of him" Matt. 14, 26; ማዕቀፍየ "an offence unto me" Matt. 16, 23; ኵነኔ ፡ ኵሉ "judgment on all" Hen. 22, 8. Even Adjectives may take such Constr. State, if they are understood rather in the sense of Substantives: ኀያላኒ ፡ ፈርዖን "Pharaoh's men of power" Gen. 50, 4; ቅዱሱ(1) ፡ ለእግዚእ "the Holy One of God" Mark 1, 24. Allied to the Possessive relation is *the relation of the Part to the Whole,* as in ሠናይቱ(1) ፡ ለሰብእ "the best part ('the best') of men" Hen. 20, 5; ቀዳሚ ፡ ወልድየ "the first of my children" Gen. 49, 3; and this relation then serves to express the Superlative (§ 187). In the same sense there may be subordinated to a Noun the same Noun in the Genitive, in order to raise the idea concerned to its very highest degree, or to exhibit it in its totality: ለዓለመ ፡ ዓለም "to eternity of eternity" (*or* 'to eternities of eternities', '*in secula seculorum*') *i. e.* "for all eternity" Hen. 10, 12; so too ትውልደ ፡ ትውልድ Hen. 10, 14; እሳተ ፡ እሳት "a sea of fire" ('an immense fire', literally 'a fire of fire') Hen. 14, 22 (2); ዕመቀ ፡ ዕመቅ ('depth of depth') βαθὺ βάθος Eccles. 7, 24; ከራሚ ፡ ከራሚ ('old store') Lev. 26, 10 &c. (*b*) But farther a Noun in the Constr. State may in a different fashion be defined by a second Noun: as when, for instance, the first Noun expresses the general notion and is limited by the second, which indicates the particular case: ሀገረ ፡ ኢየሩሳሌም "the city of Jerusalem"; በዓለ ፡ ፋሲካ "the feast of Passover"; ዕለተ ፡ ሰንበት "the Sabbath-day"; ዕፀ ፡ በለስ "fig-tree"; ሐሳዌ ፡ መሲሕ "a pretender of a Messias", "a false Christ" 1 John 2, 18; ኅብስተ ፡ ናእት "unleavened bread" Judges 6, 20. Co-ordination, it is true, may also be made use of for words which stand in this relation to one another (§ 189); but yet union by means of the Construct State is likewise of common occurrence. The latter method is even employed,—although to be sure but rarely,—to connect an Adjective with a Substantive. In fact the Substantive, by subordinating an Adjective to itself through the assumption of the Construct State, limits its own

(*b*) Genitive of Limitation.

(1) [*Cf. supra* § 153 *sqq.* for Dillmann's view of the Constr. St. relation as illustrated in the attachment of Suff. Prons. to the Noun.—tr.]

(2) [Flemming reads only እሳት, not እሳተ ፡ እሳት in this passage. tr.]

general notion by a particular determination of species. In meaning, however, a Word-group which is connected in this way, differs from one which is connected by mere co-ordination,—just as in German, *Grosskönig* differs in meaning from *grosser König*. Thus we read: ሥርወ፡ ሕሩም ("sinew of the forbidden") "sinew forbidden" Gen. 32, 26, 33; ማየ፡ ጥዑም "fresh water" Lev. 14, 50—52; Numb. 5, 17; Deut. 8, 15; ሀገረ፡ ነኪር "foreign city" Judges 19, 12; አማልክተ፡ ነኪር "strange gods" Gen. 35, 2; Josh. 24, 14, 23; ገብረ፡ ዕብራዊ "Hebrew servant" Gen. 39, 14 (F); አበ፡ አረጋዊ "old father" Gen. 44, 20 (FH); አማልክተ፡ ባዕድ "other gods", "secondary gods" Josh. 23, 16 (as contrasted with Josh. 24, 2, 16, 20, where we have ባዕደ፡ አማልክተ); Lev. 13, 37; ምድረ፡ ነኪር *Chrest.* p. 11, l. 23 *sq.*; ቃለ፡ መዐርዒር *ibid.* p. 13, line 14(¹); [for a number of other instances v. *Kebra Nag.*, '*Introd.*' p. XVIII]. The invariable mode of connecting the Possessives ዚአየ &c. by means of the Construct State of the preceding word belongs properly also to this section (§ 150, *b*). (*c*) Again, the dependent word may denote the Material or Origin of the first Noun, or some property attaching to it, and so this Genitive relation is especially employed to replace Descriptive words, *i. e.* Adjectives, Participles &c., which may be wanting: ታቦተ፡ ዕፅ "an ark of wood" ('wooden'); ሰይፈ፡ እሳት "a fiery sword" Gen. 3, 24; ብእሲ፡ ሐቅል *ἄνθρωπος ἄγροικος* Gen. 16, 12; ቈጽለ፡ ዘይት "olive-leaf" Gen. 8, 11; ነፍስ፡ ሕይወት "a living soul" Gen. 9, 12; ዕደወ፡ ስም "men of renown" Gen. 6, 4; ደቂቀ፡ ኀይል "vigorous young men" Judges 18, 2; ዕፀወ፡ መዐዛ "odoriferous trees" Hen. 24, 3; ነገረ፡ በከ "an idle word" Hen. 49, 4. And in particular, to indicate Adjectives, or other conceptional words that are wanting, the words ባዕል "lord, *or* master" and ወልድ (²) "son" are made use of,—the former in certain combinations, such as ባዕለ፡ ጸጋ "generous" (*lit.* 'master of gifts'); ባዕለ፡ መጽሐፍ "skilled in writing"; ባዕለ፡ ዕዳ "a creditor", and the latter as an expression for "old" in data of age, as ወልደ፡ ፻ወ፲ ዓመት

(c) Genitive denoting Material or Origin.

(¹) Bezold, '*Zeitschr. f. Keilschriftf.*' II, p. 316, thinks he has found something similar in Assyrian; [v. also Fleischer, '*Zeitschr. f. Ass.*' I, p. 428 *sq.* Delitzsch, '*Assyr. Gramm.*', § 122, 2]; v. on the other hand Lehmann, *Zeitschr. f. Keilschriftf.* II, p. 437.

(²) Yet perhaps only in passages where the Ground-text in Hebr. and Greek has this form of expression [or where ባዕል is a translation of the Arabic ذو or صاحب].

"110 years old" (*lit.* "son of 110 years') Judges 2,8. (*d*) Finally, the Construct State expresses also many other conceivable determinations of condition, as in ዕፀው ፡ መሥዋዕት "wood for the sacrifice" ("sacrificial wood") Gen. 22,6; and particularly, when the Noun in the Constr. State is nearly related in force to the Verb. Of this class are Participles and Verbal Adjectives, which, on taking the Constr. St., may be more exactly specified in one fashion or other, by means of Nouns following, *e. g.*: ዕቡየ ፡ ዐይን "of haughty countenance" (*lit.* 'arrogant of eye'); ሥሡዐ ፡ ልብ "of insatiable heart" Ps. 100,7; ርቱዐ ፡ ሃይማኖት ('sound in the faith') ὀρθό-δοξος; ምሉአ ፡ ጸጋ "full of grace"; ርሑቀ ፡ መዐት "far from anger" ('slow to anger') Hen. 40,9; እኍዘ ፡ ጋኔን "possessed of the devil" Mark 3,11; ርጉዘ ፡ ገቦ "pierced in the side"; ይቡሳነ ፡ ልብ "hard-hearted"; ሠናየ ፡ መዊእ "victorious", "triumphant"; ቅሩብየ "near me" Gen. 45,10; ሕያዋነ ፡ ሕይወት ፡ ዘለዓለም "living an everlasting life" Hen. 15,6; ገባርያነ ፡ ሰላም "peace-makers" Matt. 5,9(¹). To this class belong, farther, those Infinitives and conceptional words of an Infinitive character, which when in the Constr. St. may subordinate to themselves any Object that is governed in the Accusative by their respective verbs: ፍዳሃ ፡ ለኵሉ ፡ እኪት "requital for all the evil" Gen. 50,15; ሥልጣነ ፡ ኵሉ "dominion over all" Hen. 9,5; ቀቲለ ፡ ነፍስ "to take a life" (*lit.* 'to kill a soul') Matt. 19,18; አክብሮ ፡ አበ ፡ ወእሞ "to honour father and mother" Matt. 19,19; በዊአ ፡ ሀገር "to enter into the city" Mark 1,45; በጺሖ ፡ ኤፍራታ "to arrive at Ephrath" Gen. 35, 16; ከዊነ ፡ በኵር "the being first-born" Gen. 25,32 *sq.*; ወሪደ ፡ ግብጽ "to go down into Egypt" Gen. 46,3; መኑ ፡ ይክል ፡ ነጊረ ፡ ምሕረቱ፡ Sir. 18,5.

(d) Genitive indicating other Determinations of Condition.

An entire sentence may also supply the place of the dependent Noun. In particular, words conveying Notions of Time are frequently connected, in the Constr. St., with an entire sentence, and constitute thus an analogue to those prepositions, which are also used as conjunctions (v. § 170). For example: በሳኒት ፡ በልዑ "on the second day—(of the—'they have eaten')— after they had eaten" Josh. 5,12; ጊዜ ፡ ይገውሕ ፡ ጽባሕ "about the time when the

(¹) The addition of a Suffix to the Noun determining the Constr. St. is worthy of notice: thus "fair of face" is not only rendered by ላሕየ ፡ ገጽ, but also by ላሕየ ፡ ገጹ, *e. g.* in *Chrest.* p. 38, line 2.

day was dawning" ("at daybreak") Josh. 6, 15; ጊዜ ፡ የዐርብ ፡ ፀሓይ "at the time when the sun was setting" Mark 1, 32; ዕለተ ፡ ተወልደ ፡ ፈርዖን "Pharaoh's birthday" Gen. 40, 20; በዕለቱ ፡ አኅደግዎ ፡ ጥበ "on the day that they weaned him" Gen. 21, 8.

Rules observed in the Use of the Constr. St. Relation.

§ 185. Now when words are in this way bound in one group, by means of the Constr. St., it is obvious (§ 144) that the dependent word must come immediately after the governing one, seeing that a portion of the force of the entire relation lies precisely in the immediate connection of the two words. No other word then can be inserted between any two that stand in the Constr. St.-relation (1). Accordingly, if the governing word adopts an additional determination, *e. g.* an Adjective, this must come before or after the entire group: ዐቢይ ፡ ዐጸደ ፡ ወይን or ዐጸደ ፡ ወይን ፡ ዐቢይ, but not ዐጸደ ፡ ዐቢይ ፡ ወይን "a large vineyard"; or, if the governing word is associated with a Possessive which has to be expressed by a Suffix, the Suffix is not attached to the Construct State (2), like ንዋየከ ፡ ሐቅል, but either it is put at the end of the whole group, as in ንዋየ ፡ ሐቅልከ "thy field-apparatus" ('weapons') Gen. 27, 3; መሥዋዕተ ፡ መድኀኒትክሙ "your thank-offering" Josh. 22, 27; ቤተ ፡ አቡከ "thy father's house" Gen. 12, 1; ዐጽመ ፡ ገቦሁ "his ('bone of the side') rib" Gen. 2, 22; ክልኤሆሙ ፡ ሊቀ ፡ ኅፅዋኒሁ "his two chief eunuchs" Gen. 40, 2, or the Constr. St.-Relation is replaced by another mode of denoting the Genitive (v. *infra*, § 186). Farther, it is unusual for one and the same Genitive to be dependent upon two words, in such manner that both should be set in the Constr. St., and the dependent word attached only to the latter of the two.

---

(1) [Short enclitic words, however, may sometimes be found between a Constr. St. and the word which it governs (v. Praetorius, '*Aethiop. Gr.*', p. 115, where other exceptional appearances are also noticed). R. H. Charles, '*Book of Jubilees*', 1895, *Introd.*, finds fault with Dillmann for omitting to note that demonstrative prons., the pronominal adj. ኵሉ and numerals, occasionally intervene between the Constr. St. and its dependent noun. But in some of these instances, if not in all, Dillmann would probably have had respect to the Substantive-genesis of ኵሉ &c., and have regarded these words in such circumstances as being themselves governed directly by the immediately preceding Constr. St. tr.]

(2) And yet we read in Numb. 18, 31: ግብረክሙ ፡ ደብተራ ፡ ዘመርጡል "your reward for service in the tabernacle of testimony", for which other MSS. have ግብርክሙ ፡ ዘደብተራ ፡ ዘመርጡል.

"To a tribe and a family in Israel"—is not usually rendered: ለነገደ ፡ ወሕዝበ ፡ እስራኤል, but the dependent word must either be put after each of the words in the Constr. St., like ለነገደ ፡ እስራኤል ፡ ወለሕዝበ ፡ እስራኤል; or, if this arrangement seem too prolix, the word must be represented after the second of the pair by a Pron. suff. [as it is in Arabic]:—ለነገደ ፡ እስራኤል ፡ ወለሕዝቡ; or, lastly, the first governing word must stand in the Absolute State: ለነገድ ፡ ወለሕዝበ ፡ እስራኤል Judges 18, 19; እምድኅረ ፡ ኀልቀት ፡ ወተፍጻሜተ ፡ ደይን G. Ad. 39, 23; በተከ ፡ ወመተረ ፡ አሕማላት *M. Berh.* f. 9 *b*. Still, exceptions to this rule are met with: v. *Chrest.* p. XV [and Bezold, '*Zeitschr. f. Keilschriftf.*' II, p. 355, N. 1](¹). Two Genitives, however, may be dependent on one and the same Constr. St., at least if they are both of the same class, and have the same relation to the governing word, *e. g.* አድባረ ፡ ዛቡሎን ፡ ወንፍታሌም "the mountains of Zebulon and Naphthali" Matt. 4, 13; አፍራሰ ፡ ሰዶም ፡ ወጎሞር Gen. 14, 11; አምላከ ፡ ሰማይ ፡ ወምድር Gen. 24, 7; ተክለ ፡ ጽድቅ ፡ ወርትዕ Hen. 10, 16. In the very same way it is sufficient to set a Preposition once only, before a whole series of words joined together by "and", as *e. g.* in Gen. 13, 14; but it may also be repeated every time, as in Gen. 12, 1; 13, 2; 27, 16; 47, 17; and the repetition is absolutely necessary, if the word in the Genitive just preceding has been expressed by means of a Suffix, *e. g.* ለከ ፡ ወለዘርእከ "to thee and to thy seed" Gen. 24, 7 (²).

A word, dependent on a Constr. St., may itself again stand in the Constr. St., to govern another word, *e. g.* ተድባበ ፡ ቤተ ፡ መቅደስ "the pinnacle of the temple" (*lit.* 'of the house of the Sanctuary') Matt. 4, 5; ስመ ፡ አቡከ "the name of thy father" (*i. e.*, 'the name of the father of thee'); and thus, by farther extension, a longer concatenation of Nouns may be produced, bound together by the Constr. St.: መጽሐፈ ፡ ሚጠተ ፡ ብርሃናተ ፡ ሰማይ Hen. 72, 1;

(¹) *Cf.* also D. H. Müller, ZDMG XXIX, p. 117 *sqq.* on the Construct State in Minao-Sabaic.

(²) Ludolf correctly asserts, that in Poetry the Constr. St. may even be put after the word dependent upon it: v.,—besides እምወሰን ፡ ወሰነ, which he adduces as an example,—ስብሐተ ፡ መላእክት ፡ ለሐዋጺ *Chrest.* p. 36, line 9; ገድልኪ ፡ ወትሩፋተ *ibid.* p. 147, Str. 3, l. 3; and *cf. ibid.* p. XVI.

መላእክት ፡ ነገደ ፡ አብያት ፡ አበዊሆሙ ፡ ለሕዝብ Josh. 21,1; ዕበዩ ፡ ክብረ ፡ ስብሐት ፡ ቅድሳቲከ Ps. 144,5([1]).

When a word-group,—held together by the Constr. St., and answering to our Compounds in expressing only one single idea,—has to enter upon the plural, sometimes the one component is put in the plural, sometimes the other, and sometimes both([2]):—አርዌ ፡ ምድር ('beast of the earth') "serpent", forms the plural አራዊት ፡ ምድር; ዐጽመ ፡ ገቦ "rib" ('bone of the side') either ዐጽመ ፡ ገበዋት (*Org.*) or አዕጽምት ፡ ገቦ; ቤተ ፡ ክርስቲያን "Church", አብያተ ፡ ክርስቲያን or ቤተ ፡ ክርስቲያናት or አብያተ ፡ ክርስቲያናት; አበ ፡ ምኔት "abbot", አበ ፡ ምኔታት or አበወ ፡ ምኔታት; ሐሳውያነ ፡ መሲሕ "false Christs" Matt. 24,24; ሐሳውያነ ፡ ነቢያት "false prophets" Matt. 24,11; ውሉደ ፡ ዘማ "children of harlots" (*i. e.* of different ዘማ) Hen. 10,9 &c.

If the dependent word is to be thought of in our languages as furnished with the Definite Article, this determination may be expressed, in accordance with § 172, *c*, by a Suffix attached in advance to the Constr. St. and followed by ለ. *e. g.* ምሕረቱ ፡ ለእግዚአብሔር "the mercy of God"; ነገሮ ፡ ለኢየሱስ "the talk about Jesus" (*acc.*) Matt. 14,1; ከሠታ ፡ ለጠፈራ ፡ ለታቦት "he removed the covering of the ark" Gen. 8,13. In this case the dependent word which is introduced by ለ may even stand before the governing word, or be separated from it by several other words. And when several Genitives are strung together, the ለ may according to circumstances be repeated before every one, or on the other hand, when no misunderstanding can arise, it may be left out on the second occasion, as *e. g.* in Gen. 14,1. Now and then also, when the governing word assumes in addition a secondary determination, of an adjective form, Ethiopic goes so far in the freedom of its word-arrangement that the Suffix, referring to the Genitive, is appended to the Adjective instead of to the Substantive: ዝንቱ ፡ ዳግሙ ፡ ለእግዚእ ፡ ኢየሱስ ፡ ዘገብረ ፡ ተአምረ "*hoc est alterum domini Jesu, quod fecit miraculum*" John 4,54.

In Ethiopic the Definite Article of other languages is frequently expressed (v. § 172, *a*) by a Suff. Pron. appended to the

---

([1]) A remarkable arrangement is given in ቃለ ፡ ጸላኢተ ፡ ብከይ (for ቃለ ፡ ብከየ ፡ ጸላኢት) Sap. 18,10 A.

([2]) *Cf.* Hoffmann, '*Gr. Syr.*' p. 254. [*Cf.* farther Nöldeke, '*Syr. Gr.*' (*English Ed.*), p. 85 *sq.* TR.]

word which is to be determined, that is to say, by a Genitive relation. All Adjectives, in particular, when they are employed rather in the sense of Substantives, *i. e.* when they indicate a definite species of some general class of beings or objects which has been previously mentioned,—must be supplemented by a Suffix referring to the Substantive already named; and the Suffix is to be understood here in a partitive sense, *e. g.*: "the men of the city surrounded the house, both old and young" **ዐቢዮሙ ፡ ወንኡሶሙ** Gen. 19, 4, 11; "and to the second (son) he said" **ወለካልኡኒ ፡ ይቤ** (*i. e.* "to the second of it", namely 'of the family *or* pair of sons') Matt. 21, 30 ([1]); and the same usage prevails in the case of Numeral Adjectives (§ 191). But in other cases also, whenever a Noun,—standing in a partitive or possessive relation to another Noun previously mentioned,—is newly introduced into the sentence, the accuracy and nicety of the language demand that this reference be indicated by a Suffix, *e. g.* "he fled on foot" **ጕየ ፡ በእግሩ** ('with *or* on his feet') Judges 4, 15. In particular, certain conceptions, which are incomplete when they stand alone and which are dependent for their completion upon others, such as words specifying Place, Time, Measure, Number and Sort, must almost invariably be completed by another conception which they govern by means of the Construct St.; and when this latter conception is not directly combined with them, they assume a Suffix referring to it, *e. g.*: **ዑዳ ፡ ለምድር ፡ ውስተ ፡ ኑኃ ፡ ወርሕባ** "walk through the land in the length of it and breadth of it" Gen. 13, 17; "until it can no longer be numbered **እምነ ፡ ብዝኁ** for multitude" (*lit.* 'for its multitude') Gen. 16, 10; "a child, which she had born **በርሥአቲሃ** in her old age" Gen. 21, 7; v. also Gen. 37, 3; "I am small in number" **ውሑድ ፡ አነ ፡ በኍልቍየ** (*lit.* 'in my number') Gen. 34, 30; "until the end" **እስከ ፡ ተፍጻሜቱ** Hen. 2, 2 ([2]); "such is not the lawful course" **ኢኮነ ፡ ከማሁ ፡ ሕጉ** Gen. 34, 7; "the place was called in ancient time,—so-and-so" **ትካቲሁ** ('in the old time of it') Gen. 28,19, (but also **ትካት** Judges 1, 10, 11); "on the second day" **በሳኒታ**; "(it is evening), and the time of it (*i. e.* for supper) has passed by"

([1]) *Cf.* Dillmann's '*Lex.*' col. 821.

([2]) [It is noteworthy that this locution **እስከ ፡ ተፍጻሜቱ** serves to express our *etc.*, corresponding to the Arabic إِلَى آخِرِهِ, *e. g. Lit.* (ed. Bezold in C. A. Swainson's '*Greek Liturgies*') p. 383, *paen.*]

ወሰዓቲኒ ፡ ኀለፈ Matt. 14, 15; "the veil was rent in twain from the top to the bottom" እምላዕሉ ፡ እስከ ፡ ታሕቱ (*lit.* 'from the top of it to the bottom of it') Matt. 27, 51; *cf.* Gen. 35, 8 &c. Accordingly certain words of this sort are constantly furnished with a suffix, v. §§ 157, 2; 163, 2; 191.

2. Periphrastic Indication of the Genitive:— (*a*) By means of ዘ, እንተ, እለ.

§ 186. 2. The Genitive relation, however, may also be expressed, in accordance with § 145, *b*, as follows.

(*a*) By means of ዘ, እንተ, እለ. This external marking of the Genitive relation is nearly quite as extensive and manifold, in use and significance, as the subordination effected by the Constr. St.; but it is essentially distinguished from it, as regards the manner of its employment, by the circumstance that with it the words are not tied down to any fixed position. On the contrary the Genitive which is constituted by ዘ answers completely to the Genitive case of other languages; and its position with respect to the word on which it depends is just as free as that of any Genitive in Indo-European tongues. In fact the effort to attain freedom in the position of words and in the structure of the Sentence appears to be the real procuring cause of the development in Ethiopic of this peculiar denotation of the Genitive. It is applied with especial frequency in the following cases.

(*α*) When the governing word is a Proper name, which does not admit of a Constr. St., *e. g.* ቤተ ፡ ልሔም ፡ ዘይሁዳ "Bethlehem of Judah" Matt. 2, 5; or when it cannot take any special form in the Constr. St., on account of its vowel-ending, *e. g.* ምሳሌ ፡ ዘክርዳድ ፡ ገራህት "the parable of the tares of the field" Matt. 13, 36; or when it stands at the same time in the Accusative, and when accordingly the Construct State cannot be discriminated from the Absolute State, *e. g.* ቀተለ ፡ ኵሎ ፡ ሕፃናተ ፡ ዘቤተ ፡ ልሔም Matt. 2, 16.

(*β*) To avoid too long a chain of Nouns linked together by the Constr. St., or when the governing word has other determinations associated with it, from which it must not be separated, *e. g.* ትእዛዝ ፡ ቀዳማዊ ፡ ዘብርሃናት "the first ordinance of the lights" Hen. 72, 2; በዕለት ፡ ዐባይ ፡ እንተ ፡ ኵነኔ "in the great day of judgment" Hen. 10, 6; particularly when the governing word has already another Genitive depending upon it: ዝውእቱ ፡ ደምየ ፡ ዘሐዲስ ፡ ሥርዐት "this is my blood of the New Testament" Matt. 26, 28; ኮሬየ ፡ እንተ ፡ ብሩር "my silver cup" Gen. 44, 2; ምሕዋር ፡ ዘአውራኅ

"his monthly course" Hen. 74,1; አልባሲሃ ፡ ዘመበለታ "her widow's-garments" (*lit.* 'her garments of her widowhood') Gen. 38,14; ኵሎ ፡ ክብርየ ፡ ዘብሔረ ፡ ግብጽ "all my glory in the land of Egypt" Gen. 45,13; 31,7; ምሥዋዖ ፡ ለበዓል ፡ ዘአቡከ "the altar of Baal belonging to thy father" Judges 6,25; ኀበ ፡ ዕፀ ፡ በለን ፡ እንተ ፡ ላሕ "by the oak of lamentation" Gen. 35,8; ከለ ፡ ሐቅል ፡ ዘወልድኪ "thy son's mandrakes" Gen. 30,14.

(*γ*) Very frequently, also,—to avoid the repetition of the governing word, which in the Construct State relation would be indispensable, or at least desirable. If in fact several Genitives have to depend upon one and the same word, that word may no doubt be set down in the Constr. St. only once, and yet subordinate to itself more Genitives than one (v. § 185); but it is more usual in such a case to prefix ዘ to the second Genitive as well as to the third, and so on, the continuation of the Genitive relation being thereby denoted more clearly, *e. g.* መዛግብተ ፡ ፀሐይ ፡ ወዘ ወርኅ "the treasuries of the sun and (those) of the moon" Hen. 41,5; አዕጻደ ፡ ወይን ፡ ወዘዘይት "vineyards and oliveyards" Judges 15,5; or the Construct State relation may even be given up altogether, *e. g.* ኖሎት ፡ ዘሎጥ ፡ ወዘአብራም "the herdsmen of Lot and of Abram" Gen. 13,7; አብሓኵ ፡ ዘአባግዕ ፡ ወዘአጣሊ "rams and he-goats" (*lit.* 'males of the sheep and of the goats') Gen. 31,10. The possibility of denoting the Genitive in this way is of special value in those cases in which the Genitive is separated, in any fashion, rather far from its governing Noun, *e. g.* ወነሥአ ፡ ሎቱ ፡ በትረ ፡ ዘልብን ፡ ሐመልሚለ ፡ ወዘከርካዕ ፡ ዐቢየ "and he took to him a green rod of poplar and a great rod of the almond-tree" Gen. 30,37; ምህርካ ፡ ዘይኄይስ ፡ እምዘ ፡ አኀዊከ "a spoil which is better than thy brethren's" Gen. 48,22 (—in these two instances other tongues would have had to repeat በትረ and ምህርካ); or in those cases in which the Genitive supplies the place of a Predicate: ወይከውኑ ፡ ኵሎሙ ፡ ዘእምላክ καὶ ἔσονται πάντες τοῦ θεοῦ Hen. 1,8; ወራእዩ ፡ ከመ ፡ ዘመብረቅ (= ከመ ፡ ራእየ ፡ መብረቅ) "and his appearance was as that of a blaze of lightning" ("his countenance was like lightning", *E. V.*) Matt. 28,3; አንትሙ ፡ ዘክርስቶስ ፡ ወክርስቶስኒ ፡ ዘእግዚአብሔር "ye are Christ's, and Christ is God's" 1 Cor. 3,23. This ዘ serves the purpose even of rendering the Greek τὸ when followed by a Genitive: አኮ ፡ ከመ ፡ ዘበለስ ፡ ዘትገብሩ "not merely would ye be able to accomplish τὸ τῆς συκῆς" Matt. 21, 21; ሀቡ ፡ ዘነጋሢ ፡ ለነጋሢ "render to Caesar the things that are Caesar's" Matt. 22, 21; ኢትሔሊ ፡ ዘእግዚአብሔር ፡ ዘእንበለ ፡ ዘሰብእ "thou considerest not the things that be of God, but those that be of men" Matt. 16, 23.

(δ) As, according to this representation, ዘ expresses also the idea of "*the* or *those of*"(1), it is very often used in phrases which stand for Descriptive Words that are wanting, or Relative Adjectives and Derivatives of a personal nature, *e. g.* ዘጸርቅ "Raca! ('ragged one')" Matt. 5, 22; ዘመንፈስ "spiritual"; ዘወርቅ "golden"; ዘማእከል "middle" (*adj.*) Judges 16, 29; ዘውቁር "dug *or* hewn out" Deut. 6,11; ዘጋኔን "possessed" *or* "a possessed person" Matt. 9,32; [*cf.* also እንተ ፡ ውስጥ ፡ ዐይንነ "our inner eye" *Chrest.* p. 49 *ult.*]; እለ ፡ አጋንንት "those possessed with devils" Matt. 4, 24; 8, 16; ዘለምጽ "a leper" Matt. 8, 2; እለ ፡ ለምጽ "lepers" Matt. 10, 8; እለ ፡ ዐመፃ "unjust persons" Hen. 95, 7 (2); እለ ፡ ክርስቶስ "Christ's people" Mark 9, 41; ዘሕብር "speckled" Gen. 31, 8; ዘሕብረ ፡ ጸዐዳ "spotted with white" Gen. 30, 40; ዘሕብረ ፡ ሐመድ "ash-coloured" Gen. 30, 39; ዘጸጕረ ፡ ገመል "of camel's hair" Mark 1, 6; ዘበረድ "of snow" Matt. 28, 3 (3). The Collectives መንፈስ "soul", "spirit" and ሥጋ "flesh", if they are employed in the sense of "living beings" (נֶפֶשׁ, רוּחַ) and "mortal beings" (בָּשָׂר), never become Personal words till ዘ has been prefixed, *e. g.*: ኵሉ ፡ ዘመንፈስ Gen. 7, 22; ዘሥጋ Gen. 6, 12, 17; 7, 21; Matt. 24, 22; also ዘደም John 1, 13 &c.

This particle ዘ besides is used readily to bring Demonstrative, Interrogative and Relative Pronouns conveniently into the Genitive. On rare occasions it stands with words of *separation* in the sense of an Ablative, *e. g.* ወይፈልጦሙ ፡ ዘዘ ፡ ዚአሆሙ "he will separate them from one another" Matt. 25, 32 (§ 159, *g*).

(*b*) By means of ለ.

(*b*) Much less frequently is the preposition ለ,—which expresses reference in a general way —, employed to denote the Genitive relation. It is used for the most part, when the Genitive may

(1) Like the Arabic ذُو, followed by the Genitive.

(2) [For these two words Flemming's reading substitutes በዐመፃ. tr.]

(3) Many Ethiopic Proper names are also formed in the same way: ዘሥላሴ, ዘማርያም &c. [*Cf.* Nöldeke, '*Beitr. z. sem. Sprachw.*', p. 104]. In the names of Feasts, however, this ዘ is often left out: በሚካኤል for በዘሚካኤል "on Michael's (day)".

also be conceived of as a Dative, *e. g.* in ከመ ፡ ትኩኑ ፡ ውሉደ ፡ ለአቡክሙ "that ye may be children of your Father" Matt. 5,45; ይከውኑ ፡ አሐደ ፡ መርዔተ ፡ ለ፩ኖላዊ "they shall be one flock of one shepherd" John 10,16; አንትሙ ፡ ውእቱ ፡ ጼው ፡ ለምድር "ye are the salt of the earth" Matt. 5,13; ወዮሴፍሰ ፡ መልአክ ፡ ውእቱ ፡ ለብሔረ ፡ ግብጽ Gen. 42,6; እግዚእ ፡ ለኵሉ "lord of all" Gen. 45,8; 39,1; 40,1; Sap. 14,1 A; 14,15;—or when the Genitive expresses merely a *reference* to some thing or person: ትእምርት ፡ ለያዕቆብ "the sign of Jacob" ('which points to him') Gen. 30,42; ኢይትረከብ ፡ ሎሙ ፡ አሰር "no trace of them is found" Hen. 48,9 (where ሎሙ is chosen instead of አሰሮሙ in order that አሰር might remain indefinite); ዕጸቡ ፡ ለኵነኔ "the severity of the judgment" Hen. 68,2;—or to indicate the originating cause: መዐዛ ፡ ለስኂን ፡ ወከርቤ Hen. 29,2[1]; ሎቱ ፡ መዐዛ "the odour of it" Hen. 25,6;—or even to put in the Genitive a Pronoun, upon which the emphasis rests: ወላቲኒ ፡ ማይ ፡ የሐውር "and even its water is flowing" Hen. 26,3[1]. A peculiar use occurs of ለ after እለ in the sense of "the (*pl.*) of" (v. *supra a*, δ): ወአርዳኢሁ ፡ ለዮሐንስ ፡ ወእለሂ ፡ ለፈሪሳውያን "and the disciples of John and also those of the Pharisees" Mark 2,18. Similarly ለ is found besides in use to carry on the Genitive relation through farther members of a sentence, if the Genitive was expressed in the first member by means of a Suffix: ልቡ ፡ ወለዐበይቱሂ "his heart and that of his great ones" Ex. 9,35; 10,1.

(*c*) To express the Genitive relation in a Partitive sense, እምነ (§ 164, No. 3) is also employed, or the Preposition,—compounded with እም,—እምውስተ. Thus "one of them" is አሐዱ ፡ እምኔሆሙ; "which of the two?" መኑ ፡ እምክልኢሆሙ; "one of us" ፩እምኔነ Gen. 3,22; Josh. 8,37; and so, particularly, in the case of numerical data, *e. g.* Matt. 25,2; 26,47; 22,28; አመ ፡ ኮነ ፡ ፮፻ወ፩ዓመተ ፡ እምሕይወቱ ፡ ለኖሕ "in the six hundred-and-first year of Noah's life" Gen. 8,13;—also in combinations like እለ ፡ እምውስተ ፡ ጸሐፍት "certain of the scribes" ('some who were of the scribes') Matt. 9,3; እሉ ፡ ውእቶሙ ፡ እምነ ፡ ከዋክብት ፡ እለ "these are (those of) the stars which" &c. Hen. 21,6.

(c) By እምነ, to express the Partitive Genitive.

[1] [In Hen. 29,2 FLEMMING reads ስኂን without the prep., and in Hen. 26,3, ቦቲኒ instead of ላቲኒ. TR.]

(*b*) *Subordination through the Accusative or through Prepositions.*

(*b*) Subordination through the *Acc.* or through *Preps.*:— 1. Infinitives and Certain Descriptive Words governing an Accusative.

§ 187. These two kinds of Subordination are characteristic of the Verb, and they can properly occur in the department of Nouns, only when a Noun approximates the Verb in force and meaning.

1. *Infinitives* may govern a Noun in the *Accusative.* First of all, of course, the Gerund may do so; for, having already a Suffix bound up with it in the sense of Subject, it does not permit of being connected with its Object by means of the Constr. St., *e. g.* **ኀዲጎሙ ፡ ሐመረ ፡ ወአባሆሙ** "leaving the ship and their father" ('when they left the ship &c.') Matt. 4, 22; **ወኪያሁ ፡ ርእዮ** "and seeing him" ('and when he had seen him') John 21, 21; **ሰፊሖ ፡ እዴሁ** "stretching forth his hand" Matt. 8, 3. Substantive-Infinitives for the most part, it is true, take their Object to themselves after the manner of Nouns, *i. e.* by means of the Constr. St. relation, *e. g.* Matt. 22, 29; 8, 12; Mark 2, 7; 3, 4; Gen. 8, 21; 11, 8 (v. *supra* § 184); but they may take it also in the Accusative, *e. g.* Deut. 5, 22; Matt. 10, 28; 7, 11; 27, 15; **ቅንየትከ ፡ ወምልክናከ ፡ ኵሎ** Sap. 12, 16—(old version); and now and then too an abstract word, of Infinitive form, follows their lead in this proceeding, *e. g.* in **በአቱ ፡ መንግሥተ ፡ ሰማያት** "his entering into the kingdom of heaven" Matt. 19, 23. But Accusatives may be found in dependence on certain Adjectives even, and on Participial Descriptive-words, just as on a Verb, although upon the whole this is not of frequent occurrence. Active Participles, and words which signify the Agent, nearly always connect themselves with a Noun through the Constr. St. relation, *e. g.* **መፈውሰ ፡ ነፍስ** (not **መፈውስ ፡ ነፍሰ**) "a physician of souls",—and have thus already become complete Nouns(¹). On the other hand certain Adjectives, from Verbs which govern an Accusative, also take in their turn a Noun in the Accusative, particularly *Adjectives of Fulness and Want*: **ምሉኣን ፡ አዕጽምተ** "full of bones" Matt. 23, 27; **ምልእት ፡ ሕምዘ** "full of poison" Jas. 3, 8; Gen. 14, 10; **ጽዑን ፡ አፈዋተ** "laden with spices" Gen. 37, 25; even **እኁዝ** ἐχόμενος may be connected in this way: **እኁዛን ፡ መሣግረ ፡ ኀጺን** "holding iron

(¹) V. however Sir. 43, 33: **እስመ ፡ ኵሎ ፡ እግዚአብሔር ፡ ገብረ.**

fetters" Hen. 56, 1 (1). Farther, any attributive word may take to itself an Adverbial accusative (§ 174): ሠናይት ፡ ይእቲ ፡ ገጻ "she is fair of face" Gen. 26, 7; ሥቡሓን ፡ ሥጋሆሙ "fat in their flesh" Gen. 41, 2; and in the same way any Adverb (in the Accusative) may be attached to it, whether it precedes or follows: ብዕል ፡ ፈድፋደ "exceedingly rich" Gen. 13, 2; እምን ፡ ርሑቅ ፡ ብሔር ፡ ጥቀ "from a very far country" Josh. 9, 7 &c.

2. Conceptional and Descriptive Words, supplemented by Noun governed by intervening Preposition.

2. Conceptional and Descriptive words, nearly allied to the Verb, are more frequently supplemented or specifically determined by a Noun governed by an intervening *Preposition*. Thus we say: በቀል ፡ ለነፍሶሙ "revenge for their life" Hen. 22, 11; ስምዕ ፡ በሐሰት "false witness" Matt. 15, 19; ላሕ ፡ በእንተ ፡ እሙ "mourning for his mother" Gen. 24, 67; በኣት ፡ እንተ ፡ ስቍረተ ፡ መርፍእ "the going in through a needle's eye" Matt. 19, 24; also ውሉደ ፡ ትጉሃን ፡ እምሰብእ "the children of the watchmen among men" (inasmuch as ውሉድ is originally a Passive Participle, § 136, 1) Hen. 10, 9; ነዐኀኒ ፡ ድቀት ፡ በዲበ ፡ ድቀት "he has thrown me down with fall upon fall" Job 16, 14 &c. Of course these closer determinations are more usually annexed by means of the Relative pronoun. Besides, an Infinitive may at once take to itself any noun, with the help of the Preposition which its own verb governs; and it is even possible to have such combinations as ወዘእንበለ ፡ ተኀፅቦ ፡ እደውሰ ፡ በሊዕ ፡ ኢያረኵሶ ፡ ለሰብእ "but to eat without having washed the hands defileth not a man" Matt. 15, 20. Nouns may also be joined by means of Prepositions to Adjectives and Participle-like words, just as well as to any verb (2); and they are often joined to Passive Participles by means of በ "with", as in ኅኑጽ ፡ በልሳነ ፡ እሳት "built with flames ('tongues') of fire" Hen. 14, 15 (3); ጽጉባን ፡ በኵሉ ፡ ጥበብ "filled (*pl.*) with all wisdom" Rom. 15, 14; ልቡጥ ፡ በወርቅ "overlaid with gold" Ex. 28, 20; ንዙኅ ፡ በደም "sprinkled with blood" Rev. 19, 13; to other Participles and Adjectives (with intransitive conceptions) in conformity with the verb in each case, as in ንጹሕ ፡ እምነ "clear of" Matt.

(1) [FLEMMING reads here:—ይእኅዙ ፡ መቅሠፍተ ፡ ወመሣግረ ፡ ኀጺን. TR.]

(2) In this case alternating partly with the connection which is described in § 184, (*d*).

(3) [*Cf.* FLEMMING's reading: ሕኑጽ ፡ በልሳናተ ፡ እሳት. TR.]

27, 24; Gen. 24, 8; **ምሉእ ፡ እምነ** "full of" Deut. 6, 11; **ዕሩቅ ፡ እምነ** "empty of"; **ብዑል ፡ እምነ** "rich in" Gen. 13, 2; **ክልእ ፡ እምነ** "different from" Hen. 40, 2; **ውኩል ፡ በ** or **ላዕለ** "relying upon"; **ዕሩይ ፡ ምስለ** "equal to"; **ቅሩብ ፡ ለ** "near (one)" Gen. 14, 13; or with **ኀበ** 23, 13; **ልጹቅ** with **ውስተ** or **ለመንገለ** "bordering upon"; **መጋቢ ፡ ላዕለ** "steward of" Gen. 24, 2. Adjectives also, and even Substantives, may be supplemented by **ለ** with the Infinitive, for the purpose of giving a special direction to a general idea: **ሠናይ ፡ ለበሊዕ ፡ ወሠናይ ፡ ለርእይ** "good to eat and fair to look upon" Gen. 2, 9; Hen. 24, 5; **ጽልመት ፡ ለነጽሮ** "a darkness to be beheld" Hen. 22, 2; 21, 8; 24, 5.

3. Prepositions employed in intensifying and comparing Qualitative Conceptions

3. In particular, Prepositions are also employed in intensifying and comparing Qualitative conceptions (v. § 179, 2); and in this process Intransitive Verbs, which express qualities, are equivalent to Descriptive Words, inasmuch as (v. § 202) periphrases, contrived by the Relative and a finite Verb, are, in the absence of participles and adjectives, used as Adjectives; or the Verb even is itself frequently set down, when an Adjective might have been expected to stand as Predicate. To express the degrees of comparison, of other languages, a simple Adjective or Verb is often quite sufficient in Ethiopic, if it is placed in an emphatic position, or if the class of objects, among which some one is specially distinguished, is farther specially mentioned and introduced by **በ**, **በውስተ** &c., *e. g.*: **ሕጹጸ ፡ ይሰመይ ፡ በመንግሥት** "he shall be called the least in the kingdom" Matt. 5, 19; **አይኑ ፡ ትእዛዝ ፡ የዐቢ ፡ በውስተ ፡ ኦሪት** "which commandment is great ('the greatest') in the law?" Matt. 22, 36; **አነ ፡ ንኡስ ፡ በቤተ ፡ አቡየ** "I am the least of my family" Judges 6, 15; **ዘየዐቢ ፡ ትእዛዛት** "the greater commandments" Matt. 23, 23: **ዘይሤኒ ፡ ወይን** "the better wine" John 2, 10; Gen. 27, 15; and indeed some conceptional words in themselves include the degree of comparison, like **ኄሰ** "to be better"; **መብዝኀት** "the most" ('the largest portion') Ps. 77, 35; **መሠንይ** "the best" ('the best part') Numb. 31, 26.—When that, with which anything is compared, is expressly mentioned, it may be subordinated in the Accusative,—in the case of certain Verbs,—in accordance with § 176, 3, *d*, and in the Genitive (Partitive Genitive, § 184) with Adjectives, *e. g.*:—**ዐቢዮሙ** "the great one of them", *i. e.* "their greatest one"; **ቅድስተ ፡ ቅዱሳን** "the Holy of Holies", *i. e.* "the most Holy (place)". More usually, however, the Preposition

እምነ—which indicates 'a part of a whole' and also 'preference'—is associated with the Verbs and Adjectives concerned, *e. g.*: ጠቢብ ፡ እምነ "wiser than"; ይንእስ ፡ እም "he is smaller than"; ኄየሰ ፡ እም "he is better than"; ጸድቀት ፡ ትእማር ፡ እምኔየ "Tamar is more righteous than I" Gen. 38, 26; or ቡርክት ፡ እምአንስት "more blessed than women", *i. e.* "the most blessed one of women" Luke 1, 28. This phraseology for purposes of comparison may be used also with transitive Verbs, in which case እምነ means "more than": ያዕቆብ ፡ ያፈቅሮ ፡ ለዮሴፍ ፡ እምነ ፡ ኵሎሙ ፡ ደቂቁ "Jacob loved Joseph ('in preference to') more than all his (other) sons" Gen. 37, 3. Even entire clauses may be compared with each other in this way (v. *infra*, § 204). እምነ farther is frequently preceded by an intensive Adverb, such as ጥቀ "very"; ፈድፋደ "exceedingly", "much more", *e. g.* ይሠኒ ፡ ፈድፋደ ፡ እምይእቲ ፡ ሀገር "it shall be much more tolerable for them (*lit.* 'for it', *i. e.* 'the land &c.') than for that city" Matt. 10, 15; Gen. 19, 9; 29, 30; Judges 2, 19; Matt. 18, 13; 11, 9; or,—when the particular conception has to be presented in its greatest intensity,—ኵሉ is added after እምነ, *e. g.*: ትጠቢብ ፡ እምነ ፡ ኵሉ ፡ አራዊት "it is more subtle than all the other beasts" Gen. 3, 1; Mark 4, 31; Hen. 8, 1; Gen. 34, 19: but yet ኵሉ may be wanting, as in ንስቲተ ፡ እምነ ፡ እኪት "the least evil" *Chrest.* p. 45, line 5. እምነ is itself a Preposition, meaning "before"; and,—should it happen that a different Preposition is required to subordinate to the Verb the first member of the comparison, *i. e.* the word compared, this latter preposition is omitted after እምነ and before the second member of the comparison, *i. e.* before the word with which the first is compared: as in ይትፌሣሕ ፡ በእንቲአሃ ፡ ፈድፋደ ፡ እምተስዓ ፡ ወተስዐቱ "he rejoices over it more than over the ninety and nine" (*lit.* 'he rejoices over it exceedingly, before the ninety and nine') Matt. 18, 13; *cf.* also እመ ፡ ኢፈድፈደ ፡ ጽድቅክሙ ፡ ፈድፋደ ፡ እምጸሐፍት (where also እምዘጸሐፍት might have appeared, in accordance with § 186, a, γ) "unless your righteousness is greater than that of the scribes" Matt. 5, 20. Ethiopic, meanwhile, is so flexible that a Preposition of that nature may also appear after እምነ, *e. g.* in ይኄይስ ፡ ለከ ፡ አሁብ ፡ እምነ ፡ ለካልእ ፡ ብእሲ "it is better that I give (her) to thee than to another man" Gen. 29, 19, where two clauses are compared together, and where እምነ is a short expression for እምነ ፡ ዘአሁብ.

2. CO-ORDINATION OF NOUNS.

1. Co-ordination and Concord of Substantives and Demonstrative Prons., and of Substantives and Adjectives.

§ 188. In Co-ordination (Apposition) three stages may be distinguished, according to the degree of the closeness or looseness of the connection between the words.

1. *Adjectives*, as a rule, are joined to the Noun by Co-ordination. The same statement holds good for words resembling Adjectives, viz. *Demonstrative Pronouns* and *Numerals*, the Relative Pronoun also associating itself in a certain sense with them. Numerals and the Relative will be specially dealt with farther on (v. §§ 191 and 201 *sq.*). Demonstrative Pronouns are associated with the Noun exactly like Adjectives, except for the peculiarity, which they possess in contrast with the latter, of being usually placed before the Noun, as in **ይእቲ ፡ መንግሥት** Mark 3, 24; **ለውእቱ ፡ ጠፈር** Gen. 1,8; **ውእተ ፡ ላህመ** 18,8; *cf.* 50,11; **ዝንቱ ፡ ብእሲ** 24, 65; **ኆኅተ ፡ ውእቱ ፡ ቤት** "the door of that house" Judges 19, 27; **ብርሃነ ፡ ዝኩ ፡ እሳት** "the light of that fire" Hen. 71, 2. When they are placed after the Noun, they are to be regarded rather as less closely co-ordinate, *e. g.*: **ውስተ ፡ ሀገረ ፡ ኢያቡሴዎን ፡ ዛቲ** "into the city here of the Jebusites" Judges 19, 11. Several words also which were originally Substantives (Conceptional or Personal words), being used however as Adjectives, are classed with the Adjectives, as in **ላህም ፡ መግዝእ** "a fat ox" Judges 6, 28; **ትውልድ ፡ ዕሉት ፡ ወዘማ** "a perverse and adulterous race" Matt. 16, 4 (**ዘማ** is a noun, meaning "whore"); **በእንተ ፡ ሐፍሦሙ ፡ ምልአ ፡ ሕፍን ፡ ሰገም** *ἕνεκεν δρακὸς κριθῶν* Ezek. 13, 19; other examples are found in Numb. 20, 17; 21, 22; Deut. 8, 15; 9, 1; farther, in particular, **ኵሉ** "all", "every"; **ኅዳጥ** "a small quantity" and "few"; **ንስቲት** "a small thing" and "little" Jas. 3, 5; Gen. 19, 20; Judges 4, 19; Hen. 63, 6; **ሕቅ** "measure" and "moderate (in quantity)", *e. g.* **ሕቀ ፡ ማየ** "a little water" Gen. 24, 17; finally, even **ምንትሂ**, **ምንትኒ** "anything", and occasionally **ምንት** "what?" (v. § 198).

These words are set in apposition to the Noun; for the subordination of the Adjective to the Substantive, or of the Substantive to the Adjective, is upon the whole of rare occurrence, though it is certainly permissible, in accordance with § 184. The union by co-ordination is the closest possible; and in it the Adjective, as being the adventitious and less essential conception, must be regulated by the Noun, and must take Gender, Number and Case from the Noun.

The Rule of Concord in Case is observed without exception. Only, when one Noun governs another by means of the Construct State, the Adjective does not conform to such Constr. St. of the governing Noun, but is added rather as a Descriptive Word in co-ordination with the entire Word-group which is fashioned by the Constr. St. (v. § 185). If, however, the Noun stands in the Accusative, the Adjective must conform to it in that respect; and it is only in the case noted in § 143, *ad fin.*, that deviations are now and then met with, *e. g.*: **ግበር ፡ ታቦተ ፡ እንተ ፡ ዕፅ ፡ ወርብዕት** Gen. 6, 14.

On the other hand the remaining two Rules of Concord, which concern Gender and Number, although they hold good as general principles, suffer considerable limitation, to meet the peculiar fluctuations which are permitted in Ethiopic in the Gender and Number of Nouns. Since it is only actual Names of Persons that are invariably distinguished definitely as Masculine or Feminine (§ 130), while almost all other words may be regarded indifferently as Masculine or as Feminine,—the Adjective is of necessity Masculine only in the case of Names of Persons of the Masculine gender, and of necessity Feminine only in the case of like Names of Persons of the Feminine gender; while, in the case of all other Nouns, the Adjective is subject to the same fluctuations in gender that the usage of the language is exposed to as regards the gender of the Noun. Thus one says indeed **ምድር ፡ ሠናይት** Mark 4, 8, but also **ምድር ፡ ሠናይ**; **ዛቲ ፡ ምሳሌ** Mark 4, 13; **ውዴተ ፡ እኪተ** Gen. 37, 2; **ዛተ ፡ ሕይወተ ፡ ዐባየ** Judges 15, 18; **ወባዕድኒ ፡ ኵሉ ፡ ፍትወት** Mark 4, 19; **ውእቱ ፡ መስፈርት** Mark 4, 24; **ዐቢየ ፡ ፍርሀተ** Mark 4, 41; **ዝንቱ ፡ ዕቅበት**; **ዝንቱ ፡ ፍርሀት** G. Ad. 38, 15 *sq.*; **ኀጢአተ ፡ ዐቢየ** Gen. 20, 9; **ርስዐት ፡ ዐቢይ** Hen. 8, 2 (¹); **ትምህርት ፡ ሐዲስ** Mark 1, 27; **ነሥአ ፡ እብነ ፡ ዐቢየ**, and in the immediate context **ወአቀማ** Josh. 24, 26; [**ፀሐይ ፡ ብሩህ ፡ ወረደት** *K. N.* 25 b 6] &c.

Then, certainly, Personal Words in the Plural,—and particularly those Plurals of theirs, which have been formed by outer terminations—, are definitely either masculine or feminine; and, farther, official designations, which have been formed by means of *āt* (§ 133, *a*), are mostly regarded as being of the Masculine gender and in the Plural, and they are therefore generally associated with

(¹) [Flemming here adopts the variant **ርስዓን ፡ ዐቢይ**. tr.]

an Adjective in the Plural masculine, or feminine. But all other Plurals, particularly those of inner formation (Collective forms), may again be conceived of as compact collective notions, and therefore as Singulars, and either masculine or feminine,—following in fact the same fluctuation which prevails in the Gender of the Singular. In these cases a Plural may just as readily be associated with an Adjective in the Singular masculine or feminine, as with an Adjective in the Plural m. or f. (v. § 135). We meet with **ብዙኃን ፡ ኃጥአን** Mark 2, 15; **አሕዛብ ፡ ብዙኃን** Mark 3,20; **አድባር ፡ ነዋኃን ፡ ወአውግር ፡ ነዋኃት** Hen. 1,6; **ዐቢያተ ፡ ወድሩካተ ፡ ቃላተ** Hen. 5,4; **ዕፀው ፡ ብዙኃነ** Hen. 32,3; **ክልኣት ፡ አሕማር** Mark 4, 36;—but also with **ትእምራተ ፡ ዐቢያነ ፡ ወስቡሓነ** Hen. 36,4; **እሙንቱ ፡ ማያት** Hen. 67, 13; **አልባስ ፡ ሠናይት** Gen. 24, 53; **ብዙኀ ፡ አሕዛብ** Gen. 17,4; **ውእተ ፡ ቃላተ** Hen. 13,10; **ዝቃት ፡ ብሉይ** Matt. 9,17; **ማያት ፡ ብዙኀ** Ps. 92,6; **ምግባራት ፡ ሠናይ**. It may be given as a general observation, that any Plural, whatever be its form, may be joined to an Adjective in the Plural in that gender which belongs to the word in the Singular,—but also that any Plural, or even Plural of Plurals (§ 141) may be conceived of too as a Singular,—in which case it usually takes to itself the Adjective in the Singular and in the readiest gender, the Masculine, although it may also be in the Feminine. But, on the other hand, words which are Singular in form,—if they are either essentially the expression of collective notions, or even have merely a collective meaning in the particular passages concerned—, are joined to the Plural of the Adjective, and that too in the Gender which properly belongs to the individual components of the collective idea: **ብዙኃን ፡ ሰብእ** Mark 4,1; **ሕዝብ ፡ ጽኑዓን** Gen. 14,5; Deut. 9, 2; **ስብሐት ፡ ዐቢያት** "great splendours" ('great magnificence') Hen. 65, 12; **ለዘይመጽእ ፡ ትውልድ ፡ ርኁቃን** "for distant future generations" Hen. 1, 2 (1); and even **ዐውያተ ፡ ዐበይተ** Hen. 85, 6; *cf.* also **ዐበይት ፡ ዝናም** with **ዐቢየ ፡ ዝናመ** 1 Esr. 2, 49.—An Adjective which admits of an inner plural form, generally assumes it when the Noun, with which it is co-ordinated, has also the Collective form: **ዐናብርት ፡ ዐበይት** Gen. 1,21; **ተኣምር ፡ ዐበይት** Josh. 24, 17; **አሕዛብ ፡ ዐበይት ፡ ወጽኑዓን** Josh. 23,9; **አበው ፡**

---

(1) [Instead of the last two words here, Flemming reads **ርሕቅት**, the *Fem. Sing.* and does not, like Dillmann, repeat **ትውልድ**. tr.]

ቀደምት Josh. 24, 2; and sometimes even when this condition is not present, *e. g.* ብርሃናት ፡ ዐቢይት Gen. 1, 16.

ኵሉ is somewhat peculiar in its mode of junction with Nouns; *cf. supra* § 157, 2. It may stand alone, without being joined to any other Noun, with the meaning "everyone", *e. g.* Hen. 7, 1; or "everything", *e. g.* Hen. 1, 7; or "all (*pl.*)", *e. g.* Gen. 16,12; 45,1; Hen. 1, 5. When it is associated with a Noun in the Fem. Sing., it should take the form ኵላ, *e. g.* ኵላ ፡ ዛቲ ፡ ምድር Gen. 26, 4; but, seeing that it is only loosely joined to the Noun, it often keeps its own readiest gender, even with a Feminine Noun, *e. g.* ኵሉ ፡ ሠናይት ፡ እንተ Josh. 21, 43; ኵሉ ፡ ነፍስ ፡ እንተ ፡ ቦአት Gen. 46, 27. With Nouns in the Plural, it may take the Plural form: ኵሎሙ ፡ ሊቃነ ፡ ካህናት Matt. 2, 4; ኵሎሙ ፡ ሕሙማን Mark 3, 10; ኵሎን ፡ አኅማላት Mark 4, 32; ኵሎሙ ፡ ኖሎት Gen. 29, 3; but it may also remain in the Sing. Masc.: ኵሉ ፡ ተዓይን Josh. 22, 16; ኵሉ ፡ ፍና ዊሁ Josh. 22, 5; ኵሉ ፡ እለ "all, who" Josh. 23, 14; ኵሎ ፡ ሕፃናተ Matt. 2, 16; ኵሎ ፡ ዕፀወ Gen. 2, 9; ኵሉ ፡ አዝርእት Mark 4, 31:— and, as by its very nature it indicates plurality, the Noun which is associated with it does not altogether need to take the plural, but may sometimes be treated as a Collective: ኵሎ ፡ ቃለ ፡ እግዚእ "all the words (*Acc.*) of the Lord" Ex. 4, 28; ኵሉ ፡ ዐር Josh. 21, 42 &c.

The *position of the Adjective* with reference to the principal Noun is perfectly free. In this respect Ethiopic ranks with the most unrestrained of Indo-European languages. It is observable, no doubt, that in uniform and level discourse the Adjective is oftener placed after the Substantive than before it(1). But whenever any special emphasis is laid upon the Adjective, or when the distribution of the other Word-groups, or the euphony of the whole sentence, renders it desirable, the Adjective may equally well precede the Noun. With difficulty even does the Constr. St. relation introduce a restriction, to the extent of preventing an Adjective, which belongs to a Noun in the Constr. St., from intervening between the Constr. St. and the Genitive which depends upon it,— although an Adjective, belonging to the Genitive, usually falls back in such a case. On the other hand, after any Preposition the

(1) Only, ጸናፌ "exterior" is nearly always put first: v. DILLMANN's *Lex.'*, col. 1295.

Adjective may be put before the Substantive; and Demonstrative Pronouns, as well as ኵሉ, almost always precede their Substantive, even when it is dependent upon a Construct State. So too the Adjective may be separated from its Substantive by several other words, as by Relative clauses, or by intervening Adverbial or other auxiliary qualifications, *e. g.* ውስተ ፡ ፩ እምእላንቱ ፡ ግብ "into a pit of these" ('into one of these pits') Gen. 37,20,22; 26,1; ወዘአሐቲ ፡ ሐሊበ ፡ በግዕ ፡ ያጸግብ ፡ ለ፪ሰብእ Is. 7,22 (Old Vers.); or by Verbs &c., *e. g.* ገራህተ ፡ ልብየ ፡ ያንጽሑ ፡ ርሱሐ "*agrum cordis mei mundent immundum*" *Encomia Synaxarii*, Sen. 1 Enc. When more than one Adjective is connected with a Substantive, it is even more elegant and euphonious to separate them by the Substantive itself, or by other words, as in ወብእሲ ፡ ጻድቅ ፡ ውእቱ ፡ ወፍጹም Gen. 6,9; ዐቢየ ፡ ሥቃየ ፡ ወእኩየ Gen. 12,17; ግሩም ፡ ጽልመት ፡ ወዐቢይ Gen. 15,12; ሕዝበ ፡ ዐቢየ ፡ ይከውን ፡ አብርሃም ፡ ወብዙኀ Gen. 18,18.

2. Substantives in Co-ordination with Substantives. § 189. 2. A Substantive may also attract other *Substantives*, in co-ordination, in order to attain thereby a more exact determination. No doubt, when two Substantives are related to one another as Genus and Species, the General and the Particular, recourse also may be had in many cases to the process of Subordination (§ 184); thus, for instance, በውስተ ፡ ሰዶም ፡ ሀገር (Gen. 18,26) might also run በውስተ ፡ ሀገረ ፡ ሰዶም. But if the explanatory word is itself in turn determined by another,—as in ዕዋል ፡ እጓለ ፡ እድግት Matt. 21,5; ብእሲ ፡ በዕለ ፡ ቤት Matt. 21,33; ባላቅ ፡ ንጉሠ ፡ ሰዶም Gen. 14, 2, then co-ordination is the only course possible. As regards the position of the words, either the General or the Particular may be put first, according as it is desired to emphasise the one or the other:—መልአክ ፡ ዙጥኤል Hen. 32,2; መልአክ ፡ ቅዱስ ፡ ሩፋኤል Hen. 32,6; ውሉደ ፡ ረዐይተ "giant-sons" Hen. 15,3; ብእሲቱ ፡ ርብቃ Gen. 25,21; ዕቅብቱ ፡ ርሔማ Gen. 22, 24: or ፀሐይ ፡ ብርሃን Hen. 72,2; ገሃነም ፡ እሳት Matt. 18,9; ዮሐንስ ፡ መጥምቅ Matt. 14,2; ዐውሎ ፡ ዐቢይ ፡ ነፋስ Mark 4,37; ሄኖክ ፡ ብእሲ ፡ ጻድቅ ፡ ወጸሐፌ ፡ ጽድቅ Hen. 15,1. In this co-ordinate relation a Concrete even may appear alongside of an Abstract, as in ብእሲ ፡ ነጋዲት "a man, a strangeness", *i. e.* "a stranger" Judges 19,17[1]. If a Pronoun has to be interpreted in this way by

---

[1] Ex. 20,8 is also to be explained by this relation of Apposition:

a Noun co-ordinated with it, the Pronoun stands first. Agreement in Case is called for also in the forms of co-ordination described here, as *e. g.* in ብእሲ ፡ ንጉሥ Matt. 18,23; but yet this relation is somewhat less binding here, than that which is described in § 188; and a Noun in apposition with an Accusative may therefore (v. § 143, *ad fin.*) remain without any mark of the Accusative, as in አፍቅር ፡ እግዚአብሔር ፡ አምላክከ Matt. 22,37 (1). When such a Substantive-group, formed by Apposition, is subordinated to a preposition, the preposition is not, as a rule, repeated before the word in apposition. When the group,—in accordance with § 172, *c*—, is introduced by a Suffix relating to it which is followed by ለ, then the ለ is usually set down once only, provided that in the group the more specific and particular word comes first, — as in ወለዶ ፡ ለሲዶን ፡ በኵሩ Gen. 10,15; ይቤላ ፡ ለሶራ ፡ ብእሲቱ፡ Gen. 12,11; but if the more general and less specific term precedes the other, ለ is often repeated before the word in apposition:—ለእግዚእየ ፡ ለአብርሃም Gen. 24, 27, 36; the same thing occurs, if ኵሉ comes last, in loose co-ordination: ለአግማሊሁ ፡ ለኵሎሙ Gen. 24, 20; ለሰብአ ፡ ኖሎት ፡ ለኵሎሙ Gen. 43, 32. Finally, when a Substantive or an Adjective is placed in apposition to a Suffix Pronoun, it is introduced by ለ, *e. g.* ሊተ ፡ ለጻድቅ "to me, the righteous one"; እምነ ፡ እዴየ ፡ ለባሕቲትየ Judges 17, 3; Ps. 50, 5: but yet we have also ወኪያሁ ፡ ባሕቲቶ Matt. 4, 10.

3. Apposition-forms in the case of the Subject or the Object of a Sentence:— (a) When the Word in Apposition is a Simple Substantiv

3. Both the Subject and the Object (nearer or more remote) of a sentence may have new determinations added thereto, in quite loose and free co-ordination. These always admit of being resolved into full sentences, and properly are nothing but abbreviations of such sentences.

(*a*) When a word, appearing in this more remote form of apposition, is a simple *Substantive*, it may be placed in any position of the sentence, in the same Case as the noun to which it refers:—መኑ ፡ የዐርግ ፡ ለነ ፡ ኀበ ፡ ከናኔዎን ፡ መልአክ "who will go up for us as leader against the Canaanites?" Judges 1,1; የሀብ ፡ ነፍሶ ፡ ቤዛ ፡ ብዙኃን ("that) he might give his life a ransom for many" Matt. 20,28; ፈጠሮሙ ፡ ተባዕተ ፡ ወአንስተ "he created them, male and female" Gen. 5,2; 23,16; 38,18. When the word

ተዘከር ፡ ዕለተ ፡ ሰንበት ፡ አጽድቆታ "remember the Sabbath-day, to keep it holy"—, አጽድቆታ being an amending Apposition to ዕለተ.

(1) [—if this is not an old form of the Acc.; *cf.* *Kebra Nag.* p. XVI *sq.*].

in apposition refers to the Subject, and admits of being amplified by such a form as "so that he (or it) may be *this* or *that*",—then it may even take the Accusative, in accordance with § 177, 5: **መኑ ፡ የዐርግ ፡ ለነ ፡ መስፍነ** "who shall go up for us as leader?" Judges 20, 18; **ይቀርቡ ፡ ለቅሥተ ፡ ኀጢአቶሙ ፡ ፍሩሃነ** *ἐλεύσονται ἐν συλλογισμῷ ἁμαρτημάτων αὐτῶν δειλοί* Sap. 4, 20; [**ወእንዘ ፡ ትነብር ፡ ምዕስብተ** "and while she was living as a widow" *Kebra Nag.* p. 101, Note 11 (**ምዕስብት** being a form not given in D.'s '*Lex.*':—*cf. K. N., Introd.* p. XXXI)]. *Cf.* also Dillmann's '*Lex.*', col. 652 *sq.* on word **ንቡር**, and *Chrest.* p. XVI.

(b) When the Word in Apposition is an Adjective.

(*b*) When the *word in Apposition* is an *Adjective*, it is usually supplemented,—inasmuch as it occupies a comparatively independent position in the sentence,—by a Suff. Pron. referring to the Noun to which the Adjective is in apposition, and having the force noticed in § 156. Thus we find: **ምንት ፡ አቀመክሙ ፡ ዝየ ፡ ዕሩዓኒክሙ** ('what makes you stand here, idling ones that you are?') "why stand ye here idle?" Matt. 20, 6; **አኀዝዎ ፡ ለንጉሥ ፡ ሕያዎ** "they took the king alive" Josh. 8, 23; **ዕራቅየ ፡ እምፈነውከኒ** "thou wouldest have sent me away empty" Gen. 31, 42; and similarly in the case of Verbs of Perception (v. *infra*); or when the word in apposition belongs to the Subject: **ይኄይሰከ ፡ ትባእ ፡ ሐንካስከ** "it is better for thee to enter lame &c." Matt. 18, 8; [**እንዘ ፡ ሀሎኩ ፡ ንዉምየ** "while I was asleep" *Kebra Nag.* 63 a 14 *sq.*]; **ወሖረ ፡ ትኩዞ** "and he went away grieved" Mark 10, 22[1]; **ዛቡሎን ፡ ስኡኖ**[2] **፡ ይኀድር** Gen. 49, 13; **እለ ፡ ቅኑታኒሆሙ ፡ ይጸውሩ ፡ ንዋየ ፡ ሐቅል** Judges 18, 11; **አንሰ ፡ ምልእትየ ፡ ሖርኩ ፡ ወዕራቅየ ፡ አግብአኒ ፡ እግዚአብሔር** Ruth 1, 21; 3, 17 (*cf.* § 156). But yet the Suffix is now and then considered unnecessary:—**ንጉሥኪ ፡ ይመጽእ ፡ ኀቤኪ ፡ የዋህ** "thy king cometh to thee meek" Matt. 21, 5; **ሀለዉ ፡ ሰብአ ፡ ከናአን ፡ ኅዱራን** Gen. 13, 7; **አመ ፡ እሰትዮ ፡ ሐዲሰ** "when I shall drink it new" Matt. 26, 29; **ዘቀዳሜ ፡ አሥገርከ ፡ ዓሣ** "whatever fish thou catchest first ('as the first')" Matt. 17, 27; **ፈንዎቶ ፡ አግዓዜ** "to let him go free" Deut. 15, 18.

(*c*) But such an Apposition-form may be constituted even by

---

(1) V. analogous forms in Assyrian, Haupt, '*Sum. Fam.-Ges.*', p. 36 N. 2; [but on the other side, Delitzsch, '*Assyr. Gramm.*' § 80, *b*, *a* Note.]

(2) [*Cf.* Ludolf's '*Lex.*' *in voce*, col. 173, and note his exceedingly ingenious explanation of the appearance of the word in this particular passage. tr.]

an *entire clause*, or at least by some verbal conception, which should properly be expressed as a Participle, but which is expressed in another way, *viz.* by the finite Verb,—seeing that Ethiopic is no longer capable of forming all the Participles. The Apposition-form may, *first*, be attached as an abbreviated circumstantial clause, *e. g.* ወአንሶ ፡ ገጽየ ፡ ታሕተ ፡ እኔጽር "I looked, with face downward-turned" Hen. 14, 25; or,—*secondly*, it may be co-ordinated as an Imperfect by most intimate union, in accordance with § 181, *b*, *β*: ኮነ ፡ ከመ ፡ ፩እምኔነ ፡ ያአምር "he has become as one of us, knowing" Gen. 3, 22; "I will show thee all my visions . . . በቅድሜከ ፡ እነግር relating (them) in thy presence" Hen. 83, 1; "there were in that place about 3000 Philistines ይኔጽርዎ beholding him" Judges 16, 27;—*thirdly*, the Apposition-form may be rendered by እንዘ "while" and the finite verb, instead of by the Participle: ቀርቡ ፡ ኀቤሁ ፡ እንዘ ፡ ይሜህር "they came to him while he was teaching" Matt. 21, 23; ሰርሑ ፡ እንዘ ፡ የኀሥሡ "they wearied themselves searching for" Gen. 19, 11; መጽኡ ፡ እንዘ ፡ ያሜክርዎ "they came tempting him" Matt. 16, 1; የሐውሩ ፡ እንዘ ፡ ይነፍኑ "they go blowing (trumpets)" Josh. 6, 9; ፈነዎሙ ፡ እንዘ ፡ ሕያው ፡ ውእቱ። "he sent them away while he yet lived" Gen. 25, 6; 46, 30; እንዘ ፡ ምእትኑ ፡ ዓመት ፡ ሊተ ፡ እወልድ "shall I, being a hundred years old, beget (a child)?" Gen. 17, 17. When the Predicate in the clause which has እንዘ is an Adjective, even Copula and Subject may then be wanting, the clause being more closely bound to the Noun of the Principal clause which it has to qualify: ዘይመውት ፡ እንዘ ፡ ጻድቅ ፡ ወኄር "who, being righteous and good, dies" Hen. 81, 4; and if the noun which it has to qualify stands in the Accusative, the Predicate of the እንዘ-clause may even be in the Accusative: እመ ፡ አድኅፀት ፡ እንዘ ፡ ምሱለ "if she have a miscarriage with a child fully formed" Ex. 21, 23. *Fourthly*, the Apposition may be brought out by the turn of expression described in § 181, *b*, *α*.

(*c*) When an Entire Clause is in Apposition.

§ 190. (*d*) *Verbs of Perceiving, Declaring to be anything, and Turning into anything* deserve also special attention here(¹). According to Ethiopic notions, that which anything is declared as being, or is turned into, or is perceived as being, should properly, if it is to be expressed by a verb, be co-ordinated, in the form of

(*d*) Co-ordination of Predicate-Object with immediate Object, after Verbs of Perceiving, Declaring &c.

(¹) *Cf.* also § 203 with the whole of this Section.

a Participle, with the immediate Object. Since, however, such a participle cannot always be formed, other modes of expression are available at need.

1. As an Accusative of the Participle.

1. The Verbal conception, which has to indicate this Predicate-Object of the principal Verb, is co-ordinated,—as an Accusative of the Participle, with the immediate Object of the Verb (v. § 177, 4, *g*, and on the Passive construction, § 177, 5):—**ኪያከ ፡ ረከብኩ ፡ ጻድቀ** "I have found thee righteous" Gen. 7, 1; **ርኢኩ ፡ ኆኅወ ፡ ሰማይ ፡ ፍቱሓተ** "I saw the gates of heaven open" Hen. 34, 2; **ወረከብዎ ፡ ለእግዚኦሙ ፡ ውዱቀ ፡ ውስተ ፡ ምድር ፡ ምዉተ** "and they found their lord fallen on the ground, dead" Judges 3, 25; Gen. 32, 2. Such a Participle may at the same time take the Suffix, by § 189, 3, *b*: **ማእዜ ፡ ርኢናከ ፡ ርኁበከ ፡—ወ ጽሙአከ** "when saw we thee hungry,—or thirsty?" &c. Matt. 25, 37, 38, 44; **ወርእዮ ፡ ትኩዘ ፡ ኢየሱስ** "and when Jesus saw him grieved" Luke 18, 24: and in the Passive construction: **ፀምረ ፡ ጌዴዎን ፡ ተረክበት ፡ ጥልልታ** "Gideon's fleece was found bedewed" (*Org. Mar.*).

2. As an Accusative of the Gerund, with or without Suffix.

2. The Verbal expression of the Apposition takes also the form of the Gerund (Infinitive) in the Accusative, with Suffix (*cf.* § 181, *b*, *α*)(1): **ማእዜ ፡ ርኢናከ ፡ ተሞቂሐከ** "when saw we thee a prisoner?" Matt. 25, 44; **ረከበ ፡ ለቍልዔሁ ፡ ሐይዎ** "he found his servant recovered" Matt. 8, 13; and even without a Suffix:—**መኑ ፡ ትብሉኒ ፡ ከዊነ** "whom say ye that I am?" Matt. 16, 15; **አምኑ ፡ ውሉደ ፡ እግዚአብሔር ፡ ከዊነ ፡ ሕዝብ** *ὡμολόγησαν θεοῦ υἱὸν εἶναι λαόν* Sap. 18, 13; also 1 Kings 3, 21; and continued by a finite verb, in:—**ለእመ ፡ ርኢከ ፡ ከልበ ፡ ኀዲጎ ፡ እግዚኦ ፡ ወተለወከ ፡ ገሮ ፡ በእብን**—*Chrest.* p. 42, line 9 *sq.* These Accusatives with the Infinitive in the strict sense are to be found almost solely with Verbs of Perceiving and Declaring.

3. As a Finite Clause introduced by **እንዘ**, and equivalent to the Participle.

3. Very often the Participle is periphrastically expressed by **እንዘ** with the finite Verb:—**ርእየ ፡ ካልአነ ፡ እንዘ ፡ ይቀውሙ** "he saw others standing" Matt. 20, 3; Gen. 26, 8; **ረከቦሙ ፡ እንዘ ፡ ይነውሙ** "he found them sleeping" Matt. 26, 40; **ወቃለ ፡ ካልአ ፡ ሰማዕኩ ፡ እንዘ ፡ ይባርክ** "and another voice I heard praising" Hen. 40, 5; or in Passive construction:—**ተረክበት ፡ እንዘ ፡ ባ ፡ ውስተ ፡ ማኅፀና** "she was found with child" Matt. 1, 18. Even when Adjectives and participles are procurable we come upon this **እንዘ**-form of expression, as in **ርእዮ ፡ ካም ፡ እንዘ ፡ ዕሩቀ ፡ ውእቱ** "Ham saw him naked" Gen. 9, 22. The im-

(1) [V.. also PRAETORIUS' '*Aeth. Gramm.*', § 79. TR.]

mediate Object of the principal Verb is then frequently attracted, quite like a Subject, to the **እንዘ**-clause, but still it is set before it in most cases, as in **ርእየ ፡ አዕይንትየ ፡ በህየ ፡ ኵሎሙ ፡ ኃጥኣን ፡ እንዘ ፡ ይሰደዱ** "my eyes saw there all sinners driven away" Hen. 41, 2. 4. The Predicate-Object is sometimes expressed by an independent clause, and this is directly subordinated, without the aid of any conjunction, to the Verb of Perceiving. In this case the immediate Object may either stand in the Accusative, dependent on the principal Verb, or, on the other hand, it may be attracted to the dependent clause as Subject; but yet, even in the latter case, it is usually left to occupy its position between the Principal Verb and the one which is subordinated (*Attraction*). Thus we find:—**ርእዩ ፡ ጢሰ ፡ የዐርግ** "they saw smoke ascending (*lit.* 'it was ascending')" Josh. 8, 20; **ሰማዕክዎሙ ፡ ይብሉ** "I heard them say" Gen. 37, 17; **ይሬእይዎ ፡ ለወልደ ፡ እጓለ ፡ እመሕያው ፡ ይመጽእ** "they shall see the Son of Man coming" Matt. 24, 30; Hen. 32, 3; **ርእዮሙ ፡ ትኩዛነ** "he saw them sad" ('he saw them, they were sad') Gen. 40, 6; **ርኢናሃ ፡ ለይእቲ ፡ ምድር ፡ ሠናይት ፡ ጥቀ** "we saw that land to be very good" ('—it is very good') Judges 18, 9; **ርኢክዎ ፡ ለእግዚአብሔር ፡ ይነብር ፡ ዲበ ፡ መንበሩ** "I saw the Lord sitting upon his throne" Is. 6, 1, as quoted in *Gadla Yārēd*, 5, 29 *sq.*;—or with Attraction:—**ርእየ ፡ ብእሴ ፡ ይቀውም** "he saw ('a man was standing') a man standing" Josh. 5, 13; **ርኢኩ ፡ . . . ሰማይ ፡ ይትነፃኍ** "I saw . . . . the heavens destroyed" Hen. 83, 3; Mark 1, 10; also in the following position: **ወናሁ ፡ ኵሎሙ ፡ እሡራነ ፡ ርኢኩ** "and lo, all of them I saw bound" Hen. 90, 23.

4. As an Independent Clause, subordinated directly to the Verb of Perceiving, without any Conjunction. Attraction.

5. Farther, the independent Subordinate clause may, after Verbs of Perceiving and Saying, be subordinated to the principal Verb by **ከመ** "that" or "as". Here also the immediate Object of the principal verb may be attracted to the dependent clause, but the delicacy of the language demands that in such a case there shall be attached to the principal verb a Suffix Pronoun referring to that Object: **አአምረከ ፡ ከመ ፡ ድሩክ ፡ ብእሲ ፡ አንተ** (1) "I know (thee) that thou art an hard man" Matt. 25, 24, 26; **ሰምዕዎ ፡ ከመ ፡ ሀሎ ፡ ውስተ ፡ ቤት** "they heard (of him) that he was in the house" Mark 2, 1; Hen. 65, 1; 83, 4; Gen. 6, 2, 12; **ወሰበ ፡ ርእየ ፡ ከመ ፡**

5. As a Clause subordinated by **ከመ**.

---

(1) One might also have said, it is true:—**አአምር ፡ ከመ ፡ ድሩክ ፡ ብእሲ ፡ አንተ**, but **አአምረከ** is more elegant.

ሥናይት ፡ ይእቲ ፡ ዕረፍት "and when he saw that rest was good" Gen. 49, 15. If the Predicate in the subordinate clause is not a Verb, but an Adjective (or Substantive), and the immediate Object is not attracted to the Subordinate clause,—the copula may be left out in the latter: ርእዮ ፡ ለብርሃን ፡ ከመ ፡ ሥናይ "he saw the light ('that good') that it was good"(1) Gen. 1, 4, 8.

6. Predicate-Object expressed by Finite Verb in the Subjunctive, with or without ከመ, after Verbs of Causing or Making.

6. After Verbs of *Causing* or *Making*, the Predicate-Object, when it has to be expressed by a finite Verb, is put in the Subjunctive, in accordance with § 183, *b*, *c*, with or without ከመ—: thus either like ይሬስያ ፡ ትዘሙ *ποιεῖ αὐτὴν μοιχᾶσθαι* Matt. 5, 32; እመ ፡ አማን ፡ መንፈሰ ፡ ቅዱሰ ፡ ታመስልዎ ፡ ለመልክ ፡ ጼዴቅ ፡ ይኩን *Chrest.* p. 91, line 16; or like አሬስየከ ፡ ከመ ፡ ይፃእ ፡ እምኔከ ፡ አሕዛብ Gen. 17, 6; ትትአመን ፡ ከመ ፡ ያእቱ ፡ ተግባረ ፡ ማእረርከ Job 39, 12; Ps. 26, 19; Rom. 15, 14; Hebr. 6, 9. In a singular fashion this subordination by means of the Subjunctive is met with even after Verbs of Saying (which Mood serves in this case to express Possibility, like the Optative in other languages): መኑ ፡ ይብልዎ ፡ ይኩን ፡ ሰብእ "whom say the people of him, that he is?" Matt. 16, 13.

ADDENDUM: UNION OF NUMERALS AND NOUNS.

Union of Numerals and Nouns: 1. Cardinal Numbers.

§ 191. For the sake of clearness the joining of Numerals to Nouns falls to be dealt with here, rather than in the foregoing §§ 184, 185 & 188.

1. The Cardinal Numbers, with the exception of አሐዱ, are originally abstract Substantives, and accordingly should take to themselves the numbered object in the Genitive. Those forms of the Numerals, in fact, which are not increased by the Pronominal Suffix *ū*, are capable of taking the Constr. State. We find ኀምስተ ፡ ዕደወ "five men" Gen. 47, 2; ስድስተ ፡ ምእተ ፡ ብእሲ (Acc.) Judges 20, 39; ኀምሳ ፡ ምእተ ፡ ብእሲ Judges 20, 45; ክልኤተ ፡ አውራኀ Judges 11, 37; but this mode of connection is very seldom adopted"(2). Only, when the Object numbered is a Personal Pro-

(1) Instead of which we might have had ርእዮ ፡ ብርሃን ፡ ከመ ፡ ሠናይ ፡ ውእቱ.

(2) *Cf.* farther, however, Numb. 35, 14; 2 Peter 2, 5; [and v. *Kebra Nag. Introd.*, p. XVIII *sq.*].

noun, it is invariably attached as a Suffix to one or other of the Cardinal forms of the Numerals 3—10 mentioned above, and always by means of the Binding-vowel ī in accordance with § 155, 3, *a*, as these numerals are Plural notions: ሠለስቲሆሙ “the three of them” and “the three”; አርባዕቲሆሙ, ሰመንቲሆሙ &c.([1]). But if a word has to be subordinated by way of a partitive Genitive, like “three of those”, it is, in the case of all numerals without exception, attached by means of the preposition እምኔ, in accordance with § 186, *c*: ፩እምዐሠርቱ ፡ ወክልኤቱ “one of the Twelve” Matt. 26, 47; አሐቲ ፡ እምነገደ ፡ እስራኤል “one of the tribes of Israel” Gen. 49, 16 &c.

The usual mode of connecting the numbered Object with the numeral is, for all numbers, that of co-ordination (§ 188); and it has been already pointed out in § 158, that for that very reason the pronominal *ū* is commonly attached to the Numerals 1—10. They are connected with the Noun entirely like other Adjectives, or,—to be more exact,—like ኵሉ (§ 188). When the Noun is in the Accusative, they likewise take the Accusative so far as they can form such a Case: ክልኤ ፡ ምእተ ፡ ዲድረክመ Josh. 7, 21; እልፈ ፡ ብእሴ Judges 1,4; 8,4; ዐሠርተ ፡ ወሰመንተ ፡ ዓመተ “18 years” Josh. 24,33 (LXX); Judges 3, 14; Luke 13, 16; ምእተ ፡ ዲናረ Matt. 18, 28; አርባዕተ ፡ ምእተ ፡ ዓመተ Gen. 15, 13; ዐሠርተ ፡ ወክልኤተ ፡ ዓመተ Gen. 14, 4. However, the Fem. Numeral in *ū*, like ዐሥሩ, according to § 158, no longer admits of an Accusative: we have therefore ስሱ ፡ ኅዋኅወ Hen. 72, 3; ሰብዑ ፡ ኅብስተ Matt. 15, 36; ዐሥሩ ፡ ደናግለ Matt. 25,1; and occasionally the Masc.-forms, ዐሠርቱ &c., follow the same course. Even the plural forms of ምእት and እልፍ may be connected with the Object numbered, just like Adjectives; for example, in the Nominative: አእላፍ ፡ ወትእልፌት ፡ አእላፋት ፡ መላእክት Hen. 71, 13([2]).

Since definite plurality is already expressed by the Numeral, the Object numbered is most frequently connected with it in the Singular, *e. g.* ፮፻ወ፩ ፡ ዓመት Gen. 8, 13; ሠላሳ ፡ ብሩረ (Acc.) Matt. 26, 15. Yet the Plural may also be used (just as with ኵሉ § 188): ኀምሳ ፡ ጻድቃን Gen. 18, 24 *sqq.*; ዐሠርቱ ፡ ወሠለስቱ ፡ አህ

([1]) *Cf.* also ኀምሳሆሙ 4 Kings 1, 14.

([2]) [Instead of this reading of Dillmann's, Flemming gives አእላፍ ፡ ወትእልፌት ፡ መላእክት. tr.]

ጉር Josh. 21, 4; ምእት ፡ አባግዕ Matt. 18, 12; Josh. 24, 32; ዐሠርቱ ፡ ወክልኤቱ ፡ መሳፍንት Gen. 25, 16, or አርዳኢሁ (in the Gospels); እልፈ ፡ መክልየ Matt. 18, 24; ሰብዐቱ ፡ አኀው Matt. 22, 25. A Pronoun with a Numeral takes the plural, for the reason that, as a rule, it precedes it (§ 188): እልክቱ ፡ ኀምስቱ Gen. 14, 9; እሉ ፡ ሠለስቱ Gen. 9, 19; እልኩ ፡ ፬ ገጽ Hen. 40, 3; በእላንቱ ፡ ክልኤ ፡ ትእዛዝ Matt. 22, 40. Adjectives also regularly take the Plural, even when the Substantive remains Singular: ሰብዐቱ ፡ ሠዊት ፡ ቀጢናን ፡ ወዕቡራን Gen. 41, 5—7; or ሰብዐተ ፡ ካልኣነ ፡ መናፍስተ Matt. 12, 45. But we may also have ካልእተ ፡ ኀምሰ ፡ መክሊተ Matt. 25, 16; ካልእተ ፡ ሰብዐተ ፡ ዓመተ Gen. 29, 30,—in both of which cases, besides, ካልእተ has to be closely drawn to the numeral: "another 'five' talents".

As regards the Gender of Numerals we have a recurrence of the fluctuations sketched in § 188. We say, for instance, both ዐሥሩ ፡ ወሠላስ ፡ አህጉር Josh. 21, 6, 33 or ዐሥሩ ፡ ወክልኤ ፡ አህጉር &c. Josh. 21, 7, 18, 19, 22, 24, 26, 29, 32, 38—, and ዐሠርቱ ፡ ወሠለስቱ ፡ አህጉር Josh. 21, 4 &c.

The Numeral is regularly put before the Object numbered. It is only on special grounds that it may come after it, *e. g.* Gen. 32, 15, 16; 49, 28; 1 Kings 25, 5. Every Number is farther capable of standing by itself in a sentence, without being joined to any numbered Object, *e. g.* ዐሠርተ ፡ ምእተ "a thousand" (*Acc.*) Josh. 23, 10.

If the object numbered is a *Measure, Weight*, or the like, it is for the most part connected with the Numeral by the preposition በ (¹), *e. g.* ፫፻በእመት ፡ ኑኃ "its length (shall be) 300 cubits" (*lit.* 'in cubits') Gen. 6, 15; Hen. 7, 2; John 21, 8; ወኮነ ፡ ድልወተ ፡ ወርቀ ፡ አዕኑጊሁ ፡ ዘሰአሎሙ ፡ ዐሠርተ ፡ ወትስዐተ ፡ ምእተ ፡ በሰቅል Judges 8, 26. Thus also we find: ወኮነ ፡ ስገሙ ፡ በመስፈርተ ፡ ኢፍ "and the barley in it amounted to the measure of an ephah" Ruth 2, 17.

The Numeral-forms, described in § 159, *b*, which are employed to enumerate Days and Months, may also indeed be connected, as Substantives, with the object numbered, by means of the Constr. St., as in ሰቡዐ ፡ ዕለት Ex. 7, 25; but usually they take the numbered object in apposition to themselves, just like the

(¹) *Cf.* Ewald, '*Hebr. Spr.*' p. 689.

other Numerals (v. Examples, § 159, *b*). Where they stand independently for the "so-and-soth (day)", they are generally supplemented by a Suffix referring to Day or Month, as in Gen. 8,14; Lev. 23,6; Numb. 29,12; Gen. 7,11; 8,4.

2. Ordinal Numbers.

2. The *Numeral Adjectives* (*Ordinals*), must, like all other adjectives, take the Case (and Gender) of the Noun to which they are joined: **በራብዕ ፡ ትውልድ** Gen. 15,16; **በሣልስት ፡ ዕለት** Gen. 22,4. On some few occasions only the Numeral Adjective takes the Constr. St. and makes the Noun dependent upon it: **በሳኒት ፡ ዕለት** "on the following day" Josh. 10,32: this occurs oftener in denoting Fractional numbers (§ 159, *f*).

When the object enumerated is not expressly mentioned along with the Numeral Adjective, and when the latter has thus more of a Substantive character, like "the third", then it must, in accordance with § 185, *ad fin.*, be completed by a Suffix referring to the omitted Noun: **ወከማሁ ፡ ካልኡኒ ፡ ወሣልሱኒ ፡ እስከ ፡ ሰብዐቲሆሙ** "likewise the second also and the third, unto the seventh ('the seven')" Matt. 22,26; **ወካልእታኒ** "and the second (commandment)" Matt. 22, 39; Ruth 1, 4; **ከመ ፡ ካልእታ** "like the other" Matt. 12,13; **አሐዱ ፡ ይነሥኡ ፡ ወካልኡ ፡ የኀድጉ** Matt. 24,40; **በሣልስታ** "on the third (day)" Luke 2,46; **በሳኒታ** "on the following day" Matt. 27,62; so too, always:—**አሐዱ ፡ ምስለ ፡ ካልኡ** "with one another"(1). Again, the Numeral Adjective sometimes attaches to itself a Suffix with a possessive force referring to the principal Noun in the sentence: "and she said to Ruth:—**አተወት ፡ ካልእትኪ** the other (*lit.* 'thine other') has gone home; (do thou also return)" Ruth 1,15; **ኀየሰት ፡ ምሕረት ፡ ደኃሪት ፡ እምነ ፡ ቀዳሚትኪ** "the last kindness is more excellent still than the first (*lit.* 'thy first')" Ruth 3,10; **ናሁ ፡ ሣልሶሙ ፡ ዮም ፡ እንዘ ፡ ይጸንሑኒ** "behold, to-day is the third (*lit.* 'their third' *i. e.* 'day') that they have been attending upon me" Mark 8,2; "because thou saidst, 'I hate her', **ወሀብክዎ ፡ ለካልእከ** I then gave (her) to another" (*lit.* 'thine other', *i. e.* 'another than thou') Judges 15,2; "the youngest is with his father **ወካልኡሰ ፡ ሞተ** but the other ('to him') is dead" Gen. 42,13;

---

(1) But yet "one another" is frequently expressed in Ethiopic, and in Semitic generally, by the repetition of the Noun itself, as in **እብን ፡ ዲበ ፡ እብን** "one stone upon another" Matt. 24,2; **መራዕየ ፡ እመራዕይ** Gen. 32, 17 &c.

32, 20; "the same beast ሳምናሙ፡ ውእቱ፡ is the eighth ('to them')" Rev. 17, 11.—Farther, when it is said of any one that he is doing something 'for the so-and-so[th] time', this may be expressed by the Numeral Adjective, placed in apposition to the acting Subject, and supplemented by a Suffix referring to that Subject (§ 189, 3, *b*): "thou smitest me ናሁ፡ ሣልስከ፡ ዝንቱ፡ now for the third time" Numb. 22, 28; 24, 10; "he has defrauded me ወናሁ፡ ዳግሙ፡ ዮም even to-day for the second time" Gen. 27, 36. But yet we may also say, more simply: ወናሁ፡ ሣልስ፡ ዝንቱ፡ እንዘ፡ ታስተሐቅረኒ "and lo, thou art mocking me now for the third time" Judges 16, 15; Numb. 14, 22; 22, 32.

The Cardinal Number is often used for the Ordinal, or Numeral Adjective, not only in the case of the higher numbers,—which have no Adjective forms,—but also in the case of the lower ones, *e. g.* በአሐቲ፡ ኆኅት "in the first gate" Hen. 72, 25; ወሞተ፡ ዮሴፍ፡ በምእት፡ ወዐሠርቱ፡ ዓመት "and Joseph died in the hundred-and-tenth year" Gen. 50, 26; 16, 16; 17, 1, 24. Particularly when hours (of the day) are numbered, the Ethiopians prefer to employ the cardinal forms: ጊዜ፡ ሠላስ፡ ሰዓት "about the third hour" Matt. 20, 3, 5, 6; 27, 45 (yet v. በቀዳሚት፡ ሰዓት Judges 7, 19 [and *cf. Test. Ad.* (ed. Bezold, in '*Oriental. Studien*', 1906,) p. 899 *sqq.*]), just as one may also say በዓመት፡ ፭፻ "in the five hundredth year" Hen. 60, 1.

B. STRUCTURE OF THE SIMPLE SENTENCE.

§ 192. Having shown how the chief members of the Sentence,—viz., the Subject and the Predicate,—may be extended into larger groups of words, we proceed to deal with these members themselves, and with the combining of them into a Sentence.

1. The *Subject.*

1. *The Subject.* Every Sentence, which is not imperfect, must contain a Subject, *i. e.* a theme (whether person, thing, idea, fact, or relation), of which something is predicated. Such Subject is usually a Substantive (—it may also be an Infinitive, *e. g.* Matt. 15, 20; 17, 4; 1 Cor. 9, 15), or a Pronoun representing a Substantive [1]; but it may also be an Adjective if it is invested

(1) This may even be wanting, and in that case it must be supplied from the sense,—*cf. e. g.* Tobit 10, 12; አክብሪ፡ ታሕማኪ፡ እስመ፡ እም ይእዜሰ፡ ዘመድኪ αὐτοὶ νῦν γονεῖς σου εἰσίν.

with the force of a Substantive, or even an Adverb, when through the stimulus of speech the Adverb is raised to the position of a Noun-Substantive, as, for instance, ዮም in Mark 8, 2. An entire sentence even may take the place of Subject, particularly a Relative or a Conditional Sentence, *e. g.* የአክለኒ ፡ ዘረከብኩ ፡ ሞገሰ "it is enough for me that I have found favour" Gen. 33, 15; ኢያሐዝነከኑ ፡ እንዘ ፡ ንመውት "does it give thee no concern that ('when') we are perishing?" Mark 4, 38—, just as in other languages.

As, according to § 101, the finite Verb invariably contains the Person, enclosed along with the assertion, — every Sentence which is expressed by means of a finite verb is properly furnished already with its Subject, even when the latter is not distinctly mentioned. And yet that designation of the Subject which is contained in the Verb is very defective, if the Verb is in the third person, because the pronoun contained in the Verb merely points to *some* Subject, either a person, a thing or an idea; and thus it is left undetermined *what* the Subject is which is indicated in this way. In by far the greater number of sentences the Subject is therefore expressly introduced by name, or at least the context makes it clear, *who* or *what* is meant, in each particular case, by the Person which is inherent in the Verb. There are, however, sentences in which a verb in the third person stands quite by itself, neither having a Subject expressly mentioned, nor requiring a Subject to be supplied from the context. These cases fall now to be specially described.

(*a*) Indefinite Mode of Expression.

(*a*) There is *an indefinite mode of expression*, in which the speaker does not distinctly mention the Subject of an action, even though it is a living being,—a person,—because he either does not know that being or does not desire to mention it, being more concerned with the Action (Assertion) than with the person acting. In this case when the Ethiopians did not wish to put ሰብእ or ብእሲ "people" or "one" directly, for the undefined person, they employed mostly the third person Masc. Pl.:—ወአይድዕዋ ፡ ለርብቃ "and they told Rebecca" Gen. 27, 42; ኢይቀድሙ ፡ ወሂበ "they do not give first" Gen. 29, 26; 31, 26; Hen. 14, 19(1); 22, 3; 31, 3;

(1) [Flemming, however, reads here ወኢይክል ፡ ርእየ "and I could not look ('at it', *i. e.* 'at the fire')", as translating the Greek *καὶ οὐκ ἐδυνάσθην ἰδεῖν*,—instead of Dillmann's ወኢይክሉ ፡ ርእዮቶ "and people could not look at it". tr.]

Judges 16, 2 &c.; and at rare times the third person Masc. Sing., *e. g.* ከመ፡ ይእሥርከ "that he (one) bind thee" Hen. 13, 1.

(*b*) Impersonal Mode of Expression

(*b*) Then there is an *Impersonal mode of expression*, which is made use of when the speaker is concerned merely with the predication,—and not with the person or thing of which he predicates,—and therefore puts the predication in the third person Sing. Masc., without explaining whom or what he means by the pronoun which is inherent in the verb. We employ in our own tongue the impersonal "it" in such cases. Many impersonal verbs of this kind occur in Ethiopic, and always in the third pers. Sing. Masculine (not Feminine): ይዘንም "it will rain" Matt. 16, 3; መስየ "it is drawing towards evening" Matt. 16, 2; ኮነ፡ ሐዋየ "it has become evening-red" Matt. 16, 2; አከለ "it amounts to"; ኮነ "it is permitted" and "it is sufficient" (1) Deut. 3, 26; ይጸብብ "it is confining" &c. There are even impersonal clauses, in which no finite verb is contained at all, like ወሶበ፡ ለሐዊራ "and when it was about the time of her setting out" Judges 1, 14. When such impersonal clauses take the Infinitive form, they show the Suffix of the third person Sing. Masc. as Subject (v. § 181, *b*, *α*, *ad fin.*), *e. g.* ወመንፈቀ፡ ሌሊት፡ ከዊኖ "and when it was midnight" Ruth 3, 8.

Finally, *a feebly personal mode of expression* is very frequently employed, in which a verb makes its appearance at first indeed in a form seemingly impersonal, but forthwith receives a certain substitute for the missing Subject, supplied in a clause of its own. Such a substitutionary clause would, in English or German, take the form of an Infinitive with "to", or be introduced by "that", "if" or some other Conjunction. In particular we find employed in this way: ኮነ and ብውሕ "it is permitted"; ኮነ "it is enough"; መፍትው "it is necessary"; ይደሉ "it is suitable *or* becoming" (with Acc. 'for any one'); ይረትዕ "it is right"; ይቀልል "it is easy"; ይኤድም "it pleases" Josh. 9, 23; ይበቍዕ "it is profitable"; ይኄይስ "it is better"; ይሤኒ or ሠናይ "it is good"; አከለ "it is enough"; ጡበዐ "it is customary" (G. Ad.); ይቀድም (with Acc.) "it falls first to" ('any one') Ruth 4, 4; ይመስል and ያስተርኢ "it seems"; ሀለወ "it is about to happen" (with a Subjunctive following); and

(1) On the other hand the Ethiopians employ always ኮነ, with a personal reference, for our "it goes, *or* fares in such and such a way with me", *e. g.* እመ፡ ከመዝ፡ እከውን "if it will fare so with me" Gen. 25, 22.

others(1). It has already been pointed out how such verbs take to themselves the clause representing the Subject, sometimes in the form of the Accusative of the Infinitive (§ 182, *a*, *α*) or the Nominative of the Infinitive (*ibid.*), sometimes as a Subjunctive in immediate subordination (§ 182, *b*, *β*) or connected by means of **ከመ** (§ 182, *b*, *γ*). They may also introduce such representative of the Subject in some other fashion, as, for instance, in **ኢይኩንከ ፡ ዕጹበ ፡ ቅድሜከ ፡ በእንተ ፡ ውእቱ ፡ ሕፃን** "let it not seem grievous in thy sight because of the lad" Gen. 21, 12; or with **እስመ**, *e. g.* **ይኩንክሙ ፡ ለክሙ ፡ እስመ** "let it be enough for you, that" Numb. 16, 3; or through **ዘ**, *e. g.* **ኢአክለኪኑ ፡ ዘነሣእኪ ፡ ምትየ** "is it not enough for thee that thou hast taken my husband from me?" Gen. 30, 15; 33, 15. To such semi-personal sentences belongs also:—**ወለምንት ፡ እንከ ፡ ሊተ ፡ አሐዩ** "and what then shall it avail me that I live?" Gen. 27, 46.

But to this class of phrases belong quite specially the very frequently used words **ቦ** "there is *or* are" and **አልቦ** "there is *or* are not" (or **ቦቱ** and **አልቦቱ**), §§ 167, 1, *b*; 176, *h*. In distinction from **ቦ** "he has" (§ 176, *h*) the **ቦ**, which calls for description here, regularly takes to itself in the Nominative the word which in the sense of a Subject completes its meaning: **በቅድሜሁ ፡ አልቦ ፡ ማኅለቅት** "before him there is no ceasing"(2) Hen. 39, 11; 49, 2; 58, 3: this is always the case, when it is used directly for "there is", "there is not". When, on the other hand, **ቦ** has rather the force of "one finds" or "one meets with", it may take its Subject also in the Accusative (*cf.* § 176, *h*):—**ቦ ፡ ሕፅዋነ** "there are eunuchs" Matt. 19, 12; **ቦቱ ፡ ኀቤነ ፡ ሣዕረ ፡ ወእክለኒ** "we have both straw and provender" Gen. 24, 25; 42, 1 &c. This form, **ቦ** or **አልቦ**, has become so common that it is often used even to introduce a question, either alone, *e. g.* in Judges 4, 20, or along with an interrogative, *e. g.* in **ቦኑ ፡ ዐቃቢሁ ፡ አነ** "am I his keeper?" Gen. 4, 9, where it is the prop of the interrogative (v. also § 198): or it is employed with **ዘ** or **ከመ** following, in the sense of—"it is the case that . .":

---

(1) To this class belong turns of expression like **ምንት ፡ አሥሐቃ** "*cur ridere eam fecit?*"; *cf.* Dillmann's '*Lex.*' col. 188, and 4 Esr. 9, 39 (Laur. 40).

(2) Here and there, a Personal Suffix in the sense of a Dative is met with, instead of the neutral *ō* in **ቦ** and **አልቦ**, *e. g.* in **ወቀዊም ፡ አልቦሙ**, literally—"and standing is not in them", *i. e.* "there is no standing for them" Hen. 41, 2. [Flemming reads here **ወቀዊሞሙ ፡ አልቦሙ**. tr.]

—ለእመቦ ፡ ዘወለድከ "should it be the case that thou beget children" Gen. 48, 6; እመቦ ፡ ከመ ፡ ኮነ ፡ ድኅረ "if in later times it happen . ." Josh. 22, 28; Gen. 42, 38; or a periphrasis is constructed out of it and a relative following, to indicate the idea of "something", "some", "a few" (§ 173):—we even have ቦ ፡ አመ "sometimes" (¹) Matt. 17, 15; and repeated = "*modo—modo*". Lastly, ወኮነ is often used impersonally, like the Hebrew וַיְהִי and וְהָיָה, with the force of "and it came to pass",—to which introductory phrase it is better to attach what came to pass, without the ወ than with it: ወኮነ ፡ በይእቲ ፡ ዕለት ፡ በጽሑ Gen. 26, 32; 27, 1; 41, 1; Hen. 52, 7 (where the Indic. ይከውን appears); ወኮነ ፡ ሶበ ፡ ወለደት ፡ ወመንታ ፡ ሀለወ ፡ ውስተ ፡ ከርሣ Gen. 38, 27; or even by ከመ and the Subjunctive: ወኮነ ፡ እምድኅረዝ ፡ ከመ ፡ ትትከበት ፡ መንፈስየ Hen. 71, 1.

(*c*) Passive Construction. (*c*) When the Subject which performs the action is suppressed, *the Passive construction* is frequently made use of instead of the Active, and then the Object of the action becomes the grammatical Subject. This Passive construction is pretty common in Ethiopic, *e. g.* ተወልዱ ፡ ሎቱ ፡ ፵ ደቂቅ "there were born to him forty sons" Judges 12, 14; ጸሎቶሙ ፡ ለጻድቃን ፡ ተሰምዐ "the prayer of the righteous ones was heard" Hen. 47, 4; ከመ ፡ ትጸላእ ፡ ልያ "that Leah is (was) hated" Gen. 29, 31; እምትካትሰ ፡ አኮ ፡ ከመዝ ፡ ዘተገብረ "in olden times it was not so done" Matt. 19, 8; Hen. 48, 2; 50, 2; 57, 2. And yet the Passive construction, found in other languages, is frequently replaced by the indefinite mode of expression in the Active (v. *supra a*): ወይቤልዎ ፡ ለአብረሃም καὶ ἐῤῥέθη τῷ Ἀβραάμ Gen. 15, 13; ይቅትልዎ ἀποθανέτω Judges 6, 30 &c. A Passive verb may also be used in an impersonal or feebly personal way (v. *supra b*), *e. g.* ተብሀለ "it is said" Luke 4, 12; ይትፈቀድ "it is required"; ይትከሀል "it is possible"; ተስእነ "it is impossible". In the case of such verbs the clause which has to serve as Subject, is annexed to them by the same turns of phrase as in the case of other feebly personal verbs, *e. g.* ወአልቦ ፡ ዘይትከሀል ፡ ይትኀባእ ፡ እምኔከ "nothing can be concealed from thee" Hen. 9, 5. Now, seeing that a Passive Verb in the 3rd pers. Sing. Masc., used in a feebly personal sense, expresses

(¹) [*Cf.* similar phrases of Indefiniteness in Greek and Latin with ἔστι(ν) and *est*: *e. g.* ἔστιν ὅτε, *est ubi* &c. TR.]

exactly as much as an Active Verb in the 3rd pers. Pl. Masc., used indefinitely (*e. g.* ተብህለ and ይብሉ "they say"), and farther, seeing that other feebly personal verbs may take to themselves a supplementary form in the Accusative, by way of Subject (§ 182, *a*, *α*), it is not a matter of astonishment that in the Passive form of expression in Ethiopic the Object of an action,—instead of being in the Nominative as grammatical Subject,—may even be in the Accusative(1), *e. g.* ተሰምየ ፡ ስሞ ፡ ኤዶም "there was called his name, (*i. e.* "they called his name") Edom" Gen. 25, 30; Deut. 28, 10; ይትቤቀል ፡ ኵሎ "retribution will be exacted for every thing" Hen. 25, 4; Sap. 11, 4 (A); 14, 7 (A); Deut. 28, 10; 4 Esr. 2, 22 var.; 4 Esr. 6, 65 (Laur. 75); 4 Esr. 9, 24 (Laur. 27); 4 Esr. 10, 51 (Laur. 65); and even in the case of the Passive Participle: ዘረሥዩም ፡ ለነ ፡ አብያተ 4 Esr. 7, 16 (Laur. 24).

The Passive construction is not so often met with in Ethiopic, if the acting Subject is mentioned at the same time. In that case the Subject must be introduced by a Preposition denoting a relation of causality; in comparatively rare instances, by ለ, *e. g.* ትከውን ፡ ምዉእ ፡ ሎቱ፡ *Chrest.* p. 43, line 22; ወይትሌበው ፡ ለሰማዕያን *ibid.* 45, l. 24; oftener by በ, to express the instrumentality or any impersonal cause, but also said of Persons with the meaning "by" (Agency), *e. g.* ዘይትገበር ፡ በኖሎት "what is done by the shepherds" Hen. 89, 62; Matt. 14, 2 (*cf.* 2, 17; 21, 4); and by እምነ (and እም) to express the doer, *e. g.* ተበልዑ ፡ እምነ ፡ ኵሎሙ ፡ አራዊተ ፡ ገዳም "they were devoured by all the beasts of the field" Hen. 89, 57 (*cf.* § 164, 3); እመላእክት ፡ በሰማያት ፡ ትሰገድ ፡(2) ወእም አበውኒ ፡ በምድር ፡ ትሴባሕ ፡ ወእምነቢያት ፡ ትትከበር ፡ ወእምሐዋርያት ፡ ትሰበክ ፡ ወእምአብያተ ፡ ክርስቲያናት ፡ እስከ ፡ ይእዜ ፡ ትትኄበይ ፡ ወትሴባሕ *Chrest.* p. 78, line 25 *sqq.*; here and there also by Compounds of እም, *e. g.* እምቅድመ in the case of ተውህበ Hen. 37, 4, or እምኀበ.

§ 193. 2. *The Predicate* of a Sentence is usually a Verb or an Adjective (or Participle). Certain Adjectives, when used as Predicates, are in all cases, or at least in certain cases, supplemented by a Suffix (v. §§ 156; 191). Those Adjectives and Participles also, which are formed by periphrasis with the Relative Pron. (§ 202), have as Pre- 2. The *Predicate*.

(1) For the Hebrew, *cf.* Ewald § 295, *b*.

(2) On the other hand, the construction in the Active is—ሰገዱ ፡ ለ.

dicates the same construction as the ordinary Adjectives, *e.g.* **ወይከውን ፡ ደኃሪቱ ፡ ዘየአኪ ፡ እምቀዳሚቱ፡** "and his latter condition is worse than his earlier one" Matt. 12, 45; and those also which are formed by the Genitive sign **ዘ**, *e.g.* **ወልብሱ ፡ ዘጸጕረ ፡ ገመል** "and his raiment was of camel's hair" Mark 1, 6 (*cf.* § 186, *a*, δ); **እስመ ፡ እሙንቱ ፡ ዘሥጋ** "for they are mortal ('flesh')" Gen. 6, 3; and the Possessive Pronouns, described in § 150, *e.g.* **ዚአነ ፡ ማይ** "the water is ours" Gen. 26, 20; **እንተ ፡ ኢኮነት ፡ እንቲአሆሙ** "which is not theirs" Gen. 15, 13, even when they are still farther strengthened by the Relative Pronoun being prefixed to them, as in **ኵሉ ፡ ዘትሬኢ ፡ ዘዚአየ ፡ ውእቱ፡** "all that thou seest is mine" Gen. 31, 43. The Predicate also may take the form of a repetition of the Verb, as in **ወየዐቢ ፡ ወየዐቢ ፡ ጥቀ** Gen. 26, 13. In like manner the Genitives which are described in § 186, *a*, γ, when employed with the force of Adjectives, may take the position of the Predicate: **አንትሙ ፡ ዘክርስቶስ** "ye are Christ's" 1 Cor. 3, 23.

But in fact all the other classes of words may likewise take the place of Predicate, especially Nouns-Substantive (Infinitives) and Numerals, as in **ወኵሉ ፡ ነፍስ ፡ ሠላሳ ፡ ወሠለስቱ፡** "all the souls were thirty and three" Gen. 46, 15. Substantives often express the Predicate-idea more vigorously and comprehensively than an Adjective or Participle, *e. g.* **ጽዕለት ፡ ውእቱ ፡ ለነ** "it is a disgrace to us" Gen. 34, 14; **ኵሉ ፡ ምግባሪቱ ፡ ዕልወት** "all her works are apostasy (*i. e.* 'nothing but apostasy')" Hen. 93, 9. The Substantive is also used in default of an Adjective which would express exactly the same meaning, and where the Genitive of the Substantive might also in many instances be employed: **ወምድሩ ፡ በረድ** "and its floor was crystal" (=**ዘበረድ** "crystalline", *or* "of crystal") Hen. 14,10; **ወሰማዮሙ ፡ ማይ** "and their heaven was water" Hen. 14, 11; **ወፍሬሁኒ ፡ ሞገስ ፡ ጥቀ ፡ ለርእየ ፡ ገጽ** "its fruit is delightful to behold" (where an adverb even is connected with the Substantive which is used for an Adjective) Hen. 24, 5; 88, 1; 21, 8 (1); 22, 2. Farther, Nouns with Prepositions also serve as Predicate, *e.g.* **ውእቱ ፡ ኀቤየ** "he is (devoted) to me" Gen. 29, 34; **እምነ ፡ ዕጽምየ ፡ ወእምነ ፡ ሥጋየ ፡ አንተ** "of my bone and of my flesh art thou" Gen. 29, 14; **እምዕፁብ ፡ በአቱ ፡ መንግሥተ ፡ ሰማያት** "his entry

---

(1) [Flemming, however, reads here the Participle **ሕሙም**, not like Dillmann the Substantive **ሕማም**. tr.]

into the kingdom of heaven is a matter of difficulty" Matt. 19, 23 (*cf.* § 173); **እስመ ፡ ለዓለም ፡ ምሕረቱ** "for his mercy (is) for ever" Ps. 135, 1, and of frequent occurrence; **ሰይፍ ፡ ምሉኅ ፡ ውስተ ፡ እዴሁ** "a drawn sword (was) in his hand" Josh. 5, 13; **ኵሉ ፡ ግብሩ ፡ ምስለ ፡ ቅዱሳን** "all his doings (were) with the holy ones" Hen. 12, 2. And in conformity therewith even true Adverbs may form the Predicate, so far as they also express the same qualifications of condition as a Noun with a Preposition, *e. g.* **እሉ ፡ ዕደው ፡ ሰንአ ፡ እሙንቱ ፡ ምስሌነ** "these men are at peace with us" Gen. 34, 21; 42, 19; **እምነ ፡ መሬት ፡ ታሕተ ፡ ተስፋሁ** γῆς εὐτελεστέρα ἡ ἐλπὶς αὐτοῦ Sap. 15, 10. Lastly, even whole clauses serve as Predicate, particularly Relative Clauses, and abbreviated Relative Clauses, just as in other languages.

Here we must notice the peculiar use of **ብሂል** "to say", as the Predicate of a short clause: **ዝውእቱ ፡ ብሂል** "that is to say" —is the standing formula for "that is", "that means", *e. g.* in Matt. 27, 47; also in **ዘእምአቡየ ፡ ብሂል** "which is to say, 'of my father'", or "that is, of my father" Gen. 19, 37. It is then generally shortened into **ብሂል**, *e. g.* in **ይሳኮር ፡ ዐስብ ፡ ብሂል** "Issachar, ('hire', to say) that is,—'hire'" Gen. 30, 18; Mark 3, 17; 5, 41; and it is employed whenever foreign words are explained, *e. g.* in Ethiopic-Amharic lists of words [the so-called *sawāsew*].

§ 194. 3. *Union of Subject and Predicate.*

3. Union of Subject and Predicate:— (*a*) Connecting-words when Predicate is a Noun of some kind.

(*a*) When the Predicate is not a full Verb, but a Noun of some kind, we employ in our own (Western) languages the auxiliary verb "to be", to join Subject and Predicate together, or to introduce the Predicate. But in Ethiopic, as in the other Semitic tongues, such a connecting-word is, in the first place, not absolutely necessary: Subject and Predicate may be directly placed side by side; and then the sense and context show of themselves what syntactical force is attributable to the two severally in this combination, *e. g.* **ከመ ፡ ኆጻ ፡ ባሕር ፡ ብዝኆሙ** "as the sand of the sea (is) their multitude" Josh. 11, 4; **ፍሡሓት ፡ እምወይን ፡ አዕይንቲሁ** "joyous with wine (are) his eyes" Gen. 49, 12. This juxtaposition of Subject and Predicate, without any connecting-word, is in most frequent use when the Subject is a Pronoun and comes second; for in that case misunderstanding is the less likely to prevail, as the Predicate would have had to be put after the Pronoun, f such predicate had been intended merely as a word in Apposition. Accordingly we say: **መሬት ፡ አንተ** "dust thou (art)" Gen. 3,19; **ብፁዓን ፡ አንትሙ** "blessed (are) ye" Matt. 5,11; **ብዙኃን ፡ ንሕነ** "many (are) we" Mark 5,9; **ዘእግዚአብሔር ፡ አነ** "I (am) of God" Gen. 50,19; **ኅላፊት ፡ ንሕነ** "strangers (are) we" Judg. 19,18; **አይቴ ፡ አንተ** "where (art) thou?" Gen. 3,9; **ምንት ፡ ተግባርክሙ** "what is your occupation?" Gen. 46,33. But in many other cases this sense of a union between the two might not be immediately and invariably obvious; and it might then be possible to mistake the true relation of the two words for a relation of mere apposition. Accordingly in such cases Subject and Predicate are at once separated and connected by the insertion or addition of a Personal Pronoun of the third person. This Pronoun,—*the Copula*,—has in fact to discharge the function of signifying that the Subject-word and Predicate-word, although not to be bound immediately together, yet stand in a most important personal or individual relation to one another, and that the Predicate-word is nothing other than the attribute asserted of the Subject-word as the person or thing referred to. In other words, a personal Pronoun is assigned to the Predicate-word in order to turn it completely into a Predicate, precisely as the inflected Verb always encloses in its framework the Personal sign as the ligament between Subject and Predicate. Thus we say: **እስመ ፡ ረሐብ ፡ ይእቲ ፡ ምድር ፡ ቅድሜሆሙ** "for the land is spacious before them" (while the sentence, without **ይእቲ** would mean: "for a spacious land is before them") Gen. 34,21. The employment of this connecting-word is also necessary, when for special reasons (§ 196) the Subject comes first, *e. g.* in **እሉ ፡ እሙንቱ ፡ ደቂቀ ፡ ኤሌማ** "these are the children of Oholibamah" Gen. 36,14.—But, starting from those cases in which the use of the Copula was essential to clearness of meaning, it has spread to many cases in Ethiopic, in which it might have been dispensed with.—The Copula is then placed either before or after the Predicate, but preferably between Subject and Predicate: **ብዙኃን ፡ እሙንቱ ፡ ጽዉዓን** "many are called" Matt. 20,16; **ተዓይነ ፡ እግዚአብሔር ፡ ይእቲ ፡ ዛቲ** "this is the camp of God" Gen. 32,3; **መኑ ፡ ውእቱ ፡ ዝንቱ** "who is this?" Matt. 21,10; **ዛቲ ፡ ይእቲ ፡ ሥርዐትየ** "this is my covenant" Gen. 17,10; **እሉ ፡ ሠለስቱ ፡ አስካል ፡ ሠላስ ፡ መዋዕል ፡ እማንቱ** "these three clusters of grapes are three days" Gen. 40,12. Farther the Copula is necessary, when the Subject is a Relative pronoun: **ዘውእቱ ፡**

Personal Pronoun as *Copula*.

መራሒሆሙ "who is their leader" Hen. 72, 1; እንተ ፡ ይእቲ ፡ ኬብሮን "which is Hebron" Gen. 35, 37; ዘውእቶሙ ፡ ሴም ፡ ወካም ፡ ወያፌት "who are Shem, Ham and Japhet" Gen. 5, 32. The Gender and Number of the connecting pronoun, when Subject and Predicate do not agree in these points, may be regulated either by the Subject or the Predicate, but the latter method is the usual one(1): ከመዝ ፡ ውእቱ ፡ አስማቲሆሙ "their names are these" Gen. 46, 8; ምንት ፡ ውእቱ ፡ እሉ ፡ እሙንቱ "what are these?" Hen. 52, 3; መኑ ፡ ውእቶሙ ፡ እሉ ፡ ፬ ገጽ "who ('whose') are these four faces?" Hen. 40, 8. Of course the Copula may also stand when the Subject is a Pronoun of the first or second Person: አንትሙ ፡ ውእቱ ፡ ብርሃኑ ፡ ለዓለም "ye (it) are the light of the world" Matt. 5, 14; አንተ ፡ ውእቱ ፡ ዔሳው "thou art Esau" Gen. 27, 21; አነ ፡ ውእቱ ('I it') "it is I" Matt. 14, 27; አነ ፡ ውእቱ ፡ አምላከ ፡ አብርሃም "I am the God of Abraham" Gen. 26, 24; 45, 3; [*Kebra Nag.* 43 a 5 *sq.*]; አነ ፡ ውእቱ ፡ መልአክ ፡ . . . አነ ፡ ውእቱ ፡ ሚካኤል G. Ad. 138, 2—6; [አነ ፡ ይእቲ ፡ አቡከ ፡ ወእምከ, *Kebra Nag.* 27 b 11]. But yet instead of the Copula, the Subject-Pronoun may be repeated after the Predicate, *e. g.* እስመ ፡ አነ ፡ ኄር ፡ አነ "because I am good" (*lit.* 'because I, — *i. e.* as regards me, — good I') Matt. 20, 15, so that the first አነ seems to be taken as a Nominative absolute; so too አንትሙ ፡ ኢለበውያን ፡ አንትሙ Matt. 15, 16; Judges 12, 5; ወኵልነ ፡ ደቂቀ ፡ ፩ ብእሲ ፡ ንሕነ Gen. 42, 11.

Use of ሀለወ and ኮነ as Connecting-words.

On the other hand the two verbs ሀለወ and ኮነ have not yet come to be used so frequently as connecting-words between Subject and Predicate. ሀለወ has generally its full meaning, "to be present", "to exist", "to be", *e. g.* እንዘ ፡ እንተ ፡ ትልህቅ ፡ ሀለወት "so long as an elder (sister) is there" Gen. 29, 26; እንተ ፡ ሀለወት ፡ ውስተ ፡ ደብረ ፡ ከናአን "which lies in the hill-country of Canaan" Gen. 33, 18; ሀሎ ፡ ወልድ ፡ ዝየ "there is a lad here" John 6, 9; ህየ ፡ ሀሎኩ ፡ አነ ፡ ማእከሎሙ "there am I (present) in the midst

(1) [Praetorius states the rules of Concord here more clearly. He says ('*Aethiop. Gramm.*' p. 159 *sq.*): "When the Predicate contains a description or qualification of the Subject, the Pers. Pron. which serves as Copula is usually regulated in Person, Gender and Number by the Subject, and follows the Predicate; . . . but when the attachment of the Predicate seeks to show that two quite well-known things are equivalent to each other, the Pers. Pron. which serves as Copula is usually regulated by the Predicate, and precedes it". tr.]

of them" Matt. 18,20. In like manner ኮነ has generally the full signification of "becoming", "originating", "happening", "being on the point of" (*future*), *e. g.* Ps. 37,15; Mark 5,14; Gen. 29,36. Farther ኮነ standing by itself is equivalent to "it has happened", *i. e.* "it is past" Gen. 38,23. Both words, however, came to be used also as connecting-words between Subject and Predicate, either because the Predicate had at the same time to be represented as falling within the domain of the Past or Future,—a condition which cannot be expressed distinctly enough by the pronominal connecting-word (1): ወሀሎ ፡ እግዚአብሔር ፡ ምስለ ፡ ዮሴፍ "and God was with Joseph" Gen. 39,2; ወይከውኑ ፡ ኵሉ ፡ ውሉደ ፡ ሰብእ ፡ ጻድቃነ "and all the sons of men shall be (*future*) righteous" Hen. 10,21;—or for the purpose of making the Predicate negative (as if that had always to be expressed by—: 'one has not come to be—this or that'): እኁየ ፡ ጸጕር ፡ ውእቱ ፡ ወአንሰ ፡ ኢኮንኩ ፡ ጸጕረ "my brother is hairy, while I am not hairy" Gen. 27,11, 21; 42,11, 31; Matt. 10,20; ኢሀሎ ፡ ወልድ ፡ ውስተ ፡ ዐዘቅት "there was no lad (to be found) in the pit" Gen. 37,30. In all other cases in which the two verbs are employed as connecting-words, they have nearly always another significant, second meaning, *e. g.* ዘሀለወ ፡ ድልወ "who is ('stands') ready" 1 Pet. 4,5; እለ ፡ ሀለዉ ፡ ውስተ ፡ ቤት "who were ('present') in the house" Gen. 33,14; Lev. 10, 7; 21,12.

(*b*) Agreement of Predicate with Subject in Gender and Number, when Predicate is a full Verb or an Adjective.

§ 195. (*b*) *If the Predicate is a full Verb or an Adjective, it must agree with the Subject in Gender and Number.* All the variations, however, in the treatment of gender and number, which have been described in § 188, are also current here. Thus, Concord in gender and number is most strictly observed, when the Subject is a Personal Noun or Pronoun, *e. g.*, ብፁዓን ፡ አንትሙ "blessed are ye"; ኢላሐዋ ፡ ደናግሊሆሙ "their maidens did not mourn" Ps. 77,69; እስመ ፡ ብዙኃት ፡ አንስትያሁ Judges 8,30; ተወልዳ ፡ ሎሙ ፡ አዋልድ ፡ ሠናያት ፡ ወላሕያት Hen. 6,1. When the

(1) Although the pronominal Copula is found in use even in such a case: ὀψόμεθα, τί ἔσται τὰ ἐνύπνια αὐτοῦ ወንርአይ ፡ ምንት ፡ ውእቱ ፡ ሕልሚሁ Gen. 37,20; Judges 13,12. Even without any Copula, sentences are met with, which fall within the domain of the Past or the Future: ከመ ፡ ውስተ ፡ ቀዳሕያን ፡ አንተ "when thou wast among the cupbearers" Gen. 40,13; አይቴ ፡ ማኅደረ ፡ ኃጥአን "where then shall the abode of sinners be?" Hen. 38,2; Deut. 15,15.

Subject is a word denoting a thing or a conception, Concord prevails, it is true, in many instances, as in **ይኩኑ ፡ ብርሃናት** "Let there be lights!" Gen. 1, 14 (for **ብርሃን** is generally masc.); **ይትከሠታ ፡ ኅቡኣቲሆሙ ፡ ለጻድቃን** "the secrets of the just shall be revealed" Hen. 38, 3; **ርእያ ፡ አዕይንትየ** "mine eyes saw" Hen. 39, 5; but often too, the Predicate to a Subject, Fem. sing., keeps its own readiest gender (masc.): **ወኮነ ፡ ድቀቱ ፡ ዐቢየ** "and its fall was great" Matt. 7, 27; **ወኮነት ፡ እሳት ፡ ወጠነ ፡ እምቀትረ ፡ ዕለት** G. Ad. 42, 11; **እስመ ፡ ሥዩም ፡ ውስተ ፡ ልበሙ ፡ እኪት ፡ በኵሉ ፡ ጊዜ** "for wickedness is lodged in their heart at all times" Gen. 8, 21; **ወኮነ ፡ ትዕይንቶሙ ፡ ዐቢየ ፡ ጥቀ** Gen. 50, 9. Sometimes a Predicate in the Plural masc. is attached to a Subject in the Plural fem., as in **ራእያት ፡ ዱቤየ ፡ ወድቁ** "visions fell upon me" Hen. 13, 8; or the plural of the Subject is conceived of as a feminine Noun of Unity, as in **ኀጣውኢሆሙ ፡ ዐብየት** "their sins are great" Gen. 18, 20; or,—which is the most usual case,—the Predicate to a Plural stands in the Singular Masc., and that with especial frequency if it comes first: **ኀለፈ ፡ መዋዕሊሁ** Josh. 23, 1, 2; Ps. 77, 37 (in contrast with Ps. 89, 9); **ወወፅአ ፡ ስሙዓቱ** Matt. 4, 24; **ዕፀው ፡ ዘይፈሪ** Gen. 1, 11; **ይትሌዐል ፡ አቅርንተ ፡ ጻድቃን** Ps. 74, 10 (although this may also be explained in accordance with § 192, *c*); **ይኩን ፡ ኀትው ፡ መኃትዊክሙ** Luke 12, 35; **ይትባረክ ፡ ኵሉ ፡ አሕዛበ ፡ ምድር ፡ በእንቲአከ** Gen. 12, 3; [*Kebra Nag.* 4 a 21 *sqq.*]. If, however, several other predicates follow a plural Subject, without the Subject being expressly repeated, the full concord in gender and number is frequently reverted to in their case, instead of the employment of the Sing. Masc. being continued.— Notice thus cases like: **ሶበ ፡ መጽአ ፡ እማንቱ ፡ አባግዕ ፡ ይስተያ ፡ ይፀንሳ** Gen. 30, 38, followed by **ወሶበ ፡ መጽአ ፡ ወሰተያ ፡ ፀንሳ** v. 39: or **ውስተ ፡ ውእቱ ፡ ሐረግ ፡ ሠረጸ ፡ አዕጹቂሁ ፡ ወአውፅአት ፡** (not **ወአውፅአ ፡**) **አስከለ** Gen. 40, 10; Ex. 16, 22. But, *vice versâ*, collective-words in the Singular number are often associated with a Predicate in the plural(1): **አፅምኡ ፡ ሕዝብየ** "hear ye, my people" Ps. 77, 1; **ቤተ ፡ እስራኤል ፡ ተወከሉ** Ps. 113, 17, 18; **ይትዋረሱ ፡ ዘርአከ** Gen. 22, 17; **ወፅኡ ፡ ኵሉ ፡ ሀገር ፡ ይትቀበልዎ** Matt. 8, 34; Mark 1, 33.

If a sentence contains several Subjects connected by copula-

---

(1) An analogous form is furnished in the periphrasis for the Article in § 172, *c*: **ኀጢአቶሙ ፡ ለዝንቱ ፡ ሀገር** Gen. 19, 15.

tive particles, the Predicate, when it comes first, may agree either with the first Subject only, or with all of them combined together (as in § 172, *c*); but, when it comes last, it usually takes the plural, although the singular is also met with in these circumstances: **ፃእ ፡ አንተ ፡ ወብእሲትከ** &c. Gen. 8, 16; **ወወፅአ ፡ ኖኅ ፡ ወብእሲቱ** &c. Gen. 8, 18; 9, 2; **ወነሥኡ ፡ ሴም ፡ ወያፌት** Gen. 9, 23; **ወነሥኡ ፡ አብራም ፡ ወናኮር ፡ አንስቲያ ፡ ሎሙ** Gen. 11, 29; **ዘእንበለ ፡ ይትፈጠር ፡ ፀሐይ ፡ ወተአምር** Hen. 48, 3([1]); **ሰላም ፡ ወርትዕ ፡ ሱቱፋን ፡ ይከውኑ** Hen. 11, 2; **ፍርሀት ፡ ወረዓድ ፡ ነሥአሙ** Hen. 13, 3; **ሐዘን ፡ ወሕማም ፡ ወጻማ ፡ ወመቅሠፍት ፡ ኢይገስሰሙ** Hen. 25, 6([1]). In these cases much depends upon the sense: If the first word is the principal Subject, those which follow being subordinate to it in importance, so that **ወ** corresponds rather to our "accompanied by" or "along with",—as in the cases cited above, Gen. 8, 16, 18, or in **ወሐለየት ፡ ዴቦራ ፡ ወባረቅ** Judges 5, 1,—then the Predicate usually conforms only to the first of the Subjects, even though all the Subject-Words should denote persons.

Frequently also the Predicate is regulated not by the grammatical, but by the logical Subject of the sentence([2]), *e. g.* in **ምንትኑ ፡ ሕዙናን ፡ ገጽክሙ ፡ ዮም** "why is your countenance sad (*pl.*) to-day" Gen. 40, 7; **መኑ ፡ ስምከ** "what (*lit.* 'who') is thy name?" Gen. 32, 28 (v. § 198); **ይጸርኁ ፡ ነፍሳት** "the souls (of men) cry out" Hen. 9, 10.

(c) Arrangement of the Sentence. § 196. (*c*) As regards *the arrangement of the sentence*, Ethiopic exhibits greater freedom than any other Semitic language. It is capable of expressing almost any Greek sentence, with a pretty exact preservation of its word-arrangement. The entire development of the speech, during a long formative period, aimed at reaching the utmost possible freedom in the structure of the Sentence, and the ability to furnish adequate expression for the manifold forms and shades of thought. For that reason precisely, Prepositions have been formed in rich abundance, and a highly diversified employment of Suffixes has been developed, together

([1]) [In Hen. 48, 3 Flemming adopts the variant **ትትፈጠር** instead of **ይትፈጠር**, and in 25, 6, **ወጻዕር** instead of **ወጻማ**. tr.]

([2]) So too in the periphrasis of the Article, § 172, *c*: **ተዘከሮሙ ፡ ለነፍሳተ ፡ አግብርቲከ** (*Liturg.*); **ዘረዎሙ ፡ ለነገረ ፡ ኵሉ ፡ በሐውርት** Gen. 11, 9.

with the various methods, already described, of expressing Case. Behind these forms and grammatical expedients, however, a certain intellectual and mental energy is found in full vigour, which is able to hold in its grasp extended and seemingly dislocated sentences, and to assign the just relation which members of the sentence hold to each other, though separate and far apart. What form may be given, in accordance therewith, to the arrangement of the words within the individual word-groups of the sentence has already been generally indicated. In what follows we have only to discuss the arrangement of the leading members of the sentence.

(α) Usual Order.

(α) In ordinary, unimpassioned discourse, the Predicate stands at the beginning of the sentence: the Subject follows, and then the Object: **ወረከበ ፡ ዮሴፍ ፡ ሞገሰ ፡ በቅድመ ፡ እግዚኡ** Gen. 39, 4. If the Object is a Suff. Pron., it naturally precedes the Subject. When several objects appear, that which is first affected by the action comes before the others. If, however, the Object together with the verb forms only one idea, it is placed before the Subject: **ወወለደት ፡ ወልደ ፡ ይእቲ ፡ ብእሲት** Judges 13, 24; **ወወደየት ፡ አዕይንቲሃ ፡ ላዕለ ፡ ዮሴፍ ፡ ብእሲተ ፡ እግዚኡ** Gen. 39, 7. In like manner the Subject is generally put last, when farther qualifications are attached to it, as in **እሮ ፡ ኢይመይጡ ፡ ፍናዊሆሙ ፡ ብርሃናት ፡ ዘውስተ ፡ ሰማይ** Hen. 2, 1; or when it has to serve at the same time as the Subject of a (following) relative clause: **አርኀወ ፡ መስኮታ ፡ ለታቦት ፡ ኖኅ ፡ እንተ ፡ ገብረ** Gen. 8, 6. The Subject comes regularly before the Predicate, only when the latter is a Substantive (v. several examples in § 193), as well as in secondary clauses, which add the detailed circumstances of the main action, or the condition of a person or thing concerned in that action during its continuance, whether these clauses are joined to the principal clause with **ወ** or without it (Circumstantial Clauses) ([1]). In this case the person or thing, whose condition and circumstances have to be detailed, is always put at the head of the clause, and is often specially emphasised by an appended **ሰ**, thereby arresting the undivided attention, and checking the onward flow of the narrative; "he brought his present to Eglon, **ወኤግሎምሰ ፡ ቄጢጥ ፡ ብእሲ ፡ ውእቱ ፡ ጥቀ** now Eglon was a man of very refined manners" Judges 3, 17; Hen. 14, 25; "he saw a man standing before

---

([1]) V. Ewald, '*Hebr. Spr.*' § 306, *b*; '*Gr. Ar.*' § 670.

him, ወሰይፍ ፡ ምሉኅ ፡ ውስተ ፡ እዴሁ and a drawn sword (was) in his hand" Josh. 5, 13; Hen. 39, 5; ሕያው ፡ ዮሴፍ ፡ ወልድከ ፡ ወውእቱ ፡ መልአክ ፡ ለብሔረ ፡ ግብጽ Gen. 45, 26; Judges 3, 27; ነሥኡ ፡ ሎሙ ፡ አንስተ ፡ . . . ስማ ፡ ለአሐቲ ፡ ዖርፋ ፡ ወስማ ፡ . . . &c. Ruth 1, 4. Thus too the word ነዋ (or ናሁ) "lo!", when it has to point to a definite Subject, attracts this Subject to itself,—its own place being at the head of the clause,—and in this way causes it to precede the Predicate, *e. g.* in Gen. 33, 1; 41, 5; Judges 14, 5, 8; while, if it points rather to the Action than to the Subject, it leaves the original order of the words unaltered, *e. g.* in Judges 20, 40; Hen. 85, 3.

(β) Alteration of Usual Order, for Purposes of Emphasis.

(*β*) The usual order of the sentence is broken in upon, whenever any word in it, in conformity with the leaning of the thought, has to be brought into special prominence. The superior importance assigned to the word concerned is generally indicated by its position,—by its being brought to the head of the clause. Thus any word in the clause may be emphasised by being put first. For instance, the emphasis is laid upon the Subject in:—እግዚአብሔር ፡ ወሀበክሙ ፡ ዘዕለተ ፡ ሰንበት "God (himself) has given you this Sabbath-day" Ex. 16, 29; or—"and it did not stink, ወዕጼኒ ፡ ኢተፈጥረ ፡ በላዕሌሁ nor was there any worm bred in it" Ex. 16, 24: and upon the Object in:—ቃለ ፡ ዚአሁ ፡ ንሰምዕ "*his* word will we obey" Josh. 24, 24; ኃጢአትየ ፡ እዜከር ፡ ዮም "my sin do I remember this day" Gen. 41, 9; ወዘይፈክር ፡ ሊተ ፡ ኃጣእኩ "but one who can interpret to me I have not" Gen. 41, 15; ዘትግበሩ ፡ ሀለወክሙ ፡ ግበሩ "that which you have to do, do" Ex. 16, 23. Or the emphasis rests upon some qualification or other, as in:—ይኄይሰኒ ፡ ለከ ፡ አሁብ ፡ እምነ ፡ ለካልእ ፡ ብእሲ "better is it that I give (her) to thee than to another man" Gen. 29, 19; ላዕሌየ ፡ ይኩን ፡ መርገምከ "upon *me* be thy curse!" Gen. 27, 13; እመሰ ፡ ከመዝ ፡ ሀለወኒ ፡ እኩን "if it should be *so* with me" Gen. 25, 22; እምትካትሰ ፡ አኮ ፡ ከመዝ ፡ ዘተገብረ "in olden time it was not so done" Matt. 19, 8; "they gathered every morning &c., ወበዕለተ ፡ ዐርብ ፡ ያስተጋብኡ ፡ ከዕበተ ፡ ጎሞር but on the Friday they gathered a double measure" Ex. 16, 22; ሰዱሰ ፡ ዕለተ ፡ ታስተጋብኡ "for six days ye shall gather, (but) &c." Ex. 16, 26.

When a special group of words is employed to form the Subject commencing a sentence, it is generally expressed a second time in a short and emphatic form by means of a Pronoun set immediately before the Predicate:—ውእቱ ፡ ብእሲ ፡ ዘበላዕሌሁ ፡ ተረክበ ፡ ኵሬየ ፡ ውእቱ ፡ ይኩነኒ ፡ ገብረ ፡ ወአንትሙሰ (*lit.* "that man upon whom shall be found my cup, *he* shall be to me a servant, but as for you—&c.") Gen. 44, 17; ሚካኤል ፡ ወገብርኤል ፡ ሩፋኤል ፡ ወፋኑኤል ፡ ውእቶሙ ፡ ያጸንዕዎሙ Hen. 54, 6. An Accusative, Dative or Genitive,—put first by way of emphasis,—of a word determined by the Article, may, in accordance with § 172, *c*, be indicated periphrastically by ለ before the word and a Suff. Pron. after the verb or other word which governs it: ወለዝክቱኒ ፡ ሰቀልዎ "and *him* on the other hand they hanged" Gen. 41, 13; አላ ፡ ለእግዚአብሔር ፡ ትልውዎ "but the Lord do ye follow!" Josh. 23, 8; ወለብእሲትኒ ፡ ይቤላ "and to the woman in turn he said" Gen. 3, 16; ወሎሙሰ ፡ ሠረውዎሙ ፡ ለኵሎሙ "but them indeed they extirpated, one and all" Josh. 11, 14; እስመ ፡ ለእግዚአ ፡ መናፍስት ፡ ተርእየ ፡ ብርሃኑ "for of the Lord of Spirits the light appeared" Hen. 38, 4; ለጻድቃንሰ ፡ ሰላመ ፡ ይገብር ፡ ሎሙ Hen. 1, 8 (1). But in fact, any word, whatever be the rank it takes in the sentence, may be put by way of emphasis at the beginning of it, in the form of a Nominative Absolute (2); and then it is enough to have a reference to it in that part of the sentence which it would have occupied, if it had been without emphasis: አኮኑ ፡ እሙ ፡ ስማ ፡ ማርያም "is not his mother's name Mary?" Matt. 13, 55; ወያዕቆብሰ ፡ ሕሡም ፡ ራእዩ "but Jacob's face was plain-looking" Gen. 25, 27; ወወርቅክሙሰ ፡ ካዕበቶ ፡ ንሥኡ ፡ ምስሌክሙ "but as for your money, take ye the double of it with you" Gen. 43, 12; ውእቱ ፡ ዮሐንስ ፡ ልብሱ ፡ ዘይለብስ ፡ ዘጸጕረ ፡ ገመል Matt. 3, 4; ወአንትሙሰ ፡ አልቦ ፡ ዘይትቃወመክሙ "but as for you, there is no one that can resist you" Josh. 23, 9; ኵሉ ፡ ዕፅ ፡ ዘኢይፈሪ ፡ ፍሬ ፡ ሠናየ ፡ ይገዝምዎ Matt. 7, 19; ልበ ፡ ዚአሁ ፡ ትፈቅዱ ፡ ታእምርዎ Judith 8, 14. Indeed the referring Suffix itself may in certain circumstances be wanting:—ወኵሉ ፡ ዘርእ ፡ ዘይዘራእ ፡ ዲቤሃ ፡ አሐቲ ፡ መስፈርት ፡ ትገብር ፡ እልፈ Hen. 10, 19 (3).

---

(1) [FLEMMING leaves out ሎሙ here. TR.]

(2) [A Noun, introduced in this way at the head of a Sentence, unconditioned and awaiting the determination of its Case and its character by certain governing and defining words which follow, is now described usually by the term *absoluter Vorhalt* or *logischer Vorhalt*.]

(3) *Cf.* also the example given *supra*, (§ 150 *ad fin.*) of a ኪያሁ placed first as an Absolute.

Meanwhile Ethiopic is able to give special prominence to individual words, apart from position, by means of the appended particle ሰ (§ 168, 5), *e. g.* መዋዕለ ፡ ሕይወትየሰ Gen. 47, 9; እስመ ፡ መንፈሳውያንሰ Hen. 15, 7 (1); as well as by ሂ "even", ኒ "again", and several other particles of that nature.

In order to give prominence to *Nouns*, the emphatic adjoining of the Pronoun of the third Person is also made use of, or very commonly the periphrasis by means of a Suffix and ለ. A careful consideration of every possible case shows that this mode of expression (already described in § 172, *c*) is frequently employed, not only to replace the missing Article, but also to strengthen the emphasis, *e. g.* in ሐሰ ፡ ሎሙ ፡ ለአግብርቲከ "far be it from them, thy servants (that they should do this thing)" Gen. 44, 7.

To bring *Verbs* into bolder relief, the process (described in § 181, *b*, δ) of adding to their force by means of their own Infinitive is, in particular, turned to account. Now and then the place of the Infinitive is taken by other conceptional words, *e. g.* ዜና ፡ ዜነ ወኒ ፡ ኵሎ ፡ ዘገበርኪ "people have told me all that thou hast done" Ruth 2, 11; ሞተ ፡ ንመውት "die we must" Judges 13, 22; Hen. 98, 15.

How *Personal and other Pronouns* are emphasised in the Sentence, has already been pointed out in substance in §§ 150 and 148, *a*. Generally speaking, the repetition of the Pronoun also serves to give it additional prominence. When a Suffix Pronoun is attached to a Noun or a Verb, then in order to lend emphasis to it, the corresponding separate Pronoun is generally added thereto, and for the most part also in the same Case which is assigned to the Suff. Pron. in the sentence: ባርከኒ ፡ ኪያየኒ "bless me, even me" Gen. 27, 34; ሀበኒያ ፡ ኪያሃ "her do thou give me" Gen. 29, 18; ኪያኪሰ ፡ ያሐይውኪ "but thee they will save alive" Gen. 12, 12; ገብአኒ ፡ ሊተሰ ፡ ወርቅየ "to me has my money been returned" Gen. 42, 28; ሥጋነ ፡ ዘዚአነ "our own bodies" Gen. 47, 18; more rarely in the Nominative, as in:— ይቀድመከ ፡ ተሐምዎ ፡ አንተ "to thee the right of marriage as nearest kinsman first falls" Ruth 4, 4; እምአዘከሮትከ ፡ አንተ *Chrest.* p. 42, line 8; ብየ ፡ አንሰ ፡ ብዙኅ "I have plenty" Gen. 33, 9. If the Personal Pronoun stands in the Nominative, ለሊሁ or some other proper form of this class

(1) [Flemming omits the ሰ here. tr.]

(§ 150) is usually put alongside of it: አነ ፡ ለሊየ ፡ ፈርዖን "I am Pharaoh" Gen. 41, 44; ወውእቱ ፡ ለሊሁ ፡ ይኤዝዘከ "and he will command thee" Ruth 3, 4. The form ውእቱሂ is always employed to express the idea "he too", *e. g.* ወገብረ ፡ ውእቱሂ ፡ መብልዐ "and he too made ready a dish" Gen. 27, 31; and it is used even in the case of the first Person: ውእቱሂ ፡ አነሂ ፡ ኢያየድዐክሙ "neither do I tell you" Matt. 21, 27.

(γ) Other Determining Motives.

(γ) In this way the emphatic prominence, which has to be given to one member of a sentence, generally furnishes the motive for exchanging the usual arrangement of the words for a different one. But frequently the ranking of several sentences together, or their absorption into one another, also disturbs the regular order. Thus, in particular, any word, which is determined by an extended Relative Clause not admitting of insertion in the main Clause, is placed, whenever it is possible, immediately before this Relative Clause, and consequently at the end of its own proper Clause, independently even of the peculiar arrangements which result from Attraction (§§ 190 and 201). As an example, again, of the arrangement of words in Clauses which have a Verb subordinated in the Infinitive, the following passage from Ex. 16, 28 may serve: እስከ ፡ ማእዜ ፡ ተአብዩ ፡ ትእዛዝየ ፡ ሰሚዐ ፡ ወሕግየ, where ትእዛዝየ depends proximately indeed upon ሰሚዐ, but mediately upon ተአብዩ, and therefore is placed between the two. Finally, regard for the cadence and agreeable smoothness of the sentence has also a decisive influence, as, for instance, in ወናሁ ፡ ሰበዐቱ ፡ ሰዊት ፡ ዐርጉ ፡ እምነ ፡ አሐዱ ፡ ሥርው ፡ ኅሩያን ፡ ወሠናያን Gen. 41, 5,—a subject which cannot be adequately examined in detail here, within the space at our disposal. A very favourite practice is to bring together two different Case-forms of one and the same word: ዕዉር ፡ ለዕዉር ፡ ለእመ ፡ መርሖ Matt. 15, 14; እፎ ፡ ይክል ፡ ሰይጣን ፡ ለሰይጣን ፡ አውፅኦቶ Mark. 3,23; መብረቅ ፡ መብረቀ ፡ ይወልድ Hen. 43,2([1]); ኄራን ፡ ለኄራን ፡ ያየድዑ ፡ ጽድቀ Hen. 81, 7 or 81, 8; 83, 4; ትውልድ ፡ እምትውልድ ፡ ትኤብስ Hen. 107, 1 ([2]).

([1]) [መብረቅ is omitted by Flemming here, ሚጠቶሙ being made the Subject of ይወልድ. TR.]

([2]) [A good example of the influence of Verse on Word-arrangement is given in *Chrest.*, p. 16, last five lines.]

C. SPECIAL KINDS OF SENTENCES.

1. NEGATIVE, INTERROGATIVE AND EXCLAMATORY SENTENCES.

1. Negative Sentences.

§ 197. 1. *Negative Sentences.* — To express Negation, Ethiopic ordinarily makes use of the three words **ኢ**, **አኮ** and **አልቦ**.

(*a*) With ኢ.

(*a*) Of these Negatives **ኢ** comes most readily to hand and is oftenest used. It may turn an individual word into its contradictory, and then it corresponds frequently to our prefix *un* or *in*, — *e. g.* **አትውልድ ፡ ኢአማኒት** "O unbelieving generation!" Matt. 17, 17; **ኢአሚኖቶሙ** "their unbelief" Matt. 13, 58; **በኢያእምሮ ፡ መጻሕፍት** "by reason of not knowing the Scriptures" Matt. 22, 29; **በኢያእምሮ** "in ignorance" Gen. 26, 10; **ኢዘምዎ** "freedom from incontinence" ('chastity') 2 Peter 1, 6; **በኢሩካቤ** "by non-cohabitation", *i. e.* "without cohabitation". In such a case it forms a Compound with the Noun to which it is prefixed(1). **ኢ** is employed much oftener, however, to put an entire sentence in the Negative; and then it must invariably precede the Predicate, its proper position being that of a prefix to the Predicate itself: **ንሕነ ፡ ኢንክል ፡ ሐዊረ** "we cannot go" Gen. 44, 26; **ወወይነ ፡ ወሜሰ ፡ ኢይስተይ** "and of wine or mead he may not drink" Judges 13,14; **እምኢተመጠወ ፡ እምእዴነ ፡ መሥዋዕተነ ፡ ወቍርባነነ** "he would not then have accepted from us our sacrifice and our gift" Judges 13,23 (2); and so too, in expressing Infinitive clauses in the negative, Matt. 19, 18. When the sentence does not contain a full verb, **ኢ** is usually placed at the head of the sentence, *e. g.*: **ወኢጽንዐ ፡ ሰማይ ፡ ላዕሌሁ** "and there was no firmament of heaven above it" Hen. 18,12; but yet in this class of Negative Sentences, —in accordance with § 194, — the Auxiliary Verb **ኮነ** or **ሀለወ** is usually employed, and then **ኢ** is prefixed thereto,—or the help of **አልቦ** is called in (v. *infra*). But if the clause contains some individual word, following the Predicate, which has to be denied with special emphasis, the negative is prefixed both to that word

---

(1) [*Cf.* similar Compounds with *lā* in Assyrian: *ina lā-šimti* "untimely"; *Lā-Bābilū* "Non-Babylonians" &c.]

(2) An exception is furnished in Sir. 30,19: **ኢእሙንቱ ፡ ይበልዑ ፡ ወኢእሙንቱ ፡ ያጼንዉ**.

and to the Predicate, *e. g.* ወኢተርፈ ፡ ወኢአሐዱ "and there was not even one left" Judges 4, 16; Hen. 84, 3. If again the individual word which is denied comes before the Predicate, even in this case the Negative is usually repeated: ወኢማሕስዐ ፡ በግዕ ፡ ኢበላዕኩ ፡ እምአባግዒከ "not even a young ram of thy flock have I eaten" Gen. 31, 38; ወኢበአሐቲ ፡ ፍና ፡ አሆ ፡ ኢንብል *Chrest.* p. 76, line 1; ወኢ፩ዘሥጋ ፡ አልቦ ፡ (not በ ፡) ሥልጣን (1) ፡ ከመ ፡ ይግስሶ "and not a single mortal has power to touch it" Hen. 25, 4. The consequence is that in Ethiopic a double Negative is not equivalent to an affirmative. On the contrary it strengthens the negation.

But ኢ is also used as a Prohibitive, by way of subjective negation (=לֹא, μή), and then it is joined to the Subjunctive: ኢትእመኑ "believe (it) not" Matt. 24, 23; ኢትቅትሉ ፡ ነፍሶ "do not kill him" Gen. 37, 21; and in extended sentences it is usually repeated before every fresh verb, *e. g.* Judges 13, 7 (v. also *infra*). In like manner it stands in dependent, final Negative-Sentences, with or without ከመ. When ከመ cannot be dispensed with, then ከመ ፡ ኢ has the meaning "that—not", "lest" (פֶּן): — ከመ ፡ ኢትባኡ Matt. 26, 41; ከመ ፡ ኢትበል Gen. 14, 23; 26, 7, 29; ከመ ፡ ክልኤክሙ ፡ ኢይህጕል "that you may not both perish" Gen. 27, 45; it may even be rendered sometimes by "there might otherwise", *e. g.* in ከመ ፡ ኢትርከበኒ ፡ እኪት Gen. 19, 19.

(b) With አኮ. (*b*) A stronger and at the same time more independent Negative is supplied in አኮ "(in) no wise", "not" (§ 162), which often appears too in Interrogative clauses (አኮኑ, አኮሁ), and serves chiefly to deny individual members of a sentence, in which latter case አላ "but" generally stands overagainst it ("not—but —"): አኮ ፡ ለዝ ፡ ትውልድ ፡ አላ "not for this generation, but &c." Hen. 1, 2; "they will beget giants upon the earth, አኮ ፡ ዘመንፈስ ፡ አላ ፡ ዘሥጋ not spiritual, but sensual" Hen. 106, 17; አኮ ፡ በሰይፍከ ፡ ወአኮ ፡ በቀስትከ Josh. 24, 12; 22, 26, 28; and so, almost always, in abridged or incomplete sentences: ወአኮ ፡ ርሑቅ "but not far away" Hen. 30, 1; "you should petition for men, ወአኮ ፡ ሰብእ ፡ በእንቲአክሙ but not men for you" Hen. 15, 2; አኮ ፡ ሠናይ ፡ አውስቦ "then it is not good to marry" Matt. 19, 10; በሕቱ ፡ አኮኬ ፡ በበዓል "not, however, on the feast-day" Matt. 26, 5; አኮ ፡ መ

(1) [Flemming has ሥልጣኒ. tr.]

ፍትው ፡ ይሑሩ "it is not necessary that they go away" Matt. 14,16 (ኢመፍትው would rather mean "unnecessary"(1)). Regularly therefore, we have ወእመ ፡ አኮ or ወእመ ፡ አኮሰ for "and if not" (*e. g.* Gen. 18, 21), without any following verb. Farther, አኮ is often employed, when, in a sentence otherwise complete, a single word,—but not the whole sentence,—has to be put in the Negative. Now in this case, if አኮ were merely placed before the word concerned, while the rest of the sentence remained unaltered in its structure, the effect of the አኮ would be extended over the whole sentence. To meet this difficulty, አኮ with the individual word concerned is put at the head of the sentence, and the rest of it is at once interrupted and continued with the help of a relative pronoun (just as in French), *e. g.* አኮ ፡ ኵሉ ፡ ዘያገምር "not every one comprehends" ('not every one is it who comprehends') Matt. 19, 11. On the other hand አኮ ፡ ኵሉ ፡ ያገምር, even if the expression were a possible one, would mean "not any one comprehends" or "no one comprehends"; እስመ ፡ አኮ ፡ ንሕነ ፡ ዘአስቆረርናከ "for *we* have not abhorred thee" ('for it is not we who have abhorred thee') Gen. 26, 29; እምትካትሰ ፡ አኮ ፡ ከመዝ ፡ ዘተገብረ "in olden time it was not so done" Matt. 19, 8; አኮ ፡ በጽድቅ ፡ ዘአምጻእከ "not in righteousness ('is it that thou hast brought') hast thou brought" Gen. 4, 7; አኮ ፡ በኅብስት ፡ ከመ ፡ ዘየሐዩ ፡ ብእሲ "not by bread alone ('is it that man lives') does man live" Matt. 4, 4; አኮ ፡ አንትሙ ፡ ዘፈነውክሙኒ "it was not you that sent me" Gen. 45, 8; so too Gen. 3, 4; Josh. 22, 24; Matt. 7, 21; 16, 11. In the same way even a Verb is put with emphasis in the negative: አኮ ፡ ዘሞተት ፡ ሕፃን "by no means ('is it the case that the child is dead') is the child dead" Matt. 9, 24; ሶበ ፡ አኮ ፡ ዘበላዕከ ፡ ዘንተ ፡ ዕፀ "if thou hast really not eaten of this tree" Gen. 3, 11. And thus አኮ may come to be placed even immediately before the Verb, particularly when the Verb may be regarded as standing in an abridged relative or dependent clause: አኮ ፡ ትትኀብኡ ፡ ሀለወክሙ "not to hide are you obliged", (literally: 'not (that) you must conceal yourselves, —is in store for you') Hen. 104, 5.

(*c*) With አልቦ. (*c*) The Negative አልቦ signifies properly "there is not", "there does not exist" (§§ 167, 1, *b* and 192, *b*), and can only be

(1) [That is to say, the form with አኮ gives a stronger negation = "it is not at all necessary". TR.]

used when this turn of thought and expression is possible and thinkable. It stands quite independently for "no",—in opposition to እወ "yes"—, in the sense of "it is not the case", Matt. 5, 37; or in answer to a question, Matt. 13, 29; John 1, 21; or to decline or deprecate a proposal, Ex. 10, 25; Ruth 1, 13; [*Kebra Nag.* 105 a 20]. In sentences, in which a finite verb is wanting, አልቦ is used in the meaning "there does not exist": ወኢ.ማይ ፡ አልቦ ፡ ላዕሌሁ "and there is no water above it" Hen. 18, 12; ወኢ.ዕዘሥጋ ፡ አልቦ ፡ ሥልጣን ፡ ከመ ፡ ይግስስ "and there is no power in any mortal to touch it" Hen. 25, 4 (1); አልቦ ፡ ጽድቅ ፡ ውስተ ፡ አፉሆሙ "there is no righteousness in their mouth" Ps. 5, 10 (Accusative in accordance with § 192, *b*) &c. In the same way (just like אֵין), when placed before a separate Noun, it serves to form Negative Adjectives, *e. g.* አልቦ ፡ ራሕብ "not broad" ("narrow") Hen. 26, 3, and in the Plural አልቦን ፡ ራሕብ Hen. 26, 5 (*lit.* 'there is not in them any breadth'); አልቦ ፡ ኑኅ ('there is not in it height') "it is not high" Hen. 26, 4 (2). Then too, by means of አልቦ and a following Relative Pronoun, a periphrasis is formed for "no one" and "nothing" (literally, "there is not who, *or* what"): አልቦ ፡ ዘይስማዕ ፡ መኑሂ "no one must hear" Josh. 6, 10; አልቦ ፡ ዘተርፈ "no one was left" Josh. 8, 17; ወከልአ ፡ አልቦ ፡ ዘይትልዎ "and he forbade any one to follow him" Mark 5, 37; አልቦ ፡ ዘተሀበኒ "thou shalt not give me anything" Gen. 30, 31; ወኮነ ፡ ከመ ፡ ዘአልቦ ፡ ዘቦአ ፡ ውስተ ፡ ከርሦሙ "and it was as if nothing had entered their stomach" Gen. 41, 21:—and, similarly, አልቦ ፡ አመ means ('there is not, when') "never", *e. g.* Judges 19, 30. With a following ዘ, አልቦ serves to put entire sentences emphatically in the Negative: አልቦ ፡ ዘትትጋአዙ ፡ በፍኖት "see that ye fall not out by the way" Gen. 45, 24. On አልብየ &c. "I have not" v. § 176, *h*. In both of its significations—"there is not" and "I have not"—this Negative has often to make up also for Negative Adjectives which are wanting: ዐዘቅት ፡ ሐዳስ ፡ ወአልባቲ ፡ ማየ "a new and waterless pit" (liter-

---

(1) [In both passages FLEMMING has the Accus.: ማየ in Hen. 18, 12 and ሥልጣነ in 25, 4. TR].

(2) [FLEMMING has the Acc. throughout in these three passages, Hen. 26, 3, 4, 5., reading ርሕበ in 3 and 5, and ኑኀ in 4; similarly he gives the Accus.-reading instead of DILLMANN's Nom. in the next two passages cited here from 'Henoch', viz 39, 6 and 40, 1. TR].

ally: 'and water it had not') Gen. 37, 24; አውታር ፡ ሐዲስት ፡ እለ ፡ አልቦሙ ፡ ብትከተ "new, undamaged cords (or 'tendons')" Judges 16,7; ኅሩያን ፡ ኍልቈ ፡ አልቦሙ "innumerable elect" ('number was not in them') Hen. 39, 6; "I saw tens of thousands, ወአልቦሙ ፡ ኍልቈ ፡ ወሐሳብ an innumerable and incalculable multitude" ('and there was not in them number or reckoning') Hen. 40, 1; ወከዐወ ፡ ደመ ፡ ንጹሓን ፡ ብዙኃን ፡ ዘአልቦ ፡ ኍልቈ "and he shed the blood of an infinite number of holy men" *Chronique de Jean* (ed. Zotenberg), p. 70, l. 4 *sq.* [*Cf.*, farther, Hen. 103, 10, where አልቦ is found followed by a pleonastic ኢ—: ወአልቦ ፡ ዘ— . . . ኢረከብነ "we have found nobody who . . ."].

(*d*) Various Negative Phrases.

(*d*) The ideas—"nothing" and "no one",—may be expressed also by ኵሉ accompanied with a Negative, or by ኢ with a following ወኢመኑሂ or ወኢምንትኒ (§ 173), *e. g.* ኢትብልዒ ፡ ኵሎ ፡ ዘርኩስ Judges 13, 4 (*cf.* Hen. 93, 14—in a question having a negative force); አልቦ ፡ ዘርእዩ ፡ ወኢመነሂ Matt. 17, 8; Josh. 8, 17; Hen. 14, 21; ወከመ ፡ ወኢምንተ ፡ ኮነ ፡ ውስተ ፡ እዴሁ "and it was as nothing in his hand" Judges 14, 6; ወኢከመ ፡ ምንት ፡ ኮናኒ "and ('not as anything') as nothing are they to me" Gen. 47, 9; ወኢከመ ፡ ምንትሂ Sir. 17, 28; ወኢከመ ፡ ምንት ὡς οὐδέν Sir. 40, 6; ወኢበምንትኒ Amos 6, 6; v. also § 198. The idea "at all" (*omnino*) in Negative sentences is specially expressed, farther, by ግሙራ (§ 163, 2), *e. g.* ኢኀደጉ ፡ ሎሙ ፡ ሥጋ ፡ ግሙራ "they left no flesh of them at all remaining" Hen. 90, 4; ግሙራ ፡ ኢያንበብክሙኑ "have ye never read at all?" Mark 2, 25. *Not even* (*ne—quidem*) is expressed by ኢ—ጥቀ (inasmuch as ጥቀ, § 163, 1, means properly—"exactly", and then also—"even", Gen. 44, 8), *e. g.* ኢነሳሕክሙ ፡ ጥቀ ፡ እምድኅረ "ye did not even repent afterwards" Matt. 21, 32. *Cf.* also ወኢሂ ፡ ኢይክሉ(1) οὐδὲ γὰρ δύναται Rom. 8, 7 (Platt). "Not only" is አኮ ፡ ከመ, *e. g.* Matt. 4, 4; [and also ኢ or አኮ ፡—በሕቲቱ, Dillmann's '*Lex. col.* 497]. "No more", "no farther" may be expressed by ኢ—እንከ, *e. g.* ወኢደገመ ፡ እንከ Judges 13, 21; Hen. 92, 5. On እንብየ "I cannot" v. § 162, and on እንጃኒ "I know not", v. § 163, 3.

For "neither—nor" ኢ—ወኢ, or ወኢ—ወኢ (*neque—neque*) is always used; and in such cases, when Nouns are contrasted with one another by means of "neither—nor", the negation

(1) [The second ኢ is wanting in Praetorius' reprint of Platt's '*N. T.*']

must be repeated with the Verb (v. *supra*, *a*):—**ወኢይከውን ፡ ሎሙ ፡ ምሕረት ፡ ወኢሰላም** "and they shall neither meet with grace nor peace" Hen. 12, 6; **ኢመልአክ ፡ ወኢብእሲ ፡ ኢይትሜጠው** "neither angel nor man receives (it)" Hen. 68, 5; **ወኢአምጣኖ ፡ ወኢዕበዮ ፡ ኢክህልኩ ፡ ነጽሮ** "neither its extent nor its magnitude could I see" Hen. 21, 7; Luke 9, 3; **ኢይበቍዕ ፡ ብርት ፡ ወኢናእክ ፡**(1) **ኢይበቍዕ** Hen. 52, 8; **ከመ ፡ ኢይንሣእ ፡ ኢፈትለ ፡ ወኢቶታነ ፡ አሥኣን** Gen. 14, 23. **ወኢ** occurs in this way thirteen times in succession in Judges 1, 27. *Cf.* also § 206, 1 (2).

2. Interrogative Sentences: —(a) Independent Interrogation.

§ 198. 2. *Interrogative Sentences.* In Interrogation the idea, about whose existence or non-existence the questioner desires information, is thrust forward to the head of the sentence; and by the peculiar arrangement of words which is thus effected, conjoined with the character of the accentuation, the form of an interrogation may in this simple way be impressed upon the sentence. Such a simple type of interrogation, however, is of somewhat rare occurrence in Ethiopic, although illustrated in Gen. 26, 9; Matt. 12, 29 (in both passages, introduced by words which often appear in questions). If the use of any interrogative word is avoided, the question is very often introduced by **ብ ፡ ዘ** "is it the case, that?" [*est-ce que?*], *e. g.*, **ብ ፡ ዘሀለወ ፡ ዝየ ፡ ብእሲ** "is any one here?" Judges 4, 20. — But usually recourse is had to regular interrogatives.

(*a*) The interrogative which is most in use is the enclitic **ኑ** (§ 161, *a*), through which, however, the interrogative clause receives no definite colouring, seeing that it may be followed equally by an affirmative and by a negative answer:—**ዳኅንኑ ፡ አቡክሙ ፡ ዝኩ ፡ አረጋዊ ፡ ወይቤልዎ ፡ ዳኅን** "is your father, the old man, well? And they said, 'he is well'" Gen. 43, 27, 28; **ዘንተኑ ፡ ገበርኪ** "hast thou done *this*?" Gen. 3, 13. It need not be attached always to the first word:—**እምኒ ፡ ሰብአ ፡ ዚአነኑ ፡ አንተ ፡ አው ፡ እምኒ ፡ ፀርነ** "dost thou belong to our people or to our enemies?" Josh. 5, 13; and farther even **ወ**, and other conjunctions like **እስመ**, may then stand at the head of the sentence:—**ወይክሉኑ ፡ ደቂቀ ፡ ለመርዓዊ ፡ ጾዊመ** Mark 2, 19; **ኑ** may be even repeated, if the sentence consists of several clauses:—**ታማስኖሙኑ ፡ ወኢታሐዩኑ** Gen. 18, 24.

(1) [Flemming reads **ወናእክ**. Tr.]

(2) **ዘእንበለ** too is always continued by **ወኢ**.

If the force of the interrogation is meant to bear not upon a single word but upon the entire sentence, then ቦ, combined with ኑ, or ቦኑ, (= 'is it the case?') frequently appears at the head of the sentence: ቦኑ፡ እብነ፡ ይሁቦ "will he give him a stone?" Matt. 7, 9; ቦኑ፡ ዐቃቢሁ፡ አነ፡ ለእኁየ Gen. 4, 9; Josh. 22, 20; or, with still greater fulness, ቦኑ፡ ዘ ('is it the case that . . .?'), *e. g.* ቦኑ፡ ዘብክሙ፡ እኍ "have ye a brother?" Gen. 43, 7; ቦኑ፡ ዘብከ "hast thou?" Gen. 19, 12; ቦኑ፡ ካልአ፡ ዘንሴፎ "must we look for another?" Matt. 11, 3 (where ካልአ is put before the verb, because it is specially affected by the question).

Negative questions, to which an affirmative answer is expected, may be expressed, it is true, by ኢ—ኑ, *e. g.* ኢያንበብክሙኑ "have ye not read?" Mark 2, 25; but yet, instead of that form, we have at command also አኮኑ, with or without a following ዘ:—አኮኑ፡ በእንተ፡ ራሔል፡ ተቀነይኩ "have I not served for Rachel?" Gen. 29, 25; አኮኑ፡ አኀዊከ፡ ውስተ፡ ሴኬም Gen. 37, 13; and አኮኑ must be employed, when there is no verb in the sentence, or when the verb cannot begin the sentence on account of the emphasis falling upon another word. Even sentences like አልቦ፡ ብእሲት "there is no woman" may be brought into the interrogative form by attaching ኑ to አልቦ, or by placing ቦኑ before it:— ቦኑ፡ አልቦ፡ ብእሲት Judges 14, 3.

The particle ሁ (§ 161, *a*) has pretty much the same force as ኑ, and is often directly interchanged with it, but, as a rule, it seems to present farther a collateral suggestion of doubt or complete uncertainty or perplexity in the mind of the interrogator, or of the person addressed:—ይከውንሁ "is it lawful?" Matt. 19, 3; ታአምርሁ "art thou aware?" Matt. 15, 12; ይቀሥሙሁ፡ እምአሥዋክ፡ አስካለ "do men gather grapes of thorns?" Matt. 7, 16; አንተሁ፡ (another reading is አንተኑ፡) ዘይመጽእ "art thou he that should come?" Matt. 11, 3. In Ps. 93, 9 it appears in conjunction with ኑ:—ዘተከላሁ፡ ለእዝን፡ ኢይሰምዕኑ "he who planted the ear, shall he not hear?". Like ኑ it is also compounded with አኮ and አልቦ:—አኮሁ፡ መጸብሓውያንሂ፡ ከማሁ፡ ይገብሩ Matt. 5, 46; አኮሁ፡ ነፍስ፡ ተዐቢ፡ እምሲሲት Matt. 6, 25; አኮሁ፡ ሠናየ፡ ዘርአ፡ ዘራእከ Matt. 13, 27 (*cf.* አኮኑ Matt. 5, 47; 6, 26); አልቦሁ፡ አመ፡ አንበብክሙ ('is there not a time when ye have read?') "have ye never read?" Matt. 21, 16.

(*b*) The Interrogative for the Dependent Question is እመ

"whether" *or* "if", or **ለእመ** (§ 170, 1), here and there shortened into **እም**: *e. g.* **ከመ ፡ ይርአይ ፡ እመ ፡ ተኀጥገ ፡ ማይ ፡ እምነ ፡ ምድር** "to see if the water was abated from off the earth" Gen. 8, 7; **ንግርኒ ፡ ለእመ ፡ ቦቱ ፡ ማኅደረ ፡ ቤተ ፡ አቡኪ ፡ ለነ** "tell me whether there is a lodging for us in thy father's house" Gen. 24, 23; **ይትዐቀብዎ ፡ ለእመ ፡ ይፌውሶ** "they watched him whether he would heal him" Mark 3, 2:—also strengthened by **ኑ** or **ሁ**:—**እመ ፡ አንተሁ ፡ ክርስቶስ** Matt. 26, 63; **ንርአይ ፡ እመ ፡ ይመጽእኑ ፡ ኤልያስ** 27, 49; **ለእመ ፡ ዳኅናንኑ ፡ አኀዊከ** "whether thy brethren are well" Gen. 37, 14; [**እሴእሎሙ ፡ ለሰብእ ፡ እመቦ ፡ ለእመ ፡ አረክብ** *Contendings of the Apostles* (ed. Wallis Budge, 1899), Ethiop. text, p. 399, l. 11 *sq.*] (b) Dependent Interrogation.

(c) In Disjunctive Interrogation, **አው** "or" (§ 168, 2) is possible, it is true, as *e. g.* in Josh. 5, 13 and Judges 20, 28; but yet **ወሚመ** is usually employed instead of it, in independent clauses (§ 161, *a*), *e. g.* **ወሚመ ፡ ኢየሱስሃ** "or Jesus?" Matt. 27, 17; **እምኀበ ፡ ውሉዶሙኑ ፡ ወሚመ ፡ እምኀበ ፡ ነኪር** 17, 25. An additional **ኑ** may also be appended to some later word in the disjunctive interrogation: **እምሰማይኑ ፡ ወሚመ ፡ እምሰብእኑ** Matt. 21, 25; **አንተኑ ፡ ዘይመጽእ ፡ ወሚመ ፡ ቦኑ ፡ ካልእ ፡ ዘንሴፎ** "art thou he that should come, or is there another for whom we are to look?" Luke 7, 19 (—in the corresponding passage in Matt. 11, 3, we have **ወቦኑ ፡ ካልእ**). In Dependent Disjunctive Interrogation, **ወእመ** or **ወለእመ** is commonly used: **እርአይ ፡ ለእመ ፡ በከመ ፡ ጽራኆሙ ፡ . . . ይፌጽምዋ ፡ ወእመ ፡ አከሰ ፡ አእምር** Gen. 18, 21; **ለእመ ፡ አንተኑ ፡ ውእቱ ፡ ዔሳው ፡ ወለእመ ፡ ኢኮንከ** Gen. 27, 21; **እመ ፡ ይሜርሖ ፡ እግዚአብሔር ፡ ፍኖቶ ፡ ወለእመሂ ፡ አልቦ** Gen. 24, 21. The phrase "or not", coming after "whether . . .", in such dependent interrogations, is expressed by **ወእመ ፡ አልቦ**, Judges 2, 22; Hen. 89, 63. [A somewhat peculiar use of **ወኢእመ**, to introduce an alternative suggestion, is met with in the passage:—**ነደደ ፡ ልቡ ፡ ለንጉሥ ፡ በፍቅረ ፡ ዚአከ ፡ እንዳዒ ፡ ዘያአምር ፡ ለሊሁ ፡ እመ ፡ ወልዱ ፡ አንተ ፡ ወኢእመ ፡ እኁሁ ፡ አንተ** "the king's heart is filled with love for thee, that he may learn whether thou be (really) his son, or (perhaps) his brother" *Kebra Nag.* p. 30 *b* 21]. To this class of sentences belongs also the passage **ምንት ፡ ይቀልል ፡ እምብሂለ ፡ . . . ወእምብሂለ** Matt. 9, 5; Mark 2, 9 (where **እም** stands for **እመ**, *cf.* § 170, 2, and the Acc. occurs in accordance with § 182, *a*, *α*). (c) Disjunctive Interrogation.

(*d*) In order to give an additional and special shade of meaning to an interrogation, use is made of other particles, such as **መ**,

(d) Strengthening-Particles in Interrogation, and Particles of Reply.

which has been treated of already (§ 162, *ad fin.*), or እንጋ ἄρα, "indeed?" "really?" (§ 169, 3). ዮጊ also (§ 169, 10) may introduce questions denoting perplexity, which are the issue and expression of misgiving, *e. g.* ዮጊ ፡ ብእሲትከ ፡ ይእቲ፡ "is she then thy wife?" Gen. 26, 9. The affix ሰ is also applied, but merely to lend force and emphasis to the interrogation:— አሐቲኑ ፡ ክመ ፡ ለከሰ ፡ በረከትከ ፡ አበ "is there then only *one* blessing of thine, O father?" Gen. 27, 38.

እወ stands for "yea", "yes", as a reply in the affirmative, and አልቦ for "nay", "no", as the negative reply, *e. g.* Judges 4, 20. If, however, the question contains a request, አሆ is employed to express consent, and እንብየ to indicate refusal, or else the leading word in the interrogative sentence, to which has been assigned an emphatic position in the question,—is repeated, *e. g.* Gen. 43, 28; Judges 13, 11; Matt. 16, 13, 14.

(e) Definite Interrogative Words: መኑ, ምንት and others.

(*e*) Of the more definite Interrogative words, the first to be brought forward is the Pronoun መኑ, which relates always to some *person*. No doubt we meet with the phrase መኑ ፡ ስምከ "what is thy name?" Gen. 32, 28; Mark 5, 9; Judges 13, 17 (like מִי שְׁמֶךָ), but that is simply because the meaning is:—"who art thou by name?". መኑ has an Accusative form, but takes no Plural (§ 147, *b*). It may follow a Constr. St. as a Genitive:—ወለተ ፡ መኑ ፡ አንቲ፡ "whose daughter art thou?" Gen. 24, 23; Matt. 22, 42; በመብሕተ ፡ መኑ "by whose authority?" Matt. 21, 23; or the Genitive relation may be indicated by ዘመኑ, as in Hen. 22, 6, and in እንተ ፡ መኑ ፡ ዛቲ ፡ ወለት "whose damsel is this?" Ruth 2, 5. So too the Dative relation may be signified by ለመኑ, *e. g.* Matt. 22, 28. And with all the other prepositions also መኑ may be combined:— እምኀበ ፡ መኑ "from whom?" Matt. 17, 25; በእንተ ፡ መኑ "for whose sake?" Hen. 21, 5 &c. Its usual position is at the head of the clause; but if the emphasis happen to fall upon another word in the clause, that word may precede it: እሉንቱ ፡ መባዕላተ ፡ ለመኑ ፡ ያስተዳልውዎሙ "these instruments—for whom are they preparing them?" Hen. 53, 4: ዝመንፈስ ፡ ዘመኑ ፡ ውእቱ፡ "this spirit here—to whom does it belong?" Hen. 22, 6. The combination "whoever?" ("who at any place?", "who at any time?") may be expressed by the periphrasis "who is he at all that?" &c., *e. g.* መኑ ፡ ውእቱ ፡ ኀሎ ፡ ውሉደ ፡ ሰብእ ፡ ዘይክል "what man soever would be able?" ('where is there at all a son of man who could ..?') Hen. 93, 11.

The corresponding Neuter Interrogative ምንት፡ (§ 147, *b*) is very often made use of, when the enquiry is about *things*. It may take an Accusative form, combine with prepositions, and take the same positions in the sentence as መኑ, *e. g.* ዝንቱ ፡ ምንት ፡ ውእቱ፡ "what is this?" Hen. 23, 3. Notice the phrase ምንት ፡ ኮንኪ ('what hast thou (*f.*) come to?') "what is troubling thee?" Judges 1, 14. Although at first employed merely as a Substantive, it may yet take to itself, in an appositional relation, Substantives as well as Adjectives:— በእንተ ፡ ምንት ፡ ራእይ "by reason of what vision?" Hen. 60, 5;(1) ምንተ ፡ ዐስበ ፡ ብክሙ "what reward have ye?" Matt. 5, 46; ምንተ ፡ እኩየ "what evil?" Matt. 27, 23. As ምንት virtually includes a predicate, it may, like Verbs of Being, assume a Suffix in the capacity of a Dative (§ 178): ምንትከ ፡ እሉ "what are these to thee?" ('for what to thee, these?') Gen. 48, 8; ምንትከ ፡ ውእቱ ፡ ዝንቱ ፡ ኵሉ ('what is to thee &c?') "what meanest thou by all this?" Gen. 33, 8. Besides, a Dative of this kind, formed by ለ may also be applied for the purpose of adding to the force of a statement: ለምንት ፡ ለከ ፡ ትሴአል "wherefore dost thou ask (for thee)?" Gen. 32, 30; Numb. 14, 41; [*cf.* also *Kebra Nag.* 107 b 14, 16: ምንትከ ፡ ይእቲ ፡ ዛቲ *quae (tibi) haec est?*, ምንትኪ ፡ ውእቱ ዝ *quis (tibi) hic est?*].

ምንት often takes the interrogative affix ኑ, *e. g.* ምንትኑ ፡ ሤር "what is the good thing (&c.)?" Matt. 19, 16. Farther, a Verb is often associated as predicate with መኑ as well as with ምንት, not directly, but by the intervention of the relative pronoun: ምንት ፡ ዘተርፈኒ ('what is there which is left for me?') "what remains for me?" Matt. 19, 20; መኑ ፡ ዘይደልዎ ('who is there that is worthy of it?') "who is worthy of it?" Matt. 10, 11. Both interrogatives may stand equally in a direct and in an indirect interrogation, and may be rendered indefinite by affixing ሂ or ኒ, or in Negative sentences by farther placing ወኢ before the interrogative (§§ 147, *b*; 197 *d*); and then ኢምንትኒ may be combined with appositional Substantives and Adjectives, just like the interrogative ምንት, *e. g.* ኢትግበሩ ፡ ምንተኒ ፡ ዐመፃ Gen. 19, 8; ወኢምንተኒ ፡ ቃለ "not any word" Hen. 14, 7; ካልእ ፡ ምንትኒ "any other thing" Hen. 78, 17.

(1) [Flemming's reading here is ምንት ፡ ራእየ, without the preposition. tr.]

On ሚ v. § 147, *b*, and on አይ, § 147, *c*.

On አይቴ "where?", እፎ "how?", ማእዜ "when?" and ምንት, ምንተ, ለምንት "why?" *cf.* § 161, *a*. እፎ also stands frequently as a separate particle, in the same way as the other Interrogatives, and is followed by ዘ or ከመ, *e. g.* እፎ ፡ ከመ ፡ እኪተ ፡ ትፈድዩኒ "how comes it that ye requite me with evil?" Gen. 44, 4; እፎ ፡ ዘኢትሌብዉ "how is it that ye do not understand?" Matt. 16,11.

On ሚመጠን "how much?", "how many?", "how great?", and ስፍነ and እስፍንቱ "how much?", "how many?", "how often?" v. § 157, 1.

Two or more independent Interrogatives, of different signification, may be strung together, even without ወ, *e. g.* እፎ ፡ ምንተ ፡ ትትናገሩ : πῶς ἢ τί λαλήσητε Matt. 10, 19.

3. Exclamatory Sentences:— (*a*) With a single Noun.

§ 199. 3. *Exclamatory Sentences.* (*a*) In the Exclamation a single Noun may appear, detached and uninflected, *e. g.* ዳኀን ፡ ትብሉ "blameless! say ye" Matt. 23, 18; ሠናይ "well!" Ruth 3, 13; ሰላም ፡ እብል ፡ ለማርያም "Hail! say I to Mary"; ሕይወተ ፡ ፈርዖን "Life of Pharaoh!" *i. e.* "by the life of Pharaoh!" Gen. 42, 15, 16. In fact the Vocative (§ 142) is nothing other than a word uttered singly in this way as an exclamation. Such Vocative may also be preceded by the pronoun of the 2nd Pers.: አንተ ፡ እኁየ "thou! my brother!" and አንተ ፡ እግዚእየ "thou! my lord!" Gen. 33, 9, 14. On አበ "Father!" *cf. supra* § 142.

(*b*) With the Imperative in Affirmative Charges, and the Subjunctive in Prohibitions.

(*b*) The Verb in an Exclamatory sentence, and in an affirmative charge, appears in the Imperative; but with a negative it takes the Subjunctive, *e. g.* ተምዑ ፡ ወኢተአብሱ "be ye angry, but sin not" Ps. 4, 5; Eph. 4, 26; ኢትትኃሐለው ፡ ላቲ Sir. 41, 21. If one incites himself or gives a command to another, then ለ makes its appearance, followed immediately by the Subjunctive: እምይእዜሰ ፡ ለእሙት ፡ እንከ "now would I willingly die!" Gen. 46, 30; ርጉመ ፡ ለይኩን ፡ መዐቶሙ "cursed be their anger!" Gen. 49, 7; ለይኩን ፡ ብርሃን Gen. 1, 3; ውእቱ ፡ ለይዕቀብ ፡ ርእሰከ Gen. 3, 15; ለይፈጽም "let him do it!" Matt. 19, 12; ለትደምሰስ Gen. 17, 14; ጊጉየ ፡ ለእኩን ፡ ላዕሌከ Gen. 44, 32. If the sentence has two or more verbs in it, ለ either stands with the first alone, Gen. 9, 27, or with more than one, Ruth 1, 17. In Negative clauses ለኢ is not the form which is used, because ለ would be separated by ኢ from the Verb, but on the contrary ከመ ፡ ኢ, Judges 21, 1. Yet it is not absolutely necessary that this Subjunctive be introduced by

ለ or ከመ: *e. g.* we have ያውስብ Matt. 22, 24; ይቅትልዎ Matt. 26, 66; Gen. 9, 26; Ruth 4, 11; Ps. 102, 1, 2; እግዚአብሔር ፡ ይዕቀብከ ፡ እምኵሉ ፡ እኩይ Ps. 120, 7; and v. 5; ይኩን ፡ ለነ ፡ ንጉሥ ፡ መሲሓዌ ፡ በዛቲ ፡ ሀገር "let us have a Christian emperor in this city!" *Chronique de Jean*, p. 183, l. 19 *sq.* [እትፈነው "I will go" *Kebra Nag.* 113 b 1 *var.*]. ነዓ is often employed as a hortatory particle, *e. g.* ንዑ ፡ ንንድቅ Gen. 11, 4, 7; ቤተ ፡ ክርስቲያኑ ፡ ለአትናቴዎስ ፡ ሐዋርያዊ ፡ ውዕየት ፡ በእሳት ፡ ንዑ ፡ ርድኡነ ፡ ኵልክሙ ፡ ክርስቲያን "the church of the apostolic Athanasius is in flames! come and help us, all ye Christians!" *Chronique de Jean*, p. 116, l. 5 *sq.*; and it may even appear independently: ንዒ ፡ ዝየ "come thou hither!" Ruth 2, 14 (v. § 160, *a*). In the case of a strict and very emphatic command, to which no opposition is expected, the Imperfect appears, instead of the Imperative or the Subjunctive: it is, for instance, of very frequent occurrence in the ordinances of the Pentateuch. Infinitives are rarely met with in Exclamatory sentences:—there is, to be sure, the saying of common life: ዘኮነ ፡ ከዊና "what has happened,—its happening (be to it)!", that is "it is a thing finished". ኮንየ too, 3 Kings 19, 4 "enough!" ('I have had enough')—is manifestly an old Infinitive form with a Suffix: "sufficiency for me!"; for ኮነ sometimes signifies "it is enough" Deut. 2, 3; 3, 26; Numb. 16, 3.

(*c*) Entire sentences even, unfurnished with a Verb (§ 193 *sq.*), may form the Exclamation. In these, as a rule, the predicate comes first, and the copula,—between subject and predicate,—is wanting(1), *e. g.* ስብሐት ፡ ለእግዚአብሔር "praise (be) to God!"; ሰላም ፡ ለከ "peace (be) unto thee!" Judges 6, 23; እግዚአብሔር ፡ ምስሌክሙ "God (be) with you!" Ruth 2, 4; ቡሩክ ፡ ዘይመጽእ ፡ በስመ ፡ እግዚአብሔር Matt. 21, 9; 23, 39; Hen. 9, 4; ቅዱስ ፡ ቅዱስ ፡ ቅዱስ ፡ እግዚአ ፡ መናፍስት "Holy, Holy, Holy Lord of Spirits!" Hen. 39, 12; ኀበ ፡ ምትኪ ፡ ምግባኢኪ "for thy husband be thy desire!" (*lit.* 'to thy husband be thy recurring!') Gen. 3, 16. Hence the oath-formula: ሕያው ፡ አነ ፡ ወሕያው ፡ ስምየ Numb. 14, 21, 28 (—in the latter verse the last two words are omitted,

(c) Entire Sentences forming the Exclamation

(1) In Hen. 22, 14 ውእቱ is the Subject. [Besides other slight differences which FLEMMING's reading of this verse exhibits, as compared with DILLMANN's, this ውእቱ is left out. TR.]

but እመ ፡ አኮ are added—); Deut. 32,40; ሕያው ፡ አነ ፡ ወጽኑዕ ፡ (read ወጽንዐ ፡) መንግሥትየ Judith 2,12; ሕያው ፡ እግዚአብሔር (followed by ከመ) Judges 8,19; Ruth 3,13.

(d) Special Words in Exclamation.

(d) Of special words in Exclamation we have በሐ "Hail!" (1), — an Accusative, it would seem, 2 John, 10; በሐ ፡ ረቢ "Hail! Master!" Matt. 26,49; በሐ ፡ ንጉሠ ፡ አይሁድ "Hail! King of the Jews!" Matt. 27,29; and even with Suffixes: በሐክን "Hail to you! (*f. pl.*)" χαίρετε, Matt. 28,9. The opposite expression is ወይ or አሌ "Woe!", varied by ሰይል (2) "Woe! Ah!" (§§ 61 and 167,1, *a*). The first two of these words are always followed by ለ, *e. g.* ወይልኪ or አሌ ፡ ለኪ Matt. 11,21; አሌ ፡ ለክሙ Matt. 23,13 *sqq.*; [*Kebra Nag.* 67 b 4 *sqq.*]; but ሰይል invariably takes a Suffix, *e. g.* ሴልየ "Woe is me!" Ps. 119,5. To ward off anything, or protest against or deprecate anything, ሐሰ (ሖሰ), § 163,3, is made use of, either in an isolated position: ሐሰ ፡ እግዚአ ፡ ኢትግበር ፡ ዘንተ ፡ ነገረ Gen. 18,25, or more frequently, followed by a Dative: ሖሰ ፡ ሊተ ፡ እግዚአ "be it far from me, Lord!" Acts 10,14; ሖሰ ፡ ለከ ፡ እግዚአ Matt. 16,22; ሐሰ ፡ ለነ Josh. 22,29; ሐሰ ፡ ሎሙ Gen. 44,7. If a Verb has to be attached thereto, it is subordinated either by means of the Subjunctive: — Matt. 16,22; Judges 19,23; Gen. 18,25; or by means of እስከ and the Imperfect: — ሐሰ ፡ ለነ ፡ እስከ ፡ ነኅድግ "be it far from us to forsake ..!" Josh. 22,29; 24,16; ሐሰ ፡ ሊተ ፡ እስከ ፡ እገብር ፡ ለዝንቱ ፡ ነገር Gen. 44,17. To strengthen the Imperative, ሶ and እስኩ (§ 162) are used; also, ብቍዐኒ (§ 163,3), *e. g.* ብቍዐኒ ፡ ሊቀ ፡ ርኢ "I beseech thee, Master, look ..!" Luke 9,38; ብቍዐኒ ፡ እግዚአ ፡ አብሐኒ "O my lord, suffer me, I beseech thee, to ...!" Gen. 44,18; and in the plural ብቍዑኒ 2 Cor. 10,1; ብቍዑኒ ፡ አጋእስትየ "my lords, I pray you ..!" Gen. 19,18. An Interjection of joy as well as of derision is met with in እንቋዕ "bravo!", v. § 162.

(e) Optative Expressions.

(e) The Verb may likewise be put in the Subjunctive to express a *Wish*, but the Perfect also may be employed, just as in Conditional Clauses (§ 205) which are allied to Optative ones: ረከብኩ ፡ ጸጋ ፡ በቅድሜከ εὕροιμι Gen. 34,11; Ruth 2,13; ይሁዳ ፡ ሰብሑከ ፡ አኃዊከ αἰνέσαισαν Gen. 49,8; Sir. 36,4; Tob. 11,16.

(1) Corresponding to the Arabic بَخٍ, and, as regards its origin, still obscure.

(2) The ground-form seems to be ሰይ.

እመ "if!" and **እም** (§ 170) are words specially used to introduce Optative clauses, *e. g.* **እምነሣእከ** *si sumpsisses = debebas sumere* Matt. 25, 27; [**በሕቱ ፡ እምቀደምከ ፡ ነሢአ** "if thou only hadst taken" *Kebra Nag.* 66 b 2; so also **በሕቱ** in *Annal. Joh. I.* (Guidi), p. 3, l. 10; p. 6, l. 24 *sq.*], as well as the conjunction **ሶበ** "when", which is used, like לוּ, for "would that!"; **ሶበ ፡ ሞትነ** "would that we had died!" Ex. 16, 3; **ሶበ ፡ ኀደርነ ፡ ወነበርነ** "would that we had remained!" Josh. 7, 7. Farther, a *Wish* may be introduced even by the interrogatives "who? what? when? where? how?":—**መኑ ፡ ወሀበነ ፡ ዕረፍተ** "O that one would give us rest!" Hen. 63, 5; **መኑ ፡ ይሁበኒ** "O that one would give me!" Hen. 95, 1; also with **እም** = ἄν prefixed to the verb: **መኑ ፡ እምከፈለኒ** "O that one would assign to me!"; (*cf.* 2 Kings 15, 4); or with **እመ** (v. *supra*): **መኑ ፡ እመ ፡ አግብአ ፡ ለዝክቱ ፡ ሕዝብ ፡ ውስተ ፡ እዴየ** "O that one would give this people into my hand!" Judges 9, 29; Numb. 11, 29.

(*f*) Various Exclamatory Particles.

(*f*) For "how!" "how very—!" occurring in Exclamatory utterances, **ሚ** (§ 147, *b*) is employed, *e. g.* **ሚአዳም** "how charming!" Cant. 4, 10; and also **እፎ** (§ 161, *a*) and even **ከመ**, *e. g.* **ከመ ፡ ሠናይ ፡ ወፍሡሕ ፡ ርእየቱ** "how fair and pleasing is its appearance!" Hen. 32, 5. The expression of enhancement "how much more!" is rendered by **እፎ ፡ ፈድፋደ** (§ 161, *a*); for "how much less!" **እፎ** or **እፎኬ** "how then!" may also be used: "our money even we have brought back, **ወእፎኬ ፡ ንሰርቅ ፡ እምቤትከ ፡ ወርቀ** how much less would we steal money out of thy house!" Gen. 44, 8.

2. CONNECTED SENTENCES.

(*a*) COPULATIVE CLAUSES.

1. Copulative use of **ወ** and **እንዘ** and some other Particles.

§ 200. 1. The conjunction **ወ** or the enclitic **ሂ** "also" (§ 168, 3) serves to join together words, or it may be clauses, into a series. The particular discourse may be continued, it is true, by merely placing two or more of its members side by side as co-ordinates, and without the intervention, in their case, of connecting particles, *e. g.* **ልዑል ፡ ዐቢይ ፡ ወቅዱስ** Hen. 10, 1; 15, 4; but this is an unusual proceeding; even in numerical statements the individual numbers are united by special particles. If a word or a clause has not only to be connected with a preceding one, but to be emphasised at the same time as fresh material, the arrangement

ወ—ሂ or ወ—ኒ (§ 168, 3, 4) is made use of, and may often, in certain circumstances, be repeated.—If an additional Noun has to be connected with a Noun which has not been expressly mentioned, but has merely been indicated in the Verb or in a Pron. Suff., the Noun which has been thus previously indicated is again brought under notice by means of a separate Personal Pronoun, placed directly before the new Noun, as in ከመ ፡ ይንበር ፡ ውእቱ ፡ ውብእሲቱ ፡ ወደቂቁ Ruth 1, 1; Judges 19, 9; Matt. 25, 9. A Verb, Adjective or Pronoun which is referable to two or more Nouns connected by "and", and precedes the series, may either take the Gender and Number of the nearest and most important one merely, or of the whole series, the Masculine Gender being taken by preference when the members of the series are of more genders than one, *e. g.* ወወረደ ፡ ሶምሶን ፡ ወአቡሁ ፡ ወእሙ Judges 14, 5; ወነገሮሙ ፡ ለአቡሁ ፡ ወለእሙ Judges 14, 2 (v. also § 172, *c*).— When, however, the Verb, Adjective or Pronoun follows the series, it must, as a rule, take the Plural. On the other hand one and the same Noun may become the Object of two or more Verbs connected by ወ. In such a case, if the second Verb comes after the Object, it usually repeats and assumes it in the form of a Suff. Pron.;—v., however, as an exception ለምንትኑ ፡ ኅደገ ፡ ዓለመ ፡ ወመነንከ (not ወ መነንኮ) *Chrest.* p. 45, line 21 *sq.*

In Ethiopic, the most general connecting particle,—viz. ወ, —suffices to join clauses together, even in those cases in which other languages, more accurate in their expression of logical relations, make use of other uniting-words or particles. ወ is the usual equivalent in Ethiopic for the Greek particle of continuation δέ, and in many cases it serves to indicate even the adversative "but", *e. g.* Matt. 7, 3; 16, 26; only, when some individual idea in the attached sentence has to be contrasted with an individual idea in the preceding one, the form ሰ, or still more frequently ወ—ሰ (§ 168, 5), is employed. An Infinitive even may be continued by a finite Verb, as in ኀዲጎ ፡ እግዚአ ፡ ወተለወከ *Chrest.* p. 42, line 9 *sq.*; Eccl. 8, 16; and, conversely, a finite Verb may be continued by an Infinitive, *e. g.* በእንተ ፡ ዘሰማዕከኒ ፡ ሊተ ፡ ወተዐድዎትከ ፡ ለአምላክከ G. Ad. 57, 9; እንዘ ፡ የኀሥሥ ፡ ይቅትሎ ፡ ወምጽአቶ ፡ እምላዕለ ፡ ገጸ ፡ ምድር *ibid.* 78, 24. *Circumstantial Clauses* (1) also, which

(1) V. on this subject Ewald, '*Gr. Ar.*' § 670; '*Hebr. Spr.*', § 306, *c* and § 341.

are thrown in, as the discourse proceeds, for the purpose of describing more minutely some object, circumstance or situation previously mentioned,—are in like manner attached to the principal clauses by **ወ**, *e. g.* **ቦአ ፡ ቤተ ፡ ኢዮስጦስ ፡ ወቤቱ ፡ ኀረ ፡ ምኵራብ** ἦλθεν εἰς οἰκίαν Ἰούστου, οὗ ἡ οἰκία ἦν συνομοροῦσα τῇ συναγωγῇ Acts 18, 7. In these Descriptive Clauses, however,—as has already been pointed out in § 196, *c*, *α*—, the Subject must, as a rule, come first, and usually it has additional prominence given it by the attachment of the affix **ሰ**, *e. g.* "the angels came to Sodom in the evening, **ወሎጥሰ ፡ ሀሎ ፡ ይነብር ፡ ውስተ ፡ አንቀጽ** as Lot was sitting within the gate" Gen. 19, 1; 20, 4; 21, 5; 24, 62; Numb. 22, 22; Judges 13, 2. Still, Descriptive Clauses of this kind, introduced by **ወ**, are not nearly so common in Ethiopic as in Arabic. Much more frequently Ethiopic makes use of the conjunction **እንዘ** (§ 170, 5) to introduce Clauses of Circumstance, *e. g.* Gen. 18, 1; Judges 8, 11; Ex. 12, 11; Hen. 32, 3. But even without **እንዘ** or **ወ**, and merely in asyndetic apposition, a circumstantial clause may be added to the principal clause: *cf.* § 189, 3, *c*, and cases like **ወአነ ፡ ሀለውኩ ፡ እስከ ፡ ዝንቱ ፡ ዲበ ፡ ገጽየ ፡ ግልቡቤ** Hen. 14, 24; **ወነበርነ ፡ ውስተ ፡ ገዳም ፡ ኢያቀረረነ ፡ ክረምት ፡ ወኢያልሀበነ ፡ ሐጋይ** *Chrest.* p. 31, line 17 *sq.*—Finally, **ወ** is largely employed in Ethiopic to connect together clauses which stand related to one another in *Temporal* or *Logical Sequence.* No special *Waw consecutivum* is known in Ethiopic, such as we have in Hebrew, nor even a فَ as distinguished from وَ,—such as occurs in Arabic. Both in narrative diction and in the prophetic style, the individual propositions must always be strung together by the same connecting particle **ወ**; and if the succession in time or thought has to be indicated with greater exactness, this must be effected by the addition of special particles like **ወእምዝ** "and then" Judges 16, 25; 19, 8; or **ወ—እንከ** (§ 169, 2). And yet there can be no doubt that this **ወ**, although it is undistinguishable, in pronunciation or form, from the common connecting particle **ወ**, carries with it very often a more forcible signification than the latter. Coming after temporal or conditional clauses,—the apodosis of which is usually annexed to the protasis without the interposition of any Conjunction,—this **ወ** may with special effect take its place at the head of the apodosis, *e. g.* **ወሶበ ፡ ይኔጽር ፡ ወይሬኢ** "and when he looks, then he sees" Gen. 29,2; "if he brings me back again . . . safe and sound, ወይከውነኒ ፡ . . . አምላኪየ then shall he be to me my God" Gen. 28,20 *sq.*(1); and similarly after a question: ሚመጠነ ፡ ትሁቡኒ ፡ ወአነ ፡ ለክሙ ፡ አገብኦ "how much will ye give me? so shall I deliver him up to you" Matt. 26,15. When, farther, subsidiary qualifications precede the principal clause, ወ is often used to introduce effectively the principal clause itself, *e. g.*—እስመ ፡ ዓዲ ፡ ሰቡዕ ፡ መዋዕል ፡ ወአመጽእ "for there are yet seven days, and then will I bring" Gen. 7,4(2). Lastly, two actions, of which the first is the condition and premise of the second, may be connected by this more significant ወ, *e. g.*:—"I have heard say of thee ከመ ፡ ሰማዕከ ፡ ሕልመ ፡ ወፈከርከ that thou requirest merely to hear a dream, in order to interpret it at once" (*lit.* 'that thou hearest a dream and dost interpret'—*ἀκούσαντά σε ἐνύπνια συγκρῖναι αὐτά*) Gen. 41,15.—ወ is very often employed with a following Subjunctive, to supply the result contemplated in a foregoing action, especially after a summons: ተጋብኡ ፡ ወአይድዐክሙ "gather yourselves together, that I may tell you, *or* then will I tell you" Gen. 49,1; Deut. 32,1; Judges 14,13; Ps. 49,8; 80,8; or after requests, *e. g.* Matt. 26,53. In the same way a Wish or Command,—which is derived, like a consequence, from a foregoing transaction,—is associated with the foregoing clause by ወ followed by an Imperative or Subjunctive, *e. g.* "this time too hast thou told me lies, ወአይድዐኒ now tell me truly" (*ἀνάγγειλον δή μοι*) Judges 16,13; "Who has given you permission to practise hatred? ወይርከብክሙ ፡ ለኃጥአን ፡ ዘኮኔ May doom therefore light upon you sinning ones!" Hen. 95, 2(3).

But while Ethiopic may in this way employ the particle ወ, invested with a special significance, to indicate various relations, it has at command in most cases farther particles and Conjunctions, which express these relations still more definitely. Accordingly

(1) [V. also, *infra*, p. 544, Note(1); and *cf. Kebra Nag., Introd.* p. XIX.]

(2) In other cases the same end is attained by asyndetic apposition: ስኩብ ፡ ኮንኩ ፡ በቤተ ፡ መላልኤል ፡ እምሔውየ ፡ ርኢኩ ፡ በራእይ . . . "I was sleeping in the house of my grandfather Malāle'el (and then) I saw in a vision . . ." Hen. 83, 3.

(3) [Flemming reads the Indic. here, ወይረክበክሙ and not the Subj. tr.]

the use of this more forcible ወ is not so common as in some other languages. Thus,—to adduce only one instance,—the Hebrew idiom וַיְהִי כִּי is rendered in Ethiopic much oftener by ወኮነ ፡ ከመ "and it happened that", than by ወኮነ ፡ ወ.

The counterpart of the stronger connecting word "also" is furnished by ሂ (§ 168, 3) and by still more emphatic ኒ, in the sense of "also—for his part". Even in Negative Sentences the same connecting particles are in use, thus: ወኢ, ወኢ—ሂ, ወኢ—ኒ, ኢ—ሂ &c., "and not", "nor", "nor even". To express a statement in better terms and to place one thing beside another as being equally possible, use is commonly made of አው "or", on rare occasions of ወ "and" (§ 168, 1), oftener of ወእመሂ (ወእመኒ) "*sive*", "or even", and of ወለእመ, ወእመ (§ 170, 1) ([1]). ወእማእኮ serves for the disjunctive "or" (§ 170, 1). On the repetition of these particles, to express "either—or", "whether—or", v. § 206. On "or" in disjunctive interrogation v. § 198, *c*.

2. Adversative Clauses. Restrictive and Intensifying Additions to the Sentence.

2. *Adversative Clauses* are indicated by ወ (v. *supra*, No. 1), and more emphatically by the enclitic ሰ or by ወ—ሰ, *cf.* § 168, 5. To introduce an opposite statement after a negation and assert the affirmative, አላ "but" (§ 168, 6) is used, as well as እንበለ and ዘእንበለ (§ 168, 7); but yet the last two particles, in conformity with their fundamental meaning, have almost always the force rather of "but only", *e. g.* ርእየቶ ፡ ኢርኢክሙ ፡ ዘእንበለ ፡ ቃሎ "his form ye saw not, but only (heard) his voice" Deut. 4, 12; or:—"the sound in health do not need the physician, ዘእንበለ ፡ እለ ፡ የሐሙ but only they that are sick" Matt. 9,12; John 6,38; 9,31; Ps. 117, 17; 130, 3. In many passages this form answers directly to our "except" (εἰ μή), *e. g.* Matt. 5,13; Gal. 1,19; Hen. 69,11. As a correcting and affirming particle, ዳእሙ "but rather", "on the

([1]) These forms, ወእመሂ, ወለእመሂ, ወለእመ &c. may, like አው, be inserted in the sentence, without in the least disturbing the construction which has begun, *e. g.* ለእመቦ ፡ ዘሰረቀ ፡ ላህመ ፡ ወእመሂ ፡ በግዐ Ex. 21,37; [ወሶበ ፡ ይትረገዝ ፡ ሰብእ ፡ በኵናት ፡ ወእመሂ ፡ በቀስት *Miracles of the Virgin Mary* (ed. WALLIS BUDGE, 1900), Ethiopic text, p. 27 b 16 *sq.*]; but such a form may also, acting as a conditional particle, combine with the word which it attaches to what precedes,—to form an independent clause, *e. g.* ወቀተለ ፡ ብእሴ ፡ ወለእመሂ ፡ ብእሲተ Ex. 21, 29; 22, 6.

contrary" (§ 168, 9), is also often met with, *e. g.* Judges 15, 13; Gen. 35, 10.

The restrictive word ባሕቱ፡ "only" (§ 168, 8) is very frequently used in the sense of "still", "however", ἀλλά, δέ, μᾶλλον, not merely in the middle of the clause, as in 1 John 2, 19, but even connecting clauses together; and in this latter case we have mostly the compound form ወባሕቱ፡ or ወ—ባሕቱ፡, *e. g.* "I might do thee hurt, ወባሕቱ ፡ እግዚአብሔር ፡ ይቤለኒ but God said to me" Gen. 31, 29; ወእብለክሙ ፡ ባሕቱ፡ "but I say unto you" Matt. 17, 11. "Nevertheless", "notwithstanding" may be expressed by ወ—ሰ, *e. g.* Ps. 49, 17, 18; or by ምስለዝ "even with that", "in spite of that", *e. g.* 1 Cor. 14, 21; Hen. 90, 11; or by በኵሉዝ "after all", *e. g.* Hen. 89, 46. In Negative sentences the same idea is also expressed by ጥቀ ("even" § 163, 1) along with ኢ, *e. g.* "although I was continually with you, እጼንሐክሙ ፡ ጥቀ ፡ ኢሰፋሕክሙ yet you did not stretch forth your hands" Luke 22, 53; Matt. 21, 32. However, in the apodosis of conditional sentences which are introduced by "even if", "if only", "although", the idea—"yet" is usually left unexpressed; v., for instance, Matt. 26, 35.

Intensification is expressed by the Adverbs ጥቀ "even", "indeed" (§ 163, 1) and ፈድፋደ "exceedingly", "still more", particularly in Negative Clauses, in which ኢ—ጥቀ or ጥቀ—ኢ answers to *ne—quidem*, *e. g.* in Ex. 11, 7, as well as in Interrogative and Exclamatory sentences. In these last the phrase እፎ ፡ እንከ ፡ ፈድፋደ means "how much more then?" when it comes after a positive sentence, and "how much less?" when it comes after one that is negative, *e. g.* Matt. 6, 30; Heb. 12, 25. The expression ኅድጎሰ, which has been explained above (§ 163, 3), is also employed in this connection.

The purely restrictive "only" may certainly be expressed by ባሕቱ፡ (§ 163, 2), as *e. g.* in Gen. 34, 15; but, seeing that this form of the word is often used in the sense of "still", "however", ባሕቲቱ፡ (§ 163, 2) has become the usual expression for "only". Besides, even ከመ is available to indicate that idea, *cf.* § 162, and after Negative sentences እንበለ and ዘእንበለ "except" (§§ 168, 7 and 170, 4). However, just as,—in the Classical languages,—limitation is expressed not only by Adverbs, but also by inflected Adjectives (μόνος, *solus*), so Ethiopic in many cases prefers this more personal form of expression to the Adverbial one, and employs for this purpose the word ባሕቲት, already described in § 157, with Suffix pronouns attached, *e. g.* ኪያሁ ፡ ባሕቲቶ "him only" Matt. 4,10.

3. Causal and Inferential Expressions

3. Generally the Conjunction እስመ (§ 169, 4) serves to introduce a *"cause"* or *"reason"*. It is used with extraordinary frequency, corresponding first of all to our "since", "seeing that", "because", and then farther to our "for", — for which in fact Ethiopic has no other word. As it has a relative force, it may, together with the clause which it introduces, be even put before the clause containing the statement which has to be explained, *e. g.* ወእስመ ፡ አልቦ ፡ ሥርው ፡ የብሰ "and because it had no root, it withered away" Matt. 13, 6; 22, 25; Judges 15, 2. In the same way the Conjunction of comparison በከመ or ዘከመ "as" is often used also in the sense of "inasmuch as" and "as long as", *e. g.* Hen. 81, 3; Gen. 34, 7. A stronger form is found in በእንተ ፡ ዘ "for this reason, that", "on the ground, that" (§ 170, 10).

To indicate *inferences* or *conclusions*, Ethiopic has first of all the enclitic ኬ "thus", and እንከ "then", "therefore", which nearly always has a place assigned to it after the inferred idea. እንጋ "then indeed" is rather a particle of interrogation and doubt, v. *supra*, § 169, 1—3. A stronger form meets us in በእንተ ፡ ዝንቱ። or በእንተዝ "for this cause", "therefore", *e. g.* Judges 15, 19. In the Bible the form ወይእዜኒ "and now", — corresponding to וְעַתָּה, is also of pretty frequent occurrence, *e. g.* Gen. 31, 29; Judges 13, 7; 14, 2; 20, 9; — *cf.* also Hen. 94, 1, 3.

(b) ATTRIBUTIVE RELATIVE CLAUSES.

1. Presence or Absence of Introductory Relative Pronoun.

§ 201. A Relative Clause in the narrower sense is usually introduced by the Relative pronoun, which has been described in § 147, *a*. Ethiopic has no other personal Relative, but it has certainly a special Relative Adverb of Place ኀበ (§ 161, *b*) "where", "in which" (1), "whither", "to which", as well as አመ "when" or "while" (§ 161, *b*), which often at least takes the place of a Relative Adverb of Time. Relative Clauses which, without the intervention of a Relative Pronoun, add a subsidiary qualification to some word in the Principal Clause, are doubtless possible in Ethiopic, but they do not occur so often as in other Semitic tongues, and they seem to be no more than the relics of forms which belonged to a more antique stage of the language. In their case, it is all the

(1) [—and sometimes even in the sense of "while", v. *Kebra Nag.* 102 b 20.]

same whether the word, which is to be farther explained, is definite or not: አጥፍእ . . . . ሥጋ ፡ አምዐዐተከ "destroy . . . . the flesh, (which) has made thee angry" Hen. 84, 6(1); በአርአያ ፡ አርአይኩከ "according to the similitude (which) I showed thee" Ex. 26, 30; 36, 5; በዕለት ፡ ኢተሐዘበ "on a day, (on which) he looked not for (him)" Matt. 24, 50; እቶን ፡ ይነድድ (*varr.* ዘይነድድ, እንዘ ፡ ይነድድ) ኀለፈ 1 Esr. 2, 48. Even in the later speech, a Relative Pronoun may be dispensed with, and that most readily when an entire clause is dependent on a Noun standing in the Constr. St., *e. g.* in በመዋዕለ ፡ ይኴንኑ ፡ መሳፍንት "in the days (when) the judges ruled" Ruth 1, 1; Gen. 24, 11; Lev. 7, 15, 38; 13, 14; 14, 2; Numb. 6, 13; ከመ ፡ ኢትርግም ፡ ዕለተ ፡ ተወለድከ (*var.*: ዘተወለድከ) Sir. 23, 14; በብሔረ ፡ ተፄወውኩ (*var.*: በብሔር ፡ ዘተፄወውኩ) Tob. 3, 15 &c.; also in ሶበ ፡ ኮነ ፡ ጊዜ ፡ ይዕረብ ፡ ፀሓይ "when the time came, (that) the sun had to go down" Gen. 15, 17. And it has already been observed (§ 168) that not a few words, almost devoid of signification, which subordinate entire Clauses in this way, have been turned into Conjunctions.

(*a*) When Rel. Pron. is present, Supporting-Noun is sometimes merely understood.

1. (*a*) When, however, the Relative Pronoun is employed, it does not absolutely require to be supported by a Noun expressly mentioned. It may assume a more independent or substantive position, and become also correlative, *i. e.* — to use our way of speaking, — it may include its own Demonstrative, *e. g.* ዘአምን ፡ . . . . ይድኅን "who (*i. e.* 'he who') believeth . . . . shall be saved" Mark 16, 16; አልቦሙ ፡ ዘይበልዑ "they had not (anything) which they could eat" Mark 8, 1. Accordingly ዘ may signify "who", "what", "one who", "something which", "he who", "that which". Hence this simple Relative Pronoun is wont to suffice for the idea of "whoever", "whatever"; and only when it must take at the same time a distributive sense is it commonly doubled (*cf.* § 159, *g*), as, for instance, in ኵሎሙ ፡ ዘዘሐለዮሙ ፡ ልቦሙ ፡ ያምጽኡ "they are all to bring whatever their heart thinks right" Ex. 35, 5. What is said here of ዘ holds good also of ኀበ and አመ (v. *infra*). No doubt, for the sake of clearness, and particularly when ዘ has to refer to a somewhat distant Noun, the Demonstrative may farther be expressly set down before the Relative Pronoun, as in ውእቱ ፡ ዘነጽሐ "(for) him who has been subjected to cleansing" Lev. 14, 19; Gen. 15, 17; እሉ ፡ እለ "those, who" Judges 6, 10; ዝክቱ ፡ ዘአም

(1) [Flemming, however, reads እንተ between ሥጋ and the Verb. tr.]

ጽኡ Lev. 1,4; this however is by no means necessary. If on the other hand the Relative Clause comes first, especially if it is not quite short, the reference to it is frequently indicated by a demonstrative pronoun, placed at the head of the principal clause, *e. g.* እለ ፡ አነ ፡ እቤለከ ፡ እሙንቱ ፡ ይሑሩ Judges 7,4; Matt. 24,13. In the case of a Relative Pronoun, such as has been described above, which stands alone, and includes within it its own Demonstrative, the distinctions of Gender and Number are carefully attended to; and the Case-relations, which such a Relative Clause assumes within the Principal Clause, as representing a Noun Substantive, are denoted, precisely as with any Noun, *e. g.* ዘአምን ፡ . . . ይድኅን Mark 16, 16; ኢኮንክሙ ፡ አንትሙ ፡ እለ ፡ ትትናገሩ "ye are not those who speak" ('it is not ye that speak') Matt. 10, 20; ርኢኩ ፡ ዘሎቱ ፡ ርእሰ ፡ መዋዕል "I saw one who had a hoary head (*lit.* 'a head of days')" Hen. 46, 1; Numb. 23, 8; Judges 17,6; ትተልዎሙ ፡ ለእለ ፡ የዐፅዱ Ruth 2, 3; Luke 9, 11 (in accordance with § 172, *c*); ደመ ፡ ዘቀተለ "the blood of that which he has slain" Numb. 23, 24; Hen. 49, 3 (1); ምስለ ፡ እለ ፡ ሞቱ "with those who are dead" Ruth 1, 8 &c. It is worthy of remark that a Relative pronoun of the 3rd Pers. may refer even to a 1st Pers., *e. g.* ወእከውን ፡ ዘይደሉ (= ድልወ) Sap. 9, 12.

Even to a separate pronoun which is virtually in the Genitive, the Relative may be referred by means of ለ, *e. g.* *Ascensio Isaiae* 7, 20, and in the same way to a Dative (like ለጻድቃን ፡ — ለእለ), *e. g.* *Asc. Is.* 8, 26; 9, 21; 7, 21; 10, 16; 11, 16 (2).

(*b*) On the other hand when the Relative pronoun refers to a Noun expressly mentioned in the principal clause, which it qualifies like an attributive Adjective, while this noun at the same time precedes the relative clause, — then it is not indispensably necessary that the relative pronoun should agree with the Noun in Gender and Number: frequently the Relative ዘ continues to keep its readiest form, as a general Relative sign (§ 147, *a*) even when it refers to feminine and plural Nouns, *e. g.* መሳክው ፡ ርኅዋት ፡ ዘእምኔሆን "open windows, out of which" Hen. 72, 7; አንስ (*b*) Usages when Supporting-Noun is expressly mentioned.

---

(1) Flemming reads here ወመንፈስ ፡ ዘያሌቡ instead of Dillmann's ወመንፈሰ ፡ ዘ″, *i. e.* "the Spirit which bestows understanding" instead of "the Spirit of Him who bestows understanding". tr.]

(2) *Cf.* Trumpp, GGA 1877, p. 1544 *sqq. ad loca.*

34

ትያ ፡ ዘኅረዩ "wives, whom they might choose" Gen. 6,2. If the Noun, with which the Relative is associated, is a Suff. pron., the reference is contrived by prefixing ለ to the Relative: ምስሌነ ፡ ለ እለ ፡ ጾርነ "with us, who have borne" Matt. 20,12. It is not, however, absolutely necessary that the Noun, to which the Relative refers, should come before the latter: on the contrary, it may follow the Relative just like the Adjective (according to § 188), *e. g.* ኢትእርዩ ፡ ዘወድቀ ፡ እክለ "gather not up the corn which has fallen aside" Lev. 19,9; Deut. 33,11. If again the Noun has the adjunct ኵሉ, it is very common for the Relative Clause to be inserted between ኵሉ and the Noun, *e. g.* ኵሉ ፡ ዘይትገበር ፡ በእሳት ፡ ንዋይ Numb. 31,23; ኵሎ ፡ ዘትገብሩ ፡ ቃለ Deut. 1,18. Then too, the *Attraction* of the Noun to which the Relative refers, from the principal clause into the relative clause, is a favourite turn in Ethiopic, just as it is in the classical languages (1), *e. g.* ውስተ ፡ እንተ ፡ በእከሙ ፡ ሀገር "into whatsoever city ye enter" Matt. 10,11; ወአልቦ ፡ ሀየ ፡ ዘይሰቲ ፡ ማየ Ex. 17,1; ኢረከብኩ ፡ ዘመጠነዝ ፡ ሃይማኖተ "I have not found so great faith" Matt. 8,10. Or at least an adjective belonging to the leading Noun is drawn into the Relative Clause, as in ዝንቱ ፡ ደብር ፡ ዘርኢከ ፡ ነዊኀ "this high mountain, which thou hast seen" Hen. 25,3. To this class belong also cases like ወጻድቅሰ ፡ ዘይትገደፍ ፡ ኢርኢኩ Ps. 36,26; ኵሉ ፡ መቅሠፍት ፡ ዘኢኮነ ፡ጽሑፈ ፡ ውስተ ፡ ዝንቱ ፡ መጽሐፈ ፡ ሕግ ፡ ያመጽእ ፡ እግዚአብሔር ፡ ላዕሌከ Deut. 28,61. Thus also we have አመ ፡ ዕለተ "what day" ('the day on which') Gen. 3,5. In particular, ኵሉ, when it immediately precedes the ዘ, is generally combined closely with the Relative, and is regulated then in its construction, not by the principal clause, but by the Relative clause, *e. g.* ትግበሩ ፡ ኵሉ ፡ ዘጽሑፍ "('and that') ye do everything which (= whatever) is written" Josh. 23,6; Numb. 18,15; Deut. 6,1, 20; 11,3; 34,12,

Attraction of Noun.

As regards specially the Adverb of Place ኀበ, it may be employed, like ዘ, correlatively, and may signify: "in the place where", "to the place where", "in the place whither", "to the place whither", *e. g.* ሖረ ፡ ኀበ ፡ ይቀርዕ Gen. 31,19; እንበር ፡ ኀበ ፡ ረከብኩ Judges 17,9; ታስተጋብእ ፡ እምኀበ ፡ ኢዘረውከ "gatherest (from) where thou hast not strawed" Matt. 25,24; መልዕልተ ፡ ኀበ ፡ ሀሎ ፡ ሕፃን

(1) *Cf.* Ewald '*Hebr. Spr.*' § 334, *a.*

"over where the young child was" Matt. 2,9; ኢረከበት ፡ ኀበ ፡ ታዐርፍ ፡ እግራ "she found not (a place) where she could rest her foot" Gen. 8,9; ሐቅል ፡ ውእቱ ፡ ኀበ ፡ ሀለውነ "it is a desert place, where we are" Luke 9,12; [ዘቦቱ ፡ ጥሪተ ፡ ኀበ ፡ ፃፄ ፡ ወቍንቍኔ ፡ ኢያማስኖ "who has treasures there where moth and worm do not destroy them" *Chrest.* p. 47, l. 9]. But ኀበ may also be associated with some noun expressly mentioned before, — in the first place, with nouns of place, as in መካኖ ፡ ኀበ ፡ ኖመ ፡ ህየ "his place, where he sleeps" Ruth 3,4; Luke 10,5; as well as with names of things and names of persons; and in that case it fills the place of the Relative pronoun ዘ, taking a corresponding preposition of place, *e. g.* ሰረገላተ ፡ በኀበ ፡ የዐርግ "the chariots (Acc.) into which he mounts" Hen. 72,5; 73,2; መላእክተ ፡ መቅሠፍቱ ፡ በኀበ ፡ ሀለዉ ፡ ምጥዋነ "his avenging angels, to whom they had been given over" Hen. 63,1. — in a way similar to that in which ህየ may also be used in such cases, conjoined with a foregoing ዘ, *e. g.* አሕዛብ ፡ እለ ፡ ትበውእ ፡ ህየ "the nations to whom thou comest" Deut. 12,29.

2. Expression of Case-relations of the Rel. Pron. within Rel. Clause. (*a*) By supplementing Rel. Pron. by a Pers. Pron. attached as Suff. to Noun concerned

§ 202. 2. *The Case-relations of the Relative Pronoun within the Relative Clause may be expressed in various ways.*

(*a*) The ordinary way of indicating these relations of Case is by treating the Relative Pron., — though inflected according to Gender and Number, — merely as a general mark of relation which needs to be supplemented by Personal Pronouns. To be sure, when the Relative appears as the Subject of the Relative Clause, there is no necessity for its being supplemented by any Personal pronoun, because all needful supplementing is contained in the Verb itself. *e. g.* ብእሲ ፡ ዘየሐውር "the man, who goes". In like manner the supplementing process may be dispensed with, when the Relative has to take, as we would say, the Objective case or Accusative, because its Case-relation then is usually understood from the context, *e. g.* ምድር ፡ እንተ ፡ ወሀበከ "the land, which he has given thee". Still, even in this case, the supplementary Pronoun is just as often added as omitted, as in አሕዛብ ፡ ዘአንትሙ ፡ ትትወረስዎሙ "the nations whom ye shall (as heirs) succeed" Deut. 12,2: and this is particularly necessary, when the Relative pron. refers to a Pronoun of the 1st or 2nd Person. If the Relative Pron. stands related as a Genitive to a Noun in the Relative Clause, this is indicated, not by the Relative but by a Suffix attached to the Noun: ሀገር ፡ እንተ ፡ ስማ ፡ ሲኪር "a city, the name of which is Sychar" John 4, 5; ዘይበጽሕ ፡ ርእሱ "the top of which will reach" Gen. 11, 4; እለ ፡ ፍጹማን ፡ እደዊሆሙ "whose hands are consecrated" Numb. 3, 3. In case the Genitive has to be expressed by a Preposition (§ 186), the indication is given by attaching a Suffix to the Preposition; "the Church, እንተ ፡ ላቲ ፡ ተሠየምኩ ፡ ላእከ as a servant of which I have been set" Col. 1, 25; "two servants, ዘአሐዱ ፡ እምኔሆሙ one of whom". — In the same way when the relation of the Relative pronoun in the Relative clause has to be assigned to that pronoun with the help of a Preposition, the usual practice is to place the Preposition, with a corresponding Suff. pron., after the Relative, and either immediately after it or separated from it by one or two words, *e. g.* ሀገር ፡ እንተ ፡ እምኔሃ "the city, from which" Josh. 20, 6; ምድር ፡ እንተ ፡ በውስቴታ ፡ ተወልደ "the land, in which he was born" Gen. 11, 28; አዕማድ ፡ እለ ፡ ዲቤሆን ፡ ይቀውም ፡ ዝንቱ ፡ ቤት "the pillars upon which this house standeth" Judges 16, 26; ዘመጻእኪ ፡ ኀቤሁ "to whom thou art come" Ruth 2, 12; [መከን ፡ ዘተሐውር ፡ ኀቤሁ *Contendings of the Apostles* 155, 8]; ብእሲ ፡ ዘኢኀሰቈ ፡ ሎቱ ፡ እግዚአብሔር ፡ ኀጢአቶ "the man to whom God imputeth not his sin" Ps. 31, 2. — It is but very rarely, in such a case, that the reference of the Relative Pron. to the Pron. Suff. which follows, is separately indicated by a ለ prefixed to the Relative, *e. g.* in ለእለ ፡ ውስቴቶሙ ፡ ሀሎከ instead of a mere እለ Ex. 34,10.

Or by prefixing necessary Prep. to Suff. Pron.

(*b*) By prefixing Prepositions and Signs of Case to the Rel. Pron. itself.

(*b*) But the Relative Pronoun may be treated also, — in Ethiopic just as in the Indo-European languages, — as an actual Pronominal Adjective. On that view depends the second method of assigning to the Relative its Case-relations within the Relative Clause. That method consists in simply placing the signs of Case and the prepositions before the Relative, *e. g.* "money, በዘ ፡ ንሣየጥ ፡ እክለ with which we are to buy corn" Gen. 43, 22; "he enquired about the time, በዘ ፡ አስተርአዮሙ ፡ ኮከብ at which the star had appeared to them" Matt. 2, 7; ነገረከ ፡ በዘ ፡ ያስሕተከ "he hath spoken to thee that wherewith he will lead thee astray" Deut. 13, 6; Ex. 34, 35; Gen. 31, 32; Ex. 28, 4; ኵሉ ፡ ውስተ ፡ ዘወድቀ ፡ በድኖሙ "every (thing), upon which the dead body of (any of) them falleth" Lev. 11, 32, 35; ዲበ ፡ ዘርኢከ ፡ ይወርድ ፡ መንፈስ ፡ ቅዱስ "upon whom thou seest the Holy Spirit descending" John 1, 33; አእምር ፡ ለዘትገብር γνῶθι τίνι ποιεῖς Sir. 12, 1; አልቦ ፡ ለዘ ፡

አዘዘ "he has commanded no one" Sir. 15, 20; ለእመ ፡ ብከ ፡ በዘትበቍዖ "if thou hast anything, through which thou art profitable to him" Sir. 13, 14; ወሀበሙ ፡ ልበ ፡ በዘ ፡ ይሔልዩ *καρδίαν ἔδωκε διανοεῖσθαι αὐτῷ* Sir. 17, 6; ዕፅ ፡ በዘ ፡ ይትገበር Sap. 14, 7; አልቦ ፡ ለዘ የኀፍሮ ፡ ወአልቦ ፡ ለዘይፈርሆ "he (God) shuns no one, and is afraid of no one" (while, without ለ, the meaning might be: "no one shuns him, or is afraid of him") *Clem.* 204, *b*.

Occasionally the two forms of construction are so blended together, that the preposition is both placed before the Relative pronoun, and repeated after it with Suff. pron. in the Relative Clause itself, as in "blessed are they, ለእለ ፡ ኢሐሰበ ፡ ሎሙ ፡ ኵሎ ፡ ጌጋዮሙ Ps. 31, 1; ወቦ ፡ ለዘወሀቦ ፡ ኀምስተ ፡ መክሊተ Matt. 25, 15; በትረከ ፡ በዘቦቱ፡ ፡ ዘበጥከ Ex. 17, 5; 30, 4, 36; 39, 17; Lev. 11, 34 &c.

(c) By longer Prepositions placed after the Rel. Pron. which they govern.

(*c*) Meanwhile, longer prepositions are not usually placed before the Relative Pronoun; but Ethiopic has acquired the remarkable faculty of placing them after it(1): ምድር ፡ እንተ ፡ ኀበ ፡ መጻእነ "the land, to which we have come" Gen. 47, 4; እበን ፡ ዘኀበ "stones, in which" Lev. 14, 40; ኈለቍ ፡ ዘእምኔ ፡ ይወፅኡ ፡ ኆኀው "I counted the gates from which they came forth" Hen. 33, 3; ኆኀው ፡ እለ ፡ እምኀበ ፡ ይወፅእ ፡ ፀሐይ "the gates (Acc.) from which the sun comes forth" Hen. 72, 3; ብዙኀ ፡ ዘእምተጽሕፈ ፡ ዘኮነ ፡ ጸብእ ፡ ላዕለ ፡ ንጉሥ "more numerous than have been described (here) were the wars which the king had to conduct" (*lit.* 'more than what has been written of (here), (was) the warfare which was by the king') *Histoire des guerres d' ʿAmda Syōn* (ed. PERRUCHON, Paris 1890), p. 113, l. 14 *sq.* But quite short, monosyllabic prepositions are never, as far as known, placed after the Relative Pron. in this way.

The placing of the Preposition *before* the Relative, the relation of which within the Relative Clause is pointed out by the preposition, occasions no dubiety of any kind, when the Relative pron. refers to a Noun previously mentioned. But when the Relative is employed in a more correlative and substantive sense (§ 201), as in the sentence:— ዲበ ፡ ዘርኢከ ፡ ይወርድ ፡ መንፈስ ፡ ቅዱስ "upon whom thou seest the Holy Spirit descending", this mode of expression is permissible only if there is no possible doubt

(1) Like *quocum*, or *wherewith*, *whereupon* &c.

regarding the reference of the Relative pron. within the principal Clause. The Preposition occurs before the Relative with most frequency, when it depends both on the Verb of the principal clause and on that of the Relative Clause: **እእሪ ፡ እክለ ፡ ኀበ ፡ እለ ፡ ረከብኩ ፡ ሞገሰ** "I will glean ears of corn with those with whom I find favour" Ruth 2, 2.

By virtue of that freer use of the Accusative, which is described in § 174 *sq.*, the Relative pron. may, in several cases in which other languages have it preceded by a preposition, be simply subordinated in the Accusative; thus, in particular, when it is associated with an expression of time, as in **በካልእት ፡ ዓመት ፡ ዘወፅኡ** "in the second year after they had come out" Numb. 1, 1; **እምዓመት ፡ ዘተሣየጦ** "from the year, in which he bought him" Lev. 25, 50; Ps. 89, 17; and in other cases also, such as **ቅብአ ፡ ዘይትቀብኡ** "the oil (Acc.), with which they are anointed" Ex. 35,28; 38, 25 (for which, in Ex. 40, 7, we have **ዘቦቱ ፡ ይትቀብኡ**); and still more freely in **ምንት ፡ ጌጋይየ ፡ ዘዴገንከኒ** "what is my guilt that (*or* 'on account of which') thou dost pursue me?" Gen. 31, 36 (but yet v. § 203, 1, *a*).

3. Relative Construction as Periphrastic Substitute for Participles and Adjectives.

3. *The Relative construction is a favourite one in Ethiopic, and is in frequent use.* Above all, Participles which may be wanting in the language, as well as Adjectives, are periphrastically indicated by Relative clauses, *e. g.* **ዘይነድድ** "burning" Hen. 14, 12; **ዘኢያእመረ** "unwitting" Gen. 20, 4; **ዘይመጽእ** or **ዘይከውን** "future"; **ዘሀሎ** "present" Rom. 8, 38; **ዘይትነገር** "so-called" Hen. 17, 4; **ዘይዘርእ** "sower" Matt. 13, 3; **ዘይልህቅ** "the elder"; **ዘይንእስ** "the younger" Gen. 19, 31 *sqq.*; **ዘለዓለም** "everlasting"; **ዘቀዲሙ** "the earlier" Deut. 10, 4. In particular, those Adjectives, which express Capability or Incapability of any kind, are indicated in this circumlocutory fashion, such as **ዘይቀትል** "deadly" Ps. 7, 14; **ዘይመውት** "mortal"; **ዘኢይመውት** "immortal"; **ዘኢይትመጠን** "immeasurable"; **ዘኢይትኌለቍ** "innumerable"; **ዘኢያስተርኢ** "invisible" &c. In the same way the privative Adjectives of our tongues are expressed, and those which in our tongues are compounded of two or more words, *e. g.* **ኅሩያን ፡ (እለ ፡) ኍልቍ ፡ አልቦሙ** "unnumbered elect" (§ 201, *init.*); **ዘሠለስቱ ፡ ዓመቱ** "three-year-old" Gen. 15, 9; **ዘአልቦ ፡ ማየ** "waterless" Ps. 106, 4; **መጥባሕት ፡ እንተ ፡ ክልኤቱ ፡ አፈዊሃ** "a two-edged sword" Judges 3, 16; **ዘአልቦ ፡ ፈውስ** "incurable" Deut. 28, 27; **ዘአልቦ ፡ ጌጋየ** "innocent"

Ex. 23, 7. Even when a corresponding Adjective does exist in the language, the periphrastic rendering by means of a Relative clause is often preferred, as being more forcible or more elegant, as in **ዘየዐቢ ፡ ብርሃን ፡ ወዘይንእስ ፡ ብርሃን** "the greater light and the lesser light" Gen. 1, 16; **እለ ፡ ተርፉ** "the remaining" John 6, 12; Josh. 21, 26; **ዘየአኪ** (for **እኩይ**) Matt. 12, 45. Farther, an Adjective is frequently connected with its Substantive by means of the Relative pronoun,—not only when it has an adverbial adjunct along with it, as in **ዘሕያው ፡ ለዓለም** "the ever-living one" Hen. 5,1, but also when it must be emphatic: **እምነ ፡ እንስሳ ፡ ዘንጹሕ** "of *clean* beasts" (contrasted with the *unclean*) Gen. 7, 2; **ወልደ ፡ ዘበኵራ** "her firstborn son" Matt. 1, 25; Gen. 25, 25; 27, 19 (as against Gen. 38, 6)(1). That the Possessive pronouns **ዚአየ** &c. are often joined to their substantives by means of **ዘ** (*e. g.* Gen. 37, 7; 31, 18, 21), has been remarked already (v. *supra*, § 150, *b*).

The Relative style is also employed in many instances to attach any kind of subsidiary qualification to a Noun, *e. g.* **ጠየቁ ፡ ኵሎ ፡ ዘውስተ ፡ ሰማይ ፡ ግብረ** "I observed all the works (done) in Heaven" Hen. 2, 1; **አድባር ፡ ዘእምእብን ፡ ክቡር** "mountains (composed) of precious stones" Hen. 18, 6. And in almost every case our preposition "without",—for which otherwise **እንበለ** (p. 403 *sq.*) is alone available—, is expressed by **ዘአልቦ**, *e. g.* **አባግዕ ፡ ዘአልቦ ፡ ኖላዌ** "sheep without shepherds" Numb. 27, 17.

Finally, as has been pointed out already, (v. § 197, *c*), either the impersonal and adverbial Relative **ዘ** *quod*, or the personal Relative pron., is employed with special frequency after the negatives **አኮ** and **አልቦ**, *e. g.* **አኮ ፡ ኵሉ ፡ ዘይብለኒ ፡ እግዚኦ ፡ እግዚኦ ፡ ዘይበውእ ፡ ውስተ ፡ መንግሥተ ፡ ሰማያት** "not every one that saith unto me, Lord, Lord, shall enter (*lit.* "is he who shall enter") into the kingdom of heaven" Matt. 7, 21. In like manner examples will be found in § 197, *c*, which show that in the circuitous rendering of "no man", "nothing" &c. by means of **አልቦ ፡ ዘ**, the verb may occur in any mood which the connection imposes upon it, and particularly in the Subjunctive: **አልቦ ፡ ዘየሀሉ ፡** . . . "there shall be no man . . ." Lev. 16, 17; Josh. 6, 10; Matt. 16, 20.

---

(1) That **በኵር** precisely is so often joined to its substantive by the Relative pron. may doubtless be explained, besides, by the fact that its proper meaning is "first birth" not "firstborn".

4. Position of Words in a Relative Clause.

4. The position of the words in the Relative clause does not differ essentially from the arrangement in the ordinary sentence. Only, if the Relative pron. is supplemented by a preposition which has a suff. pron. attached to it, this preposition very often comes immediately after the Relative (v. examples given above). And just as in any sentence (v. § 196) a word may acquire special emphasis from being placed at the head of the sentence, so in Relative sentences too the word or words which have to be emphasised precede the Relative pron., *e. g.* **ወኢያሪኮስ ፡ ዕጹት ፡ ይእቲ ፡ ወጥቅም ፡ ዘላዕሌሃ** "now Jericho was strictly closed, and had a (good) wall round it" Josh. 6, 1; **መካን ፡ እምዝ ፡ ዘይጌርም** "a place still more frightful than this" Hen. 21, 7(1); **ወኵሎ ፡ ዘገብረ ፡ ተአምረ** "and who did all the wonders" Josh. 24, 17; **በነቢይ ፡ ዘተብህለ** "that which was said by the prophet" Matt. 21, 4; **ብእሲ ፡ ኀበ ፡ ኵሉ ፡ ሰብኡ ፡ ወሥጋሁ ፡ ዘይከውን ፡ ኢይባእ** "a man shall not go in unto any of his own near kin or of his own flesh" Lev. 18, 6. In some instances a word would seem to be put first, not entirely for the sake of emphasis, but rather with the aim of giving a certain polish to the sentence: this, accordingly, is a question of greater or less refinement in style(2).

(c) CONJUNCTIONAL RELATIVE CLAUSES.

1. Subject or Object expressed by an entire Clause:— (a) Declarative Clause introduced by ዘ.

§ 203. 1. If the Subject or Object of a Sentence cannot be expressed by a noun, but must be indicated periphrastically by an entire Clause, the Clause, which in this way declares the Subject or Object, may be attached by Relative Conjunctions, which answer, generally, to our declarative conjunction "that".

(*a*) When the Declarative Clause is pointed to even in the Principal Clause, by some demonstrative pron. or by the personal pron. inherent in the verb(3), the Relative pron. **ዘ**,—used in a

(1) [Flemming here adopts the variant **ዘየገርም**. tr.]

(2) [In the following passage an entire Relative Clause assumes in the sentence the position, and apparently the character, of an *absoluter Vorhalt*:— **ወእለሰ ፡ ይብሉ ፡ በትሕትና ፡ ልብ ፡ ኢይደልወነ ፡ ለቢሰ ፡ ክህነት ፡ ሎሙሰ ፡ ኀቤሆሙ ፡ ይኔጽር ፡ እግዚአብሔር** "and as for those who say in humility of heart—'we are not worthy of being invested with the priesthood'—, to them God has regard" *Le Livre des Mystères*, p. 35, l. 2 *sq.* tr.]

(3) But such a reference to the declarative clause is usually met with, only when that clause represents the logical Subject of the Principal Clause.

neutral sense as we would say, for "that which", "the fact, that", "I mean, that"—forms a sufficient introductory Particle for such declarative clause. Thus we have: ምንትኑ ፡ ውእቱ ፡ ዝንቱ ፡ ዘአፍጠንከ ፡ ረኪበ "how is it (*lit.* 'what *or* why is this') that thou hast found so quickly?" Gen. 27, 20; ለምንት ፡ ዝንቱ ፡ ዘአውፃእከሙነ "wherefore is it that ye have brought us out?" Numb. 20, 5; Judges 13, 18; Mark 1, 27; Gen. 12, 18; ምንተ ፡ ገበርኩ ፡ ጽምሚተ ፡ ዘትትኀጥአኒ "what have I done, that thou art secretly stealing away from me?" Gen. 31, 26 — (on the position of ጽምሚተ v. *infra*). Farther, ዘ is employed after semi-personal verbs (§ 192, *b*), to attach to them some thought which is their logical subject, *e. g.* መሰሎሙ ፡ ዘተሐውር "it seemed to them, that she was going . ." John 11, 31; Matt. 20, 10; 26, 53; Gen. 31, 31. It is also used frequently after በ, አልበ and አኮ (v. §§ 197; 198); but in the case of ይበቍዕ "it profits", the logical Subject of the verb may also be introduced to it by ለእመ, Matt. 16, 26; Gen. 37, 26 (just as in Greek). ዘ with its clause may even be placed before the principal clause, in the meaning — "as regards the circumstance, that —" or "this (fact) that", *e. g.* ወዘይቤ "and (as regards the fact) that he says" Heb. 12, 27; 4 Esra 6, 51.

(*b*) Supplementary Object-Clause introduced by ከመ, እስመ &c.

(*b*) But if the Clause, which is introduced by "that", is meant not merely as an additional declaration or explanation of an idea, already hinted at in the principal clause, but rather as the attachment of a necessary completion of the sense of the verb in that clause,—as, for instance, the Object of the Verb, after Verbs of *Saying*, *Perceiving*, *Thinking*, *Commanding*, *Fearing*, *Beginning* and so on,—then other Conjunctions and expressions are employed, and mostly ከመ and እስመ.

(α) After Verbs of Perceiving, Recognising &c.

(α) After Verbs of *Perceiving*, *Recognising*, *Thinking*, *Seeming*, *Supposing*, &c., ከመ ("how") "that"—appears the most readily: ርእየ ፡ ከመ ፡ በዝኀ "he saw that it abounded" Gen. 6, 5; Judges 16, 27; ይመስለኒ ፡ ከመ "it seems to me that . ." Hen. 106, 6; አእመረ ፡ ከመ ፡ ተንትገ ፡ ማይ "he knew that the waters were abated" Gen. 8, 11; Ps. 4, 4; also ግበር ፡ ሊተ ፡ ተአምረ ፡ ከመ ፡ አንተ ፡ ውእቱ "show me a sign (by which I may know) that it is thou" Judges 6, 17. The place of ከመ may, however, be taken by other Conjunctions having the meaning "how" (ὡς), such as ዘከመ, በከመ, እፎ, and that too not merely in cases in which the mode and manner of the transaction are of more interest than the fact of it, *e. g.* in Matt. 18, 31; Ruth 3, 16, but even in cases in which we are able to translate by "that", *e. g.* in Hen. 9, 6; Ps. 9, 13; Hen. 5, 1. **እስመ** "because" is also used, though more rarely, for "that" (ὅτι), *e. g.* **ታአምሩ ፡ እስመ** Hen. 98, 8.—It has already been explained (v. § 190), that after the Verbs named, the clause which serves as their Object may also be subordinated without the interposition of a Conjunction, as in **ርእየ ፡ ተሰጥቀ ፡ ሰማይ ፡ ወወሪዶ ፡ መንፈስ ፡ ቅዱስ** "he saw heaven rent open and the Holy Spirit descending" Mark 1, 10; Hen. 83, 3; or the Object-Clause may be put first: **ወናሁ ፡ ኵሎሙ ፡ እሡራነ ፡ ርኢኩ** "and lo, I saw all of them bound" Hen. 90, 23. Farther it has been pointed out that in such a case the Subject of the subordinate clause may also be specially brought into notice in the principal clause in the form of a Suff. Pron. attached to the verb in that clause, as in **ረከቦ ፡ ይቀውም** "he found him standing" Numb. 23, 6; or even that the subordinate clause may be introduced by the particle **እንዘ** which serves to indicate Participles by way of periphrasis, and to introduce Circumstantial clauses, *e. g.* **ርእያ ፡ አዕይንትየ ፡ በህየ ፡ ኵሎሙ ፡ ኃጥአነ ፡ እንዘ ፡ ይሰደዱ** "my eyes saw there all sinners driven away" Hen. 41, 2, where **እንዘ ፡ ይሰደዱ** answers to a Greek participle, and **ኵሎሙ ፡ ኃጥአነ**, which should be Object of **ርእያ** and should stand in the Accusative, is drawn by Attraction into the secondary clause as Subject (v. *infra*); or the subordinate clause may be introduced even by **በዘ**, *e. g. in* **በዘተወሰኩ** *Chrest.* p. 19, line 1. On the Acc. with the Infin. after such verbs, v. § 190, 2.

(β) After Verbs of Saying, Declaring &c.

(β) After Verbs of *Saying*, *Declaring*, and so on, the clause which contains their Object is, as a rule, attached by **ከመ** (§ 169, 6), *e. g.* **መሐለ ፡ ከመ ፡ ኢያአምር** "he swore that he knew not" Matt. 26, 72; more rarely by **እስመ**, *e. g.* **መሐልኩ ፡ . . . እስመ** "I swear . . . that" Hen. 98, 6; **ይብል ፡ እስመ ፡ ዝንቱ ፡ ወልድ ፡ ይከውን ፡ ንዋየ ፡ ኅሩየ** *Chrest.* p. 37, line 26 (1). If the words spoken are quoted in *oratio directa*, they generally follow without being attached by a conjunction; but still, **ከመ** or **እስመ** may be employed in Ethiopic, just like ὅτι in Greek, to introduce the *oratio directa*, *e. g.* Lev. 14, 35; Josh. 5, 6; Matt. 2, 23; 21, 16; Hen. 83, 7; *Chrest.*

(1) Very rarely by the Accus. and the Infin. (§ 190, 2), or even by the Accus. and a following Subjunctive (§ 190, 6).

p. 29, line 27; *Hexaëm.* p. 32, line 24; sometimes even ዘ is used, *e. g.* ወይቤሉ ፡ ዘአኮ ፡ ንፈርሆሙ ፡ ለደቂቀ ፡ እስራኤል Judith 5, 23. Occasionally the introductory ይቤ "he said", or other like form, is placed merely at the end of the quotation, *e. g.* እስመ ፡ አብደ ፡ ይቤልዎ "for 'he is out of his mind', they said of him" Mark 3, 21; Gen. 39, 17; Judges 21, 5; Hen. 55, 3; or else ይቤ, or the like form, even when it has been placed before the quotation, may be repeated at its close, *e. g.* Gen. 3, 3.

(γ) After Verbs of Fearing and Guarding against.

(γ) The Object-clause after Verbs of *Fearing* and *Guarding against* may, in accordance with § 182, *a*, be subordinated in the Infinitive, as in እመ ፡ ትፈርህ ፡ በሕቲትከ ፡ ወሪደ "if thou fearest to go down alone" Judges 7, 10; or in the Infinitive with ለ (§ 183, *a*), *e. g.* ኵሎ ፡ ቃለ ፡ ዕቀብ ፡ ለገቢር *πᾶν ῥῆμα φυλάξῃ ποιεῖν* Deut. 13, 1; or even by ከመ ፡ ኢ with a following Subjunctive (inasmuch as one desires that the thing, which he fears, should not happen), *e. g.* እፈርህ ፡ እምኔሁ ፡ ከመ ፡ ኢይምጻእ "I am afraid of him, lest he should come" Gen. 32, 12; 24, 9; Hen. 106, 6; ይኔጽሮሙ ፡ ዘልፈ ፡ ለአዕዋፍ ፡ ከመ ፡ ኢይረዱ ፡ ወኢይብልዑ ፡ ዘርአ ፡ ለወልደ ፡ እግዚአብሔር "he was ever on the watch against the birds, lest they should descend and devour the seed ('of') sown by the Son of God" *Chronique de Galāwdēwos* (ed. CONZELMAN, 1895), p. 62, l. 1 *sq.*; [*Chrest.*, p. 5, l. 13 *sq.*]; or even by ኢ alone, with a Subjunctive, *e. g.* ዑቅ ፡ ርእሰከ ፡ ኢታግብእ Gen. 24, 6; 31, 29; or, finally, and indeed frequently, by ዮጊ (§ 169, 10) with a following Indicative (1), *e. g.* እፈርህ ፡ ዮጊ ፡ ኢትፈቅዱ "I am afraid ye may not be willing" Hen. 6, 3; Josh. 9, 5. ዮጊ is also used without being introduced by a verb, and it answers then to our "beware lest", *e. g.* Deut. 4, 19; Lev. 10, 19; Ex. 34, 15. If the idea of fearing, &c., is negatived, then we have invariably ከመ with the Subjunctive, *e. g.* ኢተዐቀበ ፡ ከመ ፡ ይሑር "he took no heed to walk" 4 Kings 10, 31.

(δ) After Verbs of Beginning and Leaving off.

(δ) Verbs of *Beginning* and *Leaving off* may indeed take their Object-clause in the Infinitive, or even in the Subjunctive (without ከመ), *e. g.* Mark 1, 45; but the more usual construction, especially after Verbs of Beginning, is the one with እንዘ and a following Imperfect (answering to the Participle in Greek): አኀዙ ፡

---

(1) The Indicative is explained by the fundamental meaning of ዮጊ which is "perhaps": the clause which is introduced by it is thus to be regarded always as *oratio directa*.

እንዘ ፡ ይወግኡ ፡ ለለከልኡ “they began to push one another” Hen. 87, 1; 89, 15, 72.

(ε) After Verbs of Ability, Understanding &c.

(ε) On the various methods by which other Verbs,—such as, *e. g.* those of *Ability, Understanding, Custom, Command, Prohibition, Permission, Willingness* and *Unwillingness, Requesting, Demanding, Reminding,* as well as Semi-Personal Verbs,—have their Object-, and Subject-clauses attached to them, v. *supra,* § 181 *sqq.*

2. Remote Object—Design, Consequence, Cause &c.—expressed by an entire Clause.

2. When the more remote Object of an action, or its Design, Consequence, Cause, and so on, has to be expressed by an entire clause, there is doubtless available for this purpose (§ 183) the construction with the Infinitive and prefixed Prepositions, and in certain cases Subordination by means of the Subjunctive; but along with these constructions there occurs also that of connecting the clauses by Conjunctions; and in certain cases this last construction is the only permissible one.

(*a*) Final Clauses.

(*a*) For *Final Clauses,*—in so far as they are not subordinated by the Infinitive with **ለ**, or (a very common case) by the immediate and close association of the Subjunctive,—**ከመ** with the Subjunctive is made use of (v. *supra* § 183, *c*), *e. g.* **ከመ ፡ አእምር**, *var.* of **ለአእምሮ** Sap. 7, 17; or (like *qui* with the Subjunctive in Latin) the Relative Pron. **ዘ** with a following Subjunctive, *e. g.* “they sought false witnesses, **በዘ ፡ ይቅትልዎ** that through them (*or* ‘that thereby’) they might bring about his death” Matt. 26, 59; Gen. 46, 5; Ruth 4, 14. Even **ለ** is used as an equivalent for **ከመ**, *e. g.* in **ዘአንገሦ ፡ ለይንግሥ** Jer. 37, 1 (*Fref.*). Indeed in every dependent clause, which contains a purpose, a wish, an obligation or expression of will, there is such a necessity for the Subjunctive that, even after Verbs of *Saying* and *Perceiving,* it must be employed, *e. g.* **ይእዜ ፡ አእመርነ ፡ ከመ ፡ ንሰብሖ** “now do we comprehend that we have to praise him” Hen. 63, 4; **ይትበሀል ፡ ለቅዱሳን ፡ ከመ ፡ ይኅሥሡ** “it will be told the saints that they must seek” Hen. 58, 5; and thus always, when “say” is equivalent to “command” (§ 182, *b*, *β*),—indeed even when “say” conveys merely the statement of an opinion, although not very often: **መኑ ፡ ይብልዎ ፡ ይኩን ፡ ሰብእ ፡ ለወልደ ፡ እጓለ ፡ እመሕያው** “whom say the people, as to the Son of man, that he is?” (*i. e.* ‘of whom do the people say, that he is the Son of man?’) Matt. 16, 13. *Cf.* also **ኢየአምኑ ፡ ይምጽኡ ፡ ምስሌሆሙ** *G. Ad.* 62, 8; **ተናገሮ ፡ ያድኅኖ**

G. Ad. 6, 18 (where the ከመ which is added by TRUMPP is not necessary); እትአመንከሙ፡ .... ከመ፡ ትፈጽሙ Rom. 15, 14; Hebr. 6, 7; ኢተዘከረ፡ ይግበር Ps. 108, 14.

(*b*) *Consecutive Clauses* are attached (α) by እስከ (§ 169, 8) "until that", *i. e.* "so that", (1) generally with an Indicative following, *e. g.* "he answered nothing እስከ፡ ያንክር፡ መልአክ insomuch that the governor marvelled" Matt. 27, 14; Mark 1, 15; seldom with the Subjunctive, *e. g.* Gen. 16, 10 (2): or still more frequently by እስከ፡ ሶበ, § 169, 8. On እስከ after ሐሰ v. § 199, *d*. (β) ከመ too may introduce the Consequence; but even in this case it takes the Subjunctive, just as in Final conditions. Accordingly it is never used for "so that" unless the Consequence has to be set forth as being also designed or necessitated, *e. g.* "Abraham called the place so-and-so, ከመ፡ ይበሉ፡ ዮም so that it is said to this day" Gen. 22, 14 (where the Greek even has ἵνα εἴπωσι); "is there no woman among thine own people, ከመ፡ ትሑር that thou shouldest be obliged to go?" Judges 14, 3; 4 Esr. 1, 28; 2, 6. Hence in particular after Verbs of *Making*, *Effecting* &c., the Subjunctive must always follow, with or without ከመ (§ 196, 6). "So that .. not" may be expressed by the aforesaid Conjunctions with a following ኢ; but when "so that .. not" is much the same as "without that" or "except", the corresponding form in Ethiopic is እንበለ or ዘእንበለ with the Imperfect, *e. g.* "not a sparrow falls to the ground, ዘእንበለ፡ ያእምር፡ አቡክሙ without your Father knowing" ('without that your Father knows') Matt. 10, 29; also with the Subjunctive, *e. g.* "how camest thou in hither, ዘእንበለ፡ ትልበስ፡ ልብሰ፡ መርዓ without (*or* before) having put on a wedding-garment?" Matt. 22, 12; ኢይወፅእ፡ እምዛቲ፡ ሀገር፡ እንበለ፡ እሕርስ፡ ገረሀተ፡ ወእዝራእ፡ እክለ፡ ወዘእንበለ፡ አብልዕ፡ ፈረስየ፡ እምውእቱ፡ እክል "I will not leave this province, without tilling the fields and sowing the grain and making my horse eat of that grain" *Chronique de Ba'eda Mâryâm* (ed. PERRUCHON, 1893), p. 140, l. 8 *sqq*. Or again, the circumstantial determination may be attached, just like other circumstantial clauses, by እንዘ፡ ኢ, or by asyndetic apposition of the secondary clause by means of ኢ (v.

(*b*) Consecutive Clauses.

---

(1) *Cf.* حَتَّى.

(2) And, besides, not in all the manuscripts.

§ 200), or even by **ወኢ** and nothing more, as in: **የሀይጹ : ሥዕርተ : ወኢይስሕቱ፡** "they hit a hair without missing" Judges 20, 16.

(c) Causal Clauses. (c) *Causal Clauses* are attached by the Conjunction **እስመ** "because", v. *supra* § 200. So too, after Verbs of *Feeling*, the ground and occasion of the emotion are usually introduced in Ethiopic by **እስመ**, *e. g.* **ተፈሥሐ : እስመ : ተበልዑ** "he rejoiced that they were eaten" Hen. 89, 58; **ኢትሕዝኑ : እስመ** "be not ye sad, because" Hen. 102, 5; 89, 67 &c. **በእንተ : ዘ** or **በእንተ** with the Infinitive may also appear instead of **እስመ**, v. *e. g.* Gen. 6, 6, 7.

In the various clauses which are introduced by Relative conjunctions, and which have been described above, under Nos. 1 and 2, — this or that word which requires to be emphasised may be placed before the introductory conjunction of the clause, (just as in the attributive Relative-clauses. § 202, 4), *e. g.* **ርኢክዎሙ : . . . . ከዐበ : ከመ : ስሕቱ፡** "I saw . . . that they were again going astray" Hen. 89, 51; Gen. 47, 19 &c. In the same way when the clause which is introduced by the conjunction is part of a Relative clause. a portion of the words belonging to the former must precede the conjunction, *e. g.* **ምድር : እንተ : መሐልኩ : ከመ : አሀብ ክሙ** "the land, which I have sworn to give you" Judges 2, 1; **ሕዝብ : እለ : እቤ : ከመ : አውፅኦሙ** Judges 2, 3 &c. Farther, § 190 should again be called to mind here: When, — after Verbs which may govern a double Accusative, such as Verbs of *Recognising, Declaring, Making* &c.—the second Object is expressed by a clause of its own with a Relative conjunction, it is then more elegant to put the first Object in the principal clause as the Object of that clause, instead of bringing it into the dependent clause as Subject of the same, *e. g.* **ርእየ : ኖኅ : ምድረ : ከመ: አድነነት** ([1]) "Noah saw that the earth was drawing to a close" Hen. 65, 1; 83, 4; or, if that Object be indeed attracted into the dependent clause as its Subject, it must at least be placed before the conjunctions, as in **ርእየ : . . . . ኵሎሙ : ኃጥኣን : እንዘ : ይሰደዱ** Hen. 41, 2; 89, 40; 95, 1 &c.

3. Comparative Clauses. § 204. 3. *Comparative Clauses.* The Conjunctions **ከመ**, **በከመ**, **ዘከመ** are employed to introduce a *Comparison*, and also **ከመ : እንተ** before feminine Nouns, *e. g.* John 1, 32; Ps. 143, 14. The *Clause of Comparison* may be joined to another clause; and

([1]) [Flemming prefers the alternative form of the verb, **አጽነነት**. tr.]

in that case it is not essential that this latter clause should contain a reference, in the shape of a Demonstrative, to the Relative Conjunction, *e. g.* **ዘሰትየ ፡ ከመ ፡ ይሰቲ ፡ ከልብ** "he who drinketh, as a dog drinketh" Judges 7, 5; 16, 9; Gen. 6, 22; Matt. 20, 27 *sq.*; Hen. 27, 5. But if the Clause with the Relative Conjunction comes first, then a corresponding Demonstrative is generally placed at the head of the following clause, v. *infra* § 206. Of course the Conjunction of Comparison may also come before other Conjunctions, *e. g.* **ከመ ፡ ሶበ** "just as when" Judges 15, 14. On the other hand our expression "as if" or "just as if" has often a personal turn given it in Ethiopic, viz. "as he who", *e. g.* **ወነፀፆ ፡ (ለአንበሳ ፡) ከመ ፡ ዘይነፅኆ ፡ ማኅሥአ ፡ ጠሊ** "and he rent it (the lion), as one who rendeth a kid" Judges 14, 6; Gen. 41, 21; 42, 30.

For comparing Intensive Clauses the same particle **እምነ** (or **እም**) usually suffices, which we have already become acquainted with as serving this purpose (§ 187, 3). **እምነ** in fact is used, not only when the Verb of the clause compared may be expressed in the Infinitive, but also when it is put in a finite tense. As examples of the first case we have **ይኄይስ ፡ ተአምኖ ፡ በእግዚአብሔር ፡ እምተአምኖ ፡ በእጓለ ፡ እመሕያው** "it is better to trust in God than to trust in man" Ps. 117, 8, 9; Ruth 1, 12. In such a case it is not even imperative that **እምነ** should stand immediately before the Infinitive, *e. g.* "it is easier for a camel to go through the eye of a needle, **እምበዐል ፡ በዊአ ፡ መንግሥተ ፡ እግዚአብሔር** than for a rich man to enter into the kindom of God" Matt. 19, 24. The Infinitive may even be left out altogether, *e. g.* **ይኄይሰኒ ፡ ለከ ፡ አሀብ ፡ እምነ ፡ ለካልእ ፡ ብእሲ** "it is better for me that I give (her) to thee than to another man" Gen. 29, 19. In the second case **እምነ** is to be regarded, in accordance with § 168, as a Construct State, on which the entire following clause depends[1], *e. g.* **ሊተሰ ፡ ይኄይሰኒ ፡ መዊት ፡ እምይትበሀንኒ ፡ ምዝጋናየ** 1 Cor. 9, 15; **ቦኑ ፡ ይኄይሰከ ፡ ትኩን ፡ ካህነ ፡ ለ፩ብእሲ ፡ እምነ ፡ ትኩን ፡ ካህነ ፡ ለነገድ** Judges 18, 19; John 11, 50; 12, 43. Nor in this case is it essential that the Verb should immediately follow **እምነ**. On the contrary individual words or even clauses may intervene: **ይኄይሰከ ፡ ከመ ፡ ይትሐጐል ፡ ፩እምነ ፡ አባልከ ፡ እምኵሉ ፡ ሥጋከ ፡ ይትወደይ ፡ ውስ**

(1) = **እምነዘ** = **ዘእምነ** (§ 202, 2), which likewise occurs, although not often, *e. g.* Gen. 4, 13.

ተ ፡ ገሃነም "it is better for thee that one of thy members should perish than (that) thy whole body should be cast into Gehenna" Matt. 5, 29, 30; "it is better for thee that thou shouldest enter into life halt or maimed እምእንዘ ፡ ብከ ፡ ክልኤ ፡ እደ ፡ . . . . ትትወ ደይ ፡ ውስተ ፡ እሳት than that, as one having two hands . . . thou shouldest be cast into the fire" Matt. 18, 8.

1. Temporal Clauses. 4. *Temporal Clauses*. Subsidiary actions, which accompany or precede the main action, may be expressed in Ethiopic by the Gerund, whether they have or have not the same Subject as the principal clause, and whether the temporal clause comes before or after the principal clause, as also whether the action is completed or not; v. § 181.

This construction, however, is not always convenient, least of all when the subsidiary action occupies a clause of considerable length. Ethiopic has accordingly developed additional relative Conjunctions to indicate the same Time-references which may be expressed by the Gerund, particularly the references "after", "when", "in the time that", "while". The other references, such as "still", "before", "since", "so long as" &c. can in any case be expressed only by Conjunctions. All the temporal clauses, introduced by such conjunctions, are to be viewed as clauses dependent upon, or supported by, the principal clause, although it is not absolutely necessary to place them after that clause: they may also be inserted within it, or even put before it. Several of them,—especially those which are introduced by "when", "as soon as", "so long as", —occasionally possess the force of a Conditional sentence (v. § 205). Of the Temporal conjunctions which are enumerated in § 170, እምድኅረ, እምአመ, እምዘ, which answer in some degree to our "after" and "since", are, naturally, joined to the Perfect, *e. g.* Gen. 5, 4 *sqq.*; Matt. 2, 13; Gen. 11, 10; 24, 32; Ex. 19, 1; 40, 15; Deut. 2, 16 &c. ሶበ (1) and አመ, for "when" or "as", may take a verb either in the Perfect or the Imperfect, according to the context, *e. g.* Gen. 6, 1; 39, 15; Ps. 2, 5; Hen. 10, 12; Gen. 11, 10;

(1) In the 'Synaxarion' the apodosis, after ሶበ is often introduced by ወ; v. the examples given in *Chrest.*, pp. 24, 26; [v. farther *Kebra Nag.*, *Introd.* p. XIX; *Contendings of the Apostles* 214, 13 *sq.*; 154, 27 *sq.*; v. also, as an instance of the sequence እምድኅረ ፡ . . . ወ, *ibid.* 215, 1 *sq.*; and of the sequence ወ . . . ወ, ወርእዮ ፡ ሐዋርያ ፡ ወይቤሎሙ *ibid.* 371, 16 *sq.*; *cf.* also 14, 16.]

Hen. 25, 4. It is the same with እምከመ "as soon as" (also "when"): *e. g.* it is found with the Perfect in Gen. 30, 42; Numb. 21, 9; with a Perfect in a Future relation (Future Perfect) in Gen. 12, 12; Lev. 14, 34; Deut. 2, 25; Matt. 9, 21; 21, 24; and with the Imperfect in Matt. 5, 23. The very same constructions are also found with እስከ ፡ አመ, መጠነ, እምጣነ "as long as", *e. g.* Hen. 93, 3; Cant. 3, 5; Matt. 9, 15; Lev. 13, 46; Judges 18, 31; Mark 2, 19; Gal. 4, 1. On the other hand the Conjunction እንዘ (our "while" with regular tense, or "in" or "by" with the Participle), —seeing that almost invariably it introduces a circumstance or situation, falling within the time of the main action,—is chiefly construed with the Imperfect, in accordance with § 89. It occurs in this connection very frequently indeed,—in fact, nearly as often as the Participle in Greek, or *indem* and *während* in German, *e. g.* Matt. 9, 35; 13,13; 17, 3, 14; 18, 1; Luke 9, 29, 56; 11. 27; Gen. 29, 9. The occurrence of a Perfect after እንዘ is confined almost entirely to those verbs which of themselves suggest a state, condition, or circumstance, like ሀለወ itself for instance, as in Ps. 21, 9. This እንዘ may often too be translated by "although", *e. g.* in Luke 22, 53 ("although I was daily with you": E. V. "When I was &c."), particularly if it is preceded or followed by a Negative, when it may sometimes be rendered by "without", *e. g.* οὐδὲν διαφέρει δούλου, እንዘ ፡ እግዚእ ፡ ውእቱ ፡ ለኵሉ "even though he be lord of all" Gal. 4, 1; 4 Esr. 8, 67; እንዘ ፡ ኢይፈቅድ "though he consent not" ('without his consent'). With a similar force to that of እንዘ, በዘ is also used, v. § 170, 9; but yet the latter leans more to the meaning "even in the case that", *i. e.* "in spite of the fact *or* circumstance that", "notwithstanding that". "even although". It would be well, besides, to compare with this section § 200, according to which Circumstantial Clauses may even be expressed by asyndetic apposition or be introduced by ወ.—The Conjunctions እንበለ, ዘእንበለ, እምቅድመ "sooner than", "before", are joined to the Subjunctive, in accordance with § 90, *e. g.* Gen. 11, 4; 19, 4; Judges 14, 18; Gen. 24, 15; Matt. 6, 8; 26, 34; Ps. 38, 17; Hen. 9, 11; 48, 3; Gen. 2, 5; Hen. 48, 6(1); but yet the construction with the Infinitive is also possible. *e. g.* Matt. 15. 20.—Lastly. እስከ "until", may, according

(1) FLEMMING here adopts the reading ዘእንበለ, while DILLMANN has እምቅድመ. TR.]

to the particular connection, take the verb in the Perfect, as, for instance, in Matt. 12, 22; Gen. 8, 7; Hen. 13, 7; or in the Imperfect, *e. g.* Matt. 5, 18; 12, 20; Hen. 10, 12, 17; 19, 1. It is the same with **እስከ ፡ አመ** or **እስከ ፡ ሶበ** "till the time that", "until", *e. g.* Matt. 2, 9, 13; 16, 28; Gen. 39, 16; Judges 13, 7; 18, 30; Ps. 122, 3. It has been already remarked (§ 203, 2, *b*) that the signification of the three last-named Conjunctions often passes over into the meaning "so that".

3. RECIPROCAL SENTENCES AND WORDS.

(*a*) CONDITIONAL SENTENCES.

General Description. Particles and Tenses employed in Protasis and Apodosis:—

§ 205. Conditional Sentences are by their very nature double sentences; and in them one constituent of the double sentence lays down a supposition, under which the assertion of the other is realisable. No doubt there are conditional statements in which the Condition is not expressly mentioned; but these are incomplete and abbreviated sentences, which can always be developed into full sentences of two members each: farther, they must contain some hint or other, that the assertion is only to be understood conditionally.—In these double sentences the clause expressing the hypothesis usually precedes the clause containing the consequence or result; but yet inversion of that order may occur, if it is demanded by circumstances otherwise found in the context. In that case the main assertion is put first; and afterwards, by the attachment of a Condition, it is made to depend upon something else. The conditional character of the assertion is denoted generally by special conditional-particles. A Conditional Sentence may of course be found without such express marking; but it is not a common occurrence in Ethiopic. The hypothesis may be laid down, and the consequence associated therewith, either by the **ወ** of sequence, or by asyndetic apposition. Examples of the first mode may be found in § 200; and as examples of the second the following may be taken: **ኢሀሎኩ ፡ በሥጋ ፡ ሀሎኩ ፡ በመንፈስ** "if I am not in the body, yet am I in the spirit" (*Org.*); **እኌልቆሙ ፡ እምኆፃ ፡ ይበዝኁ** "if I count them, they are more than the sand"

Ps. 138, 17 ([1]). Ordinarily, however, conditional particles are made use of, and in fact **እመ** (**ለእመ**) and **ሶበ** for the Protasis, the former being employed to introduce those conditions in which some presupposition is simply advanced as such, without regard to its reality or its possibility, and the latter for those conditions in which the speaker makes a supposition which seems to him impossible or improbable. According as the hypothesis is introduced with the one or the other of these conditional particles, the Apodosis in turn is introduced in different ways. Hence, in farther dealing with the subject, we have to distinguish between two kinds of Conditional Sentences. Relative Clauses also approximate occasionally, in point of effect, to Conditional Clauses, *e. g.* **ለዘክሕደኒ ፡ እክሕዶ ፡ አነሂ** "whoever denies me (= 'if any one denies me'), him will I deny (= 'then I will deny him')" Matt. 10, 33. So also is it at times with Temporal Clauses, *e. g.* **መንፈሶሙ ፡ በማእከሎሙ ፡ ትጸንዕ ፡ ሶበ ፡ ርእይዎ ፡ ለኅሩየ ፡ ዚአየ** "their spirit will become strong within them, when they see my chosen one" Hen. 45, 3 ([2]); Gen. 38, 9; for not only is **ሶበ** a temporal conjunction as well as a conditional particle, but even **እመ** "if" is connected with **አመ** "when" (§ 170, 1).—Both in Sentences stipulating a realisable condition, and in those which merely approximate that description, the action given in the Protasis must in general be completed, or at least begun, if the consequence is to make its appearance. For that reason precisely, the tense which is commonly employed in the Protasis of a Conditional Sentence is the Perfect, inasmuch as it is made use of not only when the required condition actually falls within the Past, but even when it occurs in the Present, or belongs to the Future, in the guise of a Future Perfect. And yet we are not altogether restricted to the use of the Perfect in the Protasis, but in certain circumstances we may employ the Imperfect, or even have a Clause without any verb (§ 194). Upon the whole, Ethiopic exhibits much closer agreement with Hebrew than with Arabic, in its mode of dealing with the tenses of such clauses.

1. In *Simple Conditional Sentences,—i. e.,* Sentences, in

([1]) [But these last two examples can hardly be called Conditional Sentences. They are rather Temporal Sentences, and belong much more properly to the preceding Section, § 204, 4. TR.]

([2]) [FLEMMING's reading here varies slightly:—**ነፍሶሙ ፡** . . . **ርእይዎሙ ፡ ለኅሩያን ፡ ዚአየ**. TR.]

I. In Simple Conditional Sentences.

which a supposition is laid down without regard to its actual existence or its possibility, and a consequence is made to depend upon it,—the Protasis is introduced by እመ or ለእመ "if" (§ 170,1), and, when negative, by እመ (or ለእመ) ኢ (or አኮ). The Apodosis may be denoted by the ወ of Consequence (*e. g.* 1 Cor. 5, 3; v. also § 200), or by ወ—እንከ "in that case—then" (*e. g.* Judges 16, 7), or by እንከ alone (*e. g.* Judges 16, 11). That is not absolutely necessary, however; and in by far the greater number of cases, it is introduced without any outward marking. For "even if" or "although" እመ may suffice; but the more accurate expression is እመኒ or እመሂ ([1]), *e. g.* Ps. 22, 4; Is. 49, 15; Hen. 100, 5; Matt. 26, 35, without any antithetical particle ("yet") being made use of in the Apodosis (§ 200, 2) ([2]). If now the action or circumstance, which forms the Condition, lies in the circle of the Future,—the usual case in these Simple Conditional Sentences,—it generally stands in the Perfect (which here has the force of the Future-Perfect, § 88). In that case the action of the Apodosis likewise falls in the Future or at the utmost in the Present, and in either case it is expressed by means of the Imperfect, *e. g.* እመ ፡ ኀደጎ ፡ ይመውት "if he leaves him ('will leave him'), then he dies ('he will die')" Gen. 44, 22; 28, 20, 21; በምንት ፡ እመ ፡ አሰሩከ ፡ ትደክም "wherewith thou shalt become weak, if they bind thee therewith" Judges 16, 6; Matt. 18, 3; 26, 35; ከማሁ ፡ አቡየኒ ፡ ይገብር ፡ ለክሙ ፡ እመ ፡ ኢኀደግሙ ፡ ለቢጽክሙ "so likewise shall my Father do unto you, if ye forgive not your neighbour" Matt. 18, 34; ምንተ ፡ ይበቊዖ ፡ ለሰብእ ፡ ለእመ ፡ ኵሎ ፡ ዓለመ ፡ ረብሐ "what shall it profit a man, if he gain (will have gained) the whole world?" Matt. 16, 26; Gen. 38, 16 ([3]). And yet, in this case also, an Imperfect

---

([1]) On እንዘ ፡ ኢ "although", v. § 204, 4.

([2]) [*Cf.* እመኒ ፡ ተምዕዐ ፡ ኢየዐርብ ፡ ፀሐይ ፡ በመዐቱ፡ "even when ('though') he did become angry, the sun did not go down upon his wrath" *Chronique de Galāwdēwos* p. 58, l. 4 *sq.*; *cf.* also the following passage, giving ሂ appended to the Subject of the Apodosis, and presenting farther a curious involution:— እስመ ፡ ነፍስከሂ ፡ እመኒ ፡ ሞተ ፡ ሥጋ ፡ ኢትመውት "for even though the body dies, thy soul dies not". *Das äthiopische Maccabäerbuch* (J. Horovitz in '*Zeitschrift f. Assyr.*', 1906) p. 229, l. 31. TR.]

([3]) [*Cf.* ወአማን ፡ እመ ፡ ዐርገ ፡ ኀይል ፡ ወሞአ ፡ አእምር ፡ ከመ ፡ ፍትሐ ፡ እግዚአብሔር "and truly if a force should come up and be victori-

may occur in the Protasis, *e. g.* ለእመ ፡ እስከ ፡ ሰማይ ፡ ትትሌዐሊ ፡ እስከ ፡ ገሃነም ፡ ትወርዲ Matt. 11, 23, where, evidently, the hyperbolical nature of the expression induced the translator to apply the tense, not of actual past occurrence, but of that which was possible only, or merely thought of (almost in the meaning:—'although thou *shouldest* be exalted'): ኢንክል ፡ ለእመ ፡ ኢይትጋብኡ "we cannot, until (the shepherds) have come together" Gen. 29, 8 (where ለእመ ፡ ኢ is almost equivalent to ዘእንበለ) (1). But if the action which forms the condition falls in the Past, the Perfect alone is available, *e. g.* ለእመ ፡ ተለወ ፡ ልብየ ፡ ብእሲተ ፡ ብእሲ ፡ ወእመ ፡ ወሐይኩ ፡ ኖኅተ ፡ ቤታ ፡ ብእሲትየኒ ፡ ተአድሞ ፡ ለካልእ ፡ ብእሲ Job 31, 9: yet in such a case እመሰ, in the sense of "if really", is preferred to እመ, *e. g.* እመሰ ፡ ከመዝ ፡ ገበርኩ ፡ . . . ለያውድቁኒ ፡ ጸላእትየ Ps. 7, 3, 4. If farther the action of the Apodosis also belongs to the past, it is likewise expressed by the Perfect, *e. g.* እመሰኬ ፡ ደቂቅከ ፡ አበሱ ፡ ቅድሜሁ ፡ ወፈነወ ፡ በእደ ፡ ኀጢአቶሙ "if thy children have verily incurred guilt before him, he has delivered (them) over to the consequences of their transgressions" Job 8, 4; and thus also John 18, 23; Rom. 6, 5; Col. 3, 1. Lastly, if the action of the Condition belongs to the Present, the Imperfect, or a circumstantial clause with the force of the Present, appears in the Protasis; and in this case too እመሰ is often found instead of እመ, *e. g.* እመሰ ፡ ይትከሀል ፡ ይኅልፍ "if it is possible, —let it pass by" Matt. 26, 39; ያድኅኖ ፡ እመ ፡ ይፈቅዶ "let him save him, if he have pleasure in him" Matt. 27, 43; እመሰ ፡ ወልደ ፡ እግዚአብሔር ፡ አንተ ፡ ረድ ፡ እመስቀልከ Matt. 27, 40, 42; ወእመሰ ፡ ንጹሓን ፡ ደቂቅ ፡ እምአንስት ፡ ለይብልዑ 1 Sam. 21, 4; although an Inchoative verb may also stand in the Perfect: እመ ፡ ርኅብኩ ፡

ous, know that it is the judgment of God" *Homilia Jacobi* (ed. Fr. Pereira, in '*Oriental. Studien*', 1906) p. 892, l. 4 *sq.* tr.]

(1) [*Cf.* ወለእመ ፡ ንሴአል ፡ እስላመ ፡ ወአይሁደ ፡ ከመዝ ፡ ከመ ፡ ይፈትሑ ፡ በከመ ፡ ሃይማኖቶሙ "and if we put the question to Mohammedans or Jews, they too will give a like answer, in accordance with their faith" *Ḥatatā Zar'a Ya'qōb* (ed. Turaieff, St. Petersburg, 1904) p. 9, l. 12 *sq.* = *Philosophi Abessini* (ed. Littmann, Leipzig, 1904) p. 7, l. 21 *sq.* (except that Littmann reads እስላም ፡ ወአይሁድ); *cf.* also ለእመ ፡ ኢያምጻእክምዎሙ ፡ ለእሉ ፡ እደው ፡ መቃብያን ፡ ንሕነ ፡ ናውዕያ ፡ ለሀገርክሙ "if you do not produce these men, the Maqābīs, we will burn down your city" *Das äthiopische Maccabäerbuch* p. 199, l. 11 *sq.* tr.]

ኢይስእለከ "if I be hungry ('have become hungry') I will not beg from thee" Ps. 49, 13. Even if the action of the Protasis is one which is repeated several times, and such that **እመ** is equivalent to "as often as", the Perfect is still the better form. *e. g.* **እመ ፡ ርኢከ ፡ ሰረቄ ፡ ትረውጽ ፡ ምስሌሁ** "when thou seest a thief, thou dost run with him" Ps. 49, 19; 45, 2. Sometimes also the interrogative particles **ሁ** and **ኑ** (§ 161), adopted in the Protasis, serve a like purpose with the **ሰ** which is here and there appended to **እመ** —: for since the Condition is thus concomitantly put as a question, doubt must be awakened regarding it, such as is expressed in our "if really", "if it be the fact that", as in: **እመሰ ፡ አንተሁ ፡ እግዚኦ ፡ አዝዘኒ ፡ እምጻእ ፡ ኀቤከ** "Lord, if it be (indeed) thou, bid me come to thee" Matt. 14, 28; **እመ ፡ ይጸውዑከኑ ፡ መጽኡ ፡ እሉ ፡ሰብእ ፡ ተንሥእ** "if these men have (actually) come to call thee, arise!" Numb. 22, 20; *cf.* also **ለእመሁ** Acts 16, 15.

On rare occasions **እመ** is abbreviated into **እም**, *e. g.* **ምንትኑ ፡ ኄር ፡ ዘእምገበርኩ ፡ ሕይወተ ፡ ዘለዓለም ፡ በዘ ፡ አወርስ** "what is the good thing, the which if I do, I shall thereby gain eternal life?" Matt. 19, 16.

When two Conditional Sentences appear, the one after the other, and the second of them states negatively the presupposition, which is put affirmatively in the first, it is not obligatory to repeat the entire Protasis in the second. It is then quite sufficient to say **ወእመ ፡ አኮ** (**ወእማእኮ**) or **ወእማእኮሰ** "and if not", "if otherwise", *e. g.* **ወለእመሰ ፡ ትገብሩ ፡ ምሕረተ ፡ ላዕለ ፡ እግዚእየ ፡ ንግሩኒ ፡ ወእማእኮ ፡ እትመየጥ** "if ye now (indeed) will show kindness to my lord, tell me, but if not, then will I turn . ." Gen. 24, 49; Ex. 32, 32; Judges 9, 16—20. And this phraseology may be employed after any statement whatever, — and not merely after conditional sentences, — in order to add a representation of what will happen if the action which has just been mentioned is not realised, *e. g.* "take heed that ye do not your alms before men . . **ወእመአኮሰ ፡ ዐስበ ፡ አልብክሙ** otherwise, ye have no reward" Matt. 6, 1; Mark 2, 21; Luke 14, 32; Josh. 22, 22.

"Except" or "unless" is rendered by **ዘእንበለ** (§ 170, 4), if no new verb follows, *e. g.* Matt. 19, 9; but if it is followed by a new verb, it takes the form **ዘእንበለ ፡ እመ**, "except (that), "unless (that)" *e. g.* Matt 12, 29; or **ዘእንበለ** with the Subjunctive, *e. g.* Matt. 5,32.

On "just as if", "just as when" v. § 204, 3. "However much" is **እመ ፡ ሚመጠነ**, *e. g.* Eccles. 8,17. "If only . . not", "provided that . . . not", as a particle of *uncertainty* and *fear*, is **ዮጊ**, v. § 203, 1, *a*, *γ*.—On (**ለ**)**እመበ** *si quis* with a following **ዘ** or **ከመ** *cf.* Dillmann's 'Lex.', col. 481.

2. In Unreal Conditional Sentences(1), the Protasis is always introduced by **ሶበ**, a particle which is often employed in Optative Clauses, "would that!" (§ 199, *e*)(2). It can only be in consequence of being so employed, that it has come to be adopted as a Conditional Particle in those Conditional Sentences which present the supposition, as it were, in an Optative form. Farther, the interrogative **ሁ** or **ኑ** or the emphatic **ሰ** may be brought into use after **ሶበ**, with the same force as after **እመ** (3). As, however, **ሶበ** is also a Temporal Conjunction (§ 204, 4), a Conditional Sentence cannot be distinguished from a Temporal one by **ሶበ** alone; and therefore the Apodosis must always be introduced by the particle **እም** (4) ἄν (§ 170, 2). This **እም**, the proper mark of hypothetical statement, regularly comes immediately in front of the verb of the Apodosis, and may be repeated, if the Apodosis has more than one verb. If, however, the conditioned clause comes before the conditioning one, the **እም** is in that case sometimes omitted, *e. g.* **ኅየሰነ ፡ ሶበ ፡ ሞትነ ፡ በብሔረ ፡ ግብጽ ፡ እምነ ፡ ንመውት ፡ በዝንቱ ፡ ገዳም** "it ('was') would have been better for us if we ('died') had died in Egypt than that we should die in this wilderness" Numb. 14, 2; **ለአስሕቶ ፡ ሶበሰ ፡ ይትከሀሎሙ ፡ ለኅሩያንሂ** "to seduce, if it were possible, even the elect" Matt. 24, 24 (where **እም** is wanting, because it cannot stand between the Preposition and the Infinitive); *cf.* also G. Ad. 48, 7; [*Chrest.*, p. 86, l. 13 *sqq.*, and *Kebra Nag.*, *Introd.* p. XX. For a remarkable use of **እም** in an auxiliary clause attached to the Apodosis of such a sentence, v. *Kebra Nag.* 129 a 20 *sqq.*].

2. In Unreal Conditional Sentences.

---

(1) [—*i. e.* Sentences in which the Condition is obviously unrealisable. — Tr.]

(2) Like לוּ, لَوْ.

(3) [Occasionally, however, **ሶበ** is also replaced by **ለእመ**; v. Praetorius, '*Aethiop. Gramm*'. p. 151, l. 3; and by **ሶበ ፡ እመ**, *cf.* Bezold, *Kebra Nag.*, *Introd.* p. XX].

(4) Originally **እመ**, which still appears now and then, *e. g.* 4 Esr. 3,54 (also v. 55 in one Manuscript); 7, 20; Tobit 10, 5; [*Contendings of the Apostles* 15, 6; 151,25. *Cf.* also *Kebra Nag.*, *Introd.* p. XX].

With respect to the Tenses of Unreal Conditional Sentences it is to be observed that the Perfect prevails almost universally, both in the Protasis and the Apodosis. The Ethiopian says: "if thou didst this, then I did that"; and by the identity of Tense in the Protasis and Apodosis he at first gives expression to the circumstance merely that the two clauses exactly correspond to each other, and that the second indubitably results from the first. A conviction, however, is always found inseparably associated with this class of Conditional Sentences,—that the instances which they describe have no reality in them. Farther, this conviction can only be thoroughly relied upon, we may say, in the case of things which belong to the Past or the completed Present. Accordingly it is easy to explain why the Perfect should be used in this case,—a tense which is precisely in place, where the question turns upon occurrences which have passed away, or upon those which are completed, though not yet out of view (§ 88). But it is only from the connection or context that we can determine whether such a Perfect in an Unreal Conditional Sentence belongs truly to the circle of the Past, the Present or the Future, and whether the Protasis is concerned with the same sphere of time as the Apodosis. The connection, however, is generally sufficient to enable us so to determine: only in rare cases may there be a lingering doubt whether the Optative of the Past or of the Present should be adopted in translation,—in fact in those cases only, we may say, in which the clause concerned is just as true or as false, whether we refer it to the sphere of the Past or the Present. Accordingly we say in Ethiopic: **ሶበ፡ ነገርከኒ፡ እምፈነውኩከ** "if thou hadst told me, I would have sent thee away" Gen. 31, 27; Matt. 23, 30; Gen. 31, 42; Judges 14, 18; Matt. 11, 21; Numb. 22, 29, 33 (1); but also: **ሶበሁ፡ ተውህበ፡ ሕግ፡ ዘይክል፡ አሕይዎ፡ በውእቱ፡ ሕግ፡ እምኮነ፡ ጽድቅ** "if a law had really been given which could give life, righteousness would be by that law" Gal. 3, 21; **እምኮነ፡ ይሰሪ፡ ሎቱ** "he would forgive him" G. Ad. 90, 18; **ሶበ፡ አሕየውክምዎሙ፡ እምኢቀተልኩክሙ** "if ye had allowed them to live, I would not (now) put you to death" Judges 8, 19; Matt. 26, 24; Ps. 50, 17,—all being cases, in which the presup-

(1) In the three last-quoted passages **ወድአ** is not employed to refer the whole sentence to the past (after the manner of قَدْ), but is merely a translation of πάλαι, ἤδη, νῦν.

position belongs to the past, but the consequence to the present; or **ሶበ ፡ ፈቀደ ፡ ይቅትለነ ፡**— **እምኢተመጠወ** "if he had desired to kill us (now, or at some future time), he would not have accepted" Judges 13, 23, where the converse relation appears(¹); or, lastly: **ሶበ ፡ አኮሁ ፡ ዘኅጸሩ ፡ እማንቱ ፡ መዋዕል ፡ አልቦ ፡ ዘእምድኅነ ፡ መኑሂ** "if these (coming) days were not to be shortened, there should no man be saved" Matt. 24, 22, where the entire action, conditioning and conditioned, belongs to the future. On the other hand, in passages like Ps. 80, 12 *sq.*; 43, 22 *sq.*,—where the Protasis belongs to the past, — it is really a matter of doubt whether the Apodosis should be understood as being also of the past or as being of the present.

Only on very rare occasions does an Imperfect appear in the Protasis, instead of a Perfect; and even then **እም** with the Perfect is found in the Apodosis, *e. g.* in a proposition stating some universal truth, valid for any time: **ሶበ ፡ ያአምርሁ ፡ ባዕለ ፡ ቤት ፡ ጊዜ ፡ ይመጽእ ፡ ሰራቂ ፡ እምተግሀ ፡ ወኢእምኀደገ ፡ ይትከረይ ፡ ቤቱ** "if the master of the house had actually known at what time the thief would come, he would (assuredly) have watched, and not have suffered his house to be broken into" Matt. 24,43: *cf.* also **ሶበ ፡ አኮ ፡ ያአምሩ** "if they did not know" G. Ad. 97, 19. A Nominal Clause occurs as Protasis in *Chrest.* p. 6, line 13 *sqq.*: **ሶበ ፡ አኮ ፡ ብእሲ ፡ ልሂቅ ፡ አንተ ፡ እምጸዐልኩከ ፡ . . . . ሶበ ፡ አኮ ፡ ዘከመዝ ፡ እምእቤ** and in G. Ad. 97, 12 *sq.* **ወሶበ ፡ አኮ ፡ አንተ ፡ በኀቤየ ፡ ክቡር ፡ እምኢኮንኩ**.

In Unreal Conditional Sentences the Condition is frequently left unexpressed, as being a matter obvious from the connection; and the only announcement made is as to what must have happened if some (unexpressed) condition had been realised. It is all the more necessary that a merely hypothetical announcement of this kind should be introduced by **እም**, — always a sure sign that the clause must be translated in our languages by the Optative or the Conjunctive, *e. g.* **ወይእዜኒ ፡ እምክህልኩ ፡ ገቢረ ፡ እኩየ ፡ ላዕሌከ** "and now I might be able to do thee harm" Gen. 31, 29; **መኑ ፡ እምዜነዎ ፡ ለአብርሃም** "who would have said to Abraham?" Gen.

(¹) [—that is to say, where the presupposition (according to Dillmann) belongs to the present or future, and the inferred fact or circumstance to the past. Dillmann seems to be wrong here: It is not 'the killing' but 'the desiring to kill' which forms the presupposition in this case; and this desire—in its origin at least—belongs to the past, and is thought of as preceding 'the accepting'. TR.]

21, 7; [እፎ፡ ፈድፋደ፡ እምተፈሣሕከ "how much more wouldst thou rejoice!" *Kebra Nag.* 56 b 7]; ዘእምተሠይጠ፡ በብዙኅ "a thing which might have been sold for much" Matt. 26, 9; 16, 26; 25, 27 &c.; and even ሶበ፡ እምአዕረፈኒ "even if he should rest" (which does not happen) Sir. 34, 4 (1).

Seeing that in this way እም has the power of giving a hypothetical colouring to a sentence, it is often used also in Optative Sentences (§ 199, *e*). In a similar way it stands constantly in the phrase ሕቀ፡ ከመ፡ ዘእም with the Perfect, *haud multum abfuit quin*, *i. e.* "had nearly" (with the past part. of accompanying verb) or "came near" (with the pres. part.), *e. g.* ሕቀ፡ ከመ፡ ዘእምሰከበ "one had nearly lain" (*or* "came near lying") Gen. 26, 10; Ps. 72, 2; 118, 87.

(*b*) CORRELATED CLAUSES AND WORDS.

Various Formulae of Correlation.

§ 206. Single Words, or groups of words, as well as single Clauses, may, by means of various formulae and turns of speech, be brought into such a correlated connection with one another, that each of them postulates the other, and of itself points to the other. Of these formulae the following are to be noted:

1. "*Both—and*", or, negatively, "*neither—nor*". Such a formula is represented in a few instances by ወ—ወ—ወ, *e. g.* Gen. 33, 1; but oftener by ሂ፡ ወ, *e. g.* እሙንቱሂ፡ ወኵሉ፡ አሕዛበ፡ ቢሆሙ Josh. 10, 5; or by ሂ፡ ወ—ሂ, *e. g.* ነበበሂ፡ ወርእየሂ Matt. 12, 22; or by ኒ፡ ወ—ኒ Josh. 11, 4; Ps. 48, 2; John 2, 15; Hen. 28, 2; Gen. 24, 25; Mark 3, 32, 35 (three times); Rom. 1, 14 (four times); or by ኒ፡ ወ, *e. g.* Matt. 12, 3; or by ሂ፡ ወ—ኒ Gen. 42, 35. All these combinations may also be used with negatives. *Cf. supra*, § 197, *ad fin.*

2. "*As—so*". In Ethiopic በከመ, ከመ, ዘከመ, ከመ፡ እንተ on the one part, and ከማሁ or ከመዝ on the other, bring complete clauses,—but, for the most part, only complete clauses,—into this particular form of correlation to each other, *e. g.* Judges 15, 11;

(1) [*Cf.* cases in which the Protasis is given in a much abbreviated form,—sometimes by one word, such as እንበለዝ "without this", "but for this", "if this had not been", *e. g.*: ወእንበለዝ፡ ፍጥረት፡ ሰብእ፡ እምከነ፡ ንቱግ፡ ወእምኢረከበ፡ ኵሎ፡ ዘይትፈቀድ፡ ሎቱ፡ "if it had not been for this (disposition), the nature of man would have been imperfect, and would have failed to obtain a supply of its various wants" *Ḥatatā Zar'a Yā'qōb* p. 19, l. 20 *sq.* = *Philosophi Abessini* p. 15, l. 18 *sq.* TR.]

Numb. 5, 4: Deut. 8, 5; Matt. 12, 40; 13, 40; Hen. 98, 4; Matt. 24, 17. It is only in a few cases that single words or phrases are dealt with in this fashion, and in these cases the second member of the combination (ከማሁ) may even be left out, *e. g.* ከመ፡ መንገለ፡ መስዕ፡ መንገለ፡ ዐረብ Hen. 28, 3. በከመ፡—ወ—ኒ also occurs, Matt. 6, 10. "*The more,—the more*" or "*so much the more*" is expressed by በአምጣነ (*cf.* § 166, No. 35) with ከማሁ following, *e. g.* በአምጣነ፡ ዕበይከ፡ ከማሁ፡ አትሕት፡ ርእሰከ ('according to the measure of thy greatness, so do thou humble thyself') "the greater thou art, be thou the more humble" Sir. 3, 18; በአምጣነ፡ ይሣቅይዎሙ፡ ከማሁ፡ ይበዝኁ "the more they afflicted them, the more they multiplied" Ex. 1, 12. Farther, ከመ with some word following, expressive of *multitude*, together with ከማሁ—may represent this idea, as in ከመ፡ ብዙኀ፡ ውዕየ፡ ሥጋሆሙ፡ ከመዝ፡ በሙ፡ ተውላጥ፡ ለመንፈስ "the more their body burns, the greater change passes over their spirit" Hen. 67, 9 (1).

3. *μὲν—δέ*, for which Ethiopic has no special form,—is sometimes not translated at all, and is sometimes translated by ኒ set in the second clause. The most adequate rendering, however, is given by ሰ in the first part and ወ in the introduction of the second (v. § 200, 2).

4. "*Either—or*", in the sense of "*sive—sive*", is given in Ethiopic by እመኒ፡—ወእመኒ, or እመሂ፡—ወእመሂ. Both of these forms are used, and frequently, not only to correlate individual words, *e. g.* እመኒ፡ ሕይወት፡ ወእመኒ፡ ሞት 1 Cor. 3, 22 (repeated as many as eight times), Lev. 3, 1, Matt. 5, 37, but even to introduce two complete Conditional Sentences, which have to be confronted antithetically with one another, Luke 20, 5 *sq.*; Ps. 138, 7. If on the other hand the two sentences have to be exclusive of one another ("*aut—aut*"), then recourse is had to እማእከ or እማእኮሰ and ወእማእከ or ወእማእከሰ, *e. g.* Gen. 13, 9; 24, 29; Lev. 1, 14; Josh. 24, 15; Matt. 6, 24; 12, 33.

The Letter of Cyril to John may serve as an instance of specially involved Periods: *cf. Chrest.* p. 75, lines 2—7; 21—25; p. 76, lines 15—21.

(1) [Flemming's reading here is ተውላጠ፡ በመንፈስ. Tr.]

ADDITIONS AND CORRECTIONS.

P. 1, l. 4. The date generally accepted now, for the conversion of Abyssinia to Christianity, may be given as—the middle of the *fourth* century.

P. 13, l. 17 *sqq.* DILLMANN's strictures on the neglect of Ethiopic, however much they may have been deserved when the '*Grammar*' was first published, are happily without application to the present position of the study.

P. 17, l. 12. *Taiṭ*—should be printed—*Tait*—, as the last letter of this alphabetical name is not emphatic. In like manner, farther on in this section,—*Hauṭ*—should be—*Haut*—, and—*Paiṭ*—should be—*Pait*.

P. 23, Note ([1]), l. 3. Insert after the word—now—the following:—, at least in grammatical treatises on Ethiopic (v. PRAETORIUS' '*Aethiop. Gramm.*', *passim*),—.

P. 25, Note ([1]). Add at the end of the Note, and within the brackets, the following:—At the same time, it is true that Inscriptions do exist, which are only *half-vocalised*.—.

P. 27, l. 3 *sq.* Instead of—along with—, read—in comparison with—.

P. 27, Note ([1]). First word of line 2 should be printed—as—.

P. 33, Note ([1]), l. 2; for—Jul.—, read—Tub.—.

P. 42, l. 8; for—*p*-sound—, read—*ṗ*-sound—.

P. 43, Note ([1]) *ult.*; for—p. 578—, read—p. 518 *sq.*—.

P. 55, l. 12; for—**ኀቍጥ**—, read—**ኀቍጥ**—.

P. 65, l. 5; after—**ዐ** and **አ**,—, insert—**ሠ** and **ሰ**,—.

P. 101, l. 4 from foot; for the head-line—1. CONSONANTS.—, read—2. CONSONANTS.—.

P. 119, l. 2; for—how!—, read—how?—.

P. 121, Note ([2]), l. 2; insert a comma (,) after **የ**.

P. 173, l. 19;—Ps. 120, 4—should be—Ps. 120, 5—.

P. 207, l. 4; for—*taṣe'lka*—. read—*taṣē'lka*—.

P. 216, l. 20; for—(כֹל)—, read—(כֹּל)—.

P. 225, l. 23;—2—should be printed—(2)—.

P. 295, l. 6;—p. 173—should be—p. 53, 16 *sq.*—.

P. 317, Note (1). Add at the end of the bracketed part of the Note, and within the brackets, the following:—For a *Plural-Plural-Plural* form, v. *ibid.*, p. XXIX b: ኵሳኵሳታት.—.

P. 321, l. 24; for—Josh. 22, 23—, read—Josh. 22, 13—.

P. 325, Note (1) *ult.*; for—(through ዝ)—, read—(through ዙ)—.

P. 338. Restore the Marginal words—The Second Pers. Pron.—, which have fallen out opposite line 6 *sq.*

P. 346, l. 15;—*áhā*—should be printed—*á-hā*—.

P. 347, Note (2) *ult.*; for—S 31—, read—631—.

P. 353, Note (3), l. 3; for—*ihu*—, read—*ihū*—.

P. 361, l. 5 from foot: Add at the end of the line the following:—[For the combination **እስኩ ፡ በእስፍንቱ**, v. *Philos. Abess.*, p. 9, l. 2].—.

P. 384, l. 19; for—"frequently—, read—"frequently"—.

P. 384, l. 24;—*καί*—should be—*καὶ*—.

P. 415, l. 16; for—**ይዐቢ**—, read—**የዐቢ**—.

P. 431, l. 28; for—1906—, read—1905—.

P. 481; read last word of Marginal—Substantive.

P. 482, Note (1), l. 2; for—§ 80, *b*, *a*—, read—§ 80, *b*, *α*—.

P. 494, l. 34; for—"nothing—, read—"and nothing—.

P. 497, beginning of last line; for—f—, read—if—.

P. 499, l. 2; for—Gen. 35, 37—, read—Gen. 35, 27—.

P. 500, l. 22; for—Gen. 33, 14—, read—Gen. 39, 14—.

P. 501, Note (1), beginning of last line; read—in—.

P. 512, l. 31; for—'*Lex.*—, read—'*Lex.*',—.

P. 533, l. 3; for—Sir. 13, 14—, read—Sir. 13, 4—.

P. 540, l. 3 from foot *sq.*; substitute for the words in parenthesis the following:—*i. e.* 'whom say the people that the Son of Man is' *or* 'whom do the people take the Son of Man to be'—.

INDEX OF PASSAGES.

(THE REFERENCES ARE TO THE PAGES OF THIS EDITION).

A. SCRIPTURE.

(a) OLD TESTAMENT.

(b) APOCRYPHA.

(c) NEW TESTAMENT

(ed. PLATT, 1830; *cf.* Reprint of PLATT's Edition by PRAETORIUS, 1899).

B. ETHIOPIC COLLECTIONS AND WORKS

—APOCRYPHAL, ECCLESIASTICAL, LEGENDARY, HISTORICAL AND ETHICAL—MOST FREQUENTLY CITED IN THE GRAMMAR.

C. OTHER WORKS AND DOCUMENTS OCCASIONALLY REFERRED TO.

ADDENDUM.

References to brief Footnote-explanations of certain Terms occasionally met with in Works on Semitic Philology.

ADDITIONAL CORRECTION.

P. 52, l. 29. The first letter should be—ጕ—.

Table I.

Characters of the Ethiopic Alphabet.

	Names of the Characters according to Dillmann ('Lex.' or 'Gr.')	Names according to Isenberg	Names in the Roman N. T.	I. Ground-form pronounced with ă	II. With ū	III. With ī	IV. With ā	V. With ē	VI. With ĕ or without any Vowel	VII. With ō	Minaeo-Sabaic	Phonetic Value and Transcription	Corresponding Hebrew or Arabic Letters
1.	ሆይ *Hōi*	ሆይ	ሀውይ	ሀ	ሁ	ሂ	ሃ	ሄ	ህ	ሆ	𐩠	*h*	ה
2.	ለው *Lawe*	ላዊ	ለው	ለ	ሉ	ሊ	ላ	ሌ	ል	ሎ	𐩡	*l*	ל
3.	ሐውት *Ḥaut*	ሓውት	ሐውት	ሐ	ሑ	ሒ	ሓ	ሔ	ሕ	ሖ	𐩢	Originally strong *h* (*ḥ*); pronounced later like No. 1	ح
4.	ማይ *Māi*	ማይ	መይ*)	መ	ሙ	ሚ	ማ	ሜ	ም	ሞ	𐩣	*m*	מ
5.	ሠውት *Šaut*	ሣውት	ሠውት	ሠ	ሡ	ሢ	ሣ	ሤ	ሥ	ሦ	𐩦	Originally *sh* (*š*); pronounced later like No. 7	ש
6.	ርእስ *Re'es*	ርዕስ, ርእስ	ረእስ*)	ረ	ሩ	ሪ	ራ	ሬ	ር	ሮ	𐩧	*r*	ר
7.	ሳት *Sāt*	ሳት	ሰት	ሰ	ሱ	ሲ	ሳ	ሴ	ስ	ሶ	𐩯	*s*	ס
8.	ቃፍ *Qāf*	ቃፍ	ቀፍ	ቀ	ቁ	ቂ	ቃ	ቄ	ቅ	ቆ	𐩤	Guttural *k* (*q*)	ק
9.	ቤት *Bēt*	ቤት	ቤት	በ	ቡ	ቢ	ባ	ቤ	ብ	ቦ	𐩨	*b*	ב
10.	ተው *Tawe*	ታዊ	ተው	ተ	ቱ	ቲ	ታ	ቴ	ት	ቶ	𐩩	*t*	ת
11.	ኀርም *Ḫarm*	ኀርም	ኀርም	ኀ	ኁ	ኂ	ኃ	ኄ	ኅ	ኆ	𐩭	Originally *ch* hard (*ḫ*); pronounced later like No. 1	خ
12.	ነሃስ *Nahās*	ነሃስ	ናኅስ	ነ	ኑ	ኒ	ና	ኔ	ን	ኖ	𐩬	*n*	נ
13.	አልፍ *Alf*	አልፍ	አልፍ	አ	ኡ	ኢ	ኣ	ኤ	እ	ኦ	𐩱	*Spiritus Lenis* (')	א
14.	ከፍ, ካፍ *Kaf* or *Kāf*	ካፍ	ከፍ	ከ	ኩ	ኪ	ካ	ኬ	ክ	ኮ	𐩫	*k*	כ
15.	ወዌ, ዋዌ *Wawē* or *Wāwē* ('*Gr.*',	ዋዊ	ወዊ	ወ	ዉ	ዊ	ዋ	ዌ	ው	ዎ	𐩥	*w*	ו
16.	ዐይን *ʿAin* [*Wawe?*)	ዓይን	ዐይን	ዐ	ዑ	ዒ	ዓ	ዔ	ዕ	ዖ	𐩲	Peculiar Aspirate-Guttural (ʿ); pron. later like No. 13	ע
17.	ዘይ *Zai*	ዛይ, ዘይ	ዘይ	ዘ	ዙ	ዚ	ዛ	ዜ	ዝ	ዞ	𐩸	Soft *s* (*z*)	ז
18.	የመን, የማን *Yaman* or *Yamān*	የመን, የማን	የመን	የ	ዩ	ዪ	ያ	ዬ	ይ	ዮ	𐩺	*y*	י
19.	ድንት, ደንት *Dent* or *Dant*	ደንት	ድንት	ደ	ዱ	ዲ	ዳ	ዴ	ድ	ዶ	𐩵	*d*	ד
20.	ገምል *Gaml* ('*Gr.*' *Geml*)	ግምል, ገምል	ገምል	ገ	ጉ	ጊ	ጋ	ጌ	ግ	ጎ	𐩴	*g* hard	ג
21.	ጠይት *Ṭait* (ጤት, F.N., Guidi)	ጣይት, ጠይት	ጣይት	ጠ	ጡ	ጢ	ጣ	ጤ	ጥ	ጦ	𐩷	Emphatic *t* (*ṭ*)	ט
22.	ጰይት *Pait*	ጳይት	ጰይት	ጰ	ጱ	ጲ	ጳ	ጴ	ጵ	ጶ	—	Emphatic *p* (*p̣*)	—
23.	ጸዳይ *Ṣadāi*	ጸዳይ	ጸደይ	ጸ	ጹ	ጺ	ጻ	ጼ	ጽ	ጾ	𐩮	Emphatic, explosive Sibilant, *ts* (*ṣ*)	צ
24.	ፀጳ *Ṣ̣appā*	ፀጳ	ጸጳ	ፀ	ፁ	ፂ	ፃ	ፄ	ፅ	ፆ	𐩳	Originally a Mute (*ḍ*); pronounced later like No. 23	ض
25.	አፍ *Af*	አፍ	አፍ	ፈ	ፉ	ፊ	ፋ	ፌ	ፍ	ፎ	𐩰	*f*	ف
26.	ፐ, ፐሰ *Pa* or *Psa* (ፕሰ Praet.)	ፐ	ፐሰ	ፐ	ፑ	ፒ	ፓ	ፔ	ፕ	ፖ	—	Slightly assibilated *p* (*p'*)	—

*) Sic.

U-containing Gutturals and Palatals.

U-containing	I. With ŭ	II. With ī	III. With ā	IV. With ē	V. With ĕ	Pronunciation
ቀ	ቈ	ቊ	ቋ	ቌ	ቍ	*quă, quī, quā, quē, quĕ.*
ኀ	ኈ	ኊ	ኋ	ኌ	ኍ	*ḫuă, ḫuī, ḫuā, ḫuē, ḫuĕ.*
ከ	ኰ	ኲ	ኳ	ኴ	ኵ	*kuă, kuī, kuā, kuē, kuĕ.*
ገ	ጐ	ጒ	ጓ	ጔ	ጕ	*guă, guī, guā, guē, guĕ.*

Numerical Signs.

Ethiopic	Greek	Ethiopic				Ethiopic	Greek
1 ፩	Α	11 ፲፩	or	better	፲ወ፩	20 ፳	Κ
2 ፪	Β	12 ፲፪	„	„	፲ወ፪	30 ፴	Λ
3 ፫	Γ	13 ፲፫	„	„	፲ወ፫	40 ፵	Μ
4 ፬	Δ	14 ፲፬	„	„	፲ወ፬	50 ፶	Ν
5 ፭	Ε	15 ፲፭	„	„	፲ወ፭	60 ፷	Ξ
6 ፮	ς	16 ፲፮	„	„	፲ወ፮	70 ፸	Ο
7 ፯	Ζ	17 ፲፯	„	„	፲ወ፯	80 ፹	Π
8 ፰	Η	18 ፲፰	„	„	፲ወ፰	90 ፺	ϙ
9 ፱	Θ	19 ፲፱	„	„	፲ወ፱	100 ፻	Ρ
10 ፲	Ι					200 ፪፻	
						1000 ፲፻	
						10000 ፼	
						100000 ፲፼	

Amharic Modifications of the Ethiopic Alphabet.

I. Ground-form with ă	II. With ū	III. With ī	IV. With ā	V. With ē	VI. With ĕ or without vowel	VII. With ō
ሸ *šă*	ሹ	ሺ	ሻ	ሼ	ሽ	ሾ
ቸ *čă*	ቹ	ቺ	ቻ	ቼ	ች	ቾ
ኘ *ñă*	ኙ	ኚ	ኛ	ኜ	ኝ	ኞ
ኸ *kʰă*	ኹ	ኺ	ኻ	ኼ	ኽ	ኾ
ዠ *žă*	ዡ	ዢ	ዣ	ዤ	ዥ	ዦ
ጀ *ǧă*	ጁ	ጂ	ጃ	ጄ	ጅ	ጆ
ጨ *čă*	ጩ	ጪ	ጫ	ጬ	ጭ	ጮ

Table II.

The Formation of Verbs.

A. The Tri-radical Verb.

1. Simple Ground-Stem (I, 1).

(a) Perfect.

	Singular. 3 m.	3 f.	2 m.	2 f.	1 c.	Plural. 3 m.	3 f.	2 m.	2 f.	1 c.
Strong Verb, Transitive	ነገረ	ነገረት	ነገርከ	ነገርኪ	ነገርኩ	ነገሩ	ነገራ	ነገርክሙ	ነገርክን	ነገርነ
Strong Verb, Intransitive	ለብሰ	ለብሰት	ለበስከ	ለበስኪ	ለበስኩ	ለብሱ	ለብሳ	ለበስክሙ	ለበስክን	ለበስነ
Mediae gutturalis, Trs. and Intrs.	መሐረ	መሐረት	መሐርከ	መሐርኪ	መሐርኩ	መሐሩ	መሐራ	መሐርክሙ	መሐርክን	መሐርነ
Tertiae gutturalis, Trs. and Intrs.	ሠርዐ	ሠርዐት	ሠራዕከ	ሠራዕኪ	ሠራዕኩ	ሠርዑ	ሠርዓ	ሠራዕክሙ	ሠራዕክን	ሠራዕነ
Mediae geminatae, Intransitive	ነደ	ነደት	ነደድከ	ነደድኪ	ነደድኩ	ነዱ	ነዳ	ነደድክሙ	ነደድክን	ነደድነ
Mediae geminatae, Transitive	ነበበ	ነበበት	ነበብከ	ነበብኪ	ነበብኩ	ነበቡ	ነበባ	ነበብክሙ	ነበብክን	ነበብነ
Mediae infirmae, with u	ጾመ	ጾመት	ጾምከ	ጾምኪ	ጾምኩ	ጾሙ	ጾማ	ጾምክሙ	ጾምክን	ጾምነ
Mediae infirmae, with i	ሤመ	ሤመት	ሤምከ	ሤምኪ	ሤምኩ	ሤሙ	ሤማ	ሤምክሙ	ሤምክን	ሤምነ
Tertiae infirmae, with u / with i	ተለወ	ተለወት	(ተለውከ / ተሎከ)	(ተለውኪ / ተሎኪ)	(ተለውኩ / ተሎኩ)	ተለዉ	ተለዋ	(ተለውክሙ / ተሎክሙ)	(ተለውክን / ተሎክን)	(ተለውነ / ተሎነ)
Tertiae infirmae, Transitive	ከረየ	ከረየት	ከረይከ	ከረይኪ	ከረይኩ	ከረዩ	ከረያ	ከረይክሙ	ከረይክን	ከረይነ
Tertiae infirmae, Intransitive	ዐብየ	ዐብየት	ዐበይከ	ዐበይኪ	ዐበይኩ	ዐብዩ	ዐብያ	ዐበይክሙ	ዐበይክን	ዐበይነ
Vowel-ending & Middle-Aspirate	ርእየ	ርእየት	ርኢከ	ርኢኪ	ርኢኩ	ርእዩ	ርእያ	ርኢክሙ	ርኢክን	ርኢነ

(b) Subjunctive.

	Singular. 3 m.	3 f.	2 m.	2 f.	1 c.	Plural. 3 m.	3 f.	2 m.	2 f.	1 c.
Strong Verb, Transitive	ይንግር	ትንግር	ትንግር	ትንግሪ	እንግር	ይንግሩ	ይንግራ	ትንግሩ	ትንግራ	ንንግር
Strong Verb, Intransitive	ይልበስ	ትልበስ	ትልበስ	ትልበሲ	እልበስ	ይልበሱ	ይልበሳ	ትልበሱ	ትልበሳ	ንልበስ
Mediae gutturalis, Trs. and Intrs.	ይምሐር	ትምሐር	ትምሐር	ትምሐሪ	እምሐር	ይምሐሩ	ይምሐራ	ትምሐሩ	ትምሐራ	ንምሐር
Tertiae gutturalis, Trs. and Intrs.	ይሥራዕ	ትሥራዕ	ትሥራዕ	ትሥርዒ	እሥራዕ	ይሥርዑ	ይሥርዓ	ትሥርዑ	ትሥርዓ	ንሥራዕ
Mediae geminatae, Intransitive	ይንድድ	ትንድድ	ትንድድ	ትንድዲ	እንድድ	ይንድዱ	ይንድዳ	ትንድዱ	ትንድዳ	ንንድድ
Mediae geminatae, Transitive	ይንብብ	ትንብብ	ትንብብ	ትንብቢ	እንብብ	ይንብቡ	ይንብባ	ትንብቡ	ትንብባ	ንንብብ
Primae ወ, Strong Formation	ይወግር	ትወግር	ትወግር	ትወግሪ	እወግር	ይወግሩ	ይወግራ	ትወግሩ	ትወግራ	ንወግር
Primae ወ, Weak „	ይልድ	ትልድ	ትልድ	ትልዲ	እልድ	ይልዱ	ይልዳ	ትልዱ	ትልዳ	ንልድ
Primae ወ, Mediae gutturalis	የሐዝ	ተሐዝ	ተሐዝ	ተሐዚ	አሐዝ	የሐዙ	የሐዛ	ተሐዙ	ተሐዛ	ነሐዝ
Primae ወ, Tertiae gutturalis	ይፃእ	ትፃእ	ትፃእ	ትፃኢ	እፃእ	ይፃኡ	ይፃኣ	ትፃኡ	ትፃኣ	ንፃእ
Mediae infirmae, with u	ይኑም	ትኑም	ትኑም	ትኑሚ	እኑም	ይኑሙ	ይኑማ	ትኑሙ	ትኑማ	ንኑም
Mediae infirmae, with i	ይሢም	ትሢም	ትሢም	ትሢሚ	እሢም	ይሢሙ	ይሢማ	ትሢሙ	ትሢማ	ንሢም
Tertiae infirmae with u, Transitive	ይትሉ	ትትሉ	ትትሉ	ትትለዊ	እትሉ	ይትለዉ	ይትለዋ	ትትለዉ	ትትለዋ	ንትሉ
Tertiae infirmae with u, Intransitive	ይፍትው (ቱ)	ትፍትው (ቱ)	ትፍትው (ቱ)	ትፍትዊ	እፍትው (ቱ)	ይፍትዉ	ይፍትዋ	ትፍትዉ	ትፍትዋ	ንፍትው (ቱ)
Tertiae infirmae with u, or Mediae gutturalis	ይክዑ	ትክዑ	ትክዑ	ትክዐዊ	እክዑ	ይክዐዉ	ይክዐዋ	ትክዐዉ	ትክዐዋ	ንክዑ
Tertiae infirmae with i, Transitive	ይክሪ	ትክሪ	ትክሪ	ትክረዪ	እክሪ	ይክረዩ	ይክረያ	ትክረዩ	ትክረያ	ንክሪ
Tertiae infirmae with i, Intransitive	ይዕበይ	ትዕበይ	ትዕበይ	ትዕበዪ	እዕበይ	ይዕበዩ	ይዕበያ	ትዕበዩ	ትዕበያ	ንዕበይ
Tertiae infirmae with i, or Mediae gutturalis	ይርአይ	ትርአይ	ትርአይ	ትርአዪ	እርአይ	ይርአዩ	ይርአያ	ትርአዩ	ትርአያ	ንርአይ
Primae ወ, mediae gutturalis, tertiae infirmae (ወዐየ)	የዐይ	ተዐይ	ተዐይ	ተዐዪ	አዐይ	የዐዩ	የዐያ	ተዐዩ	ተዐያ	ነዐይ

Table III.

The Formation of Verbs.

A. The Tri-radical Verb.

1. Simple Ground-Stem (I, 1).

(c) Imperative.

	Singular. 2 m.	Singular. 2 f.	Plural 2 m.	Plural 2 f.
Strong Verb, Transitive	ንግር	ንግሪ	ንግሩ	ንግራ
Mediae gutturalis	መሐር	መሐሪ	መሐሩ	መሐራ
Mediae geminatae, Intransitive	ንድድ	ንድዲ	ንድዱ	ንድዳ
Primae ወ, Transitive	ግር	ግሪ	ግሩ	ግራ
Mediae infirmae, with ū	ኑም	ኑሚ	ኑሙ	ኑማ
Tertiae infirmae with ū, Transitive	ትሉ	ትልዊ	ትልዉ	ትልዋ
Tertiae infirmae with ū, Intransitive	ፍትው (ፍቶ)	ፍትዊ	ፍትዉ	ፍትዋ
Tertiae infirmae *mediae gutturalis*	ክዐው	ክዐዊ	ክዐዉ	ክዐዋ

	Singular. 2 m.	Singular. 2 f.	Plural. 2 m.	Plural. 2 f.
Intransitive	ልበስ	ልበሲ	ልበሱ	ልበሳ
Tertiae gutturalis.	ሥራዕ	ሥርዒ	ሥርዑ	ሥርዓ
Transitive	ንብብ	ንቢ (ንብቢ)	ንቡ (ንብቡ)	ንባ (ንብባ)
Intransitive	ለድ	ለዲ	ለዱ	ለዳ
Tertiae gutturalis.	ፃእ	ፃኢ	ፃኡ	ፃአ
with ī	ሢም	ሢሚ	ሢሙ	ሢማ
with ī, Transitive	ክሪ	ክርዪ	ክርዩ	ክርያ
with ī, Intransitive	ዕበይ	ዕበዪ	ዕበዩ	ዕበያ
Mediae gutturalis.	ረዐይ	ረዐዪ	ረዐዩ	ረዐያ

(d) Imperfect (or Indicative).

	Singular. 3 m.	3 f.	2 m.	2 f.	1 c.	Plural. 3 m.	3 f.	2 m.	2 f.	1 c.
Strong Verb, Trans. & Intrs.	ይነግር	ትነግር	ትነግር	ትነግሪ	እነግር	ይነግሩ	ይነግራ	ትነግሩ	ትነግራ	ንነግር
Primae gutturalis	የአምን	ተአምን	ተአምን	ተአምኒ	አአምን	የአምኑ	የአምና	ተአምኑ	ተአምና	ነአምን
Mediae gutturalis	ይምሕር	ትምሕር	ትምሕር	ትምሕሪ	እምሕር	ይምሕሩ	ይምሕራ	ትምሕሩ	ትምሕራ	ንምሕር
Mediae geminatae, Trans. & Intrs.	ይነድድ	ትነድድ	ትነድድ	ትነዲ	እነድድ	ይነዱ	ይነዳ	ትነዱ	ትነዳ	ንነድድ
Primae የ	ይየብስ	ትየብስ	ትየብስ	ትየብሲ	እየብስ	ይየብሱ	ይየብሳ	ትየብሱ	ትየብሳ	ንየብስ
Primae ወ	ይወልድ	ትወልድ	ትወልድ	ትወልዲ	እወልድ	ይወልዱ	ይወልዳ	ትወልዱ	ትወልዳ	ንወልድ
" " & *mediae gutturalis*	ይውሕዝ	ትውሕዝ	ትውሕዝ	ትውሕዚ	እውሕዝ	ይውሕዙ	ይውሕዛ	ትውሕዙ	ትውሕዛ	ንውሕዝ
Mediae infirmae with ū	ይነውም	ትነውም	ትነውም	ትነውሚ	እነውም	ይነውሙ	ይነውማ	ትነውሙ	ትነውማ	ንነውም
Mediae infirmae with ī	ይሠይም	ትሠይም	ትሠይም	ትሠይሚ	እሠይም	ይሠይሙ	ይሠይማ	ትሠይሙ	ትሠይማ	ንሠይም
Tertiae infirmae with ū	ይተሉ	ትተሉ	ትተሉ	ትተልዊ	እተሉ	ይተልዉ	ይተልዋ	ትተልዉ	ትተልዋ	ንተሉ
Tertiae infirmae and *med. gutturalis*	ይክሁ	ትክሁ	ትክሁ	ትክዕዊ	እክሁ	ይክዕዉ	ይክዕዋ	ትክዕዉ	ትክዕዋ	ንክሁ
Tertiae infirmae with ī	ይክሪ	ትክሪ	ትክሪ	ትክርዪ	እክሪ	ይክርዩ	ይክርያ	ትክርዩ	ትክርያ	ንክሪ
Tertiae infirmae and *med. gutturalis*	ይውዒ	ትውዒ	ትውዒ	ትውዕዪ	እውዒ	ይውዕዩ	ይውዕያ	ትውዕዩ	ትውዕያ	ንውዒ

Table IV.

The Formation of Verbs.

A. The Tri-radical Verb.

2. The remaining Verbal Stems.

		Strong	*Primae gutturalis*	*Mediae gutturalis*	*Tertiae gutturalis*	*Mediae geminatae*	*Primae* ወ	*Primae* የ	*Mediae infirmae* u	*Mediae infirmae* i	*Tertiae infirmae* u	*Tertiae infirmae* i
I, 2. Simple Intensive Stem	Perfect Subj. Imperat. Imperf.	ፈጸመ ይፈጽም ፈጽም ይፌጽም	ሐደሰ የሐድስ ሐድስ ይሔድስ	መሀረ ይምህር ምህር ይሜህር	ነስሐ ይነስሕ ነስሕ ይኔስሕ	ኰነነ ይኰንን ኰንን ይኴንን	ወለጠ ይወልጥ ወልጥ ይዌልጥ	የበበ ይየብብ የብብ ይዬብብ	ከወለ ይከውል ከውል ይኬውል	ጠየቀ ይጠይቅ ጠይቅ ይጤይቅ	ፈነወ ይፈኑ ፈኑ ይፌኑ	ሠነየ ይሠኒ ሠኒ ይሤኒ
I, 3. Simple Influencing Stem	Perfect Subj. } Imperf. } Imperat.	ባረከ ይባርክ ባርክ			ባልሐ ይባልሕ ባልሕ	ሳረረ ይሳርር ሳርር					ላሐወ ይላሑ ላሑ	ሣቀየ ይሣቂ ሣቂ
II, 1. Causative of Simple Ground-Stem	Perfect Subj. Imperat. Imperf.	አንገረ ያንግር አንግር ያነግር	አእመረ ያእምር አእምር ያእምር	አድኀነ ያድኅን አድኅን ያድኅን	አግብአ ያግብእ አግብእ ያገብእ	አንደደ ያንድድ አንድድ ያነድድ	አውለደ ያውልድ አውልድ ያወልድ	አይበሰ ያይብስ አይብስ ያየብስ	{አጸረ / አቀመ} {ያጹር / ያቅም} {አጹር / አቅም} {ያጸውር / ያቀውም}	አኬደ ያኪድ አኪድ ያከይድ	አትለወ ያትሉ አትሉ ያተሉ	አስተየ ያስቲ አስቲ ያሰቲ
II, 2. Causative of Intensive Stem	Perfect Subj. Imperat. Imperf.	አፈጸመ ያፈጽም አፈጽም ያፌጽም	አዐረየ ያዐሪ አዐሪ ያዔሪ	{አለዐለ / አልዐለ} ያልዕል አልዕል ያሌዕል	አጸብሐ ያጸብሕ አጸብሕ ያጼብሕ	አኰነነ ያኰንን አኰንን ያኴንን	አወጠነ ያወጥን አወጥን ያዌጥን		አሠወነ ያሠውን አሠውን ያሤውን	አጠየቀ ያጠይቅ አጠይቅ ያጤይቅ	አዘመወ ያዘሙ አዘሙ ያዜሙ	አሠነየ ያሠኒ አሠኒ ያሤኒ
II, 3. Causative of Influencing Stem	Perfect Subj. } Imperf. } Imperat.	አላቀሰ ያላቅስ አላቅስ		አዋሐደ ያዋሕድ አዋሕድ							(አጸመወ) (ያጸሙ) (አጸሙ)	አዋከየ ያዋኪ አዋኪ
III, 1. Reflexive-Passive of Simple Ground-Stem	Perfect Subj. } Imperf. } Imperat.	{ተንገረ / ተመሰጠ} {ይትነገር / ይትመሰጥ} {ተነገር / ተመሰጥ}		{ተግዕዘ / ተገዐዘ} ይትገዐዝ ተገዐዝ	ተመልአ ይትመላእ ተመላእ	{ተነበ / ተኀሥሠ} {ይትነበብ / ይትኀሠሥ} {ተነበብ / ተኀሠሥ}	ተወልደ ይትወለድ ተወለድ	ተየድዐ ይትየዳዕ ተየዳዕ	{ተሀውከ / ተሀወከ} ይትሀወክ ተሀወክ	ተሠይመ ይሠየም ተሠየም	{ተፈትወ / ተዐደወ} {ይትፌተው (ቶ) / ይትዐደው (ዶ)} {ተፈተው (ቶ) / ተዐደው (ዶ)}	ተኀርየ ይትኀረይ ተኀረይ
III, 2. Reflexive-Passive of Intensive Stem	Perfect Subj. Imperat. Imperf.	ተፈጸመ ይትፈጸም ተፈጸም ይትፌጸም		{ተጸአለ / ተጽእለ} ይጸአል ተጸአል ይጼአል	ተፈሥሐ ይትፈሣሕ ተፈሣሕ ይትፌሣሕ	ተአዘዘ ይትአዘዝ ተአዘዝ ይትኤዘዝ	ተወሰከ ይትወሰክ ተወሰክ ይትዌሰክ	ተየውሀ ይትየዋህ ተየዋህ ይትዩዋህ	ተፈወሰ ይትፈወስ ተፈወስ ይትፌወስ	ተጠየቀ ይጠየቅ ተጠየቅ ይጤየቅ	ተጸገወ ይጸገው (ጉ) ተጸገው (ጉ) ይጼገው (ጉ)	ተሠነየ ይሠነይ ተሠነይ ይሤነይ
III, 3. Reflexive of Influencing Stem, or Stem of Reciprocity	Perfect Subj. } Imperf. } Imperat.	ተናገረ ይትናገር ተናገር		ተማሐለ ይትማሐል ተማሐል	ተጋብአ ይትጋባእ ተጋባእ	ተናበበ ይትናበብ ተናበብ	ተዋለጠ ይትዋለጥ ተዋለጥ		ተራወጸ ይትራወጽ ተራወጽ	ተካየደ ይትካየድ ተካየድ	ተታለወ {ይታለው / ይታሉ} {ተታለው / ተታሉ}	ተጋነየ ይትጋነይ ተጋነይ

B. The Multiliteral Verb.

		Strong	With Aspirates			With Repetition of last Radical	With long Vowel as 2nd Radical		*Ultimae infirmae* u	*Ultimae infirmae* i	Weak in more than one letter	
I. Simple Stem	Perfect	ደንገፀ	ማህረከ	ገፍትአ	ብጕብጕ	ደምሰሰ	ማሰነ	ዴገነ ቶስሐ	ሰንቀወ	ጕንደየ	ጌገየ ሎለወ	ፄወወ ዐውየወ
	Subj.	ይደንግፅ	ይማህርክ	ይገፍትእ	ይብጕብጕ	ይደምስስ	ይማስን	ይዴግን ይቶስሕ	ይሰንቁ	ይጕንዲ	ይጌጊ ይሎሉ	ይፄውው የዐውዩ
	Imperat.	ደንግፅ	ማህርክ	ገፍትእ	ብጕብጕ	ደምስስ	ማስን	ዴግን ቶስሕ	ሰንቁ	ጕንዲ	ጌጊ ሎሉ	ፄውው ዐውዩ
	Imperf.	ይደነግፅ	ይመህርክ	ይገፈትእ	ይብጐብጕ	ይደመስስ	same as Subjunctive		ይሰነቁ	ይጕነዲ	like Subj.	የዐወዩ
II. Causative Stem	Perfect	አደንገፀ	አማኅፀነ	አመግዘዐ	አራህርሀ	አመርሰሰ	አማሰነ	አዴገነ አሞቅሐ	አመንሰወ	አጕንደየ	አጌገየ	አጼነወ
	Subj.	ያደንግፅ	ያማኅፅን	ያመግዝዕ	ያራህርህ	ያመርስስ	ያማስን	ያዴግን ያሞቅሕ	ያመንሱ	ያጕንዲ	ያጌጊ	ያጼኑ
	Imperat.	አደንግፅ	አማኅፅን	አመግዝዕ	አራህርህ	አመርስስ	አማስን	አዴግን አሞቅሕ	አመንሱ	አጕንዲ	አጌጊ	አጼኑ
	Imperf.	ያደነግፅ	ያመኅፅን	ያመገዝዕ	ያረህርህ	ያመረስስ	same as Subjunctive		ያመነሱ	ያጕነዲ	same as Subjunctive	
III, 1. Reflexive-Passive Stem	Perfect	ተመንደበ	ተማኅፀነ	ተመሥኰዐ	ተራህርሀ	ተዘንጐጐ	ተማሰነ	ተሞቅሐ	ተመንሰወ	ተጸምሀየ	ተሴለየ	ተቤዘወ
	Subj.	ይትመንደብ	ይትማኅፀን	ይትመሥኰዕ	ይትራህራህ	ይዘንጐጕ	ይትማሰን	ይትሞቃሕ	ይትመንሰው	ይጸምሀይ	ይትሴለይ	ይትቤዘው
	Imperat.	ተመንደብ	ተማኅፀን	ተመሥኰዕ	ተራህራህ	ተዘንጐጕ	ተማሰን	ተሞቃሕ	ተመንሰው	ተጸምሀይ	ተሴለይ	ተቤዘው
	Imperf.	ይትመነደብ	ይትመኅፀን ይትመከዐብ	ይትመሠኰዕ	ይትረሀራህ	ይዘነጐጕ	same as Subjunctive		ይትመነሰው	ይጸመሀይ	same as Subjunctive	
III, 3. Stem of Reciprocity	Perfect	ተሰናሰለ				ተጠናቀቀ			ተሰናአወ	ተሰከተየ		ተዘያነወ
	Subj., Imperf.	ይሰናሰል				ይጠናቀቅ			ይሰናአው	ይሰከተይ		ይዘያነው
	Imperat.	ተሰናሰል				ተጠናቀቅ			ተሰናአው	ተሰከተይ		ተዘያነው
IV, 1. 3. Causative-Reflexive Stem	Perfect	አስተሰንአለ							አስተሰናአወ, Imperfect ያስተሰናኡ			
V. Second or Weaker Reflexive Stem	Perfect	አንጐርጐረ		አንፈርዐጸ	አንሳዕሰዐ	አንጠለለ			አንቃዕደወ		አንጌገየ	አንሶሰወ
	Subj.	ያንጐርጕር		ያንፈርዕጽ	ያንሳዕስዕ	ያንጠልል			ያንቃዕዱ		ያንጌጊ	ያንሶሱ
	Imperat.	አንጐርጕር		አንፈርዕጽ	አንሳዕስዕ	አንጠልል			አንቃዕዱ		አንጌጊ	አንሶሱ
	Imperf.	ያንጐረጕር		ያንፈርዕጽ	ያንሰዐስዕ	like Subj.			ያንቀዐዱ		same as Subjunctive	

Table V.

The Formation of Verbs.

A. The Tri-radical Verb.

2. The remaining Verbal Stems.

		Strong	*Primae gutturalis*	*Mediae gutturalis*	*Tertiae gutturalis*	*Mediae geminatae*	*Primae* ወ	*Mediae infirmae* u	*Mediae infirmae* i	*Tertiae infirmae* u	*Tertiae infirmae* i
IV, 1. Causative-Reflexive of Simple Ground-Stem	Perfect	አስተንፈሰ አስተሰገለ	አስታሕቀረ አስተሐቀረ	አስተርሐቀ አስተረሐቀ	አስተብቍዐ አስተቀንአ	አስተኀሠሠ	አስተውሐሰ	አስተበውሐ			አስተስረየ
	Subj.	ያስተንፍስ	ያስታሕቅር	ያስተርሕቅ	ያስተብቍዕ	ያስታኀሥሥ	ያስተውሕስ				ያስተስሪ
	Imperat.	አስተንፍስ	አስታሕቅር	አስተርሕቅ	አስተብቍዕ	አስታኀሥሥ	አስተውሕስ				አስተስሪ
	Imperf.	ያስተነፍስ	ያስተሐቅር	ያስተርሕቅ	ያስተበቍዕ	ያስተኀሥሥ	ያስተውሕስ				ያስተሰሪ
IV, 2. Causative-Reflexive of Intensive Stem	Perfect	አስተጸነሰ	አስተዐገሠ		አስተፈሥሐ		አስተወከለ		አስተኀየሰ	አስተሰፈወ	አስተረሰየ
	Subj.	ያስተጸንስ	ያስተዐግሥ		ያስተፈሥሕ		ያስተወክል		ያስተኀይስ	ያስተሰፉ	ያስተረሲ
	Imperat.	አስተጸንስ	አስተዐግሥ		አስተፈሥሕ		አስተወክል		አስተኀይስ	አስተሰፉ	አስተረሲ
	Imperf.	ያስተጼንስ	ያስተዔግሥ		ያስተፌሥሕ		ያስተዌክል		ያስተኄይስ	ያስተሴፉ	ያስተሬሲ
IV, 3. Causative-Reflexive of Influencing Stem and Causative of Stem of Reciprocity	Perfect	አስተናገረ	አስተአከየ	አስተዳኀረ	አስተጋብአ	አስተፃረረ	አስተዋሀበ	አስተማወቀ	አስተሓየጸ	አስተፋነወ	አስተሣነየ
	Subj. / Imperf.	ያስተናግር	ያስተአኪ	ያስተዳኅር	ያስተጋብእ	ያስተፃርር	ያስተዋህብ	ያስተማውቅ	ያስተሓይጽ	ያስተፋኑ	ያስተሣኒ
	Imperat.	አስተናግር		አስተዳኅር	አስተጋብእ	አስተፃርር	አስተዋሁብ	አስተማውቅ	አስተሓይጽ	አስተፋኑ	አስተሣኒ

Table VI.

The Formation of Pronouns.

1. Demonstrative Pronouns.

(a) *This.*

		m.	f.		m.	f.
Sing.	Nom.	ዝ	ዛ	or	ዝንቱ	ዛቲ
	Acc.	ዘ	ዛ	or	ዘንተ	ዛተ
Plur.	Nom.	እሉ	እላ	or	እሎንቱ	እላንቱ
	Acc.	—	—	or	እሎንተ	እላንተ

(b) *That.*

	m.	f.		m.	f.
Sing. Nom.	ዝኩ	እንትኩ	or	ዝኩቱ (ዝክቱ)	እንታክቲ
Sing. Acc.	ዝኮ	—	or	ዝኩተ (ዝክተ)	እንታክተ
		c.		c.	
Plur. Nom.		እልኩ		እልኩቱ or እልክቱ	
Plur. Acc.		—		እልኩተ or እልክተ	

2. Relative and Interrogative Pronouns.

(a) *Who, which, that.*

Sing.	m.	ዘ
	f.	እንተ
Plur.	c.	እለ

(b) *Who? What?*

	m. f.	n.
Nom.	መኑ	ምንት
Acc.	መነ	ምንተ

(c) *Which?*

Sing.		አይ
Plur.	Nom.	አያት
	Acc.	አያተ

3. Personal Pronouns.

	Singular. m.	Singular. c.	Singular. f.	Plural. m.	Plural. c.	Plural. f.
I. Pers.	—	አነ	—	—	ንሕነ	—
II. Pers.	አንተ	—	አንቲ	አንትሙ	—	አንትን
III. Pers. Nom.	ውእቱ	—	ይእቲ	እሙንቱ or ውእቶሙ	—	እማንቱ or ውእቶን
III. Pers. Acc.	ውእተ	—	ይእተ			

4. Suffixed Personal Pronouns.

	I. Pers. c.	II. Pers. m.	II. Pers. f.	III. Pers. m.	III. Pers. f.
Sing.	የ as Nominal Suffix ኒ as Verbal Suffix	ከ	ኪ	ሁ	ሃ
Plur.	ነ	ክሙ	ክን	ሆሙ	ሆን

Table VII.

The Attachment of Verbal Suffixes.

		Singular.					Plural.				
		1.	2 m.	2 f.	3 m.	3 f.	1.	2 m.	2 f.	3 m.	3 f.
I. Forms which end in ă	ነገረ	ነገረኒ	ነገረከ	ነገረኪ	ነገሮ	ነገራ	ነገረነ	ነገረክሙ	ነገረክን	ነገሮሙ	ነገሮን
	ነገርከ	ነገርከኒ	—	—	ነገርኮ / ነገርከሁ	ነገርካ / ነገርከሃ	ነገርከነ	—	—	ነገርኮሙ	ነገርኮን
	ነገርነ	—	ነገርናከ	ነገርናኪ	ነገርናሁ	ነገርናሃ	—	ነገርናክሙ	ነገርናክን	ነገርናሆሙ	ነገርናሆን
II. Forms which end in ā	ነገራ	ነገራኒ	ነገራከ	ነገራኪ	ነገራሁ	ነገራሃ	ነገራነ	ነገራክሙ	ነገራክን	ነገራሆሙ	ነገራሆን
	ይነግራ / ትነግራ	ይነግራኒ	ይነግራከ	ይነግራኪ	ይነግራሁ	ይነግራሃ	ይነግራነ	ይነግራክሙ	ይነግራክን	ይነግራሆሙ	ይነግራሆን
	ንግራ	ንግራኒ	—	—	ንግራሁ	ንግራሃ	ንግራነ	—	—	ንግራሆሙ	ንግራሆን
III. Forms which end in ū	ነገርኩ	—	ነገርኩከ	ነገርኩኪ	ነገርክዎ	ነገርክዋ	—	ነገርኩክሙ	ነገርኩክን	ነገርክዎሙ	ነገርክዎን
	ነገሩ	ነገሩኒ	ነገሩከ	ነገሩኪ	ነገርዎ	ነገርዋ	ነገሩነ	ነገሩክሙ	ነገሩክን	ነገርዎሙ	ነገርዎን
	ነገርክሙ	ነገርክሙኒ	—	—	ነገርክምዎ	ነገርክምዋ	ነገርክሙነ	—	—	ነገርክምዎሙ	ነገርክምዎን
	ይነግሩ / ትነግሩ	ይነግሩኒ	ይነግሩከ	ይነግሩኪ	ይነግርዎ	ይነግርዋ	ይነግሩነ	ይነግሩክሙ	ይነግሩክን	ይነግርዎሙ	ይነግርዎን
	ንግሩ	ንግሩኒ	—	—	ንግርዎ	ንግርዋ	ንግሩነ	—	—	ንግርዎሙ	ንግርዎን
IV. Forms which end in ī	ነገርኪ	ነገርክኒ	—	—	ነገርክዮ	ነገርክያ	ነገርክነ	—	—	ነገርክዮሙ	ነገርክዮን
	ትነግሪ	ትነግርኒ	—	—	ትነግርዮ	ትነግርያ	ትነግርነ	—	—	ትነግርዮሙ	ትነግርዮን
	ንግሪ	ንግርኒ	—	—	ንግርዮ	ንግርያ	ንግርነ	—	—	ንግርዮሙ	ንግርዮን
V. Forms which end in a Consonant	ነገረት	ነገረተኒ	ነገረተከ	ነገረተኪ	ነገረቶ	ነገረታ	ነገረተነ	ነገረተክሙ	ነገረተክን	ነገረቶሙ	ነገረቶን
	ይነግር	ይነግረኒ	ይነግረከ	ይነግረኪ	ይነግሮ	ይነግራ	ይነግረነ	ይነግረክሙ	ይነግረክን	ይነግሮሙ	ይነግሮን
	ትነግር				ትነግሮ	ትነግራ				ትነግሮሙ	ትነግሮን
	እነግር	ትነግረኒ	እነግረከ	እነግረኪ	እነግሮ	እነግራ	ትነግረነ	እነግረክሙ	እነግረክን	እነግሮሙ	እነግሮን
	ንነግር		ንነግረከ	ንነግረኪ	ንነግሮ	ንነግራ		ንነግረክሙ	ንነግረክን	ንነግሮሙ	ንነግሮን
	ንግር	ንግረኒ	—	—	ንግሮ	ንግራ	ንግረነ	—	—	ንግሮሙ	ንግሮን
	ነገርክን	—	—	—	ነገርክሁ	ነገርክሃ	—	—	—	ነገርክሆሙ	ነገርክሆን
Subjunctive-Forms	ይንግር / ትንግር / እንግር / ንንግር	ይንግረኒ	ይንግርከ	ይንግርኪ	ይንግሮ	ይንግራ	ይንግረነ	ይንግርክሙ	ይንግርክን	ይንግሮሙ	ይንግሮን

Table VIII.

The Gender- and Number-Formation of Nominal Stems.

I. The Gender- and Number-Formation of Adjectives and Participles.

	1. m.	1. f.	2. m.	2. f.	3. m.	3. f.	4. m.	4. f.	5. m.	5. f.
Sing.	ሕያው	ሕያውት	ሐዲስ	ሐዳስ	ፍጹም	ፍጽምት	ባቍዕ	ባቍዕት	ሠናይ	ሠናይት
Plur.	ሕያዋን	ሕያዋት	ሐዲሳን	{ሐዳሳት ሐዲሳት}	ፍጹማን	ፍጹማት	ባቍዓን	ባቍዓት	ሠናያን	ሠናያት

	6.	6.	7.	7.	8.	8.	9.	9.
Sing.	መደንግፅ	መደንግፅት	መፍርይ	መፍሪት	መሓሪ	መሓሪት	መንፈሳዊ	መንፈሳዊት
Plur.	መደንግፃን	መደንግፃት	መፍርያን	መፍርያት	መሓርያን	መሓርያት	መንፈሳውያን	መንፈሳውያት

2. The Plural-Formation of Substantives.

(a) The Outer Plural-Formation.

(α) With Masculine Ending of the Plural.

	1.	2.	3.
Sing.	አብድ	ኃጥእ	መምህር
Plur.	አብዳን	ኃጥአን	መምህራን

For the rest, v. the Adjectives.

(β) With Feminine Ending of the Plural.

	1.	2.	3.	4.	5.	6.	7.	8.
Sing.	ዐዘቅት	ኵሊት	ዓመት	ዝብጠት	መቅሠፍት	ትእምርት	ደመና	ጽጌ
Plur.	ዐዘቃት	ኵልያት	ዓመታት	ዝብጠታት	መቅሠፍታት	ትእምርታት	ደመናት	ጽጌያት

	9.	10.	11.	12.	13.	14.	15.	16.
Sing.	ምሳሌ	ገበ	ዝቅ	ኀብር	ድልቅልቅ	ገጽ	ቃል	ዘመን
Plur.	ምሳልያት	ገበዋት	ዝቃት	ኀብራት	ድልቅልቃት	ገጻት	ቃላት	ዘመናት

	17.	18.	19.	20.	21.	22.	23.	24.
Sing.	ጥበብ	ዓለም	መንክር	ዝናም	በዓል	ሥልጣን	ትእዛዝ	ምሕራም
Plur.	ጥበባት	ዓለማት	መንክራት	ዝናማት	በዓላት	ሥልጣናት	ትእዛዛት	ምሕራማት

	Official Names. 25.	Proper Names. 26.
Sing.	ክህን	መቃሬስ
Plur.	ክህናት	መቃሬሳት

Table IX.

The Gender- and Number-Formation of Nominal Stems.

2. The Plural-Formation of Substantives.

(b) The Inner Plural-Formation.

	Plur.	Sing.		Plur.	Sing.		Plur.	Sing.
First Form	አዕዛን	እዝን	Second Form	አፍላግ	ፈለግ	Third Form	አእጹም	አጽም
	አበው	አብ		አድባር	ደብር		አህጉር	ሀገር
				አልባስ	ልብስ			
Fourth Form	አብትር	በትር	Fifth Form	አንስርት	ንስር	Sixth Form	ጸሐፍት	ጸሓፊ
				አንቅዕት	ነቅዕ		ጠበብት	ጠቢብ
				አልህምት	ላህም		ኀጥኣት	ኃጥእ

Seventh Form

	1.	2.	3.	4.	5.	6.	7.	8.
Plur.	ሰናስል	ከዋክብት	ደባትር	ተአምር	መሳፍንት	መናፍስት	መጣብሕ	[illegible]
Sing.	ሰንሰል	ኮከብ	ደብተራ	ተአምርት	መስፍን	መንፈስ	መጥባሕት	[illegible]

	9.	10.	11.	12.	13.	14.	15.
Plur.	ኀጸውንት	ክሳውድ	አጻብዕ	ሰኳንው	አራዊት	አጋንንት	አበግዕ
Sing.	ኀጺን	ክሳድ	አጽባዕት	ሰኰና	አርዌ	ጋኔን	በግዕ

3. The Attachment of Nominal Suffixes.

(a) To Singular Stems.

(α) To Stems ending in ā, ē, ō.

		1.	2 m.	2 f.	3 m.	3 f.
Nom. and Acc.	Sing.	ጸጋየ	ጸጋከ	ጸጋኪ	ጸጋሁ	ጸጋሃ
	Plur.	ጸጋነ	ጸጋክሙ	ጸጋክን	ጸጋሆሙ	ጸጋሆን

(β) To Stems ending in ī.

		1.	2 m.	2 f.	3 m.	3 f.
Nom.	Sing.	ብእሲየ	ብእሲከ	ብእሲኪ	ብእሲሁ	ብእሲሃ
	Plur.	ብእሲነ	ብእሲክሙ	ብእሲክን	ብእሲሆሙ	ብእሲሆን
Acc.	Sing.	ብእሲየ	ብእሴከ	ብእሴኪ	ብእሲሁ	ብእሲሃ
	Plur.	—	ብእሴክሙ	ብእሴክን	ብእሲሆሙ	ብእሲሆን

(γ) To Stems ending in a Consonant.

		1.	2 m.	2 f.	3 m.	3 f.
Nom.	Sing.	ሥርዐትየ	ሥርዐትከ	ሥርዐትኪ	ሥርዐቱ	ሥርዐታ
	Plur.	ሥርዐትነ	ሥርዐትክሙ	ሥርዐትክን	ሥርዐቶሙ	ሥርዐቶን
Acc.	Sing.	ሥርዐትየ	ሥርዐተከ	ሥርዐተኪ	ሥርዐቶ	ሥርዐታ
	Plur.	ሥርዐተነ	ሥርዐተክሙ	ሥርዐተክን	ሥርዐቶሙ	ሥርዐቶን

(b) To Plural Stems.

		1.	2 m.	2 f.	3 m.	3 f.
Nom. and Acc.	Sing.	መላእክትየ	መላእክቲከ	መላእክቲኪ	መላእክቲሁ	መላእክቲሃ
	Plur.	መላእክቲነ	መላእክቲክሙ	መላእክቲክን	መላእክቲሆሙ	መላእክቲሆን

Printed by Amazon Italia Logistica S.r.l.
Torrazza Piemonte (TO), Italy